COMPUTERS AND
DATA PROCESSING TODAY

COMPUTERS AND DATA PROCESSING TODAY

with BASIC   Second Edition

Steven L. Mandell
Bowling Green State University

West Publishing Company
St. Paul ■ New York ■ Los Angeles ■ San Francisco

COPY EDITOR: Elaine Linden
ILLUSTRATIONS: John Foster, Dave Pauly, Barbara Barnett
COMPOSITION: Parkwood Composition, Inc.
COVER PHOTOS: Background photo of sky, Four By Five,
Inc.; upper right photo, Michel Tcherevkoff, The Image
Bank; lower left photo, Rob Atkins, The Image Bank.

Photo credits appear following the index

A study guide has been developed to assist you in mastering
concepts presented in this text. The study guide reinforces
concepts by presenting them in condensed, concise form.
Additional illustrations and examples are also included. The
study guide is available from your local bookstore under the
title *Study Guide to Accompany Computers and Data Processing Today* **Second Edition,** prepared by Steven L. Mandell.

COPYRIGHT © 1983 WEST PUBLISHING COMPANY
COPYRIGHT © 1986 By WEST PUBLISHING COMPANY
50 West Kellogg Boulevard
P.O. Box 64526
St. Paul, MN 55164-1003

Library of Congress Cataloging-in-Publication Data
Mandell, Steven L.
    Computers and data processing today with BASIC.

    Includes index.
    1. Electronic data processing.   2. Electronic
digital computers.   3. BASIC (Computer program language)
I. Title.
QA76.M27475 1986   004   85-17769
ISBN 0-314-96079-1

CONTENTS

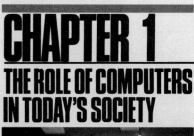

CHAPTER 1
THE ROLE OF COMPUTERS IN TODAY'S SOCIETY

Page 1

CHAPTER 2
COMPUTER EVOLUTION

Page 35

viii

CHAPTER 3
DATA PROCESSING AND COMPUTER HARDWARE

Page 69

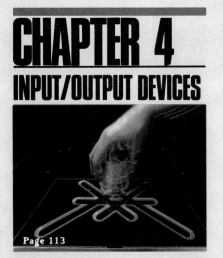

CHAPTER 4
INPUT/OUTPUT DEVICES

Page 113

A data base, therefore, could be likened to a large, centrally located room with file cabinet after file cabinet of information. Because it is kept in a central location and all personnel can have access to the information they require, information is easy to access, can be updated in one location, and is not duplicated.

A file handler, on the other hand, can be likened to a single file cabinet kept in a particular department where only the department's employees have access to the data. Another department's employees would find getting access to the data difficult, and it would therefore be duplicated across departments within the organization.

Uses

Data managers have a number of uses in the home, in business, and in specialized situations. Data managers—file handlers in particular—have proven to be very popular software packages for use in the home. The data manager can be used for just about any type of record keeping and filing done in the home (see Figure 12–2). Possible uses of data managers in the home include: keeping a personal-property inventory, creating a list of important documents and their

Figure 12–2
Electronic recipe file

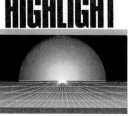

College Selection Made Simple

Prospective college students no longer have to spend hours reading catalogs or relying on someone else's advice in order to select the right college. College Explorer, a data-base package designed for microcomputers, puts students in the command seat when it comes to planning their future education. The software package comes with four disks, three of which hold a data base of 2,700 two- and four-year colleges. The fourth disk is for user input.

College Explorer was created by The College Board, the organization responsible for producing the SAT exam. Before the program will reveal the names of any academic institutions, a student must answer questions that indicate preferences in 12 major categories. Selection categories, including curriculum, degree level, athletics, school size, social programs, and religious affiliation, encourage students to specify what they want from their college experience. The task of making selection for each area helps even undirected students think seriously about their future.

Programmed explanations answer most of the likely questions about the categories. For example, when asked to select a regional location for a school, selecting "Explanation" will cause a full map of the United States and Puerto Rico to appear, with regions designated by number.

Once a student answers all criteria questions asked on the first College Explorer disk, he or she inserts one of the data-base disks. The computer searches through the data base and selects up to 30 good matches between student and institution. A student can find more information on each college in *The College Handbook,* the 1,685-page book that accompanies the data base program. College Explorer can help a student find an appropriate college much more efficiently than the book alone.

locations, keeping a computerized address book and phone listing, creating a mailing list, keeping an appointment calendar, and keeping track of works within a personal library. File handlers simply offer a means of computerizing a manual record-keeping task—that of keeping organized, readily accessible records.

File handlers are also popular with small businesses that can benefit from the conversion of manual record-keeping processes to computerized record keeping. This process of converting manual filing systems to computerized filing systems has been possibly the greatest single use of data managers. Any aspect of a business that uses some form of file system, from a Rolodex to a file cabinet, could potentially be computerized using a data manager. Business applications that are easily adapted to use with a data manager include the keeping of employee records, inventory control, and listings of suppliers and customers.

Some data managers are designed for use in special, or unique, situations. One such specialized use of data management software is in the area of mass mailing. A popular application is creating mailing lists. Mailing list data managers provide the user with the ability to store, sort, and print data that can be used for creating mailing lists or labels. Not only can these data managers be used to create mailing lists, they can be used along with word processors to generate form letters.

Features

Many of the popular data managers offer a standard group of features. In most packages, these features can be selected through choices displayed in menus (a list of options available to the user). These standard features include: adding records, deleting records, searching for and/or updating records, sorting the data file, printing, and making mathematical calculations. Additional features in some data managers include creating screen displays and displaying "help" screens with explanations to guide the inexperienced user.

Add/Delete.   Once a file has been created, data is entered into the file using the add feature. The add feature simply allows one to place a record of information in the data file. The delete, or remove, feature serves just the opposite function; it erases a record from the data file.

Search/Update.   The search feature of a data manager allows the user to search an existing data file for a record or records based on certain criteria. If, for example, one wants to find all the softball bats in a sports equipment inventory with a price of more than $15, one uses the search feature. The update feature, on the other hand, allows one to locate and change the value of a data field. If the price of the softball bats has changed from $15 to $17.50, one would use the update feature to make the change within the inventory file. In many of the data managers the search and update features are used in conjunction with each other to locate and change a record.

Sort.   The data in a file is generally stored in the order it is entered; the sort feature provides the user with a way to alter that order of storage. For example, a data file containing the names and addresses for a mailing list can be sorted according to last names before printing. This would allow the list to be printed in alphabetical order.

Print.   The print feature can be valuable, but some packages have limited printing capabilities. Some software publishers offer an independent report-generating package or package add-ons to use with the data files created using the data manager. For the purpose of printing mailing lists and mailing labels, most data managers have adequate print capabilities.

Mathematical Calculations. Some data managers are capable of making mathematical calculations on the data contained within a file. These calculations can be as simple as subtotalling or totalling a particular field within the data records, or as complex as calculating statistics such as means or averages. File handlers, for the most part, offer limited mathematical capabilities while database management packages typically permit more complex computations.

Additional Features. A special feature in many data managers allows the user to design the screen on which the data will be displayed. By designing the screen display format, the user indicates to the data manager the fields that will be contained within a record of the data file. Data managers that do not allow the creation of a display format generally require users to declare data fields that will be contained in a record.

Some data managers also display help screens upon request. If the user is confused about available choices, he or she can request a display of the available options and possibly even a brief explanation of what each option will do. This feature is valuable for inexperienced users. Since the screens are displayed only on request, the experienced user is not hampered by the additional display of menu screens and explanations of available choices.

Concept Summary 12–2 ▬ Types of Data Managers

Type	Design Purpose	Features
File Handler	Designed to duplicate traditional methods of manually filing one record at a time.	Can access only one data file at a time. May cause duplication of data between files.
Data-Base Package	Designed to consolidate independent files into an integrated whole.	Add/delete Search/update Sort Print Mathematical calculations

MODELING SOFTWARE

A Definition

Model A representation of a real-world system used in decision making.

Modeling software, as the name implies, is based on a mathematical model. A **model** is a mathematical representation of a real-world situation. For example, the relationship of a monthly payment to an amount borrowed and an annual interest rate can be shown with a mathematical equation, or model. A model used to calculate monthly payments, therefore, might look like the following:

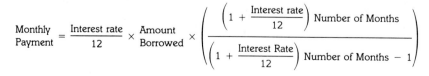

$$\text{Monthly Payment} = \frac{\text{Interest rate}}{12} \times \text{Amount Borrowed} \times \left(\frac{\left(1 + \frac{\text{Interest rate}}{12}\right) \text{Number of Months}}{\left(1 + \frac{\text{Interest Rate}}{12}\right) \text{Number of Months} - 1} \right)$$

Once the model has been developed, it can be entered into the computer using a modeling application software package. A **modeling package** uses the power and speed of a computer to perform mathematical calculations. Depending on the particular package, modeling software can also create printed reports and graphic displays.

Modeling software has a wide variety of potential uses; however, one of its most popular uses is to assist managers in decision making. By developing a model, entering it into the computer via the modeling software, and then altering values of the variables within the model, a manager can see how changes in the variables will affect the outcome of the model. This type of process is known as **simulation.**

The modeling software used on microcomputers is called an electronic spreadsheet. Modeling, or planning, packages are also used on minicomputers and mainframe computer systems. This chapter will focus on the uses and features of electronic spreadsheets.

Simulation The process used by system users to gain insight into the workings of an actual system.

Electronic Spreadsheets. A **spreadsheet,** or ledger sheet, is primarily used by accountants for performing financial calculations and recording transactions. An electronic spreadsheet is simply a computerized version of a traditional spreadsheet. Electronic spreadsheets, however, are being used for more than just financial calculations and recording of transactions. An **electronic spreadsheet** is a table of rows and columns used to store and manipulate any kind of numerical data (see Figure 12–3).

Some spreadsheets are as large as 254 rows by 64 columns. This means that a user can view only part of the spreadsheet at one time. The display screen acts as a window to view a selected portion of the spreadsheet. Vertical and horizontal scrolling are used to position a portion of the spreadsheet on the display screen.

Electronic spreadsheet An electronic ledger sheet used to store and manipulate any type of numerical data.

The point in a spreadsheet where a particular row and column meet is called a **cell.** Each cell is a unique location within the spreadsheet, and in the case of a 254 by 64 spreadsheet, there would be 16,256 cells. Cells can contain labels, values, and formulas.

Most spreadsheets also have a **status area** at the top of the display, which indicates the location of the cursor and what was entered in a particular cell.

Cell The unique location within an electronic spreadsheet where a row and a column intersect.

Figure 12–3
(a) Electronic spreadsheet.
(b) Electronic spreadsheet with labeled features

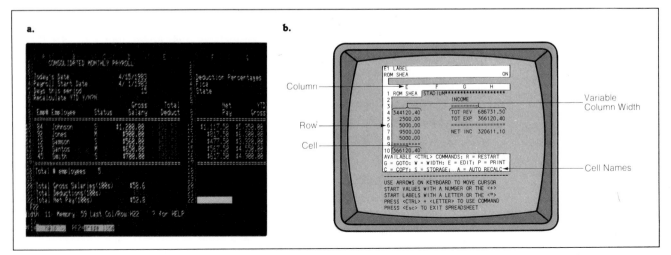

a.

b.

A **command area** at the bottom of some spreadsheets displays the commands available to the user.

Uses

Like word processors and data managers, electronic spreadsheets can be used at home as well as in business. In business, electronic spreadsheets are being used increasingly by managers as an aid to decision making. By constructing a model where inputs and outputs are identified, the manager can use the spreadsheet to predict the outcome of particular actions. This is much faster than doing this type of analysis by hand with pencil, paper, and a calculator.

At home, electronic spreadsheets can be used for a variety of purposes. Home budgeting, interest calculations, and just about any task that requires the manipulation of numeric data can be done using an electronic spreadsheet.

Features

The following are some of the most common features available on electronic spreadsheets.

Variable Column Width. Spreadsheets that have variable column widths allow the user to adjust the columns to a desired width. This can be very helpful when large values, long variable names, or large formulas are required.

Automatic Spillover. Automatic spillover is a feature of some spreadsheets that have fixed column widths. It allows extralong labels to "spill over" into the next cell.

Insert and Delete. Insert and delete features allow a user to insert or delete rows or columns as desired. If a particular cell that would be contained in a formula is inserted or deleted, the spreadsheet will automatically compensate for the row or column's addition or deletion.

Graphics. Some spreadsheets offer the user the ability to create graphs using data contained in the spreadsheet. Horizontal graphs using asterisks, simple pie charts, or line charts are often available.

Templates. A **template** is a predefined set of formulas that are used on a continuing basis. By saving the formulas as a template, they can be retrieved and new values can be substituted for calculation. This eliminates the need to enter the formulas each time the calculations are required.

Locking Cells. The locking, or protecting, of cells prevents them from being altered or destroyed. A cell that is critical to the outcome of a formula cannot be accidentally deleted or changed if the cell is locked.

Hiding Cells. Hiding cells within the spreadsheet prevents the contents of a cell from being displayed. This would prevent the user from seeing the results when data is entered for manipulation, for example. This could be used as a security measure to prevent sensitive information, such as an employee's salary, from being seen by unauthorized personnel.

HIGHLIGHT

Electronic Spreadsheets—Something for Everyone

When electronic spreadsheets were first developed, their primary use was in accounting departments of large businesses, but today, all kinds of people are finding all kinds of uses for spreadsheets.

A judge from Arizona used a spreadsheet to help detect judges' biases in terms of race, sex, or age. Judge David Phares, who taught a course in judicial applications to his peers, had each judge in his class use a spreadsheet to identify his or her patterns in sentencing. The judges could find out if they were sentencing people 18 to 22 years old much more severely than people 26 to 30 for marijuana, for example.

Jeff Conniff, a software design specialist, developed a software model to help him pursue his interest in photography. Through trial and error, he designed a model to determine f-stop and exposure time when he wanted to print enlargements of already printed photographs.

Charles Janda, chief financial officer for a large real estate firm, liked the visible trail of numbers and results that his spreadsheet generated. He did not have to remember the month-by-month growth of future value calculations in order to compare alternatives or to explain the consequences of an investment to other people in his office. Spreadsheet automatic functions for complicated interest calculations took the drudgery out of financial analysis, so Janda could concentrate on the big picture.

But Janda warns against the dangers of oversimplifying spreadsheet results, and many experienced spreadsheet users agree. Spreadsheets cannot substitute for an understanding of the functions performed by a particular package. Users will get the most out of a spreadsheet model when they develop their own model or use a model with functions they already understand.

Naming Cells. Cells can be referenced according to either their location within the spreadsheet (a cell at Column B, Row 6, for example, would be named B6), or by a name provided by the user. Naming cells is more convenient if you wish to include a cell in a formula. Rather than having to search through the spreadsheet for the cell's location, one simply refers to the cell by name in the formula.

Windows. Windows permit the user to divide the display screen into several independent displays that bring separate portions of the spreadsheet into view.

Titles. If one is using the first column of a spreadsheet for the purpose of titling the rows, the title feature allows the first column of the spreadsheet to stay locked in place while the remainder of the columns will scroll as desired.

Copy. The copy, or replication, feature allows the user to copy a cell, or group of cells, to another location within the spreadsheet. This eliminates the need to retype cells that must be duplicated throughout the spreadsheet.

Manual Recalculation. A manual recalculation feature lets the user choose when the outcome of the spreadsheet should be recalculated. Normally, when the value of a cell is changed, the spreadsheet automatically begins a recalculation. With the manual recalculation feature, more than one cell can be altered before the recalculation is started.

Sort. The sort feature in a spreadsheet provides for the ordering of information contained within the spreadsheet.

GRAPHICS SOFTWARE

A Definition

Graphics software packages are designed to allow the user to display images on a computer monitor or terminal or to print images on a printer. The images that can be created range from a bar chart to detailed designs of objects.

The operation of graphics packages can be as simple as selecting choices from a menu of available options, or as complex as being given control of the individual dots on the display screen, called **pixels,** to create images. Each display screen has a certain number of pixels that are used to make any image that is displayed on the screen. By controlling these pixels, the user can create graphic images with virtually any degree of detail desired (see Figure 12–4).

Uses

Applications for graphics software packages range from business to artistic uses. In business they are used for a number of different applications. Graphic packages that produce graphs, such as pie charts and bar graphs, are used by managers to summarize data for presentation purposes. The graphs can be

Graphics software package Application software packages designed to allow the user to display images on the display screen or printer.

Pixel The individual dot on a display screen that is combined with other dots to create characters and images.

Figure 12–4
Kaleidoscope created with a graphics package

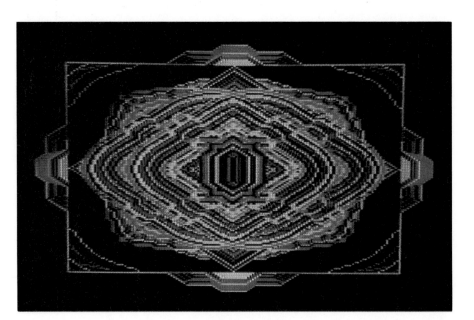

used for presentations on monitors or can be printed for distribution to those attending a presentation. The printed output from these packages can also be used to create slides or transparencies (see Figure 12–5).

Graphics packages are also being used in business to design entire objects or parts. Computer-aided design, for example, employs a graphics software package to allow an engineer to design products as complex as automobiles (see Figure 12–6). Nike, the maker of sport shoes, used a complex graphics package to help design the sole of a popular shoe.

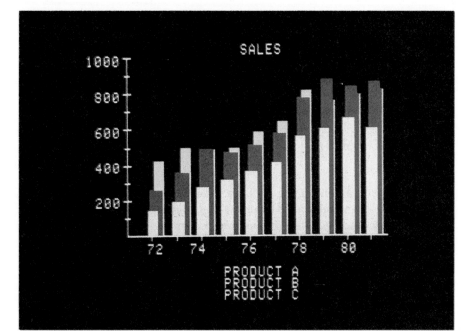

Figure 12–5
Bar graph created from a graphics package

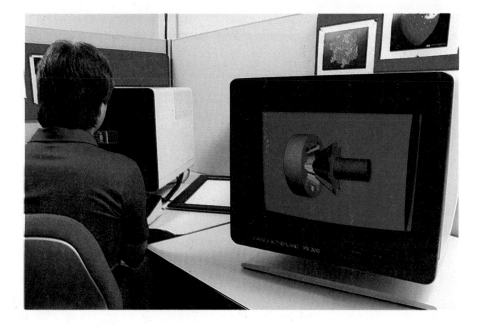

Figure 12–6
Engineering design produced with graphics software

Art is another area that is seeing increasing use of graphics packages. Computer artists can now use graphics software to "paint" images or pictures on a display screen. This technique is particularly appealing because the images on the display screen can be changed easily if the artist is dissatisfied (see Figure 12–7).

Graphics packages are also being used heavily in the creation of computer video games. Developers of these games can use the packages to create display screens that they can then save and call up for display while the game is running.

Features

Some features that are common to nearly all types of graphics software packages are discussed below.

Two- and Three-Dimensional Display. Some graphics packages are capable of only two-dimensional display, while others are capable of simulating three dimensions. Depending on the application, a two-dimensional display may be sufficient.

Save. The save feature can be particularly useful. By being able to save screen displays, a program written for a particular application can call display screens from secondary storage while the program is running. The save feature is also helpful in cases where display screens used in other applications are similar to some already saved. The saved display screens can be modified to meet the new programs' needs and saved under another name. This eliminates the need to create a new display screen from scratch each time one is needed.

Cursor Positioning. Many packages use the positioning of the cursor to create graphic images. In some cases, arrows (found on many keyboards) or control characters are used to position the cursor. In other cases, input devices such

**Figure 12–7
Computer-generated art**

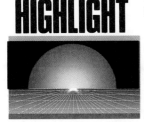

HIGHLIGHT

Software Package Hollywood's Shining STAR

One of Hollywood's most popular stars may never retire. A software program called STAR (Scene Tracking, Auto Registration) helped create special effects in the movies *2010* and *Nightmares.* The program was also used to create the ABC network logo introduced in 1984 and the Apple International commercial in which the multicolored Apple logo wisps through a computer chip.

Bo Gehring, head of Bo Gehring Associates in Venice, California, master-minded STAR. Gehring created the first computer-generated image (CGI) commercial for television in 1973. To Gehring, artist, inventor, technician and businessman, technology is only a creative tool.

Algebraic advances, perfected at the University of Utah in the 1970s, make Gehring's rich, colorful, integrated graphics possible. Using matrix mathematics, STAR converts three-dimensional pictures to two dimensions. After creating a design on a special computer equipped with a very large screen, the operator can move the design in a variety of directions with a joystick.

To integrate special effects with film, a live-action film is projected on a special screen. When the keyboard operator places the cursor at a point on the projected picture, for example, the corner of a room, STAR calculates the corresponding two-dimensional coordinates and determines what the film camera matrix was. The program then generates images that look like the camera technician shot them. When the film and the images are put together, the resulting picture appears real.

Using STAR to determine and simulate camera matrixes frees the camera operator to shoot a live scene from any angle. Previously, a scene had to be shot from a static, predetermined angle in order to impose special effects over it and make the final effect realistic.

Gehring foresees many other applications for STAR. People who lack reading skills could learn by "reading" a STAR-generated program. Gehring would also like to see flight menu graphics replaced with STAR graphics. The flight menus, now mostly charts and graphs, are for pilots. Star graphics could provide decison-making information in an easy-to-understand form that would be especially useful during split second decision making.

as joysticks, game paddles, light pens, graphic tablets, or a mouse can be used to position the cursor.

High-Resolution Graphics. High-resolution graphics capability means that the images the user can create with the software will be sharper than they would be if they were displayed in the normal display mode. High-resolution graphics offer a greater number of pixels on the display screen, which sharpens the images.

Color. Many computers also have the ability to display images in color. If a computer system has a color monitor and the capabilities to display color, the graphics package can make much more appealing images.

Animation. Animation involves the moving of an image about the display screen. The image can be moved either horizontally, vertically, or diagonally; it can also be rotated about a point. Such mobility is critical in the preparation of video games and the design of certain types of objects.

INTEGRATED SOFTWARE

In a conventional sense, integration suggests blending two or more parts into a unified whole. When the term *integration* is used in conjunction with software, however, users generally expect that the software will conform to three standards.

1. The software consists of what are usually separate application programs.
2. The software provides easy movement of data among the separate applications.
3. A common group of commands is used for all the applications in the software package.

The following discussion covers two types of **integrated software**—vertical and horizontal. Also included is a discussion of windows.

Vertical and Horizontal Integration

Horizontal software integration Application packages that are general in nature and can be used for many applications or combining various types of packages.

From the software design perspective, **horizontal integration** can be used to describe combining application packages—such as a word processor, data manager, spreadsheet, and graphics package—into one package that can share data (see Figure 12–8). The ability to combine and pass data between application packages makes integrated software very useful. By combining an electronic spreadsheet with a graphics package, for example, one obtains a very powerful, integrated application package to support decision making (see Figure 12–9).

Vertical software integration The enhancement of a single software package.

Vertical integration in a software design context is used to refer to the enhancement of a single package. For example, adding a spelling program, dictionary, or thesaurus to a word processor would be considered vertical integration.

Windows

Window/Window environment An operating system enhancement that allows more than one application software package to run concurrently.

A relatively new type of software package referred to as a window, or window environment, allows for a software design using horizontal integration. **Windows,** or **window environments,** are an enhancement to the normal operating system of a computer and allow more than one application software package to run concurrently. Windows are currently found primarily on microcomputers and are considered to be on the leading edge of microcomputer software technology.

A windowing software package gives the user the ability to split the screen into two or more miniscreens or "windows" displaying application packages that are currently in use or capable of being used. As an enhancement to or

Spreadsheet

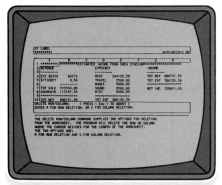

Graphics

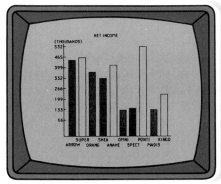

Data Base Manager

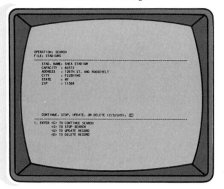

Word Processing

Figure 12–8
Integrated software

Figure 12–9
Report created from integrated software

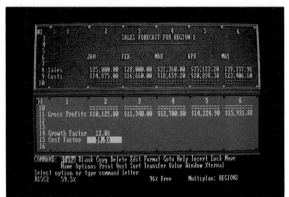

395

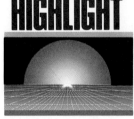

Integrated Software Reroutes Buses

When building a new school made rerouting buses necessary, school administrators in Larose, Louisiana, needed a computer program that could handle numerical analysis quickly and put the information into data bases at the same time. The Larose school staff solved the problem with an integrated software package from Lotus Development Corporation that combines a word processor, spreadsheet, data base, and graphics program.

They used the package, Lotus 1-2-3, to determine the best routes for the entire system. With a few key strokes, 1-2-3's spreadsheet calculated the outcome of different routing possibilities until administrators settled on the most efficient solution.

The electronic spreadsheet also helped administrators calculate numbers and percentages of students who did not go directly home after school. The 1-2-3 compared each student's home address with his or her afternoon destination address and counted how many variances existed between the two fields of information.

Using the program's data base, administrators sorted information by teacher name and student name. In less than a minute, 1-2-3 could sort hundreds of records and list all the students assigned to each teacher. In another minute, 1-2-3 could resort and list all students by bus number.

The school secretary could use 1-2-3's word-processing program to generate form letters and notices to parents or teachers and to type new letters and memos. Using the graphics capabilities, the staff could create charts and graphs for classroom or administrative use.

The school put the integrated program to work for financial planning and tracking disciplinary referrals, as well as for bus routing. Administrators particularly like the idea that the program encourages creative thinking. The school staff can instantly test new ideas that they might not have attempted to test without the software package.

extension of the normal operating environment, windows have a number of advantages over conventional application software packages, including the following:

- A more user-oriented, or user-friendly, environment.
- The potential for a consistent command structure across application packages.
- The ability to transfer data between applications.
- The use of a mouse or other pointing device.

Windows will undoubtedly be used to a greater extent in the future because of their ability to both simplify and enhance the environment in which the computer user has to work.

FOCUS ON MICRO-COMPUTING

Integrated Software

Ever since microcomputers first appeared on the market, software developers have been scrambling to develop software packages that meet the ever-growing needs of users. One of the most recent software developments for microcomputers is the use of integrated software. Earlier we stated that in a conventional sense, integration suggests blending two or more parts into a unified whole and that when the term *integration* is used in conjunction with software, users generally expect that the software will conform to three standards:

1. The software consists of what are usually separate application programs.
2. The software provides easy movement of data among the separate applications.
3. A common group of commands is used for all the applications in the software package.

The need for integrated software developed as microcomputers began to be used for powerful and complex computing applications. For example, a church treasurer may use a microcomputer and electronic spreadsheet primarily to keep track of the financial records of the church, but periodically it may be necessary to prepare a report for the trustees, which involves word processing (to write the report) and graphics software (to present the spreadsheet figures in an easy-to-understand form). Each time one of the above separate applications is needed to prepare a report, the treasurer has to save the current file, close the current program, eject the disk, load the needed application disk, open another file, and continue the report. If the treasurer wanted to calculate percentages from spreadsheet figures and create a pie chart that would appear in the final report, performing the necessary disk manipulations and varying program commands would be tedious at best. With some programs, complex manipulation of data from one application to another might even be impossible.

An integrated software package would facilitate the preparation of the treasurer's report. Integrated software was designed to make computers more useful by reducing and eliminating the complexities of moving from one application to another.

There are four types of integrated software. The first is the all-in-one package. This is perhaps the most widely known and used integrated software. The all-in-one package combines several common applications to make a single program. Symphony by Lotus Development and Framework by Ashton-Tate are two of the more popular all-in-one packages. Symphony combines a spreadsheet with graphics, word-processing, and data-base functions. Framework contains these four applications along with outlining and communications capabilities. These packages make moving from one application to another very convenient for the user because each application is really a component of a single program.

All-in-one packages also offer the user the benefit of a common command set. For example, the delete command would be the same whether the user

397

was deleting from the spreadsheet or the word processor. Consistency of command is especially valuable to a person who may use some applications on a limited basis. The user does not have to memorize a lot of seldom-used commands.

There are some drawbacks to all-in-one packages. The functions represented in all-in-one packages are generally not as complete as the functions offered in single application programs. An all-in-one package with complex word-processing capabilities may be weak in the spreadsheet or graphics area. Therefore, a user with highly sophisticated graphics requirements may find a package lacking in graphics capabilities and would want to use a stand-alone package for graphics needs. Power requirements are another drawback of all-in-one packages. The integrated package Jazz (by Lotus) was developed for the 512K "Fat Mac" and requires 256K of RAM to operate. Obviously, Jazz would be useless on the smaller 128K Macintosh.

The second type of integrated software is called the integrated series. These programs are actually separate application programs that share a common command set. The command set allows data to be transferred from one application to another quickly and easily. Smart Software by Innovative Software is one example of an integrated series. Programs in an integrated series offer the varied functions and data and ease of transfer of stand-alone programs without using the memory requirements of all-in-one packages.

The systems integrator is the third type of integrated software. The systems integrator makes moving data between stand-alone packages residing in memory possible. The integrator also permits simultaneous operation of stand-alone packages. IBM produces a systems integrator called Topview. One advantage of this type of integration is that it allows the user to select the stand-alone application that is best suited for the user's needs. A drawback, however, is that the stand-alone packages do not usually offer common command sets, so the user must memorize dissimilar commands. Systems integrators also use large amounts of RAM, which makes them unsuitable for use with small microcomputers.

The last type of software integration, the background utility approach, offers limited integration capabilities. This method permits the user to load a type of utility software commonly called "desk accessories" into RAM. Calculators, calendars, telephone dialers, and notepads are all types of desk accessories. Once the utility software is loaded, a stand-alone application program is also loaded into RAM. The user can then select the desk accessory needed to accompany the application program. Many microcomputer users feel background utilities more than meet their software needs. A background utility is useful with stand-alone programs, but the utility programs use so much RAM that some application programs will not load.

Individual user needs vary greatly. Each user must evaluate his or her software needs before selecting an integrated package to meet those needs.

SUMMARY POINTS

- A word processor is an application software package designed to permit the user to enter, manipulate, format, print, store, and retrieve text. Word processing involves manipulating text using a word processor.
- A word-processing system is the computer system (hardware and software), or portion of a computer system, used for the task of word processing. A dedicated word-processing system is used exclusively for word processing, while a multipurpose digital computer can be used for word processing and many other applications.
- Word processing can involve a number of different activities, but generally the activities fall into one of two categories: text editing and print formatting.
- A line editor operates on only one line of text at a time; a screen editor can operate on an entire screen of text at a time.
- A word processor that holds only one page of text in internal memory at a time is referred to as a page-oriented word processor. A document-oriented word processor treats a document as one long page.
- A few uses of word processors include creating formal reports, letters, memos, and manuscripts.
- Features included in word processors normally consist of: (1) writing and editing, (2) screen formatting, and (3) print formatting.
- Data managers are used for the same purpose as manual filing systems—the recording and filing of information.
- There are two types of data managers: file handlers and data-base packages. File handlers were developed first to replace manual filing systems, while data-base packages were developed later to organize independent files into an integrated whole.
- Data managers can be used for such tasks as creating a Christmas card list, keeping a personal calendar, maintaining inventory control, and cataloging lists of customers and suppliers.
- Features considered to be standard in nearly all data managers include: adding or deleting records, searching for and updating records, sorting records, and printing information from records. Additional features include: screen display formatting and mathematical calculation capabilities.
- A model is a mathematical representation of an actual situation. One of the most popular uses of modeling software packages is to assist business managers in decision making.
- The modeling software used most often on microcomputers is called an electronic spreadsheet. Modeling or planning packages are used on minicomputer and mainframe computer systems.
- An electronic spreadsheet is a computerized version of a traditional spreadsheet, that is, a table of columns and rows used to store and manipulate numerical data. A cell is the point at which a specific row and column intersect within the spreadsheet. Cells can contain labels, values, and formulas.
- Electronic spreadsheets assist managers in their daily decision-making tasks, and also perform financial planning and accounting tasks.
- Graphics packages allow the computer user to display images, such as graphs or pie charts on a monitor or terminal, or to print images on a printer. A pixel—the smallest element displayed on a monitor or terminal—is a small dot that is combined with other dots to create characters or images for display.

■ Graphics application software packages are used by such people as business managers, engineers, artists, and video game programmers.

■ Integrated software generally conforms to three standards: (1) The software consists of what are usually separate application programs (2) The software provides easy movement of data among the separate applications (3) A common group of commands is used for all the applications in the software package.

■ Horizontally integrated software refers to the combination of two or more application packages into a single package that is capable of sharing data.

■ Vertically integrated software refers to the enhancement of a single package.

■ Windows, or window environments, are software packages designed to accomplish horizontal integration in a software design context; they are capable of creating a more user-oriented environment for the application software user.

■ There are four types of integrated software: all-in-one packages, integrated series, system integrators, and software integrators.

REVIEW AND DISCUSSION QUESTIONS

1. Define the terms *word processor, word processing,* and *word-processing system.*
2. What are the two primary functions of a word processor? Briefly explain each.
3. How does a line editor differ from a screen editor? What is the difference between a page-oriented word processor and a document-oriented word processor?
4. What is a cursor, and how might controlling its movement help the user of a word processor edit a document? List and briefly describe five of the cursor-positioning features.
5. What is a data manager, and how is it used?
6. Give a brief explanation of the difference between a file handler and a data-base package.
7. List and briefly describe four of the common features contained in data management software packages.
8. What is modeling, and how can it be beneficial to business managers?
9. What is the process used by managers to explore possible outcomes by changing variables within the model?
10. What is a cell? What type of information can it contain?
11. What is a pixel? How is it used to create characters or images on a display screen?
12. What are some of the advantages horizontally integrated software can offer the application software user if the package has been developed using a software design perspective?
13. What three standards have users generally come to expect in integrated software?
14. What are some advantages and disadvantages of using all-in-one integrated software?

CHAPTER 13

SYSTEM ANALYSIS AND DESIGN

COMPUTERS IN OUR LIVES

A Computer System Takes Center Stage

When the Minnesota State Arts Board cut back on grant money to repertory theater companies, Phyllis Ross, the managing director of a theater company in Minneapolis, knew she had to do something about the theater's fund-raising efforts. The theater was paying two computer service bureau's for fund-raising and accounting work that Phyllis knew could be done more economically with an in-house computer system.

Phyllis had much talking to do before she persuaded the theater's board of directors to support the idea of purchasing an in-house computer system. The theater was already strapped for funds, and at first the board saw only the costs—hardware, software, and personnel—associated with computerizing the theater's operations. The benefits—improved administrative controls and a more businesslike approach to managing personnel and resources—were difficult for the board members to recognize. Most of the members were artists themselves and some of them exhibited signs of computer phobia. Wouldn't bringing high technology into the theater stifle creativity? But Phyllis finally convinced them that the efficiency of the theater's fund-raising efforts could be so dramatically increased that the system would pay for itself.

Originally, fund-raising for the theater—a direct mail campaign conducted annually by a dozen or more volunteers—was a manual operation. As the theater grew in size, that manual system was augmented by a computer service bureau, but the service was costly and the response was not as large as Phyllis had anticipated. Personalized word-processed letters cost a dollar each, so on small donations the theater actually lost money.

The high priority of donor record processing influenced the theater's hardware and software selection. Basic accounting was the second priority, and plans were laid to link other financial subsystems to the computer if the basic accounting functions were computerized successfully.

The small business system the theater eventually installed gave three offices access to files and provided each office with its own printer. The business office used the computer system primarily for raising funds, maintaining donor records, and keeping personnel files. The box office used the system for keeping track of ticket reservations and handling publicity and press releases. The scene and costume shops computerized various files including equipment maintenance schedules, purchasing plans, scenery, and costume inventory.

Phyllis is more than pleased with the system. Data processing of donor and gift records has been merged with word-processed appeal letters. Phyllis uses the system to send 10,000 to 15,000 fund-raising appeals each year. When the donations come in, she can immediately find out which donors gave more than $25 at a time and which ones have just increased their donations. Different thank-you letters according to donation size are sent to donors. Within one week a donor receives a typed thank-you letter that includes his or her name and the amount of the donation.

Installing the in-house computer system was extremely beneficial for the theater, and the board of directors did not regret its decision. Increasingly, small businesses and nonprofit organizations are turning to computer systems to help them manage their information. Accurate analysis of an organization's needs and the design of a system to meet those needs can play an important role in the success of an organization. The following chapter discusses system analysis and design.

INTRODUCTION

Every organization has specific needs that must be met by its computer system. The types of information that can be provided by a system are as diverse as the organizations that use the information. Since no two organizations are exactly alike, their computer systems are also different. Large hospitals, corporations, universities, or research laboratories usually need mainframe computers to handle their information needs. But a microcomputer with various peripheral devices might easily handle the data-processing requirements for a small retail store, restaurant, or church.

The process of choosing a computer system to meet the specific needs of an organization is not a simple task. Luckily, certain methods have been developed to help analysts design the right computer system for an organization. This chapter covers five stages of system development: system analysis, system design, programming, implementation, and audit and review. Also covered are management information systems and decision support systems, two related information systems geared toward providing managers with the information they use to make decisions.

SYSTEM THEORY

Information is data that has been processed and is useful for decision making. A manager or decision maker uses information to increase knowledge and reduce uncertainty. Most modern organizations could not function without information. An information system, therefore, is designed to transform data into information and make it available to decision makers in a timely fashion. System analysis and design is an approach used to develop and maintain information systems.

Definition of a System

A **system** is a group of related elements that work together toward a common goal. One example of a system is a single cell in a human body; each molecule in the cell performs important functions, and all the molecules work together in order for the cell to survive.

A system is made up of inputs, processes, and outputs. **Inputs** enter the system from the surrounding environment. For the cell, the inputs might be

System A group of related elements that work together toward a common goal.

Feedback A check within a system to see whether predetermined goals are being met.

oxygen and nutrients. These inputs are transformed by some **process** into outputs. The cell processes its inputs into energy and wastes. Most of the **outputs** leave the system, going back to the environment; but some may stay within the system. The energy output from cell processing is used for survival. Wastes are returned to the environment (see Figure 13–1).

In order for a system to function properly, it must be provided with **feedback.** Feedback can be either internal or external. That is, information can flow within the system or between the system and the environment. The purpose of feedback is to inform the system whether predetermined standards and goals are being met. The feedback for a cell would be the information it needs to survive. If the cell does not have enough oxygen or nutrients to survive, it tries to get more. If an attack from the outside environment threatens its survival, the cell may alter its chemistry by taking in more oxygen or nutrients to try to deter the threat. In system theory, a system's primary goal is survival, and feedback is one means used by the system to survive.

A System's Interaction with Other Systems

The body contains many different types of cells—blood cells, nerve cells, lung cells, and so on. Each of these groups can be thought of as a system. Blood cells are part of the circulatory system, nerve cells are part of the nervous system, lung cells are part of the respiratory system. Together, these systems form a still larger system called the human body. Each of the systems can be viewed in terms of its inputs, processes, outputs, and feedback mechanisms.

The boundaries between systems are not always easy to define. Neither are the elements of a system that might stand alone as systems in themselves. The determination depends on the level or scope at which one views the system.

Figure 13–1
A Cell as a System

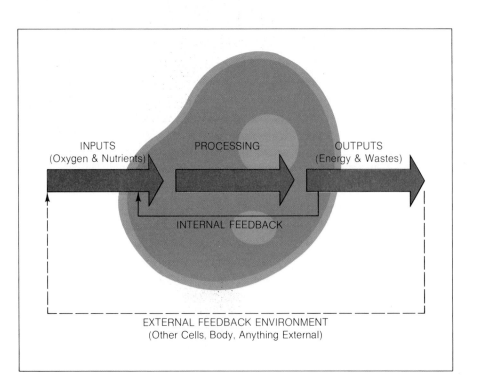

INPUTS
(Oxygen & Nutrients)

PROCESSING

OUTPUTS
(Energy & Wastes)

INTERNAL FEEDBACK

EXTERNAL FEEDBACK ENVIRONMENT
(Other Cells, Body, Anything External)

A general practitioner views the whole body as the system; an ophthalmologist views the eye as the system.

The fact that one system may belong to another, larger system is an important concept in system theory. It implies the existence of interaction among systems. All these concepts are put to good use when system theory is used to view the organization.

The Organization as a System

The concepts of system theory can also be applied to an organization. It has a group of related elements (departments and employees) working together toward a common goal (survival, growth, or profit). Figure 13–2 shows a state university as a system within a larger system, the public community. The university uses inputs from the surrounding environment and transforms them into useful outputs.

As shown in Figure 13–2, the university is affected by external environmental factors beyond its control. The economy; federal, state, and local legislation; and competition from other universities are examples of such external factors. Internal factors affecting the university include the quality of its faculty and students, the relationships between administrators, departmental relations, and internal communication channels. An analysis of the university's information needs must take into account both the internal and external environmental factors.

Each department within the university is also a system. The goal of each department is to educate students according to certain set standards. But each department must interact with other departments. For example, the history department must obtain enrollment and eligibility information from the registration department; the registration department must find out from the bursar's office which students have not paid their tuition.

Figure 13–2
The University as an Interacting System

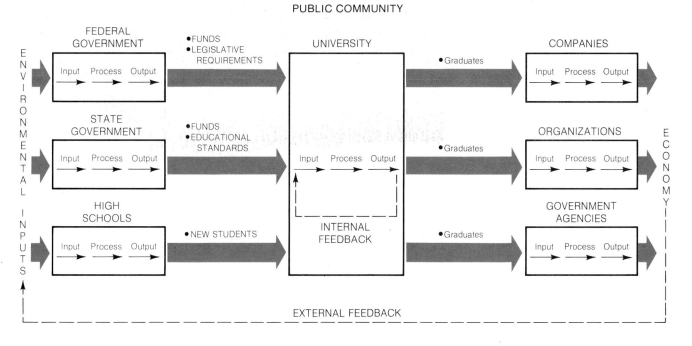

External information, such as the number of high school graduates, SAT scores, and new tax laws affecting education, comes from state agencies. Information about present and future economic conditions that will affect university enrollments is supplied by external sources such as federal agencies. A sampling of the many interactions is shown in Figure 13–3.

Analyzing an Organization Using the System Approach

An organization is too complex to study directly. Therefore, a system analyst needs tools to help analyze the complex flow of information that affects the system. In order to understand the needs of the entire organization, the analyst must step back and view the organization as a whole before focusing on the needs of each department.

The system approach provides the analyst with a way to evaluate and understand information systems by making them less complex. It is a model that attempts to mirror the actual events in an organization while reducing the complexity of the activities involved in those events. The system model highlights only the important relationships, patterns, and flows of information. Instead of defining each task performed in an organization, the model provides a general picture of the organization's functions.

When the system approach is applied to problem solving within an organization, the organization is viewed as an integrated whole, rather than as a group of independent functional areas. The assumption is that each part of an organization contributes to the overall character of the organization. If one part were removed or changed, the character of the whole organization would be altered.

Figure 13–3
The Internal and External Interactions of a University

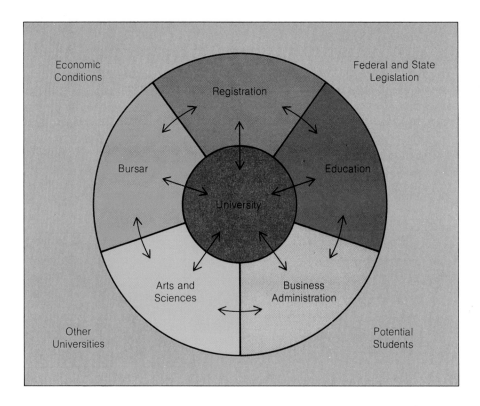

Traditionally, problem solving involved breaking an organization into parts for separate analysis. This method of problem solving involved viewing the organization from the bottom up. Interactions between parts were often overlooked. The system approach views the organization from the top down and emphasizes the importance of understanding how the organization functions as a whole, including the relationships, patterns, and information flows.

An information system is designed to meet the needs of decision makers. Some information systems are computerized; others are manual. Both must provide management with the information it needs, or they will become unused and outdated. However, even when there are reasons to review an existing system, this does not necessarily mean that a new system should be developed. Developing a new information system to replace another may cost hundreds or even millions of dollars. It is a complex and time-consuming process. The decision to develop a new system should be based on need. Developing a new system involves the following steps: analysis, design, programming, implementation, and audit and review (see Figure 13–4).

SYSTEM ANALYSIS

The first step of system analysis is to formulate a statement of overall objectives, or goals, of the system. Identifying these objectives is essential to finding out

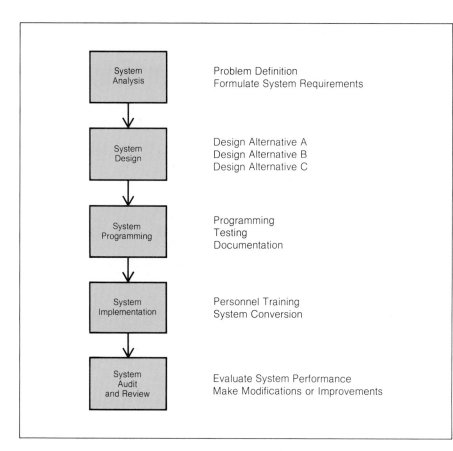

Figure 13–4
The Stages of System Development

what information the system will require. The next step is to decide how extensive the analysis needs to be to achieve the objectives.

By viewing the organization from the top down, the analyst determines the level at which the analysis should be conducted (see Figure 13–5). The persons requesting the system study and the analyst then determine the proper focus of the analysis. A well-designed focus includes the following:

- A clear and concise statement of the problem or reason for the system analysis.
- A statement clearly defining the level of the system analysis and its objectives.
- An identification of the information that must be collected and the potential sources of this information.
- A preliminary schedule for conducting the analysis.

Data Gathering

After the focus has been clearly defined, the analyst must gather data about the system. The type and amount of data gathered depend on the scope and goals of the system analysis. Data can be supplied by internal and external sources.

Internal Sources

Four common sources of internal information are interviews, system flowcharts, questionnaires, and formal reports.

Interviews. Personal interviews can be a very important source of data. Preliminary interviews provide data about current operations and procedures and the users' views of what the system should do. The analyst must be diplomatic yet probing. Often the analyst discovers informal information in the form of reports, personal notes, and phone numbers that indicate how the current information system really works. Unless interviews are conducted, these "extras" might never appear. Follow-up interviews and discussion sessions provide checkpoints to verify the accuracy and completeness of the procedures and documentation within the system.

System Flowcharts. After gathering the documents that provide the system input, the processing steps needed are illustrated in system flowcharts. The devices and files used, the resulting output, and the departments that use the output are identified. (System flowcharts are discussed in detail later in this chapter.)

Questionnaires. Questionnaires are used to collect more details about system operations. By keying questions to specific steps in a system chart, the analyst can obtain detailed data on the volume of input and output. The frequency of processing, the time required for various processing steps, and the personnel and equipment used can also be identified.

Questionnaires are useful only if they are properly constructed. Further, the analyst must be careful to make note of who filled out a particular questionnaire; a manager might respond differently from an employee. The analyst must also be sure to follow up if a questionnaire is not returned (see Figure 13–6).

Figure 13–5
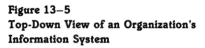
Top-Down View of an Organization's Information System

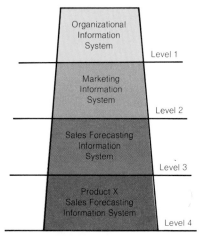

Figure 13-6
Sample Questionnaire

```
TITLE       Report Analysis—Batch Payroll Report
NUMBER      378-Batch-Pay
PURPOSE     To determine demand for and timing of Batch Payroll Report

1. Do you currently receive, or would you like to receive, the Payroll Report?
   ☐Yes     If yes, please answer the remaining questions.
   ☐No      If no, please go to the end of the questionnaire.

2. How often would you like to receive the Payroll Report?
   ☐Weekly              ☐Quarterly              ☐Annually
   ☐Monthly             ☐Semiannually

3. What would you be using the report for?
   ☐Department budgeting of payroll expenses
   ☐General information only
   ☐Other _____

4. How do you rank this report in relation to other reports you receive?
   ☐Above average       ☐Average                ☐Below average

5. Do you require more payroll information than is contained on the report?
   ☐Yes                 ☐No
   If yes, please list the additional information you require:



6. Please indicate any other information that would be useful in revising or updating
   the Payroll Report.

   _____

   _____

                                   Thank you for your cooperation.

Signed _____ Title _____

Department _____ Date _____
```

Formal Reports. Formal reports, the major outputs of many systems, should be studied carefully by the analyst (see Figure 13-7). The processing steps taken to convert data to information are usually apparent from these reports. The number of copies made and who receives them helps identify the flow of information within the organization. How and where a report is stored may indicate the degree of sensitivity and importance of the information it contains. With the advent of inexpensive paper copiers, the task of determining all users of a particular report may be extremely difficult; the ease with which copies can be made is not always an advantage in this case.

External Sources

Systems analysts should (within budgetary constraints) leave no stones unturned during the data-gathering stage. External sources of information can be very helpful. Standard external sources are books, periodicals, brochures, and product specifications from manufacturers. Customers and suppliers are some-

409

Figure 13-7
Sample Formal Report

GB ELECTRIC AND GAS COMPANY
PAYROLL REPORT
NOVEMBER, 1982

12/21/82						PAGE 2

DEPT. NO.	ID	EMPLOYEE	HOURS	GROSS PAY	TAX	NET PAY
1	12345	BUXBAUM, ROBERT	75.0	$ 750.00	$ 60.00	$ 690.00
	23488	COSTELLO, JOSEPH B	82.1	$ 623.63	$ 49.89	$ 573.74

12/21/82						PAGE 3

DEPT. NO.	ID	EMPLOYEE	HOURS	GROSS PAY	TAX	NET PAY
2	24567	ANDERSON, DAVID	80.4	$ 760.86	$ 60.87	$ 699.99
	31578	BREWER, BETTY	43.2	$ 791.85	$ 63.35	$ 728.50

12/21/82						PAGE 4

DEPT. NO.	ID	EMPLOYEE	HOURS	GROSS PAY	TAX	NET PAY
3	15432	CALDWELL, SUSAN	75.9	$ 348.38	$ 13.94	$ 334.44
	16882	CLANCY, BETTY	55.7	$ 426.10	$ 25.57	$ 400.63

12/21/82						PAGE 5

DEPT. NO.	ID	EMPLOYEE	HOURS	GROSS PAY	TAX	NET PAY
4	23451	ALEXANDER, CHARLES	90.2	$ 952.10	$ 95.21	$ 856.89
	32155	BROWN, WALLACE	77.5	$ 792.05	$ 63.36	$ 728.69
	51202	DUNIGAN, HENRY	66.5	$ 954.25	$ 86.63	$ 867.62
	70123	JACKSON, KENNETH	75.9	$ 977.59	$ 97.76	$ 879.83

		TOTAL EMPLOYEES	4
		OVERTIME EMPLOYEES	4
		TOTAL TAX	$ 352.76
		TOTAL NET PAY	$ 3,333.23

12/21/82						PAGE 6

DEPT. NO.	ID	EMPLOYEE	HOURS	GROSS PAY	TAX	NET PAY
5	20988	FOX, WILLIAM	90.0	$1,941.80	$ 233.02	$1,708.78
	31254	HALLECK, FRANCES	120.0	$4,277.20	$ 513.26	$3,763.94
	32611	HEPNER, ELMER	110.4	$ 753.80	$ 60.29	$ 693.51
	62319	HORNE, ALBERT	92.0	$ 980.00	$ 98.00	$ 882.00
	67822	SAWYER, DAVID	80.0	$ 644.00	$ 26.64	$ 617.36
	78200	SIPE, CHARLES	75.0	$1,181.25	$ 141.75	$1,039.50
	89212	SMITH, JERRY	60.0	$ 539.40	$ 32.36	$ 507.04

		TOTAL EMPLOYEES	7
		OVERTIME EMPLOYEES	4
		TOTAL TAX	$ 1,105.32
		TOTAL NET PAY	$ 9,011.93

REPORT TOTALS

		TOTAL EMPLOYEES	39
		OVERTIME EMPLOYEES	18
		TOTAL TAX	$ 4,080.61
		TOTAL NET PAY	$32,722.01

times good sources. For example, analyzing a billing system might involve asking customers what information they would like to see on an invoice. Analysts should also attempt to contact other companies that have developed or implemented similar information systems.

Data Analysis

After data has been collected, it must be organized and integrated to be seen in proper perspective. Whereas the focus during data collection is on *what* is being done, the focus during data analysis is on *why* certain operations and procedures are being used. The analyst looks for ways to improve these operations.

An analysis should be conducted to determine management's information needs and what data will be required to meet those needs. These needs will be important when input/output requirements are being determined.

Determining information needs requires the analyst to use a system approach. In a magnetic-tape-oriented, file-processing environment, creating and manipulating files is relatively easy. But many companies are rapidly moving into data-base environments. Creating and maintaining an effective data base requires that data items be independent. This means that the data must be analyzed and organized from an organizationwide perspective. A file can no longer be created for use by a single department; data must be accessible to many other departments as well. The goal is to relate data items properly, ignoring departmental boundaries.

Two of the techniques used to analyze data are grid charts and system flowcharts. These techniques are explained below. There are other methods used to analyze gathered data and analysts should use whatever tools and techniques they find useful.

Grid Charts

The **grid chart** is used to summarize the relationships among the components of a system. Figure 13–8 is a grid chart indicating which departments use which documents in an order-writing, billing, and inventory-control system.

Grid chart A chart used in system analysis to summarize the relationships between the components of a system.

Figure 13–8
Grid Chart

Document \ Department	Order Writing	Shipping	Billing	Inventory	Marketing	Accounts Receivable
Sales Order	X				X	
Shipping Order	X	X	X	X		
Invoice			X		X	X
Credit Authorization					X	X
Monthly Report					X	X

System flowchart A group of symbols that represents the general information flow.

System Flowcharts

As was discussed in Chapter 10, program flowcharts are concerned with operations on data. They do not indicate the form of input (for example, keyboard, cards, or tape) or the form of output (for example, display, document, disk, or tape); they simply use a general symbol ($\boxed{}$) for all forms of input and output.

In contrast, **system flowcharts** emphasize the flow of data through the entire data-processing system, without describing details of internal computer operations. A system flowchart represents the interrelationships among the physical system elements.

The general input/output symbol used in program flowcharting is not specific enough for system flowcharting. A variety of specialized input/output symbols are needed to identify the wide variety of media used in input/output activities. The symbols are miniature outlines of the actual media (see Figure 13–9). Similarly, specialized process symbols are used instead of the general process symbol ($\boxed{}$) to represent specific processing operations (see Figure 13–10).

The difference in emphasis in the two forms of flowcharting is due to the difference in the purposes they serve. A program flowchart aids the programmer by providing details necessary for coding the program. In contrast, system flowcharts are designed to represent the general information flow; often one process symbol is used to represent many operations.

Figure 13–11 is a sample system flowchart that shows the updating of an inventory master file. The **online storage symbol** ($\boxed{}$) indicates that the file is kept on an online external storage medium such as disk or tape. The file is used to keep track of the raw materials and finished products of the organization. How current this information is depends on how often the master file is updated. If it is updated as soon as a product is shipped or a raw material supply is depleted, the information it provides is up-to-date. Usually, however, the updating is done on a periodic basis. All changes that occur during a specific time period are batched and processed together to update the inventory master file. Reports from the shipping, receiving, and production departments are collected. The data from this set of documents is entered into the computer via a CRT. The data entered on the CRT and the inventory master file then serve as input for the updating process.

The flowchart in Figure 13–11 outlines the steps in this process. In addition to updating the inventory master file, the system generates three reports, giving management information about inventory, order shipments, and production. Notice that in the system flowchart, one process symbol encompasses the entire updating process. A program flowchart must be created to detail the specific operations to be performed within this process.

Preparing the System Analysis Report

System analysis report A report completed after the system analysis phase has been completed.

After collecting and analyzing the data, the system analyst must communicate the findings to management. The **system analysis report** should include the following items:

- A restatement of the scope and objectives of the system analysis.
- An explanation of the present system, the procedures used, and any problems identified.
- A statement of all constraints on the present system and any assumptions made by the analyst during this phase.

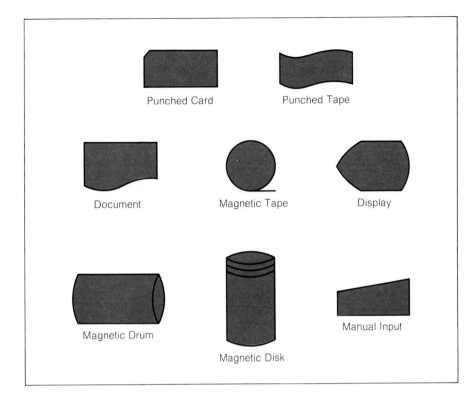

Figure 13–9
Specialized Input/Output Symbols
for System Flowcharting

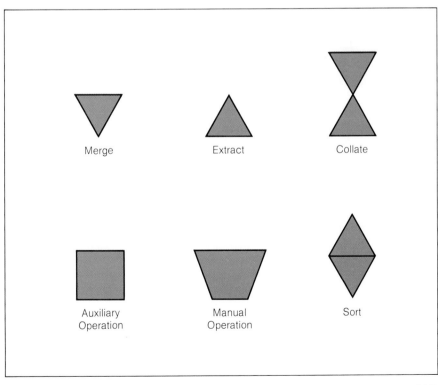

Figure 13–10
Specialized Process Symbols for
System Flowcharting

Figure 13–11
Sample System Flowchart

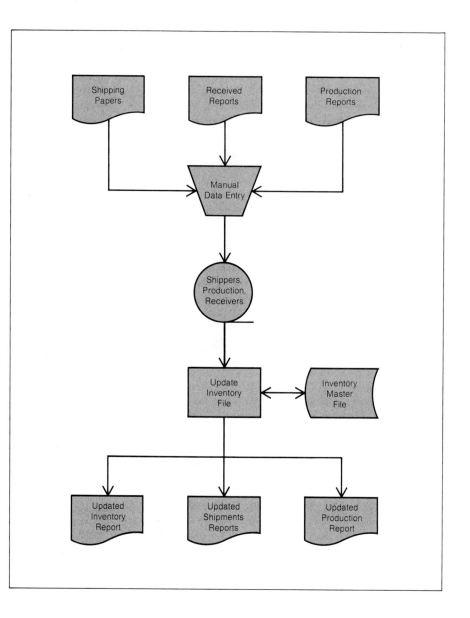

- A preliminary report of alternatives that currently seem feasible.
- An estimate of the resources and capital required either to modify the present system or to design a new one. This estimate should include costs of a feasibility study.

Only if management approves this report can the systems analyst proceed to the detailed system design.

SYSTEM DESIGN

After reviewing the system analysis report, if management decides to continue the project, the system design stage begins. Designing an information system demands a great deal of creativity and planning. It is also very costly and time-consuming. In system analysis, the analyst focused on what the current system

414

does and on what it should be doing according to the requirements discovered in the analysis. In the design phase, the analyst changes focus and concentrates on how a system can be developed to meet the information requirements.

Several steps are useful during the design phase of system development:

- Reviewing goals and objectives
- Developing system model
- Evaluating organizational constraints
- Developing alternative designs
- Performing feasibility analysis
- Performing cost/benefit analysis
- Preparing system design report

Reviewing Goals and Objectives

The system objectives that were identified during system analysis must be reviewed, since any system design offered must meet them. To maintain a broad approach and allow for flexibility in the system design, the analyst may restate the users' information requirements so that they reflect the needs of the majority of users. For example, the finance department may want a report of customers who have failed to make payments. Since this department is only one subsystem in a larger accounts receivable system, the analyst may restate the objective as (1) to maintain an accurate and timely record of the amounts owed by customers, and (2) to provide controls to detect delinquent accounts and report them as they occur.

The analyst should also try to determine any trends that may alter the objectives and goals of the organization in the future. A system must be flexible enough to allow for a certain amount of change. For instance, the system for an electric company should be flexible enough to respond to changes caused by new government regulations.

Developing a System Model

The analyst next develops a symbolic model of the system's major components and their interactions. Flowcharts or some other type of diagram can be used to represent the model.

In reviewing the model, the analyst should discover any important subsystems that have been left out. Are the major interactions among subsystems shown? Are the inputs, processes, and outputs appropriately identified? Does the model provide for appropriate feedback to each of the subsystems?

Once a satisfactory system model has been developed, the analyst has an appropriate tool for evaluating alternative designs. Each alternative can be evaluated on the basis of how well it matches the requirements of the model. Figure 13–12 is an example of a conceptual model of an accounts receivable system.

Evaluating Organization Constraints

No organization has unlimited resources; most have limitations on financial budgets, personnel, and computer facilities as well as time constraints for system development. The system analyst must recognize the constraints on system design imposed by the availability of resources.

Figure 13–12
Model of an Accounts Receivable
System

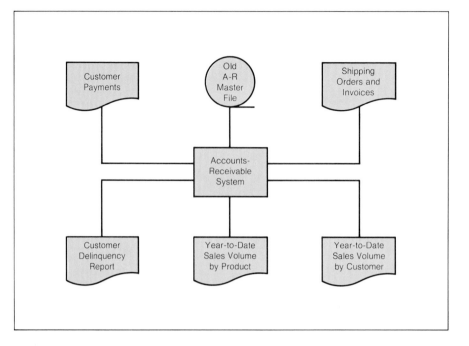

Few organizations request the optimal design for their information require-ments. Businesses are profit-seeking organizations. Only in an extremely rare case does an organization request an all-out system development with no cost constraints. (Competition or technological developments, for example, may warrant such a decision.)

The structure of an organization will also affect the designs developed by an analyst. A highly centralized organization will not be suited to distributed pro-cessing. Likewise, an organization with autonomous decision centers in many geographic locations will not function well with a centralized information system.

Human factors are other organizational constraints that must be evaluated during the system design phase. In particular, consideration must be given to the users of the system. A proposed system design must be **user friendly.** In other words, the system must be designed not only to meet the needs of the user, but also to meet those needs through an easy-to-use, understandable design.

A **menu-driven** system design, for example, guides the user through the computerized system, helping him or her to attain the needed information. A menu-driven system displays to the user "menus" explaining available choices or actions (see Figure 13–13). With the menu-driven system, the user can be guided through the process of using the system.

Technological advances such as touch-sensitive screens, the mouse, and voice recognition/voice synthesizer systems may also help make a system design more compatible with its human users. The human factors of system design, in many cases, are the most important.

Developing Alternative Designs

There is more than one way to design an information system, and system analysts are generally required to develop more than one design alternative.

User friendly A system design that is easy to use and understand.

Menu-driven A system design that guides the user through the computerized system by displaying menus that explain available choices or actions.

416

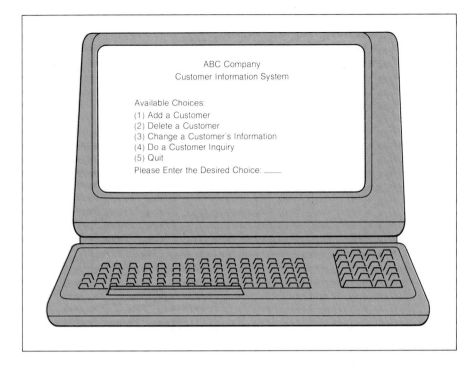

Figure 13–13
Sample Menu

ABC Company
Customer Information System

Available Choices:
(1) Add a Customer
(2) Delete a Customer
(3) Change a Customer's Information
(4) Do a Customer Inquiry
(5) Quit
Please Enter the Desired Choice: _____

This requirement is useful because it forces the analyst to be creative. By designing several possible systems, the analyst may discover valuable parts in each that can be integrated into an entirely new system. The alternative systems may also be designed in ascending order of complexity and cost; since management often desires alternatives from which to choose, designing alternative systems in this fashion is quite appropriate.

The analyst must work with a number of elements in designing alternative systems. Computerized information systems have many components. Inputs, outputs, hardware, software, files, data bases, clerical procedures, and users interact in hundreds of different ways. Processing requirements may also differ in each alternative. For example, one may require batch processing and sequential organization of files; another may provide random-access processing using direct-access storage and online terminals. The data collection, processing, storage, retrieval, and update procedures vary, depending on the alternative selected.

Each alternative developed by the analyst must be technically feasible. In some instances, analysts try to design at least one noncomputerized alternative. Although this may be difficult, it often reveals unique methods of information processing that the analyst has not considered when developing the computerized systems.

Performing Feasibility Analysis

While developing each alternative system, the analyst must keep asking the question, "Is this feasible?" A system design that requires a special operating staff will not be feasible unless the organization is willing to hire the necessary staff. Other designs may require the addition of special hardware. The analyst must decide whether to present the design to management even though the

417

hardware would have to be added. Many times, the analyst must use personal judgment and experience to eliminate infeasible alternatives.

Other factors that must be considered are the users' educational backgrounds and positions within the organization, legal constraints, and time. A system must be ready when it is needed, or it is no good at all. Probably the most common constraint is the organization's budget. The cost of each system design alternative should be within the financial constraints set by management.

Performing Cost/Benefit Analysis

Cost/benefit analysis is a procedure commonly used in business decision making. A firm has limited financial resources. They must be allocated to projects that appear to offer the greatest return on the costs of initial development. In order for cost/benefit analysis to be performed, both costs and benefits must be identified. Costs are easier to determine than benefits. Some benefits are tangible (or realizable as cash savings). Others are intangible (not necessarily giving rise to obvious reduction in costs). Naturally, intangible benefits are especially difficult to determine. How does one estimate the benefit from an improved information system that provides better customer service?

The costs of an alternative include direct costs like the initial investment required for materials and equipment; setup costs required to create computer files from old manual systems, to install data-processing equipment, and to hire personnel; and educational costs to educate the users of the new system. Ongoing expenses resulting from employee salaries, computer operations, insurance, taxes, and rent must also be identified.

Which design alternative management selects often depends on the results of cost/benefit analysis. The analyst must ensure that a comprehensive cost/benefit study has been performed on all alternatives.

Preparing the System Design Report

System design report A report given to top management after the system design phase that explains how various designs will satisfy the information requirements.

Once the analyst has completed all the steps described above, he or she must prepare a report to communicate findings to management. The **system design report** should explain in general terms how the various designs will satisfy the information requirements determined in the analysis phase. The report should also review the information requirements uncovered in the system analysis, explain in both flowchart and narrative form the proposed designs, detail the corporate resources required to implement each alternative, and make a recommendation.

Each of the alternatives should be explained in an easy-to-understand narrative form that avoids technical jargon. The purpose of the design report is to communicate; using words unfamiliar to the reader will interfere with this communication process. Flowcharts of each alternative should be provided as well.

From the detailed design work performed on each alternative, the analyst should review the important costs, benefits, and resources required for its implementation. This, more than any other portion of the report, will be carefully scrutinized by those empowered to make a design selection. Their decisions will be based on the projected benefits of each design versus the corporate resources required to implement it.

Finally, the analyst should make a design recommendation. Because of the analyst's familiarity with the current system and each alternative design, he or she is in the best position to suggest the one with the greatest potential for success. If the analyst has thoroughly and objectively analyzed resource costs, potential benefits, and corporate goals, this recommendation is apt to be adopted by management.

After evaluating the system design report, management can do one of three things: approve the recommendation, approve the recommendation with changes (this includes selecting another alternative), or select none of the alternatives. The "do nothing" alternative is always feasible. If the design of the system is approved, the analyst proceeds to implement it.

SYSTEM PROGRAMMING

After the system design has been chosen, the system must be programmed. The analyst and the programming department together will write programs to perform the tasks that meet the needs identified during system analysis and design. Software packages may also be reviewed as an alternative to writing the programs in-house.

To maintain flexibility, each program should be developed as an independent module. Independent modules make the system easy to maintain and change.

Testing

Before the system is actually installed, it must be tested and debugged. Testing occurs at various levels. The lowest level is program testing. Programs are divided into distinct logical modules. Each module is tested to ensure that all input is accounted for, the proper files are updated, and the correct reports are printed. Only after each module has been debugged should the modules be linked together and the complete program tested.

Once all program testing is complete, system testing can proceed. This level of testing involves checking all the application programs that support the system. All clerical procedures used in data collection, data processing, and data storage and retrieval are included in system testing.

Documentation

Until recently, one of the most neglected parts of system development was documentation. Many systems developed in the early 1970s were implemented with sparse documentation. This presented no problems when the systems were first implemented. Over time, however, changes in the organizations and their information requirements necessitated making system and programming changes. At that point the organizations painfully realized the need for extensive system documentation. Understanding programs written five to ten years earlier was often difficult. Changes made to them often caused errors in other programs. Thus, most organizations have begun to require adequate system documentation.

Creating system documentation requires an overview of the purpose of the entire system, its subsystems, and the function of each subsystem. Documentation of subsystems usually includes system flowcharts depicting the major processing flows, the forms and computer files input to the subsystem, and the reports and computer files output from the subsystem. This provides a frame of reference for system maintenance as information needs change.

Program documentation includes explanations of major logical portions of the program. The programmer may construct program flowcharts to allow other programmers to locate areas to be changed and to observe how the changes will affect other programs. File declarations explaining the layouts of data elements on computer files are also included as part of this documentation.

Procedure documentation instructs users how to perform their particular functions in each subsystem. These documents are designed so that users can quickly and easily get the information they need. User documentation is particularly important, since the best-designed system can fail if users perform their functions incorrectly. Procedures must be established to keep user documentation up-to-date with the latest system changes.

SYSTEM IMPLEMENTATION

In the implementation stage of the system methodology, the analyst is able to see the transformation of ideas, flowcharts, and narratives into actual processes, flows, and information. This transition is not performed easily, however. Personnel must be trained to use the new system procedures, and a conversion must be made from the old system to the new one.

Personnel Training

Two groups of people interface with a system. The first group includes the people who develop, operate, and maintain the system. The second group includes the people who use the information generated by the system to support their decision making. Both groups must be aware of their responsibilities regarding the system's operation and of what they can and cannot expect from it. One of the primary responsibilities of the system analyst is to see that education and training are provided to both groups.

The user group includes general management, staff personnel, line managers, and other operating personnel. It may also include the organization's customers and suppliers. These users must be taught the functions they are to perform and what, in turn, the system will do for them.

The personnel who operate the system must be trained to prepare input data, load and unload files on secondary storage devices, handle problems that occur during processing, and so on.

Such education and training can be provided in large group seminars or in smaller tutorial sessions. The latter approach, though fairly costly, is more personal and more appropriate for complex tasks. Another approach, used almost universally, is on-the-job training. As the name implies, the employee learns while actually performing the tasks required.

Personnel training and education are expensive, but they are essential to successful system implementation.

Conversion

The switch from an old system to a new one is referred to as a conversion. Conversion involves not only the changes in the mode of processing data but also the changes in equipment and clerical procedures.

HIGHLIGHT

Don't Blow It!

Cognitive Overload, Inc., has just completed the implementation stage of systems planning; there's a collective sigh of relief. Everything is working fine. But uh-oh!—what are these blips and glitches?

The blips, glitches, and gremlins in computer operations may be due to static electricity. Humans may not feel low-voltage static electricity, but microchips do.

Some common sources of static electricity are waxed, painted, or varnished surfaces; vinyl tile flooring; synthetic or virgin-cotton garments; styrofoam; plastic bags; electrostatic copiers; spray cleaners; and finished wood or plastic covered chairs and desks.

When completing a systems plan, a company may want to include the cost of anti-static floor mats, anti-static agents (available in spray bottles or as towelettes), or ionizers, devices that emit both positive and negative ions, which will "mate" with the charged electrons of opposite polarity and neutralize them. Protecting a system this way is much cheaper than repairing blown microcircuits or recovering lost data.

Several approaches can be used to accomplish the conversion process. The most common ones are explained below:

- *Parallel conversion.* When **parallel conversion** is used, the new system is operated side-by-side with the old one for some period of time. An advantage of this approach is that no data is lost if the new system fails. Also, it gives the user an opportunity to compare and reconcile the outputs from both systems. However, this method can be costly.
- *Pilot conversion.* **Pilot conversion** involves converting only a small portion of the organization to the new system. For example, a new system may be implemented in one department. This approach minimizes the risk to the organization as a whole, in case unforeseen problems occur, and enables the organization to identify problems and correct them before implementing the system throughout the organization. A disadvantage of this method is that the total conversion process usually takes a long time.
- *Phased conversion.* With **phased conversion,** the old system is gradually replaced by the new one over a period of time. The difference between this method and pilot conversion is that in phased conversion only one part of the new system is implemented at a time. For example, first the system's inventory control might be implemented. When it is running as planned, payroll could be implemented. In this way, each part of the system must be working before implementation of the next part is attempted. Thus, the organization can adapt to the new system gradually over an extended period while the old system is gradually being phased out. One drawback is that

Parallel conversion A system implementation approach in which the new system is operated side-by-side with the old one.

Pilot conversion A system implementation approach in which the new system is implemented in only one part of the organization at a time.

Phased conversion A system implementation approach in which parts of the new system are implemented throughout the organization one at a time.

New IRS System Converts Into Giant Headache

The Internal Revenue Service expected its new $131 million Sperry-Univac computer system to breeze through the 100 million 1984 tax returns that would arrive before April 15, 1985. But one problem after another turned the new system into a giant headache for IRS officials, not to mention an inconvenience for taxpayers expecting to see their refund checks in the mail early in the year.

The saga began in January 1980, when the IRS decided to take bids to replace its old Honeywell and Control Data computers. The contract was awarded to Sperry 18 months later. The system was supposed to be ready by the summer of 1984. In the meantime, however, the IRS twice changed the specifications on the original order, requiring more sophisticated equipment each time. As a result, the computers were not ready until November 1984, only a few weeks before the first returns began to arrive.

Problems with the hastily installed computers were apparent from the start. Of the 11 Sperry 1100/84 computers installed at IRS processing centers across the country, two had to be sent back because they would not start. In other centers, tape drives continually malfunctioned. Serious problems with some of the programs required operators to start over each time the system crashed.

Software problems also contributed to the last minute implementation of the system. While the hardware was on order, IRS officials decided to rewrite 1,500 programs, converting them from assembly language to COBOL. The conversion was turned over to a team of 300 programmers. When all the pieces involved in processing tax returns were finally assembled and tested in April 1984, processing speed was only half as fast as required. Every available IRS programmer spent the next nine months bringing the processing speed up to the required level. By then, tax returns were already coming in.

Many of these problems could have been prevented if the IRS had kept the old system around until the new system was up and running. According to the assistant commissioner of computers, Thomas Laycock, when the system was not delivered at the scheduled time, they should have waited until the next year to implement the new system. The moral of this implementation story: Never underestimate the value of a backup system.

an interface between the new system and the old system must be developed for use during the conversion process.

Crash conversion/Direct conversion A system implementation approach in which the old system is completely abandoned and the new one implemented at once.

- *Crash conversion.* **Crash (or direct) conversion** takes place all at once. This approach can be used to advantage if the old system is not operational or if the new system is completely different in structure and design. Since the old system is discontinued immediately on implementation of the new one, the organization has nothing to fall back on if problems arise. Because of the high risk involved, this approach requires extreme care in planning and extensive testing of all system components.

SYSTEM AUDIT AND REVIEW

After the conversion process is complete, the analyst must obtain feedback on the system's performance. This can be done by conducting an audit to evaluate the system's performance in terms of the initial objectives established for it. The evaluation should address the following questions:

1. Does the system perform as planned and deliver the anticipated benefits? How do the operating results compare with the initial objectives? If the benefits are below expectation, what can be done to improve the cost/benefit tradeoff?
2. Was the system completed on schedule and with the resources estimated?
3. Is all output from the system used?
4. Have old system procedures been eliminated and new ones implemented?
5. What controls have been established for input, processing, and output of data? Are these controls adequate?
6. Have users been educated about the new system? Is the system accepted by users? Do they have confidence in the reports generated?
7. Is the processing turnaround time satisfactory, or are delays frequent?

All persons involved in developing the system should be aware that a thorough audit will be performed. The anticipated audit acts as a strong incentive; it helps ensure that a good system is designed and delivered on schedule. As a result of the audit or of user requests, some modification or improvements of the new system may be required.

Making Modifications and Improvements

A common belief among system users is that after a system has been installed, nothing more has to be done. On the contrary, all systems must be continually maintained. System maintenance detects and corrects errors, meets new information needs of management, and responds to changes in the environment.

One of the important tasks of the analyst during the system audit is to ensure that all system controls are working correctly. All procedures and programs related to the old system should have been eliminated. Many of the problems that the system analyst handles during system maintenance and follow-up are problems that were identified during the system audit.

A well-planned approach to system maintenance and follow-up is essential to the continued effectiveness of an information system.

Responding to Change

A well-designed information system is flexible and adaptable. Minor changes should be easily accommodated without large amounts of reprogramming. This is one of the reasons structured programming was emphasized in Chapter 10; if each program module is independent, a minor change in one module will not affect the whole system.

No matter how flexible or adaptable a system is, however, major changes become necessary over time. When the system has to be redesigned, the entire system cycle—analysis, design, programming, implementation, and audit and review—must be performed again. Keeping information systems responsive to information needs is a never-ending process.

Concept Summary 13–1 ▪ The Purposes and Steps of System Development Stages

Stage	Purpose	Steps
Analysis	To formulate overall objectives To determine focus of analysis	Gather data from internal and external sources Analyze data Prepare system analysis report
Design	To determine how a system can meet information requirements	Review goals and objectives Develop system model Evaluate organizational constraints Develop alternative designs Perform feasibility analysis Perform cost/benefit analysis Prepare system design report
Programming	To write programs that perform information tasks according to system requirements	Test system programs Document all parts of system
Implementation	To bring the new system into use	Train personnel Switch from old system to new
Audit and review	To obtain feedback on system's performance	Compare actual performance with objectives Detect and correct errors Make changes as necessary

SYSTEM SECURITY

Computer security The technical and administrative safeguards required to protect a computer-based system against physical and nonphysical hazards.

Computer security involves the technical and administrative safeguards required to control access to information and protect a computer-based system (hardware, personnel, and data) against the major hazards to which most computer systems are exposed.

Physical computer systems and data in storage are vulnerable to several hazards—fire, natural disaster, environmental problems, and sabotage.

Physical Threats to Security

▪ *Fire.* Fire is one of the more obvious problems for computer installations that use combustible materials—punched cards, paper, and so on. Further, if a fire gets started, water cannot be used to extinguish it because water can damage magnetic storage media and hardware. Carbon dioxide fire-extinguishing systems could endanger any employees trapped in the computer room. Halon, a nonpoisonous chemical gas, can be used in fire extinguishers, but such extinguishers are costly.

- *Natural disasters.* Many computer centers have been damaged or destroyed by floods, cyclones, hurricanes, and earthquakes. Floods pose a serious threat to the computer hardware and wiring. However, water in the absence of heat will not destroy magnetic tapes unless the tapes are exposed to moisture over an extended period of time. Protection against natural disasters should be considered when the location for the computer center is chosen; for example, the center should not be located in an area prone to flooding.

- *Environmental problems.* Usually, computers are installed in buildings that were not originally planned to accommodate them. This practice can create environmental problems. For example, water and steam pipes may run through a computer room; bursting pipes could cause extensive damage. Pipes on floors above the computer room are also potentially hazardous, so all ceiling holes should be sealed. Data on magnetic media can be destroyed by magnetic fields created by electric motors in the vicinity of the computer room. Other environmental problems include power failures, brownouts (temporary surges or drops in power), and external radiation.

- *Sabotage.* Sabotage represents the greatest physical risk to computer installations. Saboteurs can do great damage to computer centers with little risk of apprehension. For example, magnets can be used to scramble code on tapes, bombs can be planted, and communication lines can be cut. Providing adequate security against such acts of sabotage is extremely difficult and expensive.

Establishing Computer Security

Besides the security measures mentioned earlier, there are several basic measures that all organizations should consider. A computer system is costly to repair or replace, and the data stored in a system are sometimes irreplaceable. When it comes to the security of a computer system, it is better to be safe than sorry.

How, then, can organizations establish computer security? First, computer users must recognize their role in security. If a high-level priority is assigned to security in the company, employees must be made aware of it and of the security measures that are being taken.

Second, many organizations recognize the need for a well-trained security force—a department of security guards who specialize in maintaining data security, conducting system audits, and asking the right kinds of questions on a daily and continuing basis. Computerized records, like handwritten books, should be scrutinized regularly to see that everything is in order.

Third, a company should exercise a great deal of care in the selection and screening of the *people* who will have access to computers, terminals, and computer-stored data. Companies should choose programmers as carefully as they select attorneys or accountants.

Finally, companies must discharge employees who stray beyond legal and ethical boundaries. Whenever these incidents occur, people must be shown that such actions will not be tolerated and that those responsible for security and protection have the intellectual and ethical integrity to follow through with the necessary disciplinary course of action, no matter how difficult it may be.

MANAGEMENT INFORMATION SYSTEMS

An information system can supply many types of information. Originally, information systems provided standard reports, such as accounting statements, sales summaries, payroll reports, and personnel reports. Recently, information systems have been designed to provide information to support decision making. This application is known as a **management information system (MIS).** An MIS is a formal information network using computers to provide management with information it needs to make decisions. The goal of an MIS is to get the correct information to the appropriate manager at the right time. This is not as easy as it might first appear.

Management information system (MIS) A formal network that uses computers to provide management with the information needed to make decisions.

Levels of Management

Three levels of management generally exist within an organization, and managers at each level make different types of decisions that require different types of information. These levels are depicted in Figure 13–14.

- *Top-level management—strategic decision making.* At the top level, activities are future-oriented and involve a great deal of uncertainty. Examples include establishing goals and determining strategies to achieve the goals. These strategies may involve introducing new product lines, determining new markets, acquiring physical facilities, setting financial policies, generating capital, and so forth.
- *Middle-level management—tactical decision making.* The emphasis in middle levels is on activities required to implement the strategies determined at the top level. Thus, most middle-management decision making is tactical. Activities include planning working capital, scheduling production, formulating budgets, making short-term forecasts, and administering personnel. Much of the decision making at this level pertains to control and short-run planning.

Figure 13–14
Levels of Management and the Decisions Made at Each Level

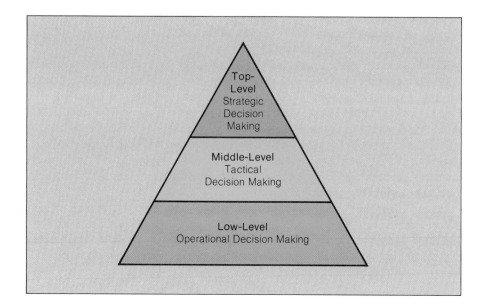

- *Lower-level management—operational decision making.* Members of the lowest level in the management hierarchy (first-line supervisors and foremen) make operating decisions to ensure that specific jobs are done. Activities at this level include maintaining inventory records, preparing sales invoices, determining raw material requirements, shipping orders, and assigning jobs to workers. The major function of lower-level management is controlling company results—keeping them in line with plans and taking corrective actions if necessary.

Managers at all levels must be provided with decision-oriented information. The fact that the nature of decisions differs at the three levels creates a major difficulty for those attempting to develop an MIS: the information system must be tailored to provide appropriate information to all levels (See Figure 13–15).

Figure 13–15
Functional Information Flow.
Information at the lowest level contains the most detail. As information flows upward, details are weeded out; only important facts are presented to top management.

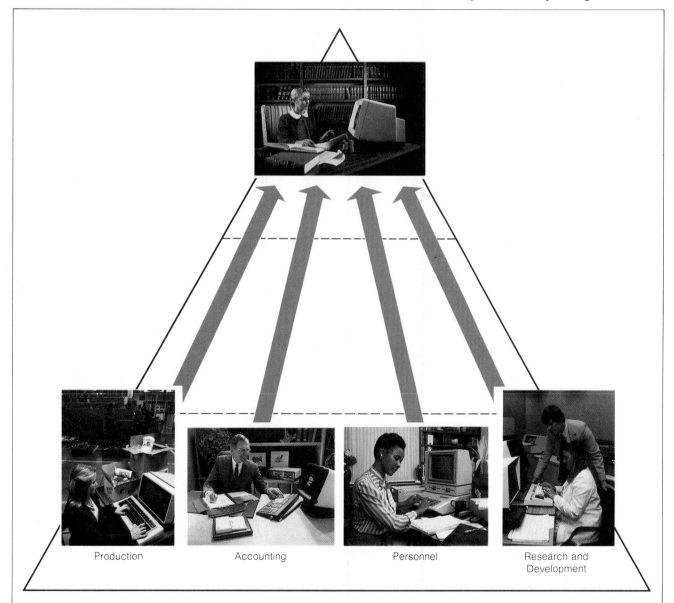

Production   Accounting   Personnel   Research and Development

Decisions made at the lower level are generally routine and well defined. The needs of first-level supervisors can be met by normal administrative data-processing activities such as preparation of financial statements and routine record keeping. Although this level of decision making is fairly basic, it provides the data-processing foundation for the entire organization. If the information system is faulty at this level, the organization faces an immediate crisis.

Tactical decision making is characterized by an intermediate time horizon, a high use of internal information, and significant dependence on rapid processing and retrieval of data. Many middle-level decisions are badly structured. The major focus of tactical decisions is how to make efficient use of organizational resources.

The main problems in MIS design arise when planners attempt to define and meet the information requirements of top-level management. Delineating these information needs clearly is extremely difficult, if not impossible. Most problems are nonrepetitive, have great impact on the organization, and involve a great deal of uncertainty. Most information systems serve the needs of the two lower levels but are not adequately designed to cope with the variety of problems encountered by top management.

Since the information needs at the three levels differ, data has to be structured differently at each level. For routine operating decisions such as payroll preparation and inventory stocking, separate employee and inventory files are adequate. To serve the middle and top levels, the data should be organized to provide inquiry capabilities across functional lines and to handle routine information reports.

Concept Summary 13–2 ▬ Differences Among Decision-Making Levels

Characteristics	Levels of Decision Making		
	Operational	Tactical	Strategic
Time horizon	Daily	Weekly/monthly	Yearly
Degree of structure	High	Moderate	Low
Use of external information	Low	Moderate	Very high
Use of internal information	Very high	High	Moderate/low
Degree of judgment	Low	Moderate	Very high
Information online	Very high	High	Moderate
Level of complexity	Low	Moderate	Very high
Information in real time	High	High	High

Decision-Oriented Reporting

Management information systems typically generate several types of reports, including scheduled listings, exception reports, predictive reports, and demand reports.

Scheduled Listings

Scheduled listings are produced at regular intervals and provide routine information to a wide variety of users. Since they are designed to provide information

HIGHLIGHT

Computers Order Food

In almost 40 percent of the nation's restaurants, there are no waitresses taking orders to the kitchen. Instead, computerized ordering devices are now being used in many restaurants to take orders back to the kitchen. This allows waiters and waitresses to spend more time in the dining room with the customers. The American Cafe in Washington, D.C., is a restaurant using one of the new systems, The Expediter. Systems like this one allow restaurant managers to learn more about their operations. For example, the Expediter told the manager that 94 cups of coffee had been sold by midafternoon and that these sales accounted for 38.12 percent of the beverage sales. With this type of system, a restaurant manager can take stock of a certain item's popularity, adjust menus, restock inventory, and analyze sales accordingly. Because eight out of ten new restaurants now fail, restaurant managers will probably find computers a helpful way to improve cost control.

The designer of The Expediter, Richard W. Hayman, foresees robot arms scooping chicken into buckets in fast-food outlets within three years.

to many users, they tend to contain an overabundance of data. Much of it may not be relevant to a particular user. Such listings constitute most of the output of current computer-based information systems.

Exception Reports

Exception reports are action-oriented management reports. The performance of an organization system is monitored, and any deviation from expected results triggers the generation of a report. Such reports can also be produced during routine batch processing. Exception reports are useful because they ignore all normal events and focus management's attention on abnormal situations that require special handling.

Predictive Reports

Predictive reports are used for planning. Future results are projected on the basis of decision models. Such models can be very simple or highly complex. Their usefulness depends on how well they can predict future events. Management can manipulate the variables included in a model to get responses to "what if" kinds of queries. Thus, such models are suited to tactical and strategic decision making.

Demand Reports

Demand reports are produced only on request. Since they are not required on a continuing basis, they are often requested and displayed through online

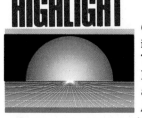 **Computers in the Leisure Industry**

Computer systems have invaded the leisure industry in a big way. A system at the Harry S. Truman Sports Complex in Kansas City, Missouri, monitors and regulates virtually every aspect of commercial activity at both Royals and Arrowhead stadiums. The system tells management, among other things, which concession stands are selling the most, what the precise state of the inventory is at any time in the supply warehouse the two stadiums share, and where cash shortages are. A particular benefit of the system is its ability to handle the facility's unionized concession workers' complicated payroll, which is subject to such variables as holiday pay rates, overtime rates, shift differentials, and bonuses. The computer's capacity to tie all the income and expenses together into a financial profile permits management to get an instantaneous summary of each event booked into the complex.

terminals. The MIS must have an extensive and appropriately structured data base if it is to provide responses to unanticipated queries (recall Chapter 6). No data base can provide everything, but the data base of a well-designed MIS should include data that may be needed to respond to such user inquiries. Providing demand reporting can be expensive, but it permits decision makers to obtain relevant and specific information when they need it.

Management and MIS

Although an MIS can help management make decisions, it cannot guarantee the decisions will be successful. One problem that frequently arises is determining what information is needed by management. To many, decision making is an individual art. Experience, intuition, and chance affect the decision-making process. These inputs are all but impossible to quantify. In designing a system, the analyst relies on the user to determine information requirements. Frequently lacking precise ideas of what they need, managers request everything the computer can provide. The result is an overload of information. Instead of helping the manager, this information overload creates another problem: how to distinguish what is relevant from what is irrelevant.

Structured Design Methodology

As the pace of technological innovation accelerates, data-processing departments must try, often in vain, to keep up. Software development is far behind existing technology, because software development is extremely labor-intensive. Thus, data-processing departments today face a productivity problem: they must obtain greater software development for each dollar invested. The basic ways of increasing productivity are: (1) to automate the software development process; (2) to require employees to work harder, or longer, or both; or (3) to change the way things are done. Structured design attempts to achieve greater productivity by focusing on the third method.

Top-Down Design

Top-down design is a structured approach to system design similar to the top-down design in structured programming (see Chapter 10). It attempts to simplify a system by breaking it down into logical functions, or modules. These, in turn, are further divided. The system is first defined in terms of the functions it must perform. Each of these functions is then translated into a module. The correct system design may require several of these modules to perform all the required tasks.

In top-down design, the most general level of organization is the main module; this overall view of the organization is most critical to the success of the system design. Modules at this level contain only broad descriptions of functions in the system. These functions are further broken down into lower-level modules that contain more detail about the specific steps to be performed. Depending on the complexity of the system, several levels of modules may be required, with the lowest-level modules containing the greatest amount of detail.

The modules of the system design are related to each other in a hierarchical manner. These relationships can be depicted graphically in a structure chart. Figure 13–16 shows a portion of such a chart for the application process at a

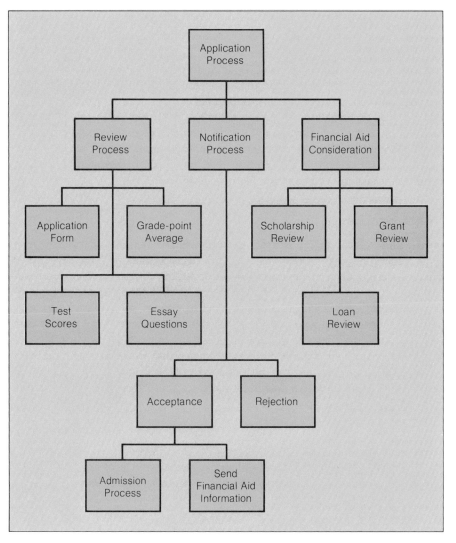

Figure 13–16
Structure Chart for the Application Process at a University

university. Using top-down design, the application process is broken down into its main modules: reviewing the applications, notifying applicants, and considering applicants for financial aid. Each of these functions can be broken down into more specific tasks. For example, the review process consists of checking the application form, obtaining transcripts to verify the grade-point average, obtaining official SAT or ACT scores, and reading the essays submitted by the applicant. These tasks may be broken down even further, if necessary.

Design Alternatives

The development of an MIS is an integrated approach to organizing a company's activities. The company's MIS must be structured in a way that will allow it to realize the full benefits of integration. When considering alternative organizational structures, the analyst faces virtually unlimited possibilities. This section describes four basic design structures: centralized, hierarchical, distributed, and decentralized. These structures should be viewed as checkpoints along a continuous range of design alternatives rather than as separate, mutually exclusive options. For example, a system design may incorporate characteristics from both the distributed system and the decentralized system.

Centralized Design

Centralized design An information structure in which a separate department is used to provide data-processing facilities for the entire organization.

Centralized design is the most traditional design approach. It involves the centralization of computer power. A separate electronic data-processing (EDP) department is set up to provide data-processing facilities for the organization. This department's personnel, like other staff personnel, support the operating units of the organization. All program development, as well as all equipment acquisition, is controlled by the EDP group. Standard regulations and procedures are employed. Distant units use the centralized equipment by a remote access communication network. A common data base exists, permitting authorized users to access information (see Figure 13–17a).

Hierarchical Design

Hierarchical design An information structure in which each level within an organization has necessary computer power.

When **hierarchical design** is used, the organization consists of multiple levels with varying degrees of responsibility and decision-making authority. In hierarchical design, each management level is given the computer power necessary to support its task objectives. At the lowest level, limited support is required, because the work is considered technical in nature. Middle-level support is more extensive, because managerial decisions at this level require more complicated analysis (hence, more information processing). Finally, top-level executives require little detailed information since they work with general issues requiring information that can be obtained only with greater processing and storage capabilities. An example of this design approach is shown in Figure 13–17b.

Distributed Design

Distributed design An information structure in which independent operating units have data-processing facilities but there is central control and coordination of computer resources.

The **distributed design** approach identifies the existence of independent operating units but recognizes the benefits of central coordination and control.

The organization is broken into the smallest activity centers requiring computer support. These centers may be based on organizational structure, geographical location, functional operations, or a combination of these factors. Hardware (and often people) are placed within these activity centers to support their tasks. Total organizationwide control is often evidenced by the existence of standardized classes of hardware, common data bases, and coordinated system development. The distributed computer sites may or may not share data elements, workloads, and resources, depending on whether they are in communication with each other. An example of the distributed design approach is given in Figure 13–17c.

Decentralized Design

In a **decentralized design,** authority and responsibility for computer support are placed in relatively autonomous organizational operating units. These units usually parallel the management decision-making structure. Normally, no central control point exists; the authority for computer operations goes directly to the managers in charge of the operating units. Since there is no central control, each unit is free to acquire hardware, develop software, and make personnel decisions independently. Responsiveness to user needs is normally high because close working relationships are reinforced by the proximity of the system to its users. Communication among units is limited or nonexistent, thereby ruling out the possibility of common or shared applications. This design approach can only be used where an existing organizational structure supports decentralized management. Further, it is not highly compatible with the MIS concept. An example of the decentralized design approach is shown in Figure 13–17d.

Decentralized design   An information structure in which the authority and responsibility for computer support are placed in autonomous operating units.

DECISION SUPPORT SYSTEMS

Closely related to the MIS is the decision support system. Whereas an MIS supplies managers with information to support structured decisions, a **decision support system (DSS)** provides managers with information to support relatively unstructured decisions. For example, an MIS may provide information about sales trends, changes in productivity from one quarter to the next, or fluctuations in inventory levels. Information such as this tells the manager what has already happened. A DSS, on the other hand, may provide financial planning models or optimal production schedules that information managers can use to determine what *might* happen.

Essentially, a DSS and an MIS do the same thing—they process data to get information that is useful to managers. What then, is the difference between a DSS and an MIS? Some professionals in the information field believe the difference is that an MIS supports only structured or operational decisions whereas a DSS supports unstructured or strategic decisions. The distinction is based on the type of decision supported. Others believe DSSs are merely subsystems of a larger MIS, capable of processing different types of data as a result of technological advances in hardware and software.

Decision support system (DSS)   An information system that provides information used to support unstructured managerial decision making.

Figure 13–17
Sample Design Structures

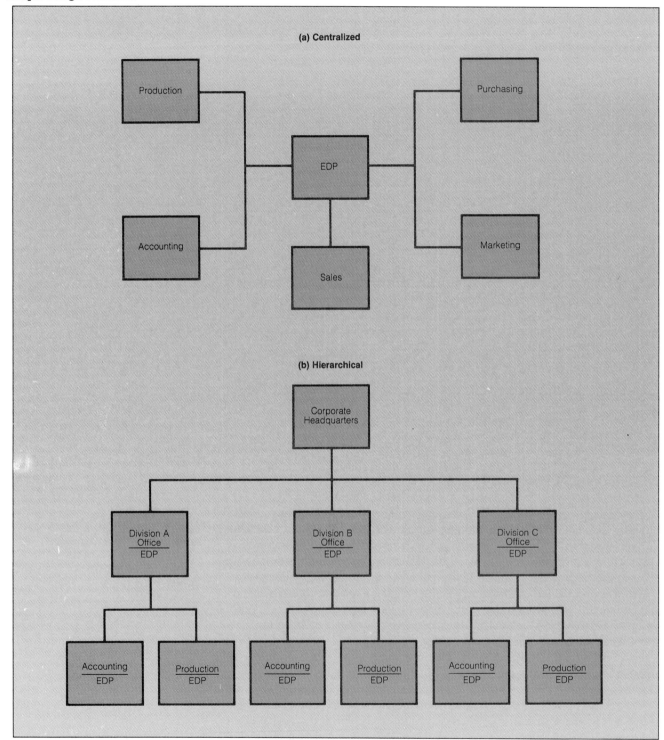

Figure 13-17
Continued

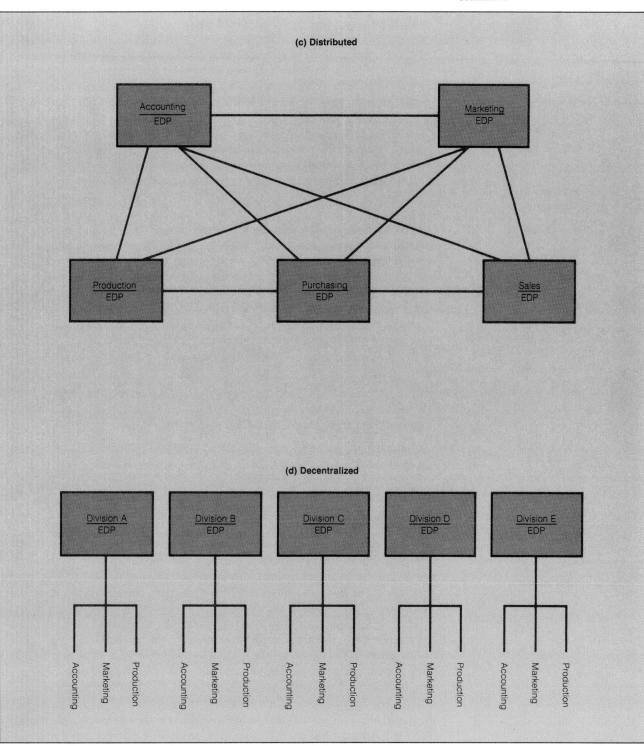

(c) Distributed

(d) Decentralized

435

DSS Turns Computerese into "Computerease"

How can computers become more usable and useful to managers? One way, according to Dr. Gerald Wagner, is through a decision support system (DSS). Wagner, president of Execucom Systems Corp. in Austin, Texas, developed a planning or modeling language called interactive financial planning system (IFPS). He calls his package an "extension of the executive mind" and says it is a "philosophy on how to do things."

DSS and IFPS packages have the ability to model—to express the relationships among variables. A DSS may need a data base to work, but a data base cannot express these very important relationships. The DSS must ask "When some numbers change, how do others?" IFPS specifically calculates how a change in a single variable affects related variables and how one variable must change to produce a desired change in another. It also simulates probability (the Monte Carlo simulation) where the value of one or more variables is unknown.

IFPS is used primarily on mainframe computers, but it is now also available for personal computers. The system helps executives wade through a sea of data and build models with a minimum of fuss while allowing them to use their basic English skills and their own logic.

The Purpose and Scope of a DSS

DSS separates structured (or operational) decision making from unstructured (or strategic) decision making. For example, a purchase order for a certain product may be generated automatically if an inventory stock level falls below a certain quantity. Such a structured decision can be handled easily by a computer.

A decision support system, on the other hand, places more emphasis on semistructured or unstructured decisions. While the computer is used as an analytical aid to decision making, the DSS does not attempt to automate the manager's decision making or to impose solutions. For example, an investment manager must make recommendations to a client concerning the client's investments. The manager's decision is based on stock performance and requires a certain amount of judgment. The computer can be used to aid the decision but cannot make the actual recommendation to the client.

The primary use of computer technology within a DSS has been to speed the processing of the large amounts of data needed for the manager to consider the full effects of a possible decision. It also allows for the consideration of a greater number of alternatives by managers—alternatives that otherwise might not have been considered due to time constraints. But as previously stated, a DSS, and within it the use of computers, must be a normal and comfortable extension of the manager's overall method of problem solving and decision making.

Advocates of DSS, therefore, claim that its emphasis is toward improving

"How much did you say we paid for this Decision Support System?"

the effectiveness and quality of decision making. The purpose of the DSS is not to replace management information systems but to enhance them. Because advances are being made in applying computer technology to the areas of tactical and strategic decision making, the rewards that can be realized are even greater than those that have occurred in the area of operational decision making. Computer applications in the areas of tactical and strategic decision making are a logical step forward in the application of computer technology to management science and a logical addition to, and advancement in, the area of management information systems.

A Model: The Heart of a DSS

As stated in the section on decision-oriented reports, predictive reports use decision models to project future results. Such models are suited to tactical and strategic decision making, which is the focus of a DSS.

A **model** is a mathematical representation of an actual system. The model contains independent variables that influence the value of a dependent variable. Think of the independent variables as the inputs and the dependent variable as the output.

In the real world, many relationships are based on the effect of an independent variable on a dependent variable. For example, the price of a sofa depends

Model A representation of a real-world system; used to construct a DSS to help managers make decisions.

on the costs of the materials needed to make it. Sales of a new brand of toothpaste depend, in part, on the amount of money spent advertising it. The number of microwave ovens sold depends on, or is a function of, the price of the oven. This relationship between price and sales could be represented by the following mathematical model:

Microwave oven sales $= f$ (Price of the oven)

The relationship could be expressed as a mathematical equation. Then a manager could plug different prices into the equation and get some idea of how many microwave ovens would be sold at each price.

The manager who will be using a DSS should be responsible for the development of the model. The model, therefore, will represent the manager's perception of the real-world system. Since the model is developed by the manager, it is based on his or her judgment of how the system works and also on the experience the manager has gained in his or her contact with the system.

The fact that each manager must have a decision model based on his or her perception of the system is what has made the implementation of DSS so difficult. Managerial styles, as well as the environments in which people manage, are unique to each manager. In order for the DSS to be useful, it must be designed to aid a manager in his or her particular decision-making style.

The Future of DSS

One of the key factors, if not the key factor, in the acceptance of DSS within an organization is management. How the management views modeling and DSS is the critical factor that determines whether they are successfully implemented and used or not. Although decision modeling is used in a large number of firms, it must still overcome obstacles such as management resistance, a lack of management sophistication, and interdepartmental communication problems if its full potential is to be realized.

Concept Summary 13–3 ▬ Comparison of MIS and DSS

	MIS	**DSS**
Purpose	To get the correct information to the appropriate manager at the right time	To provide managers with information used to determine what might happen rather than what has already happened
Type of Decision Making For Which Information Is Provided	Structured	Unstructured
Types of Reports Provided	Scheduled listings Exception reports Predictive reports Demand reports	Predictive reports
Examples of Reports Provided	Sales forecasts Report of overdue accounts List of employees who worked overtime	Financial planning models Optimal production schedule Optimal advertising plan

The acceptance and use of decision modeling and DSS in business is possibly being slowed by the resistance of top management. A skeptical attitude toward scientific management techniques and unwillingness to accept and have confidence in these techniques often slows or even prevents the implementation of DSS. In addition, management is also sensitive to a situation in which the promise of what can be done with computers is far different from what is finally accomplished. Before management will fully accept the use of computers and decision support systems, promises of what can be accomplished must be realistic. Until these promises can be realized, management's willingness to accept new decision-making aids will be hindered.

FOCUS ON MICRO-COMPUTING

Using Microcomputers in Business

When first introduced, microcomputers were generally envisioned for use in the home and small businesses as stand-alone (self-contained) systems. But recently they have begun to make their way into the management information systems of large corporations.

Perhaps the entry of major mainframe and minicomputer vendors such as IBM, Hewlett-Packard, and Xerox into the personal computer field has caught senior managers' attention and made them curious about the potential of microcomputer technology. For whatever reason, the number of microcomputers being introduced into large corporations has dramatically increased.

A corporation can take many approaches when introducing microcomputers to its managers. Ford Motor Company, for example, has gradually incorporated microcomputers into the managerial ranks. At first, Ford managers used microcomputers in a stand-alone mode only. Applications were kept in a local mode and there was no access to corporate mainframe data bases. Gradually, managers became accustomed to using their microcomputers and started acquiring software themselves so they could do more processing on their own. Ford now uses an electronic mail network that spans the country. Ford managers can use their microcomputers to communicate with other managers in more than 40 locations. Ford now has plans to implement an online information system, giving managers access to mainframe data bases through their microcomputers.

Eli Lily and Company—a manufacturer of pharmaceutical products, agricultural products, cosmetics, and medical instrument systems—has developed an extensive data-processing system to support every department. Its corporate computer center houses five large IBM computers and three Digital Equipment Corporation computers. These computers process the data sent via online teleprocessing, remote job entry, and time-sharing terminals located in user departments in the United States and abroad. Managers can also access the system with microcomputers. This extensive system gives managers access to information resources gathered and transmitted from divisions located around the world.

Now that many large organizations have accepted microcomputers, the question of how to control their use has arisen. Again, there are a number of different approaches. One approach is to centralize the purchase of personal computers under the data-processing department, which then distributes them to managers throughout the corporation. Another method is for the data-processing department to issue a list of approved models from which departments and individuals may choose. A third method is for the corporation to set up an in-house computer store to sell company-approved small computers.

Additionally, in an effort to encourage their use, many companies have made mass purchases to secure quantity discount and are allowing their employees to buy personal microcomputers at cost. Others have negotiated contracts with computer manufacturers to supply discounted systems to their employees.

Regardless of how their distribution is accomplished, the addition of microcomputers to the corporate world still faces many problems that will have to be solved before they are completely accepted. Some of these problems are deciding how to allocate information processing resources among microcomputers, minicomputers, and mainframes; assessing the effects of the use of microcomputers on organizational communications and stability; and maintaining compatibility among corporate microcomputers and between microcomputers and the larger computers. In addition, because many executives will be using their personal microcomputers to support their decision making, there is the old "garbage in—garbage out" fear that executives might use incorrect data and assumptions in making their decisions.

Even with all these uncertainties, many companies are looking to the future and seeing substantial benefits in, if not the necessity of, executives who know how these tools work.

Rockwell International Corporation's Energy Systems Group (ESG), for example, is offering financial incentives to encourage employees to acquire and learn how to operate their own personal microcomputers. ESG has separately negotiated special purchase agreements with several manufacturers allowing Rockwell employees to buy personal computers at the same corporate discount that ESG would get if it purchased the equipment in volume. The employees can pay for the computers through a payroll deduction plan, with ESG picking up any monthly finance charges. Most of the microcomputers purchased by Rockwell employees are being used in their own homes strictly as stand-alones. However, a few of these have been equipped with a dial-up communications feature that allows them remote access to some of Rockwell's mainframes. This arrangement allows employees to receive trouble calls from their offices and communicate with the corporate computing center. They can then analyze and solve business problems at home without having to drive long distances to their offices.

Probably the most limiting factor thus far in the incorporation of microcomputers into a first-rate distributed system has been the slow pace of software development. This, however, is beginning to change as microcomputers become more common.

SUMMARY POINTS

- A system is a group of related elements that work together toward a common goal. Inputs are transformed by some process into outputs. Feedback provides information to the system about its internal and external environments.
- Most systems are collections of subsystems and are themselves subsystems of larger systems.
- A business is a system made up of subsystems (departments, employees). It interacts with other systems (suppliers, customers, governments) and is also a subsystem of larger economic and political systems.
- The system model highlights important relationships, patterns, and flows of information within the organization. It is a tool often used to model reality.
- System development consists of the following phases: analysis, design, programming, implementation, and audit and review.
- Data is gathered during system analysis from internal and external sources. Interviews are an excellent way of collecting data and often lead to unexpected discoveries. System flowcharts help the analyst get a better understanding of how the components in a system interrelate. Questionnaires can be helpful, but they are sometimes difficult to design, administer, and interpret. Formal reports tell the analyst much about the present workings of the system.
- An analyst should also collect data from external sources, such as customers, suppliers, software vendors, hardware manufacturers, books, and periodicals.
- Data should be analyzed in any manner that helps the analyst understand the system. Grid charts, system flowcharts, and decision logic tables are three of the tools analysts use to accomplish this task.
- The final result of the system analysis stage is the system analysis report, a report to management reviewing the results of the analysis and the feasibility of proceeding with system design and implementation.
- If the system analysis report is approved, the analyst begins the design stage. Goals and objectives of the new or revised system are reviewed. A system model is developed, and organizational constraints are evaluated.
- Alternative designs should always be generated in the design phase. There is always more than one way to design a system, and management likes to have alternatives from which to select.
- Each alternative should undergo a feasibility analysis. This involves looking at constraints, such as those imposed by hardware, software, human resources, legal matters, time, and economics.
- A cost/benefit analysis should be conducted to determine which alternative is most economically viable. While tangible costs and benefits are easy to determine, intangible benefits are difficult to quantify.
- The final step in system design is preparing a design report to present to management. This report should explain the various alternatives and the costs, benefits, and resources associated with each. The report includes the analyst's recommendation.
- The next stage of the system methodology is system programming. Programming is one of the most time-consuming parts of the system methodology and begins almost immediately after management has approved a design.
- Testing is performed when each program module is completed. When all program testing is done, system testing commences.

- Documentation is a necessary part of system and program development. System documentation provides an overview of the entire system and its subsystems.

- During implementation, converting to a new system can be done in several ways. In parallel conversion, the old and the new system operate together for a period of time. In pilot conversion, the new system is first implemented in only part of the organization so that problems can be worked out before full-scale implementation. In phased conversion, the old system is gradually replaced with the new system a portion at a time. In crash conversion, the new system is implemented all at once.

- Once a new system is operational, it must be audited to determine whether the initial objectives of the system are being met and to find any problems in the system. System maintenance is the continued surveillance of system operations to determine what modifications are needed to meet the changing needs of management and to respond to changes in the environment.

- Management information systems seek to provide the correct information to the appropriate manager at the right time. There are three levels of management: top-level management makes strategic and future-oriented decisions, middle-level management makes tactical decisions (implementing the strategies developed by top-level managers), and lower-level management makes the day-to-day decisions that keep the organization operating efficiently.

- Decision-oriented reporting identifies various types of reports required by management. Scheduled reports are produced at regular intervals and provide routine information. Exception reports are action-oriented and monitor performance—they indicate when a particular operation is not behaving as expected. Predictive reports use models to project possible outcomes of different decisions. Demand reports are usually one-time-only requests that cover unanticipated information needs.

- Structured design is a method of breaking down a problem into logical segments, or modules. Each module performs a logical function. These modules, in turn, may be broken down further. Modules are related to one another in a hierarchical fashion, but each module is independent of the others.

- The ways in which an MIS can be designed within the structure of an organization are virtually unlimited. Common approaches are centralized, hierarchical, distributed, and decentralized structures.

- The centralized approach generally uses a single computer department to provide data processing for the entire organization.

- The hierarchical approach gives each management level the computer power needed to support its task objectives.

- The distributed approach places computer support in key activity centers, and information is shared among the various functions.

- The decentralized approach places authority and responsibility for computer support in relatively autonomous organizational units.

- Decision support systems emphasize effective decision making. Managers in strategic areas are provided with relevant information to help them make decisions. Support is provided for tasks that are not routine or structured. To be most useful, the decision support system should be compatible with the manager's decision-making processes.

- The use of computers within decision support systems has primarily been to help speed the manager's analysis of decision alternatives.

- A decision model acts as the heart of a decision support system. It is a mathematical representation of an actual system. The model should be developed by the manager who will use it so that it represents his or her perception of the actual system.
- A key factor in the acceptance of decision support systems within an organization is top management's opinions of the value of DSS and decision modeling.
- Large corporations have taken different approaches to incorporating microcomputers in their information systems. Some use microcomputers only in a stand-alone mode. Others allow either limited or full access to the corporate data bases.
- To encourage the use of microcomputers by employees, some companies have made mass purchases of microcomputers to obtain quantity discounts. Others offer special deals to employees who purchase their own microcomputers.

REVIEW AND DISCUSSION QUESTIONS

1. Think of an example of a system. Describe its inputs, processes, and outputs. What do you think its feedback mechanisms are? Using this system, see if you can picture a larger system of which it is part. What smaller systems are part of the system?
2. Name three internal information sources. How is internal information different from external? Are both types needed during the first phase of system analysis?
3. What organizational constraints can complicate a system design effort?
4. Why might a system designer initially ignore any constraints and focus instead on an "ideal" system design?
5. List and briefly explain the types of conversion available for a system implementation. Given a situation in which a new computer-based information system is replacing a manual system, what method of conversion might be best?
6. Why is a system audit important? What is the difference between system audit and system maintenance?
7. Contrast distributed and centralized system designs. Which of them is likely to be more responsive to user needs?
8. What measures can an organization take to make its computer system secure?
9. What levels of management exist in a typical organization? What are the information requirements at each level? What are some difficulties for the MIS attempting to supply needed information to each level?
10. Identify the types of reports an MIS generates. Describe the uses of each type of report and show, by examples, where each could be used.
11. What is a decision support system? How does it differ from an MIS?
12. What is the purpose of a DSS? How should it interact with the manager using it?
13. What is a decision model? Is a model an exact replica of an actual system? Why or why not?
14. Describe several approaches being taken by large corporations to incorporate microcomputers.
15. What are some of the problems facing larger organizations that have incorporated microcomputers in their information systems?

Enhancing Human Performance

Some of us who use computers find that they almost become extensions of ourselves—our minds and our bodies. Perhaps the seeds were sown in the days of video games when we reacted quickly to information on the screen by manipulating a joystick or trackball. Now we discover that computers provide immediate feedback to the data we enter, and we can improve our performance in work, education, and sports.

An executive translates his ideas into action by using an integrated package of software that permits word processing, data base formation, graphics output, and spreadsheet analysis. He learns to use the system not as if it were a foreign piece of machinery he could never master, but as if it were paper-and-pencil, calculator, library, and advisor all rolled into one ①. He has learned, for example, that writing and editing follows a cyclical path from his brain through his hands to the keyboard, through the computer to the screen, and back to his brain through his eyes. The process seems more natural than using pen or typewriter, since changes are made interactively in real time.

This computer-as-extension relationship may begin in elementary school, where children interact with computers to study, learn through

simulations, and program computer operations ②. Once students learn to type, they see the monitor displays as events they can control. They can control the rate at which they learn a lesson. They can control the outcome of a simulation. They can edit a drawing or essay until they are satisfied with the product. Students carry their computer skills into high school and college where they use the machines for writing papers, doing homework, or accessing data bases ③.

Learning with computers does not stop after formal education has ended. Future captains and pilots learn to dock a ship or fly a plane by first undergoing simulated experiences. With the MSI Ship Simulator, maneuvering and docking a vessel has the feel of the real operation. The "ship" responds to changes in speed, heading, water depth, banks, other vessels, currents, and wind ④. Most airplane pilots learn how to manage crosswinds and wind shear, banking, and landing by using a flight simulator ⑤ and ⑥. Once they are comfortable with the simulated maneuvers, they can handle in-flight experiences with greater ease.

Using computers as extensions of our bodies is not limited to learning situations. People can treat computers as machines that expand creativity or increase the quality of performance in a normal workday. Musicians use computers such as CompuPro to perform audio processing in drum machines, allowing rhythms comprised of many types of sounds to be stored and reused ⑦. Grocery store managers can check inventory and order replacement products online to keep customers happy and profits up ⑧.

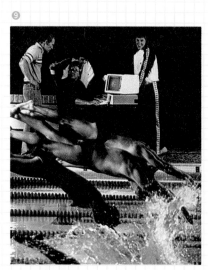

Many of us associate improvement of performance with sports. Learning correct form in running, throwing a javelin, swimming, and jumping can make the difference in a championship event. Computers can help athletes retrain their bodies to improve timing and reduce injuries. The computer becomes an extension of the athlete's body by displaying a digitized image of the body's performance. Before a swimming tournament, coaches use computers and simulation software to examine diving forms, trying to shave a few more seconds off each swimmer's time ⑨. Runners can analyze their running form to reduce time and to prevent common foot and knee injuries ⑩. Once a fault is analyzed, the runners can strengthen the proper muscles to correct an inward turn of the ankle or a pigeon-toed gait, for example. Other athletes such as pole vaulters can have their motions digitized onto computer screens to help increase the economy of every movement ⑪.

Professional athletes like the New England Patriots ⑫ and amateurs alike ⑬ benefit from training on computerized exercise systems, which measure muscular strength as the athlete exerts muscle force against a machine's force. By repeating sets of isometric and isotonic movements on the resistive exercise machines, athletes develop endurance and strengthen muscles weakened by injury or atrophy. The machines monitor progress and display immediate feedback on a screen so that athletes can judge their improvement.

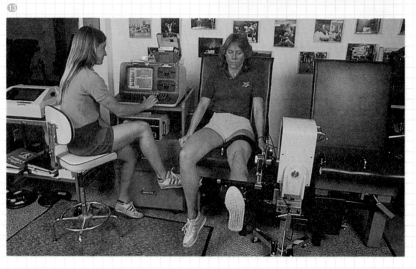

Often computers are used during sporting events to record every play for later analysis. For example, a manager uses an Apple Computer at the Yankee Stadium to record pitches, hits, and runs of the New York Yankees ⑭. After the game, players, coaches, and trainers will examine the data to see how performance could be improved. In a similar effort, New England Patriots players Ernest Gibson and Don Blackman study their player history, ⑮ while the defensive coordinator Rod Rust studies scouting reports and game statistics ⑯.

You don't have to be an athlete to enjoy computer use in recording athletic performance. Such a machine may be as close as the nearest bowling alley, ⑰ where your bowling scores are entered and compiled into one great game or a gutterball fiasco! Needless to say, the machine records your performance, but only you can improve it.

CHAPTER 14
COMPUTERS IN OUR FUTURE

COMPUTERS IN OUR LIVES

In the Year 2525 . . .

The year 2000 is just around the corner, and no matter whose crystal ball you look into, all of them clearly indicate that computers will be a significant factor in twenty-first century living. Computer hardware has developed at an incredibly rapid pace in the past two decades, a pace that will likely continue. Some futurists say advances in home computer technology will be so great that we cannot begin to predict what computers will be like—even in the next twenty years. These developments will affect the way we live, work, and play. The futurists see the effects with either optimism or pessimism.

Optimists describe a society in which passive television watchers participate in interactive computerized art forms and education becomes an interactive, self-motivating experience. The drudgery of maintaining a home will be eliminated. Human intelligence itself may be increased.

Based on current technology and research, we can already see the direction of improvement in computer hardware. The CRT screen as we know it will be obsolete. Home computer users will be able to display data, graphics, and moving video images on anything from walls to tiny screens worn on their wrist. Input will be spoken rather than typed. A "voice writer" will translate spoken words into written prose. Perhaps we will also use a "think writer" or a telepathic computer that operates with biofeedback. Through improved telecommunications, we will be able to access any television show or film from a huge library or contact anyone or anything anywhere in the world, and we will stay in contact with our home computers via voice-operated controllers as small as a wristwatch.

Of course, the home computer of the future will interface with robots that will cook, clean, do the wash, and cut the grass in response to voice commands. The robots need not be ordinary machines: with artificial personality programs, they can acquire the personality of a David Letterman or a Kermit the Frog.

Pessimists, however, describe a world filled with functional illiterates glued to video screens and lethargic family members waited on by domestic robots. Perhaps people of this future civilization will cease to interact empathetically with their own families, preferring instead robots programmed with ideal and glamorous personalities. Data bases will be so large that no one will have control over their contents, and individuals, no matter where they are, will be monitored by telepathic computer systems.

Probably the current computer revolution will lead us neither to an idealized utopia nor into a technological nightmare but to a state somewhere in between. As we come closer to a thoroughly computerized twenty-first century, however, we need to consider the moral dilemmas presented by advanced telecommunications capabilities, robotics, biological changes made possible by computers, and computerized identification cards. Some of the predicted changes may seem bizarre, but as this chapter shows, the technology that could lead to such changes is being developed today.

INTRODUCTION

Only 45 years ago, vacuum tubes controlled the electrical circuits in computers. Today scientists dream of "growing" electronic circuits from protein material. About 65 years ago, the word *robot* first appeared in the play *R.U.R.* by Karel Capek, who coined the word from the Czechoslovakian word *robota,* meaning "forced labor." In the 1930s and 1940s robots played important roles in science fiction. Today robots are no longer visions of the future. They are working in our factories and helping our young people learn in school. A February 1964 *U.S. News & World Report* article "Is the Computer Running Wild?" announced that the first computers run by integrated circuits would make their debut that year. Today Hewlett-Packard scientists have placed 450,000 transistors on a single, quarter-inch-square silicon chip. Computer technology has advanced so rapidly that computer scientists who grew up on vacuum tubes, transistors, and science fiction are performing research in the futuristic concepts of trans-puters and wafer integration.

This chapter discusses the current directions of research in chip technology, artificial intelligence, and robotics. It also presents some concerns about living in an information society.

TECHNOLOGY TODAY AND TOMORROW

In 1958 Jack S. Kilby of Texas Instruments introduced the first integrated circuit. It was a crude little piece of metal with several fine wires and other components sandwiched with solder (see Chapter 2, Figure 2–23). Later, Robert N. Noyce of Fairchild Semiconductor designed another type of integrated circuit based on the principle of "growing" an oxide layer on the silicon surface to protect the circuits on the chip. The interconnections between the circuits were then etched through the oxide layer. Soon a single chip less than one-eighth of an inch square contained 64 complete circuits. The number of circuits etched on a single chip continued to increase until, in September 1984, IBM announced a defect-free prototype of a 1 million bit (megabit) chip. Circuits have become so miniaturized that writers describe them in terms of angels dancing on the head of a pin and house-by-house maps of large cities etched on postage stamps (see Figure 14–1).

Still scientists explore the building of very high speed, ultralarge-scale integrated circuits. Experts predict that by 1990 a single chip may contain as many as 16 million transistors. Why pack so many components in such a small space? One way to achieve extremely fast computer speeds is to reduce the distance that electricity travels. However, when electronic components are crowded closer together to decrease these distances, four major problems arise.

The first problem is one that plagued the users of early computers: the generation of heat. The early computers produced heat when vacuum tubes were switched rapidly on and off and burned out the tubes; likewise, the densely packed circuits in ultralarge-scale integrated circuits create enough heat and use enough power to burn out the chips. Improved methods of etching the chips and liquid-coolant baths to house the circuitry help reduce heat generation. Even microcomputers contain a fan that circulates air to cool the circuitry.

Figure 14–1
A Computer Chip.
This chip with 450,000 transistors provides as much computing power as yesterday's room-sized computers yet is only large enough to cover Lincoln's head on a penny.

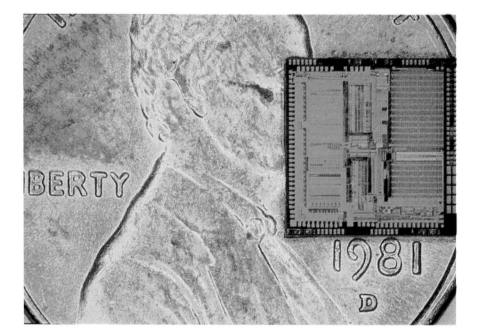

The second problem focuses on input and output from the tiny chips. Each chip rests in a ceramic or metal package; fine gold wires connect the I/O terminals around the periphery of the chip with the pins on the package (see Figure 14–2). Traditionally there are 20 to 40 pins, which in turn are connected to the printed circuit board on which the package rests. If the circuits normally found on a half dozen or more chips are integrated onto one chip, many more than 40 pins will be needed to handle the I/O operations. Some packages are designed with 164 to 180 pins linked to I/O terminals arranged in tiers around the package. Other packages, namely one produced by Honeywell, contain several chips per package, reducing the number of necessary I/O terminals.

The third problem is an offshoot of the second. As circuits are crowded closer together, the chance increases that one circuit will receive unwanted signals from nearby circuits in what is often termed *cross talk*. (Cross talk resembles the problem you may experience when making a long-distance telephone call and hearing another conversation in the background.) Using gallium arsenide chips and parallel processing may reduce cross talk. (These technologies are discussed later in this section.)

Dust particles larger than the widths of conducting paths in the circuits present a fourth problem. A path may be anywhere from two to five microns wide. (A micron is 1 millionth of a meter, 1/100 the diameter of a human hair.) A dust particle even a half micron in diameter can ruin a fragile circuit. Therefore, chip research and manufacture occurs in "clean rooms," rooms in which there are fewer than 400 half-micron or larger particles in the air.

As scientists address these four problems, they may change the materials used to make chips. For example, silicon may have met its match in a material called **gallium arsenide.** Integrated circuits made with gallium arsenide achieve speeds five to seven times those of the fastest silicon computer chips. Gallium arsenide chips also require lower voltages to operate, generate less heat, and create less cross talk than silicon chips. Although expensive, the chips are being

Gallium arsenide chip A chip made with gallium arsenide, a material that resists radiation, decreases cross talk in circuits, and creates faster circuits.

used in a variety of ways. The speed of the chips makes them suitable for use in supercomputers. Because the chips resist radiation, they can be used effectively in missile guidance, electronic warfare, radar systems, and surveillance satellites.

Perhaps the most revolutionary idea in chip development is the **biochip**—which exists in theory only. Some scientists believe that tiny computer circuits can be grown from the proteins and enzymes of living material such as *E. coli* bacteria. Like other life forms, they would require oxygen and the signals they would send would be most like those sent and received by our brains. Since biochips would be made from a living material, they could repair and reproduce themselves. They would be 10 million times as powerful as today's most advanced computers.

Biochip In theory, a chip whose circuits will be built from the proteins and enzymes of living matter such as *E. coli* bacteria.

Biochips might first be used as "microscopic noses" that could sense odors indicating unusual or dangerous conditions. The chips could also be implanted in a person's brain and linked to a visual sensor like a miniature camera in order to help the blind see. Some biochips placed in the human bloodstream could monitor and correct chemical imbalances. Although the idea of biochips may seem farfetched, scientists are already experimenting with genetic engineering, altering or designing the genetic material of plants and animals. Examples include the manufacture of human insulin and the human growth hormone, interferon. Can biochips be far behind?

In addition to chip materials, engineers are also designing ways to overcome the problem of the von Neumann bottleneck—a difficulty associated with serial processing. Based on the design of John von Neumann, computers execute instructions sequentially (or serially) by centralized program control: for this reason they are called von Neumann machines. Only a single channel carries all the data between primary storage and the control unit. Thus, a bottleneck occurs as instructions and data wait their turn to travel over the channel. The concepts of multiprogramming and virtual storage give the illusion to multiple users that a computer is performing many tasks at once. However, the computer

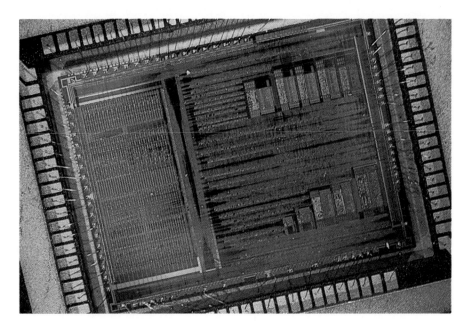

Figure 14-2
Microprocessor on a chip.
Fine gold wires connect the actual microprocessor chip to input/output terminals located on the chip carrier.

Computer Cars: Here Today, Here Tomorrow

If you ever worry about locking your keys in the car or running out of gas in the middle of rush hour traffic, you may have two fewer worries in the near future. Computerized cars are moving from the drawing board (or computer monitor, where many of today's cars are being designed) into the marketplace. And they are bringing changes in the way cars look and perform. In fact, some features of tomorrow's cars are already here.

Today's computer cars are able to figure how many miles' worth of fuel are in the gas tank. Some can estimate arrival times on long trips. Ford Motor Company's latest computerized engine control system regulates engine functions by processing as many as a million commands a second! While not as common in cars as air conditioners, computers are being included in more and more models each year.

Yet these features are only the beginning. The car of the future will need no keys. Instead, coded touchpads on the doors and dashboard will enable you to open your door and start the engine by entering the correct codes. Outside mirrors will be replaced with rear television monitors. Windshield wipers and headlights will be voice-activated. A front and rear sonar detection system will help you spot objects, such as children, animals, bikes, and toys, in the car's path.

You can also get rid of that tattered road map that's been impossible to fold ever since you first unfolded it. Tomorrow's car will locate itself on a video map in the dashboard and calculate the distance to your destination. You will be able to adjust the map to display a few city blocks or an entire state. A navigation system will bounce radio signals off a satellite to help you plot your course.

Keep in mind, however, that while the car of tomorrow may tell you where to go and how to get there, you will still have to do the driving.

is really processing several programs during the same period of time by rotating segments of the programs in quick succession.

The human brain, on the other hand, processes information in parallel sequence. It deals with large amounts of data and handles many different cognitive tasks effortlessly *and simultaneously*. Innovative forms of hardware architecture may facilitate **parallel processing** by computer. Parallel processing imitates the brain's behavior by dividing a problem into several portions and processing the portions simultaneously. The architecture would involve two or more CPUs or microprocessors.

Parallel processing provides a way to increase computer speed without further miniaturizing the circuitry and encountering the problems associated with densely packed electronic components. The first applications will most likely occur on supercomputers. Such applications include speech understanding, interpretation of data from many sensing devices, simulations, navigation uses, and artificial intelligence.

Parallel processing A type of processing in which instructions and data are dealt with simultaneously.

Recently, laser technology has offered ways to improve computer storage, telecommunications, and chip manufacture. Laser is an acronym for Light Amplification by Stimulated Emission of Radiation. A laser is a highly concentrated, tightly controlled beam of light. One way the beams are used is to record and read data from an optical disk (see Chapter 5).

The combination of optical disks and computer programming has created a promising teaching tool called **interactive video.** Some educators believe it will replace the computer, the instructional film, and perhaps even textbooks. Interactive video merges graphics and sound with computer-generated text by linking an optical disk (videodisk), a videodisk player, a microcomputer with monitor and disk drive, and computer software. Using this equipment, a student can watch news footage of historical events, learn about the most current advances in science, and listen to the music of great composers or the speeches of famous people. The interactive process begins when the student responds to computer-generated questions and forms inquiries to input into the system.

Videodisk technology will change the way we share information. As a student, you may receive a homework package consisting of software on a floppy disk and graphics on a videodisk to play on your equipment at home. As an employee, you could use the technology to learn how to show off new cars, trade shares on a stock exchange, or maintain and repair large earth-moving equipment. As a consumer, you will be able to buy huge data bases of information on any topic ranging from medical subjects to career guidance or browse through videodisk catalogs of the latest merchandise. Interactive video has become so attractive that some people believe the videodisk player will be the most important peripheral device of this decade. The technology will become even more appealing when disks are developed that can be erased and reused.

Manufacturers of computer chips may also benefit from the use of laser beams. **Wafer integration,** once abandoned because of difficulties inherent in the manufacture of large chips, is feasible once again since laser technology has been refined. In traditional chip manufacture, the circuitry for chips is etched onto one round wafer and then the individual chips are broken apart and tested (see Figure 14–3). Defective chips—sometimes 50 to 65 percent of the total—

Interactive video   A multimedia learning concept that merges computer text, sound, and graphics by using a videodisk, videodisk player, microcomputer with monitor and disk drive, and computer software.

Wafer integration   The concept of retaining the circuitry on the 5-inch silicon chip, rather than breaking the individual chips off the wafer and then packaging and relinking them.

**Figure 14–3
A wafer.**
In wafer integration, the individual chips will be retained on the 5-inch wafer rather than broken off and mounted in carriers. This technology will decrease the distance current must travel.

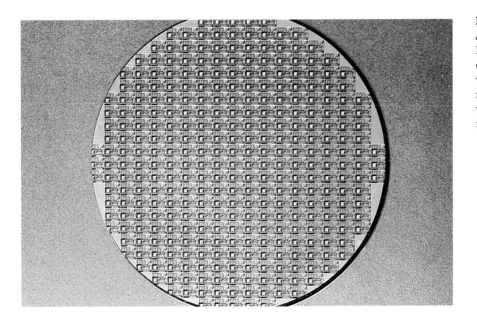

Fiber optics A data transmission concept using laser pulses and cables made of tiny threads of glass that can transmit huge amounts of data at the speed of light.

are thrown out, while usable chips are encased in carriers and wired together again on computer circuit boards. The miles of wires that connect these chips in a large computer slow down processing because electric current must travel long distances. Wafer integration would eliminate that time lag, because the circuits on many individual chips would reside on a single 5-inch wafer. With the circuitry of many chips integrated on one piece of silicon, fewer wafers, or "superchips," would be needed and less wiring would be necessary to deliver the electric signals. However, the larger the chip, the more chances for defects and the greater the number of rejected chips. With the emergence of ultraprecise lasers, wafer integration is being attempted again. A laser beam could be used as a tiny blowtorch to correct defective circuits. Eventually, researchers hope to use a computer to program the laser to build circuits on the wafers from scratch and automatically make all the interconnections between the circuits.

Lasers aid computer technology in one more important way: they carry signals through hair-thin fibers of the purest glass in a technology known as **fiber optics.** Optical fibers carry tiny staccato pulses of light that can turn on and off 90 million times per second. Fiber optic cables are being used to link computer terminals and mainframes in large industrial complexes. They are also rapidly replacing conventional telephone lines in many cities such as Fort Wayne, Indiana, and in long-distance lines across the United States. Fiber optics offers several advantages. Transmission of data by fiber optics is faster and more accurate than transmission by ordinary telephone lines. The actual cables are small: an optical cable one-half inch in diameter can carry as much data as a copper cable as thick as a person's arm. The fibers are immune to electromagnetic and noise interference and are difficult to tap. Finally, the raw material used to make the fibers is sand, a cheap and common resource. The advantages of fiber optics will increase the attractiveness of using telecommunications for banking, shopping, and medical purposes.

THE FIFTH GENERATION: ARTIFICIAL INTELLIGENCE

The term *number crunching* was born in the vacuum tube era of computing when mathematicians, scientists, and engineers used the machines to manipulate huge amounts of numerical data. Even today number crunching is what most computers do best. However, as programmers and developers of computer languages become more proficient at designing advanced software, number crunching will give way to more conceptual applications. Scientists will need faster computers with new architectures such as parallel processing to increase the power of computers. Many people call the new level of computer power the fifth generation.

The new computers and languages will, however, only begin to imitate human intelligence at higher levels of abstraction. Humanlike thinking, common sense, self-teaching, and decision-making skills are termed **artificial intelligence (AI).** Since human intelligence is not clearly understood, current AI programs incorporate just a few aspects of it. The most common AI applications are **expert systems.** These systems imitate an expert in a field, drawing conclusions and making recommendations based on a huge data base of information. An example is Dr. Lawrence Weed's medical diagnosis program, Problem-Knowledge Coupler or PKC. The patient and doctor enter history, symptoms, and test results on the computer keyboard, and, by making cross-references,

HIGHLIGHT

This Is Intelligence?

Scientists are trying to develop a fifth generation of computers with artificial intelligence. Though today's computers can perform truly amazing feats, the following story shows their limits.

In England a group of researchers studying accidents in the home decided to use a computer to help solve a problem. Statistics showed that a great majority of accidents on stairs occurred on either the top or bottom step. Probing for solutions that would reduce the number of accidents, the researchers fed statistics into a computer and eagerly awaited the results. The computer rapidly processed the data and offered this suggestion—remove the top and bottom steps.

the computer responds with a list of diseases the patient might have. This helps the doctor decide on a diagnosis and treatment. Other expert systems include Mycin, for diagnosing infectious diseases, and KEE (Knowledge Engineering Environment), a "shell," or frame on which to build a tailor-made expert system for a user. However, many experts in AI contend that expert systems do not qualify as true AI. Intelligence involves coping with change and incorporating new information to improve performance, and expert systems do neither.

If AI is to be developed further, experts need more accurate descriptions of human thought processes, improved programming to imitate those processes, large data bases, and improved hardware architecture. The advances in AI will lead to natural English communication with computers. Intelligent computers could read books, newspapers, journals, and magazines and prepare summaries of the material. They could scan mail and sort all letters but those with the most illegible addresses. Used in education, AI could help students learn to read, remember, and think and also help researchers understand how people think. Two particularly interesting applications of AI are in the fields of voice recognition and robotics.

Voice Recognition

Although the simplest way to input data into a computer is to speak, voice recognition technology is still primitive (see Chapter 4). Today's systems may recognize many words but they are usually limited to one speaker or one pitch range. "Speaker-independent" systems—those that accept a variety of voices—cost over $10,000 and have a vocabulary limited to a one or two dozen words. More versatile systems must be trained by the user to understand a particular vocabulary and recognize the user's voice pitch, accent, and inflection (see Figure 14–4). Each word must be enunciated and spoken discretely, that is, not run together with other words in a phrase. And heaven forbid that the user catch a cold!

Because of these limitations, voice recognition is best used with short-answer data. Tomorrow's systems will improve with advancements in AI and computer memory. Research in voice recognition now focuses on the ability to accept

Figure 14–4
Voice Recognition.
A voice recognition system is trained
to accept the user's voice by
matching sound wave patterns.

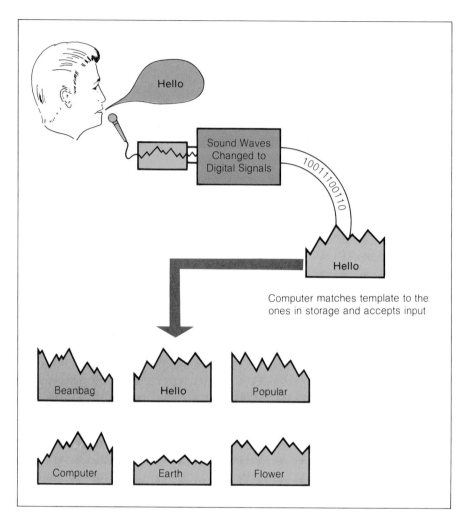

larger vocabularies, different voices, and continuous, or flowing, speech. However, a new discovery by Victor Zue, a scientist at MIT, may change the course of voice recognition research. While watching spectrograms (computer-enhanced versions of the electrical wave forms of speech), he noticed that they contained common features for each sound. For example, no matter who was speaking, the spectrogram depicted the *s* sound in *stop* as a dark rectangular wedge. Zue identified hundreds of these common features. Speech scientists at Carnegie-Mellon University in Pittsburgh believed that if Zue could read the spectograms, a computer could, too. They programmed a computer to recognize the shapes and patterns that Zue had catalogued as universal in certain words, no matter who spoke them.

An advanced system based on Zue's idea is already being used by the National Security Agency to monitor overseas telephone calls. By recognizing key words, NSA's supercomputers can isolate and record suspicious calls. On a more commercial level, Kurzweil Applied Intelligence in Waltham, Massachusetts, is testing a typewriter that will print almost 10,000 spoken words. What a boon this machine would be to handicapped people! Quadriplegics could use such a machine to write letters, make telephone calls, and communicate by radio. Advanced voice systems could also be used by elderly or handicapped people to instruct robots that would fetch things, help them with chores, or call an emergency number if an accident happened.

Some experts believe that keyboardless systems based on voice recognition and AI will become popular in the future. Users could hook the systems to their telephone lines to access just about any data base, leave messages on electronic bulletin boards, and conduct transactions—all without a single keystroke. Such systems would need to recognize natural language and overcome the problems associated with syntax and ambiguity. Users would not need to type specific codes or speak according to a standard question format but could simply request information in the same way they might ask another person. They could also direct computers to write application programs from general descriptions of needs. Natural language would provide a simple yet precise way of stating these descriptions. One experimental language is called SHRDLU, which directs robot behavior. Other natural languages include RAMIS, FOCUS, and MAPPER.

Robotics

Robotics will change as AI develops, too. Scientists are working hard to develop robots that are more mobile and sophisticated. Existing robots are deficient in four areas: vision, touch, mobility, and methods of instruction.

Perhaps the most crucial problem to overcome is that of vision. Robots interpret images in black and white with few shades of grey. They see in only two dimensions, length and width; unlike humans they do not judge depth. A robot's "eyes" are television cameras. A digitizer converts signals that come from the camera into digital code (1s and 0s). The robot then interprets the digital code to mean a certain object. Some scientists are designing robots that use fiber optic "eyes" as tiny cameras to relay images to their computers. As AI becomes more sophisticated, engineers are able to program robots to "see" objects and rotate them until recognition is possible. Robots with this capability work as bin-pickers (see Chapter 1). When special chips designed for processing and analyzing images are perfected, the robots can recognize objects much faster through parallel processing. With these advances, robots will be able to navigate throughout a person's home without bumping into objects. A robot could travel to the next room through a door, rather than being stopped by the wall. In addition, when confronted with an object in its path, a robot could decide whether to roll over it, move it out of the way, travel around it, or call for help.

A second difficulty, robot touch, has improved greatly with the development of sophisticated sensors. Some robots are equipped with several kinds of hands—after all, a robot doesn't really care what it looks like! Ichiro Kato has developed a robot hand dexterous enough to play a Schumann melody on the piano. Karen Hensley, a robot researcher, designed a hand that enables a robot to turn a doorknob. In a janitorial catalog, she found a gripper that janitors use on the end of a long pole to change light bulbs on high ceilings. Hensley's "hand" will be worn by Pluto, a robot developed by Hans Moravec, a professor at the Robotics Institute in Pittsburgh, Pennsylvania. Other robot hands can pick up an uncooked egg as easily as a heavy paperweight. Computer-driven robot arms can feed a bedridden patient and assist in nursing care. A voice-controlled robot arm designed by the engineering laboratory at Stanford University will assist the disabled.

462

Although most sensors are used to give robots skills in handling objects, scientists are experimenting with sensors that enable a robot to maintain balance while walking. Most of today's mobile robots travel on wheels, with the front two wheels providing the power to move and the back one or two wheels acting as balancers. Walking robots must maintain their own balance, and how do you program balance? Research in designing walking robots has been aided by a desk-high robot that bounces around on one leg, as if riding a pogo stick. The longer the robot can keep its balance, the more successful the engineers have been.

Finally, a robot is useless without an adequate way to receive instructions, learn new tasks, and even make rudimentary decisions. Most industrial robots are just one or two steps away from human-operated machines. The features that distinguish them are their typical crane, or arm, shape and their ability to operate by themselves once the instructions are completed. Although current software can guide a robot to perform welding jobs, drill holes, trim vinyl dashboards, paint fenders, sort parts for manufacturing processes, and assemble minute electronic components, robots cannot use a bank of programs to learn a new job or make decisions. Software is only now enabling robots to distinguish shapes in three dimensions. To pass rigorous tests for home or hospital use, a mobile robot or robot arm must be able to distinguish between a glass of water and a cup of soup. It must recognize its master's voice and respond to natural language commands. It must recognize objects in its path and determine whether to proceed or stop. It must be able to sense how fast it is moving and how tightly it is clutching. And it must be able to synthesize existing programs so that the user can program it by simple English statements to do new tasks. All these abilities stem from research into human learning behavior and AI (see Figure 14–5). Researchers at the Veterans Administration Hospital in Palo Alto, California, are only beginning to realize the potential of such robots. At the hospital, a quadriplegic learns to work with a robot that will fetch objects, help him eat, and hold a book. Perhaps one day robots will help quadriplegics the way seeing-eye dogs help the blind.

Concept Summary 14–1 ▬ Improvements in Technology

Idea	Improvements
Gallium arsenide chips	These chips are five to seven times faster than silicon chips, and help avoid the problem of cross talk.
Biochips	Although chips in theory only, biochips would be much smaller and more powerful than today's chips. They could be used to improve the condition of the human body.
Parallel processing	This concept would allow computers to use two or more CPUs to process data simultaneously rather than in sequence.
Lasers	Lasers increase efficiency of computers in several ways: laser disks can be combined with computers in interactive video to enhance learning; lasers can be used in the manufacture of chips; and the lasers in fiber optics improve telecommunications.
Voice recognition	New voice recognition systems would be able to accept larger vocabularies, different voices, and continuous, or flowing, speech.
Robotics	Research in robots is geared toward improving robot vision, touch, mobility, and methods of receiving instruction.

Figure 14–5
Synthesizing concepts of artificial intelligence into a robot

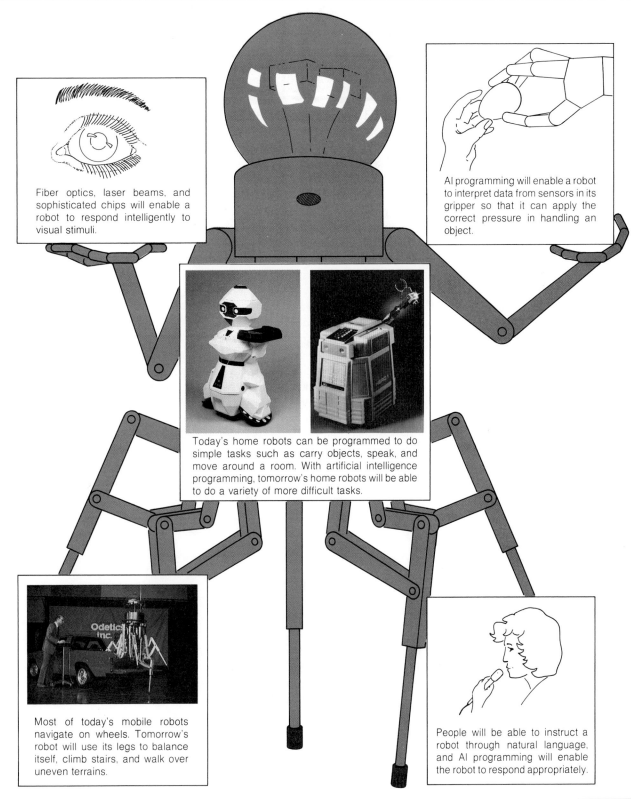

Fiber optics, laser beams, and sophisticated chips will enable a robot to respond intelligently to visual stimuli.

AI programming will enable a robot to interpret data from sensors in its gripper so that it can apply the correct pressure in handling an object.

Today's home robots can be programmed to do simple tasks such as carry objects, speak, and move around a room. With artificial intelligence programming, tomorrow's home robots will be able to do a variety of more difficult tasks.

Most of today's mobile robots navigate on wheels. Tomorrow's robot will use its legs to balance itself, climb stairs, and walk over uneven terrains.

People will be able to instruct a robot through natural language, and AI programming will enable the robot to respond appropriately.

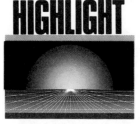

Waiterobot in Manhattan

Fast food may become even faster when a six-armed robot that prepares meals to order, takes money, makes change, sweeps floors, and clears tables goes to work at a major hamburger chain outlet in New York City. The $100,000 robot will wear the chain's uniform and a smile. Its voice-activated eyes will look at customers when they order. And it will sing if the food takes more than 15 seconds to arrive: carols during Christmas, the national anthem on Independence Day, and the chain's advertising jingle at other times.

The robot, which will have a seven-year lifespan if used 24 hours a day, was created by Peter Hughes, president of Hughes International, Inc. It is programmed to detect overcooked hamburgers and throw them away, and it will move through the restaurant on a track cleaning everything in its path with its six independently operating arms.

The robot will also help curb vandalism by sending an alarm to police when a problem has been detected. Holdups will be nearly impossible because the robot will send money to an underground vault as soon as each customer pays.

Because of the robot's efficiency, only one human engineer per shift will be needed to supervise its work. Yet, officials of the hamburger chain plan on employing only the one robot and are not anticipating large-scale unemployment in the fast food industry due to the introduction of robots.

If you're wondering who will be employing this fast food automaton, stand in line. Mr. Hughes says that he has been sworn to silence by officials of the chain. He has indicated, however, that the robot will be debuting sometime between December 1985 and February 1986.

Whether the fast food robot will be a passing fad or a growing trend is hard to say; a national pizza chain has expressed interest in employing a similar robot. We may even see a completely new chain based on the robot motif. Are you prepared for Roboburgers?

AN INFORMATION SOCIETY

A July 19, 1976, *U.S. News and World Report* article on the computer revolution began, "The changes the computer has made already in American life are insignificant compared with the startling advances predicted for the coming decade." At the time, a single microprocessor contained 3,000 transistors plus other components and provided as much power as the room-sized dinosaurs of the 1950s and 1960s. Teleconferencing was the "new kid on the block"; small banks argued that automated tellers gave an unfair advantage to the larger institutions that could afford the equipment; and people were protesting the use of scanners and the Universal Product Code in grocery stores. People who had counted on being able to send checks to creditors without sufficient funds to cover them, knowing that deposits would be made to one's account before the checks could clear, worried about electronic funds transfer. The speed of EFT would leave no time to make the proper deposits.

A decade later, the *U.S. News* statement is still true, only people are worried about different issues. Several have been discussed throughout this text: computer crime, data security, privacy, and ethics. Other concerns include monitoring people's activities by computers, using data bases, and becoming computer literate. The changes in the next decade will still be startling, particularly our increasing dependence on hardware and data processing. However, the *U.S. News* article ends by saying, "There's plenty of evidence that people won't cross the threshold of outright dependence on computers without a great deal of thought." The next three sections discuss the concerns inherent in dependence on computers.

The Card: Who's Watching Whom?

Blue Cross-Blue Shield is issuing the LifeCard, a wallet-sized card with medical history stored by laser beam. In Japan, Nipponcoinco vending machines accept laser cards in payment for food. The machine reduces the card's value, originally $40, each time the user buys food. Other cards will be used to record car repairs, guide a student's learning, and report economic news. The cards act almost like credit cards, and the owner controls their use.

Why own so many cards? Why not have just one card containing a dedicated computer that performs all personal financial transactions? Such a card may be more of a reality than we think, says George Morrow, founder and chairman of the board of Morrow, Inc., maker of personal computers and other computer equipment. Banks and creditors face mounting piles of paper, bad checks, and unpaid bills. They have already begun to solve the first problem through automatic tellers and EFT, and people now accept the use of credit cards. The next step could be a card that would identify you, provide a personal audit, balance your checkbook, and pay your utility bills. You would use the card to buy food and clothing. You would never have to balance a checkbook, worry about money being lost in the mail, or face being robbed. Banks and stores would benefit because you could not buy goods without having sufficient funds to cover your purchases. Criminals and thieves could be easily tracked: in a cashless society, they could make no purchases without their cards, and a remote computer could sense when a convicted criminal travels more than two blocks from home. People with more than four speeding tickets could no longer buy gasoline because a remote computer would program their cards to deny them that privilege. Even governments would benefit. Cash-only deals would be eliminated, guaranteeing the federal government its income tax and state and local governments their sales taxes.

Yet such cards carry ominous implications. Governments would have control of everyone's money, and could thereby ensure "correct" behavior. The cards could monitor the kinds of things we buy. Perhaps we would only be able to buy "acceptable" publications, or our tastes in reading material would be recorded and categorized as "acceptable," "suspicious," or "criminal." People in marketing research could access our records and determine purchasing and travel habits. Our cards could not be used to purchase candy and pie if we were overweight. We might have to use the cards to take breaks at work. Our lives would revolve around the cards.

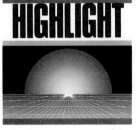

Is Big Boss Watching You?

If you've had a heart attack, you're probably thankful that a computer was monitoring your body functions while you were in the hospital. But how would you like to have your work monitored while you're on the job? Naturally, employers love the idea. But knowing that someone was watching you all the time would be unsettling. Nonetheless, computer monitoring is fast becoming an industry standard with workers linked to computers through visual display terminals (VDTs). The system connects workstations to computers to keep tabs on a worker's production. Many employers are using the technique to speed up the work pace and to determine pay raises and promotions.

"It's a little like knowing your telephone is tapped," says Harley Shaiken, a labor analyst at MIT. "You tend to act differently, which is exactly what computer monitoring is supposed to make you do."

Computer companies and employers argue that there's no difference in monitoring with or without a computer. Critics, however, maintain that keeping such a close watch over an employee's work habits leads to increased stress and high employee turnover. They also say that the system can be easily abused, citing the case of an 18-year veteran telephone operator who was fired because a computer detected she was taking more than the average 30 seconds per caller. Although she was reinstated the next day due to a high-level Communication Workers of America protest, the experience made a deep impression. "To make me responsible for the amount of time customers take is unfair," she says. "What am I supposed to do . . . I can't just cut them off."

The arguments over computer monitoring have just begun. The issue will undoubtedly become more heated as more workers are linked to company computers. But with the boss devoting so much energy to monitoring his employees, you might wonder who's monitoring the boss.

Data Base Dilemmas

The quality of information and the use of data bases present many implications for an information society. The first concern involves the future of the printed word. Students still turn to books and magazines while doing research on assigned topics. However, they are increasingly using microfilm, microfiche, and online data-base services. While embracing the new skills required to use computers and telecommunications, educators also fear that some old skills will be lost. Children learn language through listening, speaking, and trying out words again and again. They listen while stories are read out loud. Will computers interfere with these activities? Will voice recognition systems and voice synthesis eliminate the need to learn to read? Will students use information networks to the exclusion of material printed on paper?

Discussion about printed material leads to a second concern, that of copyright. Microcomputers can be programmed to download (transmit or copy from a mainframe computer, such as a network's computer) information and store it on disk. A problem can result because data bases are generally under copyright, and the people who produce the data bases depend on royalties and fees from use. Although many permit downloading for one-time use, they frown on further copying without their knowledge or payment. Many authors worry as their works become part of commercial data bases, wondering about the use, and compensation for use, of their materials.

Optical disks present a third problem for commercial data bases. The disks provide such a compact way to store data that large data bases can be sold in this form rather than by telecommunications. In addition, the disks can store graphic information, and production cost is low. Producers of online services could lose revenue when data bases are sold on disks.

A fourth problem of data bases involves transborder data flow. Some people favor free flow of information with other organizations and other countries; others want to restrict trade, business, and financial information and maintain tight control over scientific, technical, and government secrets. A company's or a country's advances in science and technology can determine competition in the marketplace or in the international military arena. Although some safeguards exist, data can be transmitted without the knowledge or permission of the data owner and without detection.

Students who access periodicals and books for facts to support a research paper thesis realize that authors have differing opinions about an event and that some books contain inaccuracies. The more sources they access, the more likely they will get a true picture of the event. What happens if the source is a data base? Who prepares the data base and how much personal bias exists in its preparation? Are the facts correct? Are several sources offered? Will material reflect current perceptions of events, public opinion polls, or trends in ethical thought? Will people develop the ability to question the validity of data, or will they believe that anything on a computer must be accurate?

The data base has many implications beyond the privacy issue. It may even partially dictate the "haves and have nots" of computer power.

The Newly Disadvantaged

While some people are worried about being monitored by computer and about who is watching the data base, others wonder what will happen to people who do not know how to use computers. Futurists believe almost every type of job will require employees to use computers. Education will certainly change through computer use and access to data bases. Most transactions will take place via computers and telecommunications. People with little computer experience will be profoundly affected. They will not be able to access a data base, read the material on the screen or enter a job that requires a great deal of computer use.

Who are these people? Most probably they will be women, older people, or members of a disadvantaged group. Often they will be people who cannot read or write, which will only exacerbate their lack of computing skills. They may fear computers because of the association with mathematics, or they may simply believe they could never learn to use the machines.

Research shows several important trends that could encourage rather than discourage the formation of a "newly disadvantaged" group of people. Parents buy computers more often for their sons than for their daughters, and send their sons to more expensive computer camps than their daughters. In schools, boys are apt to gain access to computers more often than girls, either because the girls forfeit their turns at the machines or because girls are intimidated by boys' behavior around computers. Software packaging and graphics are directed more toward the male customer than the female user, although this trend is changing. Teachers in disadvantaged school districts tend to use computers as a rote learning tool, while teachers in wealthier school districts encourage computer use to solve problems. Much of this behavior is inadvertent. Once people become aware of their behavior, the trends may change.

Although some schools have a ratio of one computer to every 165 students, more schools will be acquiring hardware and software to aid learning. The types of educational software will change, too. Rather than use programs that encourage rote learning, students will use software that offers simulations, "how-to's," concept skills, and games. They will learn by experimenting, something that Seymour Papert, the creator of LOGO, supports in his writings. By "playing" with computer software that encourages independent and creative thinking, students will establish knowledge that they can use as a frame of reference for further learning. Papert believes the learning environment will be so modified by computers that students will learn with less pain, less expense, and more success. If used correctly, computers can help remove the "mathophobias" and other phobias that may affect normal classroom learning and societal expectations.

Nevertheless, parents and teachers realize that no one innovation can prevent problems in education. Many recall the promises and the disappointments of the New Math in the late 1960s and early 1970s, and vow a more cautious approach to other innovations. By careful study, they will select the few software packages that encourage experimentation and build enthusiasm for learning. They realize that students need to learn about computers to avoid being shut out from challenges of the future.

Concept Summary 14–2 ▬ Benefits and Problems of an Information Society

Area	Benefits	Problems
Personal data cards	Eliminate need to carry cash; aid tax collection; aid payment of bills.	Can become a tool of government to monitor behavior and control money.
Access to data bases	Provides information on a wide variety of topics for personal interest, research, or job-related activity.	Causes concern about the future of printed material, violations of copyright, competition with optical disk data bases, transborder data flow, and accuracy and perspective of data.
Access to computers	Provides skills for jobs in the future, skills in telecommunications, and tools for learning.	Can, by unequal access, create a generation of "newly disadvantaged," most likely including those who are female, disadvantaged, older, or illiterate.

FOCUS ON MICRO-COMPUTING

Microcomputers and Robots

For years, robots have been working beside humans on assembly lines. Some are bin-pickers: their vision systems identify the parts that their grippers pick up to load, sort, or assemble. Other robots are welders: their cranelike arms rhythmically weld pieces of metal together. Some factories "employ" robots to spray-paint automotive parts, handle radioactive materials, or pour molten metals. These industrial workers do their jobs precisely. Many are equipped with sensors and vision systems that enable them to detect objects in their paths and pick up the correct items. If factories have robots that can do so many skillful jobs, why can't homeowners buy robots that can cut the grass, take out the garbage, vacuum the carpet, walk the dog, mind the kids, and fetch an ice-cold soda?

One major factor is, of course, the price. A robot's hand alone can cost from $4,000 to $25,000. Between $40,000 and $200,000 will buy a sophisticated, industrial robot; it will also buy several years' worth of meals out, a maid's services, lawn mowers, and babysitters. Other problems involve mobility and the complexity of the tasks. Most industrial robots are anchored to the factory floors. Only their arms sway back and forth as they perform their tasks. However, a robot for home use would have to navigate around the house and yard. It would also have to learn much more complex movements than those needed for spot welding. Artificial intelligence programming, sensors, and sight systems are still too primitive to allow a robot to do most jobs people want done.

Nevertheless, scientists and robot hobbyists are working diligently to develop home robots that can be controlled through microcomputers or "on-board" computers. Often the robots are designed to do just one task, so the scientists can study one aspect of robotics. For example, Hans Moravec, a professor at the Robotics Institute of Carnegie-Mellon University in Pittsburgh, is experimenting with robot vision using a very simple tricyclelike robot called Neptune. Once isolated aspects of robot behavior function properly, the solutions can be combined in an integrated robot that can do many jobs.

More sophisticated robots help handicapped people live more comfortable lives. Robot arms can feed disabled patients or handle jobs like twisting a lid off a bottle for people who are crippled with arthritis. At the Veterans Administration Hospital Rehabilitation Center in Palo Alto, California, a robot responds to commands like a well-trained pet to help a quadriplegic drink a glass of water or read a book.

But ordinary people don't have to wait for these complex robots to have some fun with robotics. They can buy a robot to hook up to their personal computers with an interface such as the RS232. So what do you do with the system once it's hooked up? Well, you can learn a lot about how a robot operates. Most personal robots are used in schools to help students learn computer programming or see how industrial robots work. Fifth- and sixth-graders at Stevens Creek School in Cupertino, California, are writing programs to control the movements of a robot called Topo. They have built an obstacle course in the computer lab and compete with one another to guide Topo through the maze. The "Topo Olympics" has improved students' programming skills. A high school student in Golden, Colorado, "trained" an RB5X robot to detect fire, sound an alarm, locate the fire through the smoke, and spray water on the flames.

The Topo robot made by Androbot in San Jose, California, costs about $1,500, a price more suited for a computer lab than for home use. It comes with a software program called TopoSoft for the Apple II+ or IIe computer. You can string together several commands to direct Topo to perform a series of tasks. Topo can move slowly or quickly, can speak in several volumes and pitches, and can also be governed by manipulating a joystick.

Harvard Associates, Inc., in Somerville, Massachusetts, makes the Turtle robots Turtle Tot, Tasman Turtle, and Valiant Turtle. You can use BASIC or LOGO to command these robots to trace shapes. The Tasman Turtle has a pen that permits it to draw on paper that has been taped to the floor. A variety of devices, including an arm, can be added to the turtle. An infrared transmitter sends signals from the computer to the robot so that it can move freely without being attached by cords.

A more complex robot is the RB5X, manufactured by RB Robot Corporation in Golden, Colorado. The robot contains ultrasonic and tactile sensors. You can buy optional voice synthesis equipment and a mechanical arm. Either available or under development are such additional options as a voice recognition system, vacuum cleaner, trailer, and radio communications system. RB5X can be interfaced with the Apple, Atari, TRS-80, and Commodore computers with an RS232 interface. You must also buy a terminal software package to allow the two machines to communicate. By using this robot and its software, students can learn some concepts of AI.

The most complex robot in this group is the Rhino robot arm. Prices begin at about $2,800 so this robot is more suited to high school industrial arts and computer science classes than to home recreational use. The Rhino is controlled by extensions of the BASIC language from an Apple computer or other computer with an RS232 interface.

Many other "personal" robots are available. Some contain on-board computers, and others are directed by remote control. Some give you an education in programming and geometry. All give you a taste of the future.

SUMMARY POINTS

- Four major problems arise when electronic components are packed to shorten the distance current must travel. The dense circuits generate heat; more input/output terminals are necessary; cross talk (unwanted signals from nearby circuits) occurs; and dust particles can ruin a chip. Scientists are developing new technologies to help overcome these problems.

- Gallium arsenide can be used to make chips that are faster, require less power, generate less heat, and are more resistant to radiation than silicon chips. Cross talk is not as apt to occur on gallium arsenide chips.
- Biochips are chips in name only: no prototypes have been developed. If developed, these chips will be grown from the proteins and enzymes of living material such as *E. coli* bacteria. They could repair and reproduce themselves.
- Computer chips can be linked to perform parallel processing, a form of processing that more closely resembles human brain processing. Several instructions are processed simultaneously, rather than serially (one after another). Parallel processing is a way to increase computer speed without encountering some of the problems in building very densely packed chips.
- Laser beams can be combined with computers to provide interactive video, which merges computer-generated text with sound and graphics.
- Laser beams can be used in the development of wafer integration to correct defective circuits and even build circuits from scratch on 5-inch wafers.
- Research in fiber optics aids telecommunication development because digital pulses can be sent through the glass fibers, which are immune to electro-magnetic and noise interference, and are difficult to tap.
- Today's "artificial intelligence" applications are called expert systems. These systems imitate an expert in a field, drawing conclusions and making rec-ommendations based on a huge data base. Some scientists believe expert systems are not true artificial intelligence.
- Artificial intelligence could be used to improve vision and touch systems in robots, for speech recognition systems, and for natural English communi-cation with computers. AI programs could summarize material, scan and sort handwritten addresses on mail, and help students learn.
- Principles of AI can improve voice recognition systems. Research focuses on the ability to accept larger vocabularies, different voices, and continuous, or flowing, speech.
- Natural languages and voice recognition systems will be used to help hand-icapped people, make computer interfaces more user friendly, and increase the ease of computer programming.
- Artificial intelligence will increase the powers of robot sight and touch, help robots walk, and give them the ability to make decisions and inferences.
- The information society presents new challenges. One involves cards used for financial transactions, which could become monitoring devices for peo-ple's behavior.
- Data bases present questions about the future of printed reading materials, copyrights and commercial data bases, competition between commercial data bases and data bases marketed on optical disks, transborder data flow, and accuracy of data.
- Some experts believe that people who cannot use computers will be the newly disadvantaged. They will include those who cannot read and write and therefore cannot use computers, those who have little access to com-puters in school or at home, and those who do not learn to use computers to solve problems.
- Microcomputers will increasingly be connected to robots for fun, learning, and home robot use. Some home robots include Tasman Turtle, Valiant Turtle, Turtle Tot, Topo, and RB5X.

REVIEW AND DISCUSSION QUESTIONS

1. Discuss four problems that confront scientists as they attempt to place more transistors on chips.
2. Why is gallium arsenide a better material for building faster chips?
3. If biochips were possible, what tasks could they perform?
4. How is parallel processing different from multiprogramming and virtual storage?
5. Name some uses of laser beams combined with computer technology.
6. What advantages do fiber optic cables have over the conventional copper cables in telecommunications?
7. Compare expert systems with scientists' criteria of artificial intelligence.
8. Compare today's voice recognition systems with the goals scientists hope to achieve.
9. For robots to become valuable in home use, they must be able to accomplish four types of tasks. Describe the four.
10. Discuss some problems with data bases other than privacy.
11. How can robots be used in a classroom situation?
12. How could robots connected to microcomputers change daily living in the future?

APPENDIX A
Career Opportunities

PEOPLE AND THEIR ROLES

Men and women with technical or managerial skills in data processing are employed in almost every industry. The need for data-processing personnel exists not only in business firms but also in hospitals, schools, government agencies, banks, and libraries. However, the major emphasis of this section will be on computer-related career opportunities in a business environment.

A typical computer installation in a business organization is expected to perform at least three basic functions: system analysis and design, programming, and computer operation. Personnel with the education and experience required to work in these areas are needed. Data-base technology has created the need for specialists in data-base analysis and administration. An information system manager is needed to coordinate activities, set goals for the data-processing department, and establish procedures to control and evaluate both personnel and projects in progress.

Information System Managers

Historically, data-processing managers have been programmers or system analysts who worked their way up to management positions with little formal management training. But the increasing emphasis on information systems and information management has brought a change; professional managers with demonstrable leadership qualities and communication skills are being hired to manage information system departments.

The *management information system (MIS) manager* is responsible for planning and tying together all the information resources of a firm. The manager is responsible for organizing the physical and human resources of a department. He or she must devise effective control mechanisms to monitor progress toward company goals. The following knowledge and skills are useful assets for an MIS manager:

- A thorough understanding of an organization, its goals, and its business activities.
- Leadership qualities to motivate and control highly skilled people.
- Knowledge of data-processing methods and familiarity with available hardware and software.

A man or woman seeking a career in information system management should have a college degree. A degree in business administration with a concentration in the area of management information systems is desirable for managing business data-processing centers. Some employers prefer an individual with an MBA degree. To handle high-level management responsibilities, a candidate for a position as MIS director should have at least two years of extensive management experience, advanced knowledge of the industry in which the individual hopes to work, and competence in all technical, professional, and business skills.

System Development Personnel

Programmers

Generally, three types of programming are done in an organization: *application programming, maintenance programming,* and *system programming.* Persons working in any of these areas should possess the following basic skills:

- Good command of the programming language or languages in which programs are written.
- A knowledge of general programming methodology and the relationships between programs and hardware.
- Analytical reasoning ability and attention to detail.
- Creativity and discipline for developing new problem-solving methods.
- Patience and persistence.

Application programs perform data-processing or computational tasks that solve specific problems facing an organization. This type of programming constitutes the bulk of all programming tasks. An application programmer must take a broad system design prepared by an analyst and convert it into instructions for the computer. Responsibilities of application programmers also include testing, debugging, documenting, and implementing programs.

An application programmer in business data processing must apply the capabilities of the computer to problems such as customer billing and inventory control. A business-oriented application programmer should know the objectives of an organization and have a basic understanding of accounting and management science in addition to the skills outlined earlier.

Scientific application programmers work on scientific or engineering problems, which usually require complex mathematical solutions. Thus, scientific application programming usually requires a degree in computer science, information science, mathematics, engineering, or a physical science. Some jobs require graduate degrees. Few scientific organizations are interested in applications with no college training.

Program maintenance is an important but often neglected activity. Many large programs are never completely debugged, and there is a continuing need for changes to and improvement of major problems. A responsibility of maintenance programmers is to change and improve existing programs. In some organizations, maintenance programming is done by application programmers. To be effective, a maintenance programmer needs extensive programming experience and a high level of analytical ability.

System programmers are responsible for creating and maintaining system software. System programmers are not concerned with writing programs to solve day-to-day organizational problems. Instead, they are expected to develop utility programs; maintain operating systems, data-base packages, compilers, and assemblers; and be involved in decisions concerning additions and deletions of hardware and software. Because of their knowledge of operating systems, system programmers typically offer technical help to application programmers. To be able to perform these duties effectively, a system programmer should have: (1) a background in the theory of computer language structure and syntax and (2) extensive and detailed knowledge of the hardware being used and the software that controls it.

Employers may look for specialized skills in systems programmers. For example, the increasing impact of minicomputers and microcomputers is creating a demand for programmers with experience in real-time or interactive systems using mini and micro hardware. Also, the advance technology of today's communication networks offers excellent opportunities for programmers skilled in designing, coding, testing, debugging, documenting, and implementing data communication software.

Educational requirements for programmers vary because employers' needs vary. For a business-oriented application programming job, a college degree, though desirable, is usually not required. However, most employers prefer applicants who have had college courses in data processing, accounting, and business administration. Occasionally, workers experienced in computer operation or specific functional areas of business are promoted to programming jobs and, with additional data-processing courses, become fully qualified programmers.

People interested in becoming system programmers should have at least one year of assembly language programming experience or a college degree in computer science. In addition to a degree, work experience, although not essential for a job as a programmer, is extremely beneficial.

Computer programming is taught at a number of different schools. Technical and vocational schools, community and junior colleges, and universities all offer programming courses. Many high schools offer computer programming to adults in evening classes, as well as to regular day students.

Application and system programmers will continue to be in exceptionally high demand. Application programmers with exposure to data-base management and direct-access techniques, remote processing, conversational programming, structured design, and distributed processing will be in greatest demand. As the use of minicomputers and microcomputers increases, knowledge of Assembler, C, Pascal, and BASIC will be valuable. System programmers knowledgeable in data communications, network planning and analysis, database concepts, and terminal-oriented systems will be in great demand. With these trends in mind, data processing, computer science, and business administration students may choose to direct their education toward some degree of specialization.

Programmers frequently have opportunities to advance into higher levels within an organization. A programmer who has demonstrated his or her technical competence and ability to handle responsibility may be promoted to lead programmer and given supervisory responsibilities. Some application programmers become system programmers, and vice versa.

System Analysts

The *system analyst* plays a significant role in the analysis, design, and implementation of a formal information system. The analyst has the following responsibilities:

- Helping the user determine information needs.
- Gathering facts about existing systems and analyzing them to determine the effectiveness of current processing methods and procedures.
- Designing new systems, recommending changes to existing systems, and being involved in implementing these changes.

The analyst's role is critical to the success of any management information system. He or she acts as an interface between users of the system and technical personnel such as programmers, machine operators, and data-base specialists. This role becomes more important as the cost of designing, implementing, and maintaining information systems rises.

An effective system analyst should have:

- A general knowledge of the firm, including its goals, objectives, products, and services.
- Familiarity with the organizational structure of the company and management rationale for selecting that structure.
- Comprehensive knowledge of data-processing methods and current hardware and familiarity with available programming languages.
- The ability to plan and organize work and to cooperate and interact effectively with both technical and nontechnical personnel.
- A high level of creativity.
- The ability to communicate clearly and persuasively with technical personnel as well as with persons who have little or no computer background.

Minimum requirements for a job as a system analyst generally include work experience in system design and programming and specialized industry experience. System analysts seeking jobs in a business environment should be college graduates with backgrounds in business management, accounting, economics, computer science, information systems, or data processing. An MBA or some graduate study is often desired. For work in a scientifically oriented organization, a college background in the physical sciences, mathematics, or engineering is preferred. Many universities offer majors in management information systems; their curricula are designed to train people to be system analysts.

Some organizations, particularly small ones, do not employ system analysts. Instead, *programmer/analysts* are responsible for system analysis and programming. In other companies, system analysts begin as programmers and are promoted to analyst positions after gaining experience. However, the qualities that make a good analyst are significantly different from those that characterize a good programmer. There is no clear career path *from* programming *to* analysis, though such movement is possible.

System analysis is a growing field. According to data from the United States Department of Labor, the need for system analysts will continue to increase throughout the 1980s. The need for system analysts is estimated to increase 37 percent by 1990. There is a continuing high demand for system professionals by computer manufacturers, and the increasing use of minicomputers and microcomputers will create an even greater need for analysts to design systems for small computers.

Data-Base Specialists

Data-base specialists are responsible for designing and controlling the use of data resources. A *data-base analyst*—the key person in the analysis, design, and implementation of data structures—must plan and coordinate data use within a system. A data-base analyst has the following responsibilities:

- Helping the system analyst or user analyze the interrelationships of data.
- Defining physical data structures and logical views of data.

- Designing new data-base systems, recommending changes to existing ones, and being involved in the implementation of these changes.
- Eliminating data redundancy.

A data-base analyst needs technical knowledge of programming and system methodologies. A background in system software is valuable for persons planning physical data-base structures. The job requires a college education and courses in computer science, business data processing, and data-base management system design. Many colleges offer courses in data-base management to train people to be data analysts.

A career path within the data-base specialty may lead to the position of corporate *data-base administrator (DBA).* This is a management-level position responsible for controlling all the data resources of an organization. The primary responsibilities of this position include:

- Developing a dictionary of standard data definitions so that all records are consistent.
- Designing data bases.
- Maintaining the accuracy, completeness, and timeliness of data bases.
- Designing procedures to ensure data security and data-base backup and recovery.
- Facilitating communications between analysts and users.
- Advising analysts, programmers, and system users about the best ways to use data bases.

To handle these responsibilities, a data-base administrator must have a high level of technical expertise, as well as an ability to communicate effectively with diverse groups of people. Supervisory and leadership skills developed through experience are also important.

Demand is strong for data-base specialists. With the increasing trend toward data-base management, the need for people with the technical knowledge to design data-base-oriented application systems is increasing.

ICCP

The Institute for Certification of Computer Professionals (ICCP) is a nonprofit organization established in 1973. It's purpose is to test and certify the knowledge and skills of computing personnel. A primary objective of the ICCP is to pool the resources of constituent societies so that the full attention of the information-processing industry can be focused on the vital tasks of development and recognition of qualified personnel.

The establishment of the ICCP was an outgrowth of studies made by committees of the DPMA and the ASM. The committees developed the concept of a "computer foundation" to foster testing and certification programs. In 1974 the ICCP acquired testing and certification programs, including the *Certificate in Data Processing (CDP)* examination. All candidates for the CDP examination must have at least five years work experience in a computer-based information system environment. The examination consists of five sections: data-processing equipment, computer programming and software, principles of management, quantitative methods, and system analysis and design. Any qualified person may take the examination and must successfully complete all five sections to receive the certificate. The *Certificate in Computer Programming (CCP)* recognizes experience and professional competence at the senior programmer level.

Candidates for this certification must also pass a basic five-part examination. The ICCP is involved in improving existing programs and establishing new examinations for various specialties.

SMIS

The Society for Management Information Systems (SMIS) was founded in 1968. It serves people concerned with all aspects of management information systems in the electronic data-processing industry, including business system designers, managers, and educators. The organization is an exchange or marketplace for technical information about management information systems. It also helps improve communications between MIS directors and executives responsible for the management of the business enterprise. SMIS offers educational and research programs, sponsors competitions, bestows awards, and maintains job placement programs.

Data-Processing Operations Personnel

Data-processing operations personnel are responsible for entering data and instructions into the computer, operating the computer and attached devices, retrieving output, and ensuring the smooth operation of the computing center and associated libraries. An efficient operations staff is crucial to the effective use of an organization's computer resources.

The *librarian* is responsible for classifying, cataloging, and maintaining the files and programs stored on cards, tapes, disks, diskettes, and all other storage media in a computer library. The librarian's tasks include transferring backup files to alternate storage sites, purging old files, and supervising the periodic cleaning of magnetic tapes and disks.

The librarian's job is important because he or she controls access to stored master files and programs. Computer operators and programmers do not have access to tapes or disks without the librarian's approval. This prevents unauthorized changes or processing runs.

The educational background required for a computer librarian is not extensive. A high-school diploma along with knowledge of basic data-processing concepts and clerical record-keeping skills would qualify most people for this job.

A *computer operator's* duties include setting up equipment; mounting and removing tapes, disks, and diskettes; and monitoring the operation of the computer. A computer operator should be able to identify operational problems and take appropriate corrective actions. Most computers run under sophisticated operating systems that direct the operator through messages generated during processing. However, the operator is responsible for reviewing errors that occur during operation, determining their causes, and maintaining operating records.

People seeking jobs as computer operators should enjoy working with machines. They should also be able to read and understand technical literature. A computer operator has to act quickly without error. A good operator can prevent the loss of valuable computer time, as well as the loss or destruction of files. An operator must also possess the communication skills to explain to users why programs did or did not work.

Most operators receive apprentice training. Few have college degrees. Formal operator training is available through technical schools and junior colleges. To be effective, training should include several weeks of on-the-job experience.

A *data-entry operator's* job involves transcribing data into a form suitable for computer processing. A *keypunch operator* uses a keypunch machine to transfer data from source documents to punched cards. Operators of other key-entry devices transfer data to magnetic tape or magnetic disk for subsequent processing.

A *remote terminal operator* is involved with the preparation of input data. The operator is located at a remote site, probably some distance from the computer itself. The data is entered into the computer directly, from the location at which it is generated.

Data-entry jobs usually require manual dexterity, typing or keying skills, and alertness. No extensive formal education is required; a high-school diploma is usually sufficient. However, all personnel in this category should be trained carefully to minimize the incidence of errors. Usually several weeks of on-the-job training is provided. New operators must become familiar with the documents they will be reading and the data-entry devices they will be using.

Occupations in computer operations are affected by changes in data-processing technology. For example, the demand for keypunch operators has declined as new methods of data preparation, such as direct data-entry techniques, have been developed. However, the expanding use of computers, especially in small businesses, will require additional computer operating personnel.

MANAGING INFORMATION SYSTEMS

Organization of Data Processing

Traditionally, data-processing activities have been performed within the functional departments of organizations. However, many organizations have consolidated their data-processing operations. Increased record-keeping requirements, the need for current information, and the necessity to adapt to a complex, changing environment have made this change necessary. The computer has been used increasingly as a tool to manage the paper explosion that threatens to engulf many organizations.

The rapid growth of electronic data processing (EDP) has affected the location of the EDP department in an organization's structure. In most organizations, data processing originated in the accounting area, since most record keeping was done there. However, management has recognized that information is a scarce and valuable resource used by the entire organization. Increasingly data-processing activities have been elevated in most organizational structures.

Figure A–1 shows two versions of an organizational chart for a typical manufacturing firm, each with a different general location for the EDP department. Figure A–1a shows the traditional location: the EDP manager reports to the vice-president of finance and accounting. This location is satisfactory only if the other functional areas do not demand extensive use of computer capabilities. Unless the processing requirements of the accounting and finance department are extensive, the computer is not used to its full potential under such an arrangement. This location has the following drawbacks:

- It is biased toward accounting and financial applications in setting job priorities. Since the data-processing manager reports to the controller, he or she will obviously give high priority to financial applications.
- It discourages involvement of data-processing personnel with the other functional divisions and inhibits overall integration of the data-processing function.

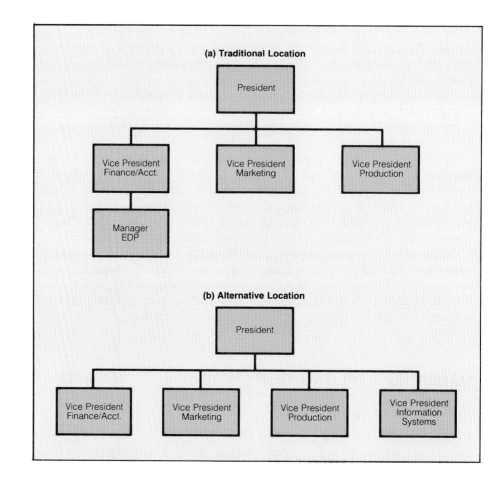

Figure A-1b shows an alternative location that overcomes these limitations. Elevating the data-processing activity to the same status as the traditional line functions (production, marketing, finance) reflects its corporatewide scope. When it occupies this position, the EDP department's name is often changed to the management information system (MIS) department, to stress the importance of its function. The independent status of the MIS department helps ensure that each functional area gets impartial service. It also helps ensure that all information requirements are integrated to meet organizational goals.

The internal organizational structure of the MIS department can take various forms. Perhaps the most common breakdown is by data-processing function—system analysis and design, programming, and computer operations (see Figure A–2).

An alternative structure emphasizes project assignments. Analysts and programmers work on specific projects in teams that include personnel from user departments. As projects are completed, teams are restructured and team members are assigned to new projects. This approach is illustrated in Figure A–3.

Managing System Development

System analysis, design, and implementation were discussed in detail in Chapter 13. Monitoring the total system development cycle to ensure that projects are completed within reasonable time schedules is the responsibility of the MIS

A–8

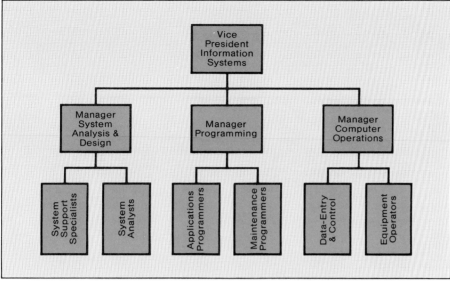

(data-processing) manager. Various formal network techniques like *PERT* (Program Evaluation and Review Technique) and *CPM* (Critical Path Method) are available for project planning and control. To use these techniques, the manager must break the project into distinct activities, determine the sequence in which the activities are to be performed, and establish a time estimate for each activity. Then, a scheduling chart can be designed. The progress of the project is monitored by comparing estimated completion times with actual times. If delays occur, the reasons behind the delays must be identified and corrective actions taken.

Managing Computer Operations

Most modern computer systems cost millions of dollars. Because of the expense of implementing a computerized system, most companies try to use the computers' CPUs and peripheral devices efficiently. Management can collect data

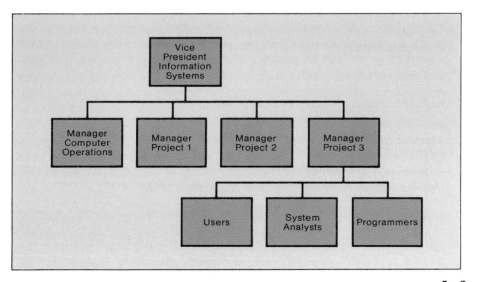

and analyze it to determine the degree of hardware use and encourage higher efficiency by proper job scheduling and balancing of hardware capabilities.

In addition to improving hardware use, the data-processing manager must monitor maintenance and reliability. Preventive maintenance must be developed for both hardware and software. Better systems can be achieved through the following practices:

- Establishing standard procedures to control actions that initiate and implement change.
- Using a modular approach for both hardware and software so that systems can be expanded; a complete switch to new equipment and new programs is a costly undertaking and should be avoided if possible.
- Strictly adhering to documentation standards. Software maintenance is impossible without extensive documentation to clarify how specific programs work.
- Implementing standard control and audit procedures to ascertain that the administrative policies and procedures established by management are followed.
- Planning for all contingencies so that data-processing interruptions are not catastrophic.

Managing an MIS is a difficult but important task. Managers must keep in mind that an MIS consists of both people and machines. No matter how sophisticated the MIS, success in using it can be achieved only through its acceptance by users at all levels of the organization.

PROFESSIONAL ASSOCIATIONS

Professional societies have been formed to increase communication among professional people in computer fields, to continue the professional education of members, and to distribute current knowledge through publications of professional journals.

AFIPS

The American Federation of Information Processing Societies (AFIPS), organized in 1961, is a national federation of professional societies established to represent member societies on an international basis. AFIPS also advances and disseminates knowledge among these groups. There are two categories of AFIPS participation: (1) member societies that have a principal interest in computers and information processing and (2) affiliated societies that, although not primarily concerned with computers and information processing, have a major interest in this area. Some of the prominent constituent societies of AFIPS are the Association for Computing Machinery (ACM), the Data Processing Management Association (DPMA), the Institute of Electrical and Electronic Engineers (IEEE), and the American Society for Information Science (ASIS). Affiliated societies of AFIPS include the American Institute of Certified Public Accountants (AICPA) and the American Statistical Association (ASA).

ACM

The Association for Computing Machinery (ACM) is the largest scientific, educational, and technical society of the computing community. Founded in 1947, this association is dedicated to the development of information processing as a discipline and to the responsible use of computers in increasingly complex and diverse applications. The objectives of the association are:

- To advance the science and art of information processing, including the study, design, development, construction, and application of modern machinery, computing techniques, and programming software.
- To promote the free exchange of ideas in the field of information processing in a professional manner between specialists and the public.
- To develop and maintain the integrity and competence of individuals engaged in the field of information processing.

The ACM has established special interest groups (known as SIGs) to address a wide range of interests in the computing field. For example, SIGSMALL was established for ACM members interested in small computers; SIGPLAN, for those interested in programming languages; and SIGCSE, for those interested in computer science education.

DPMA

Founded in Chicago as the National Machine Accountants Association, the Data Processing Management Association (DPMA) was chartered in December 1951. At that time the first electronic computer had yet to come into commercial use. The name "machine accountants" was chosen to identify people associated with the operation and supervision of punched-card equipment. The society took its present name in 1962.

DPMA is one of the largest world-wide organizations serving the information-processing and management communities. It comprises all levels of management personnel. Through its educational and publishing activities, DPMA encourages high standards in the field of data processing and promotes a professional attitude among its members.

One of DPMA's specific purposes is to promote and develop educational and scientific inquiry in the field of data processing and data-processing management. DPMA sponsors college student organizations interested in data processing and encourages members to serve as counselors for the Scout computer merit badge. The organization also presents the "Computer Sciences Man of the Year" award for outstanding contributions to the profession.

ASM

The Association for Systems Management (ASM), founded in 1947, has headquarters in Cleveland, Ohio. The ASM is an international organization engaged in keeping its members abreast of the rapid growth and change occurring in the field of systems management and information processing. It provides for the professional growth and development of its members and of the systems profession through:

- Extended programs in local and regional areas in the fields of education and research.
- Annual conferences and committee functions in research, education, and public relations.
- Promotion of high standards of work performance by members of the ASM and members of the systems profession.

■ Publication of the *Journal of Systems Management*, technical reports, and other works on subjects of current interest to systems practitioners.

The ASM has five technical departments: data communications, data processing, management information systems, organization planning, and written communications. An ASM member can belong to one or more of these departments.

APPENDIX B
Numbering Systems

INTRODUCTION

The numbering systems most commonly used with computers are binary, octal, and hexidecimal (see Chapter 3). These systems are called positional notation numbering systems. Positional notation means that each digit in a numeric representation of a number has a value, which is determined by the column placement of the digit. For example, in the base 10 system (another positional notation system), each position in a number represents a value. Consider the number 425. The 4 is located in the hundreds position and represents four 100s; the 2 is located in the tens position and stands for two 10s; and the 5 is located in the ones position and stands for five 1s.

Some numbering systems, like the Roman numeral system, are not considered positional numbering systems. The Roman numeral system does not use place value consistently. In the Roman system, the value of seven (seven 1s) is represented as VII while the value of four (four 1s) is represented as IV.

To qualify as a positional notation numbering system, the system must follow three rules:

1. The system has a base, or radix, around which the system is developed. A base is a value that indicates:
   a. The number of digits used in the system. For example, the binary system has a base (or radix) of two, and two digits (0 and 1) represent values.
   b. The positional multiplier for each digit position in a number (see Rule 3).
2. The value of a multidigit number can be determined by totaling the positional values of its digits.
3. The formula Value $= db^p$ can be used to determine the positional value of any digit. In this formula, d equals the face value of the digit, b equals the value of the base, and p equals the number of positions d is to the left of the unit (rightmost) digit.

To better understand these rules, the following example evaluates the decimal (base 10) number 6324:

We begin with the leftmost digit, 6.
$d = 6$ $b = 10$ $p = 3$
Substituting the above into the formula Value $= db^p$,
we get $6 \times 10^3 = 6000$.

The same technique can be used for evaluating the 3.
$d = 3$ $b = 10$ $p = 2$
Value $= db^p$
We get $3 \times 10^2 = 300$.

Once again the same technique is used to evaluate the 2.
$d = 2$ $b = 10$ $p = 1$
Value $= db^p$
We get $2 \times 10^1 = 20$.

Finally, the rightmost or unit digit, 4, is evaluated.

$d = 4 \qquad b = 10 \qquad p = 0$

Value $= db^p$

We get $4 \times 10^0 = 4$.

The value of 6324 equals the sum of the four positional values:
$6000 + 300 + 20 + 4 = 6324$.

In any positional numbering system, the following is true. The unit digit is multiplied by base^0; the position to the left of the unit digit is multiplied by base^1; the next position is multiplied by base^2; and so forth.

COMPUTER-RELATED NUMBER SYSTEMS

By now we are well aware that the number systems most commonly used with computers are binary (base 2), octal (base 8), and hexadecimal (base 16). In Chapter 3 we learned that binary is the only number system that is used inside a computer. The octal and hexadecimal systems are really shorthand methods of representing the binary system, but both follow the rules for positional notation numbering systems.

If we follow the first rule, 0 and 1 are the only two digits possible in binary. That means in the formula Value $= db^p$, the only two values for d are 0 and 1. When d equals 0, the value of the expression equals 0 and can be ignored. When d equals 1, however, the value of the expression is added to any other values.

For example in db^p, if $d = 0$, $b = 2$, and $p = 3$, then $0 \times 2^3 = 0$. The expression can be ignored. But, if $d = 1$, $b = 2$, and $p = 3$, then $1 \times 2^3 = 8$. In the second case, the number 8 should be added to any other values.

In binary, as in the decimal (or base 10) system, an unlimited number of digits can appear in a number. The binary number 1001101 is evaluated as follows:

$(1 \times 2^6) + (0 \times 2^5) + (0 \times 2^4) + (1 \times 2^3) + (1 \times 2^2) + (0 \times 2^1) + (1 \times 2^0) =$
$(1 \times 64) + (0 \times 32) + (0 \times 16) + (1 \times 8) + (1 \times 4) + (0 \times 2) + (1 \times 1) =$
$\qquad 64 \quad + \quad 0 \quad + \quad 16 \quad + \quad 8 \quad + \quad 4 \quad + \quad 0 \quad + \quad 1 \quad = 93_{10}$

Note: The subscript 10 stands for the base 10 number system.

Once again, when examining the first rule of positional notation, we can infer that hexadecimal notation requires 16 different symbols or digits. The numbers 0 through 9 represent ten of the digits in hexadecimal notation. The numbers 10 through 15 are represented by the letters A through F respectively.

The hexadecimal expression 17CA can be evaluated as the following:

$(1 \times 16^3) \quad + \quad (7 \times 16^2) \quad + \quad (C \times 16^1) \quad + \quad (A \times 16^0) =$
$(1 \times 4096) + (7 \times 256) + (12 \times 16) + (10 \times 1) =$
$\qquad 4096 \quad + \quad 1792 \quad + \quad 192 \quad + \quad 10 \quad = 5090_{10}$

Table B–1 presents the value equivalent to the decimal values 0 through 15 for the binary, octal, and hexadecimal number systems.

Table B–1 ▬ Value Equivalents

Decimal	Binary	Octal	Hexadecimal
0	0000	00	0
1	0001	01	1
2	0010	02	2
3	0011	03	3
4	0100	04	4
5	0101	05	5
6	0110	06	6
7	0111	07	7
8	1000	10	8
9	1001	11	9
10	1010	12	A
11	1011	13	B
12	1100	14	C
13	1101	15	D
14	1110	16	E
15	1111	17	F

CONVERSION BETWEEN BINARY, OCTAL, AND HEXADECIMAL SYSTEMS

The binary, octal, and hexadecimal systems all share a base number that is a power of 2. Binary makes use of 2^1, octal 2^3, and hexadecimal 2^4. Because the octal and hexadecimal systems are based on powers of two, binary values can be directly converted to either system. Moving from right to left in a binary number, each successive position represents the next higher power of 2 (for example, 1101 can be represented as $2^3 + 2^2 + 2^1 + 2^0$).

To convert a value from binary to octal, begin with the rightmost digit and group the digits in units of three. Next, using Table B–1, convert each unit of three into its octal equivalent. When this step has been completed, you will have octal digits with a value equal to the original binary number. For example, to convert the binary number 10011010 to octal, first group the digits into units of three, 010/011/010. Note that a leading 0 was added to the leftmost unit. g Table B–1, we can see that the octal equivalent to the binary number 10011010 is 2/3/2.

To convert the octal number into its equivalent decimal value, recall the formula Value $= db^p$. Substituting the octal digits into the formula, we get:

$$2 \times 8^2 = 128 \quad 3 \times 8^1 = 24 \quad 2 \times 8^0 \quad = \quad 16$$
$$128 \quad + \quad 24 \quad + \quad 16 \quad = \quad 168$$

To convert from octal to binary simply use Table B–1 again. The octal number 7531 has a binary value of 111/101/011/001 (leading 0s have been dropped).

To convert a value from binary to hexadecimal, begin once more with the rightmost value and group the digits into units of four. The binary number in the immediately preceding example, 111101011001, would become 1111/0101/1001 or F/5/9. Therefore, $111101011001_2 = 7531_8 = F59_{16}$.

To convert from hexadecimal to binary consult Table B–1 again. The hexadecimal number C3E becomes 1100/0011/1110.

Earlier we learned that it takes three binary digits to equal one octal digit and four binary digits to equal one hexadecimal digit. Therefore, two octal digits are used to represent the bit structure of a 6-bit byte and two hexadecimal digits are used to represent the bit structure of an 8-bit byte.

CONVERSION TO AND FROM DECIMAL NOTATION

The binary, octal, and hexadecimal systems all share a common root for their bases (2), so conversion between the systems is direct. The decimal system, however, does not share a common base with the other three, making the conversion procedures more complex.

The following steps are necessary to convert a number to decimal notation from another base.

1. Multiply the leftmost digit of the number by its base.
2. Add the next digit to the right.
3. Multiply the sum by the base.
4. Repeat Steps 2 and 3 until the unit digit has been added in. The sum is the decimal equivalent.

Examples:

a. Convert 374_8 to decimal notation:

$$
\begin{array}{rccc}
3 & 7 & 4 \\
\times\ \ 8 & & \\
\hline
24 & & \\
+\ \ 7 & & \\
\hline
31 & & \\
\times\ \ 8 & & \\
\hline
248 & & \\
+\ \ 4 & & \\
\hline
252_{10} & &
\end{array}
$$

b. Convert 1001_2 to decimal notation:

$$
\begin{array}{rccc}
1 & 0 & 0 & 1 \\
\times\ 2 & & & \\
\hline
2 & & & \\
+\ 0 & & & \\
\hline
2 & & & \\
\times\ 2 & & & \\
\hline
4 & & & \\
+\ 0 & & & \\
\hline
4 & & & \\
\times\ 2 & & & \\
\hline
8 & & & \\
+\ 1 & & & \\
\hline
9_{10} & & &
\end{array}
$$

The following steps are necessary to convert a number from decimal notation to another base:

1. Divide the decimal number by the desired base.
2. Keep the remainder as the digit of the new number.
3. Divide the quotient from the previous division by the desired base.
4. Keep the remainder as the next digit to the left.
5. Repeat Steps 2 and 3 until division yields a quotient of 0; the remainder of that step will be the high-order digit of the new number.

Examples:

a. Convert 844_{10} to hexadecimal notation:

```
16)844
  16)52                                      Rem.   12(C)
    16)3                      Rem.   4
       0      Rem.   3
Result =          3           4              C₁₆
```

Result =   3   4 C_{16}

Or $34C_{16}$

b. Convert 629 for octal notation:

```
8)629
  8)78                                    Rem.   5
    8)9                      Rem.   6
      8)1          Rem.   1
         0    Rem.   1
Result =      1         1         6         5₈
```

Result =   1   1   6 5_8

Or 1165_8

Positional values in the binary number system go as follows:

1 or 2^0	16 or 2^4	256 or 2^8
2 or 2^1	32 or 2^5	
4 or 2^2	64 or 2^6	
8 or 2^3	128 or 2^7	

The octal number system is used as a short form of representation for binary numbers. It is used mainly in computers that use a 6-bit byte as an information unit. The 6-bit byte was commonly used in computers built in the 1960s and earlier.

Examining the first rule of positional notation numbering systems, we can infer that the digits used in the octal system are 0, 1, 2, 3, 4, 5, 6, and 7. Therefore, the number 3174 is evaluated as the following:

$$(3 \times 8^3) + (1 \times 8^2) + (7 \times 8^1) + (4 \times 8^0) =$$
$$(3 \times 512) + (1 \times 64) + (7 \times 8) + (4 \times 1) =$$
$$1536 + 64 + 56 + 4 = 1660_{10}$$

Positional values in the octal number system go as follows:

1 or 8^0	512 or 8^3
8 or 8^1	4096 or 8^4
64 or 8^{32}	32768 or 8^5

The hexadecimal number system is used in computers that use an 8-bit byte to represent units of data. Like the octal system, the hexadecimal system is a shorthand form for representing binary numbers.

APPENDIX C
Program Logic Flowcharts and Decision Logic Tables

INTRODUCTION

Several common program logic problems are encountered in business applications. Six basic problems are described in this appendix. Each of these uses one or more of the four basic logic patterns discussed in Chapter 10. To understand the problems better, an example is provided for each, including a flowchart and pseudocode. Also included in this appendix is a discussion on decision logic tables.

INPUT/OUTPUT USING COUNTERS

One way to detect the end of a file when processing several input records is to use a counter. Each time an additional record is processed, the counter is incremented. When the counter equals the number of records in the file, execution stops. To use a counter effectively, the program can provide input for the number of records to be processed. This allows the number of records to change each time the program is executed. To ensure that the counter reflects the proper number of executions, the counter should be initialized to zero prior to the first execution. Initializing the counter to zero replaces any previously stored value.

Processing customer statements is one instance when the number of records may change. The number of current customers is input at the start of execution. Customer data will be read and statements will be printed the specified number of times. Figure C-1 illustrates the basic logic for this process.

Multiple Decisions

Managers make decisions daily, many of which are based on several criteria. Often, these multiple criteria and subsequent decisions are produced by a computer program. Various answers are generated depending on how many of the required criteria are met.

For instance, a used car dealer who operates several lots may wish to provide fast responses to customer inquiries about cars in stock. A master inventory listing is maintained for the cars on all lots. Inquiries can be made via a CRT for the required make, model, and year. The customer will obtain almost instantaneous results concerning the in-stock status and location of the car. This logic is shown in Figure C-2.

Figure C–1
Input/Output Using Computers

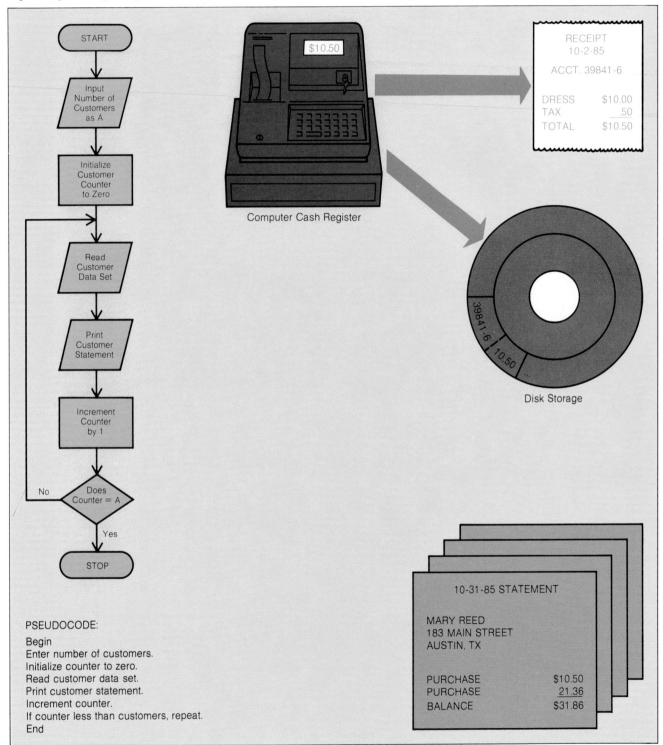

START

Input Number of Customers as A

Initialize Customer Counter to Zero

Read Customer Data Set

Print Customer Statement

Increment Counter by 1

Does Counter = A   No   Yes

STOP

$10.50

Computer Cash Register

RECEIPT
10-2-85

ACCT. 39841-6

DRESS $10.00
TAX   .50
TOTAL $10.50

39841-6   10.50   ...

Disk Storage

10-31-85 STATEMENT

MARY REED
183 MAIN STREET
AUSTIN, TX

PURCHASE $10.50
PURCHASE   21.36
BALANCE $31.86

PSEUDOCODE:

Begin
Enter number of customers.
Initialize counter to zero.
Read customer data set.
Print customer statement.
Increment counter.
If counter less than customers, repeat.
End

Figure C–2 Multiple Decisions

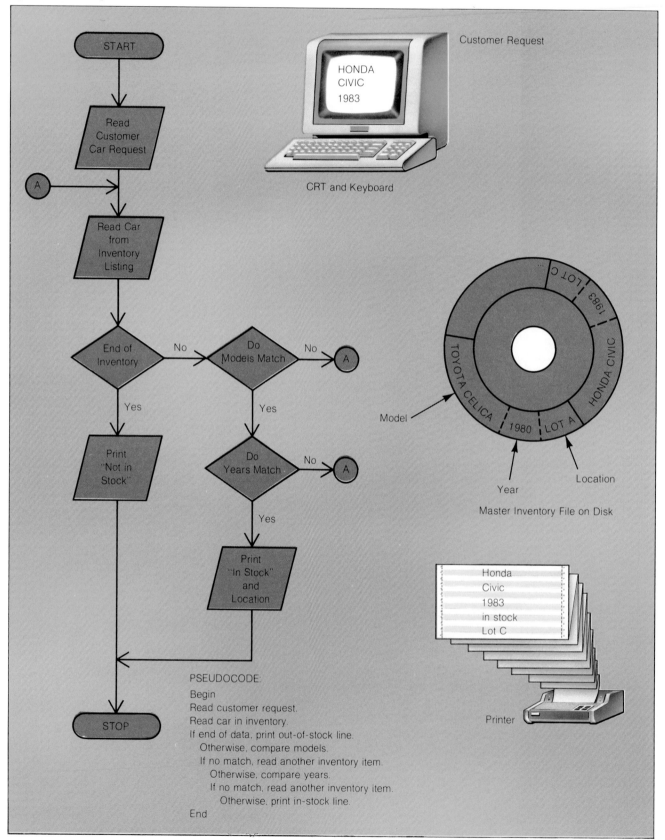

ACCUMULATING SUBTOTALS AND TOTALS

Various subtotals and totals are needed in decision making. These are indicators of business activity. The subtotals may be categorized by department, item, account classification, or otherwise. The subtotals and totals are accumulated as records are read or as values are calculated.

Figure C–3 illustrates the logic for subtotaling various types of checking accounts in a bank's files. These may include minimum balance accounts, senior citizen accounts, corporate accounts, as well as others. Each type of account is identified with a different leading digit. Checking accounts are typically ordered by number. As each account balance is read, the balance is added to both the subtotal and total. When the end of a category is reached, the subtotal is recorded and reset to zero to begin the next category. The total, however, is retained until all categories are completed.

TABLES

In some business applications, storing data in a table rather than on each individual record is more efficient. A code written on the record permits access to the table during processing. When the stored values need to be changed, the changes are made directly to the table rather than to each record. The code on the record remains the same, and the new table value is accessed with that code.

For example, a wholesaler in Indiana may service retailers in all 50 states. A table lists the freight charges for shipping to each of the states. These are identified on each shipping record by the two-letter state abbreviations. Figure C–4 illustrates the logic for generating freight statements using this table. At the start of the program, all the data from the table is read into arrays so that the data is read only once. The state code from the shipping record is compared to the state codes in the array until the correct code is located. If the freight rates change at a later date, the table is changed rather than the numerous retailer records.

MERGING FILES

Some applications may routinely or periodically require the merging of files. This process combines two or more files into one larger file. If sequential files are used, one record is read from each file and the keys are compared. If the keys are ordered from lowest to highest, for example, the record with the lowest key is written to the new file. An additional record is read from one of the original files to replace the record that was transferred. Another comparison is then made. This process continues until all records from the original files have been transferred to the new file.

An automobile insurance company may merge a new customer file with a master file daily. Figure C–5 shows the logic for this process assuming the records are ordered sequentially by policy number. Depending on the circumstances, a hard copy of the new master file may or may not be generated. In this example, a new file is in computer readable form for future processing.

Figure C-3
Accumulating Subtotals and Totals

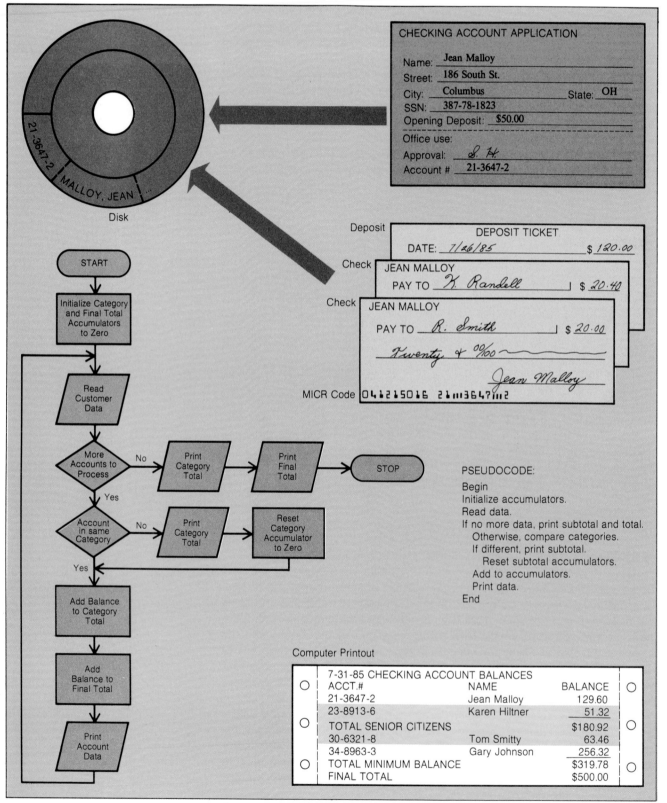

CHECKING ACCOUNT APPLICATION

Name: Jean Malloy
Street: 186 South St.
City: Columbus   State: OH
SSN: 387-78-1823
Opening Deposit: $50.00
- -
Office use:
Approval: *S. H.*
Account # 21-3647-2

Disk

21-3647-2   MALLOY, JEAN   ...

Deposit

DEPOSIT TICKET
DATE: 7/26/85 $ 120.00

Check

JEAN MALLOY
PAY TO K. Randell $ 20.40

Check

JEAN MALLOY
PAY TO R. Smith $ 20.00
Twenty & 0%₀₀
                    Jean Malloy

MICR Code 041215016 21⑈3647⑈2

Flowchart:

START

Initialize Category and Final Total Accumulators to Zero

Read Customer Data

More Accounts to Process → No → Print Category Total → Print Final Total → STOP

Yes ↓

Account in same Category → No → Print Category Total → Reset Category Accumulator to Zero

Yes ↓

Add Balance to Category Total

Add Balance to Final Total

Print Account Data

PSEUDOCODE:

Begin
Initialize accumulators.
Read data.
If no more data, print subtotal and total.
   Otherwise, compare categories.
   If different, print subtotal.
      Reset subtotal accumulators.
   Add to accumulators.
   Print data.
End

Computer Printout

7-31-85 CHECKING ACCOUNT BALANCES

ACCT.#	NAME	BALANCE
21-3647-2	Jean Malloy	129.60
23-8913-6	Karen Hiltner	51.32
TOTAL SENIOR CITIZENS		$180.92
30-6321-8	Tom Smitty	63.46
34-8963-3	Gary Johnson	256.32
TOTAL MINIMUM BALANCE		$319.78
FINAL TOTAL		$500.00

Figure C–4
Tables

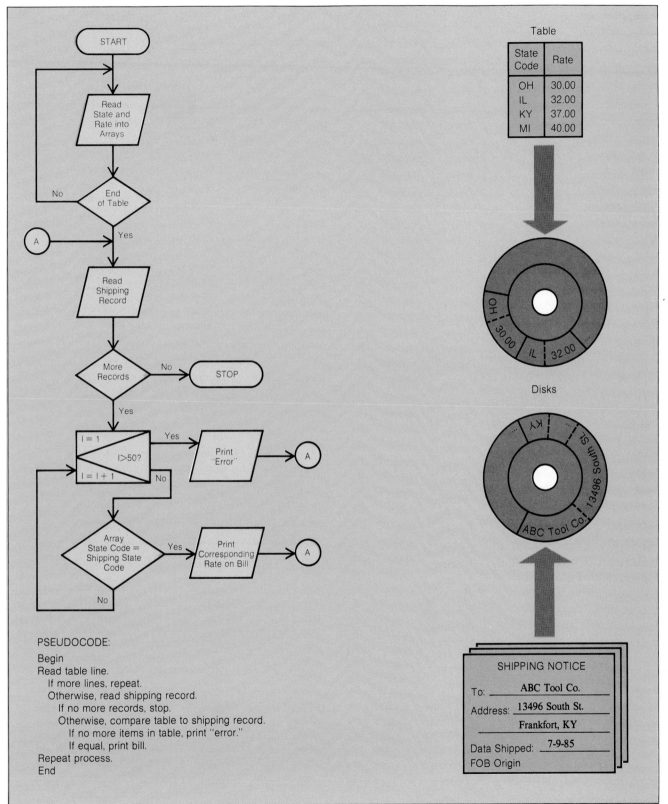

Table

State Code	Rate
OH	30.00
IL	32.00
KY	37.00
MI	40.00

Disks

START

Read State and Rate into Arrays

End of Table

No

Yes

A

Read Shipping Record

More Records

No

STOP

Yes

I = 1

I > 50?

I = I + 1

Yes

No

Print "Error"

A

Array State Code = Shipping State Code

Yes

No

Print Corresponding Rate on Bill

A

SHIPPING NOTICE

To: ABC Tool Co.

Address: 13496 South St.

Frankfort, KY

Data Shipped: 7-9-85

FOB Origin

PSEUDOCODE:

Begin
Read table line.
 If more lines, repeat.
 Otherwise, read shipping record.
  If no more records, stop.
  Otherwise, compare table to shipping record.
   If no more items in table, print "error."
   If equal, print bill.
Repeat process.
End

Figure C–5
Merging Files

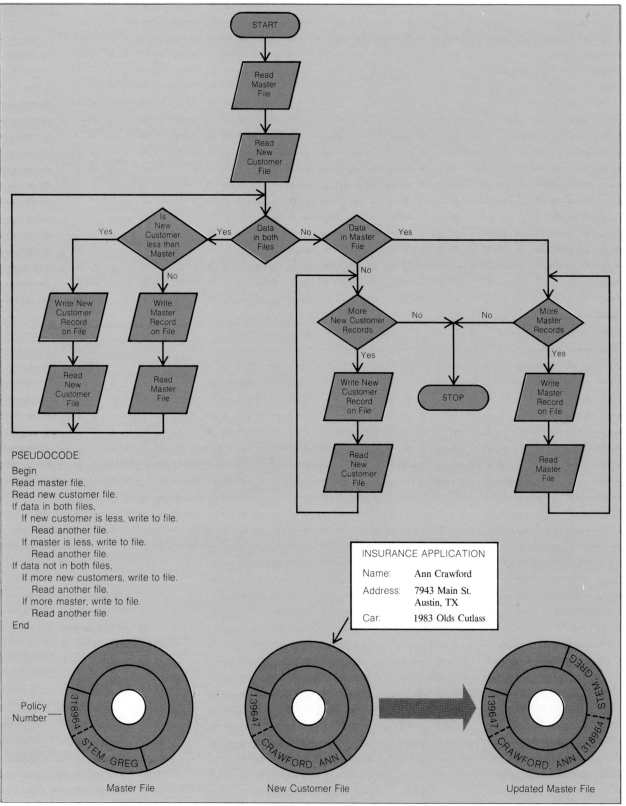

PSEUDOCODE:

Begin
Read master file.
Read new customer file.
If data in both files,
   If new customer is less, write to file.
     Read another file.
   If master is less, write to file.
     Read another file.
If data not in both files,
   If more new customers, write to file.
     Read another file.
   If more master, write to file.
     Read another file.
End

INSURANCE APPLICATION

Name: Ann Crawford

Address: 7943 Main St.
            Austin, TX

Car: 1983 Olds Cutlass

Master File   New Customer File   Updated Master File

SORTING

In many business applications, sorting, or ordering, data sets alphabetically or numerically is necessary. This can occur when data is collected or stored in an order different from that required for sequential file processing or printing reports. Arrays are used to sort the data with comparisons made between the array locations to determine which items need to be switched within a given list. This is called a bubble sort.

Figure C–6 illustrates the logic for sorting ten new employees by ascending employee number so that the new employee file can be merged with the master employee file. The new employee data was originally input as the applications were submitted and, therefore, is not in order.

There are several points to note when sorting. First, a flag is used to indicate whether any positions within the array are switched as the loop is executed. If the flag equals one, at least one switch was made. The loop is repeatedly executed until the flag remains zero throughout the execution, indicating the data is in order. Second, the loop terminal value is one less than the number of positions in the array. This prevents an error message when I equals the terminal value and the I position is compared to the I + 1 position. Finally, when ordering a set of data that includes more than one field, such as name and number, each field must be switched. Otherwise, the numbers would be in order but would not correspond to the correct names.

DECISION LOGIC TABLES

A decision logic table (DLT) is a tabular representation of the actions to be taken under sets of conditions. Thus, the decision table expresses the logic for arriving at a particular decision under a given set of circumstances. The structure within the table is based on the proposition, "If this condition is met, then do this."

The basic elements of a decision logic table are shown in Figure C–7. The upper half lists conditions to be met, and the lower half shows actions to be taken. That is, the condition stub describes the various conditions, and the action stub describes the possible actions. Condition entries are made in the top right section. Action entries are made in the bottom right section.

A decision table is not needed when conditions can be communicated and understood easily. However, where multiple conditions exist, a decision table serves as a valuable tool in analyzing the decision logic involved. Figure C–8 shows a decision table that could be used to select applicants for an assembly-line job.

The rules for selecting applicants are based on the age, education, and experience of the candidates. They must be at least 18 years old to be considered for the position. They must have at least a high school education or a year's work experience to be interviewed for further evaluation. They are hired directly if they meet both requirements. The Y's in the table mean yes, the N's mean no, and the X's indicate what actions are to be taken. The decision table is read as follows:

Rule 1: If the applicant's age is less than 18 years, then reject him or her.

Rule 2: If the applicant is at least 18 years old but has no high school education and less than one year's experience, then reject him or her.

Figure C–6
Sorting

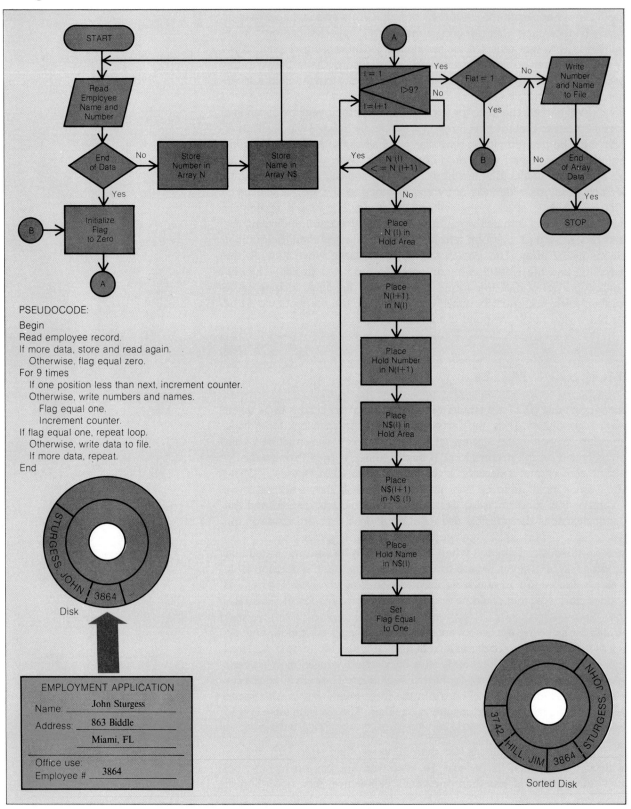

PSEUDOCODE:

Begin
Read employee record.
If more data, store and read again.
  Otherwise, flag equal zero.
For 9 times
  If one position less than next, increment counter.
  Otherwise, write numbers and names.
    Flag equal one.
    Increment counter.
If flag equal one, repeat loop.
  Otherwise, write data to file.
  If more data, repeat.
End

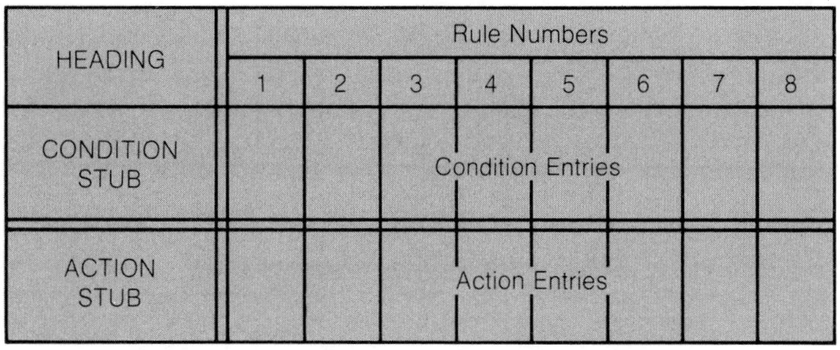

Figure C–7
Decision Logic Table

Rule 3: If the applicant is at least 18 years old, has no high school education, but has experience of more than one year, then call him or her for an interview. Once a candidate has been selected for an interview, another decision table may be needed to evaluate the interview.

Rule 4: If the applicant is at least 18 years old, has a high school education, but has less than one year's experience, then call him or her for an interview (another decision table might be used to evaluate the interview).

Rule 5: If the applicant is at least 18 years old, has a high school education, and has more than one year's experience, then hire him or her.

A more-detailed decision logic table is shown in Figure C–9. The first step in constructing such a table is to determine what conditions must be considered. In this case, these conditions are: (1) Is the customer's credit rating AAA? (2) Is the quantity ordered above or equal to the minimum quantity for a discount? (3) Is there enough stock on hand to fill the order? The conditions are listed in the condition stub section of the decision table.

The next step is to determine what actions can take place. These are: Either (1) bill at a discount price or (2) bill at a regular price; and either (3) ship the

Figure C–8
Decision Logic Table for Selecting
Applicants

SELECTING APPLICANTS		Rules				
		1	2	3	4	5
CONDITIONS	Age < 18 Years?	Y	N	N	N	N
	High School Education?		N	N	Y	Y
	Experience > 1 Year?		N	Y	N	Y
ACTIONS	Reject	X	X			
	Interview			X	X	
	Hire					X

Figure C–9
Decision Logic Table for Order Processing

ORDER PROCESSING	Rules							
	1	2	3	4	5	6	7	8
Credit Rating of AAA	Y	Y	Y	Y	N	N	N	N
Quantity Order >= Minimum Discount Quantity	Y	N	N	Y	Y	N	Y	N
Quantity Ordered <= Stock on Hand	N	Y	N	Y	N	Y	Y	N
Bill at Discount Price	X			X				
Bill at Regular Price		X	X		X	X	X	X
Ship Total Quantity Ordered		X		X		X	X	
Ship Partial and Back-Order Remaining Amount	X		X		X			X

total quantity ordered or (4) ship a partial order and backorder the rest. These possibilities go in the action stub.

Once the conditions and possible courses of action have been identified, the conditions can be related to corresponding action entries to indicate the appropriate decision. Thus, Rule 4 could be interpreted as follows: "If the customer has a credit rating of AAA, the quantity ordered is equal to or above the minimum discount quantity, and there is enough stock on hand, then bill the customer at the discount price, and ship the total order."

Decision tables summarize the logic required to make a decision in a form that is easy to understand. They are used to record facts collected during the investigation of the old system and can also be used to summarize aspects of the new system. In the latter case, they guide programmers in writing programs for the new system.

BASIC
Supplement

CONTENTS

PREFACE

BASIC has traditionally been accepted as the most effective programming language for instructional purposes. In recent years, business and computer manufacturers have recognized the vast potential for the BASIC language beyond education. Therefore, the availability and usage of BASIC has increased dramatically. Today most small business computer systems and home computer systems rely exclusively on BASIC programming support.

One major problem associated with such tremendous growth has been the lack of controls on the implementation of the language. Although there is a national standard (ANSI) version of BASIC, it is normally not followed by computer designers. Thus there are differences in the BASIC language found on various computers. The material in this book not only presents BASIC found on a typical large time-shared computer system (Digital Equipment Corp.), but also includes coverage of microcomputer implementations (PET, Apple, Apple Macintosh, IBM, TRS-80). Whenever a BASIC instruction deviates from the national standard, it is highlighted.

Color coding has been used extensively throughout the material to assist the reader. The following legend should prove valuable:

BLUE	Computer Output
BROWN SHADING	Statements Referenced in Text
RED	User Response
GREY SHADING	Nonstandard BASIC

Every program has been both class tested and run on the various computer systems. Our primary goal has been to develop a student-oriented BASIC text that is both logical and consistent in its presentation. I would appreciate receiving any suggestions that might improve the material.

BACKGROUND

BASIC was developed in the mid-1960s at Dartmouth College by Professors John G. Kemeny and Thomas E. Kurtz and has become one of the most popular programming languages. **BASIC,** short for **Beginner's All-purpose Symbolic Instruction Code,** is easy to learn, can be used for a wide variety of useful tasks, and is well suited for classroom teaching.

BASIC, like any language, includes rules for spelling, syntax, grammar, and punctuation. Just as the rules in English help us understand one another, so the rules in BASIC help the computer understand what we want it to do. In BASIC, the rules link abstract algebraic expressions with easy-to-understand English words like LET, GOTO, FOR/NEXT, INPUT, PRINT, and END.

BASIC was originally developed for use in a large, interactive computer environment: one or more BASIC users could communicate with the computer *during* processing and feel as though they had the computer all to themselves. As the demand for minicomputers and microcomputers increased, manufacturers of such computers felt pressure to develop simple but effective languages for them. Rather than create entirely new languages, most opted to offer BASIC because of its interactive capability—where the user can communicate directly with the computer in a conversational fashion. Many altered the original BASIC, however, to suit their equipment. The result is that, although the BASIC language has a universally accepted set of standard rules called **ANSI BASIC**, each manufacturer adds its enhancements, or extensions, to this standard to make use of special features of its machines.

This supplement discusses BASIC commands common to most computer systems but notes the language variations among vendors. The programming examples have been executed on seven different computers: A DECSYSTEM 20 to represent the major time-sharing systems; and the Apple II, Apple Macintosh, IBM Personal Computer, IBM Personal Computer Junior, TRS-80 Model IV, and PET/Commodore 64 to represent popular microcomputer systems. For the scope of this book, the IBM Personal Computer and the IBM Personal Computer Junior are considered the same and thus are included together under the title IBM. Most other microcomputers are capable of using a dialect called BASIC-80 from Microsoft Consumer Products and an operating system called CP/M produced by Digital Research. Since the IBM's BASIC and operating systems were also designed by Microsoft, they are similar to BASIC-80 and CP/M. Therefore, references for those systems will parallel the IBM instructions. The programming examples are run on the DECSYSTEM 20 computer, but important changes required to execute them on the other computers are noted. Although there are a variety of models and languages for the Apple and TRS-80 computers, this supplement discusses only the Apple II computer with the Applesoft language and the Apple Macintosh with Microsoft BASIC and the TRS-80 Model III computer with Model III language (essentially the same as level II BASIC for Model I).

INTRODUCTION TO COMPUTER PROGRAMMING

Computer programs (also called software) are step-by-step instructions to solve a problem. Since the computer must be able to read and interpret each instruction, each must be precisely written. To know what instructions are required to solve a problem, the programmer follows five steps (commonly called the **programming process**):

1. Define the problem.
2. Design a solution.
3. Write the program.
4. Compile, debug, and test the program.
5. Document the program (see Chapter 9).

In order to show how these steps are used in the programming process, let us take a sample data-processing problem: calculating the area of a rectangle.

The first step is to define the problem. To do so, we analyze it by using the basic flow of all data processing—**input, processing, output**—but with a twist. It is often easier to determine what processing is needed by working backwards. First, determine what output is required, and then see what input is available for the program. The gap between the available input and required output will be the processing needed in the program.

Determining the output required for the problem is quite simple—we need to know the area of a rectangle. The input available is the length and width of the rectangle. We now need to develop a series of steps, called an algorithm, that will enable us to produce the desired output from the available input. We need an arithmetic equation that translates length and width into area. Length multiplied by width equals area; hence, the algorithm to calculate area is area = length × width. We have now defined the problem.

The second step, designing a solution, requires developing a logical sequence of instructions, or statements, to solve the problem. Documentation for this step consists of written descriptions and explanations of the instructions and statements used to solve the problem. Good documentation makes the program easier for others to understand and can simplify modification or updating of the program. A tool that is commonly used at this point is the flowchart. **Flowcharts** (detail flowcharts) are a form of documentation and are composed of symbols that stand for program statements. For example, the symbol for a processing step is this:

The following is the symbol for a step that involves either input from the terminal or output to the terminal or printer:

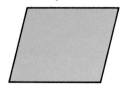

This symbol shows where the program starts or stops:

To create a flowchart for our example, we only need these three symbols. Some additional symbols that we will use later in this book include the following:

1. The symbol that shows where a comparison (decision) is to be made and where alternative processing is to occur based upon the results of the comparison is this:

2. To indicate an entry from or an exit to another part of the program flowchart, use this symbol:

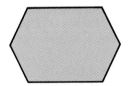

3. The following symbol represents a preparation step, such as defining the dimensions of an array (discussed in Section IX):

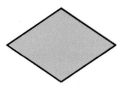

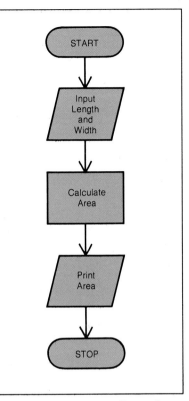

Figure I–1 ▪ Flowchart Example

Figure I–1 shows a flowchart depicting the steps of the programming example. Notice how the symbols are shown in logical order, top down, connected by flowlines (arrows). The first symbol shows the start of the program. It may correspond to one or more remarks at the beginning of the program statements. The second symbol shows an input step—we enter length and width. The third shows the processing done by the program—multiplying length by width to obtain area. After that, we want to see the result, so we output the area to the terminal. Finally, another start/stop symbol signifies the end of the program. The flowchart makes it easy to see the input, processing, and output steps of the program.

If the solution has been designed carefully, the third step—writing the program—should be relatively easy. All that is required is to translate the flowchart into BASIC statements. Figure I–2 shows this program written in BASIC. As you can see, many BASIC words, such as INPUT and PRINT, are easy to interpret. The symbol * means "multiply." The REM statement is used to document the program. Compare the coded BASIC statements in Figure I–2 to the flowchart in Figure I–1, noting the correspondence between the two.

In the program in Figure I–2, each statement starts with a **line number.** Line numbers tell the computer the order in which to execute statements.

Line 110 is a comment describing the program. The computer ignores all

Figure I–2 ▪ Area Program

```
00100 REM *************************************************************
00110 REM ***   THIS PROGRAM CALCULATES THE AREA OF A RECTANGLE   ***
00120 REM *************************************************************
00130 INPUT "ENTER THE LENGTH OF THE RECTANGLE IN CENTIMETERS";L
00140 INPUT "ENTER THE WIDTH OF THE RECTANGLE IN CENTIMETERS";W
00150 LET A = L * W
00160 PRINT "THE AREA OF THE RECTANGLE IS";A;"SQUARE CENTIMETERS"
00999 END
```

Boxes and ANSI Standards

Throughout the BASIC portion of this book, boxes are used to separate the main body of text from short discussions dealing with peculiarities, warnings, problems, and items of special interest. This, the first box, deals with the ANSI standards.

The purpose of a programming standard is to make it possible for a program to have *transportability*. In other words, if you write a program whose syntax lies completely within the BASIC standard, then this program will run correctly on *any* brand of computer that claims its BASIC meets the standards.

The American National Standards Institute, Inc., (ANSI) 1430 Broadway, New York, NY 10018, has published the ANSI Standard for Minimal BASIC. You can obtain a copy by writing the above address for document X3.60. As the title of the document suggests, the standard fails to include many features implemented by computer manufacturers. Material presented in this supplement that extends beyond the ANSI standard is shaded and identified as nonstandard.

such comment statements; they are for documentation purposes. Lines 130 and 140 tell the computer to print out a statement (shown in quotes)—the prompt (your cue) to enter the length and the width—and then to accept the input after it is typed in. Line 150 is an example of an assignment statement, which assigns values on the right side of the equal sign to special variables on the left (this is discussed in Section III). Line 160 instructs the computer to print out first a heading (shown in quotes) and then the computed area. Finally, line 999 tells the computer to stop processing. Again, you can see how the program follows the flow of input, processing, and output.

The fourth step involves sitting down at the terminal and typing the program, line for line, into the computer. Many interactive BASIC interpreters and compilers check for syntax errors as each statement is typed in. The statements necessary to use the BASIC interpreter or compiler are given in Table I–1 (found near the end of this section). **Syntax** refers to the way instructions have to be written (rules must be followed, just as grammatical rules must be followed in English). A syntax check can save considerable debugging time. Figure I–3 shows an interactive session with syntax checking.

After all syntax errors have been eliminated, the program can be tested with sample data (the fourth step). During this stage, the logic of the program is checked for correctness; for instance, were the correct statements used to determine the area? Figure I– 4 shows the execution of the area program.

During each of these five steps, it is important that adequate documentation be written and maintained. During the last step, any revisions to the documentation that may be required should be made.

This example is relatively simple, but it shows each of the steps required to complete a program. Although other problems may be more complex, the steps involved are the same; successful programming can only come about through diligent application of the five steps in the programming process.

INTERACTING WITH THE COMPUTER

An important step in BASIC programming is learning to control the computer. Although this book cannot present the full operational details for each computer, it can discuss the principles of how to turn the computer on, use the BASIC programming language, retrieve a program from secondary storage, display the program, alter the program, and save the program for future reference.

Figure I–3 ▪ Syntax Checking

```
00010 REM *** EQUAL SIGN IS IN THE WRONG PLACE ***
00020 LET L * M = N
20 LET L *
? Found "*" when expecting "="


00010 REM *** INPUT IS SPELLED I-N-P-U-T ***
00020 INPUR "MY NAME IS";N$
20 INPUR "MY NAME IS";N$

? Statement not recognized
```

Figure I–4 ▪ Execution of Area Program

```
RUNNH
ENTER THE LENGTH OF THE RECTANGLE IN CENTIMETERS ? 4
ENTER THE WIDTH OF THE RECTANGLE IN CENTIMETERS ? 3
THE AREA OF THE RECTANGLE IS 12 SQUARED CENTIMETERS
```

Manipulating Programs

BASIC programming requires the use of different types of commands. Some of the commands, like GOTO, LET, and READ, are program language statements. They are assembled into programs to solve specific business, scientific, engineering, and mathematical problems. The remainder of the BASIC supplement describes their characteristics and how they are used.

There are also **system commands,** used by the programmer to communicate with the operating system of the computer to perform functions like saving programs for future reference and making changes to programs. Some commands, like LIST, RUN, and DELETE, are almost universally used but are not covered by ANSI standards. A description of such commands as they relate to the five computer systems used in programming examples in this supplement follows.

APPLE

Hardware   The APPLE II (Figure I–5) initially contains INTEGER BASIC. Since INTEGER BASIC lacks many important features of the ANSI standard, this discussion only refers to this computer once APPLESOFT floating point BASIC has been loaded.

Starting the Computer   The power switch is located in the left rear portion of the computer. Since an external monitor or CRT is required, you must remember to turn on power to this device also. If a disk drive is attached, it

Figure I–5 ▪ Apple II Microcomputer

will whir and try to *boot* the disk operating system (DOS), so be sure that a diskette is placed in the disk drive before the computer is turned on. (When the disk drive "boots the DOS," it loads from a diskette the instructions that tell the computer how to manage the disk. This must be done before the computer can perform any disk-related tasks.)

The computer "comes up" with **floating-point BASIC,** as indicated by the use of the] character as a prompt.

Saving and Loading Programs   Programs are commonly accessed from either cassette tape or disk on this system.

■ *Cassette:* To recall a program from a cassette tape into main memory, you must first position the tape to the beginning of the program. This means that you must keep a record of where programs are located on the tape. Next, push the PLAY button and pull out the earphone plug on the recorder until you can hear the tape sounds. When you hear a constant, high-pitched tone, stop the recorder and plug the earphone jack back in. Then type LOAD, push the PLAY button, and hit RETURN. The program has been loaded when you hear a beep and the cursor appears on the screen. (The **cursor** is usually a flashing character such as an underline or a block that shows where the next typed character will appear on the screen.)

To store a program, position the tape to a blank area, type SAVE, push the PLAY and RECORD buttons simultaneously, and then press RETURN. Again you will hear a beep, and the cursor will return when the program has been written to the tape.

■ *Disk:* The Apple has a convenient file-by-name catalog system for the DOS. To save an APPLESOFT (this is Apple's name for its floating-point BASIC) program—for example, one named PROGRAM 1—on disk, type

SAVE PROGRAM1

and press RETURN. To load the same program from disk, type:

LOAD PROGRAM1

and press RETURN. You can then run the program. Alternatively, you can type RUN PROGRAM1 without loading it; this causes the DOS to both load and run the program.

APPLE MACINTOSH

Hardware   The Apple Macintosh (Figure I– 6) comes with a built-in 3 ½-inch disk drive and makes use of a pointing device called a mouse. The Macintosh runs Microsoft BASIC.

Starting the Computer   The power switch is located on the left side of the rear panel about halfway up the computer. When you turn the switch on, the Macintosh will beep to let you know it's started and then a picture (icon) representing a Macintosh disk appears on the screen. The blinking question mark shows that the Macintosh is ready for you to insert a disk. Insert a Macintosh disk (the Microsoft BASIC disk to start BASIC) into the disk drive, metal end first, label side up. The disk should be pushed in until it clicks into place. A message will then appear welcoming you to the Macintosh. You could also have inserted the disk first and then turned the power on.

To start MS-BASIC double-click the MS-Basic icon.

Figure I–6 ▪ Apple Macintosh Microcomputer

Saving and Loading Programs The commands to save and load a program on disk are found in the File Menu located at the top of the screen on the Menu Bar.

The OPEN command brings in a program from the disk so that it can be run, listed, or edited. When OPEN is chosen from the File Menu, a display box appears on the screen requesting the name of the program to be loaded. After entering the name of the file, move the pointer to the box where OK appears and then click the button on the mouse once. The program will then be loaded into memory.

The SAVE command saves a program on the disk after you have typed it or made changes to it. When SAVE is chosen from the File Menu, a dialog box appears on the screen requesting the name of the program to be saved. It assumes you want the current name, but the name can be changed.

DEC

Hardware The DECSYSTEM 2050 (see Figure I-7) is a large minicomputer that can have up to several million bytes of addressable primary storage for

Figure I–7 ▪ DECSYSTEM 2050 and VT-100 Terminal

programs—as opposed to a few tens of thousands of bytes in the microcomputers discussed here. The exact form of BASIC employed here is called BASIC PLUS 2 by the manufacturer.

The detailed hardware description very much depends on what CRT terminal is used with this computer. The one used here is the standard VT-100 terminal.

Signing On   The power switch (toggle variety) is located in the lower left on the back of the terminal. If the terminal is linked directly to the computer, press the CONTROL and C keys at the same time. If the terminal is linked to the computer by telephone, dial the correct number. When you hear a constant high-pitched tone, place the phone receiver in the modem; most modems have a light that comes on when the connection is made properly. Then press CONTROL-C.

Now a header will appear, followed by the symbol @.

```
TOPS-20 MONITOR 5.1(5622)
@
```

This is the prompt for the TOPS-20 MONITOR—the housekeeping program that controls the computer. You must now type LOGIN and account identifier followed by a password. The password should be privileged information—known only to those who need access to the programs in this particular account. For example, the programs for this manual were kept in an account called IACCT.MIS; access to the account was controlled by the password BASIC. The screen looked like this after log-in:

```
@LOGIN IACCT.MIS
```

The password did not appear on the screen, because the *monitor* knows that any characters following the blank after an account identifier are not to be made public.

After the RETURN key is pressed, the computer responds with a header giving the date and time. Then the monitor prompt (@) is displayed. To use the BASIC language, just type BASIC. When the computer is prepared to accept BASIC commands, it responds READY. To write a program, type NEW, and the computer asks for a name for the program.

```
READY
NEW
New program name--PAYROLL

READY
```

If you hit RETURN without supplying a name, the computer will call the program NONAME. You can now proceed to type in your program.

Saving and Loading Programs   We assume this computer uses disks for secondary storage. To save a program named PAYROLL, simply type SAVE PAYROLL.

```
READY
SAVE PAYROLL

READY
```

To load it at a later time, type OLD after the computer responds READY. The computer will ask for the old program's name. Type PAYROLL.

```
READY
OLD
Old file name--PAYROLL

READY
```

After the computer again responds READY, you may run or list the program or perform editing operations on it.

Signing Off   When you are finished, type GOODBYE. After the computer acknowledges your message, turn the terminal off.

IBM

Hardware   The IBM personal computer (Figure I–8) contains an enhanced version of Microsoft BASIC. We will discuss the hardware configuration using disk only. Consult your documentation for cassette commands.

Starting the Computer   Place the DOS diskette into Drive A, the left-hand drive. Then turn the computer on. The power switch is located on the right side (toward the rear) of the system unit. Don't forget to turn on the TV monitor, too. When the computer is turned on, it will try to load the DOS. (If no diskette has been placed into the disk drive, the computer will "come up" in Cassette BASIC.)

The IBM has three BASIC dialects—Cassette BASIC, Disk BASIC, and Advanced BASIC. For the purposes of this book, they are the same.

Once DOS has been booted (loaded), the computer asks for the date as follows:

```
Current date is Tue  1-01-1980
Enter new date:
```

After you have typed the date and pressed the carriage return, the computer asks for the time as follows:

```
Current time is  0:00:16.86
Enter new time:
```

Figure I–8 ▪ IBM Personal Computer

After you have typed the time and pressed the carriage return, it responds with:

```
The IBM Personal Computer DOS
Version 1.10 (C)Copyright IBM Corp 1981, 1982
A>
```

The A> is the DOS prompt. Simply type BASIC and press the carriage return to load the disk BASIC translator. The BASIC prompt is "OK." Now you are ready to start programming.

Saving and Loading Programs   The IBM has a convenient file-by-name catalog system for the DOS. To save a program on disk (for example, one named SALES), type:

```
SAVE "SALES"
```

The name of the program should be less than or equal to eight characters. Do not embed any spaces. To load the same program from disk, type:

```
LOAD "SALES"
```

You can then LIST and RUN the program. The IBM provides you with a set of predefined function keys on the left-hand side of the keyboard. These keys can be used as an alternative to typing out some system commands. The function key number and its function are given at the bottom of the screen.

PET/CBM

Hardware   The PET (Figure I–9) and CBM computers are made by the same manufacturer, Commodore Business Machines. For each number series, the two computers are nearly identical. For example, the PET 2001 and the CBM 2001 differ only as follows:

Figure I–9 ▪ PET Microcomputer

- The PET keyboard has graphics characters labeled; the CBM keyboard does not.
- The SHIFT key on a PET switches between capital letters and graphics characters, whereas the SHIFT key on a CBM switches between lower case and capital letters.

(See your manual to find out how to make the PET mimic the CBM and vice-versa with a simple POKE command.)

PET/CBM computers come in three basic styles. The oldest PETs have a small keyboard and a self-contained tape cassette. A later PET has a standard typewriter-style keyboard, but the tape cassette no longer fits inside the computer. Both of these styles have nine-inch diagonal CRT screens allowing twenty-five lines of forty characters each to be displayed. Recently, a larger screen allowing eighty-character rows has been introduced. All of these computers come with 8K, 16K, 24K, and 32K memories.

Starting the Computer The power switch is in back near the left-hand corner underneath the body of the computer. When the power switch is turned on, you see something like this:

```
***COMMODORE BASIC 4.0***
31743 BYTES FREE
READY
```

The first line tells which version of the BASIC language is available.[1] The second line tells how much memory your computer has (32K in this example). The third line indicates that you can immediately begin typing in BASIC line numbers and statements.

Saving and Loading Programs Programs are commonly accessed from either cassette tape or disk on this system.

- *Cassette:* The PET has a convenient file-by-name cataloging system. To save a program, position the tape to a blank area, and type SAVE and the program name in quotes. For example:

```
SAVE "REPORT"
```

You must also remember to press the RECORD and PLAY buttons on the cassette. If you have more than one cassette tape drive, you may have to specify the device number—otherwise, it will default to 1. For example, if you want to save REPORT on cassette tape drive 2, type

```
SAVE "REPORT",2
```

To load a stored program, you need only type LOAD and the program name (enclosed in quotes); for example:

```
LOAD "REPORT"
```

Then, when the cassette PLAY button is pressed, the computer will search for the named program. The names of other programs found during the search will be displayed on the screen. Therefore, the tape does not have to be

---

[1]All programming examples in this book were run on version 4.0; but no changes should be necessary to run them on versions 2.0 and 3.0, since the main differences are in disk commands that are beyond the scope of this book.

positioned precisely for loading. The computer will tell you when it has found the desired program and when it is loading the program into primary memory. An example—loading a program named IDIDIT, the fourth one on a tape—is shown below.

```
LOAD "IDIDIT"

PRESS PLAY ON TAPE #1
OK

SEARCHING FOR IDIDIT
FOUND COMMISSION
FOUND LAST
FOUND WEIGHT
FOUND IDIDIT
LOADING
READY.
```

■ *Disk:* The PET floppy disk system has two drives housed in one cabinet and a file-by-name catalog. To save a program named REPORT on drive 0, you type:

```
DSAVE "REPORT"
```

To specify drive 1, type:

```
DSAVE "REPORT",D1
```

If you alter a program that was read in from a disk and you want to replace the existing version on the disk, use @ as follows:

```
DSAVE "@REPORT",D1
```

To load a program from disk, you need only type:

```
DLOAD "REPORT"
```

or

```
DLOAD "REPORT",D1
```

The first example loads from drive 0, since that is the default unit.

TRS-80

Hardware These programs have all been tested on the TRS-80 Model III with the Model III BASIC language (see Figure I-10). An older computer, the Model I with Level II BASIC, is very similar to the Model III. The comments about BASIC programs here generally apply to either computer but do not deal with the Level I BASIC language.

Starting the Computer All peripherals should first be turned on. The computer is then turned on by a rocker switch located beneath the keyboard on the right hand side. All disk drives should be empty when the computer is turned on or off. If diskettes remain in the disk drives, the information on the diskettes could be destroyed. Next the TRSDOS diskette should be inserted in Drive 0. The RESET button must be pressed to enable the computer to load TRSDOS. The TRSDOS version number and date of creation will be displayed followed by the amount of RAM and the number of drives in the system. TRSDOS then prompts the user to enter the date in the form MM/DD/YY. The date in correct form must be entered and the ENTER key pressed before

TRSDOS will continue. Next the time in 24-hour for HH:MM:SS must be entered and the enter key pressed. To set the time at 00:00:00 the ENTER key may simply be pressed. The monitor will then display:

TRSDOS READY

The computer is then in the TRSDOS READY mode and TRSDOS commands may be entered.

To load the BASIC interpreter type:

BASIC

Press the ENTER key.
The computer will display:

HOW MANY FILES?

then:

MEMORY SIZE?

Press ENTER in response to each of these questions.
Next the computer will display a heading followed by:

READY

>

You may now begin to use Disk BASIC.
To use cassette BASIC hold down the reset and break keys after turning on the computer.

Saving and Loading Programs   Programs are commonly accessed from either cassette tape or disk on this system.

■ *Cassette:* The TRS-80 has a convenient file-by-name cataloging system. To save a program:

1. Position the tape to a blank area.
2. Type SAVE "program-name"; for example, SAVE "TRIAL".
3. Press the RECORD and PLAY buttons on the cassette.

To load a stored program, you need only type:

CLOAD

When the cassette PLAY button is pressed, the computer will search for the program. The names of the programs found during the search will be displayed on the screen. After the computer has found the desired program, it will load it into main memory.

■ *Disk:* To save a program (for example, TRIAL) just type:

SAVE "TRIAL"

and hit the ENTER button. To load the same program from disk, type

LOAD "TRIAL"

BASIC SYSTEM AND EDITING COMMANDS

The system and editing commands are **immediate-mode commands;** that is, they are executed as soon as the carriage control key (RETURN, ENTER) is pressed. They differ from BASIC language commands, which are not executed until the program is run. The most commonly used system commands are discussed below.

System Commands

NEW

This command tells the computer to erase any program currently in active memory. After typing this command, you can start entering a new program.

LIST

After typing in a long program, you may want to admire the finished product. Type LIST to see the program commands displayed at the terminal. If you have a very short program, LIST can display the whole program on the screen. However, if the program has more lines than the screen does, only the last part of the program will remain on the screen. Some screens permit only twenty-four lines to be displayed. You can display portions of programs by specifying the lines to be listed—LIST 250 – 400, for example. Most computers also allow you to suppress scrolling, that is, to freeze the listing temporarily (see ''Controlling the Scroll'' later in this section).

SAVE

After you have typed many program lines, you will want to avoid losing them when the computer is turned off, or if there is a power failure. To do this, you have to move a program from primary memory to a secondary storage medium such as a cassette tape or disk. This move is accomplished by the SAVE command. There are generally several options to this command; for example, you may supply a name that distinguishes this particular program from all others.

LOAD

This command moves the designated program from secondary storage to primary memory. Before moving the program. LOAD closes all open files and deletes all variables and program lines currently residing in memory.

Controlling the Scroll   If your program's output consists of forty lines of information but your screen only has a twenty-four-line capacity, how will you see all your output? The forty lines will be displayed so quickly that you will not be able to read them until the listing is finished. By then, however, the first sixteen lines will be gone—scrolled off the top of the screen.

Most computers have a means of controlling the scroll of the screen. The programmer can simply push one or two keys to freeze the display and then press the same keys to resume listing when desired. This method also can be used to freeze the output listing of a program during execution. Table I–1 summarizes the method of scroll freezing, as well as the type of editor (discussed below) used on each of the five computers.

Table I–1 ▪ Common System Commands

	DEC	APPLE	APPLE MACINTOSH	PET/COMMODORE 64
POWERSWITCH LOCATION	Left rear of terminal	Left rear of terminal	Left rear terminal	Right side panel (rear)
SIGNON PROCEDURES			No response	
User	Control-C	No response	Icon of disk with blinking question mark	No response
Computer response	TOPS-20 MONITOR	APPLE II	No response	***COMMODORE
			Insert appropriate disk	64 BASIC
Users	LOG ACCT. #	No response		V2***
	PASSWORD			No response
STARTING BASIC				
User	BASIC	Comes up in	Insert MS-BASIC disk	Comes up in
Computer response	READY	BASIC	Display directory of MS-BASIC	BASIC
User	NEW	Flashing cursor	disk	READY
Computer response	NEW FILENAME—		Double click MS-BASIC icon	(Flashing block)
User	Enter name of program; begin typing program	Begin typing program	Command box appears Begin typing program	Begin typing program
SYSTEM COMMANDS		LIST	(The following can be typed or selected from a menu)	LIST
List	LIST	RUN		RUN
Execute a program	RUN	Type line #, then	LIST	Type line #, then
Delete a line	DELETE line #	RETURN	RUN	RETURN
Store program on disk	SAVE	SAVE name	Type line #, then RETURN	SAVE "name",8
Store program on tape	Does not apply	SAVE	SAVE filename	SAVE "name"
Retrieve program from disk	OLD FILENAME—	LOAD name	Does not apply	LOAD "name",
Retrieve program from tape	Does not apply	or RUN name8	LOAD	LOAD "name"
List of file names	CATALOG	LOAD	OPEN filename	For Disk: LOAD
		CATALOG	Does not apply	"$", 8 LIST
			Files automatically appear	For Cassette: LOAD "$" LIST
SIGN-OFF PROCEDURES				
User	GOODBYE or BYE	No response	Select QUIT from File Menu	No response
Computer response	KILLED JOB	No response	Displays directory window	No response
User	Power off	Power off	Select CLOSE and then select EJECT from File Menu to quit MS-BASIC; Turn power off	Power off

Table continued on next page

Table I–1 ▪ **Continued**

	TRS-80	IBM/Cassette BASIC	IBM/disk BASIC
POWERSWITCH LOCATION	Right front under keyboard	Right rear of computer	Right rear of computer
SIGN-ON PROCEDURES			
User	No response	No response	No response
Computer response	CASS? MEMORY SIZE? RADIO SHACK MODEL III BASIC (C) 80 TANDY	IBM Personal Computer BASIC Version C1.00 Copyright IBM Corp. 1981 61404 Bytes Free OK	Enter today's date (m-d-y); time The IBM Personal Computer DOS Version 1.10 (C) Copyright IBM Corp. 1981, 1982 A >
User	Respond to CASS? and MEMORY SIZE? Queries	No response	Respond to date query
STARTING BASIC			
User	Comes up in BASIC	Comes up in BASIC	Type BASIC or BASICA (For Advanced BASIC) after computer types A >
Computer response	READY	OK	OK
User	Begin typing program	Begin typing program	Begin typing program
SYSTEM COMMANDS			
List	LIST	LIST	LIST
Execute a program	RUN	RUN	RUN
Delete a line	DELETE line #	DELETE line #	DELETE line #
Store program on disk	SAVE "name"	Does not apply	SAVE "name"
Store program on tape	SAVE "name"	SAVE "name"	Does not apply
Retrieve program from disk	LOAD "name"	Does not apply	LOAD "name
Retrieve program from tape	CLOAD "name"	LOAD "name"	Does not apply
List of file names	Return to system level and type DIR	FILES	FILES
SIGN-OFF PROCEDURES			
User	No response	No response	No response
Computer response	No response	No response	No response
User	Power off	Power off	Power off

CATALOG

A **catalog** is a program that supplies a complete alphabetical list of a user's file. This command is used to list the file names of your programs and data files. To use this command, type CATALOG or just CAT and press RETURN. The command to list the file names may vary for the different computers (see Table I–1).

Editing Commands

Everyone makes typing mistakes. You should quickly learn how to correct yours. You may find a mistake before you press the RETURN key, or you may find it later. These two conditions call for different methods of correction.

BEFORE RETURN HAS BEEN PRESSED

Suppose you type LOST when you wish to LIST a program. If you notice the error before pressing RETURN, you can move the computer's cursor back to the O in LOST by pressing the DELETE key (on the DEC), the ← key (on the Apple, IBM, and TRS-80), or the INST DEL key (on the PET/Commodore 64), or the BACKSPACE key on the Macintosh. Then you can retype LIST correctly.

AFTER RETURN HAS BEEN PRESSED

If you notice an error after RETURN has been pressed, the simplest correction, in principle, is to retype the whole line. This may get tiresome for long lines, however—especially if you need to change only one character. Each computer has a means of correcting mistakes within a given line. There is not enough space here for a full explanation of these methods, but there are two general kinds—the screen editor and the line editor.

To use the screen editor, list the portion of the program containing the error. Then move the cursor to the position of the error—typically by pressing four keys with arrows that move the cursor up, down, left, or right. The incorrect characters then can be typed over or deleted, or new characters can be inserted between existing characters.

The line editor works on individual lines. The user specifies the line containing the error and uses commands such as REPLACE, INSERT, and DELETE instead of moving the cursor to the error.

Type of Editor and Scroll Control

COMPUTER	SCREEN EDITOR?	LINE EDITOR?	SCROLL STOP/START
DECSYSTEM 20	X	X	NO SCROLL[1]
Apple	X		CTRL-S[2]
IBM/Microsoft	X		CTRL-NUMLOCK[3]
TRS-80		X	SHIFT-@[4]
PET/Commodore 64	X		None[5]
Apple Macintosh		X	Scroll bars[6]

NOTES:
[1] NO SCROLL is a separate single key.
[2] CTRL-S means hold down the CONTROL key and the S key at the same time.
[3] CTRL-NUMLOCK means hold down the control key and the NUMLOCK key at the same time.
[4] SHIFT-@ means hold down the SHIFT key and the @ key at the same time.
[5] There is no scroll stop/start key: however, pressing the shift key slows down the scroll to one line at a time.
[6] "Clicking" on the scroll bar or scroll arrow will scroll the display. "Dragging" the scroll box will also scroll the display.

SUMMARY POINTS

■ BASIC (Beginner's All-purpose Symbolic Instruction Code) was developed in the mid-1960s by Professors John G. Kemeny and Thomas E. Kurtz.

■ BASIC has rules of grammar (syntax) to which programmers must adhere.

■ The following are the five steps in the programming process: (1) define the problem; (2) design a solution; (3) write the program; (4) compile, debug, and test the program; and (5) document the program.

■ System commands are used by the programmer to communicate with the operating system of the computer. Some commonly used ones are NEW, LIST, and SAVE.

■ Editing commands help the programmer correct mistakes.

■ Table I–1 summarizes start-up procedures and common system commands.

REVIEW QUESTIONS

1. What is BASIC?
2. List the five steps of the programming process.
3. What is documentation, and why is it important?
4. What are the system and editing commands used for? List three system commands.

OVERVIEW

One of the best ways to learn any programming language is to examine sample programs. This and the remaining sections in the BASIC supplement will intersperse discussions of the language's general characteristics with program examples.

This section discusses some BASIC fundamentals: line numbers, BASIC statements, constants, character strings, and variables. All are demonstrated so that you can use them properly when you write programs.

FUNDAMENTALS OF THE BASIC LANGUAGE

A BASIC program is a sequence of instructions that tells the computer how to solve a problem. Figure II–1 is an example. This program calculates the sales tax of an item that costs $5.50.

Notice that each instruction contains a line number and a BASIC statement. BASIC statements are composed of special programming commands, numeric or character string constants, numeric or string variables, and formulas (also called expressions). Line 160 from the sample program is a typical BASIC statement. It tells the computer to multiply two values together and place the result in a location called T. T is the location in memory where the sales tax is stored.

Note that pseudocode rather than flowcharting has been used to describe the processing steps to be performed in the program. For more information about pseudocode, see Chapter 9.

On the DECSYSTEM 20 there are two commands, RUN and RUNNH, that can be used to execute (run) a program. If RUN is used, as in Figure II–1, the computer will print a header giving the name of your program, the date, and the time as well as the output of the program. The RUNNH (Run No Header) command will eliminate the header and print only the output of the program. Throughout the remainder of this book we will use the RUNNH format. (See box titled "Important Keys and Commands.")

LINE NUMBERS

The **line number** must be an integer between 1 and 99999. The upper limit for line numbers may vary according to the system being used. Program statements are executed by the computer in the sequence in which they are numbered. (Later we will explain how this sequence can be altered.) Line numbers also can be used as labels to refer to specific statements in the program.

Line numbers do not have to be specified in increments of 1. Using increments of 10, for example, makes it easier to insert new statements between existing lines at a later time without renumbering all the old statements in the program. For example, if we wanted to insert a new statement in the sample program between statements 150 and 160, we could number the new statement 155 without disturbing the order or numbering of the existing statements (see Figure II–2). The BASIC interpreter or compiler arranges all the program statements in ascending order according to line number, even though the lines actually may have been entered in some other order.

Another advantage of BASIC line numbers is that they permit changes to be made to the program as it is being entered. For example, if two lines are

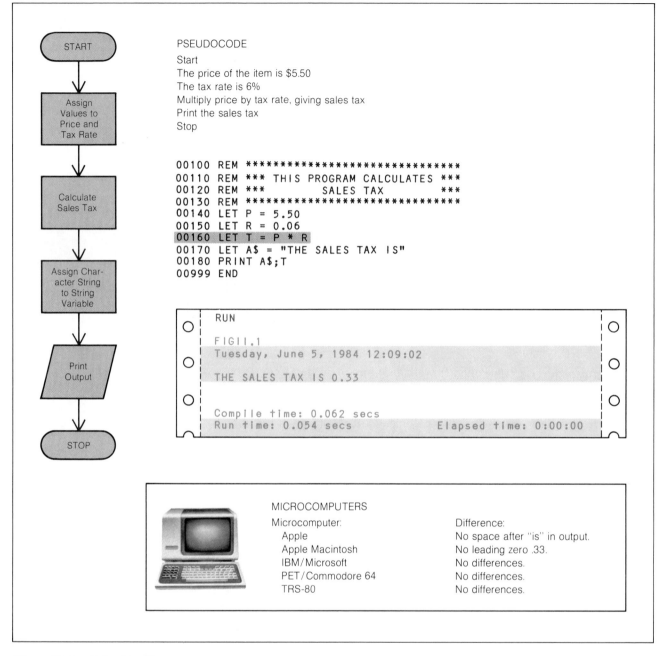

PSEUDOCODE
Start
The price of the item is $5.50
The tax rate is 6%
Multiply price by tax rate, giving sales tax
Print the sales tax
Stop

```
00100 REM *******************************
00110 REM *** THIS PROGRAM CALCULATES ***
00120 REM ***          SALES TAX       ***
00130 REM *******************************
00140 LET P = 5.50
00150 LET R = 0.06
00160 LET T = P * R
00170 LET A$ = "THE SALES TAX IS"
00180 PRINT A$;T
00999 END
```

```
RUN

FIGII.1
Tuesday, June 5, 1984 12:09:02

THE SALES TAX IS 0.33


Compile time: 0.062 secs
Run time: 0.054 secs          Elapsed time: 0:00:00
```

MICROCOMPUTERS

Microcomputer:	Difference:
Apple	No space after "is" in output.
Apple Macintosh	No leading zero .33.
IBM/Microsoft	No differences.
PET/Commodore 64	No differences.
TRS-80	No differences.

Figure II–1 ▪ Sales Tax Program

typed in with the same line number, the computer will accept the last one entered as the correct one. Thus, if we make a mistake in a statement, we can simply type in the same line number and the correct statement. Suppose that in the sales tax example, we gave P the wrong price; it should have been $6.50, not $5.50. All we have to do to correct this is type the number of the line to be changed and then retype the statement with the correct price:

```
00140 LET P = 6.50
```

The line just entered will be put into computer memory in place of the original line 140.

Important Keys and Commands

COMPUTER	EXECUTION COMMAND	CARRIAGE CONTROL KEY	COMMENTS
DECSYSTEM 20	RUN or RUNNH	RETURN	RUNNH means "RUN No Header." When RUN alone is pressed, the computer points out the date and a system-identifying label.
Apple	RUN	RETURN	
Apple Macintosh	RUN	RETURN	
IBM/Microsoft	RUN	↵	Although there is no lettering on the key, we will refer to it as *carriage return*.
TRS-80	RUN	ENTER	The ENTER key is located on the right side of the keyboard. This is the location of the RETURN key on the other computers. The two keys serve the same purpose.
PET/Commodore 64	RUN	RETURN	

Figure II-2 ▪ Sales Tax Program with Inserted Line

```
00100 REM ********************************
00110 REM *** THIS PROGRAM CALCULATES ***
00120 REM ***          SALES TAX       ***
00130 REM ********************************
00140 LET P = 5.50
00150 LET R = 0.06
00155 REM ***    TAX = PRICE * RATE    ***
00160 LET T = P * R
00170 LET A$ = "THE SALES TAX IS"
00180 PRINT A$;T
00999 END


RUNNH
THE SALES TAX IS 0.33
```

MICROCOMPUTERS

Microcomputer:	Difference:
Apple	No space after "is" in output.
Apple Macintosh	No leading zero .33.
IBM/Microsoft	No differences.
PET/Commodore 64	No differences.
TRS-80	No differences.

BASIC STATEMENT COMPONENTS

In the remaining portion of this section, we will take a closer look at numeric and character string constants and numeric and string variables.

Constants

Constants are values that do not change during a program's execution. There are two kinds: numeric and character string.

NUMERIC CONSTANTS

BASIC permits numbers to be represented in two ways: as real numbers or in exponential notation.

Real Numbers   Real numbers can be either integers or decimal fractions. The following are some examples of real numbers.

	Real	
	↙	↘
Decimals		Integers
0.91		+8765
+72.89		−103
−9.671		52

There are some rules to remember when using numbers in BASIC:

1. No commas can be embedded within numbers:

$$42305 \text{ (valid)} \qquad 1,295 \text{ (invalid)}$$

BASIC interprets the invalid example not as the number one thousand two hundred ninety-five, but as the number one and the number two hundred ninety-five.

2. If the number is negative, it must be preceded by a minus sign:

$$-1.23 \text{ (valid)} \qquad 1.23- \text{ (invalid)}$$

3. If no sign is included, the number is assumed to be positive:

$$7146 \text{ is the same as } +7146$$

Exponential Notation   Exponential notation (scientific notation) usually is used for very large or very small numbers. Some examples follow:

$$9.26347E+07 \qquad 2.984E-04$$

The E represents base 10, and the signed number following the E is the power to which 10 is raised. The number preceding the E is called the mantissa and in most systems lies between 1.000 and 9.999. A plus sign (+) by the power indicates that the decimal point is to be shifted to the right that number of places, whereas a minus sign (−) indicates that the decimal point should be shifted left the power number of places (see Figure II–3).

The following are examples of exponential notation:

Decimal	Power Equivalent	Exponential Notation
6783	6.783×10^3	6.783E+03
0.0002217	2.217×10^{-4}	2.217E−04
−4132784	-4.132784×10^6	−4.132784E+06

Figure II–3 ▪ Exponential Notation

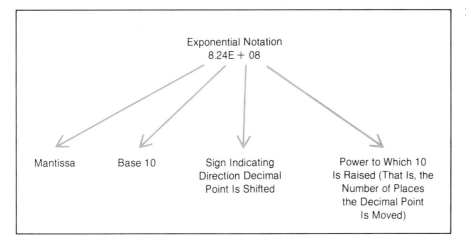

CHARACTER STRING CONSTANTS

The other type of constant is the character string. Character strings are composed of alphanumeric data—a sequence of letters, numbers, and special characters enclosed in quotation marks. The maximum number of characters allowed in a character string varies from system to system. On some systems it is not necessary to enclose character strings within quotation marks in data statements unless commas and semicolons are to be included within the character string. It is generally considered good practice to use the quotes, however. The following are examples of character strings:

```
"STEVE"
"11/12/84"
"BOWLING GREEN, OHIO"
```

The program in Figure II–1 contains a character string in line 170:

```
00170 LET A$ = "THE SALES TAX IS"
```

Variables

Any data values to be used by a program must be stored in the computer either before or during execution of the program. The computer has a great number of memory locations, which are assigned names by the programmer. These names are called variable names, because the value stored in a memory location can change as the program is executed. A variable is the name of the location or the address in memory where the value is stored and can only represent one value at a time. Memory works something like post office boxes. The variable is the P.O. box number, the memory cell is the actual box itself, and the value that is stored in memory is like the mail; however, in a computer memory "box" there can only be one piece of "mail" at a time. Each time a new piece of "mail" is put in the memory "box," the old one is taken out.

There are two types of variables: numeric and string. In our examples, P, R, and T are numeric variables, and A$ is a string variable.

NUMERIC VARIABLES

A numeric variable name represents a number that is either supplied to the computer by the programmer or internally calculated by the computer during execution of the program. A numeric variable name can be either one letter alone or one letter followed by one numeric digit. (Almost all BASICs permit the use of two letters, and many computer systems permit more descriptive variable names—see box.) The following examples show valid and invalid numeric variable names:

Valid	Invalid and Why	
X	33	(must begin with a letter)
B4	*C	(must begin with a letter)
A9	6	(cannot be a single digit)

Note lines 140,150, and 160 in the program in Figure II–2:

```
00140 LET P = 5.50
00150 LET R = 0.06
00160 LET T = P * R
```

P contains the price of the item—$5.50. R holds the tax rate, and the location of T has the result of price multiplied by rate.

STRING VARIABLES

A string variable name can represent the value of a character string—for example, a name, an address, or a Social Security number. String variable names are distinguished from numeric variable names by the use of the dollar sign ($) following a single alphabetic character. The following are examples of valid and invalid string variable names:

Valid	Invalid and Why
H$	6$ (first character must be alphabetic)
T$	X (last character must be $)

Many computer systems permit the use of more descriptive string variable names. However, all systems require that the first character be alphabetic and the last character be $. See the box for description of names permitted by other systems.

Numeric Variable Names		
MICROCOMPUTER	NUMBER OF UNIQUE CHARACTERS RECOGNIZED	ADDITIONAL CHARACTERS PERMITTED
DECSYSTEM 20	35	No
Apple	2	Yes
Apple Macintosh	40	Yes
IBM/Microsoft	40	No
TRS-80	2	Yes
PET/Commodore 64	2	Yes

String Variable Names

MICROCOMPUTER	NUMBER OF UNIQUE CHARACTERS RECOGNIZED	ADDITIONAL CHARACTERS PERMITTED
DECSYSTEM 20	34 (plus $)	No
Apple	2 (plus $)	Yes[1]
Apple Macintosh	40 (plus $)	Yes
IBM/Microsoft	40 (plus $)	No
TRS-80	2 (plus $)	Yes[1]
PET/Commodore 64	2 (plus $)	Yes[1]

[1]When additional characters are used, the last character must be a dollar sign ($).

Typical examples of the proper use of string variables can be seen in lines 170 and 180 of the sample program:

```
00170 LET A$ = "THE SALES TAX IS"
00180 PRINT A$;T
```

The character string "THE SALES TAX IS" is assigned to the string variable name A$. In line 180, the values of A$ and T are printed out. This is the output:

```
RUNNH
THE SALES TAX IS 0.33
```

Reserved Words

Reserved words are words that have a special meaning to the translator program (the interpreter or compiler) of the computer. These words cannot be used as variable names. The "Common DECSYSTEM 20 Reserved Words" box shows some of the most commonly used reserved words for the DECSYS-TEM 20. Refer to your system's manual for additional reserved words or any differences in your system.

Common DECSYSTEM 20 Reserved Words

ABS	CALL	CHR	COS
DATA	DEF	DEL	DELETE
DIM	ELSE	END	EXP
FOR	GET	GO	GOSUB
GOTO	IF	INPUT	INT
LEFT$	LET	LOG	MAT
MID$	NEXT	NOT	ON
OPEN	OR	PRINT	PUT
READ	REM	RESTORE	RETURN
RIGHT	RND	SGN	SIN
SQR	SQRT	STEP	STOP
STR$	SYS	TAB	TAN
THEN	TO	UNTIL	VAL
WHILE			

SUMMARY POINTS

■ A BASIC program is a series of instructions. Each one is composed of a line number and a BASIC statement.

■ The line numbers serve (1) as labels by which statements can be referenced and (2) as instructions to specify the order of execution of the program.

■ Using line numbers in increments of 5 or 10 permits easy insertion of new statements.

■ BASIC statements contain special reserved words (programming commands), numeric or character string constants, numeric or string variables, and formulas.

■ Constants are values that do not change. A valid numeric constant is any real number expressed as an integer, decimal fraction, or in exponential notation. Character strings are alphanumeric data enclosed in quotation marks.

■ Variable names are programmer-supplied names that specify locations in memory where data values may be stored. Numeric variable names represent numbers. String variables contain alphanumeric values, and their names are distinguished from numeric variable names by the symbol $.

■ Reserved words are words which have a special meaning to the translator program of the computer, so they may not be used as variable names.

REVIEW QUESTIONS

1. What are the two components of a BASIC instruction?
2. What types of things are BASIC statements composed of?
3. What are two main uses of line numbers? Why is it advantageous to use them in increments of five or ten?
4. What is a variable? Name two types and explain how they differ.

OVERVIEW

This section describes four elementary BASIC statements—REM, LET, PRINT, and END. The LET statement is used to input, or assign, data to variables and to perform arithmetic calculations. The PRINT statement allows the programmer to see the results of processing. Processing is stopped with the END statement. The REM statement is presented here to underscore the importance of program documentation.

THE REM STATEMENT

The remark (REM) statement provides information for the programmer or anyone else reading the program; it provides no information to the computer. The REM statement is used to document the program; the programmer generally uses it to explain program segments, to define variables used within the program, or to note any special instructions. Because they are non-executable statements, REM statements can be placed anywhere throughout the program.

The general format of the REM statement is this:

line# REM comment

Some REM statements that could be used to document or explain a program are presented next. For example:

```
00010 REM *** THIS PROGRAM CALCULATES COMPANY PAYROLL ***
```

This example illustrates the use of a REM statement to explain the purpose of a program. A REM statement such as this could be used anywhere in a program to explain the purpose of individual program segments. Notice the asterisks that surround the descriptive statement. Many programmers will use the asterisks (although any character could be used) to set off the REM statement from the other statements in a program. This technique allows the REM statements to be easily identified when the programmer is looking through long program listings.

The following example illustrates the use of a REM statement to define a variable used within the program:

```
00030 REM *** O = OVERTIME PAY ***
```

It is a good practice to define the variables used in a program, especially if other people will be using it.

It is possible to have a REM statement with no comment following it, or one followed by asterisks (*):

```
00070 REM
00080 REM ******************************************
```

In these cases, the REM statement could be used to set off comments from executable statements and thus improve the readability of the program.

THE LET STATEMENT

The purpose of the LET, or assignment, statement is to assign values to variables. It can be used to enter data into a program as well as to process it.

The general format of the LET statement is this:

line# LET variable = expression

The expression may be a constant, arithmetic formula or a variable. The following are examples:

Statement	Expression	Type
00010 LET Z = 35	35	Numeric constant
00020 LET B$ = "STEVE"	"STEVE"	Character string constant
00030 LET R = G	G	Numeric variable
00040 LET N$ = C$	C$	String variable
00050 LET Y = T * 4	T * 4	Arithmetic formula

The LET statement can be used to assign values to numeric or string variables directly or to assign the result of a calculation to a numeric variable. In either case, the value or calculated result of an expression on the right side of the equal sign is assigned to the variable on the left side. It is important to note that the statement is not evaluated in the same way as an algebraic expression.

When BASIC assigns a value to a variable on the left side of the equation, it really is putting that value in a storage location in memory labeled by that variable name. Since a storage location can only be represented by a variable name, only a variable can be on the left.

The following examples of LET statements are presented along with a short description of how they are executed.

LET Statement	Computer Execution
00010 LET N = 25	The numeric value 25 is assigned to the location called N.
00050 LET R = S + T	The values in S and T are added together and assigned to R.
00100 LET N$ = "THE WHITE HOUSE"	The character string enclosed in quotes is placed into the string variable N$ (the quotes are not).
00130 LET T = T + 1	1 is added to the current value of T, and the result is assigned to T. This result replaces whatever was in T previously. Notice that this procedure effectively counts how many times line 130 is executed.
00170 LET O = (2.25 + K - J) / (L * 20)	The arithmetic expression to the right of the equal sign is evaluated and assigned to O.

The reserved word LET identifies a statement in BASIC as an assignment statement. However, some compilers and interpreters do not require it. These versions accept the statement without the reserved word LET as follows:

00050 R = 4.55

This shorthand method can save both time and memory space.

Arithmetic Expressions

In BASIC, arithmetic expressions are composed of constants, numeric variables, and arithmetic operators. The arithmetic operators that can be used are the following:

BASIC Arithmetic Operation Symbol	Operation	Arithmetic Example	BASIC Arithmetic Expression
+	Addition	$A + B$	$A + B$
−	Subtraction	$A - B$	$A - B$
*	Multiplication	$A \times B$	$A * B$
/	Division	$A \div B$	A / B
∧ or ** or ↑ or [	Exponentiation	A^B	$A \wedge B$ or $A ** B$ or $A \uparrow B$ or $A [B$

Some examples of valid expressions in LET statements follow:

```
00010 LET A = T - U
00020 LET B = Q1 + Q2 + Q3 + Q4
00030 LET X = N ^ 5 / 2 * T
00040 LET Y = 2.5 * W
```

Hierarchy of Operations

When more than one operation is to be performed within an arithmetic expression, the computer follows a hierarchy, or priority, of operations. When parentheses are present in an expression, the operation within the parentheses is performed first. If parentheses are nested, the operation in the innermost set of parentheses is performed first. Thus, in the expression

```
(X + (Z - 2) * Y) / 15
```

the first operation to be performed is to subtract 2 from the value in Z. The result of that operation is then multiplied by Y and added to X because of the rules of priority discussed below. Once the expression within the outer parenthesis has been evaluated, that result is divided by 15.

Parentheses aside, operations are performed according to the following rules of priority:

Priority	Operation	Symbol
First	Exponentiation	∧ or ** or ↑ or [
Second	Multiplication or division	* or /
Third	Addition or subtraction	+ or −

Operations with high priority are performed before operations with lower priority (subject to our discussion on parentheses). If more than one operation is to be performed at the same level, for example,

```
5 ^ 4 ^ 2
```

the computer evaluates them from left to right. In this example, the 5 would be raised to the fourth power and then the result, 625, raised to the second power. The answer is 390,625.

The following are examples of these hierarchical rules:

Expression	Computer Evaluation
Expression 1	
2 * 5 + 1	
First: 2 * 5 = 10	Multiplication has a higher priority than addition, so it is done first.
Second: 10 + 1 = 11	Then the addition is done. The result is 11.
Expression 2	
2 * (5 + 1)	
First: (5 + 1) = 6	In this case, the addition must be done first, because it is enclosed in parentheses.
Second: 2 * 6 = 12	The result is multiplied by 2. Compare this result with the result in Expression 1.
Expression 3	
2 ∧ 3 / 4 − 2	
First: 2 ∧ 3 = 8	The priority order tells the computer to start with exponentiation.
Second: 8 / 4 = 2	Next is division.
Third: 2 − 2 = 0	Last, the subtraction is done. The result is 0.
Expression 4	
4 * 5 + 1 / 2 * 21	
First: 4 * 5 = 20	There are three operations at the same level: *, /, and *. They are performed from left to right. Last, the addition is done; the result is 30.5.
Second: 1 / 2 = 0.5	
Third: 0.5 * 21 = 10.5	
Fourth: 20 + 10.5 = 30.5	

Assigning Character Strings

The LET statement also can be used to assign a character string value to a string name. A character string is composed of alphanumeric data enclosed in quotes. For example,

```
00010 LET N$ = "MY NAME IS"
00020 LET K$ = N$
```

The following examples show valid and invalid LET statements:

Valid	Invalid and Why	
00010 LET X = Y / Z	00010 LET Y / Z = X	(Only a variable can appear on the left side of the equal sign.)
00020 LET N$ = "STEVE"	00020 LET N = "STEVE"	(A character string must be assigned to a string variable.)
00030 LET T = N1 + N2	00030 LET T = N1 + N$	(A string variable cannot be part of an arithmetic expression.)

Figure III–1, which calculates average monthly salary, illustrates several uses of the LET statement. The logic in this program is straightforward: First enter the total amount of salary for the year; second, calculate the monthly average; and third, print the results.

Line 140 is a LET statement used to enter the total amount of salary for the year, $15,000.00, into the numeric variable T. The expression in line 150 calculates the monthly average—that is, the total amount of salary for the year divided by 12, the number of months in a year. Line 160 assigns a character string to the string variable name T$. The character string and the results of the calculation are printed by line 170.

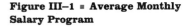

Figure III–1 ▪ Average Monthly Salary Program

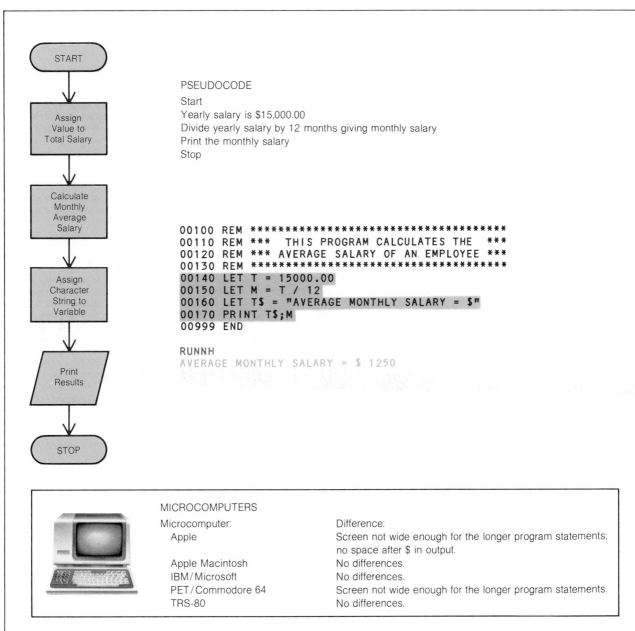

PSEUDOCODE
Start
Yearly salary is $15,000.00
Divide yearly salary by 12 months giving monthly salary
Print the monthly salary
Stop

```
00100 REM *************************************
00110 REM ***   THIS PROGRAM CALCULATES THE   ***
00120 REM *** AVERAGE SALARY OF AN EMPLOYEE ***
00130 REM *************************************
00140 LET T = 15000.00
00150 LET M = T / 12
00160 LET T$ = "AVERAGE MONTHLY SALARY = $"
00170 PRINT T$;M
00999 END

RUNNH
AVERAGE MONTHLY SALARY = $ 1250
```

MICROCOMPUTERS

Microcomputer:	Difference:
Apple	Screen not wide enough for the longer program statements; no space after $ in output.
Apple Macintosh	No differences.
IBM/Microsoft	No differences.
PET/Commodore 64	Screen not wide enough for the longer program statements.
TRS-80	No differences.

THE PRINT STATEMENT

The PRINT statement is used to print or display the results of computer processing. It also permits the formatting, or arranging, of output. The general form of the PRINT statement is as follows:

$$\text{line\# PRINT} \left\{ \begin{array}{l} \text{Variables} \\ \text{Literals} \\ \text{Arithmetic expressions} \\ \text{Combination of above} \end{array} \right.$$

PRINT statements can take several forms, depending on the output required. Let us look at some examples.

Printing the Values of Variables

We can tell the computer to print values assigned to memory locations by simply using the keyword PRINT with the variable names after it, separated by commas:

```
00200 PRINT X,Y,Z
```

The comma is used to separate one variable from another; it also is used for carriage control (more on this in Section IV).

Printing has no effect on the contents of memory. The PRINT statement is a simple reading of the value of a variable that allows the user to see what the contents are. Normally, each time the computer encounters a PRINT statement, it begins printing output on a new line. Exceptions to this are discussed in Section IV.

Printing Literals

A literal is an expression consisting of alphabetic, numeric, or special characters or a combination of all three. The following are examples of literals:

ABC	32.57	Q1B97
DEF	100	N$*#!

CHARACTER STRINGS

A character string literal is a group of letters, numbers, or special characters that you want printed on the output page. To have that done, enclose the group in quotation marks (''). Whatever is inside the quotation marks is printed exactly as it is; for example,

```
00040 PRINT "EXAMPLE - %)*&^%$#@!"
```

would appear on the output page as

```
EXAMPLE - %)*$^%$#@!
```

To print column headings, put each heading in quotes and separate each group by a comma. The comma instructs the printer to skip to the next print zone (more on this in Section IV). An example follows:

```
00070 PRINT "DATE","NAME","CLASS"
```

When line 70 is executed, the character strings are printed out exactly as typed, except that the quotation marks do not appear:

```
DATE          NAME          CLASS
```

NUMERIC LITERALS

Numeric literals do not have to be enclosed in quotation marks to be printed. For example, the statement

```
00100 PRINT 99
```

will print the following result:

```
99
```

Printing the Values of Expressions

The computer can print not only the values of literals and the values of variables but also the values of arithmetic expressions.

```
00010 LET A = 66
00020 LET B = 23
00030 PRINT A * 57 / B
```

First, the computer evaluates the expression according to the rules of priority. The result is printed as follows:

```
163.5652
```

If the value of the expression is extremely large or extremely small, the computer may print it in exponential notation.

Figure III–2 deals with the expressions in both decimal and exponential forms. When the PRINT statement in line 40 is executed, the three expressions are evaluated and their values printed. Notice that the first and last numbers are too large to be printed conventionally and are printed instead in exponential notation.

Printing Blank Lines

A PRINT statement with nothing typed after it will provide a blank line of output. For example,

```
00150 PRINT
```

To skip more than one line, simply include more than one of these PRINT statements:

```
00180 PRINT
00190 PRINT
```

THE END STATEMENT

The END statement indicates the end of the program and so must be assigned the highest line number in the program. The general format of the END statement is this:

line# END

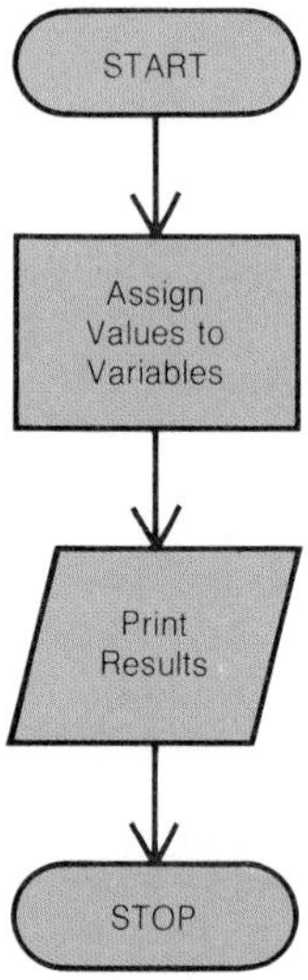

```
                    PSEUDOCODE
                    Start
                    X equals 750141
                    Y equals 523499898
                    Z equals 0.12575
                    Print X multiplied by Y
                    Print Z subtracted from X
                    Print Z multiplied by Y and added to 222


                    00010 LET X = 750141
                    00020 LET Y = 523499898
                    00030 LET Z = 0.12575
                    00040 PRINT X * Y,X - Z,Z * Y + 222

                    RUNNH
                       3.926987E+14   750140.9      6.583033E+07
```

MICROCOMPUTERS

Microcomputer:	Difference:		
	X * Y	X − Z	Z * Y + 222
Apple	3.92698737E+14	7501401.874	65830334.2
Apple Macintosh	392698736985620	750140.87425	65830334.1735
IBM/Microsoft	3.926987E+14	750140.9	6.58033E+07
PET/Commodore 64	3.92698737E+14	750140.874	65830334.2
TRS-80	3.92699E+14	750141	6.58303E+07

Figure III–2 ▪ Numeric Output

The use of an all-nines number for the END statement is a common programming practice, although it is not required. This convention serves as a reminder to the programmer to include the END statement and helps insure that it is positioned properly. See line 999 in the salary program (Figure III–1) for an example of an END statement.

A PROGRAMMING PROBLEM

Problem Definition

A university sorority was offered the following profits on candy by a local candy shop.

- 35 percent profit on pecan turtles.
- 42 percent profit on peanut clusters.
- 45 percent profit on chocolate bars.

Figure III–3 ▪ Candy Profit Program

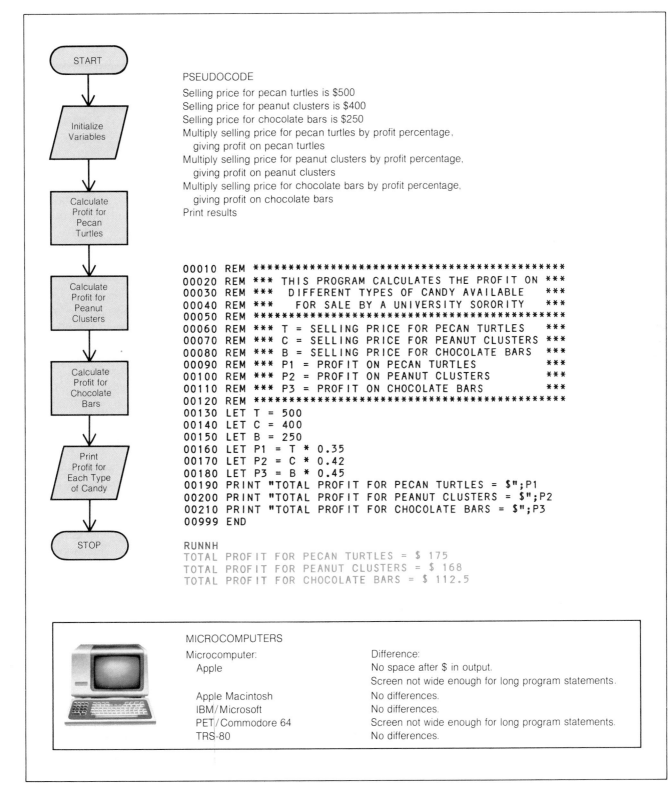

PSEUDOCODE

Selling price for pecan turtles is $500
Selling price for peanut clusters is $400
Selling price for chocolate bars is $250
Multiply selling price for pecan turtles by profit percentage,
    giving profit on pecan turtles
Multiply selling price for peanut clusters by profit percentage,
    giving profit on peanut clusters
Multiply selling price for chocolate bars by profit percentage,
    giving profit on chocolate bars
Print results

```
00010 REM ***********************************************
00020 REM *** THIS PROGRAM CALCULATES THE PROFIT ON ***
00030 REM ***   DIFFERENT TYPES OF CANDY AVAILABLE   ***
00040 REM ***    FOR SALE BY A UNIVERSITY SORORITY   ***
00050 REM ***********************************************
00060 REM *** T = SELLING PRICE FOR PECAN TURTLES    ***
00070 REM *** C = SELLING PRICE FOR PEANUT CLUSTERS  ***
00080 REM *** B = SELLING PRICE FOR CHOCOLATE BARS   ***
00090 REM *** P1 = PROFIT ON PECAN TURTLES           ***
00100 REM *** P2 = PROFIT ON PEANUT CLUSTERS         ***
00110 REM *** P3 = PROFIT ON CHOCOLATE BARS          ***
00120 REM ***********************************************
00130 LET T = 500
00140 LET C = 400
00150 LET B = 250
00160 LET P1 = T * 0.35
00170 LET P2 = C * 0.42
00180 LET P3 = B * 0.45
00190 PRINT "TOTAL PROFIT FOR PECAN TURTLES = $";P1
00200 PRINT "TOTAL PROFIT FOR PEANUT CLUSTERS = $";P2
00210 PRINT "TOTAL PROFIT FOR CHOCOLATE BARS = $";P3
00999 END

RUNNH
TOTAL PROFIT FOR PECAN TURTLES = $ 175
TOTAL PROFIT FOR PEANUT CLUSTERS = $ 168
TOTAL PROFIT FOR CHOCOLATE BARS = $ 112.5
```

MICROCOMPUTERS

Microcomputer:	Difference:
Apple	No space after $ in output.
	Screen not wide enough for long program statements.
Apple Macintosh	No differences.
IBM/Microsoft	No differences.
PET/Commodore 64	Screen not wide enough for long program statements.
TRS-80	No differences.

The selling price for each case of candy is as follows:

Item	Price
Pecan Turtles	$500
Peanut Clusters	$400
Chocolate Bars	$250

Before deciding which type of candy to sell, the sorority asks you to write a program to determine which type of candy is the most profitable (see Figure III–3).

Solution Design

The first step in the program is to enter the selling price per case for each candy type. Next, determine the profit for each type of candy by multiplying the selling price by the appropriate percentage of profit. Finally, print out the results.

The Program

Figure III–3 shows a listing and output of the program as well as a flowchart. The REM statements in lines 10 through 120 document the purpose of the program and the meanings of the variables. The REM statement in line 120 is used to set off the remarks from the executable statements. Lines 130 through 150 use LET statements to enter the selling price of each type of candy. Lines 160 through 180 calculate the profit for each type of candy. The results are printed out in lines 190 through 210.

SUMMARY POINTS

- REM statements are used to document a program; they are not executed by the computer.
- The purpose of the LET statement is to assign values to variables; LET is an optional keyword in some BASIC implementations.
- The LET statement is not evaluated as an algebraic equation. The computer first evaluates the expression on the right side of the equal sign and then assigns that result to the variable on the left side of the equal sign.
- Arithmetic expressions are evaluated according to the following hierarchy of operations: (1) operations in parentheses, (2) exponentiation, (3) multiplication or division, and (4) addition or subtraction. Multiple operations at the same level are evaluated left to right.
- The PRINT statement is used to print or display the results of processing.
- The END statement indicates the physical end of a program and stops execution.

REVIEW QUESTIONS

1. Why is it important to document your programs by using the REM statement?
2. What is the purpose of the LET statement?
3. Give the hierarchy, or priority, of operations followed by BASIC.
4. What is the purpose of the PRINT statement?

DEBUGGING EXERCISES

Debug the following program segments.

```
1. 10 *** THIS PROGRAM PRINTS A CITY ***
   15 REM *** AND ITS POPULATION ***
   20 LET C$ = 500
   25 LET P = "HICTON"
   30 PRINT C$,P


2. 40 LET 5 * X = B
   45 LET C$ = 54.7
   50 PRINT X B C$
```

PROGRAMMING PROBLEMS

1. Mr. Morley needs you to write a program for him which will calculate his gross pay if he receives his raise to $15.50 per hour. He plans to work 40 hours a week for 51 weeks. He wishes the output to appear as follows:

GROSS PAY	RATE PER HOUR
XXXXXX	15.50

Be sure to document your program.

2. You have been asked to write a program which will calculate the average score of bowling contestants and print the contestant's name, three game scores, and average score. Your output should contain column headings; be sure to document your program using the REM statement. Use the following data:

Name	Game 1	Game 2	Game 3
Bill Davis	103	136	145
Tonya Rae	150	172	167

OVERVIEW

This section will introduce new ways of entering data into a program. Although the LET statement can be used to enter small amounts of data, the INPUT statement and the READ/DATA statements are the most commonly used methods.

When programming, it is often necessary to have organized and formatted output. This yields a better appearance and readability. We will show you how to produce output with headings, columns, and appropriate spacing.

Figure IV–1 is a sample of the type of output you will be able to produce with the tools in this chapter. It also makes use of the INPUT statement.

THE INPUT STATEMENT

The INPUT statement is used for inquiry and response when a user application calls for a question-and-answer environment. The last section explained how the LET statement can be used to enter data values into a program. The INPUT statement differs from the LET statement in that it allows the user to enter data at the terminal while the program is running. The general format of the INPUT statement is as follows:

line# INPUT variable list

For example,

```
00100 INPUT H,R
00110 INPUT N$,S$,A$
```

These also could be combined into one line as follows:

```
00100 INPUT H,R,N$,S$,A$
```

or they could be on separate lines:

```
00100 INPUT H
00110 INPUT R
00120 INPUT N$
00130 INPUT S$
00140 INPUT A$
```

Figure IV–1 ▪ Formatted Output

```
RUNNH
ENTER QUANTITY AND PRICE OF SHIRTS
 ? 11,5.98
ENTER QUANTITY AND PRICE OF DRESSES
 ? 5,9.99
ENTER QUANTITY AND PRICE OF PANTS
 ? 9,7.99


                 INVENTORY LIST

          QUANTITY      PRICE          TOTAL

SHIRTS       11        $ 5.98        $ 65.78
DRESSES      5         $ 9.99        $ 49.95
PANTS        9         $ 7.99        $ 71.91
                                     $ 187.64
```

The variables listed in the INPUT statements may be string or numeric. Just be sure to enter the correct value to be assigned to each variable. In other words, the type of data must be the same as that designated by the variable.

INPUT statements are placed where data values are needed in a program. This is determined by the logic of the program. After the program has been keyed in, the user types the execution command RUNNH on the DECSYSTEM 20; the computer then starts to execute the program. Whenever the computer reaches an INPUT statement, it stops, prints a question mark at the terminal, and waits for the user to enter data. After typing in the data, the user presses the RETURN key. The computer then assigns the data value to the variable indicated in the INPUT statement and resumes processing. More than one variable can be listed in the INPUT statement; the user must know how many values to enter. When there are not enough data entered, an error message is printed, telling the user there are insufficient data. For example, when line 100 is executed with only one value entered, the result would look like this:

```
00100 INPUT H,R
RUNNH
 ? 3.35

? 59    Insufficient data at line 00100 of MAIN PROGRAM
 ?
```

If the user knew what entries to make and how many, the output would look like this:

```
RUNNH
 ? 3.35,45
```

The variable H would have the value 3.35, and R would be assigned the value 45. As you can see, the INPUT statement offers a great deal of flexibility. Each time the program is executed, new values can be entered without changing any program statements.

Prompts

The INPUT statement is usually preceded by a PRINT statement. This PRINT statement is referred to as a prompt. Since the INPUT statement signals the need for data with only a question mark, it is good programming to precede each INPUT statement with a PRINT statement that explains to the user what data is to be entered. This practice is particularly important in a BASIC program that contains numerous INPUT statements; otherwise, when users see only a question mark requesting data, they may not know what data values are to be entered and in what order.

Figure IV–2 is a program with a prompt that calculates a percentage score on a test. Lines 130 and 140 cause the program to be executed in a question-and-answer mode (also called inquiry-and-response, or conversational mode). When the program is run, line 130 causes the computer to print a message at the terminal that says, "ENTER TOTAL POINTS AND POINTS RECEIVED." A question mark then appears to signal the user that the data values are to be entered. At this point, the user types in the requested data values, separating them with commas, and then presses the RETURN key to continue execution of the program:

```
RUNNH
ENTER TOTAL POINTS AND POINTS RECEIVED       ←Program Prompt
? 75,67                                       ←Computer Prompt (?), User Data Entry
TEST PERCENTAGE = 89.33332 %                  ←Computer Continues Execution after User Pushes RETURN
```

```
00100 REM ********************************************
00110 REM ***      TEST PERCENTAGE PROGRAM       ***
00120 REM ********************************************
00130 PRINT "ENTER TOTAL POINTS AND POINTS RECEIVED"
00140 INPUT T,R
00150 LET P = R / T * 100
00160 PRINT "TEST PERCENTAGE =";P;"%"
00999 END
```

```
RUNNH
ENTER TOTAL POINTS AND POINTS RECEIVED
? 75,67
TEST PERCENTAGE = 89.33333 %
```

MICROCOMPUTERS

Microcomputer:	Difference:
Apple	No space before percent symbol.
Apple Macintosh	No differences.
IBM / Microsoft	No differences.
PET / Commodore 64	No differences.
TRS-80	No differences.

Figure IV-2 ▪ Test Percentage Program Using A Prompt And An Input Statement

Most computers permit the prompt to be an integral part of the INPUT statement. For example, the following line could be substituted for lines 130 and 140 in the test percentage program:

```
00130 INPUT "ENTER TOTAL POINTS AND POINTS RECEIVED";T,R
```

When the program is run with this new line, the question mark appears immediately after the prompt, and no separate PRINT statement for the prompt is needed:

```
RUNNH
ENTER TOTAL POINTS AND POINTS RECEIVED? 90,75
TEST PERCENTAGE = 83.33333 %
```

THE READ AND DATA STATEMENTS

The READ and DATA statements provide another way to enter data into a BASIC program. These two statements always work together. Values contained in the DATA statements are assigned to variables listed in the READ statements.

The general format of the READ and DATA statements is this:

line# READ variable list
line# DATA data list

Here some examples of READ and DATA statements:

```
00100 READ S$,N$,C
00110 READ Q,P
    .
    .
    .
00420 DATA "297-49-2210","J. DOE"
00430 DATA 25,3,2547
```

This method of entering data into a program works a little differently than the INPUT statement. The READ statement tells the computer to search through the BASIC program until it finds the first DATA statement. The computer then assigns the data values consecutively to the variables in the READ statement. Each READ statement causes as many values to be taken from the data list as there are variables in the READ variable list. Figure IV–3 illustrates this process of assigning values from the data list to variables.

Statement 40 says to the computer: "Take the value from the top of the data list and put it in the storage location named N$. (Anything that was previously in storage location N$ is destroyed when the new information is put in N$.) Next take the following value from the data list and assign it to variable P (which also destroys anything that was previously in location P). Then take the next value from the data list and place it in the storage location H (the previous contents of H are also destroyed)." After statement 40 has been executed, the character string JERRY MORRIS is in storage location N$, the number 107 is in storage location P, and the number 40 is in storage location H. This leaves the character string KENNY SANDERS at the top of the data list.

When statement 70 is executed, the character string at the top of the data list (KENNY SANDERS) is assigned to the variable N$. The character string JERRY MORRIS, which was assigned to N$ by statement 40, is replaced by the new value (KENNY SANDERS). In the same manner, the number 96 is assigned to the variable P and the number 30 is assigned to H in statement 80. When these values are assigned, the values previously stored in the variables are destroyed.

This process illustrates the basic concept of nondestructive read, destructive write. This means that, once the data items have been assigned to storage locations, they remain there and are not destroyed when read; however, when a new value is assigned to a storage location, the previous value in that location is destroyed. Thus, all four variables represent more than one value during execution, but never more than one at a time.

If a READ statement is attempted after the data list has been exhausted, a message is produced to indicate that the end of the data list has been reached. The message points out the line number of the READ statement in

Figure IV–3 ▪ READ/DATA Example

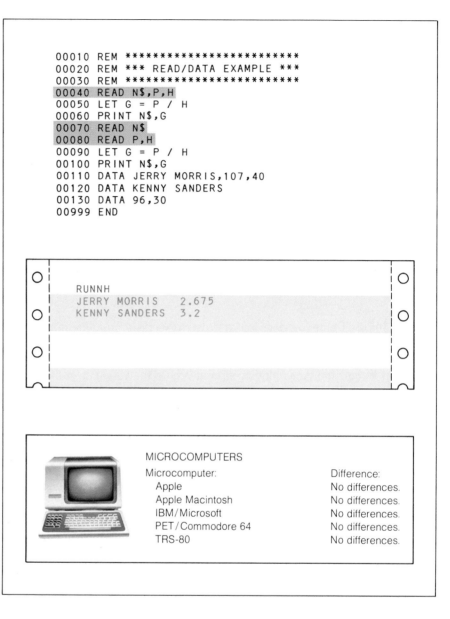

```
00010 REM ************************
00020 REM *** READ/DATA EXAMPLE ***
00030 REM ************************
00040 READ N$,P,H
00050 LET G = P / H
00060 PRINT N$,G
00070 READ N$
00080 READ P,H
00090 LET G = P / H
00100 PRINT N$,G
00110 DATA JERRY MORRIS,107,40
00120 DATA KENNY SANDERS
00130 DATA 96,30
00999 END
```

```
RUNNH
JERRY MORRIS    2.675
KENNY SANDERS   3.2
```

MICROCOMPUTERS

Microcomputer:	Difference:
Apple	No differences.
Apple Macintosh	No differences.
IBM/Microsoft	No differences.
PET/Commodore 64	No differences.
TRS-80	No differences.

error; for example, if line 80 were such a READ statement, the computer would print the following:

```
? 57 End of DATA found at line 00080 of MAIN PROGRAM
```

READ statements, like INPUT, are located wherever the logic of the program indicates the need for data. Data statements, however, are nonexecutable and may be located anywhere in the program. Although DATA statements may be anywhere in a program, it is common practice to group them together either at the beginning or the end of a program. This makes debugging easier. The BASIC interpreter or compiler simply takes all the data items in all the DATA statements and forms one combined data list, ordering the DATA statements from lowest line number to highest and then using the data from left to right. For example, the following three program segments look different, but the data lists they produce are alike:

DATA Statements	DATA List
00100 DATA 63	63
00110 DATA "EDWIN"	EDWIN
00120 DATA 21	21
00130 DATA "ALICIA"	ALICIA

or

```
00100 DATA 63,"EDWIN"
00110 DATA 21,"ALICIA"
```

or

```
00100 DATA 63,"EDWIN",21,"ALICIA"
```

Note that when two or more data values occupy a line, they are separated by commas. Character strings may or may not be enclosed in quotation marks in DATA statements. However, if the character strings are to contain leading or trailing blanks, commas, and semicolons, they must be enclosed in quotation marks.

We would assign the previous data items in the following manner:

```
00070 READ R
00080 READ S$
00090 READ C
00100 READ B$
```

or

```
00070 READ R,S$
00080 READ C,B$
```

or

```
00070 READ R,S$,C,B$
```

It does not matter in this example how many READ or DATA statements are used. However, the order of the variables and values is important. Make sure that the arrangement of values in the DATA statements corresponds to the data required in the READ statements—that is, that character strings are assigned to string variables and numeric constants to numeric variables.

Let us return to the test percentage program and change it to use READ/DATA statements (see Figure IV– 4). Lines 130 and 140 perform the same function as the INPUT statement did previously. With INPUT, the data values are assigned by the user as the program is running. With READ/DATA statements, on the other hand, the total points and points received already are contained in program line 130, the DATA statement. If we wanted to run this program again using different data, we would have to change the DATA statement.

COMPARISON OF THE THREE METHODS OF DATA ENTRY

LET, INPUT, and READ/DATA all can be used to enter data into BASIC programs. You may wonder, then, which command is best to use. That depends on the particular application. Here are some general guidelines:

1. When the data to be used by a program are constant, use the LET statement. The LET statement is often used to assign a beginning value to a variable, such as zero. This is called **initialization.** For example: LET T = 0

```
00100 REM *******************************************
00110 REM ***        TEST PERCENTAGE PROGRAM        ***
00120 REM *******************************************
00130 DATA 75,67
00140 READ T,R
00150 LET P = R / T * 100
00160 PRINT "TEST PERCENTAGE =";P;"%"
00999 END
```

```
RUNNH
TEST PERCENTAGE = 89.33333 %
```

MICROCOMPUTERS

Microcomputer:	Difference:
Apple	No space before percent symbol.
Apple Macintosh	No differences.
IBM/Microsoft	No differences.
PET/Commodore 64	No differences.
TRS-80	No differences.

Figure IV—4 ▪ Test Percentage Program Using READ/DATA Statements

2. The INPUT statement is used when a question-and-answer mode is desired. It is also a good method to use when data values are likely to change frequently. A good application for the use of the INPUT statement might be entering data about hospital patients—a situation in which people are checking in and out every day, and data about a particular patient changes frequently.

3. When many data values must be entered, READ/DATA statements are a good option. These statements often are used to read data into arrays (to be discussed in Section IX).

PRINTING PUNCTUATION

Section III explained that the PRINT statement lets us get the results of processing printed. When more than one item is to be printed on a line, commas and semicolons can be used to control the spacing of the output.

Print Zones and Commas

The number of characters that can be printed on a line varies with the system used. On some terminals, such as the DEC VT-100 used with the DECSYSTEM 20 computer, each output line consists of eighty print positions. The line is divided into five print zones, each fourteen characters wide. The beginning columns of the five print zones are shown here:

ZONE 1	ZONE 2	ZONE 3	ZONE 4	ZONE 5
COL	COL	COL	COL	COL
1	15	29	43	57

When the computer encounters the PRINT statement in this program segment:

```
00010 READ A$,B$,C$
00020 PRINT A$,B$,C$
00030 DATA "COMPUTERS","ARE","FUN"
```

the value in A$, which is COMPUTERS, will be printed starting in the first print zone. The comma between A$ and B$ tells the computer to space over to the next zone and print the value contained in B$. After ARE is printed, the comma directs the computer to space over to the third print zone and print the value in C$. The output is as follows:

Zone 1	Zone 2	Zone 3

```
RUNNH
COMPUTERS     ARE           FUN
```

If there are more items listed in a PRINT statement than there are print zones, the computer starts printing in the first zone of the next line. If the value to be printed exceeds the width of the print zone, the computer will completely print out the value, even though part of it goes into the next print zone. The comma then directs printing to start in the following print zone. Take a look at the following example and note where the value of A (30) is printed:

```
00010 LET A = 30
00020 PRINT "MY BIRTHDAY IS ON JULY",A
```

```
RUNNH
MY BIRTHDAY IS ON JULY     30
↑                ↑         ↑
```
Zone 1   **Zone 2**   **Zone 3**

Also note that since 30 is a positive number, most computers will leave a blank before the number for the sign. Of course, if the value in A were negative, the minus sign would be printed starting in the first column of Zone 3.

Table IV–1 presents the formatting differences among our five computers. The first column identifies the computer. Columns 2 and 3 give the number of columns and rows on the CRT screen. Columns 4 and 5 give the number

TABLE IV–1 ■ Computer Display Characteristics

COMPUTER	SCREEN WIDTH (CHARACTERS)	SCREEN HEIGHT (LINES)	NUMBER OF PRINT ZONES	ZONE WIDTH	SPACE FOR SIGN?	SPACE FOLLOWING?	NUMBER OF DIGITS PRINTED, SINGLE PRECISION
DECSYSTEM 20	80/312*	24/16*	5/9*	14	Yes	Yes	7
Apple	40	24	2.5	16	No	No	9
Apple Macintosh	†	**	†	†	Yes	Yes	6
IBM/Microsoft	80	24	5	14	Yes	Yes	7
TRS-80	64/32*	15	4/2*	16	Yes	Yes	6
PET/Commodore 64	40	25	4	10	Yes	Yes	9

See example
below

Example: With the Apple computer, the statement

```
10 PRINT 39;-2;9;2;-39
```

would print

```
39-292-39
```

With the Apple Macintosh, DECSYSTEM 20, IBM/Microsoft, TRS-80, and PET/Commodore 64 computers, the same statement would print

```
39 -2  9  2 -39
```

*Slash indicates both options are available to user.

**Up to 18 depending on which window is being used.

†This is determined by the WIDTH statement. Check the Microsoft BASIC Manual for the Apple Macintosh for details.

of print zones (when commas are used as spacing control in PRINT statements) and print zone widths. Columns 6 and 7 indicate whether a space is always left in front of a number for a positive or negative sign and whether a space follows a number for ease in reading. The use of semicolons is discussed next in this section. Finally, column 8 gives the maximum number of digits output to the screen. If the number to be printed contains more characters than that listed, all remaining characters will be truncated—the number will not be rounded. (The DECSYSTEM 20, IBM, TRS-80, and Apple Macintosh have provisions for double precision; however, caution must be used, because the BASIC internal functions might not be any more accurate with double precision than with single precision—see your manual.)

SKIPPING PRINT ZONES

A print zone can be skipped by the use of a technique that involves enclosing a space (the character blank) in quotation marks. This causes the entire zone to appear empty:

```
00100 PRINT "STREET"," ","PRECINCT"
```

Most computers (all five of ours) also allow the user to skip a zone by typing two consecutive commas:

```
00100 PRINT "STREET",,"PRECINCT"
```

Both of these techniques cause the literal ''STREET'' to be printed in zone 1, the second zone to be blank, and the literal ''PRECINCT'' to be printed in the third zone:

Zone 1	Zone 3

```
RUNNH
STREET                    PRECINCT
```

ENDING WITH A COMMA

As mentioned earlier, output generated by a PRINT statement normally begins in the first zone of a new line. However, if the previously executed PRINT statement ends with a comma, the output of a PRINT statement starts in the next available zone. Thus, the statements

```
00010 DATA "MY","BIRTHDAY","IS","JULY 30, 1960"
00020 READ A$,B$,C$,D$
00030 PRINT A$,B$,
00040 PRINT C$,D$
00999 END
```

produce the following output:

```
RUNNH
MY              BIRTHDAY        IS              JULY 30, 1960
```

Using Semicolons

Using a semicolon instead of a comma causes output to be packed more closely on a line. This alternative gives the programmer greater flexibility in formatting output. In the following examples, notice the difference in spacing when semicolons are used instead of commas:

Using Commas

```
00100 PRINT 409,352,-1
RUNNH
 409            352             -1
```

Using Semicolons

```
00100 PRINT 409;352;-1
RUNNH
 409  352 -1
```

The semicolon between the items tells the computer to skip to the next **column** to print the next item—not to the next print zone, as with the comma. Generally, when the number is positive, a space is left in front of the number for the sign.

SEMICOLONS AND CHARACTER STRINGS

The following example shows what happens when semicolons are used with character strings:

```
00070 PRINT "BOBBY";"LEE"
RUNNH
BOBBYLEE
```

Since letters do not have signs, they are run together. The best way to avoid this problem is to enclose a space within the quotes:

```
00070 PRINT "BOBBY ";"LEE"
RUNNH
BOBBY LEE
```

ENDING WITH A SEMICOLON

If the semicolon is the last character of the PRINT statement, carriage control is not advanced when the printing of the statement is completed; therefore, the output generated by the next PRINT statement continues on the same line; for example,

```
00070 PRINT 22435;
00080 PRINT " BOBBY";" LEE"
RUNNH
 22435  BOBBY LEE
```

Line 70 causes 22435 to be printed out. The semicolon after this number keeps the printer on the same line; then, when line 80 is encountered, BOBBY LEE is printed on the same line.

THE TAB FUNCTION

The comma causes the results of processing to be printed according to pre-defined print zones. The semicolon causes them to start printing in the next position on the output line. Both are easy to use, and many reports can be formatted in this fashion. However, there are times when a report should be structured differently.

The TAB function allows output to be printed in any column in an output line, providing the programmer greater flexibility to format printed output.

The general format of the TAB function is this:

TAB(expression)

The expression in parentheses may be a numeric constant, numeric variable, or arithmetic expression; it tells the computer the column in which printing is to occur. The TAB function (as used in a PRINT statement) must immediately precede the variable or literal to be printed out. For example, the statement

```
00100 PRINT TAB(12);N;TAB(20);N$
```

causes the printer to be spaced to column 12 (indicated in parentheses) and to print the value stored in N. The printer then spaces over to column 20, as indicated in the next parentheses, and prints the value in N$. On many computers, such as the DECSYSTEM 20, IBM/Microsoft, and TRS-80, the value in N in this example would begin in column 13 and N$, in column 21. In other words, the computer tabs to column 12 and the semicolon instructs it to begin printing in the next column (column 13, or check the systems manual for your specific system). The program in Figure IV–5 illustrates the use of the TAB function.

Note that we have used the semicolon as the punctuation mark with the TAB function. The semicolon separates the expression from the values to be printed. If commas were used instead, the printer would default and use the predefined print zones, ignoring the columns specified in parentheses. For example, if line 60 of the program in Figure IV–5 had been

```
00060 PRINT TAB(5),"NAME",TAB(20),"HIRE DATE"
```

the output would have been:

Figure IV–5 ▪ Employee Program

```
00010 REM ****************************************
00020 REM ***          EMPLOYEE REPORT        ***
00030 REM ****************************************
00040 PRINT TAB(10);"EMPLOYEE REPORT"
00050 PRINT
00060 PRINT TAB(5);"NAME";TAB(20);"HIRE DATE"
00070 PRINT
00080 READ N$,D$
00090 PRINT TAB(5);N$;TAB(20);D$
00100 READ N$,D$
00110 PRINT TAB(5);N$;TAB(20);D$
00120 READ N$,D$
00130 PRINT TAB(5);N$;TAB(20);D$
00140 DATA N. WALKER,3/12/82,S. MANDELL,5/3/79
00150 DATA T. BROOKS,9/30/83
00999 END
```

```
RUNNH
                EMPLOYEE REPORT

        NAME            HIRE DATE

      N. WALKER        3/12/82
      S. MANDELL       5/3/79
      T. BROOKS        9/30/83
```

MICROCOMPUTERS

Microcomputer:	Difference:
Apple	No differences.
Apple Macintosh	No differences.
IBM/Microsoft	No differences.
PET/Commodore 64	No differences.
TRS-80	No differences.

```
RUNNH
        EMPLOYEE REPORT

            NAME                         HIRE DATE

    N. WALKER        3/12/82
    S. MANDELL       5/3/79
    T. BROOKS        9/30/83
```

The computer spaced over the five columns indicated by the first TAB function, but when it saw the comma following the parentheses, it skipped over to the next predefined print zone to print HIRE DATE. The same thing happens again with NAME. Use semicolons rather than commas in PRINT statements containing the TAB function.

As another caution, remember that when the TAB function is used, the printer cannot be backspaced. Once a column has been passed, the printer cannot go back to it. This means that if more than one TAB function is used in a PRINT statement, the column numbers in parentheses must increase from left to right. For example,

Valid:

```
00100 PRINT TAB(8);"H";TAB(18);"I";TAB(28);"I"
RUNNH
        H         I                 I
```

Invalid:

```
00100 PRINT TAB(28);"I";TAB(18);"I";TAB(8);"H"
RUNNH
                                    I I H
```

```
00100 PRINT TAB(18);"I";TAB(8);"H";TAB(28);"I"
RUNNH
                    I H              I
```

The first invalid example tells the computer to print an exclamation point at column 28. The computer does this, but because the printer cannot backspace to column 18 and column 8, it prints letters I and H as it normally would using semicolons.

THE PRINT USING STATEMENT

Another convenient feature for controlling output is the PRINT USING statement; with it, the programmer can avoid print zone restrictions and can "dress up" the output. PRINT USING is an extension of the ANSI standards—not part of the standards. Its syntax is quite varied among different brands of computers. This section briefly describes its use on the DECSYSTEM 20 computer; the principles should be similar for other computers with this feature. Many microcomputers do not have a PRINT USING capability: The Apple and PET/Commodore 64 do not; the Apple Macintosh, IBM/Microsoft, and TRS-80 do. The general format of the PRINT USING statement is as follows:

line# PRINT USING image statement line#, expression-list

The PRINT USING statement tells which statement in the program has the print line image and what values are to be used in that print line. The expression list consists of a sequence of variables or expressions separated by commas; it is similar to the expression list in any PRINT statement. The line number of the image statement is the number of the BASIC statement that tells the computer how to print the items in the expression list.

The image statement is denoted by a colon (:) following the line number:

line#: format control characters

It is a nonexecutable statement, like DATA, and it can be placed anywhere in the program. The PRINT USING command, however, is placed where the logic demands. A single image statement can be referred to by several PRINT USING statements. Special format control characters are used in the image statement to describe the output image and to control spacing.

The major DECSYSTEM 20 formal control characters are listed in the following table (a **mask** specifies the maximum number of characters to be printed in one field):

FORMAT CONTROL CHARACTER	CONTROL IMAGE FOR	EXAMPLE
#	Numeric data; used in a mask; one symbol for each number to be printed; pads zeros to the left of decimal point	###
$	Dollar sign; printed exactly as is	$###
$$	Causes dollar sign to be printed immediately before first digit	$$##.##
**	Leading asterisks; printed in place of blanks or spaces	**###.#
	Decimal point; printed exactly as is	$##.##
E	Alphanumeric data; preceded by apostrophe ('); permits overflow to be printed to the right; left justifies; pads with blanks	'E
L	Alphanumeric data; preceded by apostrophe ('); used as a mask; left justifies; pads with blanks	'LLLLLL
R	Alphanumeric data; preceded by apostrophe ('); used as a mask; right justifies; pads with blanks	'RRRRRR
C	Alphanumeric data; preceded by apostrophe ('); used as a mask; centers in the field; pads with blanks	'CCCCCCC

Format Control Characters for Apple Macintosh, IBM, and TRS-80

APPLE MACINTOSH	IBM	TRS-80	EXPLANATION
#	#	#	Same as DECSYSTEM 20.
.	.	.	Same as DECSYSTEM 20.
		$	Same as DECSYSTEM 20.
$$	$$	$$	Two dollar signs cause the dollar sign to be floating, meaning that it will be in the first position before the number.
**$	**$	**$	Vacant positions will be filled with asterisks, and the dollar sign will be in the first position to the left of the number.
+	+	+	When a + sign is placed at the beginning or end of a number, it causes a + sign to be printed if the number is positive and a − sign to be printed if the number is negative.
−	−	−	When a − sign is placed at the end of a number, negative numbers will have a negative sign, and for positive numbers it will appear as a space after the number.
ΛΛΛΛ	ΛΛΛΛ	↑ ↑ ↑ ↑ or [[[[	This causes the number to be printed in exponential format.
\spaces\	\spaces\	%space%	This specifies a string field to be two plus the number of spaces below the characters.
!	!	!	This causes the computer to print only the first string character.
&	&		This specifies a variable-length field. The string is output exactly as it is entered.
___	___		Underscore causes the next character in the format string to be printed out. The character itself may be underscored by preceding it with two underscores (_____).
%	%		If the number to be printed is larger than the specified field, a percent sign will appear before the number. If rounding caused the number to exceed the field, the percent sign will be printed in front of the rounded number.

The program in Figure IV–6 illustrates some of these control characters on the DECSYSTEM 20.

The Apple Macintosh, IBM/Microsoft and TRS-80 PRINT USING statements are somewhat different. The general format for both of these systems looks like this:

line# PRINT USING "format"; expression-list

Figure IV–6 ▪ PRINT USING Statement on DECSYSTEM 20

```
00010 REM *************************************************************************
00020 REM ***          PROGRAM UTILIZING PRINT USING STATEMENTS          ***
00030 REM *************************************************************************
00040 PRINT
00050 PRINT
00060 PRINT USING 170,"AGENT","TICKETS SOLD","PRICE PER TICKET","TOTAL PRICE"
00070 PRINT
00080 PRINT
00090 READ N$,N,P
00100 IF N$ = "END" THEN GOTO 999
00110 LET T = N * P
00120 PRINT USING 180,N$,N,P,T
00130 GOTO 90
00140 DATA AARON,4,110.25,BURBANK,2,75.99
00150 DATA SELLERS,10,89,TRAVERS,1,150.89
00160 DATA VALE,5,125,ZINK,2,239,END,0,0
00170: 'LLLLL            'CCCCCCCCCCCC     'CCCCCCCCCCCCCCCC    'RRRRRRRRRR
00180: 'LLLLLLLLLLLLLLLL        ##           $###.##              $###.##
00999 END
```

```
RUNNH

AGENT                TICKETS SOLD      PRICE PER TICKET      TOTAL PRICE

AARON                    4                $110.25              $441.00
BURBANK                  2                $ 75.99              $151.98
SELLERS                 10                $ 89.00              $890.00
TRAVERS                  1                $150.89              $150.89
VALE                     5                $125.00              $625.00
ZINK                     2                $239.00              $478.00
```

MICROCOMPUTERS

Microcomputer:	Difference:
Apple	No PRINT USING statement.
Apple Macintosh	No PRINT USING statement.
IBM/Microsoft	See "Format Control Characters" box.
PET/Commodore 64	See "Format Control Characters" box.
TRS-80	No PRINT USING statement.

For a list of the control characters for the Apple Macintosh, IBM and TRS-80, see box.

Figure IV–7 shows examples of the PRINT USING statement on the Apple Macintosh and the IBM Personal Computer.

A PROGRAMMING PROBLEM

Problem Definition

The Clothing Store sells shirts, dresses, and pants. It needs a program to list its quantity, selling price, and total inventory price. The output should be formatted as follows:

```
                 INVENTORY LIST
           QUANTITY      PRICE           TOTAL

SHIRTS
DRESSES
PANTS
```

Solution Design

To produce the desired report, we need to ask the user to enter the quantity and price for each item. To find the inventory price, all we need to do is multiply the quantity and the price. To find the total inventory price, we just add the totals of each item.

Figure IV–7 ■ PRINT USING Statement on Apple Macintosh and IBM Personal Computer

```
PRINT USING "##.##    ";25.58,143.22,9.5,6.775         25.58  %143.22    9.50      6.78

PRINT USING "$###.##   ";927.25,34.44                  $927.25  $ 34.44

PRINT USING "$$###.##   ";927.25,34.44                   $927.25     $34.44

PRINT USING "**##.##   ";66.65,2.33                    **66.65   ***2.33

PRINT USING "**$##.##   ";66.65,2.33                   **$66.65   ***$2.33

PRINT USING "+###.##    ";-284.25,835.1,-99.99         -284.25   +835.10    -99.99

PRINT USING "###.##-    ";-284.25,835.1,-99.99         284.25-   835.10     99.99-

PRINT USING "#####,.##   ";589001,3657.75              58,900.00   3,657.75

PRINT USING "##.####^^^^   ";29.352,34.9761             2.9352E+01    3.4976E+01

PRINT USING "_$##.##_$   ";19.95,21.36                 $19.95$   $21.36$


10 LET R$ = "CANDY"
20 LET S$ = "MAN"
30 PRINT USING "!";R$;S$
40 PRINT USING "\   \";R$;S$


10 LET R$ = "CANDY"
20 LET S$ = "MAN"
30 PRINT USING "!";R$
40 PRINT USING "&";S$
```

Figure IV–8 ■ Inventory Report, Flowchart and Pseudocode (Continued on Next Two Pages)

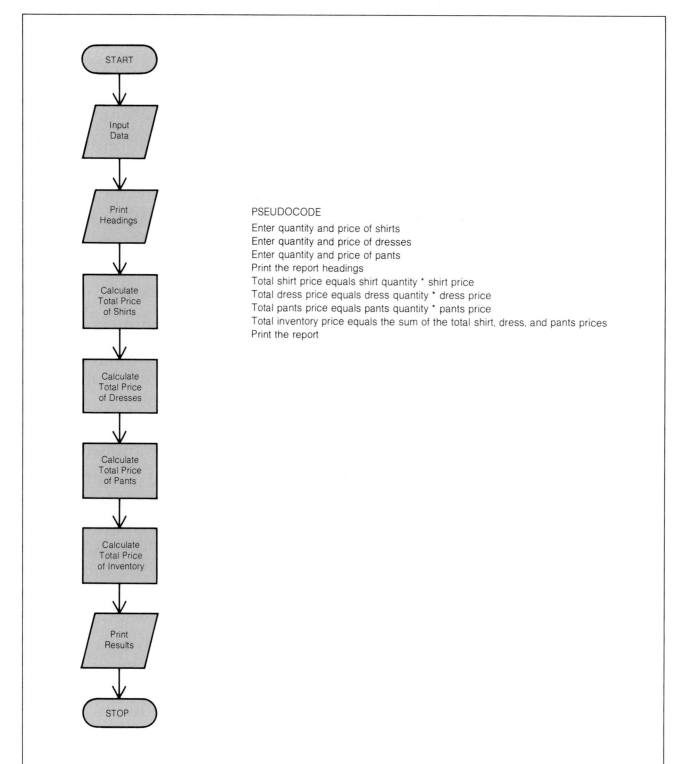

PSEUDOCODE

Enter quantity and price of shirts
Enter quantity and price of dresses
Enter quantity and price of pants
Print the report headings
Total shirt price equals shirt quantity * shirt price
Total dress price equals dress quantity * dress price
Total pants price equals pants quantity * pants price
Total inventory price equals the sum of the total shirt, dress, and pants prices
Print the report

The Program

The program in Figure IV–8 documents the major variables used in lines 40 through 70. Lines 90 through 140 request the user to enter data. Lines 90, 110, and 130 are prompts telling the user what values to enter. After the data have been entered, program execution continues. The headings are printed

Figure IV–8 ▪ Continued

```
00010 REM ******************************************************
00020 REM ***              FIGURE PRICE OF INVENTORY        ***
00030 REM ******************************************************
00040 REM *** S1,D1,P1 - QUANTITY OF THE ITEMS              ***
00050 REM *** PS,PD,PP - PRICE OF THE ITEMS                 ***
00060 REM *** TS,TD,TP - TOTALS OF EACH ITEM                ***
00070 REM *** T - TOTAL INVENTORY PRICE                     ***
00080 REM ******************************************************
00090 PRINT "ENTER QUANTITY AND PRICE OF SHIRTS"
00100 INPUT S1,PS
00110 PRINT "ENTER QUANTITY AND PRICE OF DRESSES"
00120 INPUT D1,PD
00130 PRINT "ENTER QUANTITY AND PRICE OF PANTS"
00140 INPUT P1,PP
00150 PRINT
00160 PRINT
00170 PRINT TAB(25);"INVENTORY LIST"
00180 PRINT
00190 PRINT " ","QUANTITY","PRICE","TOTAL"
00200 PRINT
00210 LET TS = S1 * PS
00220 LET TD = D1 * PD
00230 LET TP = P1 * PP
00240 LET T = TS + TD + TP
00250 PRINT "SHIRTS",S1,"$";PS,"$";TS
00260 PRINT "DRESSES",D1,"$";PD,"$";TD
00270 PRINT "PANTS",P1,"$";PP,"$";TP
00280 PRINT " "," "," ","$";T
00999 END
```

```
RUNNH
ENTER QUANTITY AND PRICE OF SHIRTS
 ? 11,5.98
ENTER QUANTITY AND PRICE OF DRESSES
 ? 5,9.99
ENTER QUANTITY AND PRICE OF PANTS
 ? 9,7.99
```

```
                           INVENTORY  LIST

               QUANTITY        PRICE          TOTAL

    SHIRTS        11         $  5.98        $  65.78
    DRESSES        5         $  9.99        $  49.95
    PANTS          9         $  7.99        $  71.91
                                            $ 187.64
```

MICROCOMPUTERS

Microcomputer:	Difference:
Apple	Screen not wide enough; output must be reformatted.
Apple Macintosh	No differences.
IBM/Microsoft	No differences.
PET/Commodore 64	Screen not wide enough; output must be reformatted.
TRS-80	No differences.

Figure IV–8 ■ Continued

in lines 150 through 200. Notice how line 170 uses the TAB statement to center the heading. The total price of shirts is figured in line 210, the total price of dresses in line 220, the total price of pants in 230, and the total price of all inventory, T, in line 240. Lines 250 through 280 print the results in the desired format.

SUMMARY POINTS

■ The INPUT statement is used to enter data into a program in a question-and-answer mode.

■ Another way of entering data into a program is to use READ and DATA statements. The READ statement causes values contained in the DATA statements to be assigned to variables.

■ READ and INPUT statements are located where the logic of the program indicates. DATA statements are nonexecutable and may be located anywhere in the program.

■ When more than one item is to be printed on a line of output, the spacing can be indicated by the use of commas and semicolons.

■ Each line of output is divided into a predetermined number of print zones. The comma is used to cause results to be printed in the print zones.

■ Using a semicolon instead of a comma to separate printed items causes output to be packed more closely on a line.

■ Using the TAB function in a PRINT statement permits results to be printed anywhere on an output line.

■ The PRINT USING feature provides a flexible method of producing output. The format control characteristics in the image statement define how the output will look.

REVIEW QUESTIONS

1. Why would you want to use the INPUT statement to enter data rather than the LET, and what is the purpose of the prompt?
2. When are the READ and DATA statements preferred to enter data?
3. LET statements are most often used for what?
4. In addition to commas and semicolons, the TAB function can also be used to format output. How does the TAB function work? Can the TAB function be used to backspace the printer?

DEBUGGING EXERCISES

```
1. 10 REM ***    READ IN DATA    ***
   20 READ P,A,T$
   30 PRINT P,A,T$
   40 READ P,T$,A
   60 DATA 5,10,ZOO,8,16
   99 END

2. 10 INPUT "ENTER YOUR NAME",N$
   20 INPUT "ENTER YOUR AGE";A$
   30 PRINT TAB(10),"NAME",TAB(25),"AGE"
   40 PRINT TAB(10);N$;TAB(5);A$
```

PROGRAMMING PROBLEMS

1. The Dairy Delight ice cream store needs a program which will calculate the amount of ice cream to order for milkshakes. Write a program which requests the user to enter the number of milkshakes he or she wishes to make. Each milkshake requires 6 ounces of ice cream. Your output should look like this:

FOR XXX MILKSHAKES YOU WILL NEED XXX OUNCES OF ICE CREAM

2. Dr. Barker wishes to find the average height in inches of his male patients. You are to write a program which will do this using the READ/DATA statements to enter the data below.

NAME	HEIGHT (in inches)
JIM GERFER	67
FRED PFEIFER	74
HENRY HOLLOW	72

Your output should include each patient's name and height. Format your output as follows:

NAME	HEIGHT
XXXX	XXX
XXXX	XXX
XXXX	XXX

AVERAGE HEIGHT IS XX INCHES

(The column of names should start in column 10, and height should start in column 25.)

OVERVIEW

The programs described to this point contained instructions that were always executed one right after the other—from the lowest line number to the highest. This section will discuss ways of transferring control to program statements out of sequence by using the GOTO, IF/THEN, and ON/GOTO statements. One of the most valuable programming techniques, looping, will also be discussed.

In the previous sections, we have been able to run a program with only one set of data without having to repeat a program segment multiple times or rerun the program. For example, if we had a program that computed a goal tender's goals against average, chances are that we probably would want to calculate the average of more than just one goal tender. Without the control statements discussed in this chapter, we would have to rerun the program for each set of data or rewrite the program segment that calculates the average as many times as we had goal tenders. Using one of these control statements, however, allows us to process multiple sets of data more efficiently. We might want, for example, the output of the goals against average program to appear as follows:

NAME	AVERAGE
PETE PETERS	3.6
JERRY MCPHEE	4.625
TOM ANDREWS	2.2

In this section we will see how these control statements allow us to obtain this output.

THE GOTO STATEMENT: UNCONDITIONAL TRANSFER

All BASIC programs consist of a series of statements that normally are executed in sequential order. Sometimes, however, it is desirable to alter the flow of execution. This is called **branching,** and the programmer can use the GOTO statement to do it. The general format of the GOTO statement is as follows:

line# GOTO transfer line#

The programming command GOTO can be written as one word or as two words, GO TO.

The GOTO statement is called an **unconditional transfer statement** because the flow of execution is altered to the transfer line number every time the statement is encountered.

A typical GOTO statement follows:

```
00210 GOTO 100
```

This statement tells the computer that the next statement to be executed is line 100. If line 100 is an executable statement, that statement and those following are executed. If it is a nonexecutable statement, execution proceeds at the first executable statement encountered after line 100.

Let us see how the GOTO statement might be used in an application by first looking at Figure V–1, which calculates the goals against average for

Figure V–1 ▪ Goals Against Average Program

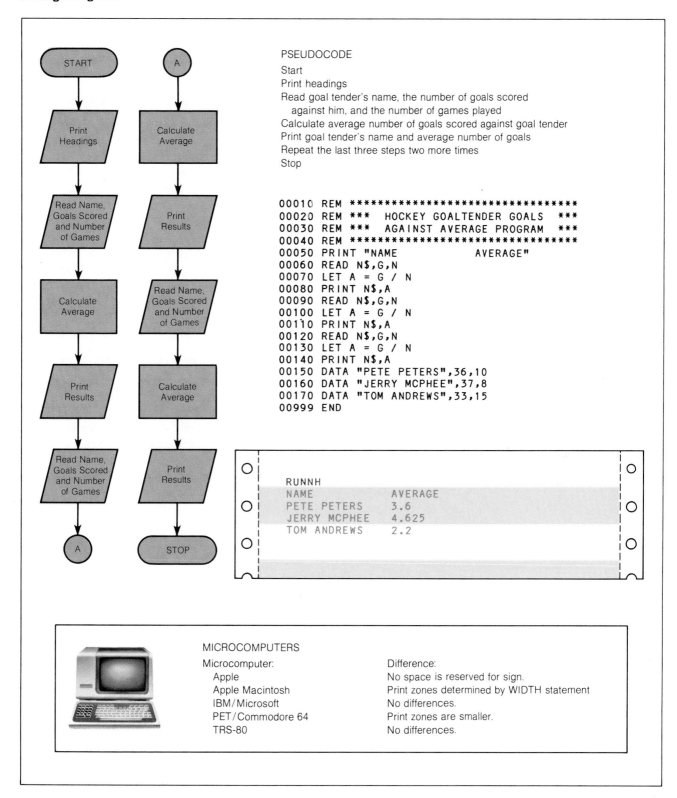

PSEUDOCODE

Start
Print headings
Read goal tender's name, the number of goals scored
   against him, and the number of games played
Calculate average number of goals scored against goal tender
Print goal tender's name and average number of goals
Repeat the last three steps two more times
Stop

```
00010 REM *********************************
00020 REM ***   HOCKEY GOALTENDER GOALS   ***
00030 REM ***   AGAINST AVERAGE PROGRAM   ***
00040 REM *********************************
00050 PRINT "NAME              AVERAGE"
00060 READ N$,G,N
00070 LET A = G / N
00080 PRINT N$,A
00090 READ N$,G,N
00100 LET A = G / N
00110 PRINT N$,A
00120 READ N$,G,N
00130 LET A = G / N
00140 PRINT N$,A
00150 DATA "PETE PETERS",36,10
00160 DATA "JERRY MCPHEE",37,8
00170 DATA "TOM ANDREWS",33,15
00999 END
```

```
RUNNH
NAME          AVERAGE
PETE PETERS   3.6
JERRY MCPHEE  4.625
TOM ANDREWS   2.2
```

MICROCOMPUTERS

Microcomputer:	Difference:
Apple	No space is reserved for sign.
Apple Macintosh	Print zones determined by WIDTH statement
IBM/Microsoft	No differences.
PET/Commodore 64	Print zones are smaller.
TRS-80	No differences.

three goal tenders and prints the results without using a GOTO statement. What we really have here is a single process (dividing the goals against the goal tender by the number of games) repeated three times. The programmer typed in the following three lines as many times as was necessary:

```
READ N$,G,N
LET A = G / N
PRINT N$,A
```

Although this is not a very difficult task with a small, uncomplicated problem, imagine how time consuming and inefficient it would be for a hundred sets of data!

The same result can be achieved much more simply by using a GOTO statement. In Figure V–2, the GOTO statement in line 90 directs the computer back to statement 60. A **loop** is formed. In this example, the error message "End of DATA found at line 00060 of MAIN PROGRAM" was printed because an attempt was made to read data after the data list had been exhausted. The execution of the program was terminated.

Note how the loop is indicated in the flowchart. A flow line is drawn from the process step immediately preceding the GOTO statement to the process step indicated by the transfer line number.

Later, this section will show how to control the number of times a loop is repeated (eliminating any error messages and the need to manually interrupt the program).

THE IF/THEN STATEMENT: CONDITIONAL TRANSFER

The GOTO statement always transfers control. Often, however, it is necessary to transfer control only when a specified condition exists. The IF/THEN statement is used to test for such a condition. If the condition does not exist, the next statement in the program is executed. The general format of the IF/THEN statement is this:

line# IF condition THEN transfer line#

A condition has the following general format:

$$\text{expression} \quad \text{relational symbol} \quad \text{expression}$$

For example, in the statement "110 IF $X < Y + 1$ THEN 230", $X < Y + 1$ is the condition.

Conditions tested can involve either numeric or character string data. Relational symbols that can be used include the following:

Symbol	Meaning	Examples
$<$	Less than	$A < B$
$< =$ or $\leq$	Less than or equal to	$X < = Y$
$>$	Greater than	$J > 1$
$> =$ or $\geq$	Greater than or equal to	$A > = B$
$=$	Equal to	$X = T$
		N\$ = "NONE"
$<>$ or $><$	Not equal to	$R <> Q$
		"APPLE" $<>$ R\$

Figure V–2 ▪ Goals Against Average Program with GOTO Statement

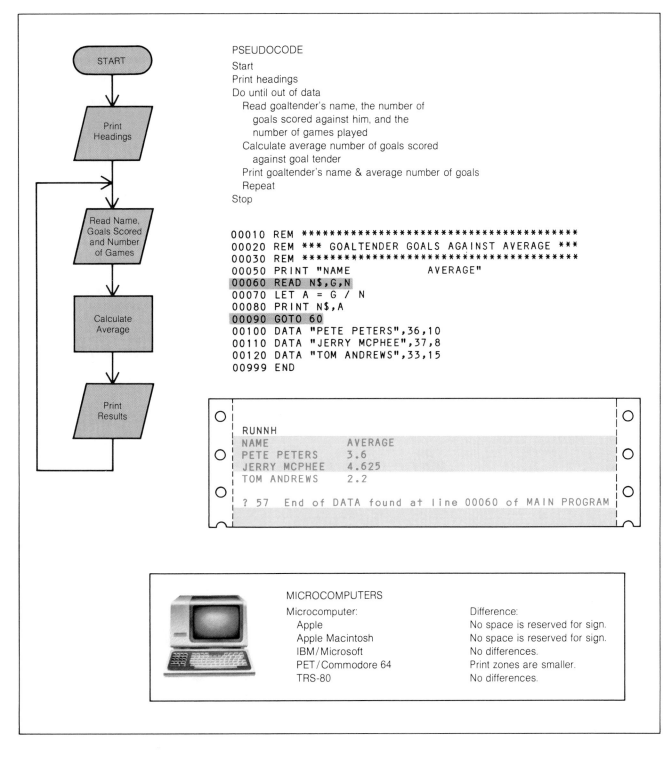

PSEUDOCODE

Start
Print headings
Do until out of data
   Read goaltender's name, the number of
     goals scored against him, and the
     number of games played
   Calculate average number of goals scored
     against goal tender
   Print goaltender's name & average number of goals
   Repeat
Stop

```
00010 REM ****************************************
00020 REM *** GOALTENDER GOALS AGAINST AVERAGE ***
00030 REM ****************************************
00050 PRINT "NAME              AVERAGE"
00060 READ N$,G,N
00070 LET A = G / N
00080 PRINT N$,A
00090 GOTO 60
00100 DATA "PETE PETERS",36,10
00110 DATA "JERRY MCPHEE",37,8
00120 DATA "TOM ANDREWS",33,15
00999 END
```

```
RUNNH
NAME            AVERAGE
PETE PETERS     3.6
JERRY MCPHEE    4.625
TOM ANDREWS     2.2

? 57  End of DATA found at line 00060 of MAIN PROGRAM
```

MICROCOMPUTERS

Microcomputer:	Difference:
Apple	No space is reserved for sign.
Apple Macintosh	No space is reserved for sign.
IBM/Microsoft	No differences.
PET/Commodore 64	Print zones are smaller.
TRS-80	No differences.

Some examples of valid IF/THEN statements follow:

Statement	Computer Execution
00050 IF Q >= 9 THEN 100 00060 LET T = T + Q 00070 PRINT Q	If the value contained in Q is greater than or equal to 9, the computer branches to line 100. If not, the computer executes the next sequential instruction, line 60.
00080 IF A < B + 54 THEN 50 00090 LET A = B + 54	If A is less than B + 54, the computer transfers to statement 50. Otherwise, it executes the next statement, line 90.
00030 IF R$ = "TRUE" THEN 100 00040 LET F = F + 1 00050 PRINT "FINISHED"	If the value contained in R$ is TRUE, control is passed to line 100. If R$ contains anything else, control goes to line 40.

The program in Figure V–3 uses numeric comparisons to search student records to find all eligible students so they can be placed on a mailing list. The program reads the name, grade point average, and major grade point average for each student. A numeric comparison is made to determine if the student is eligible to apply for an internship.

```
00080 IF GPA < 3.0 THEN 140
```

The test is stated in such a way that only if the student's grade point average is greater than or equal to 3.0 will the program continue to evaluate his or her record. Otherwise, control is transferred to line 140.

The other qualification for the mailing list is that the student's major grade point average is greater than or equal to 3.2. This is also a comparison of numbers.

```
00120 IF MGPA < 3.2 THEN 140
```

If the student's major grade point average is less than 3.2, control is transferred to line 140.

BASIC EXTENSIONS
IF/THEN/ELSE

The BASIC implementation on the Apple Macintosh and on the IBM/Microsoft allows the use of the IF/THEN/ELSE statement. This statement can be useful because it uses one IF/THEN/ELSE statement instead of many IF/THEN statements. The general format of the IF/THEN/ELSE statement is this:

line # IF condition THEN clause ELSE clause

The clause can be a BASIC statement or statements or a line number to branch to.

If the condition being tested is true, the clause following the THEN statement is executed. If the condition is false, the THEN statement is bypassed and the clause following the ELSE statement is executed.

Examples of the IF/THEN/ELSE statement are shown below:

```
10 IF A <> B THEN PRINT A ELSE PRINT B
20 IF C$ = "END" THEN 200 ELSE 150
30 IF K = 8 THEN K = -1 ELSE K = 1
40 IF T = Q / N THEN P = Q * N ELSE P = T
```

Any person who satisfies both conditions is mailed an internship application. The program output indicates that only two students, Jeff Lewis and Amy Smith, should be mailed an application.

THE ON/GOTO STATEMENT: CONDITIONAL TRANSFER

The ON/GOTO, or computed GOTO, statement transfers control to other statements in the program based on the evaluation of a mathematical expres-

Figure V–3 ▪ **Internship Program**

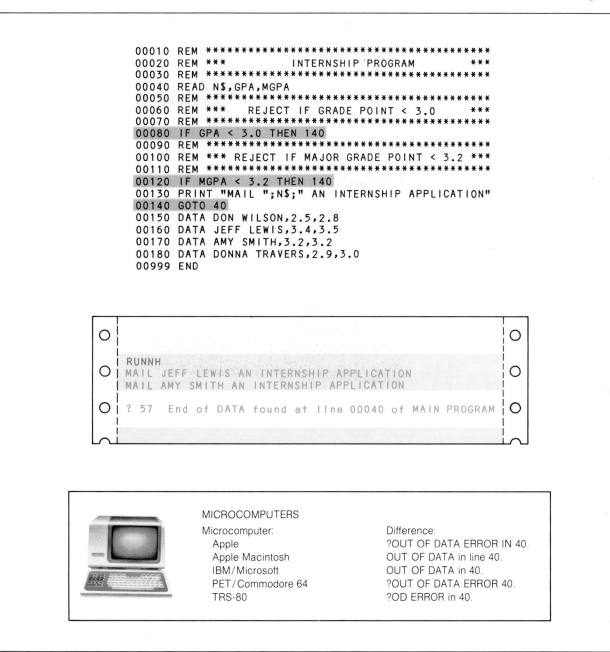

```
00010 REM *******************************************
00020 REM ***        INTERNSHIP PROGRAM         ***
00030 REM *******************************************
00040 READ N$,GPA,MGPA
00050 REM *******************************************
00060 REM ***    REJECT IF GRADE POINT < 3.0     ***
00070 REM *******************************************
00080 IF GPA < 3.0 THEN 140
00090 REM *******************************************
00100 REM *** REJECT IF MAJOR GRADE POINT < 3.2 ***
00110 REM *******************************************
00120 IF MGPA < 3.2 THEN 140
00130 PRINT "MAIL ";N$;" AN INTERNSHIP APPLICATION"
00140 GOTO 40
00150 DATA DON WILSON,2.5,2.8
00160 DATA JEFF LEWIS,3.4,3.5
00170 DATA AMY SMITH,3.2,3.2
00180 DATA DONNA TRAVERS,2.9,3.0
00999 END
```

```
RUNNH
MAIL JEFF LEWIS AN INTERNSHIP APPLICATION
MAIL AMY SMITH AN INTERNSHIP APPLICATION

? 57   End of DATA found at line 00040 of MAIN PROGRAM
```

MICROCOMPUTERS

Microcomputer:	Difference:
Apple	?OUT OF DATA ERROR IN 40.
Apple Macintosh	OUT OF DATA in line 40.
IBM/Microsoft	OUT OF DATA in 40.
PET/Commodore 64	?OUT OF DATA ERROR 40.
TRS-80	?OD ERROR in 40.

sion. The computed GOTO often operates as would multiple IF/THEN statements; any one of several transfers can occur, depending on the result computed for the expression. Since transfers depend on the expression, the computed GOTO is another **conditional transfer** statement. Its general format is this:

line# ON expression GOTO line#1,line#2,line#3, . . .,line#n

The arithmetic expression always is evaluated to an integer, and the line numbers following GOTO must identify statements in the program.

The general execution of the ON/GOTO statement proceeds as follows:

1. If the value of the expression is 1, control is transferred to the first line number indicated.
2. If the value of the expression is 2, control is transferred to the second line number indicated.

. . .
. . .
. . .

n. If the value of the expression is n, control is transferred to the nth line number indicated.

Several examples are presented here to illustrate the operation of this statement:

Statement	Computer Execution
00010 ON T GOTO 40,70,100	IF T = 1, control goes to line 40. IF T = 2, control goes to line 70. IF T = 3, control goes to line 100.
00020 ON Q / 2 GOTO 70,100	IF Q/2 = 1, control goes to line 70. IF Q/2 = 2, control goes to line 100.

If the computed expression in an ON/GOTO statement does not evaluate to an integer, the value is either rounded or truncated (digits to the right of the decimal are ignored), depending on the BASIC implementation. For example,

Statement	Value of Variable	Action
00030 ON N / 4 GOTO 20,150	N = 10	10 ÷ 4 = 2.5. The expression is evaluated as 2.5. The remainder is truncated, and the result becomes the integer 2. Control passes to statement 150.

If the expression evaluates to an integer less than 1, larger than the number of statements indicated, or greater than the maximum number of line numbers allowed, either the program will terminate with an error message or the ON/GOTO statement will be bypassed. For example,

Statement	Value of Variable	Action
00080 ON C GOTO 110,150,200 00090 LET C = Q + R	C = 5	The value of C exceeds the number of line numbers in the GOTO list. Control passes to statement 90.

ON/GOTO Errors

COMPUTER	ACTION IF NUMBER EVALUATED IS GREATER THAN NUMBER OF LINE NUMBERS	ACTION IF NUMBER EVALUATED IS LESS THAN 1 OR GREATER THAN MAXIMUM ALLOWED
DECSYSTEM 20	Execution stops/Error message displayed	"ON STMT OUT OF RANGE" error
Apple	ON/GOTO bypassed	"ILLEGAL QUANTITY" error
Apple Macintosh	Execution continues with the next executable statement	"ILLEGAL FUNCTION CALL" error*
IBM/Microsoft	ON/GOTO bypassed	"ILLEGAL FUNCTION CALL" or "OVERFLOW" error
TRS-80	ON/GOTO bypassed	"?FC" error
PET/Commodore 64	ON/GOTO bypassed	"ILLEGAL QUANTITY" error

*If the value of the expression 0 (zero), execution will continue with the next executable statement.

The box "ON/GOTO Errors" illustrates how various BASIC implementations respond to these conditions.

MENUS

A menu is a listing that displays the functions that can be performed by a program. The desired function is chosen by entering a code (typically a simple numeric or alphabetic character) from the terminal keyboard. A computer menu is like a menu in a restaurant. The user (diner) reads a group of possible selections on the screen (menu) and then enters a selection (describes the desired meal to the waiter or waitress).

The state capital menu program (Figure V–4) illustrates a common use of the ON/GOTO statement in making a menu selection. The user tells the computer which state capital she wishes to find by entering either 1, 2, 3, 4, or 5. Line 130 transfers the program execution to the appropriate operation.

In the example, the user indicates that she wishes to know the state capital of New Jersey by typing in the number 3, which is assigned to the variable N. Line 130, an ON/GOTO statement, causes program execution to branch to the third line number 180. The operation is then performed, and the result is printed.

LOOPING PROCEDURES

There are several things to consider in setting up a loop. The programmer must decide not only what instructions are to be repeated, but also how many times the loop is to be executed. There are three techniques for loop control. This section covers trailer values and counters. Section VI will discuss the other method, FOR and NEXT statements.

Trailer Value

A loop controlled by a trailer value contains an IF/THEN statement that checks for the end of the data. The last data item is a **dummy value** that is not part of the data to be processed. Either numeric or alphanumeric data can be used as a trailer value. However, the programmer must always select a trailer value that will not be confused with real data. For example, a customer account number is never 0, which implies that zero may be safely used as a dummy value.

Figure V–4 ▪ ON/GOTO Example Using a Menu

```
00010 REM ********************************
00020 REM *** STATE CAPITAL MENU PROGRAM ***
00030 REM ********************************
00040 PRINT
00050 PRINT
00060 PRINT "STATE CAPITAL MENU SELECTION, ENTER:"
00070 PRINT "        1 FOR OHIO"
00080 PRINT "        2 FOR NEW YORK"
00090 PRINT "        3 FOR NEW JERSEY"
00100 PRINT "        4 FOR PENNSYLVANIA"
00110 PRINT "        5 FOR KANSAS"
00120 INPUT N
00130 ON N GOTO 140,160,180,200,220
00140 LET C$ = "COLUMBUS"
00150 GOTO 230
00160 LET C$ = "ALBANY"
00170 GOTO 230
00180 LET C$ = "TRENTON"
00190 GOTO 230
00200 LET C$ = "HARRISBURG"
00210 GOTO 230
00220 LET C$ = "TOPEKA"
00230 PRINT
00240 PRINT
00250 PRINT "THE STATE CAPITAL IS ";C$
00999 END
```

```
RUNNH


STATE CAPITAL MENU SELECTION, ENTER:
        1 FOR OHIO
        2 FOR NEW YORK
        3 FOR NEW JERSEY
        4 FOR PENNSYLVANIA
        5 FOR KANSAS
? 3


THE STATE CAPITAL IS TRENTON
```

MICROCOMPUTERS	
Microcomputer:	Difference:
Apple	No differences.
Apple Macintosh	No differences.
IBM/Microsoft	No differences.
PET/Commodore 64	No differences.
TRS-80	No differences.

Here is how it works. An IF/THEN statement is placed within the set of instructions to be repeated, usually at the beginning of the loop. One of the variables to which data is entered is tested. If it contains the dummy value, control is transferred out of the loop. If the variable contains valid data (does not equal the trailer value), looping continues.

Figure V–5 contains a loop pattern controlled by a trailer value. The program calculates the sales price of several different flowers. Statement 140 tests the value I$ for the dummy value:

```
00140 IF I$ = "END" THEN 240
```

If the condition is true, the flow of processing drops out of the loop to line 240. If the condition is false, processing continues to the next line in sequence, line 150. Note that since we used the INPUT statement to enter the data, it is necessary to tell the user how to end the looping process. This is done in line 90. The user has to enter two dummy values, END and 0, because the INPUT statement expects two values to be entered.

Counter

A second method of controlling a loop requires the programmer to create a counter—a numeric variable that is incremented each time the loop is executed. Normally, the increment is 1. A counter is effective only if the programmer notifies the computer how many times a loop should be repeated. The following steps are involved in setting up a counter for loop control:

1. Initialize the counter to give it a beginning value.
2. Increment the counter each time the loop is executed.

Figure V–5 ▪ Flower Sales (Continued Next Page)

```
00010 REM **********************************
00020 REM ***     FLOWER SALES PROGRAM     ***
00030 REM **********************************
00040 LET D = 0.85
00050 REM **********************************
00060 REM ***       BEGINNING OF LOOP      ***
00070 REM **********************************
00080 PRINT "ENTER ITEM AND REGULAR PRICE"
00090 PRINT "ENTER END,0 WHEN FINISHED"
00100 INPUT I$,R
00110 REM **********************************
00120 REM ***    TEST FOR TRAILER VALUE    ***
00130 REM **********************************
00140 IF I$ = "END" THEN 240
00150 LET S = R * D
00160 PRINT
00170 PRINT "ITEM","SALES PRICE","REGULAR PRICE"
00180 PRINT I$,S,R
00190 PRINT
00200 GOTO 80
00210 REM **********************************
00220 REM ***          END OF LOOP          ***
00230 REM **********************************
00240 PRINT
00250 PRINT "JOB IS COMPLETED"
00999 END
```

Figure V–5 ▪ **Continued**

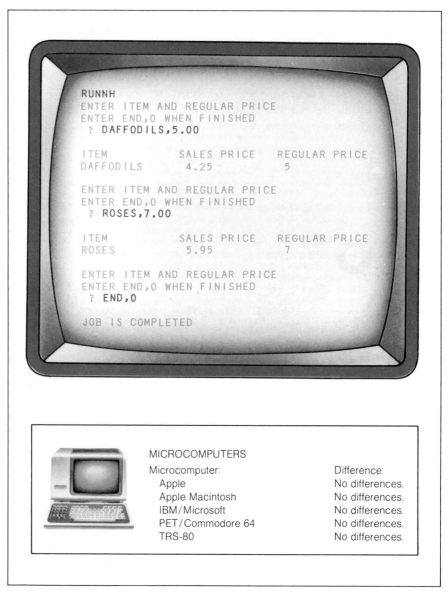

```
RUNNH
ENTER ITEM AND REGULAR PRICE
ENTER END,0 WHEN FINISHED
 ? DAFFODILS,5.00

ITEM            SALES PRICE    REGULAR PRICE
DAFFODILS         4.25              5

ENTER ITEM AND REGULAR PRICE
ENTER END,0 WHEN FINISHED
 ? ROSES,7.00

ITEM            SALES PRICE    REGULAR PRICE
ROSES             5.95              7

ENTER ITEM AND REGULAR PRICE
ENTER END,0 WHEN FINISHED
 ? END,0

JOB IS COMPLETED
```

MICROCOMPUTERS

Microcomputer:	Difference:
Apple	No differences.
Apple Macintosh	No differences.
IBM / Microsoft	No differences.
PET / Commodore 64	No differences.
TRS-80	No differences.

3. Test the counter to determine if the loop has been executed the desired number of times.

The flower sales program used in Figure V–5 can be modified to use a counter, as shown in Figure V– 6. Since there are three flowers, the loop must be executed three times. The counter in this example is C. It is initialized to 0 in line 80. The IF/THEN statement in line 140 tests the number of times the loop has been executed, as represented by the counter C. Line 190 causes C to be incremented each time the loop is executed. The loop instructions will be executed until C equals 4.

**Figure V–6 ▪ Flower Sales
Program with Counter**

```
00010 REM ******************************
00020 REM ***   FLOWER SALES PROGRAM   ***
00030 REM ******************************
00040 LET D = 0.85
00050 REM ******************************
00060 REM ***    INITIALIZE COUNTER    ***
00070 REM ******************************
00080 LET C = 0
00090 PRINT " ","REGULAR","SALES"
00100 PRINT "ITEM"," PRICE","PRICE"
00110 REM ******************************
00120 REM ***    TEST COUNTER VALUE    ***
00130 REM ******************************
00140 IF C = 4 THEN 999
00150 READ I$,R
00160 LET S = R * D
00170 PRINT
00180 PRINT I$,R,S
00190 LET C = C + 1
00200 REM ******************************
00210 REM *** UNCONDITIONAL TRANSFER ***
00220 REM ******************************
00230 GOTO 130
00240 DATA DAFFODILS,5.00,ROSES,7.00
00250 DATA CARNATIONS,4.00,DAISIES,3.00
00999 END
```

```
RUNNH
                  REGULAR        SALES
ITEM              PRICE          PRICE

DAFFODILS            5             4.25

ROSES                7             5.95

CARNATIONS           4             3.4

DAISIES              3             2.55
```

MICROCOMPUTERS

Microcomputer:	Difference:
Apple	No differences.
Apple Macintosh	No differences.
IBM / Microsoft	No differences.
PET / Commodore 64	No differences.
TRS-80	No differences.

A PROGRAMMING PROBLEM

Problem Definition

The Office of the Registrar at Ed U. K. Shun College needs a program that will assign class rank to students based on their earned credit hours. In addition, office personnel want to know how many students in each class rank are registered for a class and how many total students are in the class.

The class rank scale is as follows:

Credit Hours	Class Rank
90 or more	Senior
60 to 89	Junior
30 to 59	Sophomore
Less than 30	Freshman

The students and their credit hours earned follow:

Student	Credit Hours
Shirley Simon	66
Ed Taylor	15
Steve Dun	92
Kelly Cole	100
Gerry Hill	45
Shelly Cable	28
Beth Anderson	33
Karen Redford	89
Henry Kullen	78
Mary Mars	55

Solution Design

The first step in the program is to read each student's name and number of credit hours. Next, 1 must be added to the total number of students. The appropriate class rank should then be assigned and the total number of students in that class should be incremented. Finally, print the results.

The Program

The counter variables are initialized to 0 by the READ and DATA statements in lines 40 and 50 of Figure V–7. The name and credit hours for each student are read in line 110. Line 160 tests for the trailer value END. As long as the student's name does not equal END, the loop is re-executed. The total number of students is accumulated in line 170. The first test to determine the class rank is made in line 180. If the credit hours are less than 90, the student is not a senior. Control is transferred to line 220, where the credit hours are tested again to see if they total fewer than 60 (required for junior class status). In this fashion, credit hours less than the lowest number required for a particular class rank are passed down to the next lowest level until the correct class ranking is found. Line 300 requires no test; any credit hours fewer than 30 give the student freshman status. When the trailer value END is detected, control drops to line 380, where printing of the totals occurs.

Figure V–7 ▪ **Class Rank** (Continued on Next Two Pages)

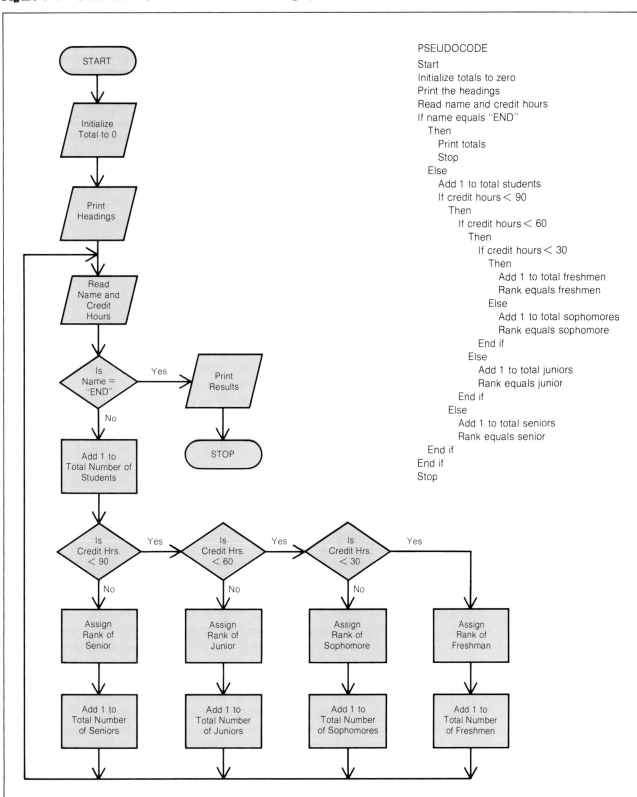

PSEUDOCODE
Start
Initialize totals to zero
Print the headings
Read name and credit hours
If name equals "END"
   Then
     Print totals
     Stop
   Else
     Add 1 to total students
     If credit hours < 90
       Then
         If credit hours < 60
           Then
             If credit hours < 30
               Then
                 Add 1 to total freshmen
                 Rank equals freshmen
               Else
                 Add 1 to total sophomores
                 Rank equals sophomore
             End if
           Else
             Add 1 to total juniors
             Rank equals junior
         End if
         Else
            Add 1 to total seniors
            Rank equals senior
       End if
   End if
Stop

Figure V–7 ▪ Continued

```
00010 REM *****************************************
00020 REM ***            ASSIGN CLASS RANK        ***
00030 REM *****************************************
00040 DATA 0,0,0,0,0
00050 READ F,S,J,SE,T
00060 PRINT "NAME"," ","CREDIT HOURS","CLASS RANK"
00070 PRINT
00080 REM *****************************************
00090 REM ***          THE LOOP BEGINS HERE       ***
00100 REM *****************************************
00110 READ S$,C
00120 REM *****************************************
00130 REM ***           TEST FOR TRAILER VALUE    ***
00140 REM ***              CONDITIONAL TRANSFER   ***
00150 REM *****************************************
00160 IF S$ = "END" THEN 380
00170 LET T = T + 1
00180 IF C < 90 THEN 220
00190 LET R$ = "SENIOR"
00200 LET SE = SE + 1
00210 GOTO 320
00220 IF C < 60 THEN 260
00230 LET R$ = "JUNIOR"
00240 LET J = J + 1
00250 GOTO 320
00260 IF C < 30 THEN 300
00270 LET R$ = "SOPHOMORE"
00280 LET S = S + 1
00290 GOTO 320
00300 LET R$ = "FRESHMAN"
00310 LET F = F + 1
00320 PRINT S$," ",C,R$
00370 GOTO 110
00380 PRINT
00390 PRINT "TOTAL # OF FRESHMAN = ";F
00400 PRINT "TOTAL # OF SOPHOMORES = ";S
00410 PRINT "TOTAL # OF JUNIORS = ";J
00420 PRINT "TOTAL # OF SENIORS = ";SE
00430 PRINT
00440 PRINT "TOTAL # OF STUDENTS = ";T
00450 DATA "SHIRLEY SIMON",66,"ED TAYLOR",15
00460 DATA "STEVE DUN",92,"KELLY COLE",100
00470 DATA "GERRY HILL",45,"SHELLY CABLE",28
00480 DATA "BETH ANDERSON",33,"KAREN REDFORD",89
00490 DATA "HENRY KULLEN",78,"MARY MARS",55
00500 DATA "END",0
00999 END
```

SUMMARY POINTS

▪ The GOTO statement is an unconditional transfer of control that allows the computer to bypass or alter the sequence in which instructions are executed.
▪ The GOTO statement often is used to set up loops.
▪ The IF/THEN statement permits control to be transferred only when a specified condition is met. If the condition following IF is true, the clause following the word THEN is given control; if it is false, control passes to the next line.

Figure V–7 ▪ Continued

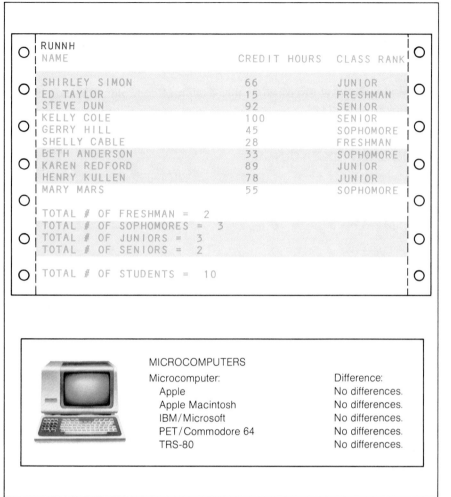

```
RUNNH
NAME                          CREDIT HOURS   CLASS RANK

SHIRLEY SIMON                      66          JUNIOR
ED TAYLOR                          15          FRESHMAN
STEVE DUN                          92          SENIOR
KELLY COLE                        100          SENIOR
GERRY HILL                         45          SOPHOMORE
SHELLY CABLE                       28          FRESHMAN
BETH ANDERSON                      33          SOPHOMORE
KAREN REDFORD                      89          JUNIOR
HENRY KULLEN                       78          JUNIOR
MARY MARS                          55          SOPHOMORE

TOTAL # OF FRESHMAN   =   2
TOTAL # OF SOPHOMORES =   3
TOTAL # OF JUNIORS    =   3
TOTAL # OF SENIORS    =   2

TOTAL # OF STUDENTS   =  10
```

MICROCOMPUTERS

Microcomputer:	Difference:
Apple	No differences.
Apple Macintosh	No differences.
IBM/Microsoft	No differences.
PET/Commodore 64	No differences.
TRS-80	No differences.

▪ The ON/GOTO statement instructs the computer to evaluate an expression and, based on its value, to branch to one of several points in a program.

▪ A menu is a listing that displays the functions a program can perform. The user selects the desired function by entering a code from the keyboard.

▪ The number of times a loop is executed can be controlled by the use of a trailer value or a counter.

▪ The trailer value is a dummy value entered at the end of all the data.

▪ A counter can be set up if the programmer knows ahead of time how many times a loop is to be executed.

REVIEW QUESTIONS

1. How do unconditional and conditional transfers differ? Give an example of each.

2. Why is the IF/THEN statement a conditional transfer? If the condition after the IF in an IF/THEN statement is false, where is control transferred to?

3. Where will control be transferred to when the following ON/GOTO statement is executed? X has the value of 270.

20 ON X/90 GOTO 90,270,310

4. What is a menu?

5. Give two methods discussed in this section of controlling the number of times a loop is executed.

DEBUGGING EXERCISES

```
1.  50 LET C = 4
    55 ON C GOTO 60,70,80
    60 PRINT "C = ";1
    65 GOTO 99
    70 PRINT "C = ";2
    75 GOTO 100
    80 PRINT "C = ";3
    99 END
```

```
2.  05 REM *** PRINT THE EVEN NUMBERS FROM 10 DOWN THROUGH Z ***
    10 LET Z = -6
    15 LET X = 10
    20 IF X THEN 99
    25 PRINT X * 10
    30 LET X = x - 2
    35 GOTO 10
    99 END
```


PROGRAMMING PROBLEMS

1. Write a program using the GOTO statement to implement a loop, and a counter to control the number of times the loop is executed. The output from this program should appear as follows:

10	20	30
40	50	60
70	80	90
100	110	120

2. Using a menu and the ON/GOTO statement, write a program which allows the user to enter his or her body weight (in pounds) and gives him or her the choice of calculating: (1) the average number of calories which should be eaten per day to maintain that body weight (weight * 16) or (2) the recommended number of grams of protein which should be consumed per day (weight * 0.453).

OVERVIEW

Section V discussed two methods of controlling loops—counters and trailer values. The IF/THEN and GOTO statements were used to implement these methods. This section presents another method for loop control—FOR and NEXT statements. In addition, it discusses nested loops (loops within loops).

Let us review what happens when a counter is used to control a loop, since the logic of FOR/NEXT loops is very similar. First, the counter variable is set to some initial value. Statements inside the loop are executed once and the counter incremented. The counter variable then is tested to see if the loop has been executed the required number of times. When the variable exceeds the designated terminal, or ending, value the looping process ends, and the computer proceeds to the rest of the program. For example, assume we want to write a program that will multiply each of the numbers from 1 to 6 by 2. The program in Figure VI–1 does this using a loop controlled by the counter method. We will see later how the FOR/NEXT loop allows us to accomplish the same steps in a more efficient manner.

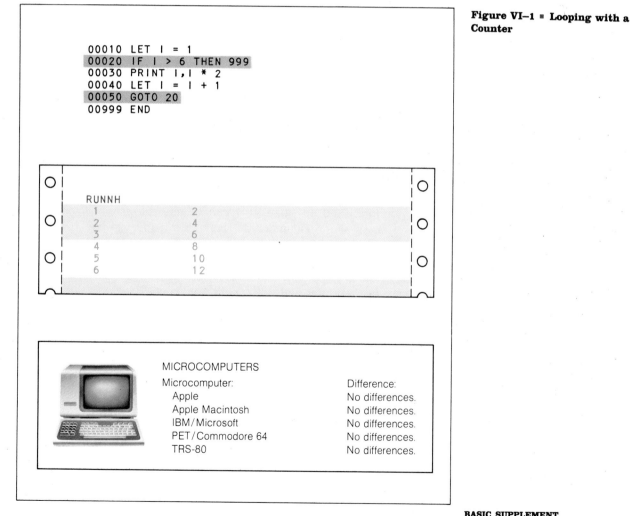

Figure VI–1 ▪ **Looping with a Counter**

```
00010 LET I = 1
00020 IF I > 6 THEN 999
00030 PRINT I,I * 2
00040 LET I = I + 1
00050 GOTO 20
00999 END
```

```
RUNNH
   1          2
   2          4
   3          6
   4          8
   5         10
   6         12
```

MICROCOMPUTERS

Microcomputer:	Difference:
Apple	No differences.
Apple Macintosh	No differences.
IBM/Microsoft	No differences.
PET/Commodore 64	No differences.
TRS-80	No differences.

THE FOR AND NEXT STATEMENTS

The FOR and NEXT statements allow concise loop definition. The general format of the FOR and NEXT loop is as follows:

line# FOR loop variable = initial value TO terminal
value STEP step value

.

.

.

line # NEXT loop variable

The FOR statement tells the computer how many times to execute the loop. The loop variable (also called the index) is set to an initial value. This value is tested against the terminal value to determine whether or not the loop should be repeated. The initial and terminal values may be constants, variables, expressions, or decimals, all of which must be numeric.

To set the initial value and test the counter took two lines (lines 10 and 20) in Figure VI–1. The FOR statement combines these two steps into one statement:

```
00050 FOR I = 1 TO 6 STEP 1
```

Loop / Initial / Terminal / Step
Variable / Value / Value / Value

Lines 40 and 50 in Figure VI–1 increment the loop variable (the counter) and send control back to line 20. The functions of these two statements are combined in the NEXT statement. In Figure VI–1, after control is transferred back to line 20, the value of the loop variable is again tested against the terminal value. Once the terminal value is exceeded, control passes to line 999. When FOR and NEXT are used, control goes to the statement immediately following the NEXT statement.

Thus, the loop used in Figure VI–1 can be set up to use FOR and NEXT statements, as shown in Figure VI–2. The FOR statement in line 10 tells the computer to initialize the loop variable, I, to one. Between the FOR and NEXT statements is line 20, the instruction that is to be repeated; it prints out I and the result of I * 2. Line 30, the NEXT statement, increments the loop variable by the step indicated in the FOR statement. The step value may be a constant, real number, variable, or expression, and it must have a numeric value.

Flowcharting FOR and NEXT loops

Figure VI–3a illustrates the standard method of flowcharting the FOR/NEXT loop. We have developed our own shorthand symbol for FOR and NEXT loops, which is shown in Figure VI–3b. This is very convenient for representing a loop, since it shows the initial, terminal, and step values for the loop variable in one symbol.

Processing Steps of FOR and NEXT Loops

Let us review the steps followed by the computer when it encounters a FOR statement:

Figure VI–2 ▪ FOR/NEXT Loop

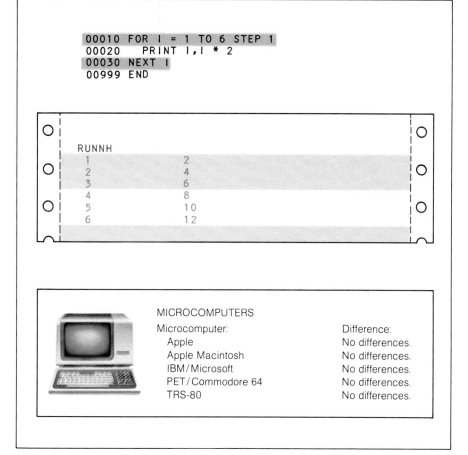

```
00010 FOR I = 1 TO 6 STEP 1
00020    PRINT I,I * 2
00030 NEXT I
00999 END
```

```
RUNNH
  1          2
  2          4
  3          6
  4          8
  5         10
  6         12
```

MICROCOMPUTERS

Microcomputer:	Difference:
Apple	No differences.
Apple Macintosh	No differences.
IBM/Microsoft	No differences.
PET/Commodore 64	No differences.
TRS-80	No differences.

Figure VI–3 ▪ Flowcharting
FOR/NEXT Loops

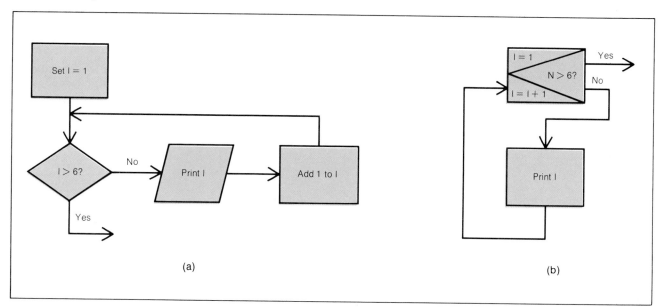

(a)

(b)

1. It sets the loop variable to the initial value indicated.

2. The first time the FOR/NEXT loop is executed, the FOR statement tests to see if the value of the loop variable exceeds the indicated terminal value. If the value of the loop variable does not exceed the terminal value, the statements in the loop are executed. Otherwise, control is transferred to the statement following the NEXT statement.

When the NEXT statement at the end of a loop is encountered, the computer does the following:

1. It adds the step value (given in the FOR statement) to the value of the loop variable. If no step value is indicated in the FOR statement, the value is assumed to be +1. Thus, the following two statements are equivalent:

```
00050 FOR I = 1 TO 6 STEP 1
```

or

```
00050 FOR I = 1 TO 6
```

2. It tests to see if the value of the loop variable exceeds the indicated terminal value.

3. If the value of the loop variable does not exceed the terminal value, the statements in the loop are executed.

4. If the value of the loop variable exceeds the terminal value, control is transferred to the statement immediately following.

Rules for Using FOR and NEXT Statements

Some rules to be aware of when you use FOR and NEXT statements follow:

1. The initial value must be less than or equal to the terminal value when using a positive step. Otherwise, the loop will never be executed; for example,

```
    Valid: FOR J = 1 TO 30 STEP 3
    Invalid: FOR J = 20 TO 10 STEP 2
```

2. There are times when it is desirable to use a negative step value, for example, to count backward from 15 by 1s (see Figure VI–4). The loop is terminated when the value of the loop variable N "exceeds" the specified terminal value, 5. In this case, though, the value of N "exceeds" in a downward sense—the loop is terminated when N is smaller than the terminal value. The initial value of the loop variable should be greater than the terminal value when using a negative step; for example,

```
    Valid: FOR K = 30 TO 20 STEP -5
    Invalid: FOR N = 20 TO 30 STEP -5
```

3. The step size in a FOR statement should never be 0. This value would cause the computer to loop endlessly. Such an error condition is known as an infinite loop:

```
    Invalid: FOR R = 1 TO 10 STEP 0
```

4. Transfer can be made from one statement to another within a loop. For example, the program in Figure VI–5 reads in five tourist attractions and their state of residence. It will print out only those tourist attractions that are not in

Figure VI–4 ▪ Using a Negative
Step Value

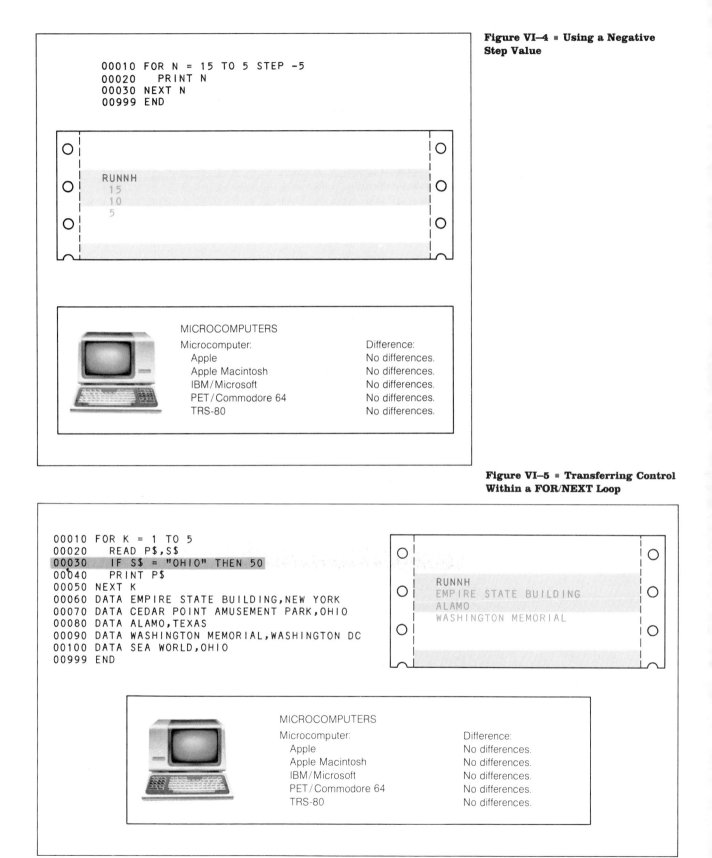

```
00010 FOR N = 15 TO 5 STEP -5
00020    PRINT N
00030 NEXT N
00999 END
```

```
RUNNH
 15
 10
  5
```

MICROCOMPUTERS

Microcomputer:	Difference:
Apple	No differences.
Apple Macintosh	No differences.
IBM/Microsoft	No differences.
PET/Commodore 64	No differences.
TRS-80	No differences.

Figure VI–5 ▪ Transferring Control
Within a FOR/NEXT Loop

```
00010 FOR K = 1 TO 5
00020    READ P$,S$
00030    IF S$ = "OHIO" THEN 50
00040    PRINT P$
00050 NEXT K
00060 DATA EMPIRE STATE BUILDING,NEW YORK
00070 DATA CEDAR POINT AMUSEMENT PARK,OHIO
00080 DATA ALAMO,TEXAS
00090 DATA WASHINGTON MEMORIAL,WASHINGTON DC
00100 DATA SEA WORLD,OHIO
00999 END
```

```
RUNNH
EMPIRE STATE BUILDING
ALAMO
WASHINGTON MEMORIAL
```

MICROCOMPUTERS

Microcomputer:	Difference:
Apple	No differences.
Apple Macintosh	No differences.
IBM/Microsoft	No differences.
PET/Commodore 64	No differences.
TRS-80	No differences.

Ohio. Note, however, that a transfer from a statement within the loop to the FOR statement of the loop is illegal. Such a transfer would cause the loop variable to be reset (rather than simply continuing the loop process):

Invalid Transfer

```
00010 FOR J = 1 TO 15
00020   IF J = 10 THEN 10
00030   PRINT J + 1
00040 NEXT J
```

If you want to continue the looping process but want to bypass some inner instruction, branch (transfer control) to the next statement, as was done in Figure VI–5 (line 30).

Transferring outside the loop before it is normally terminated should also be avoided. If such a transfer is made, the loop variable will not have the value which you would expect.

5. The value of the loop variable should not be modified by program statements within the loop. For example, line 30 here is invalid:

```
00010 FOR I = 1 TO 10
00020   LET T = T + 1
00030   LET I = T
00040 NEXT I
```

6. The initial, terminal, and step expressions can be composed of any valid numeric variable, constant, or mathematical formula. The following examples are valid where A = 7, B = 3, C = 1:

```
00010 FOR L = A TO (B + 10) STEP 2
00020   PRINT L * A
00030 NEXT L
```

```
00010 FOR N = 1 TO A STEP B
00020   LET T = T + 1
00030 NEXT N
```

```
00010 FOR J = (A * B) TO (A + B) STEP -C
00020   PRINT J,J * 3
00030 NEXT J
```

7. Each FOR statement must be accompanied by an associated NEXT statement. In addition, the loop variable in the FOR statement must be specified in the NEXT statement.

Figure VI–6 demonstrates the application of a FOR/NEXT loop. The purpose of this program is to find out the number of dropouts of a marathon race at each checkpoint of the race. There are six checkpoints. The FOR/NEXT loop is set to be executed six times—once for each checkpoint. Each time through the loop, the user enters the number of racers who have checked in at the checkpoint; then the computer prints the number of dropouts to the checkpoint, and at the end prints the total number of racers who have completed the rate and the total number of racers who dropped out.

NESTED FOR AND NEXT STATEMENTS

Loops can be nested; that is, all of one loop can be inside another loop or many other loops. An example of a nested loop follows:

Figure VI–6 ▪ FOR/NEXT Loop

```
00010 REM **************************************************************
00020 REM *** PROGRAM TO COMPUTE THE NUMBER OF MARATHON DROP-OUTS ***
00030 REM **************************************************************
00040 LET T = 100
00050 FOR J = 1 TO 6
00060    PRINT "ENTER NUMBER OF RACERS AT CHECKPOINT # ";J
00070    INPUT N
00080    PRINT "NUMBER OF DROP-OUTS AT CHECKPOINT # ";J;" = ";T - N
00090    PRINT
00100    LET T = N
00110 NEXT J
00120 PRINT
00130 PRINT "TOTAL NUMBER OF RACERS WHO COMPLETED THE RACE = ";T
00140 PRINT "TOTAL NUMBER OF RACERS WHO DROPPED OUT OF THE RACE = ";100 - T
00999 END
```

```
RUNNH
ENTER NUMBER OF RACERS AT CHECKPOINT #  1
? 100
NUMBER OF DROP-OUTS AT CHECKPOINT #  1  = 0

ENTER NUMBER OF RACERS AT CHECKPOINT #  2
? 95
NUMBER OF DROP-OUTS AT CHECKPOINT #  2  = 5

ENTER NUMBER OF RACERS AT CHECKPOINT #  3
? 85
NUMBER OF DROP-OUTS AT CHECKPOINT #  3  = 10

ENTER NUMBER OF RACERS AT CHECKPOINT #  4
? 75
NUMBER OF DROP-OUTS AT CHECKPOINT #  4  = 10

ENTER NUMBER OF RACERS AT CHECKPOINT #  5
? 70
NUMBER OF DROP-OUTS AT CHECKPOINT #  5  = 5

ENTER NUMBER OF RACERS AT CHECKPOINT #  6
? 60
NUMBER OF DROP-OUTS AT CHECKPOINT #  6  = 10


TOTAL NUMBER OF RACERS WHO COMPLETED THE RACE =  60
TOTAL NUMBER OF RACERS WHO DROPPED OUT OF THE RACE = 40
```

MICROCOMPUTERS

Microcomputer:	Difference:
Apple	Output must be reformatted.
Apple Macintosh	No differences.
IBM/Microsoft	No differences.
PET/Commodore 64	Output must be reformatted.
TRS-80	No differences.

```
 ┌─FOR K = 1 TO 5
 │ ┌─FOR L = 1 TO 4
 │ │   •                    Valid
 │ │   •
 │ └─NEXT L
 └─NEXT K
```

The inner loop often is indented to improve readability. In this case, each time the outer loop (K loop) is executed once, the inner loop (L loop) is executed four times. When the L loop is terminated, control passes to the statement immediately below it, NEXT K. When control is transferred to FOR K (and the value of K does not exceed the terminal value, 5), the FOR L statement is soon encountered again. L is reinitialized, and the L loop is again repeated four times.

In nested FOR and NEXT statements, be careful not to mix the FOR from one loop with the NEXT from another. In other words, be sure one loop is completely inside another. The following example will not execute:

```
 ┌─┬─FOR K = 1 TO 5
 │ └─FOR L = 1 TO 4
 │     •                    Invalid
 │     •
 │   ┌─NEXT K
 └───NEXT L
```

You must also be careful not to give nested loops the same index variable:

```
 ┌─FOR N = 1 TO 3
 │ ┌─FOR N = 1 TO 6
 │ │   •                    Invalid
 │ │   •
 │ └─NEXT N
 └─NEXT N
```

If you do this, each time the inner loop is executed, it changes the value of the outer loop variable. This violates Rule 5.

The following segment illustrates the mechanics of the nested loop. The outer loop will be executed four times, since I varies from 1 to 4. The inner loop will be executed three times each time the outer loop is executed once, so the inner loop will be executed a total of twelve times (3 × 4):

```
                  ┌─FOR I = 1 TO 4
                  │ ┌FOR J = 1 TO 3┐
Outer Loop ─────  │ │   PRINT I,J   ├───── Inner Loop
                  │ │ NEXT J        │
                  └─NEXT I ─────────┘
```

		I	J	
a.	First time through	1	1	First time through inner loop; J = 1
	outer loop; I = 1	1	2	Second time through inner loop; J = 2
		1	3	Third time through inner loop; J = 3
b.	Second time through	2	1	First time through inner loop; J = 1
	outer loop; I = 2	2	2	Second time through inner loop; J = 2
		2	3	Third time through inner loop; J = 3
c.	Third time through	3	1	First time through inner loop; J = 1
	outer loop; I = 3	3	2	Second time through inner loop; J = 2
		3	3	Third time through inner loop; J = 3

d. Fourth time through   4   1   First time through inner loop; J = 1
     outer loop; I = 4   4   2   Second time through inner loop; J = 2
                              4   3   Third time through inner loop; J = 3

Figure VI–7 is an application of nested loops that generates three division tables. The inner loop controls the printing of the columns in each row, and the outer loop controls how many rows will be printed.

First I is initialized to 1. Then execution of the inner loop begins. Line 30 tells the computer (when J = 1) to print "1/1 = 1." The comma at the end of that line tells the computer not to start the output of the next PRINT statement on a new line, but rather to continue in the next print zone. Line 40 increments J to 4. The value of I has not changed. The terminal value of J is not exceeded, so "¼ = 0.25" is printed in the second print zone. The inner loop executes one more time and prints out "⅟₇ = 0.1428571." After the inner loop has executed the third time, one complete row has been printed:

$$ \frac{1}{1} = 1 \qquad \frac{1}{4} = 0.25 \qquad \frac{1}{7} = 0.1428571 $$

To have printing start on the next line instead of in the next print zone, it is necessary to have the rest of the line printed with blanks. That is accom-

Figure VI–7 ▪ Nested Loops

```
00010 FOR I = 1 TO 10
00020   FOR J = 1 TO 8 STEP 3
00030     PRINT I;"/";J;"=";I / J,
00040   NEXT J
00050   PRINT
00060 NEXT I
00999 END
```

```
RUNNH
 1 / 1 = 1        1 / 4 = 0.25    1 / 7 = 0.1428571
 2 / 1 = 2        2 / 4 = 0.5     2 / 7 = 0.2857143
 3 / 1 = 3        3 / 4 = 0.75    3 / 7 = 0.4285714
 4 / 1 = 4        4 / 4 = 1       4 / 7 = 0.5714286
 5 / 1 = 5        5 / 4 = 1.25    5 / 7 = 0.7142857
 6 / 1 = 6        6 / 4 = 1.5     6 / 7 = 0.8571429
 7 / 1 = 7        7 / 4 = 1.75    7 / 7 = 1
 8 / 1 = 8        8 / 4 = 2       8 / 7 = 1.142857
 9 / 1 = 9        9 / 4 = 2.25    9 / 7 = 1.285714
10 / 1 = 10      10 / 4 = 2.5    10 / 7 = 1.428571
```

MICROCOMPUTERS

Microcomputer:	Difference:
Apple	Output must be reformatted.
Apple Macintosh	No differences.
IBM/Microsoft	No differences.
PET/Commodore 64	Output must be reformatted.
TRS-80	No differences.

plished by line 50. Finally, I is incremented when line 60 is encountered. The whole process continues until I exceeds the terminal value, 10.

A PROGRAMMING PROBLEM

Problem Definition

The Association of Business Management needs a program to display a bar chart of attendance at its annual convention. The attendance is given as follows:

MONDAY	250
TUESDAY	300
WEDNESDAY	330
THURSDAY	270
FRIDAY	140

The required output lists a three-letter abbreviation for each day in a column headed by "WEEK" and a horizontal bar chart labelled "ATTENDANCE" and marked off by units of 100.

Solution Design

The first thing which must be done is to print the headings. Then, nested loops must be set up. Each time through the outer loop the day of the week and the attendance for that day must be read, and the day printed. Then the inner loop will print the appropriate number of asterisks. Finally the key must be printed.

The Program

Figure VI–8 is a good illustration of nested FOR and NEXT loops. Statements 40 and 50 contain the names of the weekdays and their associated attendance figures. Lines 60 to 140 contain PRINT statements that adjust spacing and column headings. The outer loop (lines 150 to 220) runs five times (once for each day). Nested inside, statements 180 to 200 form a loop whose ter-

Figure VI–8 ▪ Convention Attendance Chart Program (Continued on Next Page)

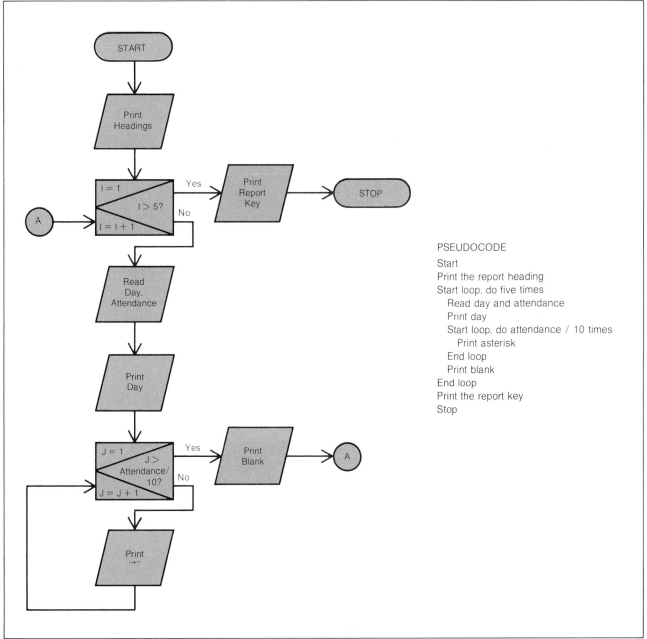

PSEUDOCODE
Start
Print the report heading
Start loop, do five times
  Read day and attendance
  Print day
  Start loop, do attendance / 10 times
    Print asterisk
  End loop
  Print blank
End loop
Print the report key
Stop

```
00010 REM ***********************************************************
00020 REM *** BAR CHART OF ANNUAL CONVENTION ATTENDANCE PROGRAM ***
00030 REM ***********************************************************
00040 DATA MON,250,TUE,300,WED,330
00050 DATA THU,270,FRI,140
00060 PRINT
00070 PRINT
00080 PRINT
00090 PRINT TAB(8);"ANNUAL CONVENTION ATTENDANCE"
00100 PRINT
00110 PRINT "DAY";TAB(8);"ATTENDANCE"
00120 PRINT
00130 PRINT TAB(7);"10";TAB(16);"100";TAB(26);"200";TAB(36);"300"
00140 PRINT
00150 FOR I = 1 TO 5
00160    READ D$,A
00170    PRINT D$;TAB(8);
00180    FOR J = 1 TO A / 10
00190      PRINT "*";
00200    NEXT J
00210    PRINT " "
00220 NEXT I
00230 PRINT
00240 PRINT "KEY"
00250 PRINT
00260 PRINT "* = 10 MEMBERS"
00999 END
```

```
RUNNH


          ANNUAL CONVENTION ATTENDANCE

DAY      ATTENDANCE

          10        100       200       300

MON      *************************
TUE      *******************************
WED      *********************************
THU      ***************************
FRI      **************

KEY

* = 10 MEMBERS
```

MICROCOMPUTERS

Microcomputer:	Difference:
Apple	Output must be reformatted.
Apple Macintosh	No differences.
IBM/Microsoft	No differences.
PET/Commodore 64	Output must be reformatted.
TRS-80	No differences.

Figure VI–8 ▪ Continued

minal value is the value of the variable A divided by 10. The value of A is the attendance during a particular day. A is divided by ten in order to print one asterisk for ten attending members. Statement 190 prints an asterisk for every ten members who attended the convention. The semicolon at the end of line 190 prevents a carriage return as long as the inner loop is executing.

After the inner loop is finished, however, it is necessary to prepare for the next day's line by the printing of a blank space in line 210, which completes the carriage return.

Many variations can be made to the basic bar chart display. The asterisk can be replaced by any other character.

SUMMARY POINTS

■ BASIC provides for concise loop definition with the FOR and NEXT statements. The FOR statement tells the computer how many times to execute the loop. The NEXT statement increments the loop variable and sends control back to the FOR statement.

■ Some rules to remember when using FOR and NEXT loops follow:
1. The initial value must be less than or equal to the terminal value when using a positive step value.
2. The step value can be negative. If it is, the initial value must be greater than or equal to the terminal value.
3. The step value should never be 0; this would cause the computer to loop endlessly.
4. Transfer can be made from one statement to another within a loop. However, transfer from a statement within a loop to the FOR statement is illegal.
5. The value of the loop variable should not be modified by program statements within the loop.
6. The initial, terminal, and step expressions can be composed of any valid numeric variable, constant, or mathematical formula.
7. Each FOR statement must be accompanied by an associated NEXT statement.
8. FOR and NEXT loops can be nested.
9. The NEXT statement of the inner loop must come before the NEXT statement of the outer loop.

REVIEW QUESTIONS

1. Give the two steps followed by the computer when it encounters a FOR statement.
2. What are the four steps followed by the computer when it encounters a NEXT statement?
3. Transfer can be made from one statement to another within a loop. True or false?
4. Name two things to be careful not to do when nesting FOR/NEXT loops.

DEBUGGING EXERCISES

```
1.  10 FOR I = 1 TO 20 STEP -2
    15    READ N
    20    IF N > 15 THEN 10
    25    PRINT N
    30 NEXT I
```

```
2. 10 FOR J = 1 TO 5
   15    FOR K = 3 TO 9
   20       LET J = J + 2
   25    NEXT J
   30 NEXT K
```

PROGRAMMING PROBLEMS

1. Write a program which will read in a list of ten names and print each one
after it is read. Use a FOR/NEXT loop. Here is the list of names.

JOHN	CANDY
KAREN	ROBERT
EDWARD	MIKE
DAVID	JOSE
TONYA	LISA

2. The Home Economics Department needs a program which will display in
a horizontal bar graph the number of students enrolled in each nutrition class,
sections 210 through 219. Use the following data.

SECTION NUMBER	NUMBER of STUDENTS
210	33
211	23
212	36
213	29
214	25
215	10
216	18
217	28
218	24
219	33

Your output should have the following format:

```
                       CLASS ENROLLMENT
SECTION
NUMBER                   STUDENTS
                1       10      20      30
210            **********************************
211            .
212
213            .
214
215            .
216
217            .
218
219            ************************************
```

OVERVIEW

BASIC has numerous built-in functions that perform specific mathematical operations, such as finding the square root of a number or generating random numbers. These functions are useful to the programmer, who is spared the necessity of writing the sequence of statements otherwise needed to perform these operations. At other times, however, it may be useful for the programmer to define a function to meet the particular needs of an application. This section discusses these two tools: library functions (also called **built-in,** or **predefined functions**) and user-defined functions.

LIBRARY FUNCTIONS

Table VII–1 lists the ANSI standard library functions found on most systems. The functions have been built into the BASIC language because many applications require these types of mathematical operations. The functions are included in the BASIC language library, where they can be referred to easily—hence, the name **library functions.**

The general format for referencing a library function is as follows:

function name(argument)

In the function references in Table VII–1, the variable X is used as the **argument.** In BASIC, the argument of a function can be a constant, a variable, a mathematical expression, or another function. These functions are used in place of constants, variables, or expressions in BASIC statements such as PRINT, LET, and IF/THEN.

Trigonometric Functions

The first four library functions in Table VII–1—SIN(X), COS(X), TAN(X), and ATN(X)—are trigonometric functions, which are very useful in mathematics, engineering, and scientific applications. They use radian measures of angles, since computers find them easier to understand than degrees. People, however, prefer to use degrees. The following examples show how to convert from one unit to the other:

Table VII–1 ▪ Common ANSI Standard Library Functions

FUNCTION	PURPOSE
SIN(X)	Trigonometric sine function, X in radians
COS(X)	Trigonometric cosine function, X in radians
TAN(X)	Trigonometric tangent function, X in radians
ATN(X)	Trigonometric arc tangent function, X in radians
LOG(X)	Natural logarithm function
EXP(X)	e raised to the X power
SQR(X)	Square root of X
INT(X)	Greatest integer less than X
SGN(X)	Sign of X
ABS(X)	Absolute value of X
RND	Random number between 0 and 1

1 radian = 57.29578 degrees	To convert 2.5 radians to degrees, multiply 2.5 by 57.29578. The product is about 143 degrees.
N radians = N ∗ 57.29578 degrees	

1 degree = 0.01745 radians	To convert 180 degrees to radians, multiply 180 by 0.01745. The result is 3.14 radians (exactly equal to π).
N degrees = N ∗ 0.01745 radians	

Exponentiation Functions

The LOG(X), EXP(X), and SQR(X) functions deal with raising a number to a particular power.

EXP(X)

The exponential, or EXP(X), function makes the calculation $EXP(X) = e^x$. The constant e is equal to 2.718. We will not dwell on e, but it is useful in advanced topics in science, mathematics, and business statistics.

LOG(X)

The **natural logarithm,** or LOG(X), function is the reverse of the EXP(X) function. For example, if $X = e^y$, then LOG(X) = Y. In other words, Y (the LOG of X) is the power e is raised to in order to find X. If we know X but need Y, we can use the following BASIC statement to find it:

```
10 Y = LOG(X)
```

SQR(X)

The square root, or SQR(X), function determines the square root of an argument. In most BASIC implementations, the argument must be a positive number. For example,

X	SQR(X)
4	2
16	4
11.56	3.4

Mathematical Functions

INT(X)

The integer, or INT(X), function is used to compute the greatest integer less than or equal to the value specified as the argument. The integer function does not round a number to the nearest integer. If the argument is a positive value with digits to the right of the decimal point, the digits are truncated (cut off). For example,

X	INT(X)
8	8
5.34	5
16.9	16

Be careful when the argument is a negative number. Remember the number line:

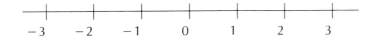

The farther left you go, the less value the number has. For example,

X	INT(X)
-2	-2
-2.5	-3
-6.3	-7

Using INT(X) to Round. Although the INT(X) function does not round by itself, it can be used in an expression that rounds to the nearest integer, tenth, hundredth, or to any degree of accuracy wanted. The program in Figure VII–1 rounds a number to its nearest dollar amount and its nearest penny amount. Since the INT(X) function returns the greatest integer less than or equal to the argument, it is necessary to add 0.5 to the argument to round to the nearest integer (see line 30). Line 40 rounds the same number to the

Figure VII–1 ▪ Rounding Program

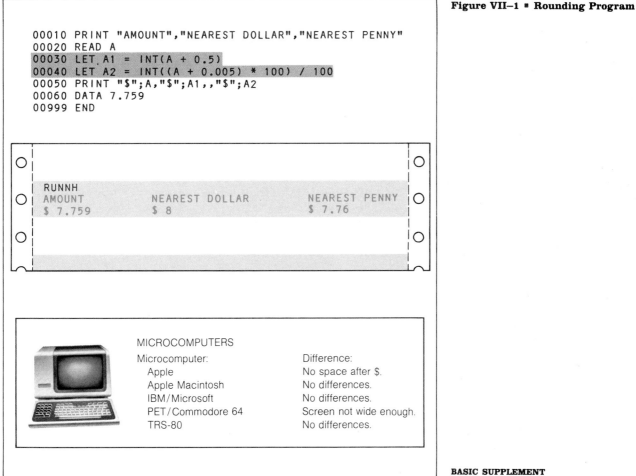

```
00010 PRINT "AMOUNT","NEAREST DOLLAR","NEAREST PENNY"
00020 READ A
00030 LET A1 = INT(A + 0.5)
00040 LET A2 = INT((A + 0.005) * 100) / 100
00050 PRINT "$";A,"$";A1,,"$";A2
00060 DATA 7.759
00999 END
```

```
RUNNH
AMOUNT                 NEAREST DOLLAR          NEAREST PENNY
$ 7.759                $ 8                     $ 7.76
```

MICROCOMPUTERS

Microcomputer:	Difference:
Apple	No space after $.
Apple Macintosh	No differences.
IBM/Microsoft	No differences.
PET/Commodore 64	Screen not wide enough.
TRS-80	No differences.

nearest hundredth. We add 0.005 to N and then multiply that result by 100. The INT(X) function is then applied, and the result is divided by 100.

SGN(X)

The sign, or SGN(X), function yields one of three possible values. If $X > 0$, $SGN(X) = +1$; if $X = 0$, $SGN(X) = 0$; and if $X < 0$, $SGN(X) = -1$. For example,

X	SGN(X)
8.34	+1
0	0
−3.5	−1
0.5	+1

This function might be used to quickly identify when a sales representative has gone over his or her allotted amount of travel expenses (15 percent of sales), as shown in Figure VII–2. After the salesperson's name, sales, and

Figure VII–2 ▪ **Travel Expense Program**

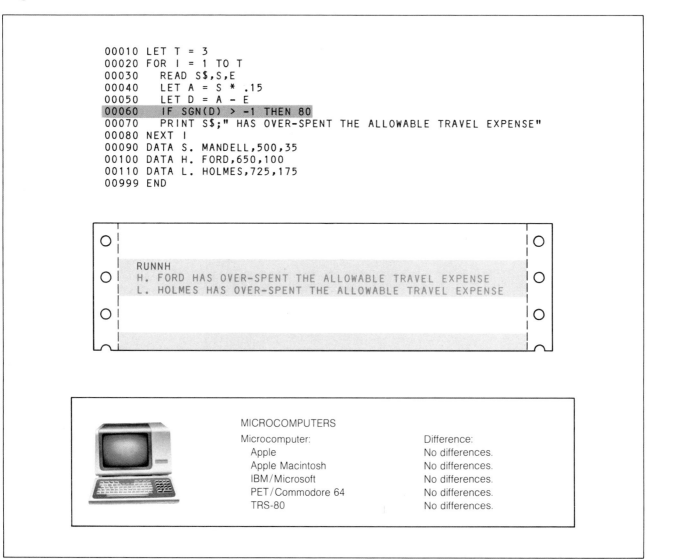

```
00010 LET T = 3
00020 FOR I = 1 TO T
00030   READ S$,S,E
00040   LET A = S * .15
00050   LET D = A - E
00060   IF SGN(D) > -1 THEN 80
00070   PRINT S$;" HAS OVER-SPENT THE ALLOWABLE TRAVEL EXPENSE"
00080 NEXT I
00090 DATA S. MANDELL,500,35
00100 DATA H. FORD,650,100
00110 DATA L. HOLMES,725,175
00999 END
```

```
RUNNH
H. FORD HAS OVER-SPENT THE ALLOWABLE TRAVEL EXPENSE
L. HOLMES HAS OVER-SPENT THE ALLOWABLE TRAVEL EXPENSE
```

MICROCOMPUTERS

Microcomputer:	Difference:
Apple	No differences.
Apple Macintosh	No differences.
IBM/Microsoft	No differences.
PET/Commodore 64	No differences.
TRS-80	No differences.

travel expenses are read, the computer calculates the allotted expenditure and then checks to see whether the balance between the allotted expenditure and the actual expenses is negative (line 60). If the balance is negative, the computer prints the overdrawn message; otherwise, the next salesperson's name is read.

ABS(X)

The absolute value, or ABS(X), function returns the absolute value of the argument. The absolute value is always positive, even if the argument is a negative value. For example,

X	ABS(X)
-2	2
0	0
3.54	3.54
-2.68	2.68

We can use this function to identify all values that differ from a given value. For example, a bank may want to know which individuals have large deposits or have loans. Figure VII–3 shows how the absolute value function

Figure VII–3 ■ Audit Search Program

```
00010 FOR J = 1 TO 3
00020    READ N$,A
00030    IF ABS(A) >= 5000 THEN 50
00040    GOTO 60
00050    PRINT "AUDIT ";N$;"'S ACCOUNT"
00060 NEXT J
00070 DATA JOY BERDAN,1999
00080 DATA JULIE PAGE,7500
00090 DATA KIM TITTLE,-10000
00999 END
```

```
RUNNH
AUDIT JULIE PAGE'S ACCOUNT
AUDIT KIM TITTLE'S ACCOUNT
```

MICROCOMPUTERS

Microcomputer:	Difference:
Apple	No differences.
Apple Macintosh	No differences.
IBM/Microsoft	No differences.
PET/Commodore 64	No differences.
TRS-80	No differences.

might be used to help identify these individuals. Line 30 tests for users who either deposited at least $5,000 or are being loaned at least $5,000.

RND

The randomize, or RND, function is used to generate a random number between 0 and 1. The term random means that any value between 0 and 1 is equally likely to occur. This function is especially important in applications involving statistics, computer simulations, and games. Some systems require that the RND function be used with an argument; other systems do not (see the "Random Numbers" box).

We can use the RND function to generate numbers greater than 1 by using it with other mathematical operations (see Figure VII– 4). Suppose we need a random number between 1 and 10 instead of between 0 and 1. Line 30 in Figure VII– 4 computes a random number between N1 (the lower limit in a selected range) and N2 (the upper limit in the range).

Lines 10 and 20 set N1 to 1 and N2 to 10. In line 30, the computer subtracts N2 from N1. The result is multiplied by a random number generated by the RND function. Finally, that product is added to N2.

USER-DEFINED FUNCTIONS

The definition (DEF) statement can be used by the programmer to define a function not already included in the BASIC language. Once the function has been defined, the programmer can refer to it as a function when necessary.

BASIC Extensions
CINT Function

The Apple Macintosh and the IBM/Microsoft allow the use of the CINT function which is useful when rounding. The format of the CINT function is shown below:

line # Y = CINT(X)

The CINT function converts X to an integer by rounding the fraction portion of the number. X must be within the range of -32768 to 32767 or else an overflow error will occur.

An example of the CINT function is shown below.

```
10 PRINT "NUMBER","INTEGER"
20 FOR I = 1 TO 3
30   READ N
40   LET C = CINT(N)
50   PRINT N,C
60 NEXT I
70 DATA 5.2980734,778.98,64.5
99 END

RUN
NUMBER          INTEGER
 5.298073        5
 778.98          779
 64.5            65
```

Figure VII–4 ▪ Random Number Program

```
00010 LET N1 = 1
00020 LET N2 = 10
00030 LET R = RND * (N1 - N2) + N2
00040 PRINT R,N1,N2
00999 END


RUNNH
8.246632        1              10
```

The DEF statement can be placed anywhere in the program before the first reference to the function. Its general format is as follows:

line# DEF function name(argument) = expression

The function name consists of the letters FN followed by any one of the twenty-six alphabetic characters. There can be only one argument. However, an argument is not required within the DEF statement. The expression can contain any mathematical operations desired, although a function definition cannot exceed one line.

When the computer encounters line 10 in the following program, it stores in memory the definition for the function FNR. Line 20 initializes T to 7. When the computer encounters line 30, it uses the definition for FNR and substitutes the value of T, which in this case is 7, for N in the expression (N * 2) + 5. The printed result is 19:

```
00010 DEF FNR(N) = (N * 2) + 5
00020 LET T = 7
00030 PRINT FNR(T)
```

```
RUNNH
 19
```

Line 10 in Figure VII–5 defines a function to round a number multiplied by 0.25 to the nearest hundredth and then to add 150 to the result. After the

Figure VII–5 ▪ Calculating Packaging Expense

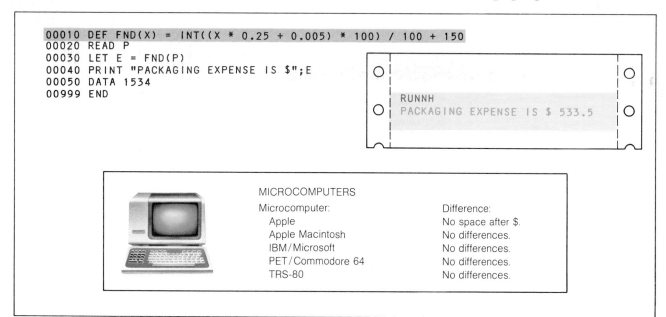

```
00010 DEF FND(X) = INT((X * 0.25 + 0.005) * 100) / 100 + 150
00020 READ P
00030 LET E = FND(P)
00040 PRINT "PACKAGING EXPENSE IS $";E
00050 DATA 1534
00999 END
```

```
RUNNH
PACKAGING EXPENSE IS $ 533.5
```

MICROCOMPUTERS

Microcomputer:	Difference:
Apple	No space after $.
Apple Macintosh	No differences.
IBM/Microsoft	No differences.
PET/Commodore 64	No differences.
TRS-80	No differences.

Random Numbers

At first it might not seem hard to make up numbers whose values are arrived at only by chance. However, this task is difficult for machines with precise structure and logic (such as computers). The various computer manufacturers use different methods for obtaining random numbers. You can obtain random numbers between 0 and 1 using each of our computers as follows.

DECSYSTEM 20

Two statements are needed with the DECSYSTEM 20 computer. The RND function needs no argument. The function used alone will give the same numbers each time a program is run; therefore, they are not truly random. Once you know that a program works the way you want it to, you should precede the statement containing RND by a RANDOMIZE statement. Now each time the program runs, RND will give a different unpredictable number. An example follows:

```
00050 RANDOMIZE

00090 LET Y = RND
```

APPLE

Only one statement is needed with the Apple microcomputer. The RND function needs an argument. A positive argument will return a random real number greater than or equal to 0 and less than 1. For example,

```
10 LET Y = RND(17)
```

If the argument is 0,

```
10 LET Y = RND(0`
```

the most recently generated random number will be returned. A negative argument generates a particular random number that is the same every time RND is used with that argument. If an RND statement with a positive argument follows an RND statement with a negative argument, it will generate a particular, repeatable sequence of random numbers.

value for the number of boxes packaged has been read, the computer is instructed to calculate the packaging expense and round it to the nearest hundredth. This is accomplished by substituting the result of P for X in the expression defined in line 10. The result is then printed out.

A PROGRAMMING PROBLEM

Problem Definition

Honesty Realty, Inc. rents apartments to college students. The apartments need new carpeting, and you have been asked to write a program to determine how many square yards of carpeting are needed. The apartment manager has given you the length and the width of each room in a standard apartment in feet.

Random Numbers

IBM/MICROSOFT

Two statements are needed to give a truly random result with the IBM/Microsoft microcomputer (works similar to the RND function on the DECSYSTEM 20). The argument for RND is optional. An example follows:

```
10 RANDOMIZE
20 PRINT RND
```

When the program is run, the computer prompts you with: Random number seed (−32768 to 32767)? You must enter a number within this range. Then the processing will continue.

PET/COMMODORE 64

Two statements are needed to give a truly random result with the PET/Commodore 64 microcomputer. The function RND needs an argument. RND(0) and RND(−N) should precede the use of RND(N). In other words, RND(0) and RND(−N) work much as RANDOMIZE does on the DECSYSTEM 20.
An example follows:

```
10 LET X = RND(-RND(0))
```

```
70 LET X = RND(2)
```

Now X should be a valid random number. Line 40 "seeds" the random number generator.

TRS-80

Two statements are needed with the TRS-80 microcomputer. An argument is needed for RND (you should use 0 to get a number between 0 and 1). An example follows:

```
40 RANDOM
```

```
90 LET Y = RND(0)
```

Solution Design

Since we know the length and the width of each room, we can use the following formula to calculate the area in square feet:

$$\text{Area} = \text{Length} * \text{Width}$$

The next step is to convert the area in square feet into the area in square yards. This is done by dividing the area in square feet by 9 (the number of square feet in a square yard). We can define a function to do this as follows:

$$\text{FNA(Area)} = \text{Area} / 9$$

The last step is to add the area of each room to give the total area of the apartment.

The Program

Figure VII–6 ▪ Area of Room Program, Flowchart, and Pseudocode (Continued on Facing Page)

Line 100 of the program in Figure VII– 6 defines a function, FNA, to convert square feet into square yards. The next several lines print the headings. Line

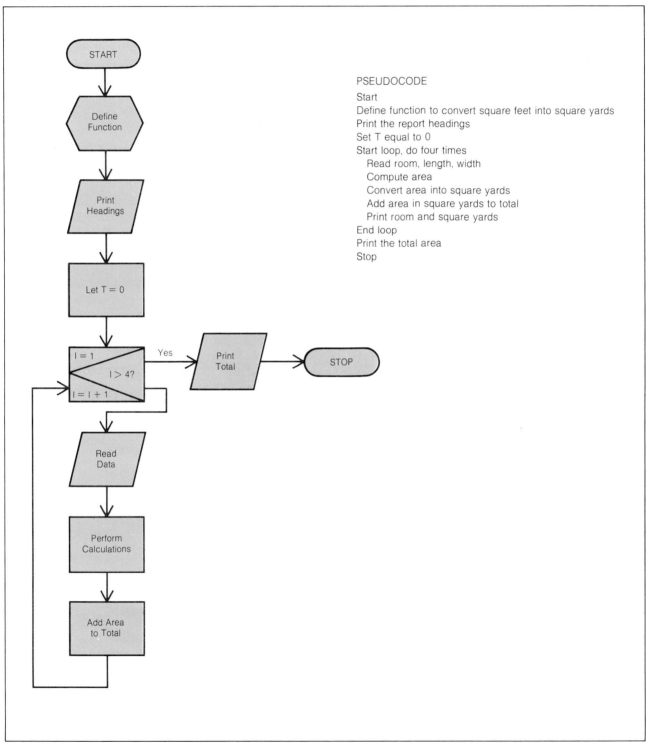

PSEUDOCODE

Start
Define function to convert square feet into square yards
Print the report headings
Set T equal to 0
Start loop, do four times
   Read room, length, width
   Compute area
   Convert area into square yards
   Add area in square yards to total
   Print room and square yards
End loop
Print the total area
Stop

Figure VII–6 ▪ **Continued**

```
00010 REM ************************************************
00020. REM *** THIS PROGRAM CALCULATES THE SQUARE YARDS ***
00030 REM ***         TO CARPET AN APARTMENT          ***
00040 REM ************************************************
00050 DATA LIVING ROOM,20,15,BEDROOM,17.5,12.5
00060 DATA DINING ROOM,15,10,BATHROOM,10,7
00070 REM ************************************************
00080 REM *** FUNCTION CONVERTS SQ FEET INTO SQ YARDS ***
00090 REM ************************************************
00100 DEF FNA(X) = X / 9
00110 PRINT
00120 PRINT
00130 PRINT "ROOM","SQUARE YARDS"
00140 PRINT
00150 LET T = 0
00160 REM ************************************************
00170 REM ***         THE LOOP BEGINS HERE           ***
00180 REM ************************************************
00190 FOR I = 1 TO 4
00200    READ R$,L,W
00210    LET A = L * W
00220    LET S = INT(FNA(A)) + 1
00230    LET T = T + S
00240    PRINT R$,S
00250    PRINT
00260 REM ************************************************
00270 REM ***             THE LOOP ENDS HERE         ***
00280 REM ************************************************
00290 NEXT I
00300 PRINT "TOTAL AREA  =",T;" SQUARE YARDS"
00999 END
```

```
RUNNH

ROOM              SQUARE YARDS

LIVING ROOM       34

BEDROOM           25

DINING ROOM       17

BATHROOM           8

TOTAL AREA  =  84  SQUARE YARDS
```

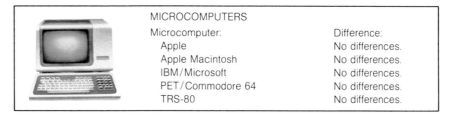

MICROCOMPUTERS	
Microcomputer:	Difference:
Apple	No differences.
Apple Macintosh	No differences.
IBM/Microsoft	No differences.
PET/Commodore 64	No differences.
TRS-80	No differences.

190 initiates the FOR/NEXT loop that reads the data, calculates the area in square feet, converts the area into square yards, and then prints the results. In line 220, the programmer refers to FNA to convert the area in square feet into square yards. Also, line 220 adds 1 to the area in order to ensure that there will be enough carpeting for each room. Line 290 marks the end of the FOR/NEXT loop. Line 300 prints the total.

SUMMARY POINTS

- The BASIC language includes several library functions that can make complicated mathematical operations easier to program.
- The trigonometric functions are SIN(X), COS(X), TAN(X), and ATN(X).
- The exponentiation functions are EXP(X), LOG(X), and SQR(X).
- Other mathematical functions are INT(X), SGN(X), ABS(X), and RND.
- It is also possible for the programmer to define functions by using the DEF statement.

REVIEW QUESTIONS

1. What are library functions?
2. What are the four trigonometric functions? When are angles used as an argument to one of the four functions? What unit of measure is used?
3. What are the three exponentiation functions and what does each function do?
4. List the four mathematical functions. What does each function do?
5. Give the general format of a user-defined function. What does the function name consist of and where are user-defined functions located in a program?

DEBUGGING EXERCISES

```
1.10 REM ***          GENERATE A RANDOM NUMBER          ***
  15 REM ***             BETWEEN 5 AND 15               ***
  20 LET R = RND


2. 10 LET R = FNAB(Y)
   15 REM ***          FUNCTION TO ROUND NUMBER          ***
   20 REM ***              NEAREST TENTH                 ***
   25 FNAB(X) = INT ((X + 0.005) * 100) / 100
```

PROGRAMMING PROBLEMS

1. Write a program which calculates the square roots and natural logarithms of the numbers from 1 to 10. Round each number to three decimal places. The output should have the following format.

NUMBER	SQUARE ROOT	NATURAL LOGARITHM
1	XX.XXX	XX.XXX
2	.	.
3	.	.
	.	.
10	XX.XXX	XX.XXX

2. Write a program to print a table giving the sine, cosine, and tangent of the following angles: 15, 30, 45, 60, 75, and 90 degrees. (Note: 1 degree = 0.01745 radians.) The table should be in the following format:

ANGLE	SINE	COSINE	TANGENT
15	XX.XX	XX.XX	XX.XX
30	.	.	.
.	.	.	.
.	.	.	.
90	XX.XX	XX.XX	XX.XX

OVERVIEW

Sometimes it is necessary to have the computer execute an identical sequence of instructions at several different points in a program. The programmer need not write the set of instructions over and over again; instead, it can be placed in a subroutine. A subroutine is a sequence of statements, typically located at the end of the main program body; it performs a particular function and may be used in several different parts of the main program. By doing this, the instructions need only be written once.

For example, oil prices are expected to increase by 10 percent. A local gas station would like a report that lists the type of gasoline, its price now, and its expected selling price after the 10 percent increase. When writing the solution to this problem, we find that the same procedure is needed to round today's prices (since gasoline prices are usually carried to four decimal places) and tomorrow's expected prices. Instead of writing this rounding procedure two different times, we have written a subroutine that will be executed twice for each type of gasoline. The program will transfer control to the subroutine and back to the main program through the use of two statements: GOSUB and RETURN. These statements, along with the STOP statement and the string functions, will be discussed in this section.

THE GOSUB STATEMENT

The GOSUB statement is used to transfer the flow of control from the main logic of a program to a subroutine. The general format of the GOSUB statement is as follows:

line# GOSUB line#

The line number following GOSUB identifies the first statement of the subroutine.

The GOSUB statement is something like an unconditional GOTO statement. The difference is that the GOSUB command also makes the computer remember where to return after the subroutine has been executed. Here is a typical example of a GOSUB statement:

```
00170 GOSUB 750
```

Figure VIII–1 uses GOSUB statements in lines 210 and 270. Notice the line number of the subroutine. Subroutines often are assigned distinctive line numbers so that they are easier to locate. Although subroutines may be placed anywhere in a program, they are usually at the end, with a line number quite a bit higher than the line numbers in the main program. This leaves sufficient room for statements to be added to the main program.

THE RETURN STATEMENT

After processing within a subroutine has been completed, control must be transferred back to the main logic flow of the program. That is accomplished by the RETURN statement. The general format of the RETURN statement is as follows:

line# RETURN

Figure VIII–1 ■ **Calculating Gas
Prices (Continued on Next Page)**

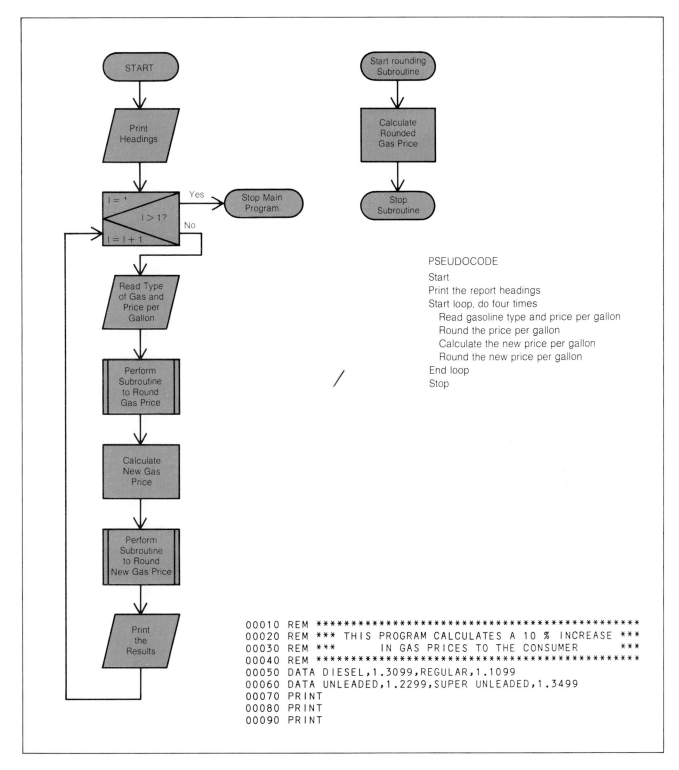

PSEUDOCODE

Start
Print the report headings
Start loop, do four times
    Read gasoline type and price per gallon
    Round the price per gallon
    Calculate the new price per gallon
    Round the new price per gallon
End loop
Stop

```
00010 REM **************************************************
00020 REM *** THIS PROGRAM CALCULATES A 10 % INCREASE ***
00030 REM ***      IN GAS PRICES TO THE CONSUMER      ***
00040 REM **************************************************
00050 DATA DIESEL,1.3099,REGULAR,1.1099
00060 DATA UNLEADED,1.2299,SUPER UNLEADED,1.3499
00070 PRINT
00080 PRINT
00090 PRINT
```

Figure VIII–1 ▪ **Continued**

```
00100 PRINT "TYPE OF GASOLINE";TAB(20);"PRICE PER GALLON";TAB(40);"NEW PRICE"
00110 PRINT
00120 REM **********************************************
00130 REM ***            LOOP BEGINS HERE          ***
00140 REM **********************************************
00150 FOR I = 1 TO 4
00160    READ G$,P
00170    REM **********************************************
00180    REM ***              ROUND PRICE            ***
00190    REM **********************************************
00200    LET X = P
00210    GOSUB 1000
00220    LET N1 = N
00230    REM **********************************************
00240    REM ***        DETERMINE NEW GAS PRICE       ***
00250    REM **********************************************
00260    LET X = P * 1.1
00270    GOSUB 1000
00280    PRINT G$;TAB(25);N1;TAB(41);N
00290    REM **********************************************
00300    REM ***             LOOP ENDS HERE           ***
00310    REM **********************************************
00320 NEXT I
00330 STOP
01000 REM **********************************************
01100 REM ***   SUBROUTINE TO ROUND THE GAS PRICES   ***
01300 REM **********************************************
01400 LET N = INT((X + 0.005) * 100) / 100
01500 RETURN
09999 END
```

```
RUNNH


TYPE OF GASOLINE      PRICE PER GALLON      NEW PRICE

DIESEL                    1.31               1.44
REGULAR                   1.11               1.22
UNLEADED                  1.23               1.35
SUPER UNLEADED            1.35               1.48
STOP at line 00330 of MAIN PROGRAM
```

MICROCOMPUTERS

Microcomputer:	Difference:
Apple	Break in 330; output must be reformatted.
Apple Macintosh	Break in 330.
IBM/Microsoft	Break in 330.
PET/Commodore 64	Break in 330; output must be reformatted.
TRS-80	Break in 330.

No line number need follow RETURN, because the BASIC interpreter remembers to return to the statement immediately following the most recently executed GOSUB statement. For example,

```
00100 GOSUB 1000
00110 PRINT T
      .
      .
01000 REM *** SUBROUTINE ***
      .
      .
01100 RETURN
```

The RETURN statement in line 1100 sends control back to the instruction following the GOSUB statement that called the subroutine, so the RETURN statement in line 1100 sends the computer back to line 110. The RETURN statement in line 1500 of Figure VIII–1 will return control to line 220 if the subroutine was called in line 210. If the subroutine was called in line 270, control will be returned to line 280.

THE STOP STATEMENT

The STOP statement halts execution of a program; it is placed wherever a logical end to a program should occur. The general format of the STOP statement follows:

line# STOP

The STOP statement differs from the END statement in that STOP can appear as often as necessary in a program, whereas the END statement can appear only once and must have the highest line number in the program.

Using STOP with Subroutines

One of the major uses of the STOP statement is with subroutines. For convenience, subroutines generally are placed near the end of a program, but the subroutine may be referred to several times in the program. A STOP statement usually is placed just before the beginning of the first subroutine to prevent unnecessary execution of the subroutine when the computer comes to the logical end of the program. Figure VIII–1 illustrates how the STOP statement is used before subroutines (line 330).

Using STOP with Exception Handling

Many programs contain **exception-handling instructions.** These sequences of statements help the computer prevent the input of invalid data, which is referred to as a **garbage in–garbage out error.** The STOP statement can be used to stop execution of a program after such a sequence has been executed.

Figure VIII–2 calculates the square root of a number. Since the computer can find the square root of positive numbers only, the program includes an exception-handling instruction in line 120. If the user of the program enters a number less than or equal to 0, the computer will branch to line 250, print an error message, and stop processing. Notice that this program also contains a stop statement in line 210; this is the logical end of the main program. In lines 180 through 200, the user is directed to input YES to continue finding the square roots of numbers. If the user does not wish to continue finding the

Figure VIII–2 ▪ Exception
Handling (Continued on Facing
Page)

```
00010 REM **********************************
00020 REM ***    ABNORMAL STOP PROGRAM    ***
00030 REM **********************************
00040 PRINT
00050 PRINT "THIS PROGRAM RETURNS THE SQUARE ROOT OF A NUMBER"
00060 PRINT
00070 PRINT "ENTER A NUMBER WHOSE SQUARE ROOT YOU WANT"
00080 INPUT N
00090 REM **********************************
00100 REM *** TEST FOR ZERO OR NEGATIVE ***
00110 REM **********************************
00120 IF N <= 0 THEN 250
00130 LET S = SQR(N)
00140 PRINT
00150 PRINT
00160 PRINT "THE SQUARE ROOT OF ";N;" IS ";S
00170 PRINT
00180 PRINT "DO YOU WANT TO TRY AGAIN? (YES OR NO)"
00190 INPUT C$
00200 IF C$ = "YES" THEN 60
00210 STOP
00220 REM **********************************
00230 REM ***     PRINT ERROR MESSAGE     ***
00240 REM **********************************
00250 PRINT "YOU HAVE ATTEMPTED TO TAKE THE"
00260 PRINT "SQUARE ROOT OF ZERO OR A NEGATIVE NUMBER"
00270 STOP
00999 END
```

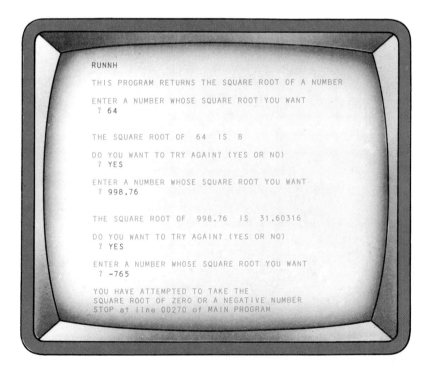

```
RUNNH

THIS PROGRAM RETURNS THE SQUARE ROOT OF A NUMBER

ENTER A NUMBER WHOSE SQUARE ROOT YOU WANT
? 64


THE SQUARE ROOT OF  64  IS  8

DO YOU WANT TO TRY AGAIN? (YES OR NO)
? YES

ENTER A NUMBER WHOSE SQUARE ROOT YOU WANT
? 998.76


THE SQUARE ROOT OF  998.76  IS  31.60316

DO YOU WANT TO TRY AGAIN? (YES OR NO)
? YES

ENTER A NUMBER WHOSE SQUARE ROOT YOU WANT
? -765

YOU HAVE ATTEMPTED TO TAKE THE
SQUARE ROOT OF ZERO OR A NEGATIVE NUMBER
STOP at line 00270 of MAIN PROGRAM
```

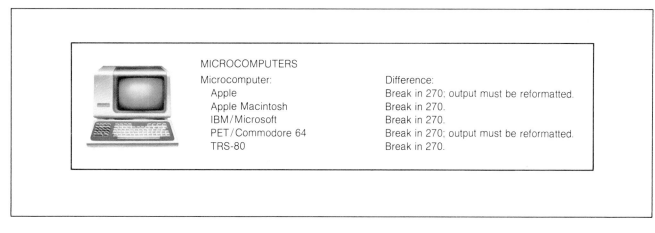

MICROCOMPUTERS

Microcomputer:	Difference:
Apple	Break in 270; output must be reformatted.
Apple Macintosh	Break in 270.
IBM/Microsoft	Break in 270.
PET/Commodore 64	Break in 270; output must be reformatted.
TRS-80	Break in 270.

Figure VIII–2 ▪ Continued

square roots of numbers, he or she types NO, and program execution ends. The STOP statement prevents subsequent lines from being executed (and thus prevents the error message from being printed unnecessarily).

STRING FUNCTIONS

Up to this point, we have manipulated numbers but have done little with strings except print them out or compare them in IF and THEN tests. Many business applications require more sophisticated manipulations of strings.

A string is simply a series of alphanumeric characters such as %#$Z, HO-NEYWELL, or TED. Usually, BASIC requires that quotation marks be placed around strings.

BASIC string functions allow programmers to modify, **concatenate** (join to-gether), compare, and analyze the composition of strings. These functions are useful for sorting lists of names, finding out subject matter in text, printing mailing lists, and so forth. For example, we can help the computer understand that Franklin Oswald III is the same as Oswald III, Franklin. The most common string functions are listed in Table VIII–1.

Table VIII–1 ▪ String Functions

BASIC STRING FUNCTION	OPERATION	EXAMPLE
string 1$ + string 2$	Concatenates; joins two string together	KUNG + FU is KUNGFU
LEN(string)	Finds the length of a string	If H$ is HELLO HOWARD, then LEN(H$) is 12
LEFT$(string,expression)	Returns the number of leftmost characters of a string specified by the expression	LEFT$("ABCDE",2) is AB
RIGHT$(string,expression)	Returns the rightmost characters of a string, starting with the character specified by the expression	RIGHT$("ABCDE",2) is BCDE
MID$(string,expression 1, expression 2)	Starting with the character at expression 1, returns the number of characters specified by expression 2	MID$("ABCDE",3,2) is CD
ASCII(string)	Returns the ASCII code for the first character in the string	If A$ contains DOG, then ASCII(A$) is 68
CHR$(expression)	Returns the string representation of the ASCII code of the expression	If CHR$(F$) > Z, then 20
VAL(expression)	Returns the numeric equivalent of the string expression	X = VAL (H$)
STR$(expression)	Converts a number to its string equivalent	STR$(123) is 123

The Concatenation Function

It is possible to join strings together using the concatenation function. In business this is often desirable when working with names or addresses. The program in Figure VIII–3 demonstrates what happens.

The LEN Function

The LEN function returns the number of characters in the string. An example of how the LEN function might be used is given in Figure VIII–4. In this example, if the value in C$ is less than ten characters long, we do not wish

Figure VIII–3 ▪ **Concatenation**

```
00010 PRINT
00020 PRINT "ENTER TODAY'S DATE"
00030 INPUT D$
00040 LET S$ = "TODAY'S DATE:   "
00050 PRINT
00060 PRINT S$ + D$
00999 END
```

```
RUNNH

ENTER TODAY'S DATE
? "OCTOBER 29, 1984"

TODAY'S DATE:   OCTOBER 29, 1984
```

MICROCOMPUTERS

Microcomputer:	Difference:
Apple	No differences.
Apple Macintosh	No differences.
IBM/Microsoft	No differences.
PET/Commodore 64	No differences.
TRS-80	No differences.

to know the length of the string. Otherwise, we wish to know the length of the string.

The LEFT$ and RIGHT$ Functions

The LEFT$ function returns the number of characters specified in the argument, starting from the beginning of the string. The RIGHT$ function returns a substring, which starts with the character specified by the expression. The LEFT$ and RIGHT$ functions are illustrated in Figure VIII–5. In this example, the computer stores a character string in G$. Line 20 tells the computer to print the first seven characters of G$. Line 30 tells the computer to start printing with the twentieth character. The microcomputer handles the RIGHT$ function differently than the DECSYSTEM20. On the microcomputers, the instruction

```
30 PRINT RIGHT$(G$,20)
```

instructs the computer to print the last twenty characters of the string. The output would look like this:

```
THE SUN
SUN IS SHINING TODAY
THE SUN IS SHINING TODAY
```

Figure VIII—4 ■ The LEN Function

```
00010 PRINT "ENTER ANY STRING LARGER THAN 10 CHARACTERS"
00020 INPUT C$
00030 IF LEN(C$) < 10 THEN 80
00040 PRINT
00050 PRINT
00060 PRINT "THE LENGTH OF ";C$;" IS ";LEN(C$);" CHARACTERS"
00070 STOP
00080 PRINT "THE LENGTH OF ";C$;" IS LESS THAN 10 CHARACTERS"
00999 END


RUNNH
ENTER ANY STRING LARGER THAN 10 CHARACTERS
? IT'S A BEAUTIFUL DAY IN THE NEIGHBORHOOD


THE LENGTH OF IT'S A BEAUTIFUL DAY IN THE NEIGHBORHOOD IS  40  CHARACTERS
STOP at line 00070 of MAIN PROGRAM
```

MICROCOMPUTERS

Microcomputer:	Difference:
Apple	Output must be reformatted.
Apple Macintosh	Output must be reformatted.
IBM/Microsoft	No differences.
PET/Commodore 64	Output must be reformatted.
TRS-80	Output must be reformatted.

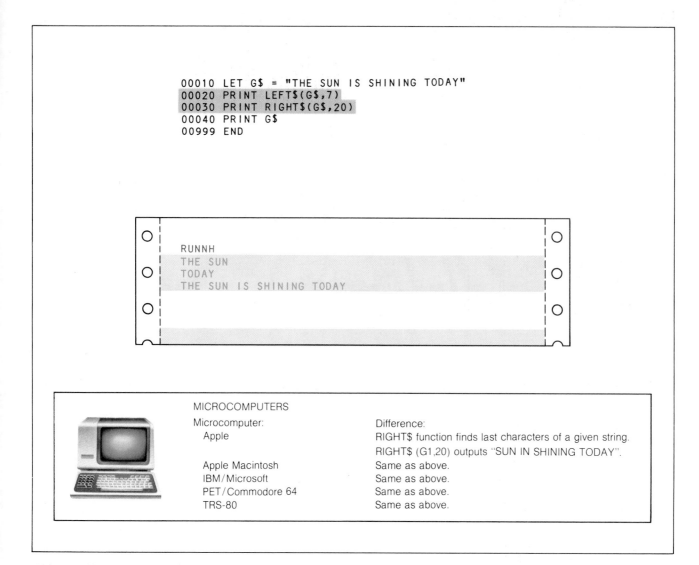

```
00010 LET G$ = "THE SUN IS SHINING TODAY"
00020 PRINT LEFT$(G$,7)
00030 PRINT RIGHT$(G$,20)
00040 PRINT G$
00999 END
```

```
RUNNH
THE SUN
TODAY
THE SUN IS SHINING TODAY
```

MICROCOMPUTERS

Microcomputer:	Difference:
Apple	RIGHT$ function finds last characters of a given string.
	RIGHT$ (G1,20) outputs "SUN IN SHINING TODAY".
Apple Macintosh	Same as above.
IBM/Microsoft	Same as above.
PET/Commodore 64	Same as above.
TRS-80	Same as above.

Figure VIII–5 ▪ The LEFT$ and RIGHT$ Functions

The LEFT$ function is often useful when comparing character strings. Suppose a program asks the user to answer a yes or no question but does not specify whether the question should be answered by typing the entire word YES or NO or just the first letter, Y or N. We can use the LEFT$ function to compare just the first character of the user's response, allowing the user to type either YES/NO or Y/N. The program in Figure VIII– 6 illustrates this.

The MID$ Function

The MID$ function is more complicated. Here is the general format:

line#   MID$(string, expression#1, expression#2)

String Constant or Variable   Starting Point in String   Numbers of Characters to Be Returned

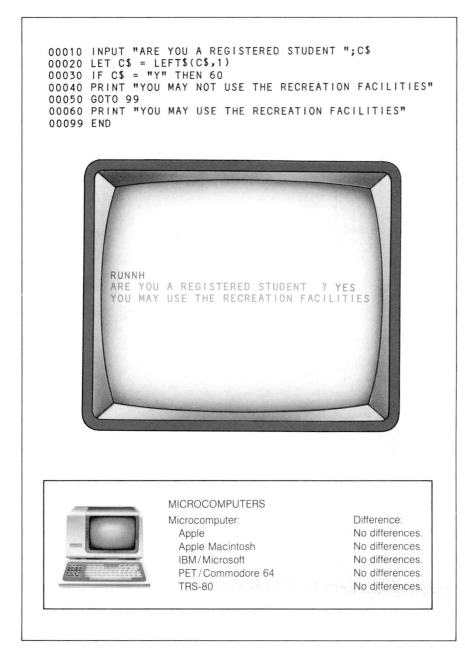

Figure VIII–6 ■ **Comparing Character Strings**

```
00010  INPUT "ARE YOU A REGISTERED STUDENT ";C$
00020  LET C$ = LEFT$(C$,1)
00030  IF C$ = "Y" THEN 60
00040  PRINT "YOU MAY NOT USE THE RECREATION FACILITIES"
00050  GOTO 99
00060  PRINT "YOU MAY USE THE RECREATION FACILITIES"
00099  END
```

```
RUNNH
ARE YOU A REGISTERED STUDENT  ? YES
YOU MAY USE THE RECREATION FACILITIES
```

MICROCOMPUTERS

Microcomputer:	Difference:
Apple	No differences.
Apple Macintosh	No differences.
IBM/Microsoft	No differences.
PET/Commodore 64	No differences.
TRS-80	No differences.

Sometimes expression 2 is omitted; in that case, the characters—from the starting point to the end of the string—are returned. This function is useful when you want to look at a string in the middle of another string. For instance, assume you have a calendar, and you want to print out the events on May 15. Here are the dates with important events.

5/2/84
5/10/84
5/15/84
5/15/84
5/17/84

The program in Figure VIII–7 will compare the day to "15" and print the events that occurred on the fifteenth.

The ASCII and CHR$ Functions

The ASCII function returns the decimal ASCII value of the first character specified in the string argument. The argument must be a variable name. Figure VIII–8 lists characters and their corresponding ASCII value. An example is shown in Figure VIII–9.

The CHR$ function works just the opposite of the ASCII function. This function returns the character that corresponds to the decimal ASCII value. The program in Figure VIII–10 illustrates the use of the CHR$ function.

The ASCII and CHR$ functions are helpful in allowing programs to respond to both lowercase and uppercase input. By using these functions, we can write a program that will allow the user to answer a yes or no question with either y or Y and n or N. Looking at Figure VIII–8, you can see that lowercase letters range from 97 to 122, and uppercase letters range from 65 to 90. An IF/THEN statement can be used to compare the ASCII value to 96. If the value

Figure VIII–7 ▪ The MID$ Function

```
00010 FOR I = 1 TO 5
00020    READ D$,E$
00030    IF MID$(D$,3,2) = "15" THEN PRINT E$
00040 NEXT I
00050 DATA 5/2/84,SALES MEETING
00060 DATA 5/10/84,MEETING WITH PRESIDENT
00070 DATA 5/15/84,SALES MEETING
00080 DATA 5/15/84,ACQUISITION
00090 DATA 5/17/84,BUSINESS SEMINAR
00999 END
```

```
RUNNH
SALES MEETING
ACQUISITION
```

MICROCOMPUTERS

Microcomputer:	Difference:
Apple	No differences.
Apple Macintosh	No differences.
IBM/Microsoft	No differences.
PET/Commodore 64	No differences.
TRS-80	No differences.

Figure VIII–8 ■ ASCII Codes

```
       32         !  33         "  34         #  35
$ 36         %  37         &  38         '  39
( 40         )  41         *  42         +  43
, 44         -  45         .  46         /  47
0 48         1  49         2  50         3  51
4 52         5  53         6  54         7  55
8 56         9  57         :  58         ;  59
< 60         =  61         >  62         ?  63
@ 64         A  65         B  66         C  67
D 68         E  69         F  70         G  71
H 72         I  73         J  74         K  75
L 76         M  77         N  78         O  79
P 80         Q  81         R  82         S  83
T 84         U  85         V  86         W  87
X 88         Y  89         Z  90         [  91
\ 92         ]  93         ^  94         _  95
` 96         a  97         b  98         c  99
d 100        e  101        f  102        g  103
h 104        i  105        j  106        k  107
l 108        m  109        n  110        o  111
p 112        q  113        r  114        s  115
t 116        u  117        v  118        w  119
x 120        y  121        z  122        {  123
| 124
```

Figure VIII–9 ■ The ASCII Function

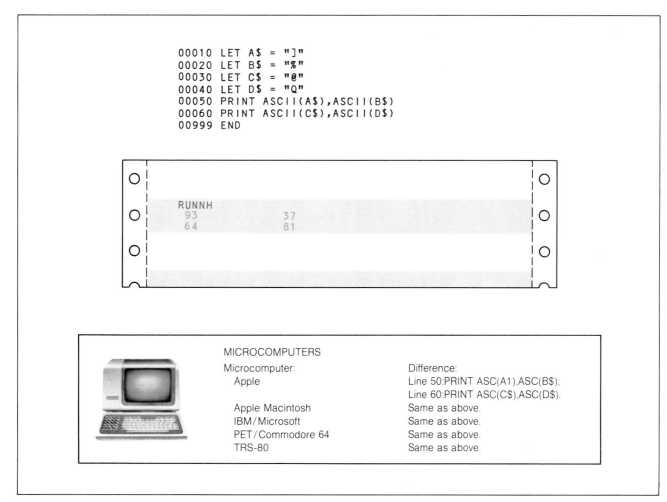

```
00010 LET A$ = "]"
00020 LET B$ = "%"
00030 LET C$ = "@"
00040 LET D$ = "Q"
00050 PRINT ASCII(A$),ASCII(B$)
00060 PRINT ASCII(C$),ASCII(D$)
00999 END
```

```
RUNNH
   93              37
   64              81
```

MICROCOMPUTERS

Microcomputer:	Difference:
Apple	Line 50:PRINT ASC(A1),ASC(B$);
	Line 60:PRINT ASC(C$),ASC(D$).
Apple Macintosh	Same as above.
IBM/Microsoft	Same as above.
PET/Commodore 64	Same as above.
TRS-80	Same as above.

Figure VIII–10 ▪ The CHR$ Function

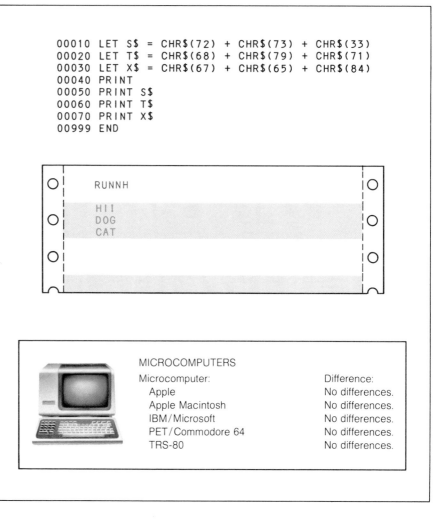

```
00010 LET S$ = CHR$(72) + CHR$(73) + CHR$(33)
00020 LET T$ = CHR$(68) + CHR$(79) + CHR$(71)
00030 LET X$ = CHR$(67) + CHR$(65) + CHR$(84)
00040 PRINT
00050 PRINT S$
00060 PRINT T$
00070 PRINT X$
00999 END
```

```
RUNNH

HI!
DOG
CAT
```

MICROCOMPUTERS

Microcomputer:	Difference:
Apple	No differences.
Apple Macintosh	No differences.
IBM/Microsoft	No differences.
PET/Commodore 64	No differences.
TRS-80	No differences.

is greater than 96, a lowercase letter has been typed; if the value is less than 96, the letter is uppercase. Once you know what type of letter you have, it can be converted to either uppercase or lowercase for comparison. An uppercase letter can be changed to lowercase by adding 32 to the ASCII value, and a lowercase letter can be changed to uppercase by subtracting 32.

The program segment in Figure VIII–11 illustrates this use of the ASCII and CHR$ functions. This program segment checks the user's reply to see if it is lowercase. If it is lowercase, 32 is subtracted from the ASCII value to give the ASCII value for the uppercase of the same letter. After subtracting, CHR$ assigns the character corresponding to the ASCII value to C$. C$ then can be compared with uppercase characters.

The VAL Function

The VAL function turns a numeric string (for example, 21893074) into a number that can be used in arithmetic calculations. Figure VIII–12 illustrates this.

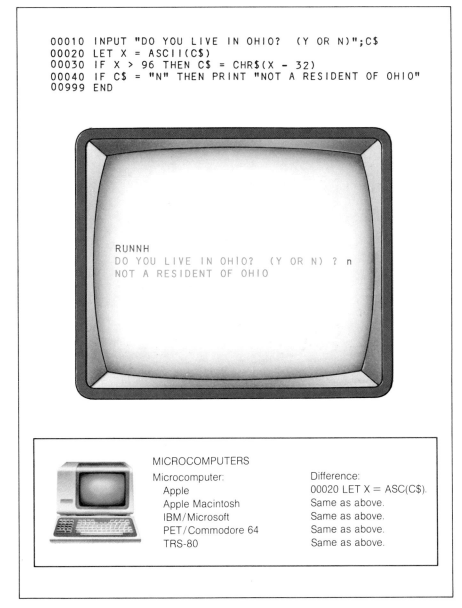

Figure VIII–11 ▪ Converting Lowercase Letters to Uppercase Letters

```
00010 INPUT "DO YOU LIVE IN OHIO?  (Y OR N)";C$
00020 LET X = ASCII(C$)
00030 IF X > 96 THEN C$ = CHR$(X - 32)
00040 IF C$ = "N" THEN PRINT "NOT A RESIDENT OF OHIO"
00999 END
```

```
RUNNH
DO YOU LIVE IN OHIO?  (Y OR N) ? n
NOT A RESIDENT OF OHIO
```

MICROCOMPUTERS

Microcomputer:	Difference:
Apple	00020 LET X = ASC(C$).
Apple Macintosh	Same as above.
IBM/Microsoft	Same as above.
PET/Commodore 64	Same as above.
TRS-80	Same as above.

By using the VAL function, it is possible to change the number in character string format to a real number so that the number can be used in mathematical computations. If the character string contains any nonnumeric characters, the VAL function will replace these with zeros.

The STR$ Function

The STR$ function is just the opposite of the VAL function; it converts a real number to a string. Figure VIII–13 illustrates the STR$ function. Remember that once a number has been converted to a character string, it no longer can be used in mathematical computations.

```
00010 PRINT "ENTER A NUMBER"
00020 INPUT N$
00030 LET N = VAL(N$)
00040 PRINT
00050 PRINT "THE NUMERIC STRING ";N$;" HAS BEEN CONVERTED TO A REAL NUMBER ";N
00999 END


RUNNH
ENTER A NUMBER
 ? 21893074

THE NUMERIC STRING 21893074 HAS BEEN CONVERTED TO A REAL NUMBER  2.189307E+07
```

MICROCOMPUTERS

Microcomputer:	Difference:
Apple	Real number = 21893074; Output must be reformatted.
Apple Macintosh	Real number = 21893074; Output must be reformatted.
IBM/Microsoft	Real number = 2.189308E+07.
PET/Commodore 64	Real number = 21893074; Output must be reformatted.
TRS-80	Real number = 2.18931E+07; Output must be reformatted.

Figure VIII–12 ▪ The VAL Function

A PROGRAMMING PROBLEM

The Problem

The goal in this problem is to write a program that accepts a bride's name and groom's name (see Figure VIII-14). The program's output will consist of the bride's name, the groom's name, and the bride's married name. For example:

INPUT	OUTPUT
Elizabeth Taylor	Elizabeth Taylor
Richard Burton	Richard Burton
	Elizabeth Burton

Solution Design

The process used to get the bride's married name can be outlined as follows:

1. Set up a loop to search the groom's name for a blank.
2. The string to the right of the blank is the last name.
3. Set up a loop to search the bride's name for a blank.
4. The string to the left of the blank is the first name.
5. Print the first name and the last name.

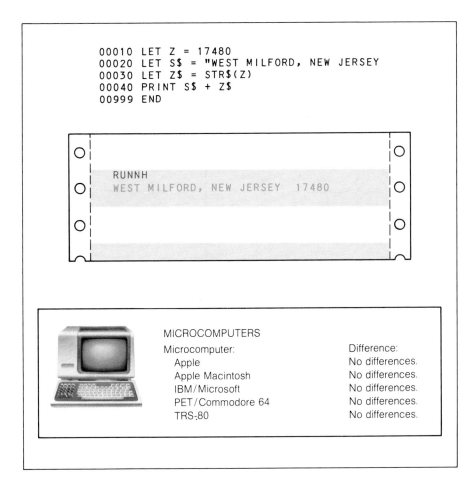

Figure VIII–13 ▪ The STR$ Function

```
00010 LET Z = 17480
00020 LET S$ = "WEST MILFORD, NEW JERSEY
00030 LET Z$ = STR$(Z)
00040 PRINT S$ + Z$
00999 END
```

RUNNH
WEST MILFORD, NEW JERSEY   17480

MICROCOMPUTERS

Microcomputer:	Difference:
Apple	No differences.
Apple Macintosh	No differences.
IBM/Microsoft	No differences.
PET/Commodore 64	No differences.
TRS-80	No differences.

The Program

Lines 40 and 60 prompt the user to enter the bride's name and the groom's name. Lines 110 to 200 form a FOR/NEXT loop that searches for a blank between the groom's first and last names. The loop is set up to look at each character. The terminal value for the loop is the length of the groom's name. Line 120 looks at each character of the string and places it in R$. In this example, the first four values of I produce the following:

I	R$
1	C
2	A
3	L
4	V

Line 160 tests whether RS$ is a blank by using the CHR$ function (the ASCII code for a blank is 32). If a blank is found, line 160 sends the computer to line 240 to search for the first name. Lines 240 to 330 form a FOR/NEXT loop which searches for the first name in the same manner as the last name

Figure VIII–14 ▪ **Married Names Program**
(Continued on Next Two Pages)

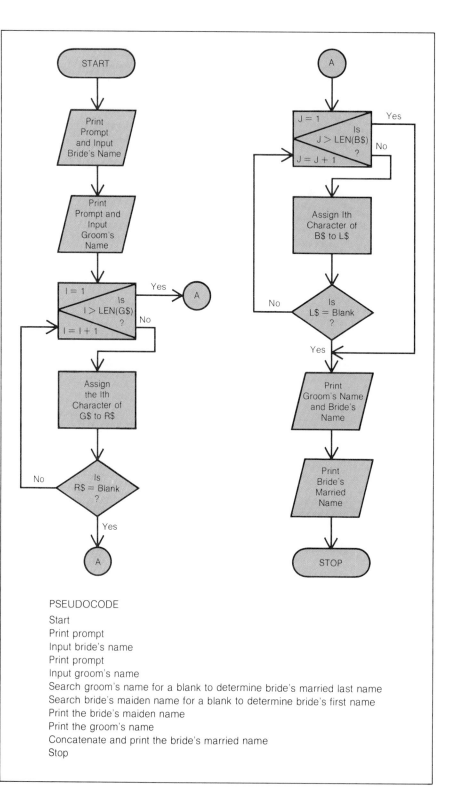

PSEUDOCODE

Start
Print prompt
Input bride's name
Print prompt
Input groom's name
Search groom's name for a blank to determine bride's married last name
Search bride's maiden name for a blank to determine bride's first name
Print the bride's maiden name
Print the groom's name
Concatenate and print the bride's married name
Stop

```
00010 REM ***************************************************
00020 REM *** PROGRAM TO PRINT OUT A BRIDE'S MARRIED NAME ***
00030 REM ***************************************************
00040 PRINT "ENTER BRIDE'S NAME"
00050 INPUT B$
00060 PRINT "ENTER GROOM'S NAME"
00070 INPUT G$
00080 REM ***************************************************
00090 REM *** SEARCH UP TO THE LENGTH OF THE GROOM'S NAME ***
00100 REM ***************************************************
00110 FOR I = 1 TO LEN(G$)
00120    LET R$ = MID$(G$,I,1)
00130    REM ***************************************************
00140    REM ***              TEST FOR BLANK               ***
00150    REM ***************************************************
00160    IF R$ = CHR$(32) THEN 240
00170    REM ***************************************************
00180    REM ***        IF NOT BLANK, THEN CONTINUE        ***
00190    REM ***************************************************
00200 NEXT I
00210 REM ***************************************************
00220 REM *** SEARCH UP TO THE LENGTH OF THE BRIDE'S NAME ***
00230 REM ***************************************************
00240 FOR J = 1 TO LEN(B$)
00250    L$ = MID$(B$,J,1)
00260    REM ***************************************************
00270    REM ***              TEST FOR BLANK               ***
00280    REM ***************************************************
00290    IF L$ = CHR$(32) THEN 370
00300    REM ***************************************************
00310    REM ***        IF NOT BLANK, THEN CONTINUE        ***
00320    REM ***************************************************
00330 NEXT J
00340 REM ***************************************************
00350 REM ***        PRINT OUT BRIDE'S MARRIED NAME        ***
00360 REM ***************************************************
00370 PRINT
00380 PRINT
00390 PRINT "BRIDE'S NAME IS ";B$
00400 PRINT "GROOM'S NAME IS ";G$
00410 PRINT
00420 PRINT "BRIDE'S MARRIED NAME IS ";LEFT$(B$,J - 1);RIGHT$(G$,I)
00999 END
```

Figure VIII–14 ▪ Continued

was found. When line 290 finds the blank between the bride's first and last name, control is sent to line 370. Lines 390 to 400 print the bride's name and the groom's name. Line 420 prints the bride's married name. Since the counter J in the second FOR/NEXT loop marks where the blank is, we use J-1 to count the number of characters in the first name of the bride's married name. The counter I in the first FOR/NEXT loop marks where the blank is, we use I to begin the RIGHT$ function for the last name of the bride's married name.

SUMMARY POINTS

▪ Two statements define a subroutine: GOSUB and RETURN.
▪ The GOSUB statement is used to transfer the flow of control from the main logic of a program to a subroutine.

```
RUNNH
ENTER BRIDE'S NAME
  ? BONNIE BELL
ENTER GROOM'S NAME
  ? CALVIN KLEIN


BRIDE'S NAME IS BONNIE BELL
GROOM'S NAME IS CALVIN KLEIN

BRIDE'S MARRIED NAME IS BONNIE KLEIN
```

MICROCOMPUTERS

Microcomputer:	Difference:
Apple	Line 420 would use RIGHT$(G$,LEN(G$) − I).
Apple Macintosh	Line 420 would use RIGHT$(G$,L(G$) − I + 1).
IBM/Microsoft	Same as Apple.
PET/Commodore 64	Same as Apple.
TRS-80	Same as Apple.

Figure VIII–14 ▪ Continued

▪ The RETURN statement transfers control from a subroutine back to the line in the main program immediately following the last GOSUB statement that was executed.

▪ The STOP statement halts execution of a program.

▪ BASIC string functions permit modification, concatenation, comparison, and analysis of the composition of strings.

REVIEW QUESTIONS

1. What is a subroutine and why is it useful?
2. What do the GOSUB and RETURN statements do? Where is the RETURN located in a program?
3. How is the STOP statement used with subroutines? What is the difference between the STOP statement and the END statement?
4. What is a string?

5. BASIC string functions allow programmers to
   a. modify strings.
   b. concatenate strings.
   c. compare strings.
   d. analyze the composition of strings.
   e. all of the above.

DEBUGGING EXERCISES

```
1.  10  READ N$,B$
    15  LET A = STR$(A$)
    20  LET A = A + 3
    25  LET A$ = VAL(A)
    30  LET C$ = B$ + A$
    35  DATA 10,30

2.  10  REM *** PRINT THE FIRST 4 CHARACTERS ***
    15  REM *** AND THE LAST 3 CHARACTERS OF A STRING ***
    20  LET A$ = "GOOD FRIDAY"
    25  PRINT LEFT(A$,4)
    30  PRINT RIGHT(A$,3)
```

PROGRAMMING PROBLEMS

1. Write a program which will use one subroutine to calculate the average number of points that the following basketball players score per game, and another subroutine to reverse the player's name so that it is in the format LASTNAME, FIRSTNAME.

PLAYER	GAME 1	GAME 2	GAME 3
Ed Miller	22	20	18
John Long	12	19	17
Joe Barros	7	3	5
Mike Hawn	15	12	12
Gary Storts	10	13	7

Your OUTPUT should include the players' names and averages with column headings.

2. Write a program to print a chart of the capital letters from A to L and their corresponding ASCII value in the following format:

CHAR	VALUE	CHAR	VALUE
A	65	B	66
.	.	.	.
.	.	.	.
.	.	.	.
K	75	L	76

OVERVIEW

So far, our programs have used simple variables such as N, C$, and T1 to represent single values. Now let us say we want to write a program that reads the weekly grocery bills for six people, calculates the average, and prints the difference between each person's weekly grocery bill and the average in the following format:

```
RUNNH
                                      DIFFERENCE
NAME              GROCERY BILL    FROM AVERAGE

F. BROCKMAN         $ 50              $ 16

T. TURNER           $ 30              $-4

G. MCMILLIAN        $ 25              $-9

J. OLSEN            $ 32              $-2

K. FISK             $ 39              $ 5

S. SPOCK            $ 28              $-6


AVERAGE WEEKLY GROCERY BILL = $ 34
```

Up to this point, we have been calculating averages by reading one value at a time into a single variable when using the READ/DATA statements and accumulating the values as they are read. In this procedure, however, each time a new value is read, the previous value stored in the variable is destroyed; thus, in the previous example, we would not be able to compare each person's grocery bill with the calculated average grocery bill. To make the comparison, each person's grocery bill would need to be stored in a separate memory location. One way of accomplishing this is by using a distinct variable name for each value. This approach will work (provided you know the number of values you will be working with beforehand) but can become cumbersome when dealing with a large number of values.

There is an easier way: BASIC permits us to deal with groups of related values as arrays. Figure IX–1 shows the coding necessary to produce the previously listed output. Array names are distinguished from simple variable names through the use of subscripts. The DIM statement tells the computer how much storage is necessary to hold an array. Arrays may be one-dimensional (sometimes called lists), two-dimensional (often called tables, or **matrices**), or of higher dimensions. A method for sorting arrays is also discussed in this section.

SUBSCRIPTS

An array is a group of storage locations in memory in which data elements can be stored. The entire array is given one name; the programmer indicates individual elements in the array by referring to their positions. The general concept is simple. Let us say there are three teachers who teach accounting classes. We would like to store the names of the teachers in an array T$. It might look like this:

```
00010 REM *******************************
00020 REM ***    GROCERY BILL PROGRAM    ***
00030 REM *******************************
00040 DIM N$(6)
00050 DIM B(6)
00060 LET T = 0
00070 FOR I = 1 TO 6
00080    READ N$(I)
00090    READ B(I)
00100    LET T = T + B(I)
00110 NEXT I
00120 LET A = T / 6
00130 PRINT " "," "," DIFFERENCE"
00140 PRINT "NAME","GROCERY BILL","FROM AVERAGE"
00150 FOR I = 1 TO 6
00160    PRINT
00170    PRINT N$(I);TAB(17);"$";B(I);TAB(31);"$";B(I) - A
00180 NEXT I
00190 PRINT
00200 PRINT
00210 PRINT "AVERAGE WEEKLY GROCERY BILL = $";A
00220 DATA F. BROCKMAN,50,T. TURNER,30
00230 DATA G. MCMILLIAN,25,J. OLSEN,32
00240 DATA K. FISK,39,S. SPOCK,28
00999 END
```

MICROCOMPUTERS

Microcomputer:	Difference:
Apple	Output must be reformatted.
Apple Macintosh	No differences.
IBM/Microsoft	No differences.
PET/Commodore 64	Output must be reformatted.
TRS-80	No differences.

Figure IX–1 ▪ Array Example

Array T$

T$(1)	ROBERT NEER
T$(2)	ANGELA LORING
T$(3)	SUSAN COOKE

We can gain access to an individual name within the array by telling the computer which position in the list it occupies. This is done through the use of subscripts. For example, Robert Neer is in the first position in the array— that is, T$(1). Angela Loring is in the second location, T$(2). Susan Cooke is in T$(3). The subscripts are enclosed in parentheses.

In BASIC, the same rules that apply to naming simple variables apply to naming arrays. Remember that only numbers can be stored in numeric variable array names, and only character strings can be stored in string variable arrays. It is good programming practice not to use the same name for both a simple variable and an array in a program.

The subscript (index) enclosed in parentheses can be any legal expression; for example, $T(Q)$, $I(15)$, and $C(X * Y)$ are valid references to array elements.

When an array element is indicated by an expression, the computer carries out the following steps:

1. It evaluates the expression inside the parentheses.
2. It translates the result to the nearest integer.
3. It accesses the indicated element in the array.

For example, if the computer encounters T(Q), it looks at the current value of Q. This value indicates the position of the desired element in array T.

Array T

10
15
16
17
32

Assume that I = 2, N = 3, and Q = 5. Then

T(I) refers to T(2)—the second element in array T, or 15.

T(N) refers to T(3)—the third element in array T, or 16.

T(I + N) refers to T(5)—the fifth element in array T, or 32.

T(Q) refers to T(5)—the fifth element in array T or 32.

References to specific elements of arrays are called **subscripted variables.** In contrast, simple variables are **unsubscripted variables.** An unsubscripted variable—say, P3—is used to refer to a single storage location named P3; the subscripted variable P(3), in contrast, represents the third item in an array called P.

THE DIM STATEMENT

When a programmer uses an array, the BASIC compiler does not automatically know how many elements the array will contain. Unless told otherwise, it makes provisions for a limited number. Usually the compiler is designed to assume that an array will have no more than ten elements (eleven elements in some systems: 0 through 10). Consequently, it reserves space for ten elements in the array. The programmer cannot write a statement that refers to an array element for which space has not been reserved.

The programmer can specify the number of elements for which space must be reserved by means of a DIM (dimension) statement. A DIM statement is not required for arrays of ten or fewer elements (or whatever number of elements the system assumes); however, many programmers will specify DIM statements for small arrays to help document the array usage.

The general format of the DIM statement follows:

line# DIM variable 1(limit 1), variable 2(limit2), . . .

The variables are the names of arrays. Each limit is an integer constant that represents the maximum number of storage locations required for a particular array.

Assume that space is needed to store fifty elements in an array named A. The following statement reserves storage for fifty elements:

```
00050 DIM A(50)
```

There is no problem if fewer than fifty values are actually read into array A, but it cannot contain more. Array subscripts can vary in the program from 0 to the limit declared in the DIM statement, but no subscript can exceed that limit. More than one array can be declared in a DIM statement; for example,

```
00040 DIM N(10),Q(55),B(125)
```

declares N, Q, and B as arrays. Array N may contain up to 10 elements; Q, up to 55 elements; and B, up to 125 elements. (If an index of 0 is used, up to 11, 56, and 126 elements can be stored, respectively.)

DIM statements must appear in a program before the first references to arrays they describe. A good programming practice is to place them at the beginning of the program. The following standard preparation symbol is often used to flowchart the DIM statement:

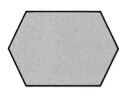

ONE-DIMENSIONAL ARRAYS

This section has been discussing lists of related values stored under a single variable name—one-dimensional arrays. Let us look at some applications involving the use of one-dimensional arrays.

Reading Data into an Array

Using FOR and NEXT statements can be an efficient method of reading data into an array. The following program segment reads and stores a list of seven prices in an array named P:

```
00010 FOR J = 1 TO 7
00020   READ P(J)
00030 NEXT J
00040 DATA 3.75,2.25,5.99,19.99
00050 DATA 1.99,0.87,4.74
```

The first time through this program loop, the loop variable J equals 1. When statement 20 is executed, the computer reads a price from the data lists and stores it in P(1)—the first storage location in array P. The second time through the loop, J equals 2. The next price is read into P(2)—the second location in the array. The loop processing continues until all seven prices have been read and stored.

Printing Data in an Array

Now assume we are to print the seven prices in array P in a single column. The following statements do just that:

```
00060 FOR I = 1 TO 7
00070    PRINT P(I)
00080 NEXT I

RUNNH
 3.75
 2.25
 5.99
 19.99
 1.99
 0.87
 4.74
```

As the loop variable I varies from 1 to 7, the index changes, and the computer prints elements 1 through 7 of array P.

Computations with Arrays

The program in Figure IX–2 generates a library book report that outlines the number of days overdue, the amount per day, and the amount due. In addition, the program prints out the total amount due from all of the overdue books.

This problem solution can be broken into the following steps:

1. Read the data into arrays.
2. Calculate the amount for each book by multiplying the amount/day and the number of days overdue.
3. Calculate the total amount due by adding the amount due from each book.

Three arrays are used in Figure IX–2. Two one-dimensional arrays are read as input: a list of the number of days each book is overdue, stored in array D, and a list of the amount due per day, stored in array A. In the main part of the program, a third array, T, is generated. It is a list of the total amount due from each book.

The program begins with a segment that establishes the number of days array, D. In lines 100 through 120, the variable L is set equal to 1, and a number is read from the data list and assigned to D(1). As the looping continues, D(2) is given a value, then D(3), and so on. When the looping is finished, array D contains the number of days each book is overdue. That is, D(1) is 5, D(2) is 3, and so on.

The next segment of the program fills array A with values in the same manner. The values read into A are the amounts due per day for each book. Thus, after execution of the loop (lines 130 through 150) has been completed, A(1) is 0.25, A(2) is 0.25, A(3) is 0.50, and so on.

Once the array elements have been stored, it is possible to manipulate them to obtain the desired information. For example, the main part of the program calculates the amount due for each book and stores the results in the array T. These computations are accomplished by multiplication of the elements in the array of the number of days overdue, D, by the corresponding elements in the amount per day array, A. All these arrays are then printed.

We also are to determine the total amount due from all of the books. We know that the array T contains the total amount due for each book. Therefore, we need to add all the elements in array T. This is accomplished in lines 200 through 230.

Figure IX–2 ▪ **Overdue Book Program (Continued on Next Page)**

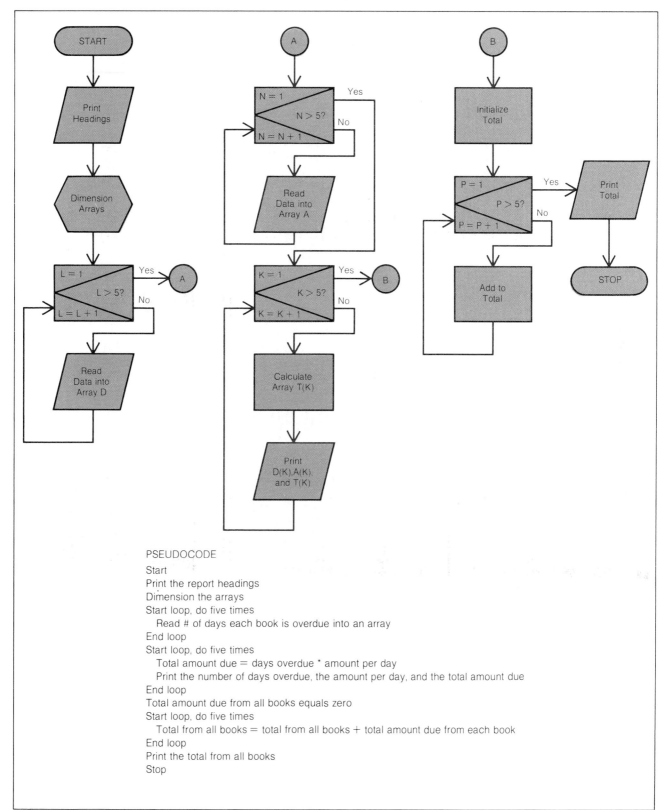

PSEUDOCODE
Start
Print the report headings
Dimension the arrays
Start loop, do five times
    Read # of days each book is overdue into an array
End loop
Start loop, do five times
    Total amount due = days overdue * amount per day
    Print the number of days overdue, the amount per day, and the total amount due
End loop
Total amount due from all books equals zero
Start loop, do five times
    Total from all books = total from all books + total amount due from each book
End loop
Print the total from all books
Stop

Figure IX–2 ■ Continued

```
00010 REM ***********************************
00020 REM *** OVERDUE LIBRARY BOOKS PROGRAM ***
00030 REM ***********************************
00040 PRINT
00050 PRINT
00060 PRINT
00070 PRINT "DAYS OVERDUE","AMOUNT/DAY","AMOUNT DUE"
00080 PRINT
00090 DIM D(5),A(5),T(5)
00100 FOR L = 1 TO 5
00110    READ D(L)
00120 NEXT L
00130 FOR N = 1 TO 5
00140    READ A(N)
00150 NEXT N
00160 FOR K = 1 TO 5
00170    LET T(K) = D(K) * A(K)
00180    PRINT D(K),A(K),T(K)
00190 NEXT K
00200 LET TD = 0
00210 FOR P = 1 TO 5
00220    LET TD = TD + T(P)
00230 NEXT P
00240 PRINT
00250 PRINT "THE TOTAL AMOUNT DUE IS $";TD
00260 DATA 5,3,14,10,2
00270 DATA 0.25,0.25,0.50,0.25,0.75
00999 END
```

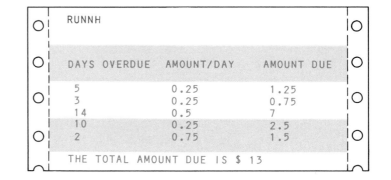

```
RUNNH


DAYS OVERDUE   AMOUNT/DAY      AMOUNT DUE

   5           0.25           1.25
   3           0.25           0.75
  14           0.5            7
  10           0.25           2.5
   2           0.75           1.5

THE TOTAL AMOUNT DUE IS $ 13
```

MICROCOMPUTERS

Microcomputer:	Difference:
Apple	No differences.
Apple Macintosh	No differences.
IBM/Microsoft	No differences.
PET/Commodore 64	No differences.
TRS-80	No differences.

If we wanted the total amount due from the first three books, we could simply alter the number of times the FOR/NEXT loop is executed:

```
00200 LET TD = 0
00210 FOR P = 1 TO 3
00220   LET TD = TD + T(P)
00230 NEXT P
```

TWO-DIMENSIONAL ARRAYS

An array does not have to be a single list of data; it can be a table or matrix. For example, assume that Connor Video, Inc. operates three video games in four different arcades. Mr. Connor has received the following table of data concerning the number of games played in each of the four arcades:

Arcade	Millipede	Star Wars	Tron
Video Madness	100	250	200
Sappy Sam's	500	600	700
Krazy Kevin's	200	225	230
City Arcade	120	520	500

The rows in the table refer to the arcades, and the columns refer to the video games. Thus, the number of games of Millipede played at Krazy Kevin's can be found in the third row, first column.

This arrangement of data—a table consisting of rows and columns—is called a **two-dimensional array.** In this case, the two-dimensional array of data comprises four rows and three columns—a total of twelve elements (4×3).

Two-dimensional arrays are named in the same way as other variables. A name used for a two-dimensional array cannot be used for a one-dimensional array in the same program (and vice versa). An individual element in a table is indicated by a pair of subscripts in parentheses. The first subscript indicates the row; the second, the column. The row and column subscripts are separated by a comma.

If we name the array G for Connor Video Inc., the number of video games played at the individual arcades can be indicated by $G(r,c)$, where r stands for the row in which a value is found, and c stands for the column in which it is found:

Array G

$G(1,1)$ 100	$G(1,2)$ 250	$G(1,3)$ 200
$G(2,1)$ 500	$G(2,2)$ 600	$G(2,3)$ 700
$G(3,1)$ 200	$G(3,2)$ 225	$G(3,3)$ 230
$G(4,1)$ 120	$G(4,2)$ 520	$G(4,3)$ 500

Thus, $G(2,3)$ represents the number of games of Tron played at Sappy Sam's, found in row 2, column 3. $G(1,1)$ indicates the number of games of Millipede played at Video Madness.

Notice that it is necessary to store the arcades' names in a separate array, because we cannot mix character string values with numeric values in the same array:

Array A$

A$(1)	Video Madness
A$(2)	Sappy Sam's
A$(3)	Krazy Kevin's
A$(4)	City Arcade

As with one-dimensional arrays, individual subscripts in two-dimensional arrays may be indicated with any legal expression:

$$G(2,3)$$
$$G(L,1)$$
$$G(L,K)$$
$$G(1, L - K)$$

As with one-dimensional arrays, the space needed to store a two-dimensional array must be stated if the array size exceeds a certain limit. Unless told otherwise, most BASIC compilers reserve enough space for an array with up to ten rows and up to ten columns. Therefore, for an array to exceed either the row limit or the column limit, the programmer must specify its size in a DIM statement. For example,

```
00070 DIM T(50,20)
```

reserves space for array T, which has fifty rows and twenty columns.

Reading and Printing Data in Two-Dimensional Arrays

Reading data into and printing data from two-dimensional arrays can be accomplished with nested FOR/NEXT statements. Thus, in Figure IX–3, we read Connor Video, Inc. data into a two-dimensional array called G. The reading of the table follows a row-by-row sequence from left to right across each column. The loops in lines 50 through 90 perform this reading process:

```
00050 FOR I = 1 TO 4
00060    FOR J = 1 TO 3
00070       READ G(I,J)
00080    NEXT J
00090 NEXT I
00100 DATA 100,250,200,500,600,700
00110 DATA 200,225,230,120,520,500
```

When the program is executed, each data value is represented by the variable G followed by a unique pair of subscripts telling its location by row, I, and column, J. As the data values are read, they fill the table row by row (that is, after row 1 has been filled, row 2 is filled, then 3, and then row 4). The outer FOR/NEXT loop controls the rows (using the variable I); the inner loop controls the columns (using the variable J). Thus, every time the outer loop is executed once, the inner loop is executed three times. While I is equal to 1, J is equal to 1, 2, and 3. The first three numbers from the data list are read into G(1,1), G(1,2), and G(1,3). Then I is incremented to 2. The inner loop again is executed three times, and the next three numbers from the data list are read into the second row, G(2,1), G(2,2), and G(2,3). I is finally incremented to 4 and the fourth row of the table is filled.

To print the entire table, a PRINT statement in a nested loop can be used.

```
00010 REM ******************************
00020 REM ***   VIDEO GAME PROGRAM   ***
00030 REM ******************************
00040 DIM G(4,3)
00050 FOR I = 1 TO 4
00060    FOR J = 1 TO 3
00070       READ G(I,J)
00080    NEXT J
00090 NEXT I
00100 PRINT
00110 PRINT "ARCADE","MILLIPEDE","STAR WARS","TRON"
00120 PRINT
00130 FOR I = 1 TO 4
00140    READ A$
00150    PRINT A$,
00160    FOR J = 1 TO 3
00170       PRINT G(I,J),
00180    NEXT J
00190    PRINT
00200 NEXT I
00210 DATA 100,250,200,500,600,700
00220 DATA 200,225,230,120,520,500
00230 DATA VIDEO MADNESS,SAPPY SAM'S,KRAZY KEVIN'S,CITY ARCADE
00999 END
```

```
RUNNH

ARCADE         MILLIPEDE     STAR WARS     TRON

VIDEO MADNESS  100           250           200
SAPPY SAM'S    500           600           700
KRAZY KEVIN'S  200           225           230
CITY ARCADE    120           520           500
```

MICROCOMPUTERS

Microcomputer:	Difference:
Apple	Screen not wide enough.
Apple Macintosh	No differences.
IBM/Microsoft	No differences.
PET/Commodore 64	Screen not wide enough.
TRS-80	No differences.

Figure IX–3 ▪ Video Game Program

This is illustrated in lines 160 through 230. Let us examine the PRINT statements in this segment:

```
00160 FOR I = 1 TO 4
00170    READ A$
00180    PRINT A$,
00190    FOR J = 1 TO 3
00200       PRINT G(I,J),
00210    NEXT J
00220    PRINT
00230 NEXT I
```

The comma in line 200 signals the computer to print the three values in predefined print zones on the same line. After the inner loop has been executed, the blank PRINT in line 220 sets the carriage return so that the next row is printed on the next line.

Adding Rows of Items

After data has been read and stored as an array, it is possible to manipulate the array elements. For example, Mr. Connor may want to find out how many video games were played at City Arcade or how many games of Star Wars were played.

Figure IX–4 ▪ Complete Video Game Program 2 (Continued on Next Three Pages)

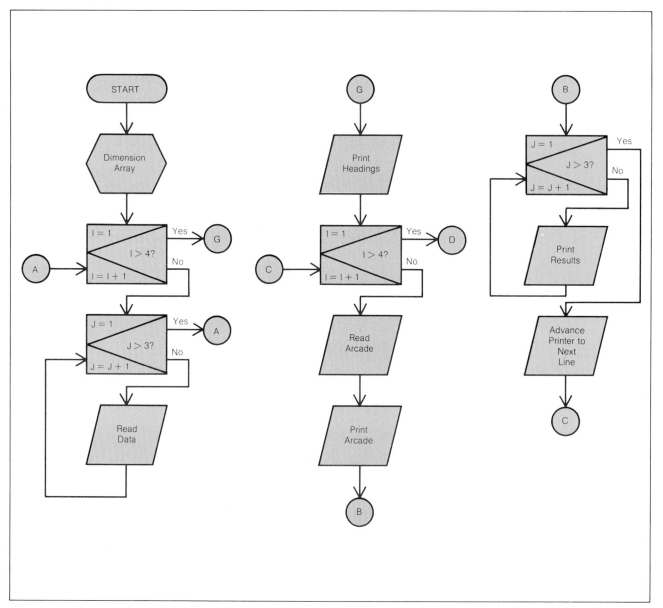

Since the data for each arcade are contained in a row of the array, we need to total the elements in one row of the array (the fourth row) to find out how many video games were played at City Arcade. This can be done with the following statements:

```
00240 LET T = 0
00250 FOR L = 1 TO 3
00260   LET T = T + G(4,L)
00270 NEXT L
```

Notice that G(4,L) restricts the computations to the elements in row 4, while the column, L, varies from 1 to 3.

Figure IX–4 ▪ Continued

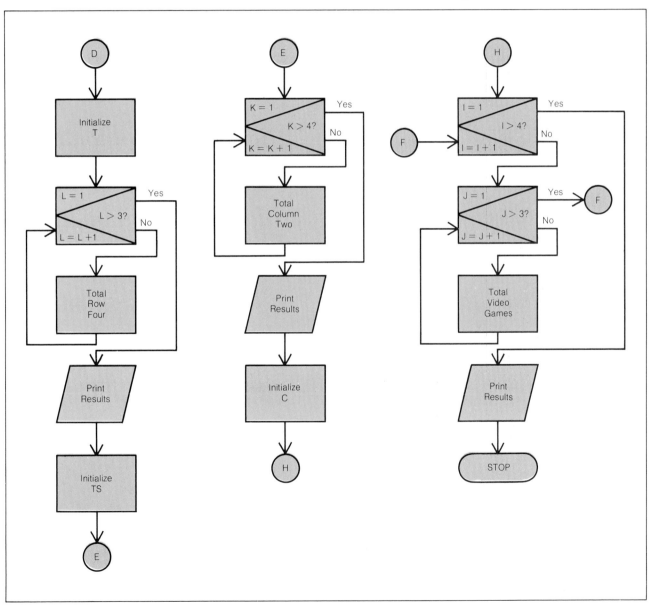

Figure IX–4 ▪ Continued

PSEUDOCODE

Start
Dimension the arrays
Start loop, do four times
  Start loop, do three times
    Read number of games into a two-dimensional array
  End loop
End loop
Print the report headings
Start loop, do four times
  Read the arcade name into an array
  Print the arcade name from the array
  Start loop, do three times
    Print the number of games from the two-dimensional array
  End loop
  Print a blank
End loop
Total of City Arcade equals zero
Start loop, do three times
  Total of City Arcade = total of City Arcade + # of each video game played at City Arcade
End loop
Print the total of City Arcade
Total of Star Wars equals zero
Start loop, do four times
  Total of Star Wars = total of Star Wars + # games of Star Wars played at each arcade
End loop
Print the total of Star Wars
Total equals zero
Start loop, do four times
  Start loop, do three times
    Total = total + # of each video game played at each arcade
  End loop
End loop
Print total
Stop

```
00010 REM *****************************
00020 REM ***   VIDEO GAME PROGRAM   ***
00030 REM *****************************
00040 DIM G(4,3)
00050 FOR I = 1 TO 4
00060    FOR J = 1 TO 3
00070       READ G(I,J)
00080    NEXT J
00090 NEXT I
00100 PRINT
00110 PRINT "ARCADE","MILLIPEDE","STAR WARS","TRON"
00120 PRINT
00130 FOR I = 1 TO 4
00140    READ A$
00150    PRINT A$,
00160    FOR J = 1 TO 3
00170       PRINT G(I,J),
00180    NEXT J
00190    PRINT
```

Figure IX—4 ▪ **Continued**

```
00200 NEXT I
00210 DATA 100,250,200,500,600,700
00220 DATA 200,225,230,120,520,500
00230 DATA VIDEO MADNESS,SAPPY SAM'S,KRAZY KEVIN'S,CITY ARCADE
00240 LET T = 0
00250 FOR L = 1 TO 3
00260    LET T = T + G(4,L)
00270 NEXT L
00280 PRINT
00290 PRINT T;" VIDEO GAMES WERE PLAYED AT CITY ARCADE"
00300 LET TS = 0
00310 FOR K = 1 TO 4
00320    LET TS = TS + G(K,2)
00330 NEXT K
00340 PRINT TS;" GAMES OF STAR WARS WERE PLAYED"
00350 LET C = 0
00360 FOR I = 1 TO 4
00370    FOR J = 1 TO 3
00380       LET C = C + G(I,J)
00390    NEXT J
00400 NEXT I
00410 PRINT C;" VIDEO GAMES WERE PLAYED ALTOGETHER"
00999 END
```

```
RUNNH

ARCADE          MILLIPEDE      STAR WARS      TRON

VIDEO MADNESS   100            250            200
SAPPY SAM'S     500            600            700
KRAZY KEVIN'S   200            225            230
CITY ARCADE     120            520            500

 1140  VIDEO GAMES WERE PLAYED AT CITY ARCADE
 1595  GAMES OF STAR WARS WERE PLAYED
 4145  VIDEO GAMES WERE PLAYED ALTOGETHER
```

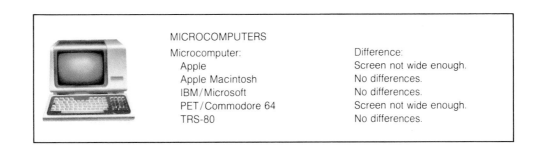

MICROCOMPUTERS

Microcomputer:	Difference:
Apple	Screen not wide enough.
Apple Macintosh	No differences.
IBM/Microsoft	No differences.
PET/Commodore 64	Screen not wide enough.
TRS-80	No differences.

Adding Columns of Items

To find the number of games of Star Wars that were played, we want to total the elements in the second column of the array:

```
00300 LET TS = 0
00310 FOR K = 1 TO 4
00320    LET TS = TS + G(K,2)
00330 NEXT K
```

In these statements, G(K,2) restricts the computations to the elements in the second column, while the row, K, varies from 1 to 4.

Totaling a Two-Dimensional Array

Now suppose we need to know how many video games were played altogether. This means we must add all the elements in the array:

```
00350 LET C = 0
00360 FOR I = 1 TO 4
00370    FOR J = 1 TO 3
00380       LET C = C + G(I,J)
00390    NEXT J
00400 NEXT I
```

C is the variable that will be used to accumulate the total. It is initialized outside the loop. To add all the elements in array G, we are going to use a nested loop. The outer loop will control the rows and the inner loop, the columns. Line 380 does the actual accumulation. The first time through the loop, both I and J equal 1; thus, G(1,1) is added to 0. J is then incremented, and G(1,2) is added to C to make 350. Then G(1,3), or 200, is added. At this point, I is incremented to 2 so that we can begin adding the second-row values and so on until all the elements in G have been totaled. Figure IX–4 shows the complete program for Connor Video, Inc. and the resulting output.

ADVANTAGES OF ARRAYS

Although it may not be obvious at this point, arrays are useful in many applications. By using arrays, we can avoid having to make up names for numerous items. Also, once data are stored in an array, the data items (elements) can be referred to over and over again without being reread. Arrays also are used extensively in file processing (discussed in Section X).

Arrays can also be manipulated in a number of ways other than the basic computational examples previously given. For instance, some of the more common manipulation techniques include array merges, array searches, and array sorts. We will discuss one method of sorting the elements of an array in this section; however, there are many other methods of sorting.

SORTING

Many applications require that data items be sorted, or ordered, in some way. For example, names must be alphabetized, Social Security numbers arranged from lowest to highest, basketball players ranked from high scorer to low scorer, and the like.

Suppose that an array, X, contains five numbers that we would like ordered from lowest to highest:

It is a simple matter for us to mentally reorder this list as follows:

Array X (Unsorted)	Array X (Sorted)
10	2
30	10
15	15
100	30
2	100

What if there were seven hundred numbers instead of five? Then it would not be so easy for us to order the number list. However, the computer is perfectly suited for such tasks. One method of sorting with the computer is illustrated in Figure IX–5.

**Figure IX–5 ▪ Sorting Program
(Continued on Next Two Pages)**

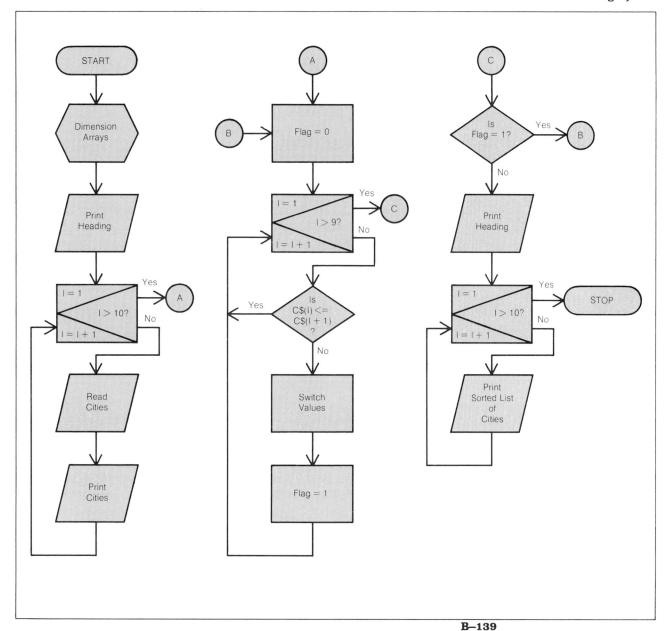

PSEUDOCODE

Start
Dimension the arrays
Print the heading for the first listing
Start loop, do ten times
  Read the cities into an array
  Print the cities from an array
End loop
Print blank lines
Flag equals zero
Start loop, do nine times
  If city$(I) > city$(I + 1)
    Then
      Switch city$(I) with city$(I + 1)
      Flag equals 1
  End if
End loop
If flag equals 1
  Then
    Flag equals zero
    Repeat preceding loop
  Else
    Print heading for the second listing
    Start loop, do ten times
      Print the cities from the array
    End loop
End If
Stop

```
00010 REM ********************************************
00020 REM ***      THIS PROGRAM SORTS THE CITIES IN    ***
00030 REM ***         THE USA INTO ALPHABETIC ORDER    ***
00040 REM ********************************************
00050 DIM C$(10)
00060 PRINT "UNSORTED LIST OF CITIES IN THE USA"
00070 PRINT
00080 REM ********************************************
00090 REM ***          READ THE NAMES INTO AN ARRAY    ***
00100 REM ********************************************
00110 FOR I = 1 TO 10
00120    READ C$(I)
00130    PRINT C$(I)
00140 NEXT I
00150 PRINT
00160 PRINT
00170 REM ********************************************
00180 REM ***               THE BUBBLE SORT            ***
00190 REM ********************************************
00200 LET F = 0
00210 FOR I = 1 TO 9
00220    IF C$(I) <= C$(I + 1) THEN 270
00230    LET H$ = C$(I)
00240    LET C$(I) = C$(I + 1)
00250    LET C$(I + 1) = H$
00260  • LET F = 1
00270 NEXT I
00280 IF F = 1 THEN 200
00290 PRINT "SORTED LIST OF CITIES IN THE USA"
00300 PRINT
00310 FOR I = 1 TO 10
00320    PRINT C$(I)
00330 NEXT I
00340 DATA LOS ANGELES,CHICAGO,DETROIT,NEW YORK CITY,DALLAS
00350 DATA CLEVELAND,BOSTON,WASHINGTON,MIAMI,DENVER
00999 END
```

Figure IX–5 ▪ Continued

The Bubble Sort

The **bubble sort** works by comparing two adjacent values in an array and then interchanging them according to the desired order—either ascending or descending order.

The program in Figure IX–5 sorts ten U.S. cities into alphabetical order. To the computer, the letter A is less than the letter B, B is less than C, and so on. Lines 110 through 140 simply read the city names into an array called C$ and print them. Lines 200 through 280 perform the bubble sort. Let us examine them carefully to see what happens.

Line 200 refers to the variable F, short for flag. It is initialized to 0. Its value is checked later by the computer to determine if the entire array has been sorted.

Notice the terminal value of the FOR/NEXT loop that sorts the array. The terminal value is one less than the number of items to be sorted. This is because two items at a time are compared. I varies from 1 to 9, which means that the computer eventually will compare item 9 with item 9 + 1. If the terminal value were 10 (the number of cities), the computer would try to compare item 10 with item 11, which does not exist in our array.

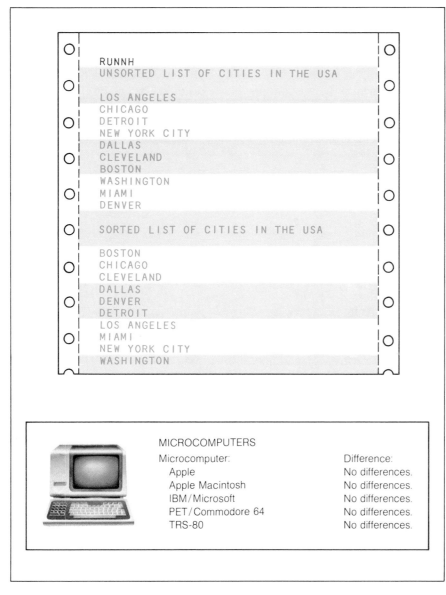

```
RUNNH
UNSORTED LIST OF CITIES IN THE USA

LOS ANGELES
CHICAGO
DETROIT
NEW YORK CITY
DALLAS
CLEVELAND
BOSTON
WASHINGTON
MIAMI
DENVER

SORTED LIST OF CITIES IN THE USA

BOSTON
CHICAGO
CLEVELAND
DALLAS
DENVER
DETROIT
LOS ANGELES
MIAMI
NEW YORK CITY
WASHINGTON
```

MICROCOMPUTERS

Microcomputer:	Difference:
Apple	No differences.
Apple Macintosh	No differences.
IBM/Microsoft	No differences.
PET/Commodore 64	No differences.
TRS-80	No differences.

Figure IX–5 ▪ Continued

The IF/THEN statement in line 220 tells the computer whether to interchange two compared values. For example, when I = 1, the computer compares LOS ANGELES with CHICAGO. Since C comes before L in the alphabet, there is need to switch these two items:

LOS ANGELES	I = 1	CHICAGO	
	Switch		
CHICAGO	I = 2	LOS ANGELES	DETROIT
	Switch		
DETROIT	I = 3	LOS ANGELES	
	No switch		
NEW YORK CITY	I = 4		

.
.
.

DENVER

Then I is incremented to 2, and LOS ANGELES is compared with DETROIT. These two names must be interchanged. This is performed by lines 230 through 250. Note that we have created a holding area, H$, so that the switch can be made. We move LOS ANGELES to the holding area, H$, and then move DETROIT to LOS ANGELES'S previous position. Now LOS ANGELES is placed in the position previously occupied by DETROIT. Whenever the computer interchanges two values, F is set to 1 in line 260. This loop continues until every item in the array has been examined. After once through this entire loop, the array C$ looks like this:

CHICAGO
DETROIT
LOS ANGELES
DALLAS
CLEVELAND
BOSTON
NEW YORK CITY
MIAMI
DENVER
WASHINGTON

Although several switches have been made, the list is not sorted completely. That is why we need line 280. As long as F equals 1, the computer knows that switches have been made, and the sorting process must continue. When the computer loops through the entire array without setting F equal to 1—that is, when no switches are made—the computer finds F equal to 0 and knows that the list is ordered.

Numbers, of course, can be sorted by this same method. Two-dimensional arrays can be sorted with nested loops.

A PROGRAMMING PROBLEM

The Problem

The *New York Times* needs to determine quickly the standings for the Patrick Division of the NHL. Six teams are included in the Division. Their names, wins, and losses follow:

New York Islanders	10	5
New York Rangers	8	7
Washington Capitals	8	7
Philadelphia Flyers	7	8
Pittsburg Penguins	2	13
New Jersey Devils	0	15

Solution Design

Since we know each team's win and loss record, the wins and losses can be introduced to the program along with the teams' names in READ and DATA statements. Last night's game should be entered by an INPUT statement. Next, the total scores must be calculated and then sorted from the highest to lowest wins (there are no ties). A crucial point is that as the win records are rearranged in the sorting section, the corresponding team's name and its loss record must be carried with each win record (although the team name and the loss record are not sorted). Finally, the results must be printed.

The Program

Figure IX–6 shows this problem's solution. Line 40 sets aside room for the variables (although this DIM statement is not strictly necessary, since the arrays have fewer than ten elements per index). Lines 130 through 150 read the data into a one-dimensional array. Lines 190 through 220 enter the win or loss for each team from last night's game. Lines 260 through 290 accumulate the wins or the losses for each team. The win records of the teams are sorted from highest to lowest in lines 330 through 470. The variables H1 and H2 in lines 370 and 380 are the holding places for the team's win record and loss

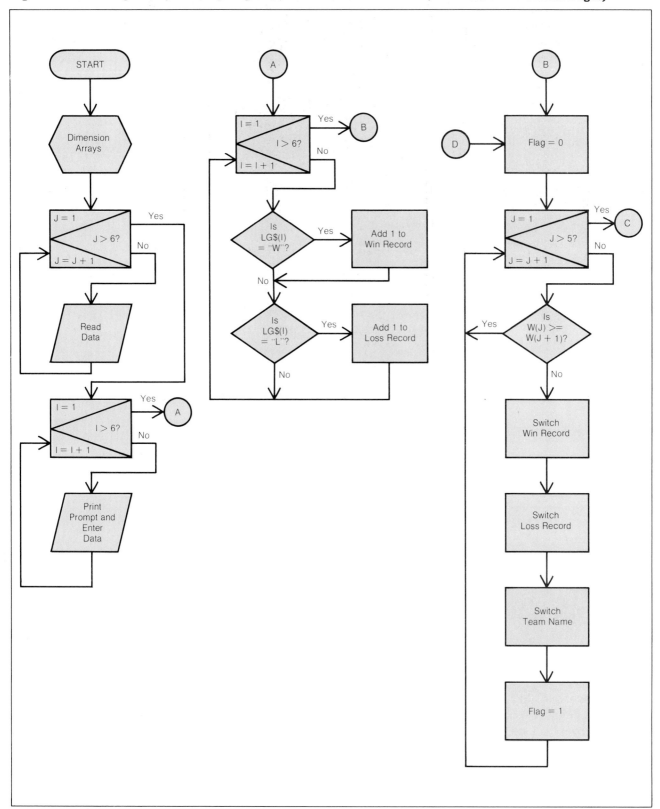

Figure IX–6 ▪ Continued

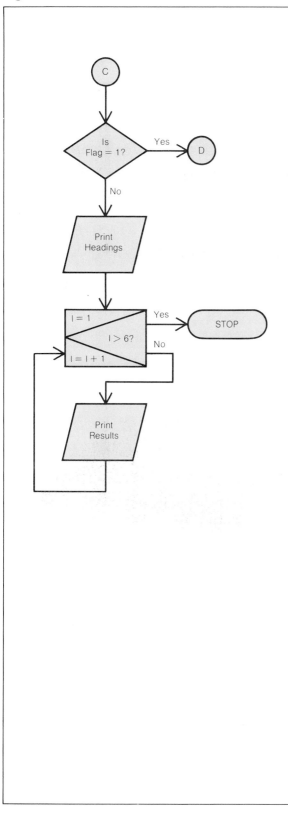

PSEUDOCODE

Start
Dimension the arrays
Start loop, do six times
    Read team, win record, and loss record into an array
End loop
Start loop, do six times
    Input win or loss for last night's game into an array
End loop
Start loop, do six times
    If win
        Then
            Add 1 to win record
    End if
    If loss
        Then
            Add 1 to loss record
    End if
End loop
Flag equals zero
Start loop, do five times
    If win record(J) < win record(J +1)
        Then
            Switch team(J) with team (J + 1)
            Switch win record(J) with win record (J + 1)
            Switch loss record(J) with loss record (J + 1)
    End if
End loop
If flag equals 1
    Then
        Flag equals zero
        Repeat preceding loop
    Else
        Print the report headings
        Start loop, do six times
            Print place, team, win record, and loss record from array
    End loop
End if
Stop

Figure IX–6 ■ Continued

```
00010 REM ****************************************
00020 REM ***    HOCKEY STANDING STATISTICS    ***
00030 REM ****************************************
00040 DIM T$(6),W(6),L(6)
00050 PRINT
00060 PRINT
00070 DATA NEW YORK ISLANDERS,10,5,NEW YORK RANGERS,8,7
00080 DATA NEW JERSEY DEVILS,0,15,WASHINGTON CAPITALS,8,7
00090 DATA PHILADELPHIA FLYERS,7,8,PITTSBURGH PENGUINS,2,13
00100 REM ****************************************
00110 REM ***   READ DATA FOR FIRST 15 GAMES    ***
00120 REM ****************************************
00130 FOR J = 1 TO 6
00140    READ T$(J),W(J),L(J)
00150 NEXT J
00160 REM ****************************************
00170 REM *** INPUT SCORES FOR THE LAST GAME   ***
00180 REM ****************************************
00190 FOR I = 1 TO 6
00200    PRINT "ENTER WIN OR LOSS (W OR L) FOR THE ";T$(I)
00210    INPUT LG$(I)
00220 NEXT I
00230 REM ****************************************
00240 REM *** CALCULATE TOTAL WINS AND LOSSES ***
00250 REM ****************************************
00260 FOR I = 1 TO 6
00270    IF LG$(I) = "W" THEN LET W(I) = W(I) + 1
00280    IF LG$(I) = "L" THEN LET L(I) = L(I) + 1
00290 NEXT I
00300 REM ****************************************
00310 REM *** SORT TEAMS INTO PROPER STANDING ***
00320 REM ****************************************
00330 LET F = 0
00340 FOR J = 1 TO 5
00350    IF W(J) >= W(J + 1) THEN 460
00360    LET H$ = T$(J)
00370    LET H1 = W(J)
00380    LET H2 = L(J)
00390    LET T$(J) = T$(J + 1)
00400    LET W(J) = W(J + 1)
00410    LET L(J) = L(J + 1)
00420    LET T$(J + 1) = H$
00430    LET W(J + 1) = H1
00440    LET L(J + 1) = H2
00450    LET F = 1
00460 NEXT J
00470 IF F = 1 THEN 330
00480 REM ****************************************
00490 REM ***    PRINT OUT THE TEAM STANDINGS   ***
00500 REM ****************************************
00510 PRINT
00520 PRINT
00530 PRINT "PLACE","TEAM",,"WINS","LOSSES"
00540 FOR I = 1 TO 6
00550    PRINT I,T$(I),W(I),L(I)
00560 NEXT I
00999 END
```

Figure IX–6 ▪ **Continued**

```
RUNNH

ENTER WIN OR LOSS (W OR L) FOR THE NEW YORK ISLANDERS
? L
ENTER WIN OR LOSS (W OR L) FOR THE NEW YORK RANGERS
? W
ENTER WIN OR LOSS (W OR L) FOR THE NEW JERSEY DEVILS
? L
ENTER WIN OR LOSS (W OR L) FOR THE WASHINGTON CAPITALS
? L
ENTER WIN OR LOSS (W OR L) FOR THE PHILADELPHIA FLYERS
? W
ENTER WIN OR LOSS (W OR L) FOR THE PITTSBURGH PENGUINS
? W
```

PLACE	TEAM	WINS	LOSSES
1	NEW YORK ISLANDERS	10	6
2	NEW YORK RANGERS	9	7
3	WASHINGTON CAPITALS	8	8
4	PHILADELPHIA FLYERS	8	8
5	PITTSBURGH PENGUINS	2	13
6	NEW JERSEY DEVILS	0	16

MICROCOMPUTERS

Microcomputer:	Difference:
Apple	Screen not wide enough.
Apple Macintosh	Screen not wide enough.
IBM/Microsoft	No differences.
PET/Commodore 64	Screen not wide enough.
TRS-80	Screen not wide enough.

record, respectively. The variable H$ in line 360 performs the same duty for the teams' names. Every time the computer switches a win record, W(J), it also must switch the corresponding team name and loss record. The computer performs the switches in lines 360 through 440. Lines 510 through 560 print the results.

SUMMARY POINTS

- Arrays are lists or tables of related values stored under a single variable name.
- Access to individual elements in an array can be gained through the use of subscripts.
- The DIM statement sets up storage space for arrays.
- Array manipulation is carried out through the use of FOR/NEXT loops.
- Two-dimensional arrays also are called tables or matrices.
- Two subscript numbers identify individual items in a matrix. The first number indicates the row; the second indicates the column.
- The bubble sort is one method of ordering values contained in an array.

REVIEW QUESTIONS

1. What is an array? Name two types of arrays and give two advantages of arrays.
2. We can reference individual elements in an array referring to their position in the array. This is done through the use of _____ _____. When the array element is referenced by an expression, what are the three steps carried out by the computer?
3. What is the purpose of the DIM statement and where is it located in a program?
4. Manipulation of arrays is often achieved through the use of _____. _____.

DEBUGGING EXERCISES

```
1.      10 DIM T$(25)
        15 FOR I = 1 TO 30
        20    READ T$(I)
        25    PRINT T$(I)
        30 NEXT I


2.      100 REM ***    TOTAL THE ELEMENTS IN    ***
        105 REM ***    ROW THREE OF ARRAY G     ***
        110 DIM G(5,6)
        115 LET T = 0
        120 FOR I = 1 TO 5
        125    LET T = T + G(I,6)
        130 NEXT I
```

PROGRAMMING PROBLEMS

1. Write a program to read fifteen data items (integers) into each of two arrays, X and Y. Calculate the products of the corresponding elements in X and Y and store the results in a third array, Z. Print a three-column table, with headings, displaying the contents of X, Y, and Z. Then compute the sum of the elements in each array and print the results. Make up your own data.

2. Write a program to accept the answers to a ten-question true/false exam given in an economics class and the corresponding student identification number. The student identifications should be placed in an array N$, and the student's answers should be entered into a two-dimensional array G. Use the following data:

STUDENT ID NO.	ANSWERS (1 = True; 0 = False)
0009	0010010010
0108	0101000011
0187	0111010011
0309	1101010101
0256	0111010010

The correct answers are: 0111010011. These answers should be entered into array A. Calculate each student's score, forming a third array, S. Find the best score, then determine each student's grade as follows: Give the best score an A; best - 1 a B; best - 2 a C; best - 3 a D; and otherwise give an F. Print a two-column table with headings, displaying the students' identification numbers and their corresponding grades.

OVERVIEW

File Processing

Business applications often involve large amounts of data. It is not uncommon for programs dealing with inventory, payroll, or customer balances to process hundreds, thousands, or millions of data items. Since the main memory of the computer is limited, users need some means of storing programs and data so that they do not have to retype them into the computer every time it is necessary to run the programs. Some microcomputers are so small that they cannot store internally all the data needed. In addition, it is useful to establish a single data file that several programs can use in different ways at different times. For example, personnel data can be used in applications such as handling payroll, processing medical claims, and printing mailing lists. For all these reasons, data often is stored on secondary storage media (secondary storage devices)—usually magnetic disks and tapes. Groups of data stored on disks or tapes are known as files.

Unfortunately, there is no standardized method for performing operations on files stored on secondary storage devices. Many BASIC implementations include unique file manipulation commands. Fortunately, the principles on which the commands are based are similar. We look first at the fundamentals of file processing and later differentiate among implementations on the computers we have been discussing.

WHAT IS A FILE?

A file is a way of organizing data. Think of a typical office, which probably has a number of file drawers. Usually each file drawer contains related information about one general topic. For example, one drawer might contain all the information about the firm's clients and be called the client file. Within this drawer might be a separate information sheet for each client giving the name, address, and so on. Each of these information sheets are referred to as a record. The individual data items, such as the client's name recorded on the information sheet, are called **fields.** A group of one or more related fields is known as a **record,** and a group of one or more related records is known as a **file** (see Figure X–1).

Figure X–1 ▪ File Organization

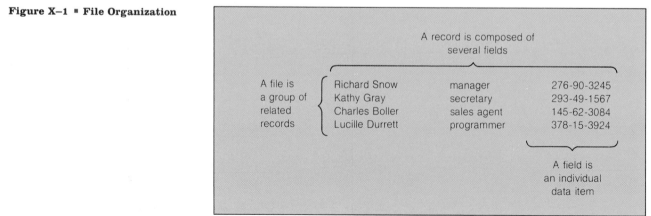

The computer has allowed us to store and manipulate files much more efficiently than its predecessor, the file cabinet. The computer uses two main types of file access methods: sequential and random access. Our discussion will concentrate mainly on accessing sequential files (opening, writing to, reading from, and closing). Random files will also be introduced. However, we will not give specific examples of random file accessing on each computer. Please refer to your system manual for more information concerning random files.

SEQUENTIAL DATA FILES

Magnetic tape is one type of sequential media (see Figure X–2). In a **sequential file,** the data items are recorded one after another and must also be read one after another in the same order in which the recording took place. For example, to recall the fifth item stored in a sequential file, you must start at the beginning of the file and read the first four items successfully to get to the fifth one.

Data also can be stored sequentially on disk (see Figure X–3). A disk is divided into concentric circles called **tracks.** The data items are recorded one after another on the tracks of the disk. Figure X–3 shows how a disk containing our client file might be organized. The number 13 is the ASCII code for the carriage return, which is used to separate fields.

In a sequential file, each field takes only the amount of space required by its length. To record data in a sequential file, the following three steps are needed:

1. *Opening a sequential data file for writing to the file.* When opening a file, the programmer must tell the computer the name of the file to which data is to be output. Using this name, the computer sets up a location on a disk or tape in which the data are to be placed.
2. *Writing data to a sequential data file.* After opening a data file, data may be written onto the disk. A special statement is used to write data onto a disk, with the processing being similar to printing output on the screen or printer, except the data are being written onto the disk instead.
3. *Closing a sequential data file.* The last step in creating a sequential data file is to close it. After all the data have been written on the disk, the file must be closed to prevent loss of its contents. Closing also indicates to the computer that the use of the file is finished for the present time.

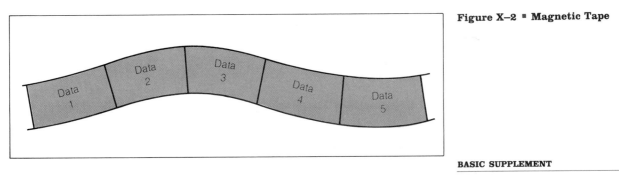

Figure X–2 ▪ Magnetic Tape

Figure X–3 ■ Disk

Reading from a sequential file also requires three steps:

1. *Opening a sequential data file for reading from the file.* The opening of a sequential file for reading may be either identical to the opening format for writing to a file or slightly modified. For example, to open a data file to write to a disk may require that a word or character be included to indicate this, such as WRITE or W. To read from the data file, these might need to be changed to READ or R.
2. *Reading data from a sequential data file.* After the file has been opened, the data can be read from the disk and placed in variables—numeric data in numeric variables and string data in string variables. Remember that in a sequential file, data are always read in the same order in which they were written.
3. *Closing a sequential data file.* Closing the file after reading the disk is identical to closing it after writing to the disk.

No matter what type of computer you are using, these general steps apply in using sequential data files. An example follows of sequential data file use on the DECSYSTEM 20 (also referred to as **terminal format files**). Following this, we will show the same example for each of our computers, the Apple, IBM/Microsoft, TRS-80, and PET/Commodore 64. Refer to the appropriate section for your computer. The discussion on implementing files will be limited to files on disk. Consult your manual for any differences in commands for tape.

DECSYSTEM 20

CREATING OR ACCESSING A SEQUENTIAL DATA (TERMINAL FORMAT) FILE

The general format of the command that creates or accesses a data file for the DECSYSTEM 20 is as follows:

line# OPEN "filename" AS FILE #number

If a file already exists with the filename specified, the computer will give us access to it. Otherwise, a new file will be created. The number can be used to refer to the file. The following is an example:

```
00010 OPEN "TELEPHONE" AS FILE #2
```

WRITING DATA TO A FILE

After the file has been created, we can write data to it:

line# PRINT #number, expression

The number is the one used in the OPEN statement. The expression is the data to be written onto the disk. For example,

```
00020 PRINT #2,"352-8952"
```

Pressing RETURN at the end of the line tells the computer that this is the end of the data item.

CLOSING A FILE

The general format of the CLOSE command is as follows:

line# CLOSE #number

The program in Figure X–4 creates a file called TELEPHONE as file #2 and writes some data to it.

Line 10 creates a file called TELEPHONE. The file number at the end of the line is used later to refer to the file. Line 20 sets up a FOR/NEXT loop to read some data items (in line 30) and write them to the file. Line 40 prints the values in T$ to file 2, TELEPHONE. Line 60 closes the file.

READING DATA FROM A FILE

To use the data stored on a file, we read it. The INPUT command can be used, and its format is as follows:

line# INPUT #file number,variable list

The following is an example:

```
00020 INPUT #2,T$
```

Figure X–4 ▪ Creating and Writing Data to a File

```
00010 OPEN "TELEPHONE" AS FILE #2
00020 FOR I = 1 TO 6
00030    READ T$
00040    PRINT #2,T$
00050 NEXT I
00060 CLOSE #2
00070 DATA "BONNIE COOK:  287-6562","TIM SMITH:  315-3537"
00080 DATA "JOHN ROGERS:  425-2920","BOB HILL:  287-7171"
00090 DATA "STEVE SIMON:  425-3172","SARAH JOHNS:  425-0061"
00999 END
```

The program in Figure X–5 reads data stored in the file called TELEPHONE.

Line 10 gives access to TELEPHONE as file 2. Line 20 sets up for a FOR/NEXT loop that reads the items from the file one by one into the array T$ and prints them out for us to see. Line 40 prints the data on the screen. Line 60 closes the file.

Apple

CREATING OR ACCESSING A SEQUENTIAL DATA FILE

The Apple system calls data files **text files.** To tell the system to use the disk, we need to cue the computer by pressing the control (CTRL) key and the D key simultaneously. Since this has to be done several times in a file manipulation program, we may want to initialize a variable, D$, to CTRL-D by doing the following:

```
10 LET D$ = CHR$(4)
```

Check section VIII to refresh your memory about what CHR$ does.

The general format of the command for creating or opening a text file is the following:

line# PRINT D$; "OPEN filename"

D$ is the CTRL-D command. The file name must begin with a letter and be less than thirty characters long. An example follows:

```
10 LET D$ = CHR$(4)
20 PRINT D$;"OPEN TELEPHONE"
```

A file called TELEPHONE now is listed in our catalog. A **catalog** is a program that supplies a complete alphabetical list of a user's files. It is designated as a text (data) file by the letter T in the catalog listing. The OPEN command is used in this manner whenever we want to gain access to data in a file.

WRITING DATA TO A FILE

After the file has been created, we can alert the computer that we want to put some data into the file by using this command:

line# PRINT D$; "WRITE filename"

Figure X–5 ▪ Reading Data from a File

```
00010 OPEN "TELEPHONE" AS FILE #2
00020 FOR I = 1 TO 6
00030    INPUT #2,T$(I)
00040    PRINT T$(I)
00050 NEXT I
00060 CLOSE #2
00999 END
```

This line is followed by the command that actually does the writing to the disk:

line# PRINT expression

This PRINT command writes the expression to the disk. Since a sequential file is simply a long list of data, the computer needs to know where one data item ends and the next one begins. Pressing the RETURN button at the end of the PRINT line tells the computer this.

CLOSING A FILE

The general format of the CLOSE command is as follows:

line# PRINT D$; "CLOSE filename"

The program in Figure X–6 opens a file named TELEPHONE, writes some data out to it, and finally closes it.

Line 10 initializes D$ to the disk command; this tells the computer we are dealing with disk files. Line 20 creates the file. Line 30 tells the computer that we are going to write some data to the disk.

In this example, the data items are different lengths: BONNIE COOK: 287–6562 is twenty-two characters long; TIM SMITH: 315–3537 is twenty characters long, and so forth. The items are separated from one another by the fact that they are on different lines. Therefore, the file is a list of items, each of which ends with the ASCII character 13, the carriage return:

TELEPHONE: BONNIE COOK: 287–656213TIM SMITH: 315–353713

READING DATA FROM A FILE

Once a file has been established, it can be read whenever the user wants to use the data. The following command alerts the computer that reading from a file on disk is to occur:

line# PRINT D$; "READ filename"

```
 10 LET D$ = CHR$(4)
 20 PRINT D$;"OPEN TELEPHONE"
 30 PRINT D$;"WRITE TELEPHONE"
 40 PRINT "BONNIE COOK:  287-6562"
 50 PRINT "TIM SMITH:  315-3537"
 60 PRINT "JOHN ROGERS:  425-2920"
 70 PRINT "BOB HILL:  287-7171"
 80 PRINT "STEVE SIMON:  425-3172"
 90 PRINT "SARAH JOHNS:  425-0061"
100 PRINT D$;"CLOSE TELEPHONE"
999 END
```

Figure X–6 ▪ Creating and Writing Data to a File

To read the data items, we use an INPUT statement, as shown in Figure X–7. After the file is opened, line 130 signals the computer that we are going to read data from a disk file. The FOR/NEXT loop then reads the data into the array T$. The file is closed by line 170.

IBM/Microsoft

CREATING OR ACCESSING A SEQUENTIAL DATA FILE

The general format for creating or accessing a sequential data file for the IBM/Microsoft microcomputer follows:

line# OPEN "filename" FOR OUTPUT AS #number
line# OPEN "filename" FOR INPUT AS #number

The filename in quotes must be less than or equal to eight characters. OUT-PUT specifies sequential output mode; it allows data to be written to the specified file on disk. INPUT specifies sequential input mode; it allows data to be read from the specified file on disk. The number after the pound (#) sign will be used later as a shorthand reference to the file in the program. An example statement creating a file called TELEPHONE follows:

```
10 OPEN "TELEPHONE" FOR OUTPUT AS #1
```

WRITING DATA TO A FILE

Once a file has been created, we can write some data to it by using a variation of the PRINT statement. Notice, however, that the following PRINT statement looks different from that used to display the results of processing:

line# PRINT #number,expression

The #number distinguishes this statement from a regular PRINT command. The number should be the same one that was specified in the OPEN statement. The expression can be any valid variable, string, numeric constant, and so on. Since a sequential file is simply a long list of items, the computer knows where one data item ends and the next one begins by the pressing of the carriage return at the end of the PRINT line.

Figure X–7 ▪ Reading Data from a File

```
110 LET D$ = CHR$(4)
120 PRINT D$;"OPEN TELEPHONE"
130 PRINT D$;"READ TELEPHONE"
140 FOR I = 1 TO 6
150    INPUT T$(I)
160 NEXT I
170 PRINT D$;"CLOSE TELEPHONE"
999 END
```

CLOSING A FILE

The general format of the CLOSE command follows:

line# CLOSE #number

Again, the number should be the same one that was used to open the file.

The program in Figure X–8 opens a file named TELEPHONE, writes some data to it, and closes the file.

Line 10 creates the file as #1. That same number is used throughout the program in the file statements as a shorthand reference to TELEPHONE. Lines 20 through 70 simply write data items to the file. Line 80 closes the file.

READING DATA FROM A FILE

Once a file has been created, it can be read to access the data using the following:

line# INPUT #number, expression

The #number distinguishes this as a file statement. The following is an example:

```
40 INPUT #1,T$
```

The program in Figure X–9 reads data stored in a file called TELEPHONE.

Line 10 accesses TELEPHONE as file #2. Line 20 sets up a FOR/NEXT loop that reads the items from the file one by one into the array T$. The items are displayed by line 40. Line 60 closes the file.

Apple Macintosh and TRS–80

CREATING OR ACCESSING A SEQUENTIAL DATA FILE

On the TRS–80, the computer will ask,

HOW MANY FILES?

```
10 OPEN "TELEPHONE" FOR OUTPUT AS #1
20 PRINT #1,"BONNIE COOK:  287-6562"
30 PRINT #1,"TIM SMITH:  315-3537"
40 PRINT #1,"JOHN ROGERS:  425-2920"
50 PRINT #1,"BOB HILL:  287-7171"
60 PRINT #1,"STEVE SIMON:  425-3172"
70 PRINT #1,"SARAH JOHNS:  425-0061"
80 CLOSE #1
99 END
```

Figure X–8 ▪ Creating and Writing Data to a File

Figure X–9 ■ Reading Data from a File

```
10 OPEN "TELEPHONE" FOR INPUT AS #2
20 FOR I = 1 TO 6
30    INPUT #2,T$(I)
40    PRINT T$(I)
50 NEXT I
60 CLOSE #2
99 END
```

Since we are going to deal with fewer than three files, we can simply press the ENTER button in response.

The following command permits access to files on both the Apple Macintosh and TRS–80.

line# OPEN "mode", buffer number, "filename"

The "mode" will be either I for sequential input (reading data from an existing file) or O for sequential output (writing data on the disk). After the "mode" is specified, we designate the number of the buffer where data will temporarily be held. The filename can be from one to eight characters long; the first character must be alphabetic (do not embed any blanks). An example follows:

```
10 OPEN "O",1,"TELEPHONE"
```

This line creates a file called TELEPHONE. After the file is opened, we can use buffer 1 to write data to the file ("mode" = O). We will see how this works later.

WRITING DATA TO A FILE

After a file has been created (opened), data can be written to it. The general format of the PRINT command is:

line# PRINT #buffer number, expression

For example,

```
20 PRINT #1,"BONNIE COOK:  287-6562"
```

prints the character string BONNIE COOK: 287–6562 as the first item in the file called TELEPHONE. The #1 is the buffer number used in the OPEN statement for TELEPHONE above.

Now we can write a simple program that creates a file and writes some data to it, as shown in Figure X–10.

Line 10 opens the file called TELEPHONE. We use buffer #1 to write data to the file. Pressing ENTER at the end of each line separates one item from another on the disk file. Line 80 closes the file.

Figure X—10 ■ Creating and Writing Data to a File

```
10 OPEN "O",1,"TELEPHONE"
20 PRINT #1,"BONNIE COOK:  287-6562"
30 PRINT #1,"TIM SMITH:   315-3537"
40 PRINT #1,"JOHN ROGERS:  425-2920"
50 PRINT #1,"BOB HILL: 287-7171"
60 PRINT #1,"STEVE SIMON:  425-3172"
70 PRINT #1,"SARAH JOHNS:  425-0061"
80 CLOSE #1
99 END
```

CLOSING A FILE

The following command closes a file:

line# CLOSE #buffer number

Make sure that the buffer number is the one specified in the OPEN statement for the file. (See lines 10 and 80 in Figure X—10.)

READING DATA FROM A FILE

To read data from a file, we first must gain access to it by using the OPEN statement. However, the mode is now I, for sequential input. The following statement should be used to gain access on an already existing file:

line# OPEN"I",buffer number,"filename"

The command that reads data from the file follows:

line# INPUT #buffer number,variable

The program segment in Figure X—11 reads data that have been stored in TELEPHONE.

Line 10 gives access to an already existing file called TELEPHONE. A FOR/NEXT loop then is established to read the data into the array T$. Data is read from the file by line 30. Note that the buffer number is the same as was

Figure X—11 ■ Reading Data from a File

```
10 OPEN "I",1,"TELEPHONE"
20 FOR I = 1 TO 6
30    INPUT #1,T$(I)
40 NEXT I
50 FOR I = 1 TO 6
60    PRINT T$(I)
70 NEXT I
80 CLOSE #1
99 END
```

designated in the OPEN statement. Lines 50 through 70 simply print out the file. Line 80 closes the file.

PET/Commodore 64

CREATING OR ACCESSING A SEQUENTIAL DATA FILE

The general format of the command for creating or accessing a data file for the PET/Commodore 64 microcomputer follows:

line# OPEN file#,device#,channel#,"0:name,type,direction"

The file number is used to refer to the file. The device number is 8, which tells the computer to open the file on disk. The channel number is a data channel, numbers 2 through 14. For convenience, it is suggested that you use the same number for both the channel and file numbers to keep them straight. The name is the file name. For our purposes here, the type is SEQ (sequential), which can be abbreviated by using just the first letter, S. The direction must be READ or WRITE, or at least the first letter of each. An example follows:

```
10 OPEN 3,8,3,"0:TELEPHONE,S,W"
```

If the file TELEPHONE already exists and we need only read what is on it, the W should be changed to R. The following example gives us access to an existing file TELEPHONE:

```
10 OPEN 3,8,3,"0:TELEPHONE,S,R"
```

WRITING DATA TO A FILE

After a filename has been created, we can write data to the file by using a PRINT command. The general format is:

line# PRINT #file number, expression

The file number is the one specified in the OPEN statement. The expression is the data to be written onto the disk. For example,

```
30 PRINT #3,"BONNIE COOK:  287-6562"
```

writes BONNIE COOK: 287–6562 to file 3. Pressing RETURN at the end of the line signals the computer that this is the end of the data item.

CLOSING A FILE

The general format of the CLOSE statement follows:

line# CLOSE #file number

Let us put these commands together in Figure X–12 to create a file called TELEPHONE, write some data to it, and close it.

Figure X–12 ■ Creating and Writing Data to a File

```
10 OPEN 2,8,2,"0:TELEPHONE,S,W"
20 PRINT #2,"BONNIE COOK:  287-6562"
30 PRINT #2,"TIM SMITH:  315-3537"
40 PRINT #2,"JOHN ROGERS:  425-2920"
50 PRINT #2,"BOB HILL: 287-7171"
60 PRINT #2,"STEVE SIMON:  425-3172"
70 PRINT #2,"SARAH JOHNS:  425-0061"
80 CLOSE #2
99 END
```

READING DATA FROM A FILE

Once a file has been established, it can be read so that manipulations can be performed on the data. First, the file should be reopened:

line# OPEN file#, device#,channel#, "O:name, type, direction"

Then we use the following command to read the data items:

line# INPUT #file number, expression

The file number, of course, must be the same as the file number in the OPEN statement. The expression is the variable that specifies where the data will be stored in internal memory.

The program in Figure X–13 reads data from the file called TELEPHONE. Line 10 opens file 2. Since the file already has been established, R is specified as the direction (that is, to read from the file). A FOR/NEXT loop is initiated in line 20. Line 30 reads data from file 2 into the array T$. Line 40 is a PRINT statement. No file number is specified; it simply prints the data items on the screen of the PET/Commodore 64. Finally, the file is closed in line 60.

RANDOM DATA FILES

Random data files are files that allow you to write to or read from a file in random order. Figure X–14 illustrates how a random file is organized on disk.

Figure X–13 ■ Reading Data from a File

```
10 OPEN 2,8,2,"0:TELEPHONE,S,R"
20 FOR I = 1 TO 6
30   INPUT #2,T$(I)
40    PRINT T$(I)
50 NEXT I
60 CLOSE #2
99 END
```

Figure X–14 ▪ Random Data Files

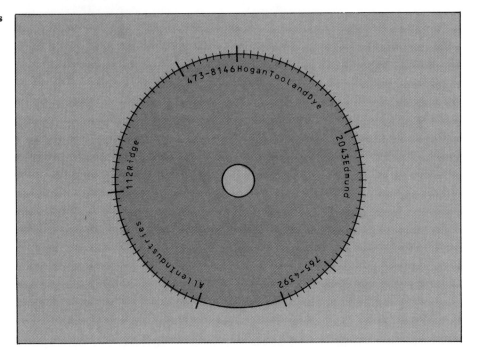

For the purposes of this book, all records must be the same length in a random file. (Check your manual for other options.) This enables the computer to find them without reading all the preceding records. Since the fields that make up each record may not be the same length, blank characters are placed after them. Because of this, random files tend to take up more disk space than sequential files, but this disadvantage is outweighed by the associated advantages, such as speed of access.

Our discussion of random files will deal with relative files. A record file with relative organization contains records that are stored in numbered locations. The number associated with a position represents its location relative to the beginning of the file. For example, record 1 would occupy the first record position; record 2, the second record position; and so forth. Thus, with a relative file we can access a record either sequentially or randomly by record number.

Like sequential files, random files have to be opened before use and closed after use. When reading or writing with a random file, the number of the record to be read or written to must be specified. Record numbers start with 1 and continue to as high as necessary to store all the records. The methods used to perform these steps vary from computer to computer.

RANDOM VERSUS SEQUENTIAL FILES

The following is a short summary of the differences between random and sequential files:

▪ Records in sequential files are written to the disk one after the other, starting with record 1.

- Records in random files may be written in any order desired.
- Records in sequential files are read from the disk one after the other, starting with record 1.
- Records in random files may be read in any order desired.
- Records in sequential files can be of varying lengths.
- Records in random files must all be the same length.

Another method of randomly accessing data in a file is through the use of indexed files. Indexed files initiate random access by means of a key, or a field within a record that uniquely identifies the contents of a particular record. For a more detailed discussion of indexed files, see your systems manual.

A PROGRAMMING PROBLEM

The Problem

Safeway National Bank keeps a file of all its customers and their account balances. They have asked you to write a program that will update their master file by using a transaction file they have processed for you.

Solution Design

The twenty customers and their account balances are described on a file called MASTER.FILE. There are ten customers and the amounts of their transactions on a file called TRANS.FILE. A negative amount on the TRANS.FILE indicates a withdrawal, while a positive amount shows a deposit. The data in these files can be read into arrays. Then the MASTER.FILE can be updated and written to a file called NEW.MASTER.

The Program

Figure X–15 gives the program listing. Line 40 sets dimensions for the arrays that will hold the data from the files. Lines 50 and 60 open the master file and the transaction file, respectively. Line 70 opens the new master file that will be an updated version of the master file. Lines 150 through 190 put data from the MASTER.FILE into arrays A$ and A. Lines 270 through 310 put the data from the TRANS.FILE into arrays N$ and T.

Now we must update the MASTER.FILE. We close files 1 and 2 with lines 320 and 330. Lines 370 through 460 determine each customer's new account balance. Lines 370 through 390 set each new account balance (B) equal to each old account balance (A). If the name from the MASTER.FILE (A$) does not equal the name from the TRANS.FILE (N$), then line processing continues at line 450 until the two names are equal. When the two names are equal, then line 430 replaces the number in B with the result of the transaction amount (T) added to the old balance (A). Lines 540 through 580 form a FOR and NEXT loop that stores each customer's name and new account balance on disk and also prints out the file listing. Line 590 closes file 3.

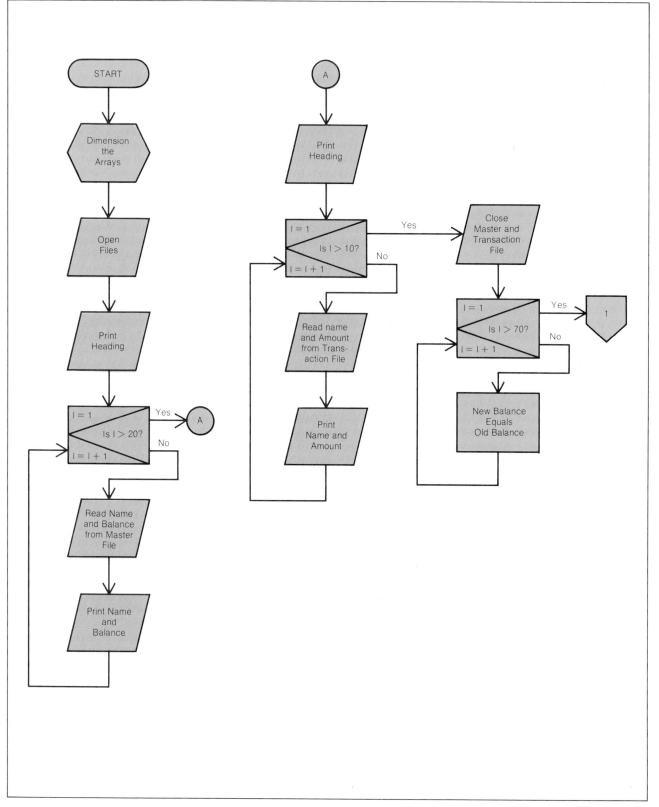

Figure X–15 ▪ Continued

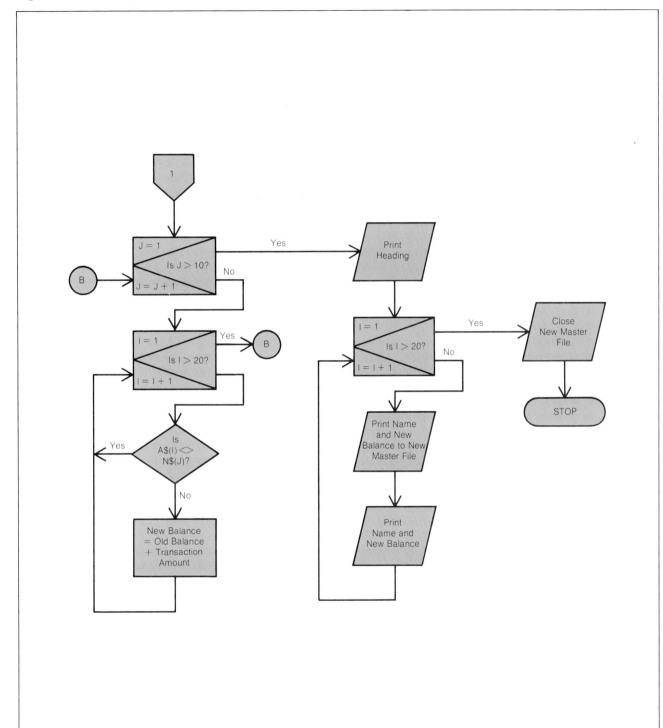

Figure X–15 ▪ Continued

PSEUDOCODE
Start
Dimension the arrays
Open master file, transaction file, and new master file
Print the master file report headings
Start loop, do twenty times
  Read name
  Read account balance
  Print name and account balance
Endloop
Print the transaction file report headings
Start loop, do ten times
  Read name
  Read transaction amount
  Print name and transaction amount
Endloop
Close master file and transaction file
Start loop, do twenty times
  New balance of each account equals its old balance
Endloop
Start loop, do ten times
  Start loop, do twenty times
    If master file name equals transaction file name
     Then
      New balance of the account equals old account balance + transaction amount
    Endloop
  Endloop
Print the new master file report headings
Start loop, do twenty times
  Write each name to the new master file
  Write each new account balance to new master file
  Print name and new account balance
Endloop
Close new master file
Stop

```
00010 REM *******************************************
00020 REM ***         FILE PROCESSING PROGRAM      ***
00030 REM *******************************************
00040 DIM A$(20),A(20),N$(10),T(10),B(20)
00050 OPEN "MASTER.FILE" AS FILE #1
00060 OPEN "TRANS.FILE" AS FILE #2
00070 OPEN "NEW.MASTER" AS FILE #3
00080 REM *******************************************
00090 REM ***      READ MASTER.FILE INTO PROGRAM   ***
00100 REM *******************************************
00110 PRINT
00120 PRINT "MASTER FILE"
00130 PRINT "ACCOUNT","BALANCE"
00140 PRINT
```

Figure X–15 ▪ Continued

```
00150 FOR I = 1 TO 20
00160    INPUT #1,A$(I)
00170    INPUT #1,A(I)
00180    PRINT A$(I),A(I)
00190 NEXT I
00200 PRINT
00210 REM *************************************************
00220 REM ***        READ TRANS.FILE INTO PROGRAM      ***
00230 REM *************************************************
00240 PRINT "TRANSACTION FILE"
00250 PRINT "ACCOUNT","AMOUNT"
00260 PRINT
00270 FOR I = 1 TO 10
00280    INPUT #2,N$(I)
00290    INPUT #2,T(I)
00300    PRINT N$(I),T(I)
00310 NEXT I
00320 CLOSE #1
00330 CLOSE #2
00340 REM *************************************************
00350 REM ***        DETERMINE NEW ACCOUNT BALANCE      ***
00360 REM *************************************************
00370 FOR I = 1 TO 20
00380    LET B(I) = A(I)
00390 NEXT I
00400 FOR J = 1 TO 10
00410    FOR I = 1 TO 20
00420       IF A$(I) <> N$(J) THEN 450
00430       B(I) = A(I) + T(J)
00440       GOTO 460
00450    NEXT I
00460 NEXT J
00470 REM *************************************************
00480 REM *** WRITE NEW BALANCE TO FILE AND PRINT OUT ***
00490 REM *************************************************
00500 PRINT
00510 PRINT "NEW MASTER FILE"
00520 PRINT "ACCOUNT","BALANCE"
00530 PRINT
00540 FOR I = 1 TO 20
00550    PRINT #3,A$(I)
00560    PRINT #3,B(I)
00570    PRINT A$(I),B(I)
00580 NEXT I
00590 CLOSE #3
00999 END
```

Figure X—15 ▪ Continued

```
RUNNH

MASTER FILE
ACCOUNT        BALANCE

CLEMMENS       7841.91
CONRAD         287.03
GIRNUS         5786.45
GOUGH          888.23
GREENE         87.55
HARRIS         45.9
HILL           443.67
KRAMMER        20.34
LEWIS          72.11
MILLER         839.89
MUGG           345.39
NEWHART        8.32
POOR           109.7
SMITH          103.28
SOMMERS        49.23
SPITERY        34.92
TWILLY         874.97
WEINSTEIN      9032.97
WILLE          656.28
YALE           834.88

TRANSACTION FILE
ACCOUNT        AMOUNT

CLEMMENS       -800
GIRNUS         -150
GOUGH          45.14
GREENE         89.23
HARRIS         99.45
HILL           443.1
KRAMMER        -10
MUGG           -175
WEINSTEIN      107.93
YALE           -200

NEW MASTER FILE
ACCOUNT        BALANCE

CLEMMENS       7041.91
CONRAD         287.03
GIRNUS         5636.45
GOUGH          933.37
GREENE         176.78
HARRIS         145.35
HILL           886.77
KRAMMER        10.34
LEWIS          72.11
MILLER         839.89
MUGG           170.39
NEWHART        8.32
POOR           109.7
SMITH          103.28
SOMMERS        49.23
SPITERY        34.92
TWILLY         874.97
WEINSTEIN      9140.9
WILLE          656.28
YALE           634.88
```

SUMMARY POINTS

■ Data is organized in the following manner. A single data item is called a field. Related fields are organized into a record. A file is composed of a group of related records.
■ There are two main types of files: sequential and random access.
■ There is no standardized method for performing operations on files stored on secondary storage devices.

REVIEW QUESTIONS

1. What are files and some of their advantages? What are fields and records?
2. Give the three steps needed to record data in a sequential file. How do these differ from the steps needed to read data from a sequential file?
3. What two things does closing a sequential file do?
4. What is the main difference between random and sequential access?

DEBUGGING EXERCISES (Designed for DECSYSTEM 20)

```
1. 100 OPEN CUSTOMER AS FILE #4
   105 FOR I = 1 TO 100
   110    READ X
   115    PRINT #2,X
   120 NEXT I
   125 CLOSE #4
```

```
2. 50 REM *** READ DATA FROM FILE ***
   55 OPEN PAYROLL FILE #3
   60 FOR I = 1 TO 5
   65    READ #3 A$(I)
   70    PRINT A$(I)
   75 NEXT I
   80 CLOSE #2
```

PROGRAMMING PROBLEMS

1. Write a program which will create a sequential file containing the following names of bodybuilders:

HANEY	BANNOUT
BERTIL	MAKKAWY
PLATZ	WILKOSZ
FULLER	BECKLES
ZANE	METZ

2. The IFBB wants to send information about the next Mr. Olympia contest to potential contestants. They need an alphabetically sorted list of bodybuilders. Write a program to read the list of names from the file you created in Programming Problem 1, sort the names alphabetically, and print them out.

BASIC Glossary

Alphanumeric data   A character set that contains any combination of letters, numbers, and special characters (such as punctuation marks).

ANSI BASIC   A programming language that has a universally accepted set of standard rules. BASIC is short for Beginners All-purpose Symbolic Instruction Code.

Argument   The quantity to be evaluated by a function. It can be a constant, a variable, a mathematical expression, or another function and is enclosed in parentheses.

Array   A one- or two-dimensional group of storage locations in memory given a single variable name. Individual elements of an array are referenced by using subscripts.

BASIC   (Beginners' All-purpose Symbolic Instruction Code) A high-level programming language commonly used for interactive problem solving by beginning programmers.

Boot   A term used to describe the process in which the disk drive loads the instructions that tell the computer how to manage the disk.

Branching   A method of transferring control from one part of the program to another by skipping past some statements in the program.

Bubble sort   A method of sorting that works by comparing two adjacent values in an array and then interchanging them according to the desired order.

Built-in function   See Library function.

Catalog   The contents of a disk.

Character string constant   A group of letters, numbers, or special characters enclosed in quotation marks; the value does not change during program execution.

Character string literal   A group of letters, numbers, or special characters assigned when a program is written that are to be printed exactly as is on the output page.

Column   Vertical segregations on the print line.

Concatenate   To append; attach; to join together two or more character strings. The addition (+) operand is used.

Conditional transfer   A transfer of control to other statements in the program based on the evaluation of a mathematical expression.

Constant   Numeric or character string value that does not change during program execution.

Conversational mode   A mode in which the user can communicate with the computer while a program is being executed.

Cursor   Usually a flashing character such as an underline or a block that shows where the next typed character will appear on the screen.

Decision block   A diamond-shaped symbol used in flowcharting to represent an IF/THEN test.

Dummy value   See Trailer value.

Exception-handling   A sequence of statements that helps the program to handle problems that would otherwise lead to a premature stop.

Expression   A valid literal, variable, or mathematical formula.

Field   A meaningful item of data, such as a student's name.

File   A grouping of related records, such as student records.

Floating-point BASIC   A version of the BASIC language that allows use of decimal fractions.

Flowchart   A symbolic chart showing the processing steps needed to solve a problem.

Garbage-in-garbage out   A phrase meaning that output can be no more accurate than the input fed into the computer.

Hierarchy of operations   The priority path a computer follows when performing more than one mathematical operation in a single formula.

Immediate mode command   A command used without a line number; executed as soon as the return key is pressed.

Index   The loop variable of a FOR/NEXT loop. This value is tested to see if the loop has been executed the desired number of times.

Infinite loop   A loop that repeats endlessly.

Initialization   Assign a beginning value to a variable; used with accumulators and counters.

Input The step in the data-processing flow where data are entered and coded for computer use.

Inquiry-and-response mode A mode in which the program requests information from the user and the user responds; see also Conversational mode.

Library function Functions that have been built into the BASIC language because many applications require these types of mathematical operations; included in the BASIC language library.

Line number The number that preceeds each statement. Line numbers tell the computer the order in which the statements are to be executed.

List See One-dimensional array.

Literal A numeric or string constant used in a PRINT statement.

Loop A series of instructions in a program that is executed repeatedly as long as specific conditions are met.

Mantissa The number preceding the "E" which in most systems lies between 1.000 and 9.999.

Mask Symbols that specify the number of characters to be printed in a field.

Matrix Another name for a one- or two-dimensional array.

Natural logarithm A function that is the reverse of the EXP(x) function.

Numeric constant A real number that does not change when a program is executed.

Numeric literal A real number assigned when a program is written (not calculated) that is to be printed exactly as is on the page. Numeric literals are used in the PRINT statement.

Numeric variable A real number that is either supplied to the computer by the programmer or internally calculated by the computer. All variables can change during the execution of the program.

One-dimensional array An array with just one column of values.

Output Information that comes from the computer as a result of processing.

Predefined function See Library function.

Processing The manipulation of data provided as input in order to generate information; includes classifying, sorting, calculating, summarizing, and storing.

Programming process A 5-step process used for problem solving: (1) Define the problem, (2) Design a solution, (3) Write the program, (4) Submit the program, and (5) Test and debug.

Prompt A message printed out to explain to the user what data should be entered. Usually used in conjunction with the INPUT statement.

Real number Numbers composed of either integers or decimal fractions.

Record A collection of data items, or fields, that are related; such as data about a single student.

Relational symbol A symbol that can be used for condition testing. These symbols include :<, >, =, >=, <=, ><, and <>.

Reserved word Words that are reserved for special purposes, such as programming commands; they cannot be used in variable names.

Sequential file A file where data items are recorded one after another and must be read one after another in the same order in which they were recorded.

Statement The fundamental building-block of a computer program. Each BASIC statement must include a line number and a BASIC command.

String variable A value composed of letters, numbers or special characters that is enclosed in quotation marks. This value may change when the program is executed.

Subroutine A sequence of statements not within the main line of the program; used primarily to avoid having to re-write program segments. All subroutines must end with a RETURN statement.

Subscripted variable Elements of an array. The subscript is the integer enclosed in parentheses that allows reference to a specific element; for example $X(3)$.

Syntax Refers to the way rules must be followed while coding instructions, just as grammatical rules must be followed in English.

System command A command used by the programmer to communicate with the operating system of the computer.

Table See Two-dimensional array.

Terminal format file See Sequential file.

Text files What the Apple system calls data files.

Tracks Concentric circles on the surface of a disk.

Trailer value A value added to the end of a data list to indicate that a loop should stop executing.

Two-dimensional array The arrangement of data in a table consisting of rows and two or more columns.

Unconditional transfer Another name for a GOTO statement. A statement that changes the flow of execution every time it is executed (unconditionally).

Unsubscripted variable Simple variables that use no subscripts, such as N1.

Variable A numerical or string value that can change during the execution of the program.

Variable name The name the programmer assigns to data stored in the computer's memory whose value can change as the program is executed.

BASIC Index

Glossary

Access mechanism The physical device that positions the read/write head of a direct-access device over a particular track.

Accounting machine Mechanically operated forerunner of the computer; could read data from punched cards, perform calculations, rearrange data, and print results in varied formats.

Acoustic coupler modem A device used in telecommunications that is attached to a computer by a cable and that connects to a telephone when a standard contoured telephone receiver is placed on two rubber cups that are built into the device.

Activity The proportion of records processed during an update run.

Address A unique identifier assigned to each memory location within primary storage.

Algorithm A set of well-defined instructions for the solution of a problem in a finite number of steps.

American Standard Code for Information Interchange (ASCII) A 7-bit standard code used for information interchange among data-processing systems, communication systems, and associated equipment.

Analog computer A computer that measures continuous electrical or physical conditions rather than operating on digits; contrast with digital computer.

Analog transmission Transmission of data over communication channels in a continuous wave form.

Analytical engine Machine designed by Charles Babbage, capable of addition, subtraction, multiplication, division, and storage of intermediate results in a memory unit; too advanced for its time, the analytical engine was forgotten for nearly one hundred years.

APL (A Programming Language) A terminal-oriented, symbolic programming language especially suitable for interactive problem solving.

Application program A sequence of instructions written to solve a specific user problem.

Arithmetic/logic unit (ALU) The section of the processor or CPU that handles arithmetic computations and logical operations.

Artificial intelligence (AI) Field of research currently developing techniques whereby computers can be used to solve problems that appear to require imagination, intuition, or intelligence.

ASCII-8 An 8-bit version of ASCII developed for computers that require 8-bit, rather than 7-bit codes.

Assembler program Translator program for an assembly language program; produces a machine language program (object program); also called assembler.

Assembly language Lower-level, symbolic programming language that uses abbreviations rather than groupings of 0s and 1s.

Atanasoff-Berry Computer (ABC) First electronic digital computer; developed by John Vincent Atanasoff and Clifford Berry.

Audio input See Voice recognition system.

Audio output See Voice response unit.

Automatic data processing (ADP) The collection, manipulation, and dissemination of data by electromechanical machines to attain specified objectives.

Automatic teller machine (ATM) Remote terminal that allows bank customers to make transactions with the bank's central computer; user can check account balances, transfer funds, make deposits, withdrawals, and loan payments, and so forth.

Auxiliary storage Also known as external storage or secondary storage; supplements primary storage but operates at slower speeds.

Back-end processor A small CPU serving as an interface between a large CPU and a large data base stored on a direct-access storage device.

Bandwidth Also known as grade; the range, or width, of the frequencies available for transmission on a given channel.

Bar-code reader A device used to read a bar code by means of reflected light, such as a scanner that reads the Universal Product Code on supermarket products.

BASIC (Beginners' All-purpose Symbolic Instruction Code) A high-level programming language commonly used for interactive problem solving by users who may not be professional programmers.

Batch file access An access method in which all transactions are accumulated for a given period of time and then processed all at once.

Batch processing A method of processing data in which data items are collected and forwarded to the computer in a group; normally uses punched cards or magnetic tape for generating periodic output, e.g. payroll.

Baud A unit used to measure transmission speeds.

Binary number system Number system used in computer operations that uses the digits 0 and 1 and has a base of 2; corresponds to the two possible states in machine circuitry—"on" and "off."

Binary representation Use of a two-state, or binary, system to represent data; as in setting and resetting the electrical state of semiconductor memory to either 0 or 1.

Biochip In theory, a chip whose circuits will be built from the proteins and enzymes of living matter such as *E. coli* bacteria.

Biomechanics Application of engineering methodologies to biological systems.

Bit (short for BInary digiT) The smallest unit of information that can be represented in binary notation.

Bit cells The name for storage locations in semiconductors.

Blocked records (blocks) Records grouped on magnetic tape or magnetic disk to reduce the number of interrecord gaps and more fully utilize the storage medium.

Blocks See Blocked records.

Boilerplating Placing the same word, phrase, or block of text in several documents.

Branch Program logic used to bypass or alter the normal flow of execution.

Broad-band channels Communication channels that can transmit data at rate of up to 120,000 bits per second; for example, laser beams and microwaves.

Bubble memory A memory medium in which data is represented by magnetized spots (magnetic domains) resting on a thin film of semiconductor material.

Bundled A way of selling computers in which the price includes training, maintenance costs, software, and other related products and services.

Bus A physical path along which data or control signals travel within a computer system.

Bus configuration A local area network (LAN) in which multiple stations connected to a communication cable can communicate directly with any other station on the line.

Byte A fixed number of adjacent bits operated on as a unit.

C A programming language that approaches assembly language in the efficiency of its object code, yet offers some of the same features of high-level language; sometimes referred to as a middle-level language.

Cache memory Also known as a high-speed buffer; a working buffer or temporary area used in primary storage to help speed the execution of a program.

Calculate To manipulate data by arithmetic or logical processes.

Capacitor The device that holds the electrical charge within a bit cell of semiconductor memory.

Cathode ray tube (CRT) A visual display device that receives electrical impulses and translates them into a picture on a television-like screen.

Cell The unique location with an electronic spreadsheet where a row and a column intersect.

Central processing unit (CPU) Acts as the "brain" of the computer; composed of three sections—arithmetic/logic unit (ALU), control unit and primary storage unit.

Centralized design An information structure in which a separate data-processing department is used to provide data-processing facilities for the entire organization.

Chain The logical path linking records according to one common field.

Chain printer An output device that has the character set engraved in type and assembled in a chain that revolves horizontally past all print positions; prints when a print hammer (one for each column of the paper) presses the paper against an inked ribbon that presses against the characters on the print chain.

Charge-coupled device (CCD) A storage device made of silicon; nearly 100 times faster than bubble memory devices.

Check digit An additional bit determined by performance of some calculation on the code; used to catch input errors.

Chief programmer team (CPT) A method of organization and evaluation used in managing system projects by which a chief programmer supervises the programming and testing of program modules; programmer productivity and program reliability are increased.

Classify To categorize data according to certain characteristics so that they are meaningful to the user.

Clock speed The number of electronic pulses a microprocessor can produce each second.

COBOL (COmmon Business-Oriented Language) A high-level programming language generally used for accounting and business data processing.

Code To translate data into machine-readable form so they can be entered into the computer system.

Collect To gather data from various sources and assemble them at one location.

Command area The area at the bottom of some electronic spreadsheets that displays the available commands to the user.

Commercial data base A collection of information accessible over communication lines to paying subscribers; also called information service and information utility.

Communicate To transfer information in intelligible form to a user.

Communication channel A medium for carrying data from one location to another.

Communication software Programs that assist in the transfer of data across communication channels by "tricking" a computer into acting as if a microcomputer terminal is part of that system.

Compatibility The ability to use equipment or software produced by one manufacturer on a computer produced by another manufacturer.

Compatible Descriptive of hardware and/or software that can work together.

Compiler program Translator program for a high-level language such as FORTRAN or COBOL; translates source-program statements into machine-executable code; also called compiler.

Computer General-purpose electronic machine with applications limited only by the creativity of the humans who use it; its power is derived from its speed, accuracy, and memory.

Computer crime Criminal act that poses a threat to those who use computers or is accomplished by using a computer.

Computer ethics Term referring to the standard of moral conduct in computer use; way in which the spirit of the law is applied to computer-related activities.

Computer literacy General knowledge about computers; includes some technical knowledge about hardware and software, the ability to use computers to solve problems, and awareness of how computers affect society.

Computer output microfilm (COM) Miniature digitized photographic images of output placed on magnetic tape, which serves as input to a microfilm processor.

Computer security The technical and administrative safeguards required to protect a computer-based system against physical and nonphysical hazards.

Computer store A retail store that sells microcomputers and is structured to meet the needs of small business and personal computer owners.

Computer-aided design (CAD) Process of designing, drafting, and analyzing a prospective product using computer graphics on a video terminal.

Computer-aided manufacturing (CAM) Use of a computer to simulate or monitor the steps of a manufacturing process.

Computer-assisted instruction (CAI) Use of a computer to instruct or drill a student on an individual or small-group basis.

Computerized axial tomography (CT or CAT) scanning Form of noninvasive physical testing that combines X-ray techniques and computers to aid diagnosis.

Concentrator A device that systematically allocates the use of communication channels among several terminals.

Control program A routine, usually part of an operating system, that helps control the operations and management of a computer system.

Control unit The section of the CPU that directs the sequence of operations by electrical signals and governs the actions of the various units that make up the computer.

Convert To translate information into a form people can read.

Coprocessor A microprocessor that can be plugged into a microcomputer to replace or work with the microcomputer's original microprocessor.

Counter A value in a program that indicates the number of times a loop is to be executed; the value is tested each time the loop is executed and when the stated value is reached, the loop is terminated.

Crash conversion Also known as direct conversion; a system implementation approach in which the old system is completely abandoned and the new one implemented at once.

Cursor A flashing character on a computer display screen that shows where the next typed character will appear.

Daisy-wheel printer An output device resembling an office typewriter; it employs a flat disk with petal-like projections, each having a character at its tip; printing occurs one character at a time.

Data Facts; the raw material of information.

Data base Collection of data that are commonly defined and consistently organized to fit the information needs of a wide variety of users in an organization.

Data communication The electronic transmission of data from one site to another usually over communication channels such as telephone/telegraph lines or microwaves.

Data manager/data-management package An application software package that computerizes the everyday tasks of recording and filing information.

Data processing A systematic set of procedures for collecting, manipulating, and disseminating data to achieve specified objectives.

Data structures The relationships between the data elements in a computer file.

Data-base analyst The person responsible for the analysis, design, and implementation of the data base.

Data-base management system A set of programs that serves as the interface between the data base and the programmer, operating system, and users.

Debugging The process of locating, isolating, and resolving errors within a program.

Decentralized design An information structure in which the authority and responsibility for computer support are placed in relatively autonomous organizational operating units.

Decimal number system A number system based on the powers of 10.

Decision logic table (DLT) A table that depicts the logic used to arrive at a particular decision given a certain set of circumstances.

Decision support system (DSS) An information system that provides information used to support unstructured managerial decision making.

Dedicated word-processing system A computer system designed solely for word processing.

Deletion A feature of a program that allows removal of

characters, data, words, sentences, or blocks of text.

Demodulation   The process of retrieving data from a modulated carrier wave.

Desk-checking   A method used in both system and application program debugging in which the sequence of operations is mentally traced to verify the correctness of the processing logic.

Detail diagram   Diagram used in HIPO to describe the specific function performed and data items used in a module.

Difference engine   Machine designed by Charles Babbage in 1822 to compute mathematical tables with results up to five significant digits in length (In Babbage's time, the word *engine* meant invention).

Digital computer   Type of computer commonly used in business applications; operates on distinct data (for example, digits) by performing arithmetic and logic processes on specific data units.

Digital transmission   The transmission of data as distinct "on"/"off" pulses.

Direct access   Method of processing in which data are submitted to the computer as they occur, and located, retrieved, and updated without reading all preceding data.

Direct-access file design   Records are organized in a file in any order, with record keys providing the only way to access data.

Direct-access storage   A method of storing data whereby the data can be retrieved in any order, at random.

Direct-access storage device (DASD)   Auxiliary storage device that allows data to be stored and accessed either randomly or sequentially.

Direct-connection modem   A device used in telecommunications that is attached to a computer by a cable and which connects directly to a telephone line by plugging into a standard phone jack.

Directory   Contains record keys and their corresponding addresses; used to obtain the address of a record with a direct-access file design.

Disk address   The method used to uniquely identify a data record on a magnetic disk; consists of the disk surface number, the track number, and the record number.

Disk drive   The mechanical device used to rotate a disk pack during data transmission; common speeds range between 40 and 1,000 revolutions per second.

Disk pack   A stack of magnetic disks.

Distributed data processing (DDP) system   A system in which data processing is done at a site other than that of the central computer.

Distributed design   An information structure in which independent operating units have some data-processing facilities but there is still central control and coordination of computer resources.

Document-oriented word processor   A word processor that treats a text file as a single document, rather than as a series of pages.

Dot-matrix printer   A type of impact printer that creates characters through the use of dot-matrix patterns.

Downtime   The time a system is not working because of equipment problems.

Drum printer   An output device consisting of a metal cylinder that contains rows of characters engraved across its surface; one line of print is produced with each rotation of the drum.

Dumb terminal   A terminal that cannot be programmed.

Dummy module   A temporary program module inserted at a lower level to facilitate testing of the higher-level modules; used in top-down design to enable higher-level program modules to be coded prior to completion of lower-level modules.

Dump   A hard-copy printout of the contents of computer memory; valuable when debugging programs.

EDSAC (*Electronic Delay Storage Automatic Computer*)   Developed in England; the first stored-program computer.

EDVAC (*Electronic Discrete Variable Automatic Computer*)   A stored-program computer developed at the University of Pennsylvania.

EEPROM (*Electrically Erasable Programmable Read-Only Memory*)   A form of read-only memory chip that can be reprogrammed with special electrical pulses while remaining inside the computer.

Electronic data processing (EDP)   Data processing performed largely by electronic equipment, such as computers, rather than by manual or mechanical methods.

Electronic funds transfer (EFT)   Cashless method of managing money; accounts involved in a transaction are adjusted by electronic communication between computers.

Electronic mail   Transmission of messages at high speeds over telecommunication facilities.

Electronic spreadsheet   An electronic ledger sheet used to store and manipulate any type of numerical data.

Electrostatic printer   A nomimpact printer in which electromagnetic impulses and heat are used to affix characters to paper.

Electrothermal printer   A nonimpact printer that uses special heat-sensitive paper; characters are formed when heated rods in a matrix touch the paper.

ENIAC (*Electronic Numerical Integrator And Calculator*)   First general-purpose electronic digital computer; developed by John W. Mauchly and J. Presper Eckert Jr. at the University of Pennsylvania.

EPROM (*Erasable Programmable Read-Only Memory*)   A form of read-only memory that can be erased and reprogrammed, but only by being submitted to a special process such as exposure to ultraviolet light.

Even parity   A method of coding in which an even number of 1 bits represent each character; used to increase the detection of errors.

Expert system   Form of artificial intelligence software that imitates the same decision-making processes of experts on a specific field.

Extended Binary Coded Decimal Interchange Code (EBCDIC)   An 8-bit code for character representation.

Family of computers Mainframes of differing sizes built by the same manufacturer and having the same processor.

Feedback A check within a system to see whether predetermined goals are being met.

Fiber optics A data transmission concept using laser pulses and cables made of tiny threads of glass that can transmit huge amounts of data at the speed of light.

Field A meaningful item of data, such as a social security number or a person's name.

File A grouping of related records, such as all student records; sometimes referred to as a data set.

File handler A data-management application package capable of operating on only one file at a time.

First-generation computers Computers that used vacuum tubes; developed in the 1950s; much faster than earlier mechanical devices, but very slow in comparison to today's computer.

Fixed scanner An input device used to scan and read source data in bar-code form or in human-readable form.

Fixed-length records A record format in which a maximum number of character positions are assigned.

Flexibility The degree to which a computer system can be adapted or tailored to the changing requirements of the user.

Flexible disk A low-cost, random-access form of data storage made of plastic; a flexible magnetic disk currently made in 3½-, 5¼-, and 8-inch diameter sizes; also called diskette or floppy disk.

Flowchart A graphic representation in which symbols represent the flow, operations, logic, data, and equipment of a program or system; a program flowchart illustrates the structure and sequence in a program and a system flowchart illustrates the components and the flow of data through an entire system; also called a block diagram or logic diagram.

Flowlines The lines that connect flowchart symbols.

FORTH A middle-level programming language that offers advantages of assembly language and high-level languages.

FORTRAN (FORmula TRANslator) A high-level programming language used primarily for programming mathematical, scientific, or engineering operations.

4-bit Binary Coded Decimal (BCD) A 4-bit computer code that uses 4-bit groupings to represent digits in decimal numbers.

Fourth-generation computers Computers that use chips made by large-scale integration and offer significant price and performance improvements over earlier computers.

Front-end processor A small CPU serving as an interface between a large CPU and peripheral devices.

Full-duplex A type of communication channel through which data can be transmitted in both directions simultaneously.

Fully distributed network configuration A network design in which every set of nodes in the network can communicate directly with every other set of nodes through a single communication link.

Gallium arsenide chip A chip made with gallium arsenide, a material that requires lower voltage, generates less heat, and operates much faster than computer chips made from silicon.

Garbage in-garbage out Phrase illustrating the fact that the meaningfulness of computer output relies on the accuracy or relevancy of the data fed into the processor.

General-purpose computers Computers that can be used for a variety of purposes.

Grade See Bandwidth.

Graphic display device A visual display device that projects output in the form of graphs and line drawings and accepts input from a keyboard or light pen.

Graphics software package Application software package designed to allow the user to display images on the display screen or printer.

Graphics tablet A flat board-like object, that when drawn on, transfers the image to a computer screen.

Grid chart A chart used in system analysis to summarize the relationships between the components of a system.

Half-duplex A type of communication channel through which data can be transmitted in both directions, but in only one direction at a time.

Hard copy Printed output.

Hardware Physical components that make up a computer system.

Hexadecimal number system A base 16 number system commonly used when printing the contents of primary storage to aid programmers in detecting errors.

Hierarchical configuration A network design for multiple CPUs, in which an organization's needs are divided into multiple levels that receive different levels of computer support.

Hierarchical data structure Also called tree structure; the data structure in which one primary data element may have numerous secondary data elements linked to it at lower levels.

Hierarchical design An information structure in which each level within an organization has necessary computer power; responsibility for control and coordination goes to the top level.

High-level programming languages Englishlike coding schemes that are either procedure-, problem-, or user-oriented.

HIPO (Hierarchy plus Input-Process-Output) A documentation or design technique used to describe the inputs, processing, and outputs of program modules.

Hollerith code Method of data representation named for the man who invented it; delineates numbers, letters, and special characters by the placement of holes in 80-column punched cards.

Horizontal software integration The combining of two or more software applications into one package that can share data.

Impact printer A printer that forms characters by physically striking a ribbon against paper.

Indexed-sequential file design Records organized

sequentially and also listed in an index; allows for both sequential and direct-access processing.

Information   Data that has been organized and processed so it is meaningful.

Ink-jet printer   A nonimpact printer that uses a stream of charged ink to form dot-matrix characters.

Input   Data submitted to the computer for processing.

Input/output management system   A subsystem of the operating system that controls and coordinates the CPU while receiving input from channels, executing instructions of programs in storage, and regulating output.

Insertion   A feature of a program that allows characters, words, sentences, or blocks of text to be inserted into a document.

Instruction set   The fundamental logical and arithmetic procedures that the computer can perform, such as addition, subtraction, and comparison.

Integrated circuit   An electronic circuit etched on a small silicon chip less than 1/8-inch square, permitting much faster processing than with transistors and at a greatly reduced price.

Integrated software   Two or more application programs that work together to allow easy movement of data between the applications; they also use a common group of commands among all of the applications.

Intelligent terminal   A terminal with an internal processor that can be programmed to perform specified functions, such as data editing, data conversion, and control of other terminals.

Interactive processing   A data-processing method where the user enters input via a keyboard during processing.

Interactive   Descriptive of computer languages that allow the programmer or program user to communicate directly with the computer in a conversational fashion.

Interactive video   A multimedia learning concept that merges computer text, sound, and graphics by using a videodisk, videodisk player, microcomputer with monitor and disk drive, and computer software.

Interblock gap (IBG)   A space on magnetic tape that facilitates processing; records are grouped together and then separated by interblock gaps.

Internal modem   A modem built into the internal circuitry of a computer; no external cables or connections are needed.

Interpreter program   High-level language translator that evaluates and translates a program one statement at a time; used extensively on microcomputer systems because it takes less primary storage than a compiler; also called interpreter.

Interrecord gap (IRG)   A space that separates records stored on magnetic tape; allows the tape drive to regain speed during processing.

Inverted list   A list that has an index for every field in a file

Job-control language (JCL)   A language that serves as the communication link between the programmer and the computer operating system.

Job-control program   A control program that translates the job-control statements written by a programmer into machine-language instructions that can be executed by the computer.

Josephson junction   A primary storage unit that, when completed, will be housed in liquid helium to reduce the resistance to the flow of electricity that currently exists in semiconductor memory.

K (kilobyte)   Symbol used to represent 1,024 (2^{10}) storage units (1024 bytes) when referring to a computer's main memory; often rounded to 1,000 bytes.

Key   The unique identifier or field of a record; used to sort records for processing or to locate specific records within a file.

Keypunch   A keyboard device that punches holes in a card to represent data.

Key-to-disk   Hardware designed to transfer data entered via a keyboard to magnetic (hard) disk.

Key-to-diskette   Hardware designed to transfer data entered via a keyboard to a floppy disk instead of the conventional (hard) disk.

Key-to-tape   Hardware designed to transfer data entered via a keyboard to magnetic tape.

Language-translator program   Software that translates English like programs written by programmers into machine-executable code.

Large-scale integration (LSI)   Method by which circuits containing thousands of electronic components are densely packed in a single silicon chip.

Laser printer   A type of nonimpact printer that combines laser beams and electrophotographic technology to form images on paper.

Laser storage system   A secondary storage device using laser technology to encode data onto a metallic surface; most often used for mass storage.

Librarian program   Software that manages the storage and use of library programs by maintaining a directory of programs in the system library and appropriate procedures for additions and deletions.

Library program   A user-written or manufacturer-supplied program or subroutine that is frequently used in other programs to perform a specific function; it is written and stored on secondary storage and called into primary storage when needed.

Light pen   A pen-shaped object with a photoelectric cell at its end; used to draw lines on a visual display screen.

Line editor   A word processing feature that allows operation on only one line of text at a time.

Linkage editor   A subprogram of the operating system that links the object program from the system residence device to primary storage.

Linked list   A file using pointers to maintain the sequence of the records.

Links Transmission channels that connect modes.

LISP (LISt Processing) A high-level programming language commonly used in artificial intelligence research and in processing of lists of elements.

Local-area network (LAN) A specialized network of computers that operates within a limited geographic area, such as a building or complex of buildings, with the stations being linked by cable.

Loop Program logic that causes a series of instructions to be executed repeatedly as long as specified conditions remain constant.

Machine language The only set of instructions that a computer can execute directly; a code that designates the proper electrical states in the computer as combinations of 0s and 1s.

Magnetic core Iron-alloy, doughnut-shaped ring about the size of a pinhead of which memory can be composed; an individual core can store one binary digit (its state is determined by the direction of an electrical current); the cores are strung on a grid of fine wires that carry the current.

Magnetic disk A direct-access storage medium consisting of a metal platter coated on both sides with a magnetic recording material upon which data is stored in the form of magnetized spots.

Magnetic domain A magnetized spot representing data in bubble memory.

Magnetic drum Cylinder with a magnetic outer surface on which data can be stored by magnetizing specific positions on the surface.

Magnetic tape A sequential storage medium consisting of a narrow strip of material treated with a magnetizable coating upon which spots are magnetized to represent data.

Magnetic-ink character reader A device that reads characters composed of magnetized particles; often used to sort checks for subsequent processing.

Magnetic-ink character recognition (MICR) The process that allows magnetized characters to be read by a magnetic-ink character reader.

Main memory See Primary memory/storage.

Main storage See Primary memory/storage.

Mainframe A type of large, full-scale computer capable of supporting many peripherals.

Management information system (MIS) A formal network that uses computers to provide information used to support structured managerial decision making; its goal is to get the correct information to the appropriate manager at the right time.

Mark I First automatic calculator.

Mark sensing See Optical-mark recognition.

Master file A file that contains all existing records organized according to the key field; updated by records in a transaction file.

Megahertz (MHz) One million times per second; the unit of measurement for clock speed.

Memory Part of the computer that stores data.

Memory management/memory protection In a multiprogramming environment, the process of keeping the programs in primary storage separate from each other.

Menu-driven A program design that provides the user with "menus" displaying available choices or selections to help guide the user through the process of using a software package.

Message switching The task of a communications processor of receiving messages and routing them to appropriate destinations.

Microcomputer A smaller, low-priced computer used in homes, schools, and businesses; also called a personal computer or home computer.

Microprocessor A programmable processing unit (placed on a silicon chip) containing arithmetic, logic, and control circuitry; used in microcomputers, calculators, microwave ovens, and for many other applications.

Microprogram A sequence of instructions wired into read-only memory; used to tailor a system to meet the user's specific processing requirements.

Minicomputer A type of computer with the components of a full-sized system but with smaller primary storage capacity.

Mnemonics Symbolic names or memory aids used in assembly language and high-level programming language.

Model A representation of a real-world system; used to construct a DSS to help managers make decisions.

Modeling package An application software program that uses the power and speed of a computer to simulate a real world situation.

Modem A device that modulates and demodulates signals transmitted over communication lines.

Modular approach A method of simplifying a project by breaking it into segments or subunits.

Modulation A technology used in modems to make data processing signals compatible with communication facilities.

Module Part of a whole; a program segment or subsystem; set of logically related program statements that perform one given task in a program.

Mouse A desk-top input device that controls cursor movement, allowing the user to bypass the keyboard.

Move A feature of a program that allows an entire block of text to be shifted from one location to another.

Multiphasic health testing (MPHT) Computer-assisted testing plan that compiles data on patients and their test results, which are compared with norms or means to aid the physician in making a diagnosis.

Multiplexer A device that permits more than one I/O device to transmit data over the same communication channel.

Multiprocessing A multiple CPU configuration in which jobs are processed simultaneously.

Multiprogramming A technique that places several programs in primary storage at the same time, giving the illusion that they are being executed simultaneously; this results in increased CPU active time.

Narrow bandwidth channel A communication channel that can only transmit data at a rate of 45 to 90 baud; for example, telegraph channels.

Natural language/query language A language, designed primarily for novice computer users, that uses Englishlike sentences, usually for the purpose of accessing data in a data base.

Network The linking together of several CPUs.

Network data structure The data structure in which a primary data element may have many secondary elements and the secondary elements may have numerous primary elements.

Next-sequential-instruction feature The ability of a computer to execute program steps in the order in which they are stored in memory unless branching takes place.

Node The endpoint of a network; consists of CPUs, printers, CRTs, and other physical devices.

Nondestructive read/destructive write The feature of computer memory that permits data to be read and retained in its original state, allowing repeated reference during processing.

Nondestructive testing (NDT) Testing done electronically to avoid breaking, cutting, or tearing apart a product to find a problem.

Nonimpact printer The use of heat, laser technology, or photographic techniques to print output.

Nuclear magnetic resonance (NMR) A computerized diagnostic tool that involves sending magnetic pulses through the body to identify medical problems.

Numeric bits The four rightmost bit positions of 6-bit BCD used to encode numeric data.

Object program A sequence of machine-executable instructions derived from source-program statements by a language-translator program.

Octal number system Number system in which each position represents a power of 8.

Odd parity A method of coding in which an odd number of 1 bits is used to represent each character; facilitates error checking.

Office automation Integration of computer and communication technology with traditional office procedures to increase productivity and efficiency.

Offline Not in direct communication with the central computer.

Online In direct communication with the computer.

Online file access An access method in which records are updated when transactions are made; current information can be retrieved at any time.

Online storage symbol A symbol that indicates that the file is kept on an online external storage medium such as disk or tape.

Operand The part of an instruction that tells the computer where to find the data or equipment on which to operate.

Operating system (OS) A collection of programs used by the computer to manage its operations; provides an interface between the user or application program and the computer hardware.

Operation code Also known as op code; the part of an instruction that indicates what operation is to be performed.

Optical disk Also known as a laser disk; stores data as the presence or absence of a pit burned into the surface of the disk by a laser beam.

Optical-character recognition (OCR) A method of electronic scanning that reads numbers, letters, and other characters and then converts the optical images into appropriate electrical signals.

Optical-mark page reader A device that senses marks on an OMR document as the document passes under a light source.

Optical-mark recognition (OMR) Mark sensing; a method of electronic scanning that reads marks on a page and converts the optical images into appropriate electrical signals.

Output Information that comes from the computer as a result of processing into a form that can be used by people.

Overview diagram A diagram used in HIPO to describe in greater detail a module shown in the visual table of contents.

Page In a virtual storage environment, the portion of a program that is kept in secondary storage and loaded into real storage only when needed during processing.

Page frame In a virtual storage environment, one of the equal-sized physical areas into which primary storage is divided.

Page-oriented word processor A word processor that treats a document as a series of pages; contrast to document-oriented word processor.

Paging A method of implementing virtual storage; data and programs are broken into equal-sized blocks, or pages, and loaded into real storage when needed during processing.

Parallel conversion An approach to system implementation in which the new system is operated side-by-side with the old one until all problems are worked out.

Parallel processing A type of processing in which instructions and data are handled simultaneously.

Parent The primary data element in a data structure.

Parity bit A bit added to detect incorrect transmission of data; it conducts internal checks to determine whether the correct number of bits are present.

Partition In multiprogramming, the primary storage area reserved for one program; may be fixed or variable in size; see also Region.

Pascal A high-level language developed for education purposes, to teach programming concepts to students; named after French mathematician Blaise Pascal.

Peripheral device Device that attaches to the central processing unit, such as a secondary storage device or an input-output device.

Phased conversion An approach to system implementation in which parts of the new system are implemented throughout the organization one at a time.

Pilot conversion An approach to system implementation in which the new system is implemented in only one part of the organization at a time.

Piracy The unauthorized copy of a copyrighted computer program.

Pixel The individual dot on a display screen that is combined with other dots to create characters and images.

PL/1 (Programming Language One) A structured, general-purpose programming language used for both scientific and business applications.

Plotter An output device that converts data emitted from the CPU into graphic form; produces hard-copy output.

Pointer An additional field in a record that contains the address of the next record to be accessed.

Point-of-sale (POS) terminal Computerized system that records data for such tasks as inventory control and accounting at the location where goods are sold.

Primary key A unique field for a record; used to sort records for processing or to locate a particular record within a file.

Primary memory/storage Also known as internal storage or main storage; the section of the computer that holds instructions, data, and intermediate and final results during processing.

Print formatting The manner in which the word processor communicates with the printer to tell it how the text should be printed.

Printer A device used to produce permanent (hard copy) computer output; impact printers are designed to work mechanically; nonimpact printers use heat, laser, or chemical technology.

Printer keyboard An output device similar to an office typewriter; prints one character at a time and is controlled by a program stored in the CPU of the computer.

Print-wheel printer An output device consisting of 120 print wheels, each containing 48 characters. The print wheels rotate until an entire line is in the appropriate position, then a hammer presses the paper against the print wheel.

Privacy An individual's ability to control the collection, processing, storage, dissemination, and use of data about personal attributes and activities.

Process To transform data into useful information (by classifying, sorting, calculating, summarizing, storing).

Processing program A routine, usually part of an operating system, used to simplify program preparation and execution.

Processor The term used to refer collectively to the ALU and control unit.

Program A series of step-by-step instructions that tells the computer exactly what to do; of two types, application and system.

Programmable communications processor A device that relieves the CPU of the task of monitoring data transmission.

Programmer The person who writes step-by-step instructions for the computer to execute.

PROM (Programmable Read-Only Memory) Read-only memory that can be programmed by the manufacturer or by the user for special functions to meet the unique needs of the user.

Propagation delay A time delay in a satellite communication system.

Proper program A program using the structured approach and top-down design, and having only one entrance and one exit.

Pseudocode An informal, narrative language used to represent the logic patterns of structured programming.

Punched cards Heavy paper storage medium in which data is represented by holes punched according to a coding scheme much like that used on Hollerith's cards.

RAM disk A portion of RAM memory that is temporarily turned into a storage device through software control; it appears like a disk to the computer but is not actually a disk.

Random-access memory (RAM) Form of primary storage into which instructions and data can be read, written and erased; directly accessed by the computer; temporary memory that is erased when the computer is turned off.

Randomizing (hashing) A mathematical process applied to the record key that produces the storage address of the record.

Read-only memory (ROM) The part of computer hardware containing items (circuitry patterns) that cannot be deleted or altered by stored-program instructions.

Read/write head An electromagnet used as a component of a tape or disk drive; in reading, it detects magnetized areas and translates them into electrical pulses; in writing, it magnetizes appropriate areas, thereby erasing data stored previously.

Real storage Primary storage; contrast with virtual storage.

Real time Descriptive of a system's capability to receive and process data, providing output fast enough to control the outcome of an activity.

Record A collection of data items, or fields, that relates to a single unit, such as a student.

Region In multiprogramming with a variable number of tasks, a term often used to mean the internal space allocated; a variable-sized partition.

Register An internal computer component used for temporary storage of an instruction or data; capable of accepting, holding, and transferring that instruction or data very rapidly.

Relational data structure The data structure that places the data elements in a table with rows representing records and columns representing fields.

Remote network A system where terminals are connected to the central computer by a communication channel.

Remote terminal A terminal that is placed at a location distant from the central computer.

Resident routine One of the most frequently used components of the supervisor, which is initially loaded into primary storage.

Retrieve To access previously stored data.

Ring configuration A network design in which a number of computers are connected by a single transmission line in a ring formation.

Ring list A linked list containing pointer fields indicating the end of a chain; the last record contains a pointer back to the first record.

Robot Machine that performs any of several tasks (such as moving or manipulating materials, parts, or tools) under stored-program control.

RPG (Report Program Generator) An example of a problem-oriented language originally designed to produce business reports.

Run book Program documentation designed to aid the computer operator in running a program; also known as the operator's manual.

Screen editor A word-processing feature that allows the text on the entire screen to be edited.

Screen formatting Word-processing features that control the way in which text appears on the display screen.

Scrolling The process of moving a portion of a text file on to or off of the display screen; used to view portions of a document.

Search A feature of a program that permits the user to locate a word or set of characters throughout a file.

Second-generation computers Computers that used transistors; smaller, faster, and had larger storage capacity than first-generation computers.

Secondary key Fields that are used to gain access to records on a file; may not be unique identifiers.

Secondary storage Also known as external or auxiliary storage; supplements primary storage and is external to the computer; data is accessed at slower speeds.

Segmentation A method of implementing virtual storage; involves dividing a program into variable-sized blocks, called segments, depending on the program logic.

Selection Program logic that includes a test; depending on the results of the test, one of two paths is taken.

Semiconductor memory Memory composed of circuitry on silicon chips.

Sequential file Data (records) stored in specific order, one right after the other.

Sequential file design Records that are organized in a file in a specific order based on the value of the key field.

Sequential processing The process of creating a new master file each time transactions are processed; requires batch file access.

Sequential-access storage Auxiliary storage from which records must be read, one after another, in a fixed sequence, until the needed data is relocated; for example, magnetic tape.

Service bureaus A business that provides data-processing services such as system development and computer operations.

Silicon chip Solid-logic circuitry on a small piece of silicon used to form the primary storage of third-generation computers.

Simple list A file without pointers.

Simple sequence Program logic in which one statement after another is executed in the order in which they are stored.

Simplex A type of communication channel that provides for unidirectional, or one-way, transmission of data.

Simulation Duplication of conditions likely to occur in a real-world situation when variables are changed.

6-bit binary coded decimal A data representation scheme that is used to represent the decimal digits 0 through 9, the letters A through Z, and 28 special characters.

Soft copy Data displayed on a CRT screen; not a permanent record.

Software Program or programs used to direct the computer for solving problems and overseeing operations.

Software compatibility The ability to use programs written for one system on another system with little or no change.

Sort To arrange data elements into a predetermined sequence to aid processing.

Sort/merge program A utility program used to sort records to facilitate updating and subsequent combining of files to form a single, updated file.

Source program A sequence of instructions written in either assembly language or high-level language that is translated into an object program.

Source-data automation The use of special equipment to collect data at its point of origin.

Spatial digitizer An input device that can graphically reconstruct a three-dimensional object on the computer display screen.

Spreadsheet Also known as a ledger sheet; used by accountants for performing financial calculations and recoding transactions.

Star configuration A network design in which all transactions must go through a central computer before being routed to the appropriate network computer.

Status area A portion of an electronic spreadsheet that appears at the top of the display and shows the location of the cursor within the spreadsheet and what was entered into a particular cell of the spreadsheet.

Storage register The register that holds information being sent to or taken from the primary storage unit.

Store To retain processed data for future reference.

Stored program Instructions stored in the computer's primary memory in electronic form; can be executed repeatedly at the computer's own speed.

Stored-program computer Computer that stores in main memory instructions in electronic form for operations to be performed.

Stored-program concept The idea that program instructions can be stored in primary storage (computer memory) in electronic form so that no human intervention is required during processing; allows the computer to process the instructions at its own speed.

Structure chart A graphic representation of top-down programming, displaying modules of the problem solution and relationships between modules; of two types—system and process.

Structured flowchart Graphic representation of the logic patterns depicting the function of a program or module; the diagram is compactly arranged in a partioned box; also called Nassi-Shneiderman chart.

Structured programming A top-down modular approach to programming that emphasizes dividing a program into logical sections to reduce testing time, increase programmer productivity, and bring clarity to programming.

Structured walkthrough A formal evaluation of the documentation and coding of a program or system by a group of managers, analysts, and programmers to determine completeness, accuracy, and quality of design.

Subroutine A sequence of statements outside the main part of the program; saves the programmer time by not having to write the same instructions over again in different parts of the program.

Subscripts The row and column numbers that identify the location of a data element in a table.

Summarize To reduce large amounts of data to a more concise and usable form.

Supercomputer The largest, fastest, most expensive type of computer in existence, capable of performing millions of calculations per second and processing enormous amounts of data; also called maxicomputer or monster computer.

Supervisor program Also known as the monitor or executive; the major component of the operating system; coordinates the activities of all other parts of the operating system.

Swapping In a virtual storage environment, the process of transferring a program section from virtual storage to real storage, and vice versa.

Syntax Rules of a programming language that must be followed when coding instructions, just as syntactical rules must be followed in English.

System A group of related elements that work together toward a common goal.

System analysis report A report given to top management after the system analysis phase has been completed; includes a statement of objectives, constraints, and possible alternatives.

System analyst The person who is responsible for system analysis, design, and implementation of computer-based information systems and who is the communication link or interface between users and technical persons.

System design report A report given to top management after the system design phase that explains how various designs will satisfy the information requirements; includes flowcharts, narratives, resources required to implement alternatives, and recommendations.

System flowchart A group of symbols that represents the general information flow within an information system; focuses on inputs and outputs rather than on internal computer operations.

System library A collection of files in which various parts of an operating system are stored.

System program A sequence of instructions written to coordinate the operation of computer circuitry and to help the computer run quickly and efficiently.

System residence device An auxiliary storage medium (disk, tape, or drum) on which operating system programs are stored and from which they are loaded into primary storage.

Tape cassette A sequential-access storage medium (similar to a cassette used in audio recording) used in small computer systems for high-density digital recording.

Tape drive A device that moves tape past a read/write head.

Telecommunications The combined use of communication facilities, such as telephone systems and data-processing equipment.

Telecommuting Method of working at home by communicating via electronic machines and telecommunication facilities.

Teleconference Method of conducting meetings between two or more remote locations via electronic and/or image-producing facilities.

Template A predefined set of formulas for use on an electronic spreadsheet.

Terminal An input/output device through which data can be input to or output from a system.

Terminal software See Communication software.

Text editing The process of making changes to a document after the text has been entered into the computer.

Third-generation computers Computers characterized by the use of integrated circuits, reduced size, lower costs, and increased speed and reliability.

Thrashing A situation in virtual storage in which little processing occurs in comparison to the amount of locating and swapping of pages or segments.

Time-sharing An arrangement in which two or more users can access the same central computer resources and receive what seems to be simultaneous results.

Top-down design A method of defining a solution from general to specific in terms of major functions to be performed, and further breaking down the major functions into subfunctions; the further the breakdown, the greater the detail.

Touch screen A computer screen that can detect the point at which it is touched by the user; it allows the user to bypass the keyboard.

Touch-tone device A type of terminal used with ordinary telephone lines to transmit data.

Track A horizontal row stretching the length of a magnetic tape on which data can be recorded; one of a series of concentric circles on the surface of a magnetic disk; one of a series of circular bands on a magnetic drum.

Trailer value A value used to control loop execution in which a unique item signals the computer to stop performing the loop.

Transaction file A file containing changes to be made to the master file.

Transient routine A supervisor routine that remains in secondary storage with the rest of the operating system.

Transistor An on/off switch connecting the data line to the capacitor; a type of circuitry characteristic of second-generation computers; smaller, faster, and more reliable than vacuum tubes but inferior to third-generation, large-scale integration.

Transponders Small amplifiers located on satellites which receive signals from the earth station and reflect them to the receiving stations.

Transputer A small, complete computer that contains the control unit, arithmetic/logic unit, memory, and communications circuitry and can easily be linked to other transputers to share processing functions.

Unbundled A way of selling computers in which vendor support and training items are priced separately.

Undo A feature of a program that allows the user to recover text that has been accidentally deleted.

UNIVAC I (*UNIVersal Automatic Computer*) One of the first commercial electronic computers; became available in 1951.

Universal Product Code (UPC) Machine-readable code consisting of 30 dark bars and 29 spaces that identify a product and its manufacturer, commonly used on most grocery items.

User friendly Describes computers or software that are easy to use and understand.

User's group An informal group of owners of a particular brand of microcomputer who meet to exchange information about hardware, software, service, and support.

Utility program A program within an operating system that performs a specialized function.

Vacuum tube Light bulb-like device from which almost all air has been removed and through which electricity can pass; often found in old radios and televisions; used in first-generation computers to control internal operations.

Variable A meaningful name assigned by the programmer to storage locations of which the values can change.

Variable-length records A record format in which the unused character spaces are eliminated from the record.

Verify To check the accuracy and completeness of data.

Vertical software integration The enhancement of a single software package. For example, adding a spelling checker to a word processing program.

Very large-scale integration (VLSI) Further miniaturization of integrated circuits, offering even greater improvements in price, performance, and size of computers.

Videodisk Medium of storage, usually optically encoded, on a platter that stores high-quality visual images; read by a videodisk player and often used as a peripheral device with computers.

Virtual storage An extension of multiprogramming in which portions of programs not being used are kept in secondary storage until needed, giving the impression that primary storage is unlimited; contrast with real storage.

Visual display terminal A terminal capable of receiving output on a cathode-ray tube (CRT) and, with special provisions, is capable of transmitting data through a keyboard.

Visual table of contents Similar to a structure chart; each block is given an identification number used as a reference to other HIPO diagrams.

Voice recognition system An input system that allows the user to "train" the computer to understand his or her voice and vocabulary. The user must follow only the patterns the computer is programmed to recognize.

Voice response unit A device through which the computer "speaks" by arranging half-second records of voice sounds or prerecorded words.

Voice-grade channel A communication channel that has a wider frequency range and can transmit data at a rate of forty-five to ninety bits per second; for example, a telegraph channel.

Volatility The frequency of changes made to a file during a certain period of time.

Wafer integration The concept of retaining the circuitry on the five-inch silicon chip, rather than breaking the individual chips off the wafer and then packaging and relinking them.

Wand reader An input device used in reading source data represented in optical bar-code form or in human-readable characters.

Window (window environment) An operating system enhancement that allows more than one application software package to run concurrently.

Wire-matrix printer See Dot-matrix printer.

Word A memory location within primary storage; varies in size (number of bits) from computer to computer.

Word processing The manipulation of text data to achieve a desired output.

Word processor An application software package that performs text-editing functions.

Word processing system The computer system (hardware and software), or portion of the system, used for the task of word processing.

Word wrap A feature of a program that automatically positions text so that full words are positioned within declared margins.

Xerographic printer A type of nonimpact printer that uses printing methods similar to those used in common xerographic copying machines.

Zone bit Used in different combinations with numeric bits to represent numbers, letters, and special characters.

Index

Abacus, 37
Aberdeen Proving Ground, 44
Access mechanism, 152
Accounting machine, 42–43
Acoustic coupler modem, 201
Activity, 180–181
Ada, 354
Address, 85
Aiken, Howard H., 42
Algorithm, 290
Alkoff, Larry, 316
Amdahl, Gene, 55, 62
American Standard Code for Information
    Interchange (ASCII), 100
Analog computer, 71–72
Analog transmission, 200
Analytical engine, 39–40
APL (A Programming Language), 356–357
Apple Computer Inc., 57, 64, 252
Apple Education Foundation, 17
Application program, 330
Ariel, Gideon, 36
Arithmetic/logic unit (ALU), 83–84
Artificial Intelligence (AI), 61, 458; robotics,
    461–463; voice recognition, 459–461
ASCII, 100
ASCII-8, 100
Ashford, Evelyn, 36
Asimov, Isaac, 72
Assembler program, 307
Assembly language, 49, 307, 344–345
Atanasoff, John Vincent, 42–44
Atanasoff-Berry Computer (ABC), 42–44
Audio input, 135, 459–461
Audio output, 135
Automatic data processing (ADP), 74
Automatic teller machine (ATM), 5
Auxiliary storage, 74

Babbage, Charles, 39, 42
Back-end processor, 340
Backus, John, 48, 50

Bandwidth (grade), 205; broad-band, 205;
    narrow, 205; voice-grade, 205
Bar-code reader, 120–122
Bardeen, John, 51–52, 62
BASIC (Beginner's All-purpose Symbolic
    Instruction Code), 352–354, 362
Batch file access, 175–176
Batch processing, 53, 78
Baud, 201–203
Beginner's All-purpose Symbolic Instruction
    Code (BASIC), 352–354, 362
Bell, Gordon, 48
Bell, Gwen, 48
Berman, Jerry, 191
Berry, Clifford, 42
Binary code, See Machine language
Binary number system, 40, 93–95
Binary representation, 93–95
Biochip, 455
Bit, 90
Bit cells, 90–91
Blocked records (blocks), 146–148
Blocks, See Blocked records
Boilerplating, 379
Braittain, Walter, 51–52, 62
Branch logic pattern, 297
Bricklin, Dan, 58, 62
Broad-band channels, 205
Bubble memory, 91
Bundled, 240
Burks, Arthur W., 300
Burroughs Adding Machine Company, 42
Burroughs Corporation, 42
Burroughs, William S., 42
Bus configuration, 211
Byron, Augusta Ada, 40–41, 354
Byte, 100

C, 362–363
Cache memory, 88
CAD (Computer-aided design), 6
Calculate, 76

CAM (Computer-aided manufacturing), 6
Capacitor, 91
Cathode ray tube (CRT), 125
CBA (Computerized biomechanical analysis),
    36
Cell, 387
Central processing unit (CPU), 83–88
Centralized design, 432
Chain, 171
Chain painter, 128
Charge-coupled device (CCD), 157
Check digit, 101
Chief programmer team (CPT), 292–294.
    See also Structured walkthrough
Clark, Arthur C., 204
Classify, 76
Clock speed, 254
COBOL (Common Business-Oriented
    Language), 348–351
Code, 76
Code checking, 100–101
Collect, 76
COM (Computer output microfilm),
    134–135
Command area, 388
Commercial data base, 272; connect time,
    272; flat fee, 272
Commodore Business Machines, Inc., 57,
    63–64, 252
Common Business-Oriented Language
    (COBOL), 348–351
Communicate, 77
Communication channel, 199–200
Communication software, 203
Compact disk, 158
Compatibility, 258
Compatible, 55
Compiler program, 307
CompuServe, 218–219
Computer crime, 22
Computer ethics, 23, 466–467; See also
    Privacy

I-1

Memory management/memory protection, 336
Menu-driven, 416
Message switching, 206
MICR (Magnetic-ink character recognition), 119–120
Microcomputer, 4, 56, 249–280; in business, 439–440; care and maintenance, 278; in communications, 218–219; compatibility, 257–259; computer stores, 276–277; data security, 192–193, 241–243; impact of, 267–277; integrated software for, 397–398; languages for, 368–369; operating system (OS), 255–257; peripherals, 259–264; popularity of, 229; portable/transportable, 264–266; power, 101–103; programs for, 316–318; robots and, 469–470; storage, 162–163, 255; supermicrocomputers, 266–267; telecommunications, 272–275; user's groups, 275–276; uses, 268–270
Microprocessor, 56, 83, 250–251; clock speed, 254; static electricity and, 421; word size, 254
Microprogram, 91–92
Middle-level languages, 362–363. See also Programming language
Minicomputer, 55, 225–230; applications, 226–227; flexibility, 226; software sales, 227
Minsky, Marvin, 61–62
MIS, See Management information system
Mnemonics, 49, 307
Model, 386–387, 437–438
Modeling package, 387
Modem, 200–201, 203; acoustic coupler, 201; direct-connect, 201; full-duplex, 201, half-duplex, 201; internal, 201; simplex, 201
Modular approach, 289
Modulation, 200
Module, 289–290
Monster computer, See Supercomputer
Moore, Charles, 363
Mouse, 136, 260
Move, 379
Multiphasic health testing (MPHT), 14
Multiplexer, 205
Multiprocessing, 336, 340–342
Multiprogramming, 336–337

Napier, John, 37
Napier's Bones, 37, 48
Narrow bandwidth channel, 205
Nassi, Isaac, 301
Nassi-Shneiderman charts, 301–303
National Submicron Facility, 94
National Weather Service, See Computers, weather forecasting

Natural language (query language), 363–365
Network, 206, configuration, 209–211; data structure, 168–169; local-area, 206–208; remote, 206; See also Distributed data processing
Network configuration: bus, 211; fully-distributed, 211; hierarchical, 209–211; ring, 209; star, 209
Network data structure, 168–169
Next-sequential-instruction feature, 85
Nishi, "Kay", 259
NMR (Nuclear magnetic resonance), 15
Node, 209
Nondestructive read/destructive write, 85
Nonimpact printer, 128–131
Norfolk Southern Railway Company, 213–215
Nuclear magnetic resonance (NMR), 15
Number crunching, 458
Numeric bits, 99

Object program, 307
OCR (Optical-character recognition), 122
Octal number system, 95–97
Odd parity, 101
Office automation, 7
Offline, 82
Olsen, Kenneth H., 48
OMR (Optical-mark recognition), 120–122
Online, 82
Online file access, 176
Online storage symbol, 412
Opel, John, 252-253
Operand, 85, 344
Operating system (OS), 55, 331–336; components of, 332–336; control programs, 332–333; processing programs, 334–336; purpose of, 331–332
Operation code, 85, 344
Operator's manual, See Run book
Optical disk, 159
Optical-character recognition (OCR), 122
Optical-mark page reader, 120
Optical-mark recognition (OMR), 120–122
OS, See Operating system
Output, 76–78, 88, 404; new developments, 137–139
Output devices, 125–131; computer output microfilm 134–135; plotters, 132–134; printers, 125–131; special purpose, 131–136
Overlapped processing, 336
Overview diagram, See HIPO

Page, 339
Page frame, 339
Page-oriented word processor, 376
Paging, 339
Parallel conversion, 421

Parallel processing, 456
Parent, 167–168
Parity bit, 100–101
Partition, 336
Pascal, 359–361
Pascal, Blaise, 38–39, 359
Pascaline, 38–39
Peripheral device, 258–264; input/output devices, 259–262; storage media, 262–264
Personal computer, See Microcomputer
Phased conversion, 421–422
Pilot conversion, 421
Piracy, 366–367
Pixel, 390
PL/1 (Programming Language One), 354–356
Plotter, 132–134
Pointer, 171
Point-of-sale (POS) terminal, 123–124
Powers, James, 41
Primary key, 184
Primary memory/storage, 74
Print formatting, 377, 381
Printer, 125–131; daisy-wheel, 127; dot-matrix, 126–127; drum, 128; electrostatic, 129; electrothermal, 129; impact, 126–128; keyboard, 126; laser, 130–131; print-wheel, 127–128; wire-matrix, 126–127; xerographic, 131
Printer keyboard, 126
Print-wheel printer, 127–128
Privacy: issue of, 19–22, 191; in law enforcement, 13, 191; legislation, 18, 21–22
Problem-solving, See Programming
Process, 3, 404
Processing program, 334–336
Processor, 84
Program, 4, 285–318; application, 330; compiler, 307; control, 332–333; design aids, 297–303; desirable qualities, 286–287; maintenance, 311–312; object, 307; processing, 334–336; proper, 305; statements, types of, 305–306; system, 329–330; utility, 335
Programmable communications processor, 206
Programmable read-only memory (PROM), 12
Programmer, 72
Programming: case study, 312–315; compiling, 306–308; debugging and testing, 308–310; documentation, 291; process, 287; structured, 287; team, 292–294; testing, 291–292; top-down design, 289
Programming language: Ada, 354, APL, 356–357; assembly, 49, 307, 344–345; BASIC, 352–354, 362; C,

PHOTO CREDITS
Chapter Opening Photos

1 Michel Tcherevkoff, The Image Bank; **35** Rob Atkins, The Image Bank; **69** Michel Tcherevkoff, The Image Bank; **113** Michael Rochipp, The Image Bank; **141** Don Carroll, The Image Bank; **165** Michael Rochipp, The Image Bank; **197** Michel Tcherevkoff, The Image Bank; **223** Don Caroll, The Image Bank; **247** Ken Cooper, The Image Bank; **283** "Two Chairs" (1984) by Kevin McMahon; **327** Michael Rochipp, The Image Bank; **373** Steve Dunwell, The Image Bank; **401** "Minnechunks" (1983) by Kevin McMahon; **451** Michael Rochipp.

"Computers in Our Lives" Photo "Globe" (1983) by Kevin McMahon and Scott Walter.
"Highlight" Photo by Michael Rochipp, The Image Bank.
"Focus On Microcomputing" Photo by Geoffrey Gove, The Image Bank.

Computers Illustrated Photos

Enhancing Creativity and Entertainment: **1,** courtesy of Cranston/Csuri Productions, Inc.; **2** "KULA-LITE," FM 92, Honolulu; **3** Product of Paul Xander, CGL at NYIT; **4** courtesy of Ramtek Corporation; **5** courtesy of IBM Research Division; **6** courtesy of CompuPro, Hayward, CA; **7** and **8** courtesy of Don Bluth Animation; **9** and **10** Robert Abel and Associates; **11** and **12** courtesy of Autodesk, Inc.; **13** courtesy of T/Maker Graphics; **14** courtesy of Sight and Sound Music Software; **15** courtesy of IBM Research Division; **16** courtesy of National Computer Camps, Box 585, Orange, CT 06477; **17–19** courtesy of Sperry Corporation; **20** courtesy of Astroworld.

Enhancing Research and Technology: **1** courtesy of IBM; **2** courtesy of AT&T, Bell Laboratories; **3–5** courtesy of Motorola, Inc., **6** courtesy of Sperry Corporation; **7** courtesy of Motorola, Inc., **8** courtesy of Electro Scientific Industries, Portland, Oregon; **9** courtesy of AT&T, Bell Laboratories; **10–11** courtesy of IBM; **12** courtesy of Pfizer, Inc.; **13** courtesy of NASPA/JPL; **14** courtesy of Aero Service Division, Western Geophysical Company of America; **15** and **16** courtesy of Jet Propulsion Laboratory; **17** and **18** courtesy of Marathon Oil Company; **19** and **20** courtesy of MSI Data Corporation.

Enhancing the Quality of Life: **1** and **2** courtesy of Bio-Logic Systems Corporation; **3** courtesy of Pfizer, Inc.; **4** courtesy of Baxter Travenol Laboratories, Inc.; **5** courtesy of IBM; **6** Permission by Honeywell, Inc.; **7** courtesy of Wright State University; **8** courtesy of the University of Utah; **9** courtesy of National Biomedical Research Foundation, Georgetown University Medical Center, Washington, D.C.; **10** courtesy of Officer OPD II, Orlando Police Department; **11–13** courtesy of Phoenix Fire Department; **14** and **15** courtesy of Club Med; **16** courtesy of Best Western International; **17** courtesy of Apply Computer, Inc.

Enhancing Human Performance: **1** courtesy of Xerox Corporation; **2** courtesy of Radio Shack, a division of Tandy Corporation; **3** courtesy of Apple Computer, Inc., **4–6** courtesy of Flight Safety International, Inc., **7** courtesy of CompuPro, Hayward, CA; **8** courtesy of MSI Data Corporation; **9** courtesy of IBM; **10** and **11** courtesy of John Morgan; **12** Photos by Tom Croke—New England Patriots; **13** courtesy of John Morgan; **14** courtesy of New York Yankees; **15** and **16** Photos by Tom Croke—New England Patriots; **17** courtesy of Brunswick Corporation.

Text Photos

vii courtesy of Apple Computer, Inc.; **viii** courtesy of Storage Technology Corp.; **ix** courtesy of IBM; **x** courtesy of National Semiconductor; **xi** courtesy of IBM; **xii** courtesy of The Chicago Tribune; **xiii** courtesy of American Satellite Corporation; **xix** courtesy of Control Data Corporation; **xv** courtesy of Apple Computer, Inc.; **xvi** courtesy of Apple Computer, Inc.; **xvii** courtesy of IBM; **xviii** courtesy of Texas Instruments; **xix** courtesy of Ford Motor Company; **xx** courtesy of the Jet Propulsion Laboratory; **5** courtesy of Ohio Citizens Bank; **6** (top) courtesy of Evans & Sutherland; **6** (bottom) Photo courtesy of U.S. Steel; **7** General Dynamics photo; **8** courtesy of CPT Corporation; **9** Photo courtesy of American Satellite Company, Rockville, Maryland; **10** courtesy of Digital Equipment Corporation; **11** U.S. Army Photos by Sp4 Fred Sutter; **12** Photograph provided courtesy of Aydin Controls, a division of Aydin Corporation; **13** courtesy of FBI; **15** courtesy of Philips Corporation; **16** courtesy of Floating Point Systems; **17** courtesy of Apple Computer, Inc.; **20** courtesy of FBI;

Figure 1–2
Computer-Aided Design.
Using CAD software, an engineer can design a three-dimensional image of a product and rotate it in any direction desired to make adjustments and test it.

peared so far. First-generation robots possess mechanical dexterity but no external sensory ability—that is, they cannot see, hear, feel, or smell. Such a robot typically consists of a mobile arm ending in some sort of viselike grip, claw, or other tool. The arm is attached to a box that houses the control unit and the entire device is anchored to a stationary base on the factory floor (see Figure 1–4).

Second-generation robots, however, possess more human qualities, including tactile sense or crude vision. They can "feel" how tightly they are gripping an object or "see" whether there are obstacles in their path. The combination

Figure 1–3
Computer-Aided Manufacturing.
The entire steel rolling operation of this U. S. Steel mill is supervised and monitored from this computerized control center.

6

communication between computers and/or computer **terminals.** No cash or checks actually change hands.

One popular form of EFT is the **automatic teller machine (ATM).** ATMs are unattended remote devices that communicate with a bank's computer (see Figure 1–1). Many banks have installed the machines in the outside walls of the bank buildings. Customers identify themselves by inserting plastic cards (often their credit cards) and entering identification codes. The cards contain account numbers and credit limits encoded on strips of magnetic tape. Once identification is approved, the customers select transactions by pushing a series of buttons.

Manufacturing

The computer revolution has done much to increase the productivity of manufacturing plants. Manufacturing involves designing and building products.

A fast-growing use of computers in industry involves **computer-aided design (CAD)** and **computer-aided manufacturing (CAM).** The major benefit of CAD has been quicker completion of design and testing processes. Using CAD, an engineer can design and draft a product model in color and three dimensions on a video terminal (see Figure 1–2). The model can be turned to expose any side or angle, and cross-sectional cuts show interior details on the display screen. The computer model also detects the strengths and weaknesses of a product, unwanted vibrations on an airplane wing for example, before the first sample is ever built.

Often CAD is paired with CAM, which simulates, or imitates, the manufacturing process, allowing engineers to spot and correct problems in the process. The adjustments they make can save the manufacturer large amounts of money and time. In addition CAM is used to monitor the actual assembly line work (see Figure 1–3).

Computer controlled **robots** are being used in industry to replace workers in routine, dull, heavy or dangerous jobs. Two generations of robots have ap-

Terminal An input/output device through which data can be input to or output from a system.

Automatic teller machine (ATM) Remote terminal that allows bank customers to make transactions with the bank's central computer.

Computer-aided design (CAD) Process of designing, drafting, and analyzing a prospective product using computer graphics on a video terminal.

Computer-aided manufacturing (CAM) Use of a computer to simulate or monitor the steps of a manufacturing process.

Robot Machine to perform any of several tasks (such as moving or manipulating materials, parts, or tools) under stored-program control.

Figure 1–1
Automatic Teller Machine.
This customer of Ohio Citizen's Bank can use the bank's automatic teller machine at any time of day that is convenient for him.

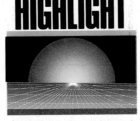

HIGHLIGHT

Help For Managers

Is Mr. X overly sensitive to criticism? Does Ms. O appear to be shy? Would the manager of Department C benefit from training in how to handle interpersonal relations?

Where do managers get help in dealing with such problems? Once, the answers came from personnel departments or training sessions. Today, managers can get help from computer programs.

One such program is the Management Edge, developed by Human Edge Software Corp., Palo Alto, California. The program asks questions about the personalities of employees and offers hints to help managers deal with employees. Employee problems can range from coping with spouses and children to improving production.

Wilson Learning Corp., a unit of John Wiley & Sons, Inc., is developing a system to train managers to deal with people. The program combines computers and video disk machines. It leads managers through a series of simulations dealing with how to react to and talk with employees.

With such software available, some companies are replacing humans with computers for training and counseling.

By the way, the answer to the first question above is "Don't let this worry you. Mr. X gets angry easily, and may even appear angry before you begin speaking."

Hardware Physical components that make up a computer system.

Program Series of step-by-step instructions that tells the computer exactly what to do.

Microcomputer A computer small in size, but not in power; now available in 8-, 16-, and 32-bit configurations.

Software Program used to direct the computer for solving specific problems and overseeing operations.

Real-time Descriptive of a system's capability to receive and process data, providing output fast enough to control the outcome of an activity.

Electronic funds transfer (EFT) Cashless method of managing money; accounts involved in a transaction are adjusted by electronic communication between computers.

Until recently, computer capabilities were limited to large businesses and corporations. As the cost of computer **hardware** decreases, however, more small businesses are able to use computers. Many computer **programs** for small computers are now available to handle typical business activities. The advent of the **microcomputer** has made it possible for any entrepreneur to purchase the hardware and **software** needed for a complete accounting system.

Computers in the business field provide many other services. Airlines, travel agencies, and hotels use extensive networks of computer equipment to schedule reservations. Branches of a business may be connected by communication lines across the country. Businesses are installing computers in offices to make clerical duties more efficient. Since computers work very fast, they can handle large amounts of data, and can provide results within **real-time** constraints, they seem almost indispensable in banking, manufacturing, and office functions.

Banking

Many banks now offer automated services, such as direct deposit of checks into customers' accounts by their employers and automatic payment of bills. Customers can also request that a regular amount be transferred from checking accounts to savings accounts each month. This type of service illustrates a concept called **electronic funds transfer (EFT).** In an EFT system, the accounts of the party or parties involved in a transaction are adjusted by electronic

Stevie's use of computers is one of hundreds of ways computers have been used to redefine common tasks—and some not so common ones. Computers run businesses, teach children, tally votes, test water, and monitor air. They track inventory, control costs, monitor sales, and regulate production lines. They diagnose diseases, design cars, automate labs, and predict weather. They guide missiles, send shuttles into space, steer ships, drive trains, and fly planes. They eliminate drudgery and save time. Computers, as we see in this chapter, are becoming an indispensable part of our society.

INTRODUCTION

Because of computers, our lives have changed drastically. Computers have expedited everyday transactions in banking and shopping. They have invaded the workplace, affecting the operation of factories, offices, schools, hospitals, and laboratories. They have aided in complex activities such as weather forcasting and disease diagnosis. Although they have made life easier, computers have created problems, too. Job automation has increased fears about unemployment. Huge data bases have led to difficulties in ensuring individual privacy. The proliferation of computers has fostered entire systems to secure data, hardware, and software from natural or accidental problems and from people who would err, snoop, steal, sabotage, embezzle, falsify, or destroy.

It is not difficult to see that our society will become increasingly dependent on computers. This chapter examines current computer applications in business, government, medicine, education, and entertainment. The chapter also discusses the problems of privacy and computer crime. Material in this chapter is intended to present a broad picture of the impact computers have had on our society. The reader is encouraged to learn about other uses of computers through magazines, periodicals, or television.

COMPUTERS IN BUSINESS

Hardly a day goes by when we are not confronted by a computer-generated business transaction. Each time we visit the bank, use a credit card, pay a bill, or buy groceries, a **computer** lurks behind the scene, recording each transaction. Even a visit to a fast-food restaurant involves computer transactions. Whenever business data is to be recorded, more than likely a computer is performing the task.

Computers can **process** data in a fraction of the time it would take to perform the same jobs manually. In any business, computers can help reduce paperwork and costs associated with performing routine transactions. Business activities include controlling inventory levels, billing customers for services and products, calculating payroll and taxes, paying for inventory and supplies, reporting for decision making by managers, and supporting a host of other business functions. Computer systems can be implemented to perform all these transactions and increase the efficiency of an organization's operations.

Computer General purpose electronic machine with applications limited only by the creativity of the humans who use it.

Process Transform data into useful information (by classifying, sorting, calculating, summarizing, storing).

3

COMPUTERS IN OUR LIVES

Stevie's Wondrous Computers

When Stevie Wonder premiered his album People Move Human Plays *at New York's Radio City Music Hall, the event was sold out for six nights. At this concert Stevie, integrating some of the latest computer technology with his music, brought down the house.*

As the house lights dimmed, a band member pressed a button on Stevie's keyboard rack. Suddenly, Radio City Music Hall was alive with a computer-controlled drum machine and synthesizer rapping out the beat of "It's Growing." A computerized machine called a PPG Wave 2 sequencer controlled the drum machine and electronic keyboards while the Wonderlove band came on stage with their instruments and started playing to the music's rhythm. Stevie, who is blind, was then guided onto the stage and the audience erupted into deafening applause. This spectacular opening introduced an evening filled with electronic and computerized sound.

Superstar Stevie Wonder has been using computers for more than five years. On his 1979 album The Secret Life of Plants, *Stevie used a custom-built digital synthesizer called a Melodeon to create a variety of sound effects, including strange jungle and bird noises. The Melodeon is unsophisticated compared with some of the other computerized instruments Stevie now uses—the Fairlight, the Emulator, and the PPG Wave 2.2. The unique sonic textures produced by these instruments, along with the programmability of keyboards and digital drum machines, inspired the musical structure of "It's Growing" and "Broken Glass."*

Because Stevie is blind, computers are an important part of his personal life, too. Stevie "reads" with his Kurzweil Reading Machine (KRM), which includes a computer that scans words on a printed page and a speech synthesizer that speaks those words out loud. He uses the KRM for business and pleasure, reading synthesizer manuals and popular novels such as Frank Herbert's Dune *books.*

Stevie also uses the Versabraille, a portable computer that stores Braille characters on a data cassette. The data can then be sent to another Versabraille via modem, a device that converts signals transmitted over communication lines, or it can be translated into speech by a KRM. The Versabraille's printout even creates Braille characters. People experienced with Braille can easily read these characters by running their fingertips over them. Since the Versabraille is lap size, Stevie uses it both on and off the road, conducting business, taking notes, or writing song lyrics and letters.

Stevie is learning to interface his Versabraille, KRM, and instruments so that he and his musical tools will be able to fully communicate. His instruments can "talk" to him either through the Versabraille's readout strip or KRM's synthetic voice, or he can "talk" to them and control what they do by writing in Braille on the Versabraille.

Stevie still plays piano as well as synthesizer, and harmonica as well as drum machine. But computers, without any question, enrich his music and his life.

2

CHAPTER 1

THE ROLE OF COMPUTERS IN TODAY'S SOCIETY

COMPUTERS AND
DATA PROCESSING TODAY

In preparation of this second edition, the following people provided invaluable comments based on their experience using COMPUTERS AND DATA PROCESSING TODAY:

Professor Beverly Blaylock
Grossmont College, California

Bruce A. Boraas
Mankato State University, Minnesota

Marvin L. Daugherty
Indiana Vocational Technical College

Robert M. Denmark
Seaton Hill University, New Jersey

Orlynn R. Evans
Stephen F. Austin State University, Texas

Lorinda Hite
Owens Technical College, Ohio

Kaila Katz
Montclair State College, New Jersey

Raymond C. Marves
Florida Junior College

Thomas A. Parkinson
Oakland Community College, Michigan

Leesa Pohl
Park College, Missouri

R. B. Purse
University of Regina/Canada

Richard G. Schenck
Antelope Valley, California

Many individuals and companies have been involved in the development of the material for this book. Numerous corporations and government agencies provided the color pictures found in this book in addition to applications material. Many professionals provided the assistance required for completing a text of this magnitude: Sarah Basinger, Laura Bores, Susan Moran, and Robert Szymanski on student material; Allan Johnson on instructor material; Sue Bauman with Pascal and Karen McKee with BASIC; Russell Thompson on software development; Meredith Flynn and Norma Morris on manuscript development; and Shannan Benschoter, Ann Bressler, Linda Cupp, Melissa Landon, and Sally Oates on manuscript preparation. The design of the book is a tribute to the many talents of William Stryker. One final acknowledgment goes to my publisher and valued friend, Clyde Perlee, Jr., for his encouragement and ideas.

Steven L. Mandell

Answers). The format for the student materials supporting the language supplements is slightly different. For each section in the language supplement the *Study Guide* includes Structured Learning, a Worksheet, and Programming Problems.

A complete instructor's resource package has been designed to reduce administrative efforts. In the *Instructor's Manual,* the classroom support includes: Learning Objectives, detailed Outlines, Answers to Review and Discussion Questions, Additional Review and Discussion Questions and an Answer Key to the *Study Guide.* Extensive materials have been included for language versions of this text. For each section in the language supplement, there is an average of four programming problems; each problem in the BASIC supplement is accompanied by a flowchart and a list of any differences for microcomputers.

A Test Bank of over 1,000 multiple choice questions is also included in the *Instructor's Manual.* In addition, the WESTEST or MICROTEST computerized testing service is available from West Publishing Company with these questions in machine-readable form.

There are 100 Transparencies (25 in color) available to qualified adopters. Most of these visuals are unique, and not mere reproductions of artwork found in the text. Additionally, a narrative script of a tour of a modern computer facility augments a set of color slides available to adopters from West Publishing Company.

In keeping with the extraordinary growth of microcomputers and application software, two software packages are available to qualified adopters of this text. The first package consists of an educational version of a word processor, electronic spread sheet, data manager, and graphics package. This software is available for a number of microcomputers providing hands-on experience and guidance with these four popular types of application packages. These instructional packages will acquaint students with the basic concepts of commercial software packages in a simple, easy-to-follow format. The second software package includes five hands-on projects to get the students involved with using simulated home banking, an information network, computerized ticket purchasing, a psychological traits analysis package, and a dental office data base. A *Users Guide and Laboratory Workbook* accompanies both software packages and includes numerous exercises for the four application programs and the five user oriented programs.

Also available is WestTutor™, a computer-assisted instruction package developed from the BASIC Supplement of the textbook. Instructions are provided at the bottom of each screen to direct the student through the tutorial. Instructions are also provided for the instructor.

ACKNOWLEDGMENTS

I wish to thank the people who helped shape the first edition of this text through their comments, criticisms and suggestions: Don Cartlidge, New Mexico State University; James W. Cox, Lane Community College, Oregon; Richard H. Harms, Santa Ana College, California; Fred L. Head, Cypress College, California; Kathleen Ott, New Mexico Junior College; Curtis G. Rawson, Kirkwood Community College, Iowa; Al Stehling, San Antonio College; Rein Turn, California State University, Northridge; Kenneth W. Veatch, San Antonio College; Louis A. Wolff, Moorpark College, California.

The basic pedagogical format found in this book is designed to aid in the clear, straightforward presentation of the material, while including motivational real-world examples. Each chapter begins with "Computers in Our Lives" which describes how computers are used in areas familiar or fascinating to students. Next is a brief introductory section that provides a logical link with the previous material. The chapter outline that follows permits the student to develop a frame of reference for the text material. This outline also provides a useful guide when preparing for exams. At the conclusion of the chapter material, there is a point-by-point summary in sentence form followed by approximately ten review questions.

Two additional features in the pedagogical design warrant special attention, and are also related to the title of this book, *Computers and Data Processing Today*. Several Highlight boxes are included in each chapter that present material of current interest. They are designed to be motivational and entertaining, while at the same time providing current perspectives that enrich the book's content.

Secondly, because of the tremendous proliferation of microcomputers today, it became apparent that adequate attention had to be devoted to their special requirements. This arose both from my own teaching experience as well as from comments received from instructors all around the country. The decision was made to include separate chapters on microcomputers and application software as well as to integrate microcomputer information throughout the book in the "Focus on Microcomputers" section at the end of each chapter. This section integrates microcomputer concepts and applications into the material discussed in that particular chapter. This combination should prove to be valuable for students entering a "micro world."

In addition to the new appendix, "Numbering Systems," we have again included "Career Opportunities," to give students a practical insight into computer-related careers. The importance of good flowcharting techniques can never be underestimated. This was also made clear to me in reviews of the text. Therefore, the flowcharting material presented in the text and in the BASIC/Pascal supplements is augmented through the use of a separate appendix entitled "Program Logic Flowcharts and Decision Logic Tables." Individuals with courses utilizing a computer language laboratory will find this addition provides significant flexibility in teaching program design. Finally, at the end of the text is a comprehensive glossary and a separate index.

In order to provide appropriate materials for the widest variety of teaching situations, there are three versions of this book available—first, a version with a very complete BASIC language supplement with microcomputer implementation; second, a version with a standard Pascal supplement; and finally a language-free version.

SUPPLEMENTARY EDUCATIONAL MATERIAL

The *Study Guide* to accompany this text includes numerous materials for student reinforcement. Each chapter in the *Study Guide* contains the following: Key Terms; a narrative Summary of the chapter; a Structured Learning section; and an extensive set of questions and answers (True/False, Matching, Short

PREFACE

The revision work associated with this edition has been one of my most enjoyable and rewarding efforts. Feedback from instructors using the text has provided an excellent source of ideas for improvement. Nothing can replace the actual classroom testing of material when attempting to create a new edition. The final result is a new, second edition of a textbook vastly improved in structure and substance.

NEW FEATURES

Readers familiar with the first edition of the text will notice several changes incorporated into the second edition. These changes include the following:

- Three new chapters: Data Structures and File Design; Microcomputers; Application Software.
- New appendix on Numbering Systems
- Computers in Our Lives—short, high-interest, student-oriented applications which open each chapter
- Marginal Definitions
- Concept Summaries
- Computers Illustrated—thematic photo essays dealing with creativity, entertainment, research and technology, human performance and the quality of life
- Restructuring of chapters to provide greater flexibility
- Newly developed software support
- Updated and revised "Highlights"
- Updated and revised "Focus on Microcomputers"

In the last few years, there has been an explosion in the number of students taking beginning courses in computers and data processing. This explosion has resulted in the need for a wide variety of books and teaching materials. The goal of this book is to provide an introductory text that is concise while maintaining clarity and teachable style. I believe that this book continues my philosophy of presenting the educational material in a logical, uncluttered manner while including relevant real-world examples. Additionally, by virtue of its full-color format and extensive use of graphics, I believe this book is one of the most visually appealing introductory computer books yet published. The book remains modular and flexible so that an instructor may reorder the topics according to his or her approach.

CHAPTER 14
COMPUTERS IN OUR FUTURE

Page 451

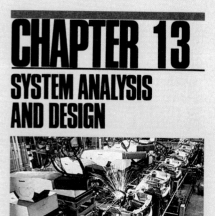

CHAPTER 13

SYSTEM ANALYSIS AND DESIGN

Page 401

CHAPTER 12
APPLICATIONS SOFTWARE

Page 373

Page 327

CHAPTER 10
THE PROGRAMMING PROCESS

Page 283

xvi

CHAPTER 9
MICROCOMPUTERS

CHAPTER 8
COMPUTER SYSTEMS

Page 223

CHAPTER 7
DATA COMMUNICATION

Page 197

CHAPTER 6
DATA STRUCTURES AND FILE DESIGN

CHAPTER 5
STORAGE DEVICES

Page 141

Figure 1–4
Robotics.
Robots anchored to the factory floor do routine, but perhaps dangerous welding jobs.

of touch-sensitive grippers and computerized vision has created a robot capable of reaching into a bin of mixed parts, finding a certain object, and picking it up. These actions may sound simple, but they involve a complex series of judgments and movements. Collectively, these robots are called bin-picking robots.

Office Electronics

Recent developments in computer technology have changed the office environment. Organizations are realizing that computer technology is efficient, cost effective, and in fact necessary to handle the exploding information revolution.

Every office function—typing, filing, and communications—can be automated. Among the specific applications are word processing, electronic mail, teleconferencing, and telecommuting. The term applied to the processes that integrate computer and communication technology with traditional office procedures is **office automation.**

Word processing is the most widely adopted office automation technology; an estimated 75 percent of U. S. companies employ some type of word processing. It provides a mechanism to prepare text, and bypasses the shortcomings of traditional writing and typing. A user enters text on a typewriterlike keyboard, and the words appear on a display screen rather than on paper. The user can edit, rearrange, insert, and delete material until the document is exactly as desired. Then a printer produces a letter-perfect document with much less

Office automation Integration of computer and communication technology with traditional office procedures to increase productivity and efficiency.

Word processing Manipulation of text data to achieve a desired output.

7

Electronic mail Transmission of messages at high speeds over telecommunication facilities.

Teleconferencing Method of conducting meetings between two or more remote locations via electronic and/or image-producing facilities.

effort than it takes to produce the same document on a typewriter. Furthermore, the system can print as many perfectly typed copies as desired. The text can be stored on cassette tape or disk and can be changed at any time (see Figure 1–5).

Transmitting text at high speeds over telecommunication facilities is referred to as sending **electronic mail.** The simplest form of computer-based mail systems allows one user of the service to send a message to another by placing it in a special storage area in the electronic system. The second user retrieves the message by printing it on paper or the display screen. The parties need not use the system at the same time in order to send and receive messages. The mail can be duplicated, revised, incorporated into other documents, passed along to new recipients, or filed like any other document in the system.

Office communications can be facilitated by another electronic technology— **teleconferencing.** Teleconferencing enables people in different geographical locations to participate in a meeting at the same time. Satellite technology has enabled corporations with offices in different countries around the world to take advantage of teleconferencing. Businesses can benefit in two ways: reduction in travel time and reduction in travel costs. However, few organizations are willing or able to spend the millions of dollars required to install and upgrade the more elaborate teleconferencing systems.

The most basic form of conducting electronic meetings, audio conferencing, consists of a conference call linking three or more people. Ideal for impromptu meetings, audio conferencing requires no major equipment investment but is limited to voice communication.

Figure 1–5
Word-Processing System.
A stand-alone word-processing system provides enough equipment that people who use the system do not have to access a central computer to accomplish a task. The system is inexpensive enough to allow organizations to acquire one without investing in large computers.

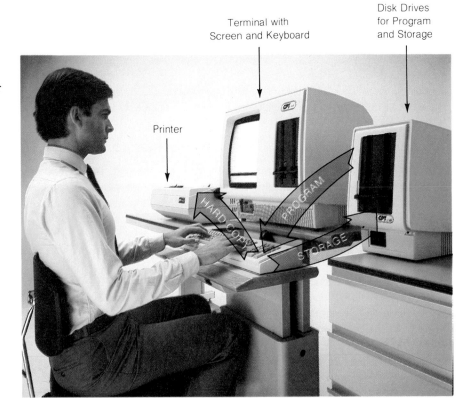

Printer

Terminal with Screen and Keyboard

Disk Drives for Program and Storage

The most advanced teleconference—the videoconference—allows two-way, full-motion video and two-way audio communication. The participants are able to see and hear each other's responses (see Figure 1–6).

Perhaps the most exciting prospect for the automated office involves **telecommuting**—commuting to the office by computer rather than in person (see Figure 1–7). The system offers advantages in cities where office rent is high and mass transit systems or parking facilities are inadequate, and in businesses that do not require frequent face-to-face meetings among office workers. Telecommuting also provides greater flexibility for disabled employees and working parents.

Telecommuting does have disadvantages, however. Some employees may not have the discipline to work away from the office. They may enjoy the social aspects of going to work. They may fear that "out of sight is out of mind,"

Telecommuting Method of working at home by communicating via electronic machines and telecommunications facilities.

Concept Summary 1–1   Computers in Business

Computers and Computer Processes in Business	
Banking	Electronic Funds Transfer Automatic Teller Machines
Manufacturing	Computer-aided design (CAD) Computer-aided manufacturing (CAM) CAD/CAM Robotics
Office Electronics (The automated office)	Word processing Electronic mail Teleconferences Telecommuting

Figure 1–6
Videoconference.
A videoconference can often save money for corporations that depend on frequent meetings between people at distant branches.

particularly when promotions and raises are considered. In addition, managers may be uneasy about the amount of control they have over employees who work away from the office.

COMPUTERS IN GOVERNMENT

The largest user of computer systems in the United States is the federal government. This fact is not surprising when one considers the many government agencies that collect, process, and store information about the population. A typical example is the U. S. census, taken every ten years. In 1980, about 120 million census forms were mailed to individual residences. The forms contained a total of 3.3 billion questions, which had to be processed by January 1, 1981, so that state population figures would be available for congressional reapportionment. Without computers, the task could never have been finished in time. Other primary uses of computers by the federal government include military planning, Internal Revenue Service data processing, weather forecasting, and law enforcement.

Every branch of the armed forces is involved in military planning and decision making. High-level officials use computer-generated information to keep records of all the military personnel employed by the government, plan defenses, practice battle strategies, and maintain vigilance over potentially dangerous offensive manuevers. The North America Air Defense Command near Colorado Springs, Colorado, shelters a huge **data base** for military control purposes. This data base accepts data from radar and satellite equipment positioned throughout the world. The data can be updated and retrieved at a moment's notice. For example, the computer can calculate the position of rockets and missiles within several seconds after they are launched and can signal and perform the appropriate actions in case of attack.

Data base Collection of data defined and organized to allow a wide range of retrieval methods and uses.

Computers are also used by military planners to **simulate** wars (see Figure 1–8). Military commanders can practice making decisions based on the lifelike situations presented by the computer. This allows them to gain experience without engaging in real battles, sharpening their skills in case a real threat should arise.

Simulate Duplicate conditions likely to occur in a real-world situation when variables are changed.

Every person living in the United States who earns more than a minimal amount of money must report to the federal government for tax purposes. In addition, corporations and businesses file annual tax returns on the earnings of their businesses. Each year the Internal Revenue Service (IRS) uses computers to monitor and record the data on the millions of tax returns received. Without the aid of computers, it would take many years to process just one year's worth of returns.

The IRS also performs detailed audits on returns selected by the computer on the basis of conditions identified as unusual or likely to contain errors or fraud. By reducing the manual operations required to perform the audits, the IRS can audit more returns each year.

The forecasting of weather is one of the most interesting applications of computers in government. Several variables, such as air pressure, wind velocity, humidity, and temperature, are fed into huge computers for the processing of complex mathematical equations. The equations describe the interaction of these variables. By combining the data with mathematical models, forecasters can predict the weather.

Figure 1–8
War Simulation.
This participant uses the computer for war simulation exercises. The display screens represent various situations that might be encountered in an actual war.

Although local forecasters use radar data directly, they also rely on national and international weather information. The world's weather information is col-

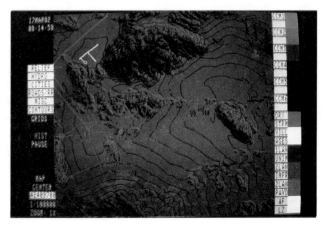

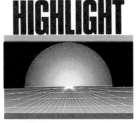

Computers and Recreational Aesthetics

Computers are often considered tools for smoothing out our work. But in Colorado, the United States Forest Service is using computers to *add* bumps and obstacles to our play.

In the past, ski resorts have been marked by scarred mountainsides where ski trails have simply been cut through the trees in a straight line down the mountain. The trails, plainly visible for miles around, were an eyesore. Now, concern for the environment and for skiers' safety has prompted the use of computers to design trails. Fed with detailed information about the mountainside (the position of every tree, rock, and gully—data carefully collected and recorded by Forest Service employees over a number of years) the computers generate pictures suggesting the best and safest trails for skiers.

The improved trails mean more business for the ski resorts. And a trail that follows a natural course down the mountain, around stands of trees instead of through them, is easier both on the land and on the eye.

lected by the National Weather Service in Maryland from a variety of locations: hundreds of data-collection programs (DCPs) placed on buoys, ships, weather balloons, and airplanes; about 70 weather stations; and four satellites (see Figure 1–9). Two of the satellites orbit the earth over the poles to send pictures revealing the movement and shape of clouds. The other two satellites are in stationary orbits above the equator.

The Weather Service's "brain" consists of 14 computers housed at the meteorological center. These computers receive information from some of the DCPs whose data are beamed up to the two "stationary" satellites above the equator. The computers also receive information from other DCPs: the infor-

Figure 1–9
Weather Forecasting Display.
Weather satellite display of a hurricane system generated on an Aycon/16 System.

mation travels from ground station to ground station. The 14 computers use all of this incoming data to construct a mathematical description of the atmosphere. These weather reports—2,000 daily—are sent to local weather offices. Manual processing would take so much time that the results would not be available until the weather conditions had already occurred!

Law enforcement agencies like the FBI and intelligence-gathering agencies like the CIA use computer systems to store information, plan their operations, and track criminals. One government agency, the National Crime Information Center, uses a national network of computer terminals to keep track of police and law enforcement information. The Justice Department is using the system to monitor people who are considered a threat to officials but have never been convicted of a crime (see Figure 1–10). Under the plan, the Secret Service can place in the center's computer the names of persons considered to be threats to the president and vice president, presidential candidates, visiting heads of state, or anyone else the service must protect. Records are also kept about people who are associated with other types of terrorist activities.

Among the most elaborate communication systems in the world, the center is linked to 64,000 federal, state, and local law enforcement agencies. Any local law enforcement agency can quickly determine if a person they want to arrest or have already arrested is recorded in the center's files.

This network has drawn a great deal of criticism—some of it from members of Congress. No complaints are heard about the system as it pertains to tracking known criminals. But those concerned with protecting civil liberties express fears that anyone's name might find its way into the computer, possibly causing damage to an innocent person.

Figure 1–10
FBI Data Base.
The ease with which computerized information about people can be stored and retrieved has led to an increasing concern that computers may pose a threat to personal privacy. Here FBI computer operators are preparing magnetic tapes for storage in the bureau's huge tape library.

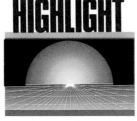

Monitoring Chemical Spills

Since a recent chemical spill at the Union Carbide plant in Bhopal, India resulted in the deaths of more than 2,000 people, chemical companies have become much more interested in computerized tracking and warning systems designed to protect communities around their plants. The old method for predicting the path and level of toxicity of a chemical cloud (still in use at most chemical plants) involves the use of lengthy charts and tables and relies on human calculations.

Safer Emergency Systems, Inc., has designed computerized emergency systems for 25 chemical plants. The system combines a computer, a 19-inch color graphics screen, and a printer with sensors placed at key locations in the plant to detect leaks early and sound alarms in the central computer. A tower placed on a rooftop or in a nearby open field has sensors that help plot the temperature and direction of a chemical cloud.

When the computer detects a leak, it begins closely monitoring its sensors, and requests information from its operator about what sort of chemical has been released. The computer plots the direction the chemical cloud is taking and how toxic the cloud is. The computer also prints out telephone numbers for police, fire departments, hospitals, and other agencies that need to be called.

Using the computerized system saves valuable time in an emergency, making it possible for necessary evacuation and cleanup operations to begin more quickly. With increased use of such computerized emergency systems, chemical companies hope to prevent another incident like the one in Bhopal.

COMPUTERS IN MEDICINE

Medical personnel diagnose illnesses, provide treatments, and monitor patients. Computer technology is used to facilitate the timeliness and accuracy of these jobs.

Computers are increasingly combined with testing equipment to provide diagnostic tools in hospitals and clinics (see Figure 1–11). Three common forms—multiphasic health testing, computerized axial tomography, and nuclear magnetic resonance scanning—help with preventive health care and offer non-invasive (nonsurgical) testing techniques. In **multiphasic health testing** computer equipment aids in performing a series of tests, stores the results of the tests, and reports the results to doctors. Physical examinations are performed by trained technicians and paramedics using the computer equipment. Procedures include electrocardiograms, X-ray tests, blood tests, vision and hearing tests, blood pressure tests, and height and weight measurement. The computer system compares the results of the tests to predetermined standards of normal health. The patient's physician receives a report of the test results before meeting with the patient. Multiphasic testing permits the doctor to spend more time on diagnosis and treatment, and can be valuable in preventive health care.

Multiphasic health testing (MPHT) Computer-assisted testing plan that compares data on patients and their test results with norms; aids in making a diagnosis.

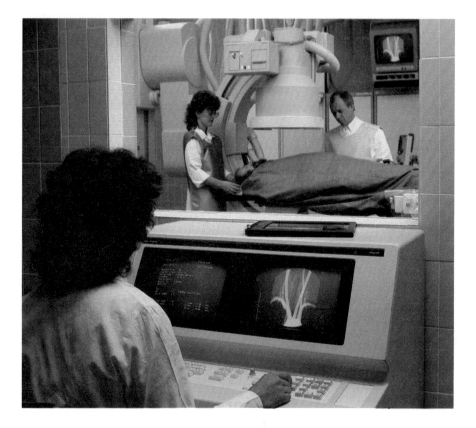

Figure 1–11
Computer-Assisted Diagnosis.
Many hospitals are using computers
to assist doctors in diagnosis. Here, a
radiologist views a computerized
image to assist in the diagnosis.

Computerized axial tomography, commonly known as CAT scanning, is a diagnostic aid that joins two tools—X rays and computerized evaluations of X-ray pictures. A CAT scan can do something that ordinary X-ray tests cannot: it can provide clear pictures of cross-sections of the body. Using many cross-sections together, it is possible to make a three-dimensional composite of an organ or bone (see Figure 1–12).

Computerized axial tomography (CT or CAT scanning) Form of noninvasive physical testing that combines X-ray techniques and computers to aid diagnosis.

Medical Data Systems of Ann Arbor, Michigan, has taken the CAT scan one step further. The company markets a computer system that constructs a three-dimensional image of an organ on a video monitor and also recreates the actual movement of the organ in the simulated organ on the screen. Doctors are able to identify parts of the organ that are not functioning normally.

Nuclear magnetic resonance (NMR) scanning may soon replace the CAT scan in hospitals. Unlike X-ray tests or CAT scans, NMR can "see" through thick bones. Moreover, NMR works without radiation. Magnetic pulses sent through the body react differently when they come into contact with different parts of the body. A computer is used to collect the results and create a detailed picture of the inside of the body.   Often NMR scanning is more successful in detecting problems than CAT scanning. Since the procedure does not use radiation, it can be used for testing children and pregnant women. There are some drawbacks to NMR scanning, however. For example, it does not produce clear images of bones or spot breast cancer.

Nuclear magnetic resonance (NMR) scanning Diagnostic tool that involves sending magnetic pulses through the body to identify medical problems.

Both CAT scans and NMR scans allow doctors to conduct tests without invading the body through surgery. This prevents the infections and fatigue associated with surgery.

Figure 1–12
CAT Scan.
Computerized axial tomography enables a physician to "view" the inside of a patient's body, often eliminating the need for exploratory surgery.

Computers also help ensure the success of reconstructive surgery. One of the primary concerns in reconstructive surgery is how the patient will look after the surgery. Computer-generated pictures can predict the results of reconstructive surgery. In the case of a patient with a deformed skull, CAT scan cross-sections are used to produce three-dimensional pictures of the skull. The computer studies the results of the CAT scan and presents a picture of the skull after reconstruction. Models based on the computer picture help the doctor plan the proper surgical techniques. It also helps the patient visualize the outcome of the surgery.

The applications of computers in medicine are almost limitless. Perhaps by the end of the 1980s computers will be used to test the skills and efficiency of doctors. Computers are already used to keep records on the performance of doctors at one California hospital. Part of the push for using computers to obtain efficiency will come from Medicaid officials who are diligently trying to reduce hospital expenses.

EDUCATION

A popular question in the past ten years has been "Will the computer replace the teacher?" The answer is "no," but computers can help teachers with their work. The number of computers used in schools has increased dramatically.

16

Encendiendo Una Llama!

Cross an Apple with a bunch of creative, bilingual kids and what do you get? Urban Adventure, of course! In Hartford, Connecticut, some 175 bilingual children in grades 3 through 6 benefit from the project, funded by money from the Apple Education Foundation and a federal program called Encendiendo Una Llama (Lighting a Flame). The goal of Urban Adventure is to let players explore the educational resources of the city (museums, parks, and government buildings) and help them develop language skills. Students are creating the games to explore the city. Since most of the students are Hispanic, they improve language abilities in both English and Spanish.

For the first adventure game, students explored the Hartford Public Library. Then they created their game using a graphics tablet and light pen. They wrote both Spanish and English versions of the game. This was accomplished with the Mountain Computer Super-Talker, which changes the sound waves of a voice into digital signals to store on a computer disk. The game teaches other students about the library and it also teaches correct pronunciations in Spanish and English so the player can build language skills. The bilingual students are "lighting a flame" for many other bilingual students to follow through the maze of languages.

Many schools are emphasizing **computer literacy.** People who are computer literate know what a computer can and cannot do, how a computer works, and how computers evolved. Educators believe that computers will play an important part in our lives in the future. If people know how to use computers, they will be better prepared to cope with the changes technology brings.

Computer literacy   General knowledge about computers; includes some technical knowledge, ability to use computers to solve problems, and awareness of how computers affect society.

This student uses a computer to help him with a chemistry experiment.

Computer-assisted instruction (CAI) Use of a computer to instruct or drill a student on an individual or small-group basis.

Computers were first used in classrooms in the 1960s to drill multiplication tables, names of state capitals, and other facts to be memorized. The concept of using computers or computer-imitating devices as teaching tools was called programmed learning. **Computer-assisted instruction (CAI)** still teaches by programmed learning, or drilling. Teachers realize the advantages of allowing students to use computers, because students learn at their own rates, receive immediate feedback, and feel comfortable with their impersonal "teacher." Students who need repeated drills find this patient teacher very helpful.

Students in kindergarten through twelfth grade are not the only people who benefit from CAI. Adults enrolled in colleges or vocational schools or in night classes can learn computer literacy skills and improve their chances of getting better jobs. Often corporations use the concepts of CAI to train or retrain employees in company policies, new computer uses, or new manufacturing or office procedures.

A wide selection of CAI software is available for computers. The software consists of drills, tutorials, and simulations. Drills quiz the student. The student learns by memory. Tutorials are programs that introduce students to new material and quiz them on their understanding of the material. Some CAI programs are simulations that imitate real-world situations, allowing students to learn through experience and induction without having to take actual risks.

Concept Summary 1–2   Privacy Legislation

Legislation	Provisions
Fair Credit Reporting Act of 1970	Gives individuals the right to access credit data about themselves
	Gives individuals the right to challenge and correct erroneous data
Privacy Act of 1974	Provides individuals with the right to determine what data is recorded by a government agency and how it will be used
	States that individuals must be provided with a method of correcting or amending incorrect data
	Requires organizations to ensure the reliability of collected data and take precautions to prevent misuse
	States that data collected for one purpose should not be used for another without the consent of the individual involved
Right to Financial Privacy Act of 1978	Limits government access to customer records of financial institutions
	Protects confidentiality of personal financial data
Education Privacy Act	Regulates access to computer stored records of grades and behavior evaluations in public and private schools

Bring on the Band, Switch on the Synthesizer!

The hottest sounds in pop and rock come from electronic synthesizers. You don't just plunk on a keyboard or strum a few strings. You twiddle knobs and plug in extra wires to produce the new sounds. The synthesizer bends sound waves to create brand-new sounds—sounds you would not normally hear in nature. And Thomas Dolby is at the forefront of computerized music.

Dolby, a 25-year-old Englishman, tapes real jungle noises, violin sounds, or singers, and alters the sound with his computer system nicknamed "Henry II." With the system, Dolby has changed tempos, merged fragments of two songs into a giant musical jigsaw puzzle, and broken voices into drum beats.

Henry II consists of an Australian-made digital synthesizer called a Fairlight which governs electronic keyboards, drum machines, and a German-made computer called a PPG 340/380 Wave. With the system, Dolby creates complex sounds on the Wave and edits them using the Fairlight's sophisticated commands. Samples of Dolby's work are recorded on the album *The Flat Earth* and hit singles such as "She Blinded Me with Science."

BEHAVIORAL ASPECTS OF COMPUTER USE

As computer use increases, certain aspects of behavior must be addressed. People fear impersonalization, and privacy violations. They are uneasy about using newfangled machines. And they realize that computers open one more arena for crime.

Privacy

The widespread use of computers, information systems, and telecommunication systems has created a major concern in recent years—the invasion of individual privacy. **Privacy** involves an individual's ability to determine what, how, and when personal information is communicated to others. With computers becoming the main means of storing personal information relating to credit, employment, taxes, and other aspects of a person's life, the issue of privacy assumes great importance (see Figure 1–13).

Data can be easily obtained and stored using computers. An individual's data stored in one main file can be accessed easily by entering his or her social security number. The increased ease of obtaining data tempts organizations to collect more data than necessary. People have less control over who has access to personal data. They are unaware whether their files are complete and accurate. They may not even be aware that such data is being kept. There must

Privacy An individual's ability to control the collection, processing, storage, dissemination, and use of data about personal attributes and activities.

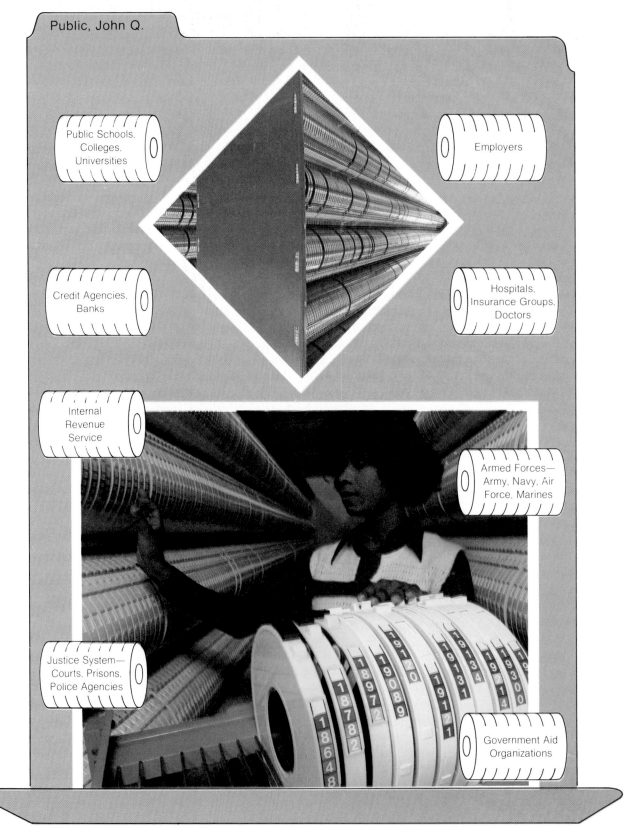

Public, John Q.

Public Schools, Colleges, Universities

Employers

Credit Agencies, Banks

Hospitals, Insurance Groups, Doctors

Internal Revenue Service

Armed Forces— Army, Navy, Air Force, Marines

Justice System— Courts, Prisons, Police Agencies

Government Aid Organizations

be an appropriate balance between the legitimate needs of organizations for information about people and the rights of individuals to maintain their privacy.

The main concerns of the privacy issue can be summarized as follows:

- Too much personal data is collected and stored in computer files.
- Organizations are increasingly using these files to make decisions about individuals.
- Much of the personal data collected about individuals may not be relevant to the purposes for which it is to be used.
- The accuracy, completeness, and currency of the data may be unacceptably low.
- The security of stored data is a problem.

Since the early 1970s, several laws have been enacted to protect privacy by controlling the collection, use, dissemination, and transmission of personal data. By far the most numerous have been passed by the federal government to protect against abuse of the government's own record-keeping agencies. The Freedom of Information Act of 1970 allows individuals access to data about themselves in files collected by federal agencies. It was passed because of the potential for the government to conceal its proceedings from the public.

The most sweeping legislation was the Privacy Act of 1974. Signed on January 1, 1975, this act is designed to protect the privacy of individuals about whom the federal government maintains data. The act names these provisions:

- People must be able to determine what data about themselves is recorded by government agencies and how it will be used.
- Individuals must be provided with a method of correcting or amending incorrect data.
- Data collected for one purpose should not be used for another without the consent of the individual.
- Any organization creating, maintaining, using, or disseminating personal data must ensure the reliability of the data and must take precautions to prevent its misuse.

Several other laws have been passed by the federal government in an attempt to control data-base misuse. The Education Privacy Act is designed to protect privacy by regulating access to computer-stored records of grades and behavior evaluations in both private and public schools. The act provides that no federal funds will be made available to an educational agency that has a policy of denying parents and students access to the student's relevant educational records. The Right to Financial Privacy Act of 1978 provides further protection by limiting government access to the customer records of financial institutions, protecting to some degree the confidentiality of personal financial data.

Many state laws regarding government record-keeping practices are patterned after the Privacy Act of 1974. Most states have enacted some controls on such practices in the public sector. Many of these laws require notices describing the records that each government agency maintains; provide for the collection and storage only of data that is relevant, timely, and accurate; and prohibit unauthorized disclosures of data relating to individuals.

The only significant federal attempt to regulate the information practices of private organizations is the Fair Credit Reporting Act of 1970, a law intended to deter privacy violations by lending institutions that use computers to store and manipulate data about people's finances. This legislation gives individuals

Figure 1–13 *(opposite page)*
Storage of Data.
The stacks and rows of magnetic tapes show how easily just one corporation can accumulate and store huge amounts of data using computer systems. Mutliply one corporation's data base by the many data bases kept by other organizations including the federal government, and you can see how John Q. Public could be completely unaware of what data is recorded about him. The ease by which organizations can record, store, and access data has led to concerns about data privacy and correct use of data.

21

the right of access to credit data about themselves and the opportunity to challenge and correct erroneous data. States have also begun to regulate the information activities of nongovernmental organizations. Much legislation in this area strengthens the protections afforded by the Fair Credit Reporting Act of 1970.

Relatively few information privacy violation cases have been litigated. Since one problem of privacy violation is that data is transferred and disclosed without the knowledge or consent of the subjects, people are not likely to know how their personal data is used and probably will not realize they may have a claim to take to court. Furthermore, privacy litigation is something of a contradiction in terms: by taking claims to court, litigants may expose private aspects of their lives to a far greater extent than the initial intrusion did.

Computer Crime

Computer-related crime is more of a problem than most people realize. Americans are losing billions of dollars to high-technology crooks whose activities go undetected and unpunished; estimates of losses range from at least $2 billion to more than $40 billion a year. While no one really knows how much is being stolen, the total appears to be growing fast.

Computer crime Criminal act that poses a threat to those who use computers or is accomplished by using a computer.

What is meant by the term **computer crime?** Although there is no consensus on definition, a broad but practical view defines computer crime as a criminal act that poses a greater threat to a computer owner than it would to a nonowner or a crime that is accomplished by using a computer. The perpetrator may manipulate input to the computer; change computer programs; or steal data, computer time, and software. Sometimes the actual hardware or software is damaged. Because computer crimes are often committed by professional people or office employees—people who have easy access to computer systems—they are called white-collar crimes.

The unique threat of computer crime is that criminals often use computers to conceal not only their own identities but also the existence of the crimes. Law officers worry that solving computer crimes seems to depend on luck. Many crimes are never discovered because company executives do not know enough about computers to detect them. Others are hushed up to avoid scaring customers and stockholders. It is difficult for a company to admit that computer systems cannot be made "crime-proof."

Perhaps 15 percent of computer thefts are reported to police. Many of these do not result in convictions and jail terms because the complexities of data processing mystify most police officials, prosecutors, judges, and jurors. To make matters worse, courts are often lenient in sentencing computer criminals.

Computer crimes can be classified in four categories: sabotage, theft of services, property crimes, and financial crimes. Sabotage of computers results in destruction or damage of computer hardware. In some cases, the computer itself is not used to carry out the destruction. However, sabotage may require some sophistication if computer-assisted security systems must be thwarted or the system is to be manipulated to harm itself.

Computer services can be abused in a variety of ways, too. Employees may acquire mailing lists from a city's computer to use for private mailings, for example, or they may use an organization's computers to conduct their own free-lance services after working hours. Wiretapping is another technique used to gain unauthorized access to a computer system. By "piggybacking" onto a legitimate user's line, one can have free access to the user's privileges whenever the line is not being used by the authorized party.

Computerizing banks and businesses creates a situation in which employees and customers could manipulate computer programs to acquire money. These financial crimes seem even more easy to commit since the advent of electronic funds transfer. Often employees detect ways to siphon small amounts—a few cents—from many accounts. A program can be altered to round off the fractions of cents from accounts when the interest is figured. These tiny amounts are transferred to another account, where they are allowed to accumulate and collect interest. Sometimes gaining access to bank records allows a group to change credit records. At least one group of people in California engaged in the business of creating favorable credit histories to clients seeking loans. Often an employee can manipulate a company's funds by causing multiple checks to be made out to the same person or by rerouting legitimate checks to false addresses.

Companies can implement many security measures to protect their computers and their funds (see Chapter 13). But often the security of systems depends upon the ethics of individuals. **Computer ethics** is a term used to refer to the standard of moral conduct in computer use. Ethics can govern an individual's attitude toward use of data in data bases, toward behavior on the job, and toward the copying of software.

Perhaps the most well-known matters involving ethics are the activities of hackers (computer enthusiasts) who feel challenged to break the security measures designed to prevent unauthorized access to a particular computer system. Regardless of the innocence claimed in meeting such a challenge, hackers have sometimes erased valuable data or caused a system to break down or malfunction.

Often employees also have the opportunity to use a company's computers and software for personal use. Some companies allow employees to use equipment on their own time, and most have adopted standards of behavior regarding personal use. But often the standards are only as effective as the personal ethics of each employee. Gaining access to a data base for illegitimate use or copying copyrighted software may be easy, but it is also unethical and illegal. It is the responsibility of each computer user to evaluate his or her own actions and determine the standard of morals to be followed. Only through ethical behavior will the ultimate security and privacy of computers and computer data be assured.

Computer ethics Term referring to the standard of moral conduct in computer use or computer-related activities.

FOCUS ON MICRO-COMPUTING

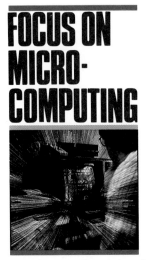

A Chicken in Every Pot and a Microcomputer on Every Desk

Electricity, automobiles, air travel, and television have changed our everyday lives in years past. Two cars in every garage and three televisions in every home seem to be the rule rather than the exception today. Perhaps tomorrow's promise will be "a computer for every family member."

The Subeck family, near Chicago, illustrates tomorrow's promise today. Mrs. Subeck once questioned the worth of owning personal computers. But once the first home computer was purchased, more followed quickly. Today the family of four owns ten computers—four Atari 800s, four Atari 400s, two TRS-80s, and an assortment of peripheral devices. Eventually the family started an electronic bulletin board that is maintained 24 hours a day.

The daily lives of the Van Slyke family in Forest City, Iowa, have changed, too, since each family member uses a computer at work or school. Jeff, the father, sits at a terminal connected to an IBM 4341 mainframe at the town's Winnebago plant to plan "just-in-time" inventory, patterned after the Japanese-inspired system of keeping just enough supplies on hand to maintain production without stockpiling the supplies. Jeff's wife, Becky, uses an Apple Lisa for her job as a word processor in the engineering department. Alyson and Jesse use Texas Instruments computers at school. Alyson also composes music on her Texas Instruments machine at home. She subscribes to *Enter*, a computer magazine for children and teenagers. Already Alyson and Jesse are comfortable with their home systems; they are growing up playing with microcomputers, just as children of the 1960s and 1970s grew up watching television.

People use microcomputers for tasks as ordinary as bookkeeping or as creative as composing music. Microcomputers can control home environments and security, bring Wall Street into the home or office via telecommunications, help prepare genealogical records, or enhance college careers. Microcomputers can change plans for summer vacations, too, if you decide to attend a camp that incorporates study of computers and programming.

Once people went to summer camp to swim to the raft in the center of the lake, play "tipsy canoe," watch for fresh bear tracks, and get poison ivy. Today many camps focus their curricula on microcomputers and programming languages. There are camps for children, teenagers, adults, and families. Some camps are set in exotic places like Mexico, Hawaii, Lake Tahoe, or even the riverboat Mississippi Queen. Others are more like school and are located in institutions like Amherst College in Massachusetts, Duke University in North Carolina, and Lincoln College in Illinois. Many camps include activities other than those generated on microcomputers. One for adults only at Jackson Hole, Wyoming, mixes computer business applications on the IBM PC with white water rafting and skiing. Another camp for families, nestled on Mt. Rainier in Washington, combines microcomputers with seasonal activities such as sleigh rides, skiing, and fishing.

Camps offer a relaxing atmosphere for learning about computers, but computer education is also offered in the fast-paced, often stressful environment of college. Following Drexel University's initiative in 1982, many colleges demand that each student take at least one computer course, and some are requiring students to buy microcomputers to use during their college careers. At some universities, students are even able to access the school's main computer after graduation. Researchers are trying to determine the difficulty students have in using microcomputers or campus computer systems. Some of the responses at Carnegie-Mellon University in Pittsburgh indicate that computers have indeed governed student campus life. Of the students questioned, 78 percent found out that learning to use the computer took longer than they expected, and 76 percent felt overwhelmed by the amount of work required in computer classes. Many students discovered that their schedules were governed by the computer: so many students were using the computers that each student slotted time for computer use before planning other activities in order to complete assignments on time.

While microcomputers may increase certain kinds of stress, they can make running a business easier. Everyday business applications center on such procedures as business graphics, word processing, accounting, and financial analyses. Yet there seems to be no limit to the creative aspects of microcomputing in business. Chef Terence Dicker is surrounded by copper kettles hanging from racks, fresh vegetables and meats, and soup brewing on the stove. But he has to be careful to wash his flour-dusted hands before looking up inventory, menus, or recipes on his Apple IIc computer. Dicker is the food and beverage director of the Williamsburg Hospitality House in Virginia. He uses the Apple IIc to track costs, inventory, and future needs in order to run the kitchen efficiently. When he first became interested in microcomputers, there was no software for kitchen management. He designed some programs and wrote a book called **Computer Programs for the Kitchen,** which tells how to set up a kitchen management data base. Truly his entire approach toward kitchen management has been influenced by the advent of the microcomputer.

Microcomputers will increasingly affect the lives of the elderly and disabled, too. Computers can sense intruders, monitor a person's location, or permit someone to phone from a remote location in case of trouble. Some home computers can even be programmed to monitor blood pressure and pulse. Others automatically dial preset telephone numbers to notify a fire or police department of break-ins, floods, or fire. By establishing security systems and telecommunication links to accomplish these tasks, microcomputers can help elderly people stay in their own homes longer.

Combined with special sensory devices, microcomputers will also enable the disabled to work at home. Such capabilities will increase feelings of self-worth in handicapped individuals and help them focus on personal goals. John Boyer of Madison, Wisconsin, is deaf and blind, yet he runs his own company, Computers to Help People, Inc. His objective is to write software to help the disabled and show employers that hiring the disabled can be profitable.

These and many other examples illustrate how microcomputers can change our lives. There is no doubt that computers are becoming far more integrated into our daily lives as we begin to shop, manage our households, run our businesses, and entertain ourselves by computer.

SUMMARY POINTS

- Computers are used in almost every phase of business. Even small businesses can benefit from computer use, now that costs of computers and programs have decreased.
- Through electronic funds transfer (EFT) in banking the computer permits 24-hour banking services, banking from home, and other automated services, such as direct deposit of paychecks and automatic payment of bills.
- Manufacturers also have taken advantage of computer-aided design and computer-aided manufacturing (CAD/CAM), which help their engineers and technicians to design, test, and manufacture products.
- Robots have also helped manufacturers to compete. Robots do routine, dull, heavy, or dangerous jobs. Two generations of industrial robots have appeared so far.
- Offices benefit from computer systems by implementing applications such as word processing, electronic mail, teleconferencing, and telecommuting.
- Military personnel in the federal government use computers to collect and analyze data related to defense, aid military planning, and simulate wars.
- The Internal Revenue Service (IRS) uses computers to record tax data reported by individuals and businesses and to audit selected tax returns.
- Complex calculations with vast amounts of data collected and processed by computers enable weather forecasters to predict weather.
- Huge data bases help the FBI and CIA solve crimes, prevent terrorism, and protect public figures.
- Physicians use computerized procedures to diagnose and monitor patients. The procedures include computerized axial tomography (CAT scans), multiphasic health testing, nuclear magnetic resonance (NMR) scanning, surgery by computer-controlled lasers, and life-support monitoring for critically ill patients.
- An important aspect of many curricula in today's schools is computer literacy. Computer literacy courses vary in their content, but most frequently stress technical knowledge about hardware and software, computer history, programming, ethics, problem-solving, and social impact of computer use.
- Software that drills, instructs, and simulates comprises computer-assisted instruction (CAI).
- Privacy and crime are major concerns since the creation of large data bases has led to less individual control over private aspects of living and since computers have created an electronic arena for criminals to exchange money, steal funds, and destroy or alter data.
- Legislation that helps protect individuals includes the Privacy Act of 1974, the Education Privacy Act, The Right to Financial Privacy Act of 1978, the Freedom of Information Act of 1970, and the Fair Credit Reporting Act of 1970.
- Types of crime include sabotage to hardware or software, theft of services, property crimes, and financial crimes.
- Although certain measures can aid in preventing computer crime and securing confidential data, security really depends upon the ethics of the individuals who have access to computer systems.
- Microcomputers affect people's lives, too. The smaller computers aid in business and school activities. Vacations may center around which computer camp sounds most attractive. College students may be required to purchase

microcomputers to use while taking classes. People who are disabled or elderly can hook up complex systems to monitor their health or permit them to communicate with people in the outside world.

REVIEW AND DISCUSSION QUESTIONS

1. Name some ways that computers aid manufacturers and other businesses.
2. What are some advantages of office automation?
3. What workers might take advantage of full or partial telecommuting?
4. What impact has computer technology had on some of the functions of the federal government?
5. What private data may be too sensitive or particularly subject to abuse in government data bases?
6. Show how the advantages of the computer can be put to good use in the diagnosing and treating of medical ailments.
7. Explain why computer literacy has become such an important issue in education. At what point do you feel children should be exposed to computers? Is there a danger in exposing them to computers at too young an age?
8. Why has the issue of privacy become so important? How can the problems associated with the storage of personal data be resolved?
9. What is computer crime? Describe some ways that computers are related to the perpetration of crimes.
10. What is meant by the term *computer ethics*? Describe some situations in which individuals apply their personal codes of ethics.
11. How can microcomputers influence the lives of disabled or elderly people?
12. How do you think microcomputers will be used in connection with telecommunications in the future?
13. Talk to some people who are employed by companies that use large mainframe computers. Are microcomputers being used more frequently at these places of business? Why?

Enhancing Creativity and Entertainment

Computers have redefined the limits of art and music. They have made possible the creation of images and sounds once found only in dreams. Professional artists and entertainers use minicomputer and mainframe equipment to create animation and surrealistic scenes and to superimpose human actors upon computer-generated backgrounds. However, advances in microcomputer technology and software provide increased computer power to any of us who want to explore our ideas.

Perhaps the most visible and dramatic computer-generated effects appear in television, movies, and advertising. When we watch sporting events, the networks display animated logos such as those created for Superbowl XVIII① by Cranston/Csuri Productions, Inc. Other artists take advantage of the surrealistic effects that computer graphics permit, like the pink clouds bubbling in the background of an FM radio station advertisement ② or the seaweed drifting under water ③. Even mathematics plays a role in generating graphics. A new word, *fractal,* was coined in 1975 to describe the mathematics used to create realistic forms by computer. Fractal geometry can be used to create such realistic forms as mountains, tree bark, broccoli spears or mud cracks in a dry riverbed. Some computer art is so realistic that it looks like a photograph ④. Fractal geometry can also generate surreal images such as a "dragon" ⑤.

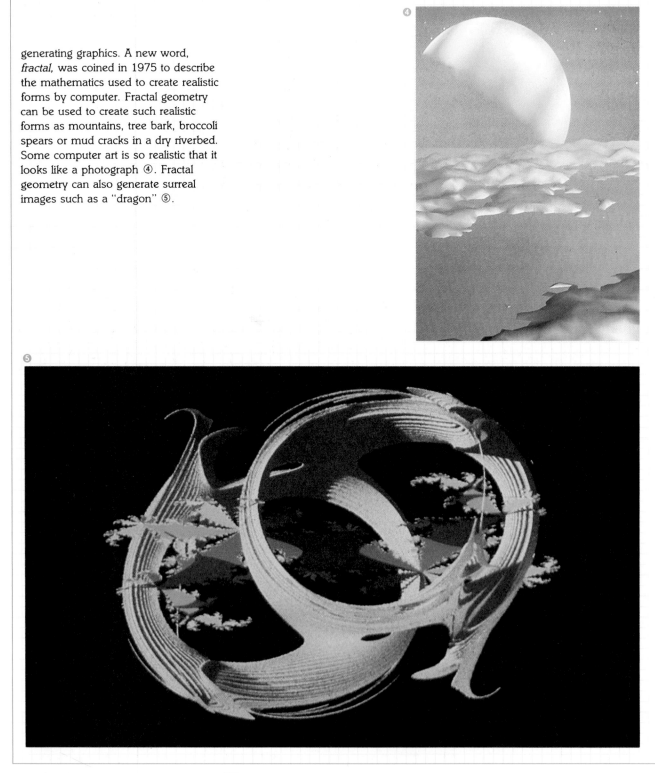

30

Behind the scenes in television and advertising are teams such as San Francisco's public TV station, KQED, which uses a multi-user CompuPro system to supply information about schedules, publicity releases, logs, and more ⑥. Also behind the scenes are animation creators like Don Bluth, surrounded by his friends Borf, Ace, and Kimberly from "Space Age," an animated laser-disc arcade game ⑦. Don Bluth's artistry is also evident in the video game "Dragon's Lair," which features Dirk the Daring and his worst enemy, The Dragon ⑧. Examples of the work done by Robert Abel and Associates in Hollywood, who supplied some of the graphics for the movie *Tron,* include both an animated umbrella dance for software called "High Fidelity" and a 90-second spot for Panasonic's three-dimensional television system called "Glider." In the umbrella scene, red and white two-dimensional textures were mapped onto three-dimensional geometric shapes ⑨. The room in "Glider" features computer-generated perspective drawing ⑩.

⑥

⑦

⑧

⑨

⑩

Although we are impressed by some of the more spectacular graphics effects seen in television, videos, and movies, graphics is used in the planning stages of design, too. Graphics capabilities are used by engineers and architects for more practical applications such as designing homes and bridges ⑪ and ⑫. AUTOCAD software was used to plan these structures.

However, computer graphics and sound effects are not limited to professional artists, producers, and musicians. Anyone can purchase equipment and software in many price ranges to experiment with graphics and sound effects at home. Some software allows you free reign on your own creative ideas, while other software, such as the click art available for the Apple Macintosh computer, allows you to incorporate prepared art—like this portrait of Albert Einstein—in your own documents ⑬. You can also compose melodies and add other rhythms and sound effects using a synthesizer and personal computer. Many packages offer menus from which you choose the effects you want, as seen on this screen display guiding the use of a Kawasaki synthesizer ⑭. Even the common printer is no longer a simple dot matrix or daisy wheel typing machine. An IBM color ink jet printer can reproduce foods so realistically that the result looks like a photograph ⑮.

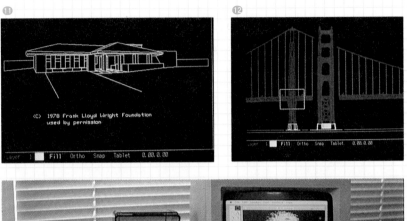

Computers have become so popular in the entertainment field that you can plan your vacation around using them. Many people attend computer camps, offered by National Computer Camps, Orange, Connecticut, ⑯ where they learn to program, use simulation software, and prepare graphic designs. Computers are also an integral part of vacations at Disney World and EPCOT, where hands-on experiences with computers and robots such as SMRT-1 are not to be missed ⑰,⑱, and ⑲. At AstroWorld in Houston, Texas, tourists delight in computer-operated characters that talk, sing and dance. The Udder Delights—harmonizing heifers who "ooh" and "moo" their way into the hearts of the audience—are just a few of the performers in The Great Texas Longhorn Revue. This state-of-the-art family entertainment is produced by "theatronics," a combination of theater and electronics ⑳. Wherever you go, you can be on the lookout for computer-generated effects in the entertainment field.

CHAPTER 2
COMPUTER EVOLUTION

COMPUTERS IN OUR LIVES

Going for the Gold with Computers

With our increased awareness of the importance of exercise in maintaining good health, we have become a nation of weekend athletes. Even though the toughest competition we may ever enter is a 10K race, we still have that drive to extend our abilities and become as good as the pros. Computers are helping many of us to do this.

Evelyn Ashford, winner of the gold medal in the 100-meter track event at the 1984 Summer Olympics, has helped all women runners— amateur and professional—improve their running style through her own experience with computerized biomechanical analysis, CBA for short. Ashford, like many athletes, went to the Coto Research Center in Coto de Caza, California, to get help from CBA. Ashford wanted to be a better runner. The Coto Research Center analyzed Ashford's running style by filming her running stride with a high-speed camera from front, back, both sides, and above. Ultrasensitive pressure plates attached to her feet electronically measured the force on all parts of her soles as they touched the ground. As she moved, the angles of her joints were calculated, along with the effort made by her muscles. All this information was then fed into a computer. The end result was a series of three-dimensional figures that displayed Ashford's fluid motion on a monitor. Examination of the CBA showed Ashford that women's wider-angle thighbone attachment to the pelvis causes too much hip sway when running. By bringing her feet closer to the midline to compensate for this, Ashford—and all women runners—can run more efficiently.

The U.S. women's volleyball team also got help from CBA that enabled it to cover the distance from notably poor performer to winner of a silver medal at the 1984 Summer Olympics. One way team members used CBA was to analyze the differences between themselves and their opponents. CBA allowed them to compare, for example, Flo Hyman of the U.S. team with Yokayama, her counterpart on the Japanese women's volleyball team. The computer showed that even though Yokayama is 11 inches shorter than 6-foot 5-inch Hyman, she was a more powerful spiker, hitting the ball at the strongest point in her leap whereas Flo hit it too late. The team took the information CBA provided and designed a training program to help Flo and the team improve.

After CBA shows athletes how they can improve, the next step is a lot of hard training. Dr. Gideon Ariel, director of the Coto Research Center, has developed a computerized exercise machine to help athletes with their training programs. This exercise machine, which is similar to a Nautilus or Universal machine, monitors muscle tension, fatigue, work force, and speed, and the computer automatically adjusts the load to the capability of the user, always providing a maximum workout. Originally designed for professional athletes, the machine will soon be benefiting amateurs as well thanks to the decreasing cost of computer chips. A computerized exercise system for the home gym may be something no serious fitness buff will want to be without.

Biomechanical analysis is just one example of the new sophistication of computer techniques used to gather, input, and process data. In their earliest uses, computers were confined to simply performing mathematical calculations on equations that were entered by hand. Before computers, calculations were completed using even cruder methods. Chapter 2 traces the development of computers from early mechanical devices to the present state-of-the art-machines.

INTRODUCTION

The history of the computer is a story of human ingenuity used to develop tools to calculate answers to problems and record the results. Early humans used their fingers for counting but quickly developed methods that would also aid in maintaining a permanent record of inventory. Ancient shepherds tied knots in pieces of rope or laid out pebbles to keep exact count of their herds. Merchants once carved marks on clay or stone tablets to represent transactions. Then came the abacus, a device made of beads strung on wires, which was used for addition and subtraction (see Figure 2–1).

The abacus, along with hand calculations, was adequate for computation until the early 1600s, when John Napier (1550–1617) designed a portable multiplication tool called Napier's Bones, or Napier's Rods (see Figure 2–2). The device was made of ivory rods. The user slid the rods up and down against each other, matching the numbers printed on them to figure multiplication and division problems. Napier's idea, which was based on the concept of logarithms, led to the invention of the slide rule in the mid-1600s.

These tools were anything but automatic. People had to manipulate the devices much as if they were counting on their fingers. How did subsequent inventions develop to the point of automatic data processing?

Figure 2–1
The Abacus

Figure 2-2
Napier's Bones

Figure 2-2
Napier's Bones

EARLY MECHANICAL DEVICES

As business became more complicated and tax systems expanded, people saw the need for faster, more accurate aids to computation. The idea for the first mechanical calculating machine grew out of the many tedious hours a father and his son spent preparing tax reports.

The Pascaline

In the mid-1600s, Blaise Pascal, a mathematician and philosopher, and his father, a tax official, were compiling tax reports for the French government in Paris. As they agonized over the columns of figures, Pascal decided to build a machine that would do the task much faster and more accurately. His machine—called the Pascaline—was based on the decimal system and could add and subtract (see Figure 2–3).

Figure 2-3
Blaise Pascal and the Pascaline

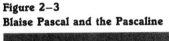

Much as an odometer keeps track of a car's mileage, the Pascaline functioned by a series of eight rotating gears, or notched wheels. Each wheel stood for one place: the ones place, tens place, hundreds place, and so on. As the first wheel counted out ten digits (one complete revolution, from 0 to 9) a pin on its edge would turn the next wheel, which stood for the number of tens. This second gear would rotate the next, and so on.

Unfortunately, a market for the Pascaline never grew. Only 50 Pascalines were built. Not only was Pascal the only person who could repair his machine, clerks and accountants would not even use it. They were afraid it might replace them at their jobs! Today we remember Pascal's role in computer history: the computer language Pascal was named in his honor.

About 50 years later in 1694, the German mathematician Gottfried Wilhelm von Leibniz improved Pascal's machine. In addition to adding and subtracting, the Leibniz mechanical calculator could also multiply, divide, and figure square roots. The user would enter the numbers and set the machine to the desired operation. Although the machine could have helped scientists with time-consuming manual calculations, it did not become widely used.

The Punched Card Concept

Machines designed before the early 1800s required human intervention to operate. One of the first advances in programmable instructions benefited the weaving industry. In an attempt to automate the weaving process, a French weaver named Joseph Marie Jacquard built a loom controlled by **punched cards** (see Figure 2–4). Heavy paper cards, linked in a series, passed over a set of rods on the loom. The pattern of holes in the cards determined which rods were engaged, thereby adjusting the color and pattern of the product. Before Jacquard's invention, a loom operator had to adjust the loom settings by hand before each glide of the shuttle. That process was tedious and time-consuming.

Jacquard's invention emphasized three concepts that became important in computer development. One was that information could be coded on punched cards. A second was that the cards could be linked to present a series of instructions—essentially, a program—that would allow a machine to perform its work without human intervention. A third concept was that such "programs" could provide job automation.

The first person to propose the concept of the modern computer was Charles Babbage, a professor at Cambridge University in England. As a mathematician he realized the time-consuming and boring nature of constructing mathematical tables (squares, square roots, logarithms, and so on). Babbage proposed a machine that could compute the properties of numbers. With a grant from the British government, he designed a working model of the **difference engine** (see Figure 2–5). However, he was unable to build a larger version. Even slight flaws in the brass and pewter rods and gears threw the difference engine out of whack. In Babbage's day, the technology was too primitive to build more accurate parts.

Babbage lost interest in the project when he began designing a new machine, the **analytical engine.** The design for this steam-powered machine was amazingly similar to the design of modern computers. It would have four components: a "mill" to manipulate data; a "store" to hold data; an "operator" or system to carry out instructions; and a separate device to read and "write" processed information by punched cards. In addition, Babbage's collaborator,

Punched cards Heavy paper storage medium in which data is represented by holes punched according to a specific coding scheme.

Difference engine Machine designed by Charles Babbage to compute mathematical tables. (In Babbage's time the word *engine* meant "invention").

Analytical engine Machine designed by Charles Babbage that could perform calculations and store intermediate results in a memory unit.

**Figure 2–4
The Jacquard Loom**

Figure 2–5
Charles Babbage and the Difference Engine

Augusta Ada Byron, Countess of Lovelace, suggested that Babbage use the **binary number system** rather than the decimal number system to code his machine.

Although Babbage died before he could construct the analytical engine, his son built a model from Babbage's notes and drawings in 1871. Because of the concepts used in the two engines, Babbage is known today as the father of computers.

Punched cards played an important role in the next important advance toward automatic machines. Dr. Herman Hollerith, a statistician, worked for the U.S. Census Bureau to develop a mechanical method of tabulating census data (see Figure 2 – 6). Counting the 1880 census had taken 7½ years. Since the population

Binary number system Number system using the 0 and 1; corresponds to the ''on'' and ''off'' states in electric circuits.

Figure 2–6
Herman Hollerith and the Tabulating Machine

40

HIGHLIGHT

Augusta Ada Byron, Countess of Lovelace

While Charles Babbage was struggling through the development of his difference engine in the mid-1800s, he was not alone. Working by his side was Augusta Ada Byron, daughter of the poet, Lord Byron, and later, Countess of Lovelace. Lady Lovelace was considered a mathematical genius and her work with Babbage has earned her the title of the first programmer.

Lady Lovelace began working with Babbage in 1842 after translating from French to English a paper about his difference engine. Her interest heightened as she worked on the project, and the following year, when she was 28 years old, Lady Lovelace had added some of her own ideas to Babbage's. The paper, as it turned out, tripled in length due to her additions.

One of Lady Lovelace's ideas that earned her the title of first programmer was what we now refer to as the concept of a *loop*. She had observed that the same sequence of instructions were often necessary to perform a single calculation. She discovered that by using a single set of cards, and a conditional jump facility, the calculation could be performed with a fraction of the effort.

Lady Lovelace continued to work with Babbage until her tragic death from cancer at the age of 36. Babbage was once again left alone to continue with his labor. Neither Lady Lovelace nor Babbage lived to see the fruits of their efforts. In honor of her work, a high-level programming language (used chiefly by the U.S. government) was named Ada.

had increased significantly during the intervening years, the job of taking the 1890 census seemed formidable.

Hollerith designed a tabulating machine that would read and sort data from punched cards. The holes in the paper cards conformed to a special code, the **Hollerith code,** arranged on a grid of 12 rows and 80 columns. Once data was punched, a tabulator read the cards as they passed over tiny brushes. Each time a brush found a hole, it completed an electrical circuit and caused special counting dials to increment the data. The cards were then sorted into 24 compartments by the sorting component of the machine. These cards were the forerunners of today's standard computer card.

Hollerith's invention was so efficient that the 1890 census was completed in 2½ years, despite an increase of 13 million people since 1880. Encouraged by his success, Hollerith formed the Tabulating Machine Company in 1896 to supply equipment to census takers in western Europe and Canada. The U.S. Census Bureau continued to be a major user of his equipment in 1900. A disagreement with the census director, however, caused Hollerith to lose the bureau's business. Meanwhile, his successor at the bureau, James Powers, redesigned the machines and eventually formed his own company, which was later to become Remington Rand and later, Sperry Univac.

Hollerith energetically sought new clients. The railroad industry implemented his machines, followed by other mercantile and manufacturing clients. In 1911

Hollerith code Method of data representation that delineates characters by the placement of holes in 80-column punched cards.

Figure 2–7
Thomas J. Watson Sr.

Accounting machine   Forerunner of the computer; could mechanically read data from punched cards, calculate and sort data, and print results.

Mark I   First automatic calculator.

Digital computer   Type of computer that operates on distinct data, (for example digits) by performing arithmetic and logic processes on specific data units.

Atanasoff-Berry Computer (ABC)   First electronic digital computer; developed by John Vincent Atanasoff and Clifford Berry.

Vacuum tube   Light bulb-like device through which electricity can pass, such as those found in old radios and televisions.

Hollerith sold his company, which later combined with 12 others to form the Computing-Tabulating-Recording (CTR) Company.

In 1924 Thomas J. Watson Sr. became president of CTR and changed its name to the International Business Machines Corporation (IBM) (see Figure 2–7). The IBM machines made extensive use of punched cards. After Congress set up the Social Security System in 1935, Watson won for IBM the contract to provide machines needed for this massive accounting and payment distribution system. During World War II, Watson's company was also asked to finance two projects to aid the government in ballistics research. One was a computing device proposed by Howard H. Aiken. The other was an electronic computer suggested by John W. Mauchly and J. Presper Eckert. Watson chose to finance only Aiken's project, a mistake that resulted in the establishment of a leading competitor, Remington Rand, today Sperry Corporation.

EARLY DEVELOPMENTS IN ELECTRONIC PROCESSING

About the time that Hollerith's tabulating machines were working on the census, William S. Burroughs began marketing his mechanical adding machines. The key-driven, hand-cranked machines calculated numbers and printed them on paper tape. His company, the Burroughs Adding Machine Company, is a direct ancestor of Burroughs Corporation.

From this time on, it becomes more difficult to sort the advances preceding the modern computer because they were occurring so fast. **Accounting machines** built in the late 1920s and early 1930s supported full-scale record-keeping and accounting functions (see Figure 2–8). They did little more than manipulate vast quantities of punched cards. The first real advance toward modern computing was made by Aiken's team at Harvard University. Backed by money and engineers from IBM, the team built the **Mark I** (also called the Automatic Sequence Controlled Calculator) (see Figure 2–9). Unfortunately, Aiken neglected to credit IBM's role in developing the machine, and IBM never again collaborated with him on a project.

Aiken's machine could store 72 words, perform three additions a second, and multiply two 10-place numbers in three seconds. The U.S. Navy used it to figure data needed to design and fire weapons until the end of World War II. The Mark I was controlled by paper tapes and results were obtained in the form of punched cards. The mammoth machine was three times the size of a living room and weighed five tons. It consisted of 78 accounting machines and contained 500 miles of wiring. Its parts made a loud, clacking noise during processing. Aiken realized that, in many ways, the Mark I was like the analytical engine drafted by Charles Babbage more than 100 years earlier.

Meanwhile John Vincent Atanasoff and his assistant, Clifford Berry, had built the first electronic **digital computer** (see Figure 2–10). A professor of mathematics and, later, physics at Iowa State University, Atanasoff needed a machine that would solve large equations and perform other complex calculations. Existing calculators were too slow and inaccurate. On the other hand, the **Atanasoff-Berry Computer,** or **ABC,** was capable of solving 29 simultaneous linear equations with 29 variables. It was based on the binary number system and used **vacuum tubes** for storage and arithmetic – logic functions.

The ABC was a limited-purpose computer. Atanasoff was unable to market or patent his computer, and for many years other people got credit for devel-

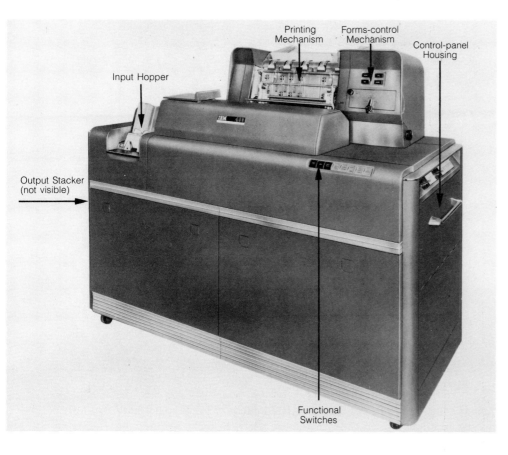

Input Hopper

Printing Mechanism

Forms-control Mechanism

Control-panel Housing

Output Stacker (not visible)

Functional Switches

Figure 2–8
An Accounting Machine

Figure 2–9
Howard Aiken and the Mark I

Figure 2–10
John Atanasoff, Clifford Berry, and the ABC

ENIAC (Electronic Numerical Integrator and Calculator) First general-purpose electronic digital computer; developed by John W. Mauchly and J. Presper Eckert Jr.

General-purpose computers Computers that can be used for a variety of purposes.

oping the first electronic computer. In 1974 a federal judge ruled that Atanasoff was the true inventor of the concepts required to build a working electronic digital computer. Those ideas laid the foundation for the next advances in the development of the computer.

In December 1940 John W. Mauchly attended a meeting of the American Association for the Advancement of Science (AAAS) to speak about the use of vacuum tubes to speed up computations electronically. There he met Atanasoff and learned of the ABC. He accepted Atanasoff's invitation to see the machine. After studying the ABC, Mauchly enrolled in a course at the University of Pennsylvania's Moore School of Engineering—a government program designed to train engineers in electronics in the hope of recruiting researchers. His laboratory instructor for the course was J. Presper Eckert Jr., then a young graduate student.

Mauchly joined the staff at the Moore School, which was engaged in a project with the U.S. Army Ordnance Department's Aberdeen Proving Ground. He teamed with Eckert to design a machine that would generate precise artillery trajectory tables for the ballistics research going on at Aberdeen. The tables accounted for gravity, air movement, and the size and material of the weapons.

At first, Mauchly and Eckert sought financial backing from IBM. However, the project was funded by the U.S. Army. In June 1946 the pair introduced their machine, the **Electronic Numerical Integrator and Calculator (ENIAC),** the first **general-purpose** electronic **computer** (see Figure 2–11). The ENIAC was huge. Its 18,000 vacuum tubes required housing that was 10 feet high, 10 feet wide, and some 100 feet long. It could perform in .003 of a second a calculation that the Mark I could do in 3 seconds.

Since the ENIAC was finished after World War II ended, it was used to study weather, cosmic rays, and atomic energy. Dr. Edward Teller used the ENIAC in his work on the hydrogen bomb at Los Alamos in 1946. At the time, scientists

44

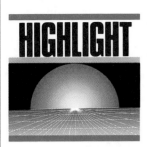

HIGHLIGHT

Alan Turing and the Enigma

We have studied the scientists and mathematicians who invented a variety of devices that led to the development of the modern computer. But until very recently, one person had been left out of the historical accounts. The reason for the omission has to do with war and security. The man is Alan Turing. The war was World War II.

Alan Turning was an Englishman who had formulated the logical basis for computable numbers in a paper written in 1936. His ideas laid the foundation for the United States machine, ENIAC. In fact, Turing even traveled secretly to the United States to help with the development of ENIAC.

Why the hush-hush about Alan Turing?

His ideas contributed to breaking the code of German war messages, and breaking the code meant winning the war for the Allies. But since Turing's work involved a top-secret war effort, his name was not associated with the work until 1974, 20 years after his death.

The British government feared it might lose the war, so MI6, Britain's CIA, urgently began to work on a machine that could break the coded messages sent by Enigma, the German encoding, or scrambling, machine. The patterns set up in Enigma seemed foolproof. If necessary, they could be changed every day. The Germans were so sure that their codes were safe that they sent radio messages about their most secret plans. Also, the Germans were so sure that they would win the war, they did not press research to develop their own digital computer.

According to Turing's theory, the Enigma could be emulated mathematically by using 0s and 1s. So MI6 sent the men, including Turing, who studied the Enigma to the small town of Bletchley to try to develop such a code-breaking machine. The Turing team built several machines before eventually building the Colossus, code-named ULTRA, a single-purpose computer that worked with vacuum tubes. ULTRA quickly unscrambled German messages and was instrumental in defeating the Germans.

The decoding projects were so secret that Winston Churchill, then prime minister of England, allowed the German bombing of Coventry to take place without warning the people or planning strategic defense moves. Any such actions would have given the Germans a hint that their codes were being broken.

---

thought that seven computers like the ENIAC could handle all the calculations the world would ever need.

One problem, however, loomed large: operating instructions had to be fed into the ENIAC by setting external switches and connecting wires on control panels called plugboards. If a mistake occurred in setting even one switch, the program would be incorrect. John von Neumann, a mathematical genius and

Figure 2–11
The ENIAC

member of the Institute for Advanced Study in Princeton, New Jersey, began to study ways to overcome this difficulty. The solution involved the **stored-program concept.** Von Neumann, along with Mauchly and Eckert, believed that both the instructions and the data could be written in binary code and stored in computer memory. Binary code, or **machine language,** is based on the binary number system, which used two digits, 0 (zero) and 1 (one). The language suits the computer because electronic components are in one of two states, "on" or "off"—that is, conducting or nonconducting. Strings of 1s and 0s could specify the desired electrical states—on and off, respectively—of the computer's circuits and memory banks.

Von Neumann's principles spurred development of the first **stored-program computer** in the United States. As it turned out, two groups of people were working simultaneously to create such a machine. Maunchly and Eckert were working with others at the University of Pennsylvania on the **EDVAC (Electronic Discrete Variable Automatic Computer)** (see Figure 2–12); scientists at Cambridge University in England were building the **EDSAC (Electronic Delay Storage Automatic Computer).** The EDSAC received the title of first stored-program computer, although it was completed only a few months before the EDVAC.

The two machines marked the end of the quest to develop a self-sufficient calculating machine. They performed arithmetic and logic operations without human intervention, depending solely on instructions stored in computer memory. These computers really introduced the computer age and the information society. Refinements of the computer concept have focused on speed, size, and cost. These developments are commonly categorized as the four generations of computers.

THE FIFTIES: PIONEERS IN THE INDUSTRY

In the 1950s, the ramifications of computer technology were only beginning to be recognized. Mauchly and Eckert were expanding their work with EDVAC,

Figure 2–12
John von Neumann and the EDVAC

Concept Summary 2–1 ■ Motivations for Data Processing Developments and the Machines that Resulted

Person	Motivations	Machine
Pascal	Needed a faster, more accurate way to compute tax reports	Pascaline
von Leibniz	Wanted a faster way to compute scientific calculations	Mechanical calculator
Jacquard	Thought changing loom settings by hand was tiresome and time-consuming	Jacquard's loom
Babbage	Realized the time-consuming and boring nature of constructing mathematical tables (squares, square roots, logarithms, etc.)	Difference engine; analytical engine
Hollerith	Knew the government was worried that the 1890 census would not be finished in time.	Tabulating machine
Atanasoff	Needed a machine that would help him solve large equations and other complex calculations.	Atanasoff-Berry Computer (ABC)
Aiken	Helped in designing a machine that aided the aiming and firing of weapons.	Mark I
Eckert, Mauchly	Designed a machine to solve weapons problems.	ENIAC
von Neumann	Realized the problem with setting computer instructions by moving switches and wires.	EDVAC

Old Computers Don't Die; They Just Sto(re) Away!

Everyone was quite emotional on that memorable day in fall 1980. The staff at Brigham Young University gathered for a ceremony at which the director of the computer center, Willard Gardner, made a farewell speech. "Stretch" was to be retired. But the staff knew that Stretch would be well cared for: Stretch would be exhibited at the Computer Museum, now located on Boston's Museum Wharf.

Stretch was an IBM 7030 machine built in the 1950s. It contained 150,000 transistors, read 1000 punched cards per minute, and used almost $1000 worth of electricity per month. So the university sent Stretch to the Computer Museum, which stores and displays old calculating and computer equipment.

The collection began when Kenneth H. Olsen, president of the Digital Equipment Corporation, decided to save the Whirlwind, a computer about to be junked. Whirlwind was stored in a DEC warehouse, but in 1979 Olsen and Gordon Bell, a DEC vice president, displayed the computer and Bell's collection of old calculating instruments in the lobby at DEC. Bell's wife, Gwen Bell, became director of the museum. She set out to present computer history from the dinosaurs of the vacuum-tube age to today's microchips.

Along with the Whirlwind Computer, Gwen Bell exhibited her husband's Napier's Bones, seventeenth-century slide rule, and early pocket calculator that sold for $395. The display grew to include a Hollerith Tabulating Machine; a UNIVAC I; an early IBM RAMAC disk that was 2½ feet in diameter and stored all of 100K; an Enigma, and the AN/FSQ-7, a vacuum tube machine that grew out of the Whirlwind project and was the backbone of the U.S. Air Force air defense system from 1958 to 1983. Today the museum is a nonprofit organization independent of DEC. The exhibits appear in galleries according to technology: the Vacuum Tube Era, the Transistor Era, the Integrated Circuit Era, and the Image Gallery, which exhibits state-of-the-art technology.

completing the first UNIVAC, a name that became as synonymous with *computer* as *Kleenex* was with *tissue*. The first translating programs and high-level languages were being developed by such people as Commodore Grace Murray Hopper and John Backus. And Thomas J. Watson Jr. was establishing IBM's ("Snow White") position among the other corporate giants (the "Seven Dwarfs") in the computer industry: Sperry Rand, Control Data Corporation, Honeywell, RCA, NCR, General Electric, and Burroughs.

First-generation computers were huge, expensive, and often undependable. They were very slow compared to today's computers, and their internal storage capacity was limited. Vacuum tubes controlled their internal operations (see Figure 2–13). The masses of vacuum tubes took up a lot of space and generated considerable heat. Special air conditioning had to be installed to cool the sur-

First-generation computers Computers that used vacuum tubes; much faster than earlier mechanical devices.

directly in the path of a funnel cloud, they can supply data that allow the supercomputers to process better storm models. They also hope to gather measurements about all types of atmospheric conditions to forecast accurately within zero to twelve hours and precisely within a mile. To do this, meteorologists need more sophisticated chip technology, processing architecture that allows many items to be processed simultaneously, and even more advanced primary memory systems.

Weather forecasting is only one example of data-processing applications. Other applications that rely on data-processing include payroll preparation, accounting, sales forecasting, statistical analysis, inventory control, and budgeting. This chapter discusses the most common and current computer functions, data processing, input and output, and primary storage.

INTRODUCTION

One can acquire a general understanding of electronic data processing without making a detailed study of the computer technology involved. However, a basic understanding of how the computer operates better equips the student of data processing to appreciate the computer's capabilities and limitations and to relate this knowledge to data-processing activities.

This chapter identifies the basic functions a computer can perform and the reasons a computer's power seems so marvelous. The key components of a computer and their functions are described in relation to the data-processing stages. The chapter also discusses input and output, the central processing unit (CPU), and internal storage (read-only memory, ROM, and random-access memory, RAM). The chapter concludes with a discussion of data representation—the binary number system and computer codes.

DIGITAL AND ANALOG COMPUTERS

Earlier in this book when we used the term *computer,* we were referring to a specific type—the **digital computer.** However, there are also **analog computers.** It is important to distinguish between these two types.

In a digital computer, data is represented by discrete "on" and "off" states of its electronic circuitry. Numbers, letters, and other special symbols are represented by a unique code of 1s (on) and 0s (off). This is referred to as binary notation. The digital computer must convert all its input to binary form and, after processing the data, output the results in the same form. The 1 and 0 states used for both numeric and alphabetic data can be represented by holes in punched cards or paper tape, as well as by magnetic spots on tapes and disks. This binary data can be converted to regular print so that the computer user can easily understand it.

Digital computers achieve varying degrees of precision, depending on their

Analog computer A computer that measures continuous electrical or physical conditions rather than operating on digits.

particular construction and machine characteristics. For example, some digital computers can provide results accurate to hundreds or even thousands of decimal places. Such computers are often used in scientific applications. For business applications, results accurate to only a few decimal places are sufficient. Therefore, computer manufacturers build various models of digital computers to meet the varied needs of the ultimate users of these machines.

In contrast to digital computers, analog computers do not operate directly on "on" and "off" states represented by binary digits. Instead, they measure continuous physical or electrical magnitudes, such as pressure, temperature, current, voltage, length, or shaft rotations. For example, a gasoline pump is an analog device that measures (1) the quantity of gasoline pumped (to the nearest tenth of a gallon) and (2) the price of that gasoline (to the nearest penny). Another example of an analog device is a car speedometer. Here, driveshaft rotations are measured and converted to a number that indicates the speed of the car.

While numerical results can be obtained from analog computers, they are arrived at indirectly. Because digital computers are commonly used in the applications discussed in this book, the remainder of the book focuses on digital computers.

COMPUTER FUNCTIONS

Science fiction has given computers human powers. Isaac Asimov's story "Robbie" tells how a robot baby-sitter saves the life of an 8-year-old girl. Hollywood has personalized computers by giving them superhuman powers in space odyssey movies. After reading about and seeing these mythical powers of computers, it is hard to believe that today's computers are really quite limited in what they can do. Computers can perform just three basic functions:

- Perform arithmetic operations (addition, subtraction, multiplication, and division).
- Compare numeric or alphabetic values (test the relationship of two values to see if they are equal or if one is greater than the other).
- Store and retrieve data.

The number of unique instructions required to direct a computer to perform these functions is limited, often fewer than 100. Together, these instructions constitute the **instruction set** of the computer. Engineers design the instruction set into the electronic circuitry of the machine. By manipulating this small instruction set, **programmers** can write computer programs that harness the computer's power to help them achieve desired results.

The functions listed above are simple enough to do. A person can add, subtract, decide whether one value is greater than another, or look up some data from a written file. A computer just does the tasks much faster. The three features that make computers so remarkable are: (1) speed; (2) the accuracy with which they follow directions; and (3) their ability to store vast amounts of data.

Two physical factors determine the speed of a computer: the switching speed of its electronic circuits and the distances that electricity has to travel. Recent advances in technology have vastly increased the switching speed of electronic circuits. Other advances have made it possible to reduce the distances current

Instruction set Fundamental logical and arithmetic procedures that the computer can perform, such as addition, subtraction, and comparison.

HIGHLIGHT

Intrigue and the Superchip

Don't tell anyone, but Superchip is coming! How it's made is a carefully guarded secret. Superchip will make possible the creation of computers that are hundreds of times faster and more powerful than anything now existing. With Superchip, the government will be able to do a better job of forecasting the weather, designing weapons, breaking codes, and finding new sources of energy; and industry will be able to build better airplanes, weapons, and other products. No wonder all the secrecy is necessary!

The old way of making chips involves etching circuitry on thin wafers of silicon. Each tiny chip is tested. The ones that pass are broken off the wafer, placed in carriers and then hooked back together on printed circuit boards. It takes time for electrical signals to travel through all the wires between the chips.

The new method would save that miniscule amount of time. All the circuitry would be placed on the five-inch wafer, eliminating the breaking apart step and the need for the wiring that increases the travel time of the signals.

The major problem is flaws. New ultraprecise lasers will help eliminate errors. The lasers will act as tiny blowtorches, allowing direct etching and correction of the circuits, one by one. Ultimately, a computer will program the laser to build the circuits from scratch, make the corrections, and build any interconnections needed for full wafer-scale integration. Science fiction? Maybe—but watch the news to see if any semiconductor company or research laboratory pulls it off!

must travel—and, therefore, the time required for electricity to travel those distances—by packing circuits closer together. Modern computers are capable of performing millions of calculations in one second. Today's computer speeds are often measured in terms of nanoseconds and other small units (see Table 3–1). In the past, the time required to perform one addition ranged from 4 microseconds to 200 nanoseconds. The time will probably be 200 to 1,000 times faster in the future.

The accuracy of computers applies only to the inherent reliability of the electronic circuits that make up a computer. The same type of current passed through the same electrical circuits will yield the same results each time. When

Table 3–1 ▬ Divisions of a Second

Unit	Symbol	Fractions of a Second
Millisecond	ms	one-thousandth (1/1,000)
Microsecond	μs	one-millionth (1/1,000,000)
Nanosecond	ns	one-billionth (1/1,000,000,000)
Picosecond	ps	one-trillionth (1/1,000,000,000,000)

Garbage in–garbage out Phrase illustrating the fact that the meaningfulness of output relies on the reliability of data or programs.

Primary memory/storage Section of the computer that holds instructions, data, and intermediate and final results during processing.

you turn on a light switch, you expect the light to go on, not the radio or a fan. The computer is reliable for the same reason: its circuitry—or internal operation—is reliable. Of course, if the data or programs submitted to the computer are incorrect, the computer will not be able to produce correct results. The output will be useless and meaningless, illustrating the principle of **garbage in—garbage out.**

The part of the computer that stores data to be operated on is the computer's memory. This memory, however, is the **primary memory,** or **primary storage,** that resides in the computer itself. Other data can be stored on magnetic disks or tapes, making computer memory seem almost limitless. When data is needed, it is brought from these **secondary storage** media to internal memory. The data can be retrieved in a fraction of the time humans require to search through paper files.

The ability of the computer to store, retrieve, and process data, all without human intervention, separates it from a simple calculator and gives it its magnificent power and appeal. So while humans may be able to perform the same functions as the computer, the difference is that the computer can reliably and accurately execute millions of instructions in a second and store the results in an almost unlimited memory.

DATA PROCESSING

Data processing A systematic set of procedures for collecting, manipulating, and disseminating data to achieve specified objectives.

Data processing is nothing new. People have processed data ever since they have had things to count. **Data processing** refers to the collection, manipulation, and distribution of data to achieve certain objectives. As technology developed, electromechanical machines were developed to perform these functions. The term **automatic data processing (ADP)** described the use of such machines. Today, the electronic computer is used to achieve results in a procedure called **electronic data processing (EDP).** But the term *data processing* is often the phrase used to describe EDP.

Electronic data processing (EDP) Data processing performed largely by electronic equipment, such as computers.

Data Facts; the raw material of information.

The objective of all data processing, whether manual, electromechanical, or electronic, is to convert data into information that can be used in making decisions. **Data** refers to raw facts that have been collected from various sources but not organized or perhaps even defined. The number 747 is a raw fact. What it describes is not known. Perhaps it is the type of jet that will take you to Switzerland. Perhaps it is the winning number of pennies in a jar for a guessing game. Maybe it is a house number. Once you know what 747 stands for and you have a use for that number, it becomes **information.** On a larger scale, a bank manager may have very little use for a daily list of amounts of all checks and deposit slips from one branch office. But manipulating the data in one fashion or another may provide useful information: perhaps a summary of the total number and dollar value of deposits and withdrawals at the branch for one day. Information, then, is data that has been organized and processed (see Figure 3–1). Information increases understanding and helps people make intelligent decisions.

Information Data that have been organized and processed so they are meaningful.

To be useful to decision makers, information must be delivered to the right person, at the right time, in the right place. It must be accurate, timely, complete, concise, and relevant. If information fails to meet these requirements, it fails to meet the needs of those who must use it and thus has little value.

To derive information from data, the data is processed. To make data pro-

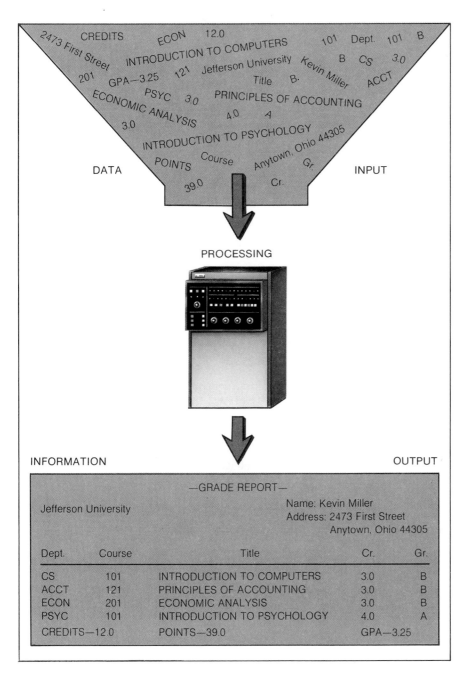

Figure 3–1
The Data-Processing Flow

DATA   INPUT

PROCESSING

INFORMATION   OUTPUT

—GRADE REPORT—

Jefferson University

Name: Kevin Miller
Address: 2473 First Street
Anytown, Ohio 44305

Dept.	Course	Title	Cr.	Gr.
CS	101	INTRODUCTION TO COMPUTERS	3.0	B
ACCT	121	PRINCIPLES OF ACCOUNTING	3.0	B
ECON	201	ECONOMIC ANALYSIS	3.0	B
PSYC	101	INTRODUCTION TO PSYCHOLOGY	4.0	A
CREDITS—12.0		POINTS—39.0	GPA—3.25	

cessing effective, the data should be organized in an integrated way so that anticipated needs of users for information can be met. Therefore, data items are placed in groups from the smallest unit, the field, to the largest unit, the data base. A business firm may maintain specific data about its employees, such as home address, social security number, hourly wage, withholding tax, gross income, and so on. Each of these categories is called a **field.** A collection of fields that relate to a single unit (in this case, a single employee) is a **record.** A grouping of all related records (in this case, all employee records) is a **file.** The development of more-sophisticated software has provided a method of

Field   A meaningful item of data, such as a social security number or a person's name.

Record   A collection of data items, or fields, that relates to a single unit, such as a student.

File   A grouping of related records, such as all student records; sometimes referred to as a data set.

structuring data to satisfy a wider variety of information needs, in a form called a **data base.** This book consistently uses the terms *field, record, file,* and *data base* as described (see Figure 3–2).

All data processing follows the same basic flow: input, processing, and output. **Input** describes the process of capturing data and getting it into a form that the computer can "understand." Input involves three steps:

- **Collect** the raw data.
- **Verify** or check the accuracy of data. (This step helps eliminate the possibility of garbage in—garbage out.)
- **Code** the data into a machine-readable form for processing.

Once all the data has been input, it is processed. **Processing** entails several types of manipulations:

- **Classifying.** Data can be organized according to characteristics that are meaningful to the user. At the bank, the amount of each transaction can be classified as a deposit, withdrawal, loan, or payment.
- **Sorting.** Data can be arranged alphabetically or numerically into a particular sequence. Bank deposits can be sorted according to account number, or the people attending an aerobics class can be sorted alphabetically by last names.
- **Calculating.** Data can be figured arithmetically or logically. For example, if the data are 20 feet for length and 10 feet for width, the area of the room (length times width) is calculated to be 200 square feet. To calculate a comparison, one can determine the total cost of carpeting the room with carpet that costs $25.95 per square yard, or a cheaper grade that costs $12.95 per square yard.
- **Summarizing.** A large amount of data can be reduced to a concise, usable form. All grades for all students in all classes can be summarized by grade-point averages, naming those students who deserve to be on the dean's list.
- **Storing.** Data can be retained on a storage medium such as disks, tapes, or microfilm to facilitate later processing or retrieval.

Output provides the computed results of processing in a form that humans can use. Three steps are necessary in the output phase of data flow:

- **Retrieval.** Information is pulled from storage for use by the decision maker.

Figure 3–2
Organization of a Data Base

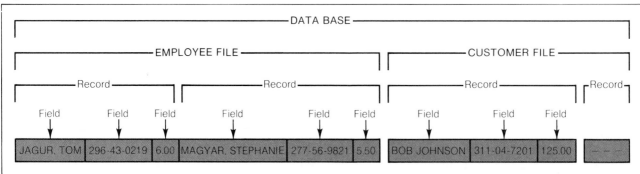

- **Conversion.** Information is translated from the form used to store it to a form understandable by the user—that is, words, charts, or pictures.
- **Communication.** When the right information is in the right place at the right time, communication occurs, and the information has been useful.

Concept Summary 3–1 ▬ Processing Functions

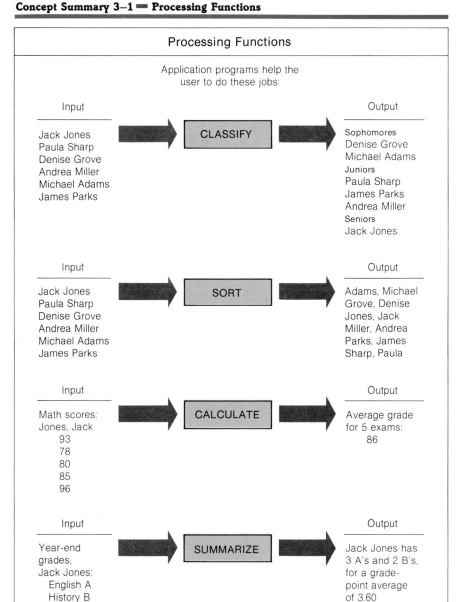

Processing Functions
Application programs help the user to do these jobs:

Input

Jack Jones
Paula Sharp
Denise Grove
Andrea Miller
Michael Adams
James Parks

→ CLASSIFY →

Output

Sophomores
Denise Grove
Michael Adams
Juniors
Paula Sharp
James Parks
Andrea Miller
Seniors
Jack Jones

Input

Jack Jones
Paula Sharp
Denise Grove
Andrea Miller
Michael Adams
James Parks

→ SORT →

Output

Adams, Michael
Grove, Denise
Jones, Jack
Miller, Andrea
Parks, James
Sharp, Paula

Input

Math scores:
Jones, Jack
   93
   78
   80
   85
   96

→ CALCULATE →

Output

Average grade
for 5 exams:
   86

Input

Year-end
grades,
Jack Jones:
   English A
   History B
   Algebra B
   Biology A
   Latin A

→ SUMMARIZE →

Output

Jack Jones has
3 A's and 2 B's,
for a grade-
point average
of 3.60

Input

Jones, Jack
GPA = 3.60

→ STORE →

Output

Data processing is monitored or evaluated in a step called **feedback.** Over time, the information provided through data processing may lose its effectiveness. Feedback is the process of evaluating the output and making adjustments to the input or the processing steps to ensure that processing results in good information (see Figure 3–3).

For data processing to occur electronically, four hardware components are necessary: input devices, a central processing unit, output devices, and media for secondary storage. All this equipment is coordinated by instructions, or programs, that govern the data flow through a computer system. The next section examines how the hardware is coordinated with the data-processing flow to achieve EDP.

THE ROLE OF COMPUTERS IN PROCESSING DATA

Two general types of computer processing can occur (see Figure 3–4). One type is **batch processing,** in which data items are collected in a group over time and processed all at once. In a bank, all transactions—deposits, withdrawals, loans, or loan payments—are entered into the computer system as they occur. However, a summary of the number and dollar amounts of all transactions for a day may not be processed until night, when the bank is closed. Then the computer processes all the data and reports the day's business in summary form. Batch processing is the most convenient type of processing when magnetic tapes are used to store data (see Chapter 5, which describes how data is processed from tapes).

Sometimes a large computer can process data very quickly and provide the user with results by batch processing in a short time. The problem is the user may have to wait "in line" for hours to have a job processed. In many cases, the user wants to see results of processing at his or her convenience. If the computer is being used for word processing or writing software for personal computers, the user needs immediate feedback. This feedback occurs during **interactive processing.** The user can type in a memo, for instance, see the words on a screen, and immediately correct typing mistakes or edit awkward sentences. The user writing a BASIC program can try the program as soon as a portion or all of it is written, not eight hours later.

Interactive processing is often used for individual transactions. A person making a plane reservation wants to know immediately what's available and at what cost. Not only that, the computer system must record the transaction immediately, or a travel agent in another office may sell the same seat to another customer. A bank customer putting money in a savings account wants the result entered in a bank book now, not tomorrow or next week. Often individual transactions are completed by interactive processing but summarized by batch. Although the bank customer has an immediate record of a deposit, the summary of a day's similar transactions will not be produced until the bank is closed.

To perform either method of computer processing, three elements are needed: hardware, software, and data. Hardware consists of the computer and peripheral devices. Software refers to the instructions, or programs, entered into a system. And data refers to the raw facts. Let's see how these elements work together in EDP.

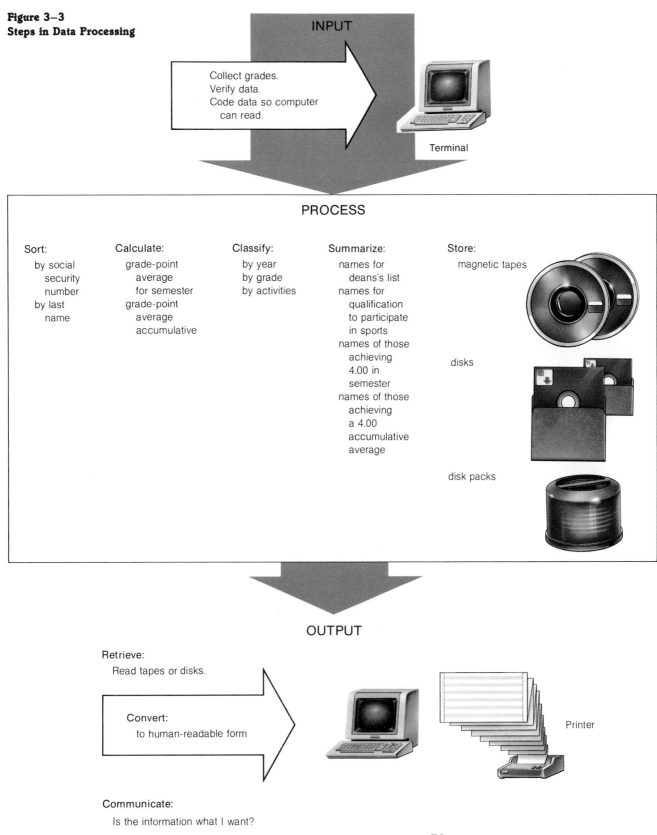

Figure 3–3
Steps in Data Processing

INPUT

Collect grades.
Verify data.
Code data so computer
can read.

Terminal

PROCESS

Sort:
  by social
    security
    number
  by last
    name

Calculate:
  grade-point
    average
    for semester
  grade-point
    average
    accumulative

Classify:
  by year
  by grade
  by activities

Summarize:
  names for
    deans's list
  names for
    qualification
    to participate
    in sports
  names of those
    achieving
    4.00 in
    semester
  names of those
    achieving
    a 4.00
    accumulative
    average

Store:
  magnetic tapes

  disks

  disk packs

OUTPUT

Retrieve:
  Read tapes or disks.

Convert:
  to human-readable form

Printer

Communicate:
  Is the information what I want?

79

Figure 3–4
Batch Processing versus Interactive
Processing

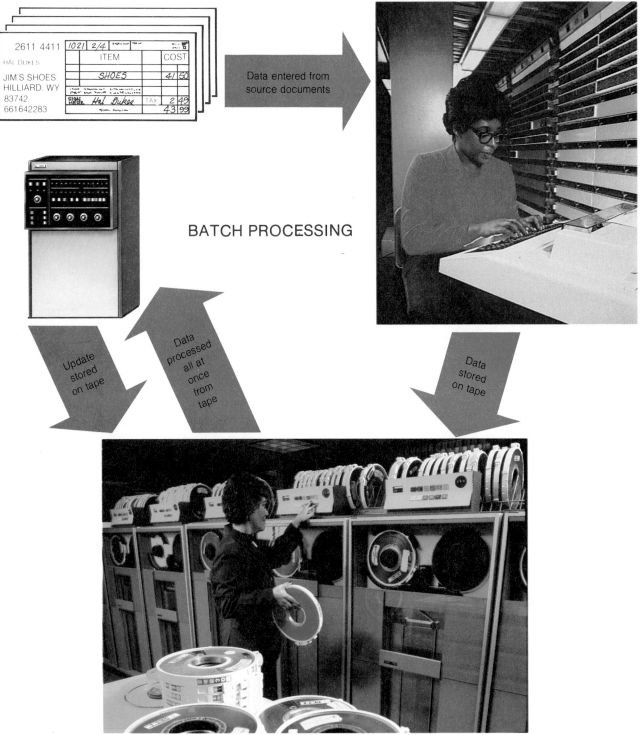

BATCH PROCESSING

Figure 3–4
Continued

An architect prepares presentation graphics to show clients samples of his firm's work.

Students use computers to learn through PLATO® courses.

Using a light pen with her computer, this woman modifies the computer program that produced the woven design.

INTERACTIVE PROCESSING

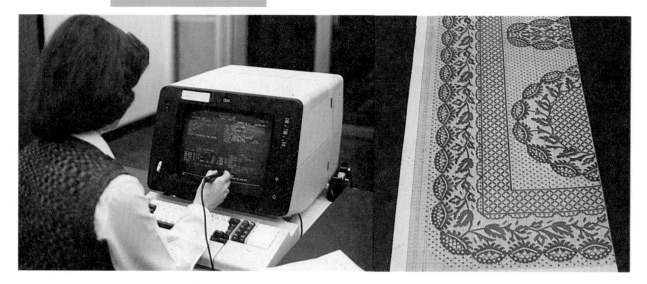

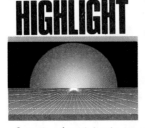

Static Can Zap a Microprocessor!

When you were little, you probably scuffled along the carpet to build up static electricity and then "zapped" somebody. The snap that was felt and heard—to the chagrin of its receiver—is called electrostatic discharge (ESD). Ten steps on a nylon rug can build up 10,000 to 20,000 volts of static electricity in your body.

While humans may not feel a low-voltage ESD, a microprocessor surely can! A glip, gremlin, or glitch in computer operations can be caused by a discharge of only 2,000 volts of static electricity. During winter months, when indoor temperature is high and humidity low, a stroll across an office carpet can generate up to 30,000 volts of static electricity—enough to do permanent damage to your computer, disk drive, or software.

Static can be transferred to the system either by contact charging (for example, a person touching the keys on a computer terminal), or by induction charging—electric fields radiating from such items as clothing or polyethylene bags. A shirt sleeve, for example, can generate enough static electricity to destroy most PROM (programmable read-only memory) chips. Other sources of static electricity include waxed, painted, or varnished surfaces; vinyl flooring; synthetic garments; styrofoam; electrostatic copiers; spray cleaners; and plastic-covered chairs and desks.

When completing a computer system plan, a company should include the cost of antistatic floor mats, antistatic agents in spray bottles or towelettes; and ionizers, devices that neutralize charged electrons. Protecting a system this way is much cheaper than repairing blown microcircuits or recovering lost data.

Offline Not connected to the central computer.

Input and Input Devices

Data must be entered into the computer in some way. Data entry can occur online or offline. **Offline** entry occurs when a device set apart from the computer is used to store data on cards, disks, or tape. A person types in all the data he or she reads from sales slips, credit card receipts, hand-written time cards, or similar documents. Later the data is read in batches by another machine directly connected to the computer.

Online entry occurs when the device used is directly connected to the computer. The device may read punched cards, disks, or tapes. It may read data optically from codes printed on products or from a page of printed text. A person may speak into a microphone for voice input or enter data manually by using the keyboard of a terminal, probably the most common device used in online entry. Often in the online method, some type of processing occurs at various points during the data entry. Chapter 4 discusses input devices in detail.

Input of data can consist of entering new data, changing old data, or deleting data. The source documents must be reliable, the data entry must be accurate, and the data timely, for processing to result in meaningful information. Regardless of the method of input, the data is now coded in a form that the computer can use. The computer can read the patterns of holes in punched cards, detect the magnetized spots on tape or disk, or interpret the electric impulses of data stored temporarily in primary storage. The data has now been collected, verified, and coded.

Central Processing Unit

The computer itself stores data temporarily and acts on it. The component that is responsible for this is the **central processing unit (CPU).** The CPU consists of three parts that function together as a unit. These parts are the control unit, the arithmetic/logic unit, and primary storage (also referred to as internal storage or memory).

While the CPU incorporates all three components, the control unit and the arithmetic/logic unit are often referred to collectively as the **processor.** A processor may incorporate one or more circuit elements, or "chips." In a large computer, the processor may be built on several circuit boards in boxlike structures or frames, hence the term *mainframe* (see Figure 3–5). Processors in microcomputers have been shrunk in size to fit onto a single plug-in chip and are referred to as microprocessors (see Figure 3–6). Primary memory typically resides on separate circuit boards and is linked to the processor via a common data path called a "bus."

Central processing unit (CPU) Acts as the "brain" of the computer; composed of three sections—arithmetic/logic unit (ALU), control unit, and primary storage unit.

Processor The term used to refer collectively to the ALU and control unit.

**Figure 3–5
Circuit Boards.**
This manufacturing facility includes an automatic system for inserting components into circuit boards. The system accurately inserts 7,000 components per hour and "senses" the presence or absence of a component on the circuit board.

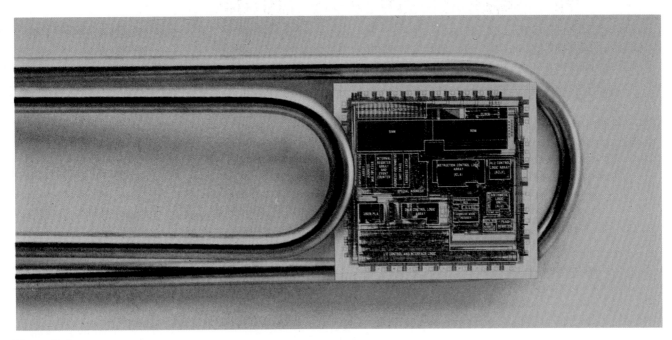

Figure 3–6
Microcomputer with CPU Chip, ROM Chip, and RAM Chip

Random-access memory (RAM) Form of primary storage into which instructions and data can be read, written, and erased.

Control unit Section of the CPU that directs the sequence of operations and governs the other units that make up the computer.

Arithmetic/logic unit (ALU) The section of the processor or CPU that handles arithmetic computations and logical operations.

Operation code (op code) The part of an instruction that tells what operation is to be performed.

Operand The part of an instruction that tells where to find the data or equipment to be operated on.

Next-sequential-instruction feature Ability of a computer to execute program steps in the order in which they are stored unless branching occurs.

Address A unique identifier assigned to each memory location within primary storage.

When data and programs enter the CPU, they are held in primary storage. Generally the primary storage that holds the data and programs is a form of semiconductor memory called **random-access memory (RAM).** RAM is the working area of the computer. Since RAM is volatile, or nonpermanent, data or programs will be erased when the electric power to the computer is turned off or disrupted in any other way. When any changes or results are to be saved, they must be saved on an external form of storage—on disks or magnetic tapes, for example.

To begin work, data and programs to be manipulated are written into RAM. What happens to the contents of RAM depends on the processor (see Figure 3–7). The processor is the heart of the computer and as stated earlier consists of two processing units: the control unit and the arithmetic/logic unit. The **control unit,** as its name implies, maintains order and controls activity in the CPU. It does not process or store data. Rather, it directs the sequence of operations. The control unit interprets the instructions of a program in storage and produces signals that act as commands to circuits to execute the instructions. Other functions of the control unit include communicating with an input device in order to begin the transfer of instructions and data into storage and, similarly, communicating with an output device to initiate the transfer of results from storage.

The manipulation of the data occurs in the **arithmetic/logic unit (ALU)** of the CPU. The ALU does not store data but performs arithmetic computations and logical operations. Arithmetic computations include addition, subtraction, multiplication, and division. Logical comparisons include six combinations of equality: equal to, not equal to, greater than, less than, equal to or greater than, and equal to or less than. Since the bulk of internal processing involves these calculations or comparisons, the capabilities of a computer often depend on the design and capabilities of its ALU.

The processor receives instructions on what to do with data from programs that reside in the primary storage portion of the CPU. A computer program is a series of instructions to be executed by the computer. These instructions can be written in any programming language but must be translated into machine language for execution. Remember that machine language is the only language the computer can "understand." It consists of the 1s and 0s that designate the proper electrical states ("on" or "off") in the computer. Each machine language instruction has two basic parts: the operation code and the operand. The **operation code (op code)** tells the CPU what function is to be performed (such as ADD, SUBTRACT, MOVE DATA, or COMPARE). The **operand** indicates the primary storage location of the data to be processed.

The computer performs instructions sequentially, in the order they are given, unless instructed to do otherwise. This **next-sequential-instruction feature** requires that instructions be placed in consecutive locations in memory. Otherwise the computer would be unable to differentiate between instructions and data.

In order to direct processing operations, the control unit of the CPU must be able to locate each instruction and data item in primary storage. Therefore, each location is assigned a unique number **address.** The addresses are assigned during the engineering of the processor unit. When a program is loaded into primary storage, each byte of data receives a location. Sometimes data at some locations must be changed, added, or deleted during execution of the program. Using numbers instead of symbolic names could be quite tedious. A **variable,** or symbolic name for the kind of data to be changed, represents a location to the programmer who writes the stored-program instructions. Suppose the computer is instructed to add a 5½ percent sales tax to each purchase. The program must be able to locate the amount of the purchase entered and the 5½ percent figure it is to use to manipulate the data. The programmer assigns the variables TAX and COST to these amounts. Then the computer finds the variable COST, multiplies the value stored there by the 5½ percent sales tax, and adds the result to the cost. The computer may then store the result in a new location that the programmer has named TOTAL.

The important thing to remember about what is stored in primary storage is that the data and programs will remain at their assigned locations until some other data or programs are written into the same locations. This basic characteristic of RAM memory is known as **nondestructive read/destructive write.** This means that the computer can use the same data and programs over and over until they are changed. It also means that the same program can manipulate different data over and over again. Each series of instructions placed into this memory is called a **stored program.** This is the stored-program concept discussed earlier under Computer Evolution in Chapter 2. This concept enables the computer to process data at its own speed with no human intervention.

The three parts of the CPU interact as follows:

Step 1—Initially, the control unit directs the input device to transfer instructions and data to primary storage.

Step 2—The control unit takes one instruction from storage and interprets it.

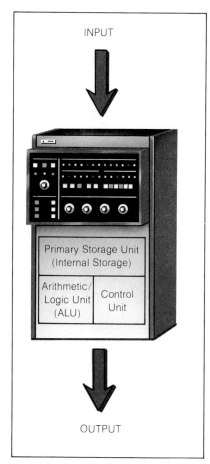

Figure 3–7
Computer System Components

Variable Meaningful name assigned by the programmer to storage locations of which the values can change.

Nondestructive read/destructive write Feature of computer memory that permits data to be retained in its original state, allowing repeated reference.

Stored program Instructions stored in the computer's primary memory in electronic form; can be executed repeatedly at the computer's own speed.

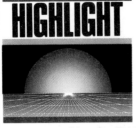

The British Chip

Somehow microprocessors don't fit the stereotype of England—tea, Shakespeare, double-decker buses, and snooty butlers. But a British company may soon leap into the microprocessor market with its "transputer." Inmos P.L.C., a $56-million-a-year company once owned by the British government, has already earned a place in the microchip world with its high-speed RAM chips for military and scientific uses. The company, now owned by Thorn EMI P.L.C., has announced that it will market the transputer by mid-1985.

The transputer is a chip that uses the principles of parallel processing. It is engineered to work more like the human mind. Parallel machines break problems into many small parts and solve them simultaneously with many small processors. A transputer is a building block for these machines. It contains a processor, a memory, and communications circuitry. A few computer architects have tried building parallel machines out of conventional and homemade chips. These engineers are delighted at the prospect of the transputer. Yet acceptance of the transputer is not assured. The chip has its drawbacks. It works best when it is programmed in its own language, called Occam.

The commercial advantages of using parallel processing are still not great enough to merit spending large sums of money acquiring a system. And Inmos does not yet have the money to promote the transputer. Furthermore, computer manufacturers tend to look to their current suppliers for new designs that are consistent with the old ones. We have yet to see if the transputer will make an impact in computerdom.

Step 3—The control unit sends the appropriate electronic signals to the ALU and to storage to cause the instruction to be executed.

Step 4—The signals sent to storage may tell it to transfer data to the ALU, where it is mathematically manipulated or comparisons are performed.

Step 5—The result may then be transferred back to primary storage. After an instruction has been executed, the control unit takes the next instruction from primary storage. Data may be transferred from storage to the ALU and back several times before all instructions are executed.

Step 6—When all instructions have been executed, the control unit directs the storage unit to transfer the processed data (information) to the output device (see Figure 3–8).

During the processing of data, data items or instructions may be placed in temporary storage areas known as **registers.** They are considered part of the control unit, and are not considered primary storage. Registers receive data, hold it, and transfer it very quickly as directed by the control unit of the CPU. They increase the speed of execution.

Some registers perform specific functions and are named according to the functions they perform. An accumulator is a register that accumulates results

Register An internal computer component used for temporary storage of an instruction or data.

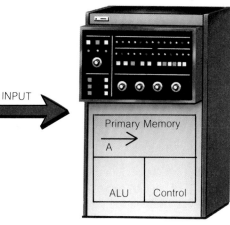

INPUT →

Step A:
Instruction and data from the input device are stored in primary storage under direction of the control unit.

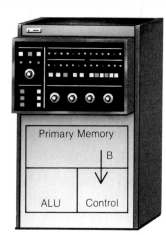

Step B:
The control unit examines one instruction and interprets it.

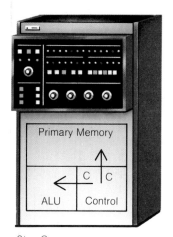

Step C:
The control unit sends appropriate electronic signals to the ALU and to primary storage.

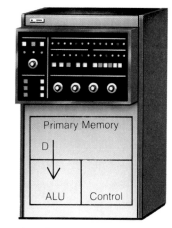

Step D:
The required data items are transferred to the ALU, where calculations and/or comparisons are performed.

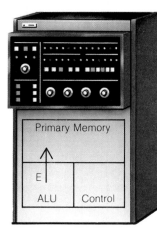

Step E:
The result is transferred back to the primary storage unit. B—E are continued until all instructions have been executed.

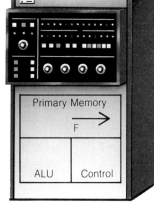

OUTPUT →

Step F:
The control unit signals the primary storage unit to transfer results to the output device.

Figure 3–8
Computer Operations

of computations. A storage register holds data being sent to or taken from the primary storage unit. During program execution, each instruction is transferred to an instruction register, where it is decoded by the control unit. The address of a data item called for by an instruction is kept in an address register. Some computers do not have registers with specific uses but instead have general-purpose registers that can be used for both arithmetic and addressing functions.

Cache memory Also known as a high-speed buffer; a working buffer or temporary area used to help speed the execution of a program.

Cache memory, also referred to as a high-speed buffer, is a portion of primary storage used to help speed the processing operations of the computer. Cache memory serves as a working buffer or temporary area to store both instructions and data that must be accessed a great deal by the program being executed. Storing the data in a temporary area of primary storage eliminates the need for constant accessing of secondary storage for the data or instructions. Although more expensive than primary storage, cache memory increases processing speeds, which sometimes justifies its use.

Output and Output Devices

In order for humans to understand the results of data processing, the computer must instruct output devices to prepare the information in human-readable form. First of all, the computer retrieves the needed information from storage. Then the computer converts the information to words, graphs, or charts that humans can read. This output may be printed on the display screen of a terminal or on paper. The final phase of output is communication, and communication occurs only if the information is accurate, timely, concise, complete, relevant, and readable. (See Figure 3–9 for a summary of data flow with input and output.)

Output devices include many different kinds of printers, plotters, voice systems, and display screens of terminals. These devices are discussed in detail in Chapter 4.

TYPES OF PRIMARY STORAGE

Primary storage consists of all storage considered part of the processor. It is sometimes called primary memory, main memory, or main storage. Second- and third-generation computers contained primary storage units composed of

These electron devices on a seashell are made by NEC, one of the world's top producers of semiconductor devices.

Figure 3–9
Data Flow

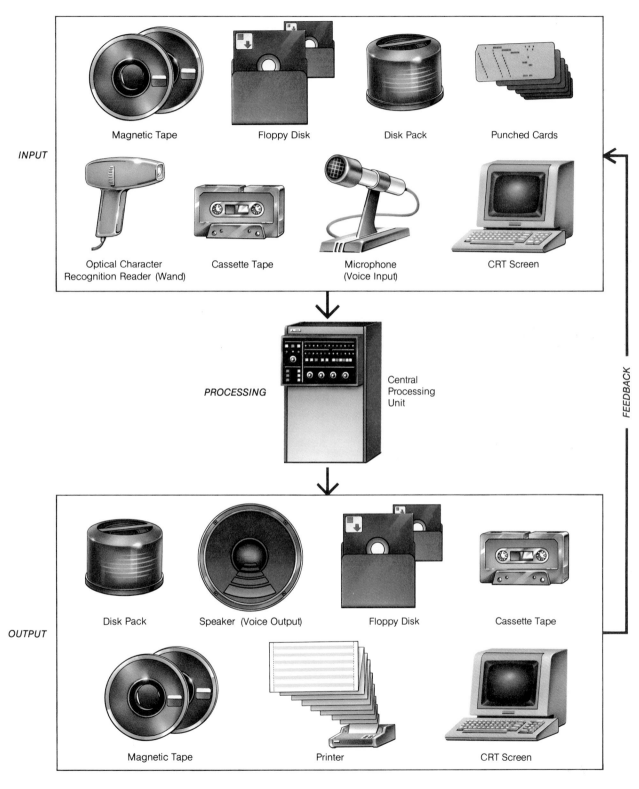

INPUT

Magnetic Tape

Floppy Disk

Disk Pack

Punched Cards

Optical Character
Recognition Reader (Wand)

Cassette Tape

Microphone
(Voice Input)

CRT Screen

PROCESSING

Central
Processing
Unit

OUTPUT

Disk Pack

Speaker (Voice Output)

Floppy Disk

Cassette Tape

Magnetic Tape

Printer

CRT Screen

FEEDBACK

Bit (short for BInary digiT) The smallest unit of information that can be represented in binary notation.

Semiconductor memory Memory composed of circuitry on silicon chips.

Bit cells The name for storage locations in semiconductors.

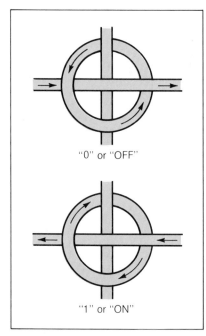

Figure 3–10
Magnetizing a Core

Figure 3–11
A Memory Chip That Holds Up to 64,000 Pieces of Information

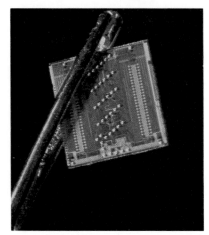

magnetic cores. Each core could store one binary digit, or **bit** (short for *binary digit*). The operation of the cores was based on the principle that a magnetic field was created when electricity flowed through a wire (Gauss's law). The direction of the magnetic field, which depended on the direction in which the electric current flowed, determined which binary state a core represented. Magnetization of a core in a clockwise direction indicated an "on" (1) condition; a counterclockwise direction of magnetization represented an "off" (0) condition (see Figure 3–10).

Technological developments have led to the use of semiconductors in primary storage units. **Semiconductor memory** is composed of circuitry or silicon chips. One silicon chip, only slightly bigger than one core, may hold as much data as thousands of cores (see Figure 3–11). Also, the speed of processing is significantly faster with semiconductors than with cores. The main storage of recent computers consists mostly of semiconductors.

Semiconductors are designed to store data in locations called **bit cells,** which are capable of being in an "on" or "off" state. "On" is represented by a 1, and "off" by a 0. The bit cells of semiconductor memory are arranged in eight-row by eight-column matrices (see Figure 3–12). Unlike core memory, semiconductor memory does not store data magnetically. The bit cells indicate an "on" state when holding a charge and an "off" state when not containing a charge. The bit cell at which the current intersects, therefore, is holding a charge, while the remaining bit cells along the two lines are not holding a charge. As indicated by Figure 3–12, bit cells 2,3 and 6,4 are holding a charge and would be considered to be "on," while the remaining cells would be "off."

The bit cells of a semiconductor are arranged so that they can be written to

Figure 3–12
A Portion of Semiconductor Memory

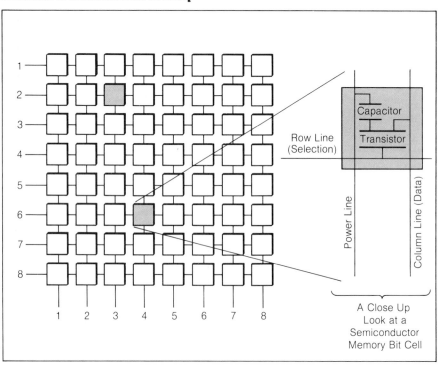

or read from as needed. They have an inherent nondestructive read capability (since they either do or do not pass current). A diagram highlighting the actual makeup of a bit cell is also shown in Figure 3–12. The selection line is the row line, while the data line is the column line. Once current is passed through the selection line, all transistors along the row are turned on. The **transistor** is an on/off switch connecting the data line to the **capacitor,** which holds the electrical charge. Once the data line and selection line both receive a charge, current passes through the transistor, causing the capacitor to take on a charge. If the selection line is not turned on, no current will pass through the transistor and the capacitor will have no charge.

One disadvantage of most semiconductor memory units is that they require a constant power source. Since they rely on currents to represent data, all their stored data is lost if the power source fails and no emergency (backup) system exists. This temporary memory is the random-access memory (RAM) discussed earlier.

Recently, a device called **bubble memory** was introduced as a replacement medium, not only for primary storage, but also for auxiliary storage. This memory consists of magnetized spots, or **magnetic domains,** resting on a thin film of semiconductor material. The magnetic domains (called bubbles) have a polarity opposite that of the semiconductor material on which they rest. Data is stored by shifting the bubbles' positions on the surface of the material (see Figure 3–13). When data is read, the presence of a bubble indicates a 0 bit. The bubbles are similar to magnetic cores in that they retain their magnetism indefinitely. Bubbles are much smaller than magnetic cores, and more data can be stored in a smaller area. A bubble memory module only slightly larger than a quarter can store 20,000 characters of data. In addition, primary storage consisting of bubble memory is not volatile, that is, data is preserved even if the electric power fails.

Some manufacturers have introduced bubble memory in portable computers; however, a more common use of bubble memory is for limited storage capabilities in input/output devices. High cost and production difficulties have been major factors limiting industry and user acceptance of bubbles.

Computers are capable of performing complex manipulations that result in finding square roots and evaluating exponents. Such functions can be built into the hardware or software of a computer system. Building them into the hardware provides the advantages of speed and reliability, since the operations are part of the actual computer circuitry. Building them into software allows more flexibility, but carrying out functions built into software is slower and more prone to error.

When functions are built into the hardware of a computer, they are placed in **read-only memory (ROM).** Read-only memory instructions cannot be changed or deleted by other stored-program instructions. Since ROM is permanent, it cannot be occupied by common stored-program instructions or data. Sometimes ROM chips are called firmware. Building instructions into ROM makes the distinction between hardware and software less clear-cut.

A direct result of this characteristic is microprogramming. **Microprograms** are sequences of instructions built into ROM to carry out functions (such as calculating square roots) that otherwise would have to be directed by stored-program instructions at a much lower speed. Microprograms are usually supplied by computer manufacturers and cannot be altered by users. However, microprogramming allows the basic operations of the computer to be tailored

Figure 3–13
Bubble Memory Section Magnified 1,500 Times

Transistor An on/off switch connecting the data line to the capacitor.

Capacitor The device that holds the electrical charge within a bit cell of semiconductor memory.

Bubble memory Memory medium in which data is represented by magnetized spots (magnetic domains) resting on a thin film.

Magnetic domain A magnetized spot representing data in bubble memory.

Read-only memory (ROM) Part of computer hardware containing items (circuitry patterns) that cannot be deleted or altered by stored-program instructions.

Microprogram Sequence of instructions wired into read-only memory; used to tailor a system to meet the user's processing requirements.

Figure 3–14
Erasable Programmable Read-Only Memory.
(a) This chip is Intel 2764—a 5V only, 54,536-bit ultraviolet erasable and electrically programmable read-only memory (EPROM). Its standard access time is 250 ns with speed selection available at 200 ns. Chip size is 153.5 square mil.

(b) A chip is mounted in a plastic carrier with a number of pins that allow it to be plugged into a circuitry board. This one is an Intel 2816 memory, a 16,384-bit electrically erasable programmable read-only memory (E²PROM). It can be electrically erased and reprogrammed through the use of a 21-volt pulse.

to meet the needs of users. If all instructions that a computer can execute are located in ROM, a complete new set of instructions can be obtained by changing the ROM chip. When selecting a computer, users can get the standard features of the machine plus their choice of the optional features available through microprogramming. Many minicomputers and microcomputers today are directed by instructions stored in ROM.

A version of ROM that can be programmed is **programmable read-only memory (PROM).** PROM can be programmed by the manufacturer, or it can be shipped "blank" to the end user for programming. Once programmed, its contents are unalterable. With PROM the end user has the advantages of ROM along with the flexibility to meet unique needs. A problem with it, though, is that mistakes programmed into the unit cannot be corrected. To overcome this drawback, **erasable programmable read-only memory (EPROM)** has been developed (see Figure 3–14). This memory unit can be erased, but only by being submitted to a special process, such as being bathed in ultraviolet light.

DATA REPRESENTATION

If a computer can only understand the states of its electric circuits in terms of 0s and 1s, how is data processing accomplished? People communicate information by using symbols that have specific meanings. Most likely they enter data and instructions into the computer by using English words or at least by using some less tedious and easier-to-understand symbols than machine language.

To use a computer, people must convert their symbols to a form the computer can recognize. Some people use this direct form when working with computers. Others depend on special programs that translate their words and symbols into

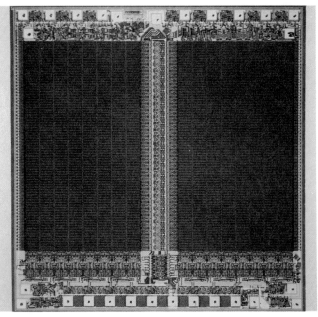

a

b

RAM	ROM
Stands for random-access memory	Stands for read-only memory
Used as primary storage for holding temporary data	Used for holding permanent data, for example, programs built into ROM by the manufacturer
Volatile: any changes or results must be saved on disk or tape or they will be lost	Permanent: data remains intact even when the power is off

	Other forms of ROM are:
	  PROM—programmable ROM
	  EPROM—erasable PROM

the 1s and 0s that represent "on" and "off." In either case, the computer can recognize instructions and data in the form of binary representation.

Binary Representation

Data is represented in the computer by the state of the machine's circuitry: magnetic states for core storage, current for semiconductor storage, and the position of magnetic bubbles for bubble memory. In all cases, only two states are possible, "on" and "off." The use of this two-state system to represent data is known as **binary representation.**

The **binary (base 2) number system** operates in a manner similar to the way the familiar **decimal (base 10) number system** works. For example, the decimal number 4,672 can be analyzed as follows:

Binary representation Use of a two-state, or binary, system to represent data.

Binary number system Number system using the digits 0 and 1 and having a base of 2; corresponds to the "on" and "off."

```
4   6   7   2
            └→ 2 × 10⁰ =      2    or    4   6   7   2
        └────→ 7 × 10¹ =     70          │   │   │   │
    └────────→ 6 × 10² =    600          │   │   │   │
└────────────→ 4 × 10³ =   4000    or   10³  10²  10¹  10⁰
                          ─────
                           4672
```

Each position represents a certain power of 10. The progression of powers is from right to left; that is, digits further to the left in a decimal number represent larger powers of 10 than digits to the right of them (see Figure 3–15).

The same principle holds for binary representation. The difference is that in binary representation each position in the number represents a power of 2 (see

10^5	10^4	10^3	10^2	10^1	10^0
100,000	10,000	1,000	100	10	1

**Figure 3–15
Decimal Place Values**

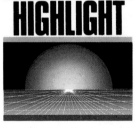

The Clean Room

You enter the clean room through an airlock, a special passage that isolates the laboratory from the dirt of the outside world. Any dust particles are blown away from the laboratory when the door is opened: air pressure inside the airlock is greater than that in the reception area. No smoking, eating, or drinking occurs here. You can't wear cosmetics, write with anything other than ballpoint pens, or wear cleated hiking boots. And you must wear a special "bunny" suit: booties, a bonnet, and a lab coat.

You have just entered the clean room of the Knight Laboratory, housed at Cornell University's National Research and Resource Facility for Submicron Structures—National Submicron Facility, for short. Here research is being conducted, not in electronics, but in microelectronics, to build new and better integrated circuits. Measurements are taken in microns: a micron is 1/100 the diameter of a human hair.

There are 12 small rooms around the larger laboratory. Each of these smaller rooms rests on its own pad of "floating" concrete, 2½ feet thick, isolated from the foundation and adjacent rooms. The slightest vibration from nearby traffic could ruin a delicate experiment. What kinds of things happen here: Well, a few of them produced these stunning results:

- Letters so tiny that, using them, you could put all 30 volumes of the *Encyclopaedia Britannica* on a postage stamp;
- A device that can measure the change in the earth's magnetic field caused by the blink of an eye;
- Electronic devices so small that 30,000,000 of them would fit on a single ¼-in-square chip; and
- Experimental chips that can perform more than a million calculations in a single second.

Compare these marvels with the 30-ton, 20,000-square-foot calculator called ENIAC: it could perform only 5,000 calculations per second! Quite a change in 40 years!

"I want to go home, the tin man wants a heart, the lion wants courage, and the scarecrow wants an electrically programmable read-only memory chip coupled with 256K of memory."

Figure 3–16). For example, consider the decimal number 14. In binary, the value equivalent to 14 is written as follows:

$$
\begin{array}{l}
1\ \ 1\ \ 1\ \ 0 \\
\quad 0 \times 2^0 = 0 \\
\quad 1 \times 2^1 = 2 \\
\quad 1 \times 2^2 = 4 \\
\quad 1 \times 2^3 = \underline{8} \\
\qquad\qquad\quad 14
\end{array}
\quad \text{or} \quad
\begin{array}{cccc}
1 & 1 & 1 & 0 \\
| & | & | & | \\
2^3 & 2^2 & 2^1 & 2^0
\end{array}
$$

As further example, the value represented by the decimal number 300 is represented in binary form below:

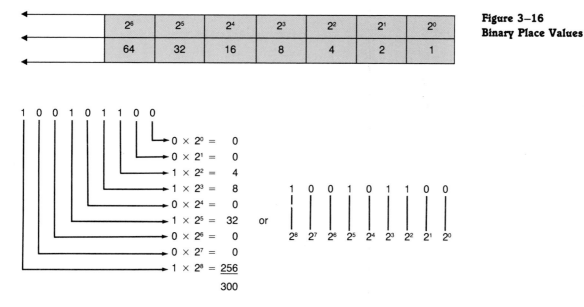

Figure 3-16
Binary Place Values

2^6	2^5	2^4	2^3	2^2	2^1	2^0
64	32	16	8	4	2	1

1 0 0 1 0 1 1 0 0

$$0 \times 2^0 = 0$$
$$0 \times 2^1 = 0$$
$$1 \times 2^2 = 4$$
$$1 \times 2^3 = 8$$
$$0 \times 2^4 = 0$$
$$1 \times 2^5 = 32$$
$$0 \times 2^6 = 0$$
$$0 \times 2^7 = 0$$
$$1 \times 2^8 = \underline{256}$$
$$300$$

or

1 0 0 1 0 1 1 0 0

2^8 2^7 2^6 2^5 2^4 2^3 2^2 2^1 2^0

As indicated by the examples above, the binary number system uses 1s and 0s in various combinations to represent various values. Each digit position in a binary number is called a bit, as defined previously. A 1 in a bit position indicates the presence of a specific power of 2; a 0 indicates the absence of a specific power. As in the decimal number system, the progression of powers is from right to left.

Octal Number System

Although all digital computers must store data as 0s and 1s, the sizes of the storage locations do vary. These storage locations within primary memory are referred to as **words,** and one word is equal to one location (see discussion on storage locations and addresses in this chapter). Word sizes are measured in bits and are typically 8, 16, 24, 32, 48, and 64 bits in length.

The **octal (base 8) number system,** which uses digits 0 to 7, can be employed as a shorthand method of representing the data contained within one word, or addressable memory location. In the case of 24- and 48-bit word size computers, the octal number system provides a shorthand method of representing what is contained in memory. This is true because three binary digits, or bits, can be represented by one octal digit and both 24 and 48 are divisible by three.

As was noted above, three binary digits can be represented by one octal digit. This is done by considering the first three binary place values from right to left that sum to 7—the highest single digit value in the octal number system.

Word A memory location within primary storage; varies in size (number of bits) from computer to computer.

Octal number system Number system in which each position represents a power of 8.

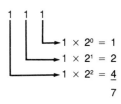

1 1 1

$$1 \times 2^0 = 1$$
$$1 \times 2^1 = 2$$
$$1 \times 2^2 = \underline{4}$$
$$7$$

95

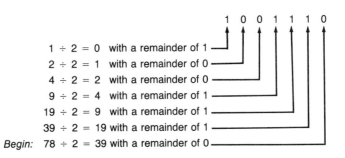

HIGHLIGHT

Easy-to-Do Conversion

It's easy to convert whole decimal numbers to binary numbers, or to numbers in any other base, for that matter. Simply get out your handy-dandy pocket calculator, and push the buttons for conversions!

Seriously, there is an easier way than the subtraction method. It's the division/multiplication method. All you do is divide the number by the value of the base until nothing is left to divide. The remainders of each division—written in each place starting with the ones place—form the new equivalent numeral. Here's how it works in base 2:

```
                              1  0  0  1  1  1  0
        1 ÷ 2 = 0  with a remainder of 1
        2 ÷ 2 = 1  with a remainder of 0
        4 ÷ 2 = 2  with a remainder of 0
        9 ÷ 2 = 4  with a remainder of 1
       19 ÷ 2 = 9  with a remainder of 1
       39 ÷ 2 = 19 with a remainder of 1
Begin: 78 ÷ 2 = 39 with a remainder of 0
```

Now convert the decimal number 325 to a base 2 number. Did you get 101000101? Very good! So try something more difficult: change 325 to a base 8 number. Was your answer 505? Good! That means 5 in the 64s place, 0 in the 8s place, and 5 in the 1s place. Try some more problems you make up. Check them with your calculator!

If we wanted to represent a binary value contained in a 24-bit word as an octal value, it could be converted as follows:

```
000  000  000  000  001  111  000  010
 ↓    ↓    ↓    ↓    ↓    ↓    ↓    ↓
 0    0    0    0    1    7    0    2
```

If we then wanted to convert the octal value to its decimal equivalent, it could also be done. The octal number 1,702 is equivalent to the decimal number 962. Consider the conversion below, keeping in mind that each digit of the octal number represents a power of 8.

```
1  7  0  2
         → 2 × 8⁰ =   2      or   1   7   0   2
      → 0 × 8¹ =   0
   → 7 × 8² = 448
→ 1 × 8³ = 512              8³  8²  8¹  8⁰
            962
```

For another example, the value represented by the decimal number 10,000 is displayed in octal form below:

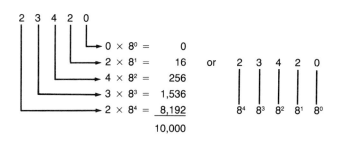

Hexadecimal Number System

When a program fails to execute correctly, examining the contents of certain memory locations to discover what went wrong may be necessary. In such cases, the programmer often finds having a printout, or **dump,** of the contents of the memory locations is useful (see Figure 3–17). If everything were printed in binary representation, the programmer would be staring at page after page of 1s and 0s. Detection of errors would be difficult, since binary numbers are difficult to read, write, and remember.

To alleviate this problem, the contents of storage locations in computers can be represented by symbols of the **hexadecimal (base 16) number system.** In the hexadecimal number system, 16 symbols are used to represent the digits 0 through 15 (see Figure 3–18). Note that the letters A through F designate the numbers 10 through 15. The fact that each position in a hexadecimal number represents a power of 16, allows for easy conversion from binary to hexadecimal, since 16 is equal to 2^4. A single hexadecimal digit can be represented in four binary digits.

As was noted above, four binary digits can be represented by one hexadecimal digit. This is done by considering the first four binary place values (from

Dump A hard-copy printout of the contents of computer memory; valuable in debugging programs.

Hexadecimal number system A base 16 number system used when printing the contents of primary storage to help programmers detect errors.

```
9000D203   9000C11E   41330004   4650C05A
0010E020   C1220064   E020C186   006407FE
40F0F740   40F0F840   4040F540   40F2F340
40404040   40404040   40F2F340   40F2F340
40F4F640   40F2F540   40F1F240   40F2F440
4040F640   40F6F640   40F8F540   40404040
40F0F840   40F2F540   40F3F140   4040F540
F2F5F640   F7F8F940   F1F2F540   F6F2F440
00000005   00000005   00000006   00000007
0000000F   00000010   00000015   00000017
00000018   00000018   00000019   00000019
00000035   00000035   00000037   00000038
00000055   00000055   00000060   0000007D
0000022B   0000022B   0000022B   0000022B
0000022B   00000315   F0E3C8C5   40E4D5E2
E2D6D9E3   C5C440C1   D9D9C1E8   F1F5F5F5
F5F5F5F5   F5F5F5F5   F5F5F5F5   F5F5F5F5
F5F5F5F5   F5F5F5F5   F5F5F5F5   F5F5F5F5
```

Figure 3–17
Core Dump

Figure 3-18
Binary, Hexadecimal, and Decimal
Equivalent Values

BINARY SYSTEM (PLACE VALUES)				HEXADECIMAL EQUIVALENT	DECIMAL EQUIVALENT
8	4	2	1		
0	0	0	0	0	0
0	0	0	1	1	1
0	0	1	0	2	2
0	0	1	1	3	3
0	1	0	0	4	4
0	1	0	1	5	5
0	1	1	0	6	6
0	1	1	1	7	7
1	0	0	0	8	8
1	0	0	1	9	9
1	0	1	0	A	10
1	0	1	1	B	11
1	1	0	0	C	12
1	1	0	1	D	13
1	1	1	0	E	14
1	1	1	1	F	15

right to left) that sum to 15—the highest single digit value in the hexadecimal number system.

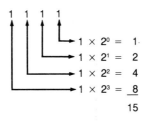

$$1 \times 2^0 = 1$$
$$1 \times 2^1 = 2$$
$$1 \times 2^2 = 4$$
$$1 \times 2^3 = \underline{8}$$
$$15$$

If we wanted to represent a binary value contained in a 32-bit word as a hexadecimal value, it could be converted as follows:

0000 0000 0000 0000 0000 0010 0010 1011

0   0   0   0   0   2   2   B

If we then wanted to convert the hexadecimal value to its decimal equivalent, it could also be done. Keep in mind that each digit of the hexadecimal number represents a power of 16.

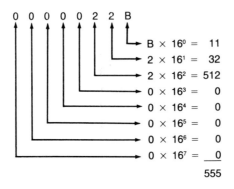

0 0 0 0 0 2 2 B

$$B \times 16^0 = 11$$
$$2 \times 16^1 = 32$$
$$2 \times 16^2 = 512$$
$$0 \times 16^3 = 0$$
$$0 \times 16^4 = 0$$
$$0 \times 16^5 = 0$$
$$0 \times 16^6 = 0$$
$$0 \times 16^7 = \underline{0}$$
$$555$$

Computer Codes

Many computers use coding schemes other than simple binary notation to represent numbers. One of the most basic coding schemes is called **4-bit binary coded decimal (BCD).** Rather than represent a decimal number as a string of 0s and 1s (which gets increasingly complicated for large numbers), BCD represents each decimal digit in a number by using four bits. For instance, the decimal number 23 is represented by two groups of four bits, one group for the 2, the other for the 3. Representations of the number 23 in 4-bit BCD and in binary are compared below:

|0 0 1 0| |0 0 1 1|
                          4-bit BCD

    2   3

0000000000010111   Binary

The representation of a three-digit decimal number in 4-bit BCD consists of three sets of four bits, or 12 binary digits. For example, the decimal number 637 is coded as follows:

|0 1 1 0| |0 0 1 1| |0 1 1 1|
                                       4-bit BCD

    6   3   7

0000001001111101   Binary

Use of 4-bit BCD saves space when large decimal numbers must be represented. Furthermore, converting a 4-bit BCD to its decimal equivalent is easier than converting a binary representation to decimal.

The 4-bit code allows 16 (2^4) possible unique bit combinations. We have already seen that 10 of them are used to represent the decimal digits 0 through 9. Since that leaves only 6 remaining combinations, this code is used only to represent numbers.

To represent letters and special characters as well as numbers, more than four bit positions are needed. Another coding scheme, called **6-bit BCD,** allows for 64 (2^6) unique bit combinations. Thus, 6-bit BCD can be used to represent the decimal digits 0 through 9, the letters A through Z, and 28 characters, such as the period and the comma.

The four rightmost bit positions in 6-bit BCD are called **numeric bits.** The two leftmost bit positions are called **zone bits** (see Figure 3–19). The zone bits are used in various combinations with the numeric bits to represent numbers, letters, and special characters.

Another approach to data representation is an 8-bit code known as **Extended Binary Coded Decimal Interchange Code (EBCDIC).** An 8-bit code allows 256 (2^8) possible bit combinations. Whereas 6-bit BCD can be used to represent only uppercase letters, 8-bit EBCDIC can be used to represent uppercase and lowercase letters and additional special characters, such as the cent sign and

4-bit binary coded decimal (BCD) A 4-bit computer code that uses 4-bit groupings to represent digits in decimal numbers.

6-bit BCD Data representation scheme used to represent the decimal digits, the letters, and 28 special characters.

Numeric bits The four rightmost bit positions of 6-bit BCD used to encode numeric data.

Zone bit Used in different combinations with numeric bits to represent numbers, letters, and special characters.

Extended Binary Coded Decimal Interchange Code (EBCDIC) An 8-bit code for character representation.

ZONE BITS		NUMERIC BITS			
B	A	8	4	2	1

Figure 3–19
Bit Positions in 6-Bit BCD Representation

American Standard Code for
Information Interchange (ASCII) A
7-bit standard code used for information
interchange among computer
equipment.

ASCII-8 An 8-bit version of ASCII
developed for computers that require
8-bit codes.

Byte A fixed number of adjacent bits
operated on as a unit.

the quotation mark. The EBCDIC bit combinations for uppercase letters and numbers are given in Figure 3–20.

In EBCDIC, the four leftmost bit positions are zone bits, and the four rightmost bit positions are numeric bits. As with 6-bit BCD, the zone bits are used in various combinations with the numeric bits to represent numbers, letters, and special characters.

The **American Standard Code for Information Interchange (ASCII)** is a 7-bit code developed with the cooperation of several computer manufacturers whose objective was to develop a standard code for all computers. Because certain machines are designed to accept 8-bit rather than 7-bit code patterns, an 8-bit version of ASCII, called **ASCII-8** was created. ASCII-8 and EBCDIC are similar, the key difference between them being in the bit patterns used to represent certain characters.

Bits, as described, are very small units of data; combining them into larger units is often useful. A fixed number of adjacent bits operated on as a unit is called a **byte.** Usually, one alphabetic character or two numeric characters are represented in one byte. Since eight bits are sufficient to represent any character, 8-bit groupings are the basic units of memory. In computers that accept 8-bit characters, a byte is a group of eight adjacent bits.

When large amounts of storage are described, the symbol K is often used. Generally, one K equals 1,024 (2^{10}) units. Thus, a computer that has 256K bytes of storage can store 256 × 1,024 or 262,144, characters.

Code Checking

Parity bit Means of detecting
erroneous transmission of data by
determining if the number of 1 bits in a
bit pattern is either odd or even.

Computers do not always function without errors. When errors occur, they must be detected immediately to keep the data from being changed.

Most computers include an extra bit at each storage location to check for certain kinds of internal errors. This extra bit is called a **parity bit.**

Figure 3–20
EBCDIC Representation: A–Z, 0–9

Character	EBCDIC Bit Configuration		Character	EBCDIC Bit Configuration	
A	1100	0001	S	1110	0010
B	1100	0010	T	1110	0011
C	1100	0011	U	1110	0100
D	1100	0100	V	1110	0101
E	1100	0101	W	1110	0110
F	1100	0110	X	1110	0111
G	1100	0111	Y	1110	1000
H	1100	1000	Z	1110	1001
I	1100	1001	0	1111	0000
J	1101	0001	1	1111	0001
K	1101	0010	2	1111	0010
L	1101	0011	3	1111	0011
M	1101	0100	4	1111	0100
N	1101	0101	5	1111	0101
O	1101	0110	6	1111	0110
P	1101	0111	7	1111	0111
Q	1101	1000	8	1111	1000
R	1101	1001	9	1111	1001

Computers can be set to either **odd parity** or **even parity.** If a computer is set for odd parity, each character is represented by an odd number of 1 bits. The parity bit is set to 0 if the number of 1 bits in the character is already odd. If the number of 1 bits is even, the parity bit is set to 1, making the total number of 1 bits odd. With even parity, the parity bit is set to either 0 or 1 so that the total number of 1 bits is even.

When the computer checks each character for errors, it checks for the proper number of 1 bits. For example, a computer set for even parity will check for an even number of 1 bits and will detect an error in any character having an odd number of 1 bits.

If an error is detected, the computer may try to redo the read or write operation in which the error occurred. If the error remains, the computer will inform the operator. The computer cannot correct these errors; it can only detect them.

A **check digit** is also used in detecting errors. While the parity check is an internal operation, performed in the computer's circuits, a check digit is used in program instructions to catch input errors. The check digit is determined by some mathematical calculations on the code, specified by the programmer. The resulting digit becomes part of the code. Credit cards, banking cards, and employee ID cards generally use check digits. For example, assume that calculations performed on the employee number 93976 resulted in the check digit 4. The computer could tell when an operator mistakenly entered 93996 instead of 93976 because the calculations on the digits would not result in 4, the check digit.

Check digit A digit added to an existing number, such as an inventory number, determined by performing some calculation on the code; used to catch input errors.

Odd parity Method of coding in which an odd number of 1 bits is used to represent each character; facilitates error checking.

Even parity Method of coding in which an even number of 1 bits represent each character; used to enhance detection of errors.

FOCUS ON MICRO-COMPUTING

How Much Power Does a Micro Need?

When people discuss the differences between microcomputers and mainframes, the most obvious difference is physical size. The largest mainframes, known as supercomputers, can fill an entire room, while the typical microcomputer fits nicely on a desk. Yet as chips are designed to hold more and more transistors, microcomputers are becoming more powerful.

The microprocessor is the heart of the microcomputer. It usually contains the control unit and the arithmetic/logic unit and is directly linked to primary storage. The insides of a personal computer (single user–oriented microcomputer) also reveal other storage chips: some RAM chips for primary storage and some ROM chips for other functions. Personal computers require less primary memory to manipulate data and computer instructions because they are dedicated to one person or one task. Programs and primary storage are not shared among many users as is done in mainframe systems. Personal computers also transfer smaller words— groups of bits—at a time.

However, immediate results and ease of use have increased the popularity of personal computers in the business office. Executives can use their personal computers with spreadsheet software to help make financial decisions quickly. Business uses have fostered more powerful machines. To run sophisticated business software, personal computers should have 512K of RAM. RAM memory requirements just to hold instructions are often in the 300K range. Then the executive will also enter data, which requires even more memory.

In the various science fields, micros are used to record data and monitor equipment and experiments around the clock. Even the less-powerful Timex-Sinclair at $100 fills the need for plotting data. At Virginia Commonwealth University in Richmond, Dr. George W. Gander used the Timex-Sinclair to plot the temperatures of laboratory rabbits being injected with particular drugs.

At many universities, use of the mainframe computer is not free. Students may pay as much as $500 per quarter, or even per month, to run programs on the school's mainframe computer. Results are not immediate, and an incorrect program can cost a lot of money. Using microcomputers gives immediate results at less cost. There is no waiting time because the computer is dedicated completely to one task. In addition, microcomputers give students the confidence to experiment and make mistakes in private.

Now the question is, how much power is needed in a personal computer? Software seems to expand to fit the amount of storage available; therefore, no memory capacity is too large. On the other hand, when the prices of new chips decrease, the semiconductor manufacturers develop newer, more powerful chips.

Personal computer users can also get expansion cards—and the more power available, the more power users seem to want. A recent unit is a multifunction expansion card offering up to 3Mbytes (megabytes, or million bytes) produced by AST Research in Irvine, California. This unit is built for the IBM PC AT. Capabilities such as this blur the distinctions between microcomputers and some larger computers.

Let's study a historical example. The IBM 360 Model 30 mainframe was introduced in the 1960s. The machine required air conditioning and a room 18 feet square to house the CPU, the control console, a printer, and the desk for a keypunch operator. It cost $280,000 in 1960s dollars and could perform 33,000 additions per second at full speed. Today's base model of the IBM Personal Computer (PC) contains 256K of memory for $1,995. A fully equipped IBM PC can perform 700,000 additions per second at full speed. If expansion boards up to 3Mbytes are used, more users will be able to do several tasks with a personal computer as the heart of a system.

The more powerful microprocessor chips enable microcomputers to address more data. IBM used the Intel 80286 in its IBM PC AT, and Apple used the Motorola 608020 in the updated Macintosh computer. Having this kind of power has allowed users to perform CAD tasks on their personal computers. Intel has been working on an even more powerful chip, the 80386, which can make a personal computer seem even more intelligent. Implementing the 80386 chip would enable a computer to address 4 gigabytes—4 billion bytes—of data. Computers of this power could handle voice recognition and sophisticated AI programs.

Although microcomputers are not as powerful as today's larger computers, the differences will continue to diminish as microcomputers acquire more speed, larger word sizes, larger memory, and more complex software. For people in business and science, running applications on personal computers is more convenient than waiting a long time to receive results from a large mainframe computer. When microcomputers are linked in a network to allow data sharing, the personal computer becomes even more powerful. The wide range of capabilities necessitates deciding exactly how much power is required for each application.

SUMMARY POINTS

- Computers are classified as either digital or analog. Digital computers operate on distinct data in steps and are the computers commonly used in business applications. Analog computers measure continuous physical or electrical magnitudes, such as pressure, temperature, current, or voltage and are less accurate than digital computers.
- All computer processing involves the basic machine functions of performing simple arithmetic (addition, subtraction, and so on), comparing values (either numeric or alphabetic), and storing and retrieving data.
- The computer derives its power from its speed, accuracy, and memory capacity.
- The speed of computer processing is limited by the switching speed of its electronic circuits and the distances that current must travel through these circuits. Advances in technology have made building computers that can perform operations in nanoseconds (billionths of a second) possible.
- The accuracy of computers refers to the reliability of electrical circuits. Although the internal operations of the computer are essentially error free, output will not be valid unless the data and instructions are valid. Understanding this "garbage in—garbage out" concept is fundamental to understanding computer "mistakes."
- The collection, manipulation, and dissemination of data is known as data processing. When computer equipment is used to process data, the procedure is known as electronic data processing (EDP).
- *Data* refers to raw, unorganized facts. *Information* is data that has been organized and processed for use in making intelligent decisions. For information to be useful, it must be accurate, timely, complete, concise, and relevant.
- Data must be organized to be processed effectively. A data item is called a field; a collection of fields relating to a single unit is a record; and a grouping of related records is a file. The structuring of data to support the information needs of a wide variety of users creates a data base.
- The conversion of data to information follows this pattern: input through processing to output. Input involves collecting, verifying, and coding data. Processing may include classifying, sorting, calculating, summarizing, and storing data. Information retrieved and converted so that it can be communicated to the user in an intelligible form is output.
- Two types of processing are batch (in which data is submitted all at once) and interactive (in which the user may enter data during execution of a program).

- Some data is entered offline through a device not directly connected to the computer; other data is entered online through a device directly connected to the computer.
- The processing part of a computer is the central processing unit (CPU). The CPU is made up of the control unit, which maintains order and controls what is happening in the CPU, the arithmetic/logic unit (ALU), which performs arithmetic and logical operations and primary storage which holds all data and instructions necessary for processing.
- Instructions are placed in consecutive locations in memory so they can be accessed consecutively. This is called the next-sequential-instruction feature.
- Each location in storage has a unique address, which allows stored-program instructions and data items to be located by the control unit as it directs processing operations. Programmers often use variables—names for storage addresses—to indicate data locations.
- The stored-program concept involves storing both data and instructions in primary memory, thus eliminating the need for human intervention during processing. The nondestructive read/destructive write characteristic of primary memory allows a program to be reexecuted as many times as needed since the program remains intact until another is stored over it.
- Registers are devices that facilitate execution of instructions. They act as temporary holding areas and are capable of receiving information, holding it, and transferring it very quickly as directed by the control unit of the CPU.
- Cache memory is a portion of primary storage designed to speed the CPU's processing of instructions or data.
- One method of storing data in primary storage uses electrical currents to set magnetic cores to "on" and "off" states. Another form of storage is semiconductor memory, which uses circuitry on silicon chips. A new form of primary storage, called bubble memory, creates magnetic domains on a thin film of semiconductor material. The part of memory that is the working area of the computer is called random-access memory (RAM).
- Read-only memory (ROM) is part of the hardware of the computer. It stores microprograms or other items in a form that cannot be changed. Functions built into ROM can be carried out more quickly than stored-program instructions. If the ROM can be programmed once, it is called programmable read-only memory (PROM); if it can be corrected and reprogrammed, it is called erasable programmable read-only memory (EPROM).
- Data representation in the computer is based on a two-state, or binary, system. A 1 in a given position indicates the presence of a power of 2, and a 0 in a given position indicates the absence of a power of 2. This binary system can be used for indicating the state of computer circuits by assigning 0 to "off" (or no current flowing) and 1 to "on" (or current flowing).
- The 4-bit binary coded decimal (BCD) system uses groups of four binary digits to represent the decimal digits 0 through 9. The 6-bit BCD system allows for 64 unique bit combinations; alphabetic, numeric, and 28 special characters can be represented. Both EBCDIC and ASCII-8 are 8-bit coding systems and are capable of representing up to 256 different characters. ASCII is a 7-bit coding system. The ASCII codes were developed to create some standardization among products of different manufacturers.
- Octal (base 8) and hexadecimal (base 16) notation can be used to represent binary data in a more concise form. For this reason, the contents of computer

memory are sometimes viewed or printed in one of these notations. Programmers use these number systems to help them locate errors.
- Parity bits are used to detect errors in data transmission. Check digits are used to determine the correctness of data entry.
- The capabilities of personal computers are beginning to blur the distinctions between microcomputers and larger computers, such as mainframes or minicomputers.
- Microcomputers can aid businesspeople and scientists by making available computer power for immediate results, eliminating waiting periods between runs to check the correctness of programming, monitoring specific data of science experiments, and increasing the privacy of computer use.

REVIEW AND DISCUSSION QUESTIONS

1. Distinguish between analog and digital computers, giving examples of each.
2. Although computer processing is essentially error free, mistakes can and do occur. Explain how. What is meant by the phrase "garbage in—garbage out"?
3. Distinguish between data and information. Give some examples.
4. What are some of the functions performed in converting data into information? Given an example of how a computer can be used to perform these functions.
5. Describe the relationship that exists among data within a data base—that is, what is a field, a record, a file, and a data base?
6. Name the three parts of the CPU, and discuss the function of each.
7. Explain what is meant by the stored-program concept, and show why it is significant to EDP.
8. Describe three types of primary storage.
9. Explain the concept of ROM. How does it relate to microprogramming? What implications does it have in the issue of software piracy?
10. Why are computer codes necessary? What advantages does EBCDIC offer compared to 6-bit BCD?
11. What is meant by the next-sequential-instruction feature?
12. What relationship do the first four binary place values (from right to left) have with the hexadecimal number system?
13. Convert these binary values to decimal numbers:
    (a) 10010100
    (b) 11111
    (c) 1001101
14. Convert the following binary value to a hexadecimal value. Then convert the hexadecimal value to a decimal value.
    00110111
15. Convert the following binary value to an octal value. Then convert the octal value to a decimal value.
    101100101
16. What is the purpose of code checking? Can incorrect data be detected by using either a parity bit or a check digit?
17. How does a microcomputer seem more convenient than a mainframe system for certian business, science, and study applications?

18. What sociological implication is attached to having a personal computer on your desk at work or to owning a personal computer with much greater RAM than necessary for your purposes?

19. Read computer magazines and interview people who own personal computers to help you set up a system of computer hardware that you would like for your personal use.

Enhancing Research and Technology

Computers have made a major impact in laboratories around the world. They can simplify complex or time-consuming experiments and have opened up new areas of research never imagined until the advent of computers. Ironically, computers themselves have revolutionized the manufacturing of microchips, the miniature components that give all computers their power.

The metal or plastic cabinets that look like computers merely house the intricate system of chips and wires that do the work. Originally, the cabinets took up as much space as a two-car garage in order to hold all the vacuum tubes, transistors, wiring, and switches that made up early computers. However, large-scale and very large-scale integration made possible the etching of microscopic circuits on tiny pieces of silicon and consequently the manufacturing of smaller cabinets.

Once hand-drawn on huge pieces of paper and converted into computer memory by a process called digitizing, computer circuits are now planned by computer-aided design (CAD) technology. A designer enters data by drawing with a light pen at a graphics terminal, shown with the chip design superimposed in the foreground ①. Sometimes the circuits are displayed in color on the monitor ②. And sometimes the circuits are automatically generated by computer drafting equipment.

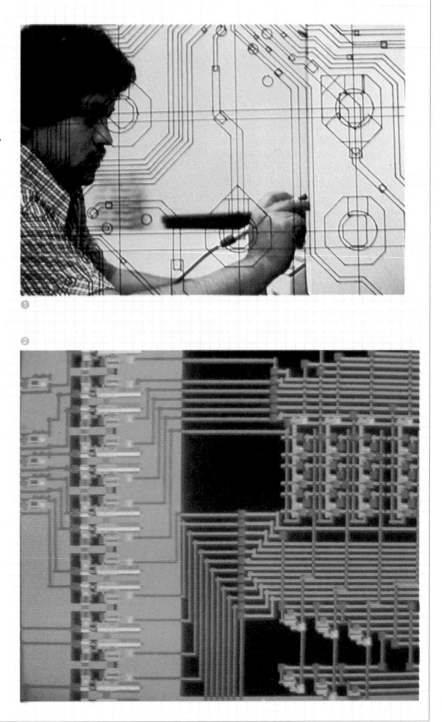

107

Before the designs can be reduced and etched on the chips, the silicon must be prepared. The raw material, polycrystalline silicon ③, is processed in a large crystal-growing furnace operating at 1440 degrees Centigrade. After two hours, the material emerges as a two-foot-long ingot of single crystal silicon, with a diameter of two to six inches ④. The ingots are sawed into wafers about 25 mils thick, which are polished to a mirrorlike finish ⑤. Now the wafers are ready for the photolithographic processing, in which the pattern of the circuits is reproduced over the face of the wafer. The circuit patterns are transferred to glass masks ⑥. The masks act like photograph negatives: light is passed through them onto photosensitive materials coating the wafer. Unexposed areas are washed away in a developing process, and the remaining design is etched by acid into the thin oxide layer on the wafer. These coating and etching procedures are carried out in "clean rooms" where the number of dust particles is meticulously regulated and where workers must wear "bunny-suits ⑦." In addition, specific elements are implanted that give silicon the ability to carry electrical current.

③

④

⑤

⑥

⑦

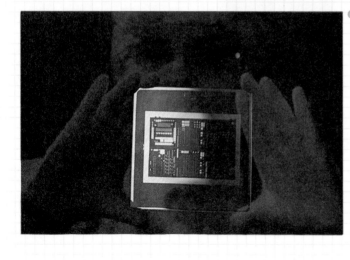

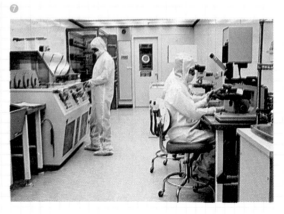

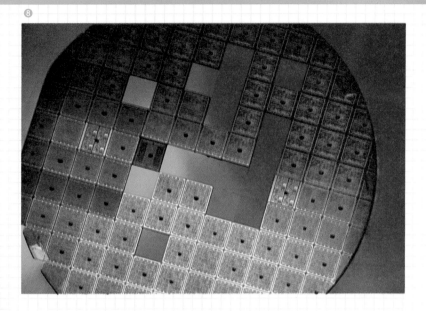

The wafer is inspected and only the best chips are cut out of it to package in carriers ⑧. Two that passed the test are the Bellmac-32A microprocessor (top) and 256K Ram chip (bottom) ⑨. Some chips are mounted singly in carriers and connected to other chips and circuitry by gold wires. Other chips are mounted in multi-chip carriers such as the IBM module of four 1K-bit chips ⑩. New ways of making chips will allow designers to program an electron beam gun to etch circuits directly into the silicon, eliminating the need for masks ⑪.

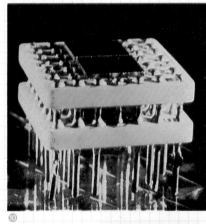

109

The chips form the computer, which—with the proper software—enable scientists and engineers to study our universe from molecular structure to our galaxy. For example, at Pfizer Inc.'s research center in Groton, Connecticut, scientists examine a computer's rendition of the molecular structure of Cardovar, the company's newest drug for treating hypertension ⑫. On the other hand, the Jet Propulsion Laboratory in Pasadena, California, identified a new mass in space, detected by the Infrared Astronomical Satellite. In an image that uses different colors to show light intensity, that object appears as a red patch in the lower left ⑬. The right-hand image was produced by equipment that did not detect the unknown object. Whether the mass is a star in our galaxy or star activity in a distant galaxy remains to be seen.

Other computerized processes enable researchers to study land, forest, and ocean topology. By using Aero Service's Interactive Digital Image Manipulation System (IDIMS), scientists can manipulate data in a terrain map with selected colors representing different elevations, slope, or terrain vegetation ⑭. Seasat satellites collect data that can be coded by color to produce images of the elevations of the ocean's floor ⑮ and ⑯.

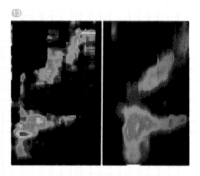

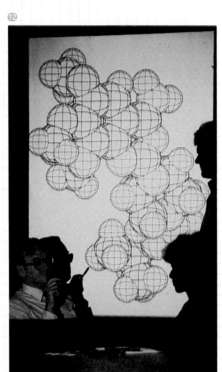

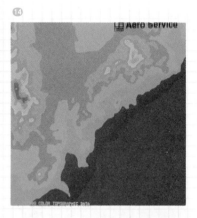

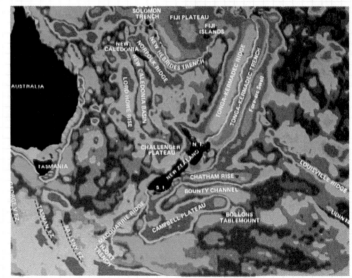

110

Computers help organizations such as Marathon Oil Company and other energy-producing companies carry on research needed for everyday business. Through computer technology, Marathon Oil Company directs all tanker and pipeline movements for LOOP—the Louisiana Offshore Oil Port—which is owned by a consortium of oil companies, with Marathon holding the largest interest ⑰. Similar computer systems enable Marathon to perform research and keep in touch with their South Brae production platform in the North Sea ⑱. Other energy-producing companies rely on computers to read meters and monitor pipelines for flaws ⑲ and ⑳. Computers will continue to aid research and technology by decreasing time-consuming manual processes and increasing the areas that can be studied.

CHAPTER 4

INPUT/OUTPUT DEVICES

COMPUTERS IN OUR LIVES

Technology Talks

Kendall College in Evanston, Illinois, is ideally suited for Tony Lacotta, and when he received his acceptance letter, no future college student could have been happier. Tony chose Kendall because the college's commercial art school is nationally recognized as one of the best in the country; its graduates are frequently cited for their excellent training and creative achievement. Tony has been dreaming of becoming a commercial artist for years, and Kendall College can help him realize that dream. But Kendall's excellent reputation for training commercial artists is only one reason Tony is attending the school. Tony has cerebral palsy, and Kendall College is equally known for its sensitivity in accommodating students with special needs.

Although Tony has good control over his hand and arm movements, he has difficulty walking, and his speech is almost impossible for most people to understand. To help overcome the communication problems that Tony has struggled with all his life, Kendall, through a special endowment fund, has provided Tony with an Apple Macintosh computer equipped with a DECtalk voice synthesizer. The computer and synthesizer are usually located in Tony's dorm room enabling him to "talk" with his roommates. When special oral presentations are required for a class, Tony, with help from a friend, takes his computer and synthesizer to class or, as many of the classrooms at Kendall are equipped with Macintosh computers, carries just his synthesizer to class in a backpack and simply plugs the device into the classroom computer.

To use the synthesizer Tony types on the computer keyboard and the synthesizer converts his typed sentences into understandable speech. The DECtalk synthesizer is one of the more expensive on the market, but the quality of the computerized speech is so good that MCI Communications, one discount long distance telephone service, is using the synthesizer with its electronic mail service so that messages received via their service can be communicated through spoken words rather than words printed on a monitor. Tony enjoys being able to vary the pitch, tone, and speed of the synthesizer while talking with friends, and the synthesizer's unlimited vocabulary has given Tony the freedom to easily express a full range of thoughts and feelings for the first time in his life. The synthesizer's dial-up capability makes it possible for Tony to call home and talk to his parents just like nonhandicapped college students—and like all students his calls are more frequent when he is running short of funds at the end of the month!

Speech synthesizers are only one example of the many ways in which Kendall College is using computers with special input/output devices to make life easier and success more achievable for its special-needs students. Keyboard adapters are available for students with poor motor control in the hands and arms. Quadriplegics can use optical head pointers or light-beam switches. One student even uses a brow-wrinkle switch to control her computer. Braille keyboards with programs to convert English to Braille are used by visually impaired students. Special modems allow deaf students to communicate with both those who are deaf and those who can hear.

114

The development of input/output devices has not only brought computer use to people with special educational needs but also to handicapped people in noneducational situations. For example, a graphics tablet (an input device that, when drawn on, transfers the image to a computer screen) can be used for art therapy and specially adapted joysticks can be used for playing video games. The following chapter discusses input/output devices and explains how they work.

INTRODUCTION

A computer system includes much more than just a central processing unit (CPU). Data must be provided to the computer in a form it can recognize, and output must be translated into a form humans can understand. Input and output are important activities in any computer-based system because they are the communication links between people and machines. If these people/machine interfaces are weak, the overall performance of the computer system suffers.

This chapter discusses the various forms of input to the computer and newer developments that use input devices to communicate directly with the computer (a phenomenon called source-data automation). The chapter concludes with a discussion of output devices, including printers and special-purpose input and output.

PUNCHED CARDS

As we saw in Chapter 2, punched cards were used in data processing long before the digital computer was developed. Punched cards were used with early digital computers as a means of entering data. Today's uses of punched cards are limited. They are often found as user-oriented documents, such as time cards, invoices, checks, and turnaround documents. A turnaround document is frequently used for utility bills. The document consists of two parts, often with a perforation in the middle. One part is the customer's record of the bill and the other part contains information for the utility company about the customer's account. When the customer receives the bill, he or she tears the card on the perforation, keeps the designated portion, and returns the other portion along with a payment.

The standard punched card has 80 vertical columns and 12 horizontal rows (see Figure 4–1). Data is recorded as holes punched in a particular column to represent given characters. The pattern of holes used to represent characters is known as the Hollerith code, after its inventor, Herman Hollerith. Figure 4–2 shows an example of a punched card that records the sale of an item.

Data is most commonly recorded on punched cards with the use of a **keypunch** (see Figure 4–3). An operator reads a source document (document from which data originates) and transcribes the data from the document onto cards by pressing keys on a keyboard, much as if he or she were using a typewriter. The machine automatically feeds, positions, and stacks the cards, thus allowing

Keypunch A keyboard device that punches holes in a card to represent data.

115

Figure 4–1
Eighty-Column Punched Card and
Hollerith Code

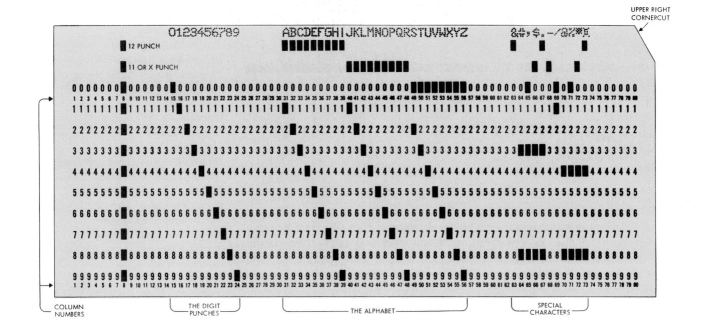

Figure 4–2
Punched-Card Record

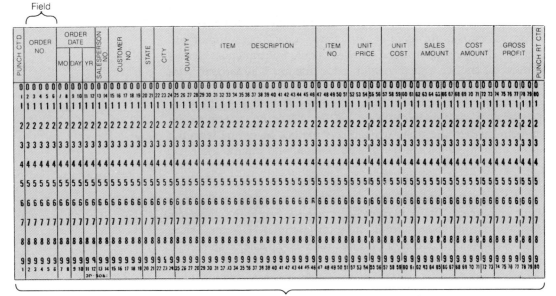

Record

116

the operator to concentrate on the keying operation. Even with these automatic functions, keypunching can be quite costly. One person is needed to operate each machine, and much time is spent keying data.

KEY-TO-MAGNETIC MEDIA

Punched-card systems require much mechanized movement and have many limitations. To overcome those limitations, methods were developed to record and enter data using magnetic media such as **magnetic tape** or **magnetic disks** rather than cards. In this process, data is entered in much the same fashion as with the keypunch, but it is stored not as punches on cards but as magnetized spots on the surface of a tape or disk. The data can be stored indefinitely because the spots retain their magnetism. Unlike punched cards, which cannot be reused, data can be replaced with new data when desired. Tapes and disks can also store much more data in a smaller space; for example, between 1,600 and 6,250 characters are commonly stored on one inch of magnetic tape. Data stored on tape or disk can be read into the CPU hundreds of times faster than data on cards. Thus, use of magnetic tape or disk significantly increases the efficiency of data-processing operations. Many **key-to-tape** systems were replaced by disks or diskettes as a result of advancing technology.

A typical **key-to-disk** configuration consists of several keying devices, all of which are connected to a computer. Data is recorded on magnetic disks (see Figure 4–4). Before that, however, it is usually edited by the computer. This editing is directed by the computer's stored-program instructions. If an error is detected, the system interrupts the operator and "stands by" until a correction has been entered. The correct data is then stored on the magnetic disk for input to the computer.

A popular data-entry system for microcomputers is the **key-to-diskette** system. A flexible (or floppy) diskette is used instead of the conventional (hard) disk. The data is entered on a keyboard, displayed on a screen for the operator to check, and recorded on the diskette. A key-to-diskette system can operate by itself or with a group of similar devices as described above. Advances in

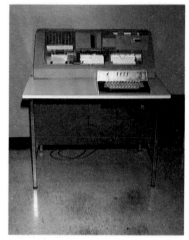

Figure 4–3
Keypunch

Magnetic disk A metal platter coated on both sides with a magnetic recording material upon which data is stored in the form of magnetized spots.

Key-to-disk Hardware designed to transfer data entered via a keyboard to magnetic disk or diskette.

Figure 4–4
Key-to-Disk System

117

disk technology and the subsequent reduction in prices of key-to-disk and -diskette systems have made them the method of data storage chosen by most computer users.

SOURCE-DATA AUTOMATION

Data entry has traditionally been the weakest link in the chain of data-processing operations. Although data can be processed electronically at extremely high speeds, significantly more time is required to prepare data and enter it into the computer system.

One approach to data collection and preparation that is gaining in popularity is called **source-data automation**. The purpose of this method is to collect data about an event, in computer-readable form, when and where the event takes place. By eliminating the intermediate steps used in preparing card input, source-data automation improves the speed, accuracy, and efficiency of data-processing operations (see Figure 4–5).

Source-data automation The use of special equipment to collect data at its point of origin.

Source-data automation is implemented by a variety of methods. Each requires special machines for reading data and converting it into machine language. The most common approaches to source-data automation are discussed below.

Figure 4–5
Methods of Source-Data Automation

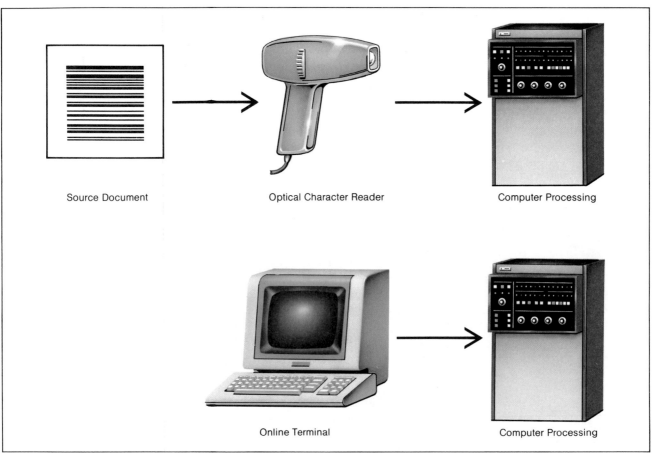

Source Document   Optical Character Reader   Computer Processing

Online Terminal   Computer Processing

The Songwriter's Helper

David McLey, a young Canadian musician, has invented a computer-based instrument that could be a boon to every songwriter. He calls his invention the McLeyvier and says it will sell for between $22,000 and $55,000, depending on the additions each buyer demands. Featuring a pianolike keyboard and a magnetic disk memory that can store at least six hours of music, the McLeyvier remembers all the sounds the musician plays and all the modifications made in the creative process. It also displays the actual musical score on a video screen as it is being composed. The user need not even know how to read and write music.

Magnetic-Ink Character Recognition

Magnetic ink was introduced in the late 1950s to facilitate check processing by the banking industry. Because magnetic-ink characters can be read by both humans and machines (see Figure 4–6), no special data conversion step is needed. Magnetic-ink characters are formed with magnetized particles of iron oxide. Each character is composed of certain sections of a 70-section matrix (see Figure 4–7). The characters can be read and interpreted by a **magnetic-ink character reader;** this process is called **magnetic-ink character recognition (MICR).**

Magnetic-ink character reader A device that reads characters composed of magnetized particles; often used to sort checks for subsequent processing.

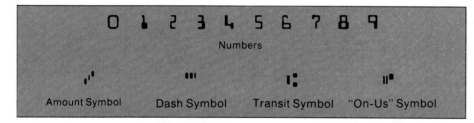

Figure 4–6
Magnetic-Ink Character Set

Figure 4–7
Matrix patterns for Magnetic-Ink Characters

All magnetic-ink characters on checks are formed with a standard 14-character set. Other character sets may be used in other applications. As the checks are fed into the MICR device, it reads them and sorts them by bank number at a Federal Reserve Bank and by account number at the issuing bank. In this manner, checks are routed back to each issuing bank and then back to its customers. Between 750 and 1,500 checks per minute can be read and sorted by an MICR system (see Figure 4–8).

Optical Recognition

Optical recognition devices can read marks or symbols coded on paper documents and convert them into electrical pulses. The pulses can then be transmitted directly to the CPU or stored on magnetic tape for input at a later time.

The simplest approach to optical recognition is known as **optical-mark recognition (OMR)**, or **mark sensing.** OMR is often used for machine scoring of multiple-choice examinations (see Figure 4–9). In this application, the person taking the examination makes a mark with a heavy pencil in the location corresponding to the desired answer. The marks on an OMR document are sensed by an optical-mark page reader as the document passes under a light source. The presence of marks in specific locations is indicated by light reflected at those locations. As the document is read, the optical-mark data is translated into machine language. When the optical-mark page reader is directly connected to the computer, up to 2,000 forms of the same type can be read and processed in an hour.

Another type of optical reader, known as a **bar-code reader,** can read special line or bar codes (patterns of optical marks). Some bar codes in use today are shown in Figure 4–10. They are suitable for many applications including credit-card verification and freight identification to facilitate warehouse operations.

Optical mark recognition (OMR) A method of electronic scanning that reads marks and converts the optical images into appropriate electrical signals.

Bar-code reader A device used to read a bar code by means of reflected light, such as a scanner.

Figure 4–8
Sample Check with Magnetic-Ink Characters

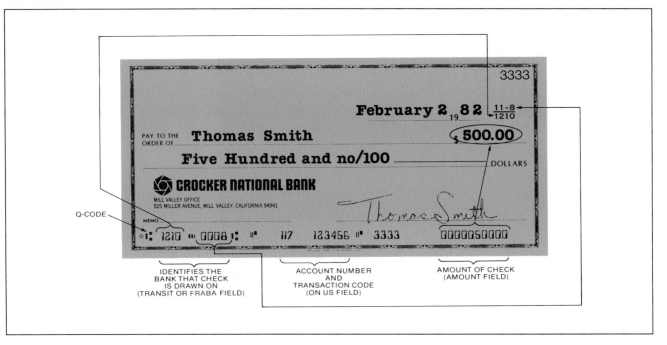

Figure 4–9
Optical-Mark Recognition

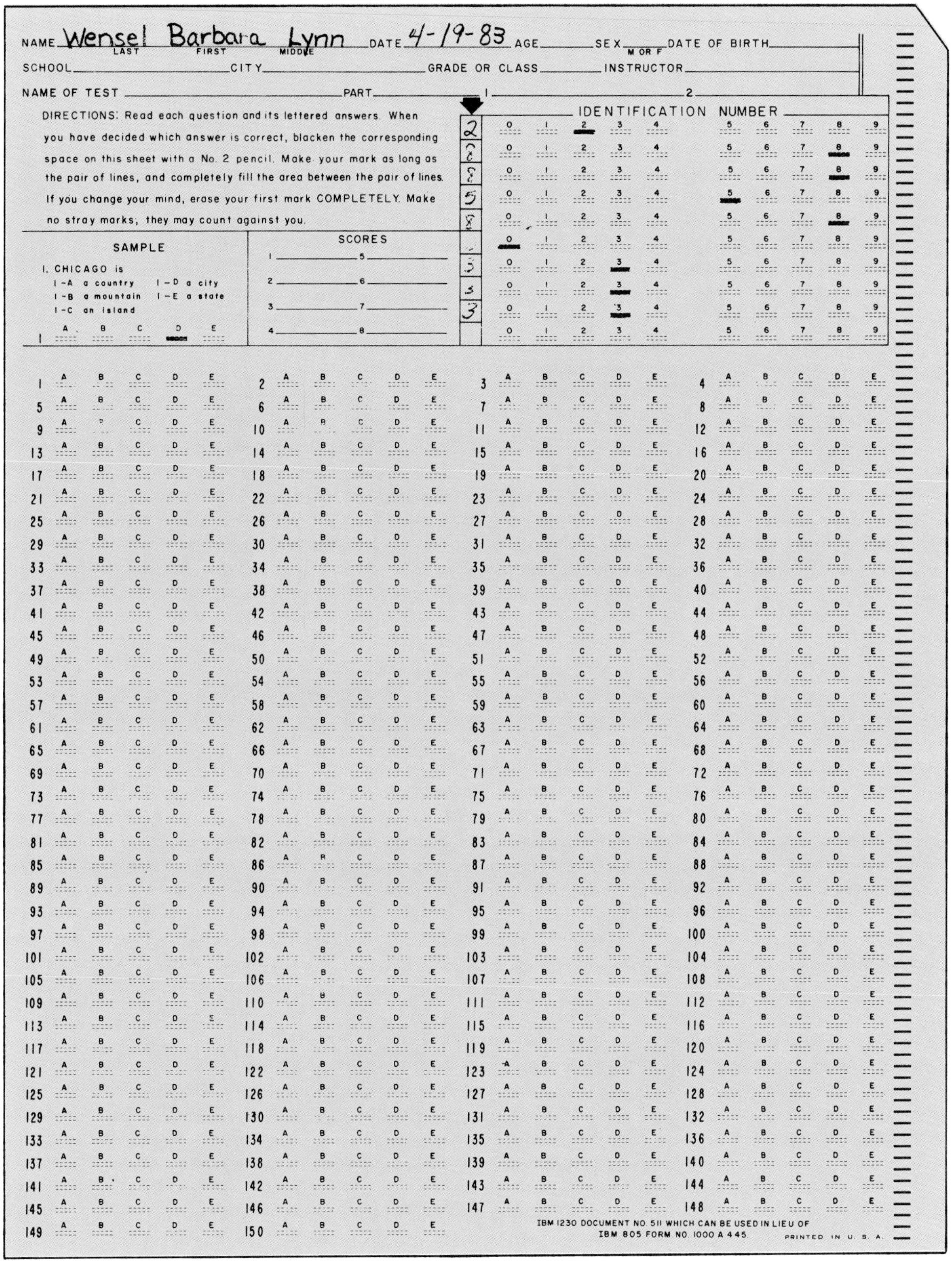

Figure 4–10
Types of Bar Codes

Data is represented in a bar code by the widths of the bars and the distances between them. Probably the most familiar bar code is the **Universal Product Code (UPC)** found on most grocery items. This code consists of vertical bars that represent both the manufacturer's identity and the identity of the item but not the item's price. The code for each product is a unique combination of these vertical bars.

Optical-character readers can read special types of characters known as optical characters. Some **optical-character recognition (OCR)** devices can read characters of several type fonts, including both uppercase and lowercase letters. The most common font is shown in Figure 4–11.

A major difference between optical-character recognition and optical-mark recognition is that optical-character data is represented by the shapes of characters rather than by the positions of marks. However, both OCR and OMR devices rely on reflected light to translate written data into machine-readable form.

Remote Input

Remote terminal A terminal placed at a location distant from the central computer.

Online In direct communication with the computer.

Remote terminals collect data at its source and transmit it to a central computer for processing **(online).** Generally, data is transmitted over telecommunication

122

Jeans and Beams

What do blue jeans and computers have in common? A lot, if the jeans are made by Levi Strauss & Co. and the computers by Light Signatures, Inc. Light Signatures has been working with Levi Strauss to protect the jeans manufacturer from counterfeiters. That's right, counterfeiters! Not the money kind, but the jeans kind.

Makers of counterfeit jeans manufacture a product that closely resembles the Levi line. To add authenticity to the fake pants, a counterfeit label is stitched on the rear of the jeans.

Light Signature uses a high-intensity light beam to spot fakes. Each label on a genuine pair of Levis jeans has a unique fiber composition. When a high-intensity light beam is focused on a label, the unique fiber pattern appears like a shadow. The fiber pattern is focused on a solid-state sensor in a hand-held computer with light-sensitive elements. The computer analyzes the fiber pattern and compares it to a numeric code, also on the label. If the two match, the jeans are authentic. Levi Strauss is so pleased with the success of the Light Signature system that they have expanded its use to other product lines.

The next time you pull on a pair of Levi jeans check out that label. It could be hiding some top secret information!

equipment. This process is described more fully in Chapter 7. The many types of remote terminals available can increase the versatility and expand the applications of the computer. Types of remote terminals discussed here are point-of-sale terminals, touch-tone devices, voice-recognition devices, and intelligent terminals.

Remote terminals that perform the functions of a cash register and also capture sales data are **point-of-sale (POS) terminals.** These terminals have a keyboard for data entry, a panel to display the price, a cash drawer, and a printer that provides a cash receipt. A POS terminal typical of those found in many supermarkets is shown in Figure 4–12.

Figure 4–12
Point-of-Sale Terminal

Figure 4–11
OCR Characters

ABCDEFGHIJKLMN
OPQRSTUVWXYZ , .
$ / * – 1234567890

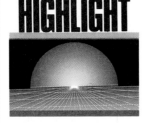

Psychiatric Programming

Research programmers in Philadelphia have created "Chris," a computerized mental health simulator. Chris will be called into action to train students in the art of psychiatric interviewing; but Chris is the schizophrenic patient, not the well-organized, rational doctor as we might expect. Students must figure out how to deal with Chris when he takes off into chaotic, irrational reveries. Should the computer run into a bug or misinterpret the student's query, the student often cannot distinguish the response from general schizophrenic symptoms.

Another psychiatric research product, "Eliza," recently operated in an interactive mode with Chris. Their conversation was unusually striking, since Eliza is a simulated psychiatrist program designed to train students in a particular diagnostic technique. Using this technique, a psychiatrist takes the patient's statement and responds with a leading question to keep the conversation going. (For example, the patient claims, "My mother hates me," and the interviewer replies, "Why do you think so?")

Researchers report that the script of this computer-to-computer session reads uncannily like some human interactions.

Wand reader A device used to scan and read source data represented in optical bar-code form or in human-readable characters.

Some POS terminals have **wand readers** or a **fixed scanner** that reads the UPC (bar code) stamped on an item. The sale is registered automatically as the checkout clerk passes the wand reader over the code; there is no need to enter the price via a keyboard unless the wand malfunctions. Using the UPC symbol, the computer system identifies the product and uses this data to find the item's name and price. Thus, POS terminals enable retailers to collect sales data at its source. If the terminals are directly connected to a large central computer, retailers can call up useful inventory and sales information almost instantaneously.

Touch-tone devices are remote terminals used with ordinary telephone lines to transfer data from remote locations to a central computer. The data is entered via a special keyboard on the terminal. Generally, slight modifications must be made to the telephone connection to transfer data over the line (see Figure 4–13).

Intelligent terminals, still another type of remote device, can be programmed by use of stored instructions. This capability distinguishes them from the ter-

Concept Summary 4–1 ▬ Types of Input

Types of Input		
Punched Cards	**Key-to-Magnetic Media**	**Source Data Automation**
Keypunch	Key-to-tape	Magnetic-ink character recognition (MICR)
	Key-to-disk, diskette	Optical-mark recognition (OMR)
		Remote input

minals discussed earlier in this chapter (sometimes called **dumb terminals**), which cannot be programmed. Intelligent terminals have the same kinds of components as full-sized computers but are limited in their storage capability and in the set of instructions they can perform. They are useful for editing data prior to transmitting it to a central computer; editing and other manipulating functions are directed by programs stored in the terminal's primary storage unit. Most intelligent terminals have a **cathode-ray tube (CRT)** and/or a printer built into them.

Cathode-ray tube (CRT) A visual display device that receives electrical impulses and translates them into a picture on a television-like screen.

PRINTERS

Computer **printers** have a straightforward basic function—printing processed data in a form humans can read (see Figure 4–14). This permanent, readable

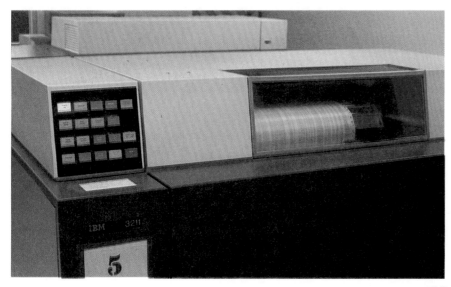

Figure 4–14
Printer

copy of computer output is called **hard copy.** To produce hard copy, the printer first receives electronic signals from the central processing unit. In an **impact printer,** these signals activate print elements that are pressed against paper. **Nonimpact printers,** a newer development, use heat, laser technology, or photographic techniques to produce output.

Impact Printers

Impact printers come in a variety of shapes and sizes. Some print a character at a time, while others print a line at a time. Printer-keyboards, dot- or wire-matrix printers, and daisy-wheel printers are the three principal character-at-a-time devices.

The **printer-keyboard** is similar to an office typewriter (see Figure 4–15). All instructions, including spacing, carriage returns, and printing of characters, are sent from the CPU to the printer. The keyboard allows an operator to communicate with the system—for example, to enter data or instructions.

Dot-matrix (also called **wire-matrix**) **printers** are based on a design principle similar to that of a football or basketball scoreboard. The matrix is a rectangle composed of pins, usually seven pins high and five pins wide. Certain combinations of pins are activated to represent characters. For example, the number 4 and the letter L are formed by a combination of pins being pressed against paper as seen in Figure 4–16. The dot combinations used to represent various

Impact printer   A printer that forms characters by physically striking a ribbon against paper.

Figure 4–15
Printer Keyboard.
This Dataproducts 3–50™ KSR (Keyboard-Send-Receive) terminal produces 50 high-quality characters per second.

Figure 4–16
Character Patterns for Solid and Dot-matrix Patterns

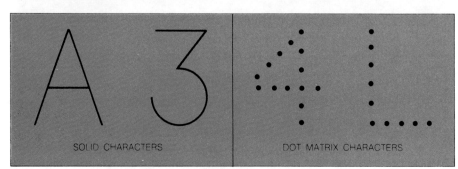

SOLID CHARACTERS   DOT MATRIX CHARACTERS

Figure 4–17
Dot-Matrix Character Set

ABCDEFGHIJKLM
NOPQRSTUVWXYZ
0123456789—.:
&/♦$*!%@=(+)

numbers, letters, and special characters are shown in Figure 4–17. High-quality characters produced by dot-matrix printers contain more dots placed closer together. Dot-matrix printers can typically print up to 15 characters per second or 900 characters per minute.

Daisy-wheel printers use a daisy wheel that is a flat disk with petal-like projections (see Figure 4–18). Daisy wheels come in several type fonts that can be interchanged quickly to suit application needs. The daisy-wheel printer offers high-quality type and is often used in word-processing systems to give output a typewriter quality appearance. Daisy-wheel printers can produce up to 50 characters per second.

Types of line-at-a-time printers include print-wheel, chain, and drum printers. A **print-wheel printer** typically contains 120 print wheels, one for each of 120 print positions on a line (see Figure 4–19). Each print wheel contains 48 alphabetic, numeric, and special characters. Each print wheel rotates until the desired character moves into the corresponding print position on the current print line. When all wheels are in their correct positions, a hammer drives the

Figure 4–18
Daisy Wheel.
The daisy wheel is the font carrier used in daisy wheel printers. The wheel has a set of spokes, each with a single character placed at the tip. The hub of the wheel rotates to bring the desired character into position, and the character is then struck by a hammer mechanism to form an image on paper.

127

Figure 4–19
Print Wheel

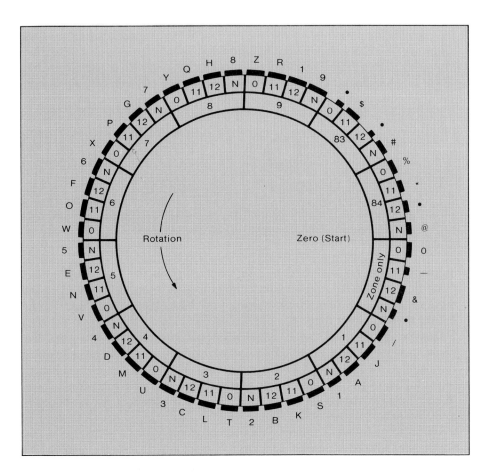

paper against the wheels and an entire line of output is printed. Print-wheel printers can produce about 150 lines per minute, which makes them comparatively slow.

A **chain printer** has a character set assembled in a chain that revolves horizontally past all print positions (see Figure 4–20). There is one print hammer for each column on the paper. Characters are printed when hammers press the paper against an inked ribbon, which in turn presses against appropriate characters on the print chain. Type fonts can be changed easily on chain printers, allowing a variety of fonts, such as italic or boldface, to be used. Some chain printers can produce up to 2,000 lines per minute.

A **drum printer** uses a metal cylinder with rows of characters engraved across its surface (see Figure 4–21). Each column on the drum contains a complete character set and corresponds to one print position on the line. As the drum rotates, all characters are rotated past the print position. A hammer presses the paper against the ink ribbon and drum when the appropriate character is in place. One line is printed for each revolution of the drum, since all characters eventually reach the print position during one revolution. Some drum printers can produce 3,000 lines per minute.

Nonimpact Printers

Nonimpact printer A printer that uses heat, laser technology, or photographic techniques to produce output.

As mentioned earlier, nonimpact printers do not print characters by means of a mechanical printing element that strikes paper. Instead, a variety of other

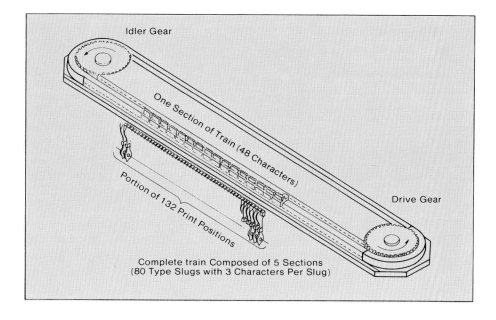

Figure 4-20
Chain Printer

Idler Gear

One Section of Train (48 Characters)

Portion of 132 Print Positions

Drive Gear

Complete train Composed of 5 Sections
(80 Type Slugs with 3 Characters Per Slug)

methods are used. Electrostatic, electrothermal, ink-jet, laser, and xerographic printers will be discussed here.

An **electrostatic printer** forms an image of a character on special paper using a dot matrix of charged wires or pins. The paper is moved through a solution containing ink particles that have a charge opposite that of the pattern. The ink particles adhere to each charged pattern of the paper, forming a visible image of each character.

Electrothermal printers generate characters by using heat and heat-sensitive paper. Rods are heated in a matrix; as the ends of the selected rods touch the heat-sensitive paper, an image is created.

Both electrothermal and electrostatic printers are relatively quiet in operation. They are often used in applications where noise may be a problem. Some of these printers are capable of producing 5,000 lines per minute.

Figure 4-21
Print Drum

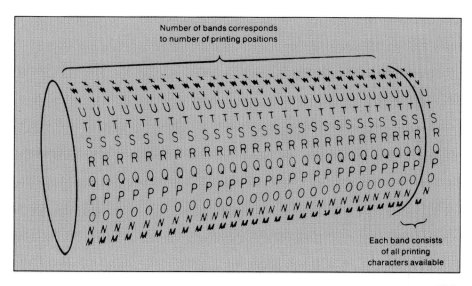

Number of bands corresponds
to number of printing positions

Each band consists
of all printing
characters available

Computers and Sports

Even the world of sports is being invaded by computers. The Milwaukee Bucks of the National Basketball Association have entered the computer age. The Bucks purchased a microcomputer to computerize team statistics.

Traditionally, keeping game stats meant entering hash marks on a scorecard, followed by many hours of adding columns and typing results. The system used by the Bucks now virtually eliminates this time-consuming manual process.

The system is a standard, off-the-shelf microcomputer with a special basketball keyboard. The statistics are entered with the touch of a button, and the specially developed statistics programs do the rest of the work. Accurate up-to-date statistics are displayed on video monitors for radio and television broadcasters. Seconds after the game ends, the stats are totaled and printed in box-score form. Later the system produces cumulative information, along with season highs and lows, in printed form suitable for press releases.

This system can produce enough statistics to inundate even the most statistically oriented sports fan.

In an **ink-jet printer,** a nozzle is used to shoot a stream of charged ink toward the paper. Before reaching it, the ink passes through an electrical field that arranges the charged particles into characters.

Laser printers combine laser beams and electrophotographic technology to create output images (see Figure 4–22). A beam of light is focused through a rotating disk containing a full font of characters. The character image is projected

Figure 4–22
Laser Printer.
The 9800 series laser printer from Datagraphix, Inc., operates at speeds of up to 21,000 lines per minute.

onto a piece of film or photographic paper, and the print or negative is developed and fixed in a manner similar to that used for ordinary photographs. The output consists of high-quality, letter-perfect images—the process is often used to print books. Laser printers, which can operate up to 21,000 lines per minute, are being considered as a solution to the slower printing speeds of word-processing systems.

Xerographic printers use printing methods much like those used in common xerographic copying machines. For example, Xerox, the pioneer of this type of printing, has one model that prints on single 8½-by-11-inch sheets of plain paper rather than on the continuous form paper normally used. Xerographic printers operate at 4,000 lines per minute.

Since nonimpact printers involve less physical movement than impact printers, they are generally much faster. They also offer a wider choice of type faces and better speed-to-price ratios than impact printers, and their technology implies a higher reliability because they use fewer movable parts in printing. The disadvantages of nonimpact printers include the special paper requirements and/or poor type image quality of some printers and their inability to make carbon copies. However, nonimpact printers can produce several copies of a page in less time than it takes an impact printer to produce one page with several carbon copies.

New printing systems now on the market combine many features of the printing process into one machine. For example, collating, routing, hole punching, blanking out of proprietary information, and perforating may be performed. Some printers produce both text and form designs on plain paper, reducing or eliminating the need for preprinted forms.

SPECIAL-PURPOSE INPUT AND OUTPUT

In many instances, traditional input/output devices cannot provide the appropriate form of output. At these times, special devices are required.

Visual Display Terminals

Visual display terminals in common use display data or information on cathode-ray tubes (CRTs) which are similar to television screens (see Figure

Concept Summary 4–2 ■ Impact and Nonimpact Printers

Impact Printers	Speed	Nonimpact Printers	Speed
Printer-keyboard printer	Very slow	Electrostatic printer	Up to 5000 lines per minute
Dot-matrix printer	Up to 900 characters per minute	Inkjet printer	Up to 200 characters per second
Daisy-wheel printer	Up to 50 characters per second	Laser printer	Up to 21,000 lines per minute
Chain printer	Up to 2000 lines per minute	Xerographic printer	Up to 4000 lines per minute
Drum printer	Up to 3000 lines per minute		

4–23). A typical screen can hold 24 lines, each containing 80 characters. Some of the newer terminals have 25 lines, one reserved for special messages. These terminals supply **soft-copy** output. That means the images that appear on the screen are temporary. Visual display terminals are well-suited for applications involving inquiry and response where no permanent (printed) records are required. They can be used for capturing data that will be transmitted from remote offices to a central computer. Data can be entered on the keyboard and verified on the display screen as it is keyed.

Visual display terminals can display output more quickly than printers; some CRT terminals can display up to 10,000 characters a second. In addition, they operate more quietly than printers. A printer can be connected to a CRT terminal to produce a hard copy of the screen contents.

Graphic display device A device that projects output in the form of graphs and line drawings.

Another type of CRT, known as a **graphic display device,** is used to display drawings as well as characters on a screen (see Figure 4–24). Graphic display devices are generally used to display graphs and charts, but they can also display complex curves and shapes. With some terminals, data displayed on the screen can be altered by using a **light pen,** a pen-shaped object with a light-sensitive cell at its end (see Figure 4–25). Users can "draw" lines on the screen by specifying the ends of the lines with the light pen and can quickly alter graphs and line drawings by applying the pen at the appropriate locations on the screen. Graphic display devices are being used in highly technical fields, such as aerospace engineering, where they aid in the design of new wing structures.

Light pen A pen-shaped object with a photoelectric cell at its end; used to draw lines on a visual display terminal.

Plotters

Plotter An output device that converts data emitted from the CPU into graphic form; produces hard copy.

A **plotter** is an output device that converts data or information from the CPU into graphic form. It can produce lines, curves, and complex shapes. The major difference between a plotter and a graphic display device is that the plotter

Figure 4–23
Visual Display Terminal

Figure 4–24
Graphic Display Device

HIGHLIGHT

Liquid Crystal Display

Do you own a calculator or a digital watch? If you do, chances are good that the numbers on the display are formed by a liquid crystal process. Imagine a television or computer screen that displays images in the same way!

How does a liquid crystal display work? Picture a layer of tiny bits of confettilike material placed between two thin pieces of glass. When a piece of confetti or crystal is electrically charged or "turned on," it changes from transparent to opaque and a dot appears on the screen.

Liquid crystal display screens are much flatter than CRT screens, and they are now being used in portable computers like those made by Sharp and Hewlett-Packard. A Japanese manufacturer, Suwa Seikosh, produced a two-inch color liquid display screen for pocket-sized televisions. The screen could also be used in computers. Liquid crystal displays have many advantages over traditional CRTs. Liquid crystal displays do not flicker, produce radiation, nor use much electric power.

There are still problems with liquid crystal displays, but scientists are working hard to eliminate problem areas and improve the technology. Many people predict that CRT screens will soon be artifacts of the past, much like buggy whips.

Figure 4-25
Visual Display Device.
This operator at Lockheed makes changes on the design of an airplane using a light pen and a keyboard to alter the design.

produces hard copy (paper), whereas the graphic display device produces soft copy (screen image).

A typical plotter has a pen, movable carriage, drum, and chart-paper holder (see Figure 4–26). Shapes are produced as the pen moves back and forth across the paper along the y-axis while the drum moves the paper up and down along the x-axis. Both the upper movement and the pen movement are bidirectional. The pen is raised and lowered from the paper surface automatically.

The plotter can be used to produce line and bar charts, graphs, organizational charts, engineering drawings, maps, trend lines, supply and demand curves, and so on. The figures are drawn precisely, because the pen can be positioned at up to 45,000 points in each square inch of paper. Some plotters can produce drawings in eight colors. The usefulness of the plotter lies in its ability to communicate information in easy-to-understand picture form.

Computer Output Microfilm

Computer output microfilm (COM) Miniature photographic images of output placed on magnetic tape, which serves as input to produce microfilm.

In situations where large volumes of information must be printed and stored for future reference, conventional paper output is not appropriate. Paper uses a great deal of storage space, and it is often difficult to find needed information quickly in conventional paper files. One alternative to paper output is **computer output microfilm (COM)**. COM consists of photographed images produced in miniature by the computer. In some cases, the output is first recorded on magnetic tape. Special photocopying equipment is then used to reproduce the information on microfilm. Often COM equipment is used to display output on a CRT screen, and then the screen is exposed to microfilm. Microfilm copy can be produced as a roll of film or a four-by-six-inch microfiche card.

The main advantage of COM is that large quantities of data can be stored compactly, reducing both space requirements and storage costs. Further, both character and graphic output can be recorded. The use of a transparent forms-overlay permits headings to be printed and lines superimposed so that output is highly readable. The cost of producing additional microfilm copies is very low. In the past, high initial investment costs and the inability of the computer

Figure 4–26
Plotter.
Business information can be transformed into graphic form for printed presentation on this Hewlett-Packard desktop plotter.

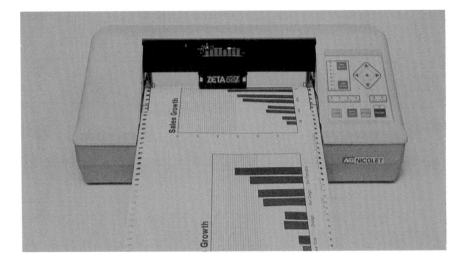

to retrieve microfilmed data directly have been disadvantages. However, costs are declining and the number of COM systems in use is increasing.

Voice Input and Output

Remote terminals that use **audio input,** or **voice recognition systems,** are suitable for low-volume, highly formal input. Instead of entering data into the computer by punching keys on a terminal, the computer is programmed to recognize a specific voice pattern. The user must follow only the speech patterns the computer is programmed to recognize (see Figure 4–27).

Computer **audio output,** or **voice response units,** "speak" by arranging half-second records of voice sounds (phonemes) or prerecorded words. This approach is being used in the banking industry to report customer account balances and in supermarkets to inform customers of the amount of each purchase. Many phone companies use voice response units to answer calls for directory assistance. Often the audio response units are coupled with touch-tone terminals for remote data entry as in super markets. An entire unit can weigh less than ten pounds, and some are even built into briefcases for easy portability.

Graphics Tablets

Graphics tablets are flat, board-like surfaces connected to a computer CRT screen. The user draws on the tablet using a pencil-like device, and the resulting image appears on the screen with colors, textures, and patterns (see Figure 4–28).

Spatial Digitizer

Three-dimensional graphics can be created on the display screen by use of a **spatial digitizer.** With a spatial digitizer the user can enter the X, Y, and Z coordinates of any three-dimensional object by tracing the object with the

Figure 4–27
Voice Recognition.
This lab technician is using an Interstate Electronics voice recognition terminal for voice data entry. Direct data input using the human voice replaces conventional keystroke entry, thereby keeping the user's hands free for other tasks.

Voice response unit A device through which the computer "speaks" by arranging half-second records of voice sounds or prerecorded words.

Figure 4–28
Graphics Tablet Used with Microcomputer

Concept Summary 4–3 ▬ Special-Purpose Input and Output

Type of Device	Advantages	Disadvantages
Visual display terminal	Fast, quiet, well suited for inquiry and response	Not a permanent record of output
Plotter	Stores large quantities of data compactly; stores both character and graphic output	Initial equipment investment cost is high
Computer output microfilm	Produces hard copy; produces information in easy-to-read form	Output appears more slowly than with a visual display terminal
Voice input and output	Allows users to bypass keyboard, freeing hand movement	Computer recognizes only limited speech patterns

digitizer's arm or pointer. The precise measurements are taken electronically, and the object is reconstructed graphically on the screen.

Touch Screen

A **touch screen** looks like a normal computer screen, but it can detect a touch by the user and can identify the point at which the user actually touches the screen. The touch screen is especially useful when the user has a list of alternatives from which to choose. When the user touches the desired alternative, the computer registers the choice made and continues processing accordingly.

Mouse

The **mouse** is a hand-movable input device that controls the position of the cursor (the mark on the display screen that indicates the current location at which data will be entered). The mouse is connected to the computer by an input cord (see Figure 4–29). When the mouse is rolled on a flat surface, it sends electronic signals through the cord to the computer to move the cursor on the screen quickly and easily.

**Figure 4–29
Mouse**

FOCUS ON MICRO- COMPUTING

Input and Output

As microcomputers become increasingly popular, many different applications are being developed to make the most of their potential. New applications have created a demand for new input and output devices. Improvements on traditional devices are also needed.

Data entry has been the weakest link in the data-processing operation. Much time and effort has been directed toward improving present and creating new technologies to increase the speed, accuracy, and effectiveness of the input process.

The many firms entering the microcomputer business have presented a variety of input device designs as each firm tries to gain a competitive edge for its product.

One area in which wide differences can be found is keyboard input. For example, the arrangement of letters, numbers, and special characters on the Apple keyboard closely resembles that of a conventional typewriter, both in appearance and function. In contrast, the IBM PC keyboard divides its keys into three separate sections: one for standard character keys; one for special function keys; and a third for numeric keys. Both the Apple and the IBM PC keyboards are of the standard tactile type, where you can feel the keys move under your fingers.

Another type of keyboard, designed for use by the very young and the physically disabled, is the pressure-sensitive membrane-covered keyboard, which is more durable than standard keyboards. To enter data, users simply press the appropriately marked points on the membrane cover. The cover provides excellent protection against spills and other forms of contamination. The membrane keyboard may also be appropriate for computer-hostile environments, such as factories, where dust may pose a problem for conventional keyboards. Users accustomed to traditional keyboards may miss the key movement associated with the traditional boards. Because users cannot feel key movement under their fingertips input must be constantly verified by looking at the screen.

Keys that perform special functions or can be programmed for multiple uses are another keyboard feature common to many microcomputers. The Commodore 64 has a special function key that can be programmed to do many different tasks. The Apple Macintosh has a key that, when pressed with a combination of one or more keys, allows the user to bypass the mouse to cut, delete, copy, or "paste," among other things.

With the advent of video games, joysticks and game paddles have become almost indispensable when purchasing a home computer. These devices input an electrical response that controls the movement of a cursor appearing on the screen in such diverse forms as paddles, missiles, and frogs.

As microcomputers continue to grow in popularity, more and more people are looking for other ways to use their microcomputers. For those of you with a bit of the artist in your blood, the development of the graphics tablet lets you turn your microcomputer into a canvas. With the appropriate software, a graphics tablet—which uses an electronic drawing pen—lets you create your very own masterpiece on your microcomputer's display terminal. Software for the graphics tablet is also available for architects and engineers who use personal computers professionally.

Engineers using computers to aid the design process often find that their initial design can use some modifications. The idea of making changes directly through the CRT screen gave rise to another input device, the light pen, described earlier. An engineer can use the light pen to modify a computer-aided design (CAD) quickly and easily.

On the leading edge of microcomputer input innovations are spatial digitizers and voice-recognition systems. Micro Control Systems, Inc., has developed a spatial digitizer for Apple and for IBM PC microcomputers that allows users to record x, y, and z coordinates of any three-dimensional object. The device consists of a clear lucite tablet (Space Tablet) that is mounted on a precision-machined arm. Data is given to the computer by tracing the point of the arm around a three-dimensional object; the three-dimensional nature of the object will be displayed on the screen. The device also allows for two-dimensional use.

One example of a voice-entry system is the Shadow/VET made by Scott Industries. Since the voice-entry system is "trained" to recognize a given vocabulary, the spoken vocabulary reportedly may be anything from English, to Ancient Egyptian, to the tonal variations given by a severely speech-impaired person.

Voice data entry has many possible applications. Scott Industries already has several installations of its Shadow/VET in place with handicapped people who would be unable to use a computer except by voice. Other applications of voice-recognition systems include actually telling the computer to turn off the lights or turn on the oven.

Output devices for microcomputers include not only the standard devices such as impact and nonimpact printers and CRTs, but also plotters and graphic display devices. The latter two can display charts, graphs, and complex curves and shapes in a multitude of colors to enhance the analysis of your output.

Because a computer can send information to a printer much faster than the printer can accept it, your computer can be tied up for quite some time as it waits to feed its output to the printer. For those of you who have experienced the frustration of waiting until the printing of one job is completed before you can use the computer again, there is now a special device called a spooler that alleviates this problem. Connected to your computer and printer, the spooler buffers (accepts and holds) the output and transmits it to the printer at the printer's specific print rate. It allows you to continue using your computer while your printer does its job.

Devices such as Videx Enhancer II for the Apple allows the keyboard to memorize words or phrases that can then be entered by pressing a single key. A type-ahead buffer allows the keyboard to remember what you typed while the computer is printing or attending to some other function. It also allows entry and display of uppercase and lowercase letters with fully functional shift keys. With more people using microcomputers for word processing, devices like the Enhancer II will be a welcome addition. In line with this thought is an innovation by Corvus Systems. They have developed a single-unit, dual-orientation screen that can be flipped on its side, allowing a vertical format for word processing and a horizontal format for spread sheets. If your screen doesn't allow for a full 80-column display, devices such as Vista's Vision 80 for Apple computers give your terminal a standard 80-column by 24-line display screen.

Another special-purpose device is the Votrax's Type-N-Talk (TNT), a text-to-speech synthesizer. It can read ASCII test characters from your computer files and pronounce these characters as spoken English words. Devices like this could become a valuable aid in the learning process, providing vocal prompts, exception conditions, and user dialogs with microcomputers.

As development of new and present technologies in the area of input/output devices continues, we are seeing an improvement in the speed, accuracy, and effectiveness of the data-processing operation. As a result, microcomputers can be expected to have a wide variety of new and innovative applications.

SUMMARY POINTS

- Punched cards represent data by the position of holes punched in the cards. One card can store up to 80 columns of data.
- Key-to-tape and key-to-disk systems use a magnetic medium to store data. New data can be stored over old data that is no longer required.
- Source-data automation refers to capturing data about an event when and where it occurs. Examples include magnetic-ink character readers; optical recognition (optical mark and optical character); and remote input using point-of-sale (POS) terminals, touch-tone devices, and voice-recognition systems. Intelligent terminals can verify and edit data before submitting input to the main computer.
- Printers can be either impact or nonimpact. Impact printers can be categorized as line-at-a-time and character-at-a-time printers. Nonimpact printers use electrostatic, electrothermal, ink-jet, laser, and xerographic methods.
- Special-purpose output provides information in a particular way or format. Visual display terminals (CRTs) provide soft-copy output of computer information. Plotters provide information summarized and interpreted in graphic form. Computer output microfilm (COM) stores data in reduced size on photographic film.
- New applications for microcomputers have created a need for new input and output devices. Improvements are also needed on traditional devices.
- Spatial digitizers and voice recognition systems are two types of improved input devices used with microcomputers. The convenience of producing printed output with microcomputers has improved with the creation of spooler buffers, which make it possible to continue using the microcomputer during the printing process.

REVIEW AND DISCUSSION QUESTIONS

1. What are some advantages of using magnetic tapes or magnetic disks rather than punched cards to record data?

2. What type of key-to-magnetic media is commonly used with microcomputers?
3. What is source-data automation? How is it beneficial to information systems?
4. Describe two forms of source-data automation.
5. What is the UPC?
6. Explain the difference between impact and nonimpact printers. What are some advantages and disadvantages of the two types of printers?
7. Other than printing, what routine tasks can be performed by a modern printing system?
8. Differentiate between hard copy and soft copy.
9. In what situations would visual display terminals be used?
10. What is a plotter, and how does it differ from a graphic display device?
11. Describe how computer output microfilm (COM) might be useful to a large bank.
12. What are special function keys on a microcomputer keyboard, and what do they do?
13. How does a spooler operate with a microcomputer?
14. Describe some situations in which a membrane-covered keyboard might be appropriate.
15. Why do you think so much emphasis has been placed on the new input/output devices?

CHAPTER 5

STORAGE DEVICES

COMPUTERS IN OUR LIVES

Interactive Multi-Media Graphics

Animation and motion pictures had fascinated Marsha Johnson ever since she was a child. When she was ten years old she began to make up cartoons with water colors, oil paints, chalk, pen and ink—any art medium she could get her hands on. Later, begging the use of her family's movie camera, she created comic home movies. Excitedly, she watched the splendid animation in Walt Disney films, and tried some original animation in high-school art class. When video games became a near craze, she was more interested in watching the graphics of the game than in winning.

A trip to EPCOT (Environmental Prototype Community of Tomorrow) opened a new world of art forms for Marsha. The center, near Orlando, Florida, offers exhibits that show how our future world might look. During her visit to EPCOT, Marsha created her own roller coaster ride, reviewed a mixed-media show on a light-wave, fiber-optic system, and saw how Disney artists had combined graphics, speech synthesis, and music. The entire system was stored on videodiscs—discs that could hold so much data they made magnetic discs seem primitve.

But videodiscs were not the last word. A year later Marsha was introduced to Dragon's Lair, a laserdisc arcade game combining animation, three-dimensional illusions, and interaction. The story was about Dirk the Daring, a heroic but clumsy knight who tries to rescue Princess Daphne from an evil dragon but whose quest is hampered by the Giant Chicken Foot, the Acid Creature, a scalding geyser, skulls, slime, and The Mudmen. Marsha was fascinated. Again, although she rarely won the game, she rarely played to win. Instead she studied the animation. The laserdisc provided the speed and clarity Marsha knew would be vital in future laserdisc-based graphics.

At Columbus College of Art and Design in Columbus, Ohio, Marsha is majoring in graphic art. Since the university provides many types of microcomputers, peripherals, and a powerful minicomputer for its art students to use, Marsha hopes to learn more about storing her work on laserdiscs. Although the technology does not yet allow her to modify her work once it is stored on the discs, Marsha believes future videodisc technology will offer that capability.

In most schools today programs are stored on floppy discs; music is stored on grooved, vinyl platters; text is stored in books; and paintings, sculpture, and architecture are stored at distant locations. No wonder videodisc storage seems so attractive. If artists like Marsha can learn to combine the graphics, sound, text, and far-away places in one medium, the benefits to education in enhanced motivation and interaction will be enormous. This chapter discusses all the various kinds of computer storage devices and their uses.

INTRODUCTION

Business organizations maintain a considerable amount of data regarding production, employees, customers, inventory levels, and other data required to perform their business functions. Each application will have specific job requirements—for timing, costs, and volume of data processed—that will largely influence the design of the computer-based files.

This chapter examines the two most popular types of data storage media, magnetic tape and disk, and the three most common types of file arrangements using tapes and disks (sequential, direct-access, and indexed-sequential). Finally, the chapter covers considerations about the use of mass storage in file design and future trends in storage.

CLASSIFICATION OF MEDIA

A computer system generally includes two types of storage: **primary storage** and **secondary,** or **auxiliary storage.** Primary storage, discussed in Chapter 3, is part of the CPU and is used to store instructions and data. Semiconductor memory, the circuitry on silicon chips that speeds up processing, is the most widely used form of primary memory. Bubble memory is also in limited use.

In many instances, the amount of data required by a program or set of programs exceeds the capacity of primary storage. In these cases, the data is stored in secondary storage. Secondary storage is not part of the CPU. The most common types of secondary storage are magnetic tapes and magnetic disks. Media such as punched cards, mass storage, and magnetic drums are also used. These secondary storage media cost much less than primary storage and thus make storage of large volumes of data economically feasible.

The secondary storage media are connected to the CPU. Once data has been placed in secondary storage, it can be retrieved as needed for processing. However, the retrieval of items from secondary storage is slower than from primary storage. After processing has been completed, the data or results can be written back onto the secondary medium (see Figure 5–1).

Access to data in secondary storage can be either direct or sequential. The method depends on the storage medium used. Storage media such as magnetic tape and cassette tape provide **sequential-access storage.** The computer must start at the beginning of a tape and read what is stored there until it comes to the desired data. In contrast, storage media such as magnetic disks or magnetic drums do not have to be read sequentially; the computer can access the desired data immediately—thus the name **direct-access storage.** Direct-access media, then, provide faster retrieval than sequential-access media.

SEQUENTIAL-ACCESS MEDIA

Magnetic Tape

A **magnetic tape** is a continuous plastic strip wound on a reel, quite similar to the tape used in reel-to-reel audio recorders. The magnetic tape's plastic base

Primary storage The section of the CPU that holds instructions, data, and intermediate and final results during processing.

Secondary storage Also known as external or auxiliary storage; supplements primary storage but operates at slower speeds.

Sequential-access storage Auxiliary storage from which records must be read in a fixed sequence until the needed data are located.

Direct-access storage A method of storing data from which data can be retrieved in random order.

Magnetic tape A storage medium consisting of a narrow strip on which spots of iron-oxide are magnetized to represent data.

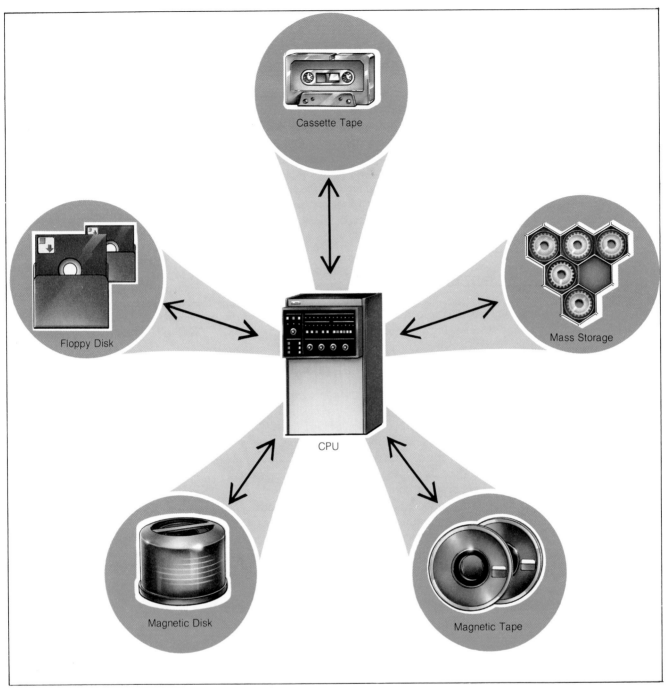

Figure 5-1
Secondary Storage Devices

is treated with a magnetizable coating. Typically, the tape is one-half inch in width. It is wound in lengths from 400 to 3,200 feet. Magnetic tapes are also packaged in cartridges for use with small computers.

Data is stored on magnetic tape by magnetizing small spots of the iron oxide coating on the tape. Although these spots can be read by the computer, they are invisible to the human eye. Large volumes of information can be stored on a single tape; densities of 1,600 characters per inch are common, and some

144

tapes are capable of storing up to 6,250 characters per inch. A typical tape reel of 2,400 feet can store as much data as 400,000 punched cards.

The most common method of representing data on tape uses a nine-track coding scheme, although other coding schemes are also used. When the nine-track method is used, the tape is divided into nine horizontal rows called **tracks** (see Figure 5–2). Data is represented vertically in columns, one character per column. This method of coding data is identical to the Extended Binary Coded Decimal Interchange Code (EBCDIC) used to represent data in primary storage. In this way, eight bits, and eight of the nine tracks, are used to represent each character. The ninth bit functions as a parity bit.

A magnetic tape is mounted on a **tape drive** when the information it contains is needed by a program. The tape drive has a **read/write head** (actually an electromagnet) that creates or reads the bits as the tape moves past it (see Figure 5–3). When it is reading, the read/write head detects the magnetized areas and converts them into electrical pulses to send to the CPU. When writing, the head magnetizes the appropriate spots on the tape, erasing any previously stored data.

Individual records on magnetic tape are separated by **interrecord gaps (IRGs)**, as shown in Figure 5–4. These gaps do not contain data but perform another function. A tape is rarely read in its entirety, all at once. Rather, it is stopped

Track One of a series of concentric circles on the surface of a magnetic disk.

Tape drive A device that moves tape past a read/write head.

Interrecord gap (IRG) A space on a magnetic tape that facilitates processing; records are separated by interrecord gaps.

**Figure 5–2
Nine-Track Tape with Even Parity**

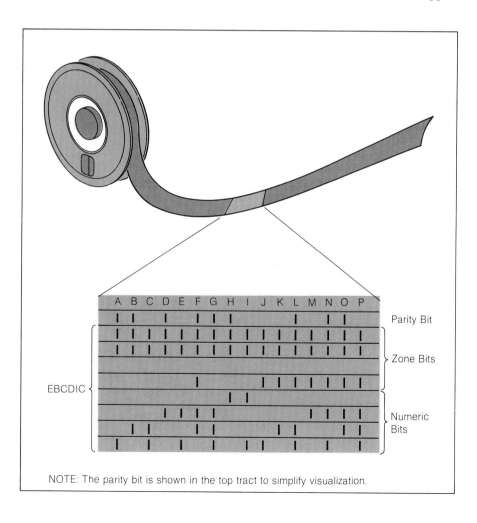

NOTE: The parity bit is shown in the top tract to simplify visualization.

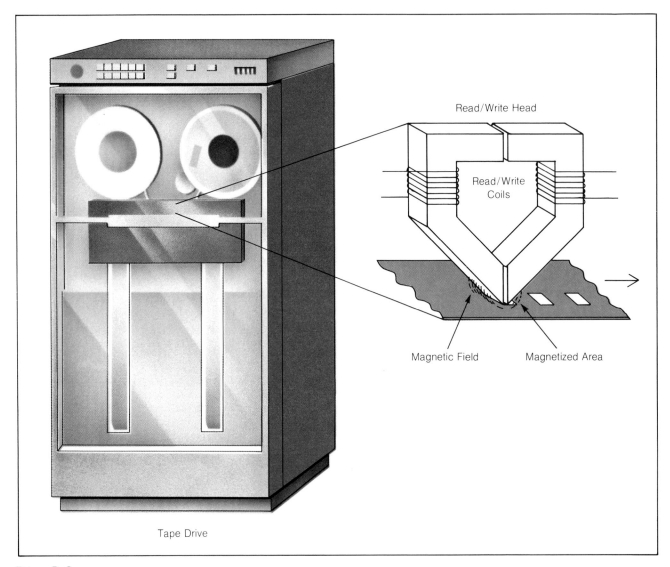

Figure 5–3
Recording on Magnetic Tape

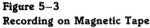

Blocked records (blocks) Records grouped on magnetic tape or magnetic disk to reduce the number of interrecord gaps.

Interblock gap (IBG) A space on magnetic tape that facilitates processing; records are grouped together and separated by interblock gaps.

after the end of a record is reached. The tape must then be accelerated to the correct speed before the next record can be read correctly; otherwise the result would be similar to what happens when a phonograph record is played at the wrong speed. The IRG allows the tape to regain the proper speed before the next record is read. The length of the interrecord gap depends on the speed of the tape drive; if the tape drive is very fast, longer gaps are needed, while slower speeds require shorter gaps.

If records are very short and divided by equally long IRGs, the tape may be more than 50 percent blank, causing the tape drive to be constantly stopping and accelerating. To avoid this possibility, records may be grouped, or blocked. These **blocked records,** or **blocks,** are separated by **interblock gaps (IBGs),** as in Figure 5–5. Instead of reading a short record and stopping, then reading another short record and stopping, the read/write head reads a block of short

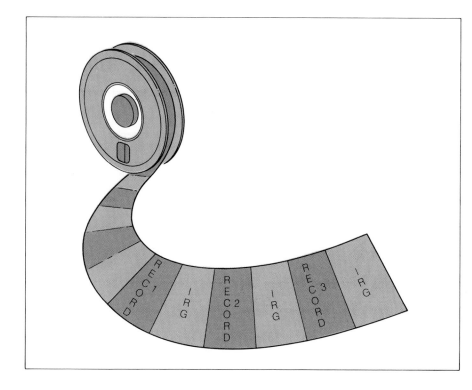

Figure 5-4
Magnetic Tape with Interrecord Gaps

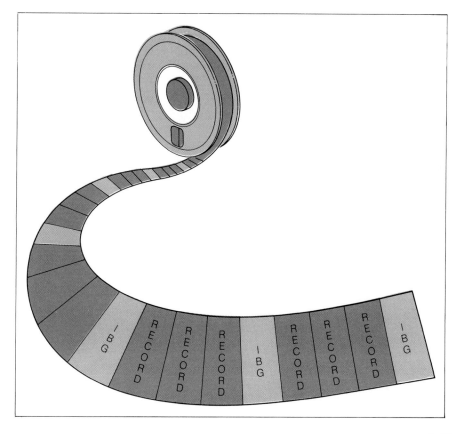

Figure 5-5
Magnetic Tape with Interblock Gaps

147

records at once and then stops, reads another block and stops, and so forth. This method serves two purposes:

1. The amount of storage available on the tape is used more efficiently.
2. The number of read/write (input/output) operations required is significantly reduced, which makes the use of computer resources much more efficient.

Concept Summary 5–1 ▬ Magnetic Tape

Features	Advantages	Disadvantages
A continuous plastic strip of tape is wound on a reel Tape is treated with a magnetizable coating Data are represented as magnetized spots on the surface of the tape Data are accessed sequentially	Transfers data between tape and the CPU rapidly Records can be any length Stores large amounts of data in a small space Erasable and reusable Low-cost backup Well-suited for sequential processing	Must be read sequentially Tapes require proper labels for content verification Environmental factors can distort data stored on magnetic tape Humans cannot read the data on magnetic tape

Cassette Tape

Small computer systems may not need a large amount of secondary storage. For these systems **tape cassettes** and tape cartridges have been developed. Tape cassettes look like those used in audio recording, and some can even be used with a typical cassette player/recorder. The major difference between the two types of tape cassettes is the tape itself: tape cassettes used for storing data use higher-quality, high-density digital recording tape (see Figure 5–6).

Figure 5–6
Tape Cassette

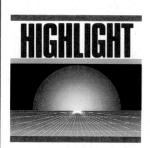

HIGHLIGHT

Computer Decorating

Have you ever spent days traveling from one store to another trying to coordinate fabric samples, wallpaper, and paint? If you have, you are probably familiar with the frustration of being told that the wallpaper pattern you finally selected has been discontinued or the price of your chosen drapery fabric has increased 100 percent.

Robert Sherman, an interior designer for over 25 years, is so familiar with and frustrated by the above story that he has developed a new business. His company, Search and Source, produces electronic libraries that store listings of products used in the interior design business. Besides such standard information as color, fiber, and price, the electronic library includes information about shipping and delivery dates.

There is a color video electronic photograph for each item listed in the electronic library. The system uses a color chip display with 1,200 different shades, and the quality of the colors represented is excellent. When a customer selects a fabric or floor covering, the system indicates compatible colors and products and tells which companies in the system offer the desired items.

Mr. Sherman's idea has been implemented by design centers and department stores all over the country, and satisfied customers feel the savings in time and money have more than offset the cost of the service.

The recording densities for tape cassettes range from 125 to 200 characters per inch, and the common length is between 150 and 200 feet. Tape cartridges, on the other hand, can store from 200 to 800 characters per inch, and come in standard lengths of 300, 450, and 555 feet.

The advantages of using magnetic tape are as follows:

- Data can be transferred between magnetic tape and the CPU at high speeds.
- Magnetic-tape records can be any length, while card records are usually limited to 80 characters.
- Because of their high recording densities, magnetic tapes can store a large amount of data in a small amount of space.
- Magnetic tape can be erased and reused.
- Magnetic tape can provide high-capacity storage and backup storage at a relatively low cost. A 2,400-foot magnetic tape costs from $20 to $30.
- Magnetic tape is perfectly suited for sequential processing. It is the most common storage medium in these types of systems.

Use of magnetic tape has the following disadvantages:

- Since tape is a sequential medium, the entire tape must be read from start to finish when being altered. The amount of time required precludes its use where instantaneous retrieval of data is required.
- All tapes and reel containers must be properly labeled and identified.

- Humans cannot read the data on magnetic tape. When the validity of such data is questioned, the contents, of the tape must be printed.
- Environmental factors can distort data stored on magnetic tape. Dust, moisture, high or low temperatures, and static electricity can cause improper processing. Therefore, the environment must be carefully controlled.

DIRECT-ACCESS MEDIA

Magnetic Disks

Magnetic disk A storage medium consisting of a metal platter coated with a magnetic recording material on which data is stored.

The conventional **magnetic disk** is a metal platter 14 inches in diameter, coated on both sides with a magnetizable material like iron oxide. In many respects, a magnetic disk resembles a phonograph record. However, it does not have a phonograph record's characteristic grooves; magnetic disk surfaces are smooth. A disk unit does store and retrieve data in much the same fashion as a phonograph. The disk is rotated while a read/write head is positioned above its magnetic surface. Instead of spiraling into the center of the disk like the needle of a phonograph, however, the read/write head stores and retrieves data in concentric circles. Each circle is referred to as a track. One track never touches another (see Figure 5–7). A typical disk has from 200 to 500 tracks per surface.

Disk pack A stack of magnetic disks.

In most disk storage devices, several disks are assembled to form a **disk pack** (see Figure 5–8) mounted on a center shaft. The individual disks are spaced on the shaft to allow room for a read/write mechanism to move between them (see Figure 5–9). The disk pack in Figure 5–9 has 11 disks and provides

Figure 5–7
Top View of Disk Surface Showing 200 Concentric Tracks

Figure 5–8
Disk Pack

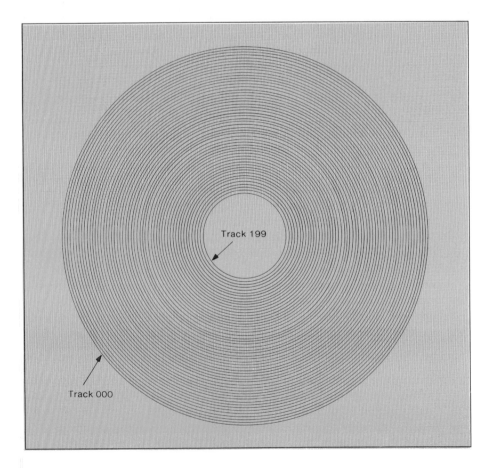

Track 199

Track 000

Figure 5-9
A Disk Pack
a. Side View
b. Top View

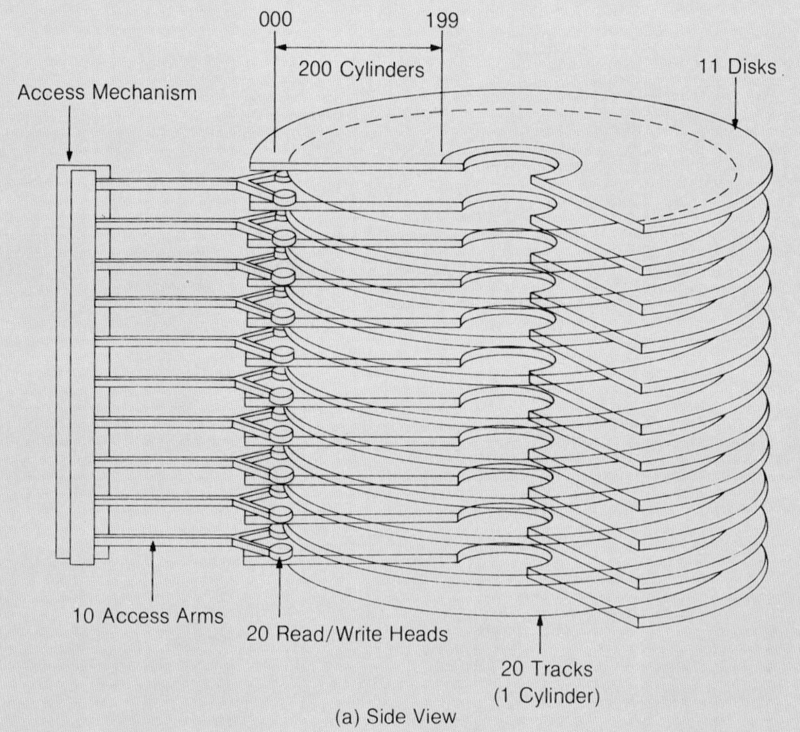

Access Mechanism

000   199

200 Cylinders

11 Disks

10 Access Arms

20 Read/Write Heads

20 Tracks
(1 Cylinder)

(a) Side View

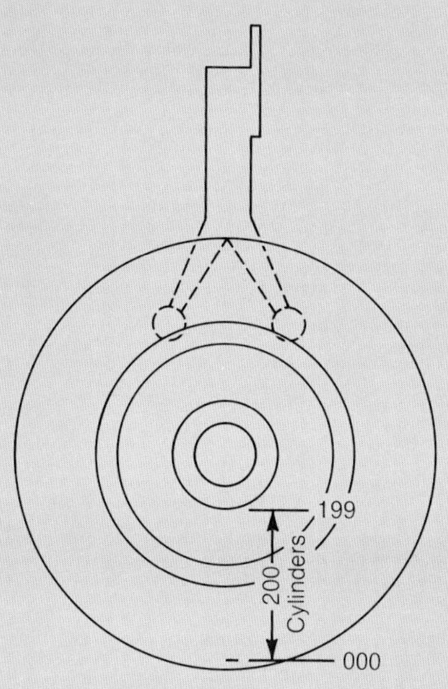

199

200 Cylinders

000

(b) Top View

Disk drive The mechanical device used to rotate a disk pack during data transmission.

Access mechanism The physical device that positions the read/write head of a direct-access device over a particular track.

20 usable recording surfaces; the top and bottom surfaces are not used for storing data because they are likely to become scratched or nicked. A disk pack may contain anywhere from 5 to 100 disks.

A disk pack is positioned in a disk drive when the data on the pack is to be processed. The **disk drive** rotates all disks in unison at speeds up to 3,600 revolutions per minute. In some models, the disk packs are removable; in others, the disks are permanently mounted on the disk drive. Removable disk packs allow disks to be removed when the data they contain is not needed. Users of removable disk packs typically have many more disk packs than disk drives (see Figure 5–10).

The data on a disk is read or written by the read/write heads located between the disks. Most disk units have one read/write head for each disk recording surface. All the heads are permanently connected to an **access mechanism.** When reading or writing occurs, the heads are positioned over the appropriate track by the in-and-out movement of the access mechanism (see Figure 5–9).

When data on the surface of one disk in the disk pack is required, all the heads move to the appropriate track, because they are connected to the same access mechanism. Because all the read/write heads move together, they are positioned over the same tracks on all disk surfaces at the same time. All the number-one tracks on the disk surfaces form a cylinder; the number-two tracks on all surfaces form another cylinder enclosed within the first; and so on. The number of cylinders per disk pack equals the number of tracks per surface.

Some disk units have one read/write head for each track. The access time is much faster with this type of disk unit since the access mechanism does not need to move from track to track. Units like this are rarely used because of their high cost. The placement of data on the disk pack, therefore, can be an important factor if the amount of access time is critical. If access time is a factor, storing the data being accessed most frequently in the same cylinder or adjacent cylinders is best, because this will reduce the motion of the read/write heads and, therefore, the access time.

Figure 5–10
Disk Storage Units with Removable Disk Packs

HIGHLIGHT

Computers Blend the Old and the New

Are you interested in finding the answer to an obscure point of ancient Hebrew law? Then travel to Bar Ilan University in Tel Aviv, Israel, and pose your question to the "Responsa Project"—a data base that stores the contents of 250 volumes of rabbinical statements and judgments on legal questions. That's the equivalent of 50 million words!

Responsa are questions and answers about religious issues. There are over 3,000 volumes of responsa altogether, and eventually 500 volumes will be stored on disks. The volumes stored thus far contain information on Jewish life in Europe and North Africa. The information covers a time span from the Middle Ages to the 20th century.

Scholars use the data base to find information about a variety of topics that affected Jewish life in earlier times. But scholars are not the only users of this unusual data base. Sociologists, historians, economists, and linguists have all made use of the Responsa Project. Information that once would have taken months of devoted research can now be located in minutes. Graduate students, quick to accept the new technology that made the project possible, are using the data base to write dissertations that otherwise would not be written.

Many Orthodox rabbis were not as quick to embrace the blending of the ancient and the modern. But Ovadiah Yosef, former chief rabbi in Israel, gave the system his approval; seven volumes of his responsa were computerized!

Lawyers are among the most enthusiastic users of the data base. Until a few years ago, Israeli law was based on British common law. Currently, in the event of a conflict, Hebrew law takes precedence. Attorneys use the data base to find evidence that will support their clients' positions.

Care has been taken to preserve the information contained in the data base. Five backup copies are stored in bank vaults in the United States and Europe.

Each track on a disk can store the same amount of data (even though the tracks get smaller toward the center of the disk). Consider a disk pack on which a maximum of 7,294 characters can be stored per track and 4,000 usable tracks (20 surfaces × 200 tracks per surface) are available. Such a disk pack could conceivably store 29 million characters of data.

Data stored on a magnetic disk is located by disk surface number, track number, and record number; this information constitutes a **disk address.** The disk address of a record immediately precedes the record (see Figure 5–11). Disk records are separated by gaps similar to the interrecord gaps on magnetic tape. Thus, although more data can be stored on a track by blocking several records together and reducing the number of gaps, the presence of gaps does reduce the amount of information that can be stored on a disk. In the disk pack described above, the usable storage capacity would be somewhat less than the potential capacity of 29 million characters of data.

Figure 5–11
Disk Address

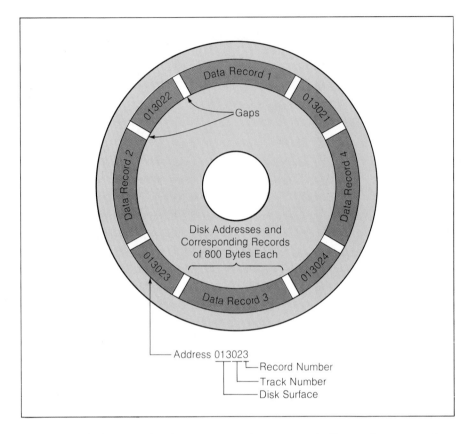

Because disks provide direct access, they are typically used to store data about which frequent inquiries are required. Depending upon the disk drive, read speeds of up to 850,000 characters per second are possible.

Floppy Disks

Flexible disk A low-cost random-access form of data storage made of flexible plastic; also called diskette or floppy disk.

The **flexible disk, diskette,** or **floppy disk** was introduced in 1973 (see Figure 5–12a and 12b) to replace punched cards as a medium for data entry, but it

Concept Summary 5–2 ▪ Magnetic Disks

Features	Advantages	Disadvantages
Disks are treated with a magnetizable coating	Files can be organized for sequential or direct-access storage	More expensive than magnetic tape
Data are represented as magnetized sports on the surface of the disk	Data can be accessed quickly	Requires backup files or data may be lost during alterations
Disks come in varying sizes	Software allows files to be altered simultaneously	Requires complex programming to gain access to files
		Easy access to data may pose security problems

Figure 5–12a
Floppy Disks of 8 inches and
5¼ inches

Figure 5–12b
3½ inch Floppy Disk

can also store programs and data files. These floppy disks are made of plastic and coated with an oxide substance. They are, in most respects, miniature magnetic disks. The diskettes often sell for as little as $3 and are very popular for use with microcomputer systems and point-of-sale terminals. They are reusable, easy to store, and weigh less than two ounces. They are readily interchangeable and can even be mailed. Because flexible disks are removable, they provide added security for a computer system. A typical disk can store as much data as 12,000 punched cards.

The floppy disk comes in three standard sizes—8 inches, 5¼ inches, and the more recently introduced 3½-inch size. The larger disks are permanently sealed in a paper jacket (see Figure 5–12a). The 3½-inch disks are enclosed in a tough plastic case (see Figure 5–12b). Data is stored as magnetized spots in tracks, as on conventional (hard) magnetic disks, and is addressed by track number and sector number. There are 77 tracks and 26 sectors on a standard 8-inch disk, and 40 tracks and 18 sectors on a 5¼-inch disk. The 3½-inch disks have 135 tracks and 80 sectors. The read/write head moves back and forth in the rectangular opening (the read/write notch) and can be placed on any track. Unlike the one in hard disk systems, this read/write head actually rides on the surface of the disk rather than being positioned slightly above it. The disk rotates at 360 revolutions per minute (as compared to as many as 3,600 revolutions per minute for hard disk drives).

Magnetic disks have several advantages over magnetic tape:

▬ Disk files can be organized sequentially and processed in the same way as magnetic tape, or they can be organized for direct-access processing.

155

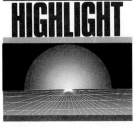

Nutrition on a Disk

Computers have made our lives easier or more fun by making it possible for us to play video games, learn French, balance our checkbooks, or write a paper. In many cases, we simply slip a disk into a disk drive and begin. Now computers can even be used to tell us how and what to eat! Grab-a-Byte by the National Dairy Council of Rosemont, Illinois, is a computer disk that does just that.

The disk contains an educational program designed to help students learn about nutrition. The program is divided into three sections. In the first section, students are quizzed about their knowledge of calories, food groups, and nutrition. Then a Nutrition Sleuth challenges students by presenting "nutrition mysteries" for them to solve. Finally, the program allows students to select their own meals from a list containing a variety of foods. Once meals are selected, the computer analyzes the selections and determines if the student choices will provide a balanced meal. Students are given an opportunity to change their selections when the computer indicates that the choices will not provide a wholesome meal. The program offers students a fun way to learn about good eating habits.

- The fast access time offered by magnetic-disk storage allows data files to be changed immediately.
- Quick response can be made to inquiries (normally, response is made in seconds).
- With the appropriate software, a single transaction can simultaneously update or alter several files that are stored on disks.

The major disadvantages of magnetic-disk storage are:

- Magnetic disk is a relatively expensive storage medium; it may cost ten times as much as magnetic tape in terms of cost per character stored. However, reductions in disk costs and the introduction of flexible disks are making these storage devices more attractive from a cost standpoint.
- When data that exists on disk is altered, the original data is erased and the new data put in its place. Therefore, there is no backup file. If there are no other provisions for error checking and backup files, data can be lost.
- Disk storage requires more complicated programming for gaining access to records and updating files. The hardware itself is also highly complicated, and skilled technicians are required to maintain it.
- Security may be a problem because of the ease of gaining access to data on disk files.

MASS STORAGE

As stated earlier using primary storage is very fast because access to data is direct and requires no physical movement. The speed of electricity is, in effect, the only limiting factor. However, primary storage is also very expensive. Disk storage is less expensive and provides direct-access capabilities, but even disk storage tends to be too expensive when very large amounts of data must be stored for direct-access processing.

To meet the need for a low-cost method of storing mass amounts of data, mass storage devices have been developed. They allow rapid access to data, although their access times are much slower than those of primary storage. Large files, backup files, and infrequently used files can be placed in mass storage at a relatively low cost.

One type of mass storage uses a cartridge tape as the storage medium. The cartridges are similar to cassette tapes and permit sequential access of data. The high-density tape used requires 90 percent less storage space than common magnetic tape. A mass storage system such as this can hold the equivalent of up to 1,000 tape reels. The mounting of the tapes is controlled by the system, rather than an operator, and tends to be faster than the traditional operator-controlled mounting of magnetic tapes (see Figure 5–13).

Mass storage is not limited to high-density magnetic tape. A mass storage system for minicomputers using small floppy disks as the storage medium was introduced. However, unlike the cartridge system described above, most mass storage devices require extensive physical movement because the needed files must first be found and then mounted mechanically before data can be read or written. Although direct access is possible, the retrieval time is relatively slow (normally measured in seconds).

Figure 5–13
Mass Storage Device using Cartridge Tape

Charge-coupled device (CCD) A storage device made of silicon; nearly 100 times faster than bubble memory devices.

Laser storage system A secondary storage device using laser technology to encode data on a metallic surface; often used for mass storage.

TRENDS IN DATA STORAGE

Charge-Coupled Devices

As technology continues to advance, smaller, faster, and less-expensive storage devices will become commonplace. Advances are rapidly being made in semiconductor and laser technology. An innovation in semiconductor technology is the development of **charge-coupled devices (CCDs)** for use in data storage. CCDs are made of silicon similar to semiconductor memory. They are nearly 100 times faster than magnetic bubble memory but are somewhat slower than semiconductor RAM. As in semiconductor memories, data in CCDs can be lost if a power failure occurs. CCDs are used primarily with large computer systems such as minicomputers and mainframes.

Laser Technology

Laser technology provides an opportunity to store massive quantities of data at greatly reduced costs. A **laser storage system** can store nearly 128 billion characters of data at about one-tenth the cost of standard magnetic media. In a laser storage system, data is recorded when a laser beam forms patterns on the surface of a polyester sheet coated with a thin layer of rhodium metal. To read data from this sheet, the laser reflects light off the surface, reconstructing the data into a digital bit stream. Laser data resists alteration, and any attempt to alter it can be detected readily, so it provides a secure storage system. Furthermore, unlike magnetic media, laser storage does not deteriorate over

157

A New Job for an Old Disk

Are you looking for a compact way to store 100,000 typewritten pages? Then perhaps you should consider storing those pages on a compact disk.

In the past, compact disks have been used mainly for reproducing high-quality music recordings. Compact audiodisks have not been the tremendous success that their manufacturers had predicted. But now makers of the disks believe that the digital storage devices could also be used to store computer data.

A standard compact disk is 4.7 inches in diameter. That is enough storage space for 500 million bytes of data. By comparison, the standard single-sided, single-density floppy disks used with many microcomputers is capable of storing only 500,000 bytes 1,000 times more bytes than a floppy disk!

Information stored on a compact disk is encoded by pinpoint laser beams that burn tiny pits on the surface of the disk. Each disk can store vast amounts of information, but once the information has been stored on the disk, it cannot be changed or erased. This limits its use.

Makers of compact disks are searching for new markets for the disks. Many disk makers think that the compact devices are well suited for electronic publishing. Large data bases or many smaller data bases could be stored on one disk. Once a data base was recorded on a disk, it could be sold to users. This approach would allow users to bypass current data-base systems that require access through a commercial network. A commercial network stores data on a central computer through which users must access the data. With a compact disk, users would not have to pay the service charges associated with a commercial system.

In the educational market, compact disks could hold an entire curriculum for a course such as a foreign language. Another use for the disks involves software. Due to the vast storage capacity of compact disks, both a program and its documentation could fit on the same disk. When a user had a problem with a program, he or she could consult the documentation stored on the disk for help in solving the problem.

time and is immune to electromagnetic radiation. Another advantage is that there is no danger of losing data because of power failures.

A more recent development is a laser system to be used as a mass storage device for minicomputers. This system uses a helium-neon laser, delivering about ten milliwatts of optical power to a disk coated with a film of nonmetallic substance (tellurium). Data is recorded when the laser creates a hole approximately one micrometer in diameter in the film. The disk used in this system is 30 centimeters in diameter and can store ten billion bits on its 40,000 tracks. The data cannot be erased once it is written, so this system is best suited for archival storage or for a great volume of data that must be maintained online.

Another development in laser technology is the optical, or laser, disk. **Optical disks** are much faster than hard disks but are still fairly slow when compared to semiconductor RAM. One big advantage, though, is their capacity. A single optical disk the size of a 12-inch stereo record can hold the text equivalent of 1,735 books per side (see Figure 5–14). Bits of data are stored on an optical disk as the presence or absence of a tiny pit burned into the disk by a pinpoint laser beam. A line one inch long contains about 5,000 pits, or bits, of data.

Optical disk A storage medium on which a laser beam encodes data by burning tiny pits on the surface of the disk.

RAM Disks

Accessing data on disks is a relatively slow process compared to the speed at which a microprocessor can manipulate data. **Random-access memory (RAM) disks** are currently the only type of storage device that can approximate the speed of a microprocessor. A new peripheral storage device using RAM chips is now available (see Figure 5–15). A RAM card that contains RAM chips plugs into the computer in the same slot as the disk drive card. It is indistinguishable from a disk drive to the computer. RAM disks function like storage diskettes. Even though a RAM disk functions like a regular diskette, it is not actually a separate physical disk. It is simply storage space in RAM that has been given the job of functioning like a disk. A typical RAM disk used with a microcomputer

RAM disk A portion of RAM memory that is temporarily turned into a storage device.

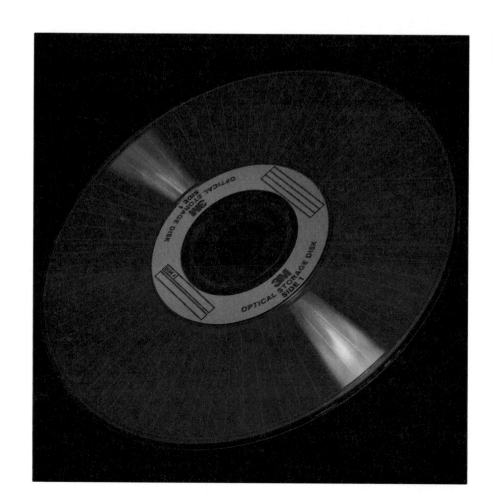

Figure 5–14
Optical Disk

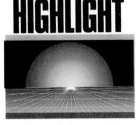

Powerful Duo

Optical disks and microcomputers are being teamed to create "the most effective communications technology that ever existed," according to Allen Adkins the president of Interactive Arts of Mountain View, California. Of course, some people may feel Mr. Adkins is a bit prejudiced; his company has used optical disks and microcomputers in a series of lessons designed to teach both adults and children. The series is called *I Can*.

I Can uses videodisks that combine pictures and written explanations to teach reading and writing to functionally illiterate students. A controller box directs the computer, which in turn directs a videodisk player to place images on the screen. A program replaces the picture taken from the disk with a new image when necessary. The visual image on the screen is coordinated with the written text throughout the lesson.

Videodisks offer an advantage over other storage media. A 12-inch disk can hold 54,000 images—enough images to prepare a lesson lasting a half hour.

The disks are especially effective for use with hearing-impaired children, who rely heavily on graphics in learning. The excellent quality of the images produced on the disks creates very lifelike pictures on the computer screen.

The educational field is not the only area in which optical disks are being put to use. For example, Alaska is storing fingerprint files on optical disks. NEC Information Systems of Boxborough, Massachusetts, developed the Automated Fingerprint Identification System used by Alaska. The new system will save the police hours of time in checking for fingerprint matches. It permits up to 2,750 prints to be checked in less than five minutes.

---

has up to 256K of storage and has a retrieval rate 50 times faster than a floppy disk.

The advantage of using RAM disks is speed. Data stored in RAM can be transferred from one part of RAM to another faster than it can be transferred from a disk to RAM.

The disadvantage of RAM disks is that they require a continuous power supply. As with any RAM, when the power source is removed the data will be erased from memory. Some manufacturers are providing battery backup units for use with RAM disks in case of a power failure.

Josephson Junction

The **Josephson junction** is a form of primary storage named for Brian Josephson, a British Nobel Prize winner. Josephson junctions are in their early stage of development. When the technology is perfected, the speed at which primary

Josephson junction A type of primary storage currently undergoing development.

Figure 5–15
RAM Disk Chip

storage operates is estimated to increase tenfold. Current semiconductor memory is slower than that proposed with Josephson junctions because of the environment in which it is housed. By housing the circuits in liquid helium, the Josephson junction will eliminate the resistance to the flow of electricity that exists in semiconductor memory. The use of the Josephson junction, along with other technological advances, is expected to lead to further reduction in the size of computer hardware.

Technology advances so rapidly that accurate prediction of what future storage media will be like is nearly impossible. The objectives of making storage less expensive, faster, and smaller will continue to be pursued. The state of the art changes almost from day to day.

FOCUS ON MICRO-COMPUTING

Data Storage

For a computer system to be of much use, the programs and data must be instantly available. Since the amount of internal memory in a microcomputer is generally not adequate for the storage of all the applications you might have for it, secondary or peripheral forms of storage are necessary.

An inexpensive form of storage for microcomputers is magnetic tape in cassettes and cartridges. These cassettes and cartridges are similar to those used in audio recording, but they use a higher-quality, higher-density digital recording tape.

Magnetic tape cassettes and cartridges are well suited for temporary storage of short programs and data that are suitable to sequential processing. For those who have no greater need or whose budget won't allow more, the relatively low cost of the equipment and medium offers an affordable alternative to the more expensive disk drives. Disadvantages of cassettes and cartridges are their relative slowness compared with other secondary storage formats and the fact that programs and data must be stored and accessed sequentially. It can become tedious loading cassettes and cartridges into memory for long programs or for manipulation of large amounts of data.

Floppy disks, the most widely used form of secondary storage for microcomputers, overcome these drawbacks. A single disk can hold relatively large chunks of programs and data and can access them directly at many times the speed of magnetic tape. They are available in two standard sizes—8 inches and 5¼ inches—and a new 3½-inch microdisk has been introduced by Sony, Apple, and Hewlett-Packard. Their storage capacity presently extends from 100K to 1 megabyte (one million bytes) on 5¼-inch disks and 125K to 1.2 megabytes on 8-inch disks. However, increased storage capacity can be expected in the near future, pushing the upper boundaries even further.

The format for data storage on a floppy disk can take any of the following combinations: single-sided/single-density, single-sided/double-density, double-sided/single-density, and double-sided/double-density. Double-sided means that the system allows using both sides of a disk. Double-density means that the system permits "doubling" the amount of data, no matter how many sides are used.

As long as disks are used on the drives for which they are designed, there is usually no problem. If your system allows for a variety of disk drives to be used, a disk designed for a specific type of drive may cause problems if you try to use it on a different type of drive. Unless otherwise specified, some good rules of thumb are: data on double-sided disks cannot be used by single-sided drives; data on double-density disks cannot be used by single-density drives; however, data on single-sided/single-density disks can be used by double-sided/double-density drives. An innovation by Omni is a reversible disk for use on single-sided 5¼-inch disk drives. It performs like single-sided disks, except that it can be flipped over, allowing you to record on the reverse side.

Some users, though, may have storage requirements greater than those provided by even the largest-capacity floppy disks. Some personal computing systems allow the use of hard disks that offer, in addition to more storage, greater speed in accessing data. There are two forms, the hard-disk pack—a totally sealed unit with no user access—and the removable disk pack. The hard-disk pack has a number of positive features: relatively low price, reliability, security from damage by untrained users (because of the sealed unit), small size, and large storage capacity. The removable system, however, provides easier and quicker backup. For example, a "standard" basic hard-disk system consists of a floppy disk for backup and the enclosed hard-disk unit. If the floppy disk has a storage capacity of 500,000 characters and the hard-disk unit is capable of holding 5 million characters, there will be a marked imbalance when it comes to copying the data from the hard disks to floppy disks. To complete backup would require a box of ten disks and at least 20 minutes. This may not seem too great a problem; however, standard software for file copying will deal only with complete files. Any file greater than the size of the floppy disk cannot be backed up without a special "backup routine." It is advisable to make sure that this is available before purchasing a hard-disk system. The disks in the removable disk pack are physically detachable from the system and, therefore, avoid this problem since spare disks can be inserted for backup purposes. Currently, the use of hard-disk packs predominates because of the high cost of removable disk packs.

SUMMARY POINTS

- Secondary storage, which is not part of the CPU, can store large amounts of data and instructions at a lower cost than primary storage. The most common secondary storage media are magnetic tapes and magnetic disks.
- Access to data in secondary storage can be either sequential or direct. Magnetic tapes on reels and in cassettes provide sequential-access storage. Hard disks, magnetic disks, and floppy disks provide direct-access storage.
- Magnetic tape consists of a plastic base coated with iron oxide. Data is stored as small magnetized areas on the surface of the tape.
- Usually data is represented on tape by a nine-track coding scheme, such as 8-bit EBCDIC with a ninth bit for parity.
- Tape density refers to the number of characters that can be stored on one inch of tape.
- Data is often recorded on magnetic tape in groups of records called blocks. Blocks are separated from each other by interblock gaps (IBGs). Blocking reduces overall input/output time and also makes more efficient use of available storage.
- Tape cassettes are similar to audio cassettes. They can store up to 200 characters per inch and are used when small amounts of storage are required.
- A disk pack is positioned on a disk drive, which rotates all disks in the pack in unison. Some disk packs are removable; others are permanently mounted on disk drives.

■ Magnetic disks provide direct access. Any record can be located by referring to its address—disk surface number, track number, and record number.

■ Flexible or floppy disks provide low-cost, direct-access storage. Floppy disks are easy to store, and are frequently used with minicomputers and microcomputers.

■ Direct-access processing is most often used when changes are frequent, but only a small proportion of the master records must be updated at a time.

■ Mass storage devices are appropriate when large amounts of data must be stored at low cost. Commonly used mass storage media are cassette and cartridge tapes and floppy disks. Floppy disk mass storage devices provide direct access, but retrieval time is much slower than with standard disk storage.

■ Advances in technology continue to make storage devices faster, smaller, and less expensive. Two recent innovations are charge-coupled devices and laser storage systems.

■ Optical disks allow faster access to data than hard disks, but they are a fairly slow form of data retrieval compared to RAM. The advantage of optical disks as a storage medium is their storage capacity.

■ A RAM disk is an area of RAM that temporarily functions like a storage diskette.

■ Josephson junction technology allows primary memory to be housed in helium to eliminate the resistance to the flow of electricity in semiconductor memory.

■ Since the amount of internal storage in a microcomputer is not adequate for all the applications the user might need, peripheral forms of storage are necessary. Magnetic tapes and floppy disks are used for secondary storage with microcomputers; floppy disks are the most widely used form of peripheral storage with microcomputers.

REVIEW AND DISCUSSION QUESTIONS

1. Distinguish between primary and secondary storage. Name some common secondary storage devices.
2. Which storage media provide direct access, and which provide sequential access?
3. What is the purpose of blocking records with an interblock gap?
4. Describe two types of mass storage devices.
5. What is a RAM disk?
6. What is the most widely used form of peripheral storage for microcomputers?
7. What is the difference between single-sided and double-sided floppy disks?
8. Discuss the advantages and disadvantages of magnetic tape storage.
9. Discuss the advantages and disadvantages of magnetic disk storage.
10. If you were purchasing a microcomputer system, what type of data storage device would you choose for your system?
11. For what application might hard-disk storage be a good choice for a microcomputer user?

CHAPTER 6

DATA STRUCTURES AND FILE DESIGN

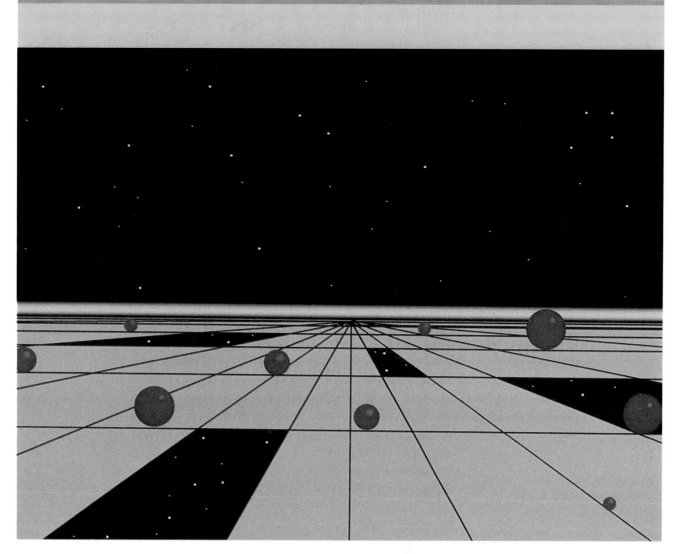

COMPUTERS IN OUR LIVES

Data Base to the Rescue!

When the city of New York announced its plans to close Engine Company 212, a firehouse serving two Brooklyn communities, a determined group of residents refused to let it happen. With the help of a Texas Instruments Portable Professional personal computer, volunteers from Greenpoint and Northside rallied to save the local firehouse.

The volunteers took over the firehouse, occupied it, and ran it for sixteen months. During those months, Engine Company 212 became known as the "People's Firehouse." The city, responding to the group's firm stand and to public pressure, reopened the firehouse. But the volunteer People's Firehouse stayed on, gained financial support through grants, and evolved into a computer-assisted operation with forty-one employees.

Its goal is fire prevention. The People's Firehouse collected data on structural fires over the last five years. Using dBase II data-base software, data such as the locations of all buildings in the neighborhood and names of each building's owner, insurance company, and tenants are stored in a data base. Important statistics on housing, fires, and industry trends are also included. The files are designed so that employees of the People's Firehouse can quickly access information on potential arson targets.

A data base is a collection of different types of information. Each piece of data in a data base is recorded and stored one time only. The data is organized in a way that allows related data to be easily accessed. In the People's Firehouse data base, for example, by entering one owner's name, all buildings owned by that person can be retrieved. Entering the location of a particular building will reveal the number and names of its tenants, the owner's name and insurance company, and any complaints registered about it.

Besides identifying potential arson targets, the People's Firehouse data base also helps keep track of properties that are becoming run down and are therefore fire prone. When the group becomes aware of a negligent owner, it tries to persuade the owner to sell the property. For example, when two rundown buildings were researched through the data base, it was found they were owned by the same person who also owned thirteen other buildings in the neighborhood. The People's Firehouse pressured him to sell the buildings. Now new owners have begun repairing the buildings to bring them up to fire and safety standards.

Data bases are becoming popular with personal computer owners, collectors and hobbyists in particular. For example, Edward Mair, an avid bird-watcher and president of Newburyport Birder's Exchange, records his bird sightings using dBase II and an Apple computer. His data base includes each bird's common and Latin name, its location when seen, age, sex, and notes about its behavior. The data base also automatically classifies each bird according to its order, genus, and species.

Joanna Posey, a genealogist, uses PFS:File and an Apple computer to store closets full of family records. Because her computerized data base sorts

166

and retrieves data so fast, she has been able to uncover traits and trends in her family's history that were buried deep within the large volumes of paper records. The data base allows her to search for a specific family name, birthdate, or hometown and retrieve data in seconds. She can then find links between family members that may have taken weeks or months to find otherwise.

These few examples show the usefulness of data bases as research tools. Their real power comes from the way data is structured and files are designed. Data bases, data structure, and file design are the topics of this chapter.

INTRODUCTION

The way in which data elements are arranged within a data file (data structure) and the manner in which the data file itself is organized (file design) are especially important for the users of an information-processing system. Before a computerized information-processing system can be implemented, the data structures and file design must be determined.

Chapter 5, Storage Devices, discussed the physical design of data stored on magnetic tape and magnetic disk. The physical design is primarily the concern of programmers. This chapter focuses on the logical organization of data, which mostly concerns the people who will use the data. It also covers the methods used to access data in a file since the access method is directly related to the logical organization of data.

DATA STRUCTURES

Data elements in a computer file can be arranged in many ways according to how they relate to one another. The relationships, called **data structures,** represent the ways in which data elements can be linked in a logical way, as determined by the user. The most common data structures are the hierarchical, network, and relational structures.

Data structures The relationships between the data elements in a computer file.

Hierarchical Data Structures

When a primary data element has many secondary data elements linked to it at various levels, it is called a **hierarchical** (or tree) **data structure.** The primary data element is the **parent** element. Each parent may have many children (secondary elements) related to it, but each child may have only one parent. For example, in Figure 6–1, A is the parent of B and C; B is the parent of D and E; and D is the parent of H, I, and J.

A school system may use the hierarchical data structure for its student files. Figure 6–2 shows the relationship between data elements of a student's course

Hierarchical data structure Data structure in which one primary data element may have numerous secondary elements linked to it at lower levels.

167

Figure 6–1
Hierarchical Data Structure

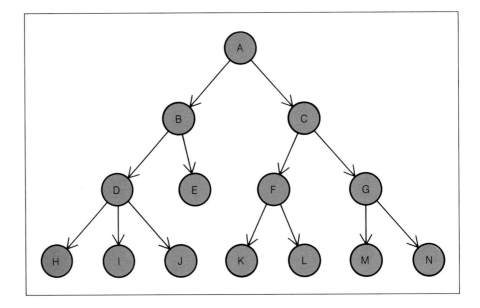

schedule. A student's social security number is linked to the courses in which the student is enrolled. Each course is linked to one teacher, a meeting time, and a room number. Therefore, if the principal needed to know where a particular student was at 1:00, for example, he or she could enter the student's social security number into the computer and the student's course schedule would be displayed.

Network data structure Data structure in which primary data elements may have many secondary elements, and secondary elements may have numerous primary elements.

Network Data Structures

Similar to the hierarchical data structure, a **network data structure** allows a parent data element to have many children, but it also allows a child to have

Figure 6–2
Student Course Schedule Shown in a Hierarchical Data Structure

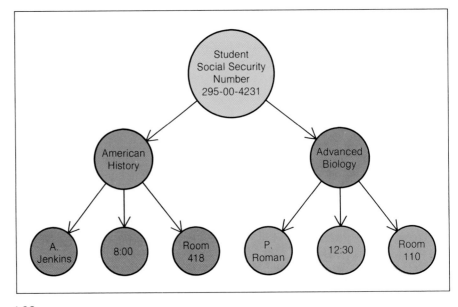

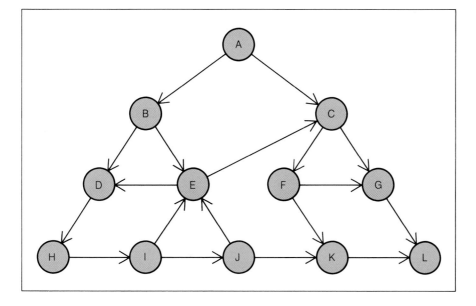

Figure 6–3
Network Data Structure

more than one parent. With this structure, any data element can be related to any other data element. There is no longer a simple hierarchy of data elements with relationships flowing only from a high level to a lower level. Data elements at a lower level can be related to elements at a higher level although these structures are quite complex (see Figure 6–3).

Figure 6–4 shows the relationship between data elements of a student course file. Each course is related to a student, a teacher, a meeting time, and a room number. Courses may have two parents, a student social security number and a teacher. With this relatively simple example, the principal could locate either a student or a teacher by entering the student's social security number or the teacher's name.

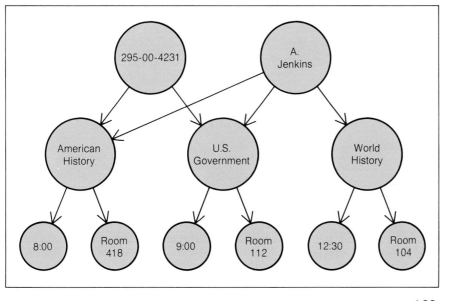

Figure 6–4
Student Course Schedule Shown in a
Network Data Structure

Relational data structure Data
structure that places data elements in a
table with rows representing records
and columns representing fields.

Relational Data Structures

A **relational data structure** places the data elements in a table with columns and rows. The rows represent records, and the columns represent fields or individual data elements. (Records and fields were discussed in Chapter 3.) With this structure, a data element can be related to other elements in the column in which it is located or to elements in the row in which it is located. With a relational data structure, the user can access either the data elements that comprise a record (one row) or the data elements contained in one field (one column).

Table 6–1 shows a relational data structure of authors, books, publishers, and copyright dates. A record contains an author, book, publisher, and copyright date. For example, Ernest Hemingway, *The Sun Also Rises,* Charles Scribner's Sons, and 1926 make up one record. Each record has an author field (Hemingway), book field *(The Sun Also Rises),* publisher field (Charles Scribner's Sons), and copyright date field (1926).

Each data element has a unique location in the table identified by the column number and row number. The row and column numbers are called **subscripts.** For example, the subscript (1,5) identifies the data element, James Joyce, located in Column 1 and Row 5.

This sample data structure might be used at a bookstore. A clerk could then obtain the record with J. R. R. Tolkien data, for example, or a list of all book titles carried at the store (the data elements in one field).

Logical Organization of Data

Pointers and Chains

Data records in a file can be linked according to some order that is meaningful to the user. Linking records in some specified order is necessary so the user can access data from a file by asking specific questions. For example, a school secretary may wish to obtain lists of students in alphabetical order, students with junior status, or students taking Introductory Psychology this term. Without some way to link all students enrolled in Introductory Psychology, the secretary could not obtain that list without searching each record in the file.

Table 6–1 ▬ Relational Data Structure

		COLUMNS (FIELDS)			
		Author (1)	Book (2)	Publisher (3)	Copyright (4)
ROWS (RECORDS)	(1) Ernest Hemingway	The Sun Also Rises	Charles Scribner's Sons	1926
	(2) F. Scott Fitzgerald	The Last Tycoon	Charles Scribner's Sons	1941
	(3) Richard Adams	Watership Down	Avon	1972
	(4) J. R. R. Tolkien	The Silmarillion	George Allen & Unwin	1977
	(5) James Joyce	Ulysses	Random House	1934
	(6) William Faulkner	The Sound and the Fury	Random House	1946
	(7) J. D. Salinger	The Catcher in the Rye	Bantam Books	1945

Concept Summary 6-1 ▪ A Comparison of Data Structures

Type of Data Structure	How Elements Are Logically Linked in a File
Hierarchical	Parent element may have many children
Network	Parent element may have many children and child element may have more than one parent
Relational	Elements in a table are linked to elements in the same row and the same column

Records can be linked by adding an extra field that points to the next record in the sequence. This extra field is called a **pointer.** The pointer contains no data describing the record. It contains the address of the next record to be accessed. In Figure 6-5, the pointer for record number 1 directs the computer to record Number 6. It links hotels that are located in Cleveland. The pointer for record Number 6 directs the computer to record number 10, the next hotel located in Cleveland. The logical path linking records according to one common field, such as city, is called a **chain.**

An asterisk (*) indicates to the computer the end of the chain has been reached. In Figure 6-5, the asterisk in record number 10 indicates that there are no more Cleveland hotels in the file.

Records in a file may also be linked by more than one chain. With multiple chains, records can be linked according to any number of fields. Multiple chains will be covered in the following sections.

Pointer An additional field in a record that contains the address of the next record to be accessed.

Chain The logical path linking records according to one common field.

Record Number	Hotel	City	Number of Rooms	Children Free	City Pointer
1	Holiday Inn	Cleveland	230	No	6
2	OK Inn	Nashville	84	Yes	9
3	Trails End	Omaha	62	No	5
4	Quality Inn	Austin	112	Yes	
5	Red Carpet	Omaha	96	Yes	*
6	Radisoon	Cleveland	218	No	10
7	Hilton	Tampa	204	Yes	
8	Holiday Inn	Toronto	320	No	
9	Red Roof	Nashville	90	Yes	*
10	Quality Inn	Cleveland	106	No	*

Figure 6-5
Records Linked by a Pointer

Simple list A file without pointers.

Linked list A file using pointers to maintain the sequence of the records.

Ring list A linked list with pointer fields indicating the end of a chain; the last record contains a pointer back to the first record.

Inverted list A list that has an index for every field in a file.

Lists

A **simple list,** such as the one shown in Table 6–2, is a file without pointers. To group records by a common characteristic, such as city, or to place them in sequential order according to record number, the file would have to be sorted.

Adding pointer fields forms **linked lists,** like the one shown in Table 6–3, that easily show these relationships without sorting the records. The linked list in Table 6–3 contains multiple chains, one linking cities and one linking record numbers. Linked lists are useful when sequential access is needed and also when records are updated often. When a record is added or deleted, the file does not need to be resorted. Only the pointers need to be updated. For example, if record number 20 were added to the file in Table 6–3, it could simply be added as the last record. As shown in Table 6–4, the record number pointer 23 in record number 18 is changed to 20, and record number 20 now contains pointer 23. Also, record number 20 is linked to record number 5 because of their relationship by city (Dayton).

Ring lists are similar to linked lists except there are no asterisks in the pointer field to indicate the end of a chain. The last record in a chain contains a pointer back to the first record in the list or chain. As shown in Table 6–5, there is no beginning or ending city pointer or record number pointer. Because the list is an endless ring, updating the pointers is more difficult than in a linked list.

When records are linked according to many different fields, the use of pointers and chains becomes very complicated and inefficient. With **inverted lists,** an index is created for each field used to link records. A fully inverted list has an

Table 6–2 ▬ Simple List

Record Number	Name	Address	City	Zip Code	Account Balance
10	Wendt, Wendy	16 Central	Columbus	42712	417.89
5	Jones, Jeff	5 Madison	Dayton	52133	634.19
23	Wincki, Laurie	34 Turney	Cleveland	45857	112.44
47	Golden, Tom	111 Eastern	Columbus	43368	245.75
15	Evans, Brad	56 Wellton	Columbus	42751	98.17
18	Powers, Emily	191 Parkway	Findlay	42711	42.31
27	Langley, Wes	78 Montana	Toledo	43611	451.04

Table 6–3 ▬ Linked List with Two Pointers (for City and Record Number)

Record Number	Name	Address	City	Zip Code	Account Balance	City Pointer	Record Number Pointer
10	Wendt, Wendy	16 Central	Columbus	42712	417.89	47	15
5	Jones, Jeff	5 Madison	Dayton	52133	634.19		Start 10
23	Wincki, Laurie	34 Turney	Cleveland	45857	112.44		27
47	Golden, Tom	111 Eastern	Columbus	43368	245.75	15	*
15	Evans, Brad	56 Wellton	Columbus	42751	98.17	*	18
18	Powers, Emily	191 Parkway	Findlay	42711	42.31		23
27	Langley, Wes	78 Montana	Toledo	43611	451.04		47

Table 6–4 ▬ Revised Linked List After the Addition of One Record

Record Number	Name	Address	City	Zip Code	Account Balance	City Pointer	Record Number Pointer
10	Wendt, Wendy	16 Central	Columbus	42712	417.89	47	15
5	Jones, Jeff	5 Madison	Dayton	52133	634.19	*	Start 10
23	Wincki, Laurie	34 Turney	Cleveland	45857	112.44		27
47	Golden, Tom	111 Eastern	Columbus	43368	245.75	15	*
15	Evans, Brad	56 Wellton	Columbus	42751	98.17	*	18
18	Powers, Emily	191 Parkway	Findlay	42711	42.31		20
27	Langley, Wes	78 Montana	Toledo	43611	451.04		47
20	Cramer, Karen	88 Longford	Dayton	43001	157.68	5	23

index for every field in a file. It would allow the user to access records according to any common field. A partially inverted list contains an index for selected fields. The partially inverted list in Table 6–6 shows indexes created for the fields *last name* and *city*.

Inverted lists are most useful when large files must be searched for a small amount of data. They allow files to be searched for certain fields very quickly. A disadvantage of inverted lists is that the indexes require a lot of storage, sometimes more than the records themselves. For this reason, determining how the file will be accessed so that indexes are not created unnecessarily is important.

FILE DESIGN

Before a file can be designed, several factors must be considered, including the type of logical record to be used, the access method required, and the organization of the file.

Logical Records

A logical record consists of a group of data fields. Recall from Chapter 3 that a data field is a meaningful unit of data, such as a name, social security number,

Table 6–5 ▬ Ring List

Record Number	Name	Address	City	Zip Code	Account Balance	City Pointer	Record Number Pointer
10	Wendt, Wendy	16 Central	Columbus	42712	417.89	47	15
5	Jones, Jeff	5 Madison	Monroe	52133	634.19		10
23	Wincki, Laurie	34 Turney	Cleveland	45857	112.44		27
47	Golden, Tom	111 Eastern	Columbus	43368	245.75	15	5
15	Evans, Brad	56 Wellton	Columbus	42751	98.17	10	18
18	Powers, Emily	191 Parkway	Findlay	42711	42.31		23
27	Langley, Wes	78 Montana	Toledo	43611	451.04		47

Table 6–6 ▬ Partially Inverted List

Characteristic	Record Number
Last Name:	
Wendt	10
Jones	5
Wincki	23
Golden	47
Evans	15
Powers	18
Langley	27
City:	
Columbus	10, 47, 15
Dayton	5
Cleveland	23
Findlay	18
Toledo	27

Key The unique identifier or field of a record.

or address. The length of each data field must be determined before a file can be designed. A data field's length is determined by the number of characters contained in the field. Also, one data field should be chosen to serve as the unique **key** that will identify the record. For example, social security number could be used as a key since no two people should have the same social security number.

Fixed-Length Records

Fixed-length records A record format in which a maximum number of character positions are assigned.

After the data fields to be contained in a logical record and a unique key have been determined, deciding whether the records will be of fixed or variable length is necessary. **Fixed-length records** are easier to design and work with in a data file. But there may be one major problem in using fixed-length records. When a fixed-length record is used, each data field in the record is assigned a certain number of characters. A problem arises when the number of characters needed in a data field is uncertain. If too few characters are assigned, there may not be enough character spaces to handle some data. For example, in Figure 6–6 the data field for customer name allows for 20 characters. A customer name such as Federated Aviation Systems, which has 26 characters (including spaces), would not fit in the allotted space. This would cause a problem if the entire name of the customer is needed. In some cases, another customer name, such as Federated Aviation Suppliers, would appear the same if only part of the name could be stored.

Customer names could be abbreviated when they exceed the fixed record length. However, this approach has disadvantages, especially when dealing with large files. Appropriate abbreviations must be decided upon and a list, or directory, of the abbreviations maintained so the user can positively identify the abbreviated form of each customer name.

One might think a simple solution to the problem would be to assign a large number of characters to data fields that will contain an uncertain number of characters. But this can waste space in the data file if data do not fill the space allotted in each data field.

Variable-Length Records

Variable-length records A record format in which the unused character spaces are eliminated from the record.

Variable-length records eliminate wasted space in a file. Variable-length records still require a certain number of characters to be specified for each data field. However, before a record is stored in a file, the unused character spaces are eliminated. For example, 50 character spaces could be assigned to a customer name data field, which should be enough to accommodate all possible customer

Figure 6–6
Fixed-Length Records

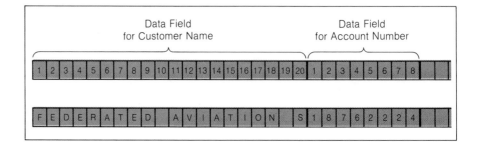

Caltrans, Intelligent Traffic

The roads in Los Angeles—among the most traveled in the world—have a mind of their own. And it's located in the traffic control center downtown where the region's 700 or so miles of freeways are monitored and controlled by Caltrans (California Department of Transportation).

The Caltrans system uses a computer network that communicates with video monitors and wire loop coils embedded in the roads to check traffic density and speed. The entire freeway system is represented by an electronic map covering one wall of the control center. Lights on the map, which mark the length of each freeway, shine green for traffic moving faster than 40 miles per hour, amber for traffic moving between 20 and 40 miles per hour, and red for traffic moving slower than 20 miles per hour. When serious accidents occur, lights blink red at the appropriate places on the map.

Traffic is directed on the freeways by electronic message boards controlled by the Caltrans computer. The message boards inform drivers of traffic conditions ahead. Traffic signals at the on-ramps, also controlled by the computer, allow only so many new cars per minute into the flow of traffic.

Traffic engineers and scientists are always working on ways to improve existing freeway systems. Some suggest that traffic can be considered a problem in fluid dynamics, one fluid being the moving vehicles and the other fluid being vehicles that are stopped. Someday traffic analysts hope to be able to determine the rate of fuel consumption resulting from any layout of streets and highways.

names. Then if only 12 spaces are used, the remaining 38 will be eliminated from the record, not wasted.

Variable-length records make the best use of file space but are not always the most efficient to use. Some software systems simply cannot use variable-length records, and fixed-length records are better suited to applications with known file space requirements.

Methods of File Access

Another consideration in determining the best file design is the manner in which data will be retrieved. The access method can be either batch or online, depending on how fast data must be retrieved.

Batch File Access

With **batch file access,** all transactions to be processed are gathered for a period of time and then processed at one time. The period of time for which trans-

Batch file access An access method in which all transactions are accumulated for a given period of time and then processed all at once.

actions are gathered before processing may be one work shift (8 hours), one calendar day (24 hours), or any other logical length of time dictated by the information needs of the user.

Batch file access is most useful when current information is needed only at set times, rather than at all times. For example, student grades can be processed at the end of a term or customer orders at the end of a day.

Online File Access

Online file access
An access method in which records are updated when transactions are made.

Online file access provides the ability to retrieve current information at any time. Each time a transaction is made, the affected records are updated at the same time. Online file access is often used for inventory control, airline reservations, and banking transactions.

Logical File Designs

Sequential file design   Records organized in a file in a specific order based on the value of the key field.

Indexed-sequential file design   Records organized in sequential order and also listed in an index.

Direct-access file design   Records organized in a file in any order, with record keys providing the only way to access data.

Different access methods require different file designs. If a data file requires batch file access, the best file design may be a **sequential file design.** If online access is needed, an **indexed-sequential file design** or **direct-access file design** must be used.

Sequential File Design

A group of records ordered according to their key values form a sequential file. Figure 6–7 shows a portion of an employee file with the records arranged

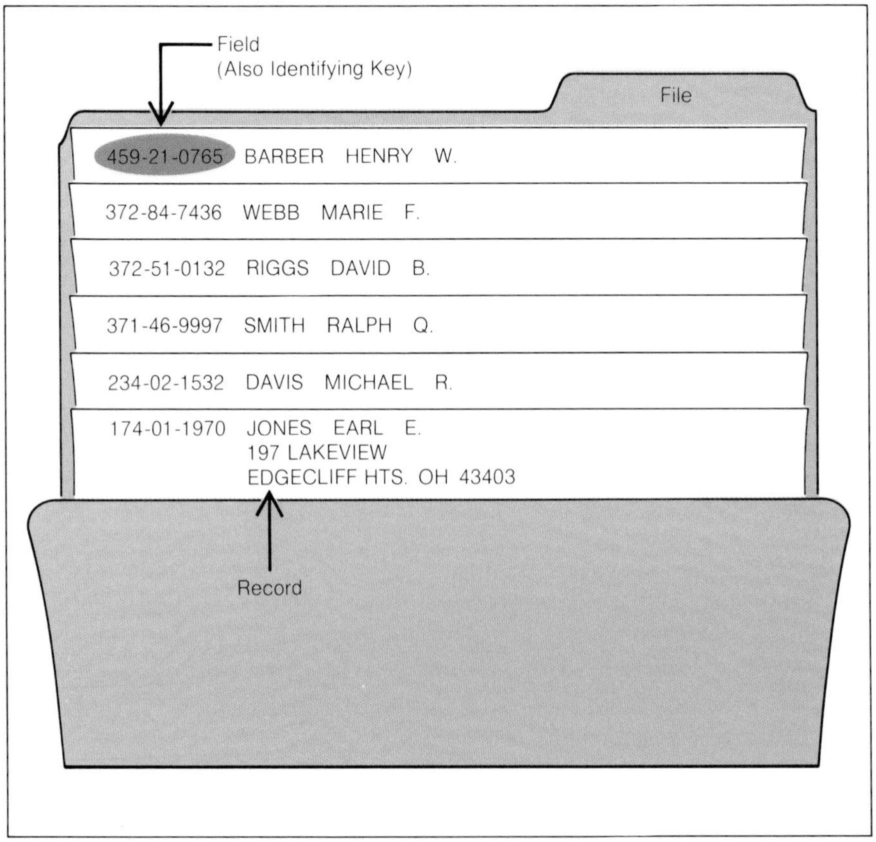

Figure 6–7
Employee File Using Social Security Number as the Key

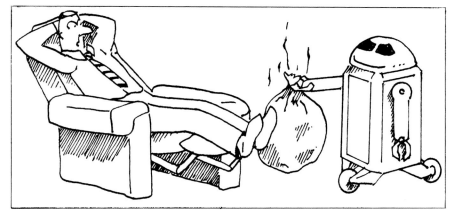

". . . and I suppose my slippers are out on the curb."

according to social security number. Sequential file design is useful when a particular record must be updated and the number of records in a file is very small. To update a particular record, the file is searched from the beginning until the record is found.

Updating involves two sets of files: the **master file** and a **transaction file.** The master file is the file containing all existing records. The transaction file is the file containing the changes to be made to the master file. During the updating process a third file, the new master file, is created. The old master file is organized in sequential order according to the key field but the transaction file may be organized in any order. To speed up the updating process, the transaction file should first be sorted according to the same key as the master file.

To update a file, the computer compares the key of the first master file record with the key from the first record in the transaction file. If the keys do not match, the computer writes the record to the new master file as is and reads the next record on the master file. When a match between the master and transaction records occurs, the computer updates the master record. If a transaction record has no matching master record, the computer may generate an error message.

Some transactions may add a new record, while others may delete an existing record. Since records are stored one after another on a sequential file, these types of transactions cannot be handled using the old master file alone. To allow for the insertion or deletion of records, a new master file is created whenever changes are made to the old master file. Each master record not deleted from the file must be written into a new master file, whether or not it is changed during the update. The process of creating an entirely new master file each time transactions are processed is called **sequential processing.**

With sequential processing, there is no direct way to locate the matching master record for a transaction. Each time a certain master record is to be updated, the entire master file must be read and a new master file created. Since this makes updating one record in a file very time-consuming, transactions are collected over a period of time and processed in one run (see Figure 6–8). Therefore, batch file access must be used with sequential file design.

The amount of time required to update a record with sequential processing includes the time needed to process the transaction, read and rewrite the master file until the proper record is reached, update the master record, and finish rewriting the master file. To reduce the time needed, the transactions are sorted

Master file A file that contains all existing records organized according to the key field; updated by records in a transaction file.

Transaction file A file containing changes to be made to the master file.

Sequential processing The process of creating a new master file each time transactions are processed; requires batch file access.

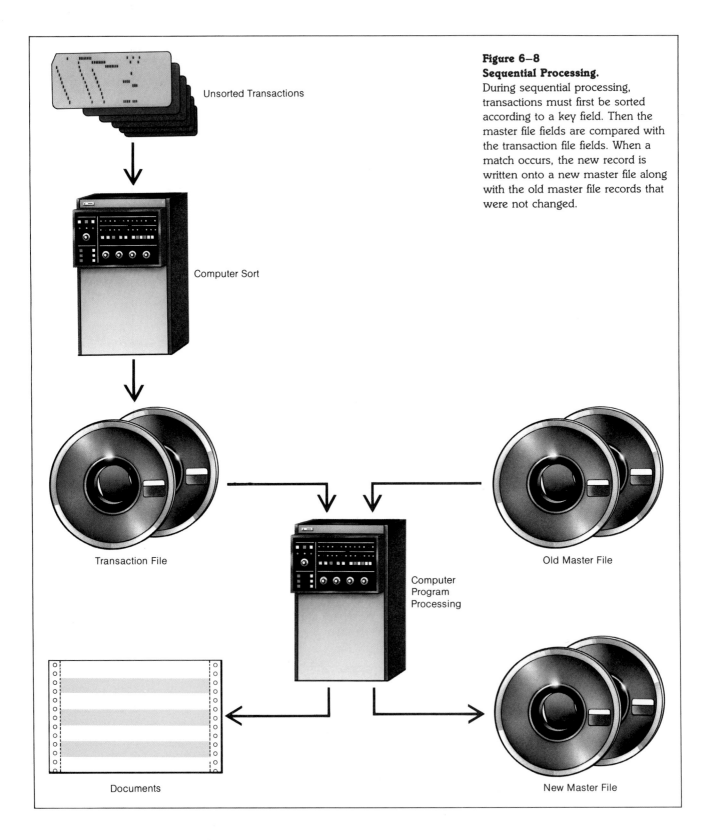

Unsorted Transactions

Computer Sort

Transaction File

Old Master File

Computer Program Processing

Documents

New Master File

Figure 6–8
Sequential Processing.
During sequential processing, transactions must first be sorted according to a key field. Then the master file fields are compared with the transaction file fields. When a match occurs, the new record is written onto a new master file along with the old master file records that were not changed.

in the same order as the master file. For security, the old master file and the transaction records are kept for a period of time; then, if the new master file is accidentally destroyed, it can be reconstructed from the old master and the transaction files. In many instances, two generations of old masters are kept, giving rise to "father" and "grandfather" backup copies.

Example of Sequential Processing. The preparation of customer bills is well suited to sequential processing. Customers' bills are usually prepared only at scheduled intervals. Standard procedures apply and large numbers of records must be processed.

Processing customer records results in the preparation of bills for customers and updates of the amounts they owe. Magnetic tape is an appropriate medium for this application because the customer records can be arranged in customer number order and processed in sequence accordingly.

The procedure for preparing the billing statements involves the following steps:

1. The transaction records indicating which items have been shipped to customers are keypunched and verified. One card is used for each item shipped. The key-to-tape operation also provides a report of invalid transactions so that they can be corrected (see Figure 6–9a).
2. The transaction records are sorted according to customer number because the customer master file is arranged in customer number order (see Figure 6–9b).
3. The sorted transactions are used to update the customer master file. The process involves reading the transaction records and master records into primary storage (there may be more than one transaction record for a master record). The master record is updated to reflect the final amount owed by the customer, and a report is usually printed for management. For example, during the billing update, the computer may print a listing of customers who have exceeded their credit limits (see Figure 6–9c).
4. The customers' bills are prepared from the data generated in Step 3 (see Figure 6–9d).

Making Inquiries to Sequential Files. How inquiries into a sequential file on magnetic tape are handled depends on the type of inquiry. Consider the following inquiries into the employee file shown in Figure 6–7.

1. List the records of employees with social security numbers 234-02-1532 and 372-84-7436.
2. List all employees from the area with zip code 43403.

The employee file is sequenced according to social security number. In the first case the file will be searched for the correct social security numbers from the beginning of the file, but only the key of each record will be checked. As soon as the required social security numbers are located and the required records listed, the search is stopped. Of course, if the numbers are in the last two records on the file, then the entire file must be searched.

For the second inquiry, the entire file will again have to be searched. In this case, the zip code field of each record must be checked to see if it matches 43403. This illustrates one problem with referring to a nonkey field on sequential files. If an inquiry is based on a field other than the key, a great deal of time

Figure 6–9
Billing Operation Using Sequential
Processing

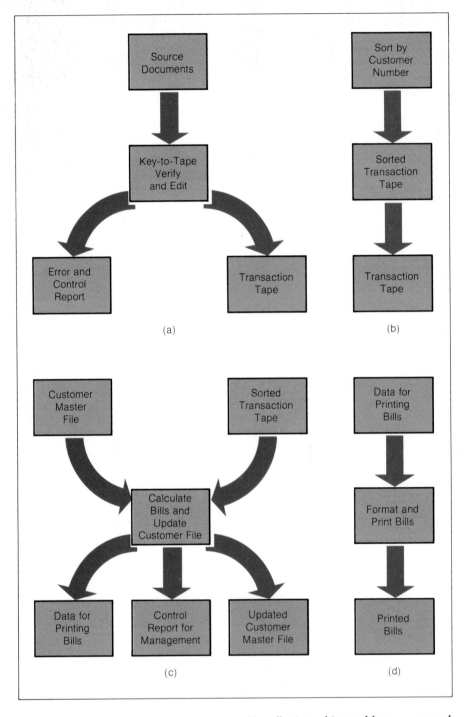

may be wasted in the search process. To alleviate this problem a second employee file, ordered by zip code, could be created; however, this approach requires multiple files with duplicate data.

Assessment of Sequential File Design. Sequential processing and file design are suitable for applications with high **activity** and low **volatility.** Activity refers to the proportion of records processed during an updating run, and volatility

Activity The proportion of records processed during an update run.

Volatility The frequency of changes made to a file during a certain period of time.

180

refers to the frequency of changes to a file during a given time period. Examples of applications with high activity and low volatility (requiring large numbers of records to be updated at specific times) include payroll processing, updating the addresses of magazine subscribers, and preparing student grades.

Advantages of sequential processing and file design include the following:

- It can be cost effective when at least half the records in a master file are updated during one processing run.
- The design of sequential files is simple.
- Magnetic tape, a low-cost medium, can be used to maximum advantage.

The disadvantages of this mode of processing include the following:

- The entire master file must be processed and a new master file written even when only a few master records have to be updated.
- Transactions must be sorted in a particular sequence; this takes time and can be expensive.
- The master file is only as up to date as the last processing run. In many instances, using information from a master file that has not been recently updated results in the use of old, and sometimes incorrect, information.
- The sequential nature of the file organization makes it difficult to provide information for unanticipated inquiries such as the status of a particular record.

Direct-Access File Design

Direct-access file designs also use the key field of the records but in a different way from sequential design. The key field provides the only way of accessing data within a direct-access file design. Therefore, records are stored in no particular order.

The data record being sought is retrieved according to its key value, so records before or after it are not read. Usually, a mathematical process called **randomizing** or **hashing** is applied to the record key, with the result of the process being the storage addresses of the record. The address is usually a number of five to seven digits that is related to the physical characteristics of the storage medium. When a file is created, this address determines where the record is written; during retrieval, the address determines where to locate the record. Another way to obtain the address of a record is to place the record keys and their corresponding addresses in a **directory** (see Figure 6–10). During processing, the computer searches the directory to locate the address of a particular record.

Direct-access file design is much more efficient than searching an entire data file for a particular record. It is useful when information must be updated and retrieved quickly and when accurate information is crucial. A common application of direct-access file organization is for airline seat reservations. Accurate information about available flights and seats must be available at all times so that flights are not overbooked.

In contrast to a batch-processing system, a direct-access system does not require that transaction records be grouped or sorted before they are processed. Data is submitted to the computer in the order it occurs usually using an online access method. **Direct-access storage devices (DASDs),** such as magnetic-disk drive units, make this type of processing possible. A particular record on a master file can be accessed directly, using its assigned keys, and updated

Randomizing (hashing) A mathematical process applied to the record key that produces the storage address of the record.

Directory Contains record keys and their corresponding addresses; used to obtain the address of a record with a direct-access file design.

Figure 6–10
Sample Directory for Social Security Number

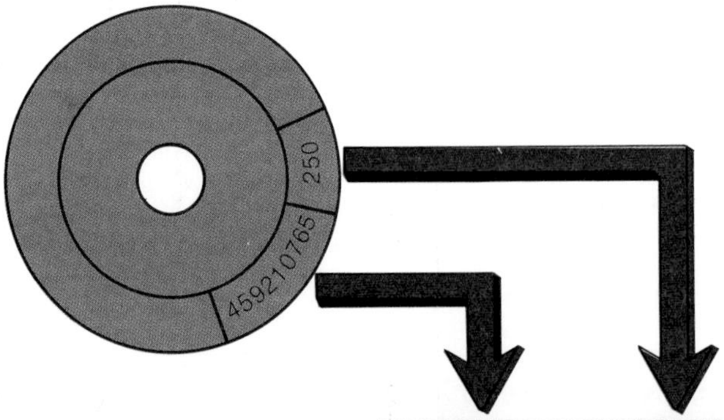

Social Security Number	Address
459210765	250
372847436	829
372510132	301
371469997	677
234021532	425
17401970	712
⋮	⋮
⋮	⋮

without all preceding records on the file being read. Only the key to the record need be known. Thus, up-to-the-minute reports can be provided. For example, assume Ralph Smith's address in the employee master file in Figure 6–7 had to be changed. With direct-access processing, the computer can locate the record to be updated without processing all records that precede it. Figure 6–11 shows how direct-access processing would be used in a business.

Making Inquiries to Direct-Access Files. To see how direct-access files handle inquiries, refer to the two inquiries discussed in connection with sequential files:

1. List the records of employees with social security numbers 234-02-1532 and 372-84-7436.
2. List all employees from the area with zip code 43403.

With regard to the first inquiry, the records of the two employees can be located directly, assuming the social security number is used as the key.

The approach used for the second inquiry will depend on the organization of the file. If the file is large and much processing is done based on a geographic

182

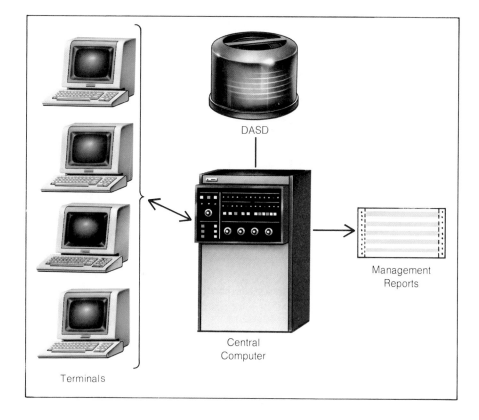

DASD

Management
Reports

Central
Computer

Terminals

Figure 6–11
Direct-Access Processing.
During direct-access processing, the master record is updated when the transaction occurs. There is only one master record. It contains only the most recent updated records.

breakdown of employees, a directory relating zip codes and their record addresses can be created (as in Figure 6–12). However, if there are not many employees and processing is seldom based on the geographic breakdown of employees, a directory to locate employee records by zip code may have little value. In this case, the situation is the same as with sequential files: the entire file must be read to obtain the desired information.

Assessment of Direct-Access File Design. Direct-access processing and file design is suitable for applications with low activity and high volatility. Examples of applications with low activity and high volatility (requiring only a few records to be updated frequently) include banking operations, and hotel and airline reservation systems.

Advantages of direct-access processing and file design are the following:

- Transaction data can be used directly to update master records via online terminals without first being sorted. Transactions are processed as they occur.
- The master file is not read completely each time updating occurs; only the master records to be updated are accessed. This saves time and money.
- Gaining access to any record on a direct-access file takes only a fraction of a second.
- Direct-access files provide flexibility in handling inquiries.
- Several files can be updated at the same time by use of direct-access processing. For example, when a credit sale is made, the inventory file can be updated, the customer file can be changed to reflect the current accounts

Figure 6–12
Directory for Zip Codes

ZIP CODE	ADDRESS
43403	12043
43403	12140
44151	12046
44153	12143
44200	12146
44201	12045

183

receivable figure, and the sales file can be updated to show which employee made the sale. Several runs would be required to accomplish all of these operations if sequential processing was used.

Disadvantages of direct-access design include the following:

- During processing, the original record is replaced by the updated record. In effect, it is destroyed. (In batch processing, a completely new master file is created, but the old master file remains intact.) Consequently, to provide backup, an organization may have to make a magnetic-tape copy of the master file weekly and also keep the current week's transactions so that master records can be reconstructed if necessary.
- Since many users may have access to records stored on direct-access devices in online systems, the chances of accidental destruction of data are greater. Special programs are required to edit input data and to perform other checks to ensure that data is not lost. Also, there exists the possibility of confidential information falling into unauthorized hands; additional security procedures are necessary to reduce this risk.
- Implementation of direct-access systems is often difficult because of their complexity and the high level of programming (software) support that such systems need.

Indexed-Sequential File Design

Sequential processing is suitable for applications where the proportion of records processed in an updating run is high. However, sequential files provide slow response times and cannot adequately handle file inquiries. On the other hand, direct-access processing is inappropriate for applications like payroll where most records are processed during a single run. When a single file must be used for both batch processing and online processing, neither direct-access nor sequential file organization is appropriate. The same customer file that is used in a weekly batch run for preparing bills by the accounting department may be used daily by order-entry personnel to record orders and check credit status. To some extent, the limitations of both types of file design can be minimized by using another approach to file organization—indexed-sequential design.

In this structure, the records are stored sequentially on a direct-access storage device according to a primary key. A **primary key** is a field that will be unique for each record on the file. In addition, secondary keys can also be established. **Secondary keys** are fields that are used to gain access to records on the file but may not be unique. For instance, if zip code is chosen as a secondary key, there may be several records with the same value. Records on an indexed-sequential file can be accessed randomly by using either the primary or one of the secondary keys, or the file can be read sequentially—in primary-key sequential order.

The method used to gain access to a record on an indexed-sequential file is a little different from the method for a direct-access file. Every record on an indexed-sequential file may not have its own unique address. Rather, several records may be grouped together and one address given for the entire group. An index table is created for all fields that are primary or secondary keys. The index table lists the value of the key (such as social security number) and the corresponding address on the direct-access storage device at which the group containing that record can be found. A key given by the user is matched against the index table to get an approximate address for the required record. The computer then goes to that location on the direct-access storage device and checks records sequentially until the desired record is found. In the case of secondary keys, all records with that key may be retrieved.

Figure 6–13 shows the employee file from Figure 6–7 set up as an indexed-sequential file. The primary key is a social security number, while zip code is

Figure 6–13
The Physical Layout of Records on a Disk for Indexed-Sequential Design

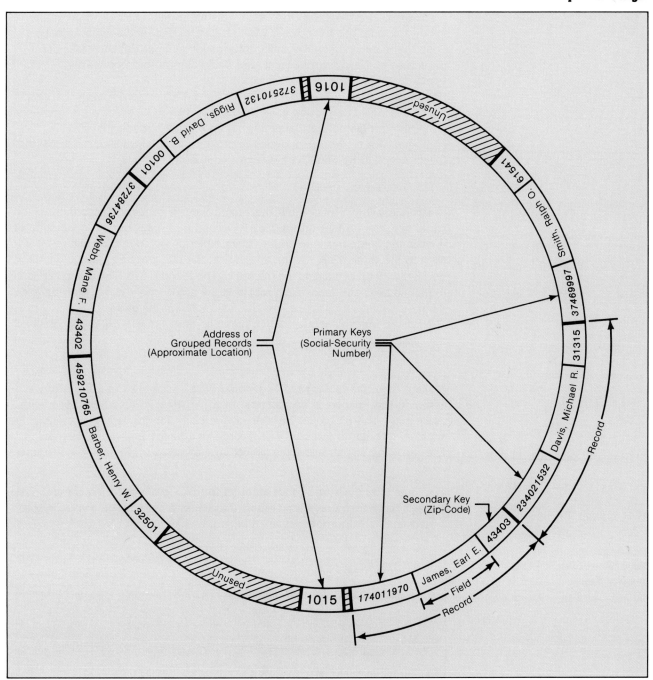

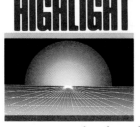

HIGHLIGHT

A Dating Service for Horses

A computerized dating service for horses? With data-base management software, Brad Baker of Moondrift Farms, a Colorado horsebreeding ranch, matches horses.

Detailed information is kept on all horses at the ranch. This information includes how many times a mare has been bred, what she's been fed, and even information on the mare's personality traits. Information such as this increases the success of the system because a mare's traits can be more easily matched to an appropriate stallion.

Baker has a similar program for stallions. This system makes checking any stallion's background easy for mare owners.

Other programs that Baker has set up include a medical history program for his horses and even a program to keep track of repair work that needs to be done on the farm's equipment.

a secondary key. Notice how the records are in sequence according to the social security number on the file. To locate an employee with a zip code of 43403, the computer goes to the index table for zip code (see Figure 6–14). Next to the value 43403 is the address on the direct-access storage device at which the group containing that record can be found, 1015. The computer goes to that address and reads each record in the group until the one with zip code 43403 is found. In this case, it is the first record in the group.

Thus, an indexed-sequential file provides direct-access capability. Since all the records are ordered according to a primary key, it also allows efficient sequential processing.

Making Inquiries to Indexed-Sequential Files. The customer file referred to earlier in this chapter is an example of a file suitable for indexed-sequential processing. The file could be read sequentially for the billing operation. In addition, it could be accessed one record at a time for order-entry transactions. The following steps outline the procedures involved in preparing a customer order:

1. A customer mails or phones an order to ABC Company for equipment. The clerk receives the order and enters the customer number on a visual display terminal. This number acts as a key to the file.

Figure 6–14
Index Tables of Primary and Secondary Keys

PRIMARY KEY (Social Security Number)		SECONDARY KEY (Zip Code)	
Number	*Address*	*Number*	*Address*
174–01–1970	1015	00101	1016
234–02–1532	1015	31315	1015
371–46–9997	1015	32501	1016
372–51–0132	1016	43402	1016
372–84–7436	1016	43403	1015
459–21–0765	1016	61541	1015

2. The index to the customer number on the customer file is searched until it is located. The record's approximate address is used to begin the search on the disk file. Once at that location, records are looked at sequentially until a match is found between the number entered and the appropriate record. Once the appropriate record is found, the information appears on the terminal's screen. The clerk verifies shipping and billing addresses.

3. The order is entered on the keyboard, and a sales order is generated by a printer connected to the system.

4. The customer's record is updated to reflect the current order.

Assessment of Indexed-Sequential File Design. Indexed-sequential files have a built-in flexibility that is not available with either sequential or direct-access designs. They work well in an environment where transactions are batch processed and inquiries require the fast response of direct-access processing.

Advantages of indexed-sequential design include the following:

■ Indexed-sequential files are well suited for both inquiries and large processing runs.

■ Access time to specific records is apt to be faster than it would be if the file were sequentially organized.

Disadvantages of indexed-sequential design include the following:

■ More direct-access storage space is required for an indexed-sequential file than for a sequential file holding the same data because of the storage space required for indexes.

■ Processing time for specific record selection is longer than it would be in a direct-access system.

Data Bases

Organizations such as hospitals, banks, retailers, and manufacturers have special information needs. Usually, data is collected and stored by many depart-

Concept Summary 6–2 ■ Comparison of File Designs

	Sequential	Direct-Access	Indexed-Sequential
Types of Access	batch	online	batch or online
Data Organization	sequentially by key value	no particular order	sequentially and by index
Flexibility in Handling Inquiries	low	high	very high
Availability of Up-to-Date Data	no	yes	yes
Speed of Retrieval	slow	very fast	fast
Activity	high	low	high
Volatility	low	high	high
Examples	payroll processing billing operations	airline reservations banking transactions	customer ordering and billing

Data base A single collection of related data that can be used in many applications.

Figure 6–15
Data Bases Meet Many Needs.
This company's data base is designed to provide information for management reports to such persons as the marketing manager and the director of human resources. Without leaving their offices, these people can make inquiries to the data base to obtain data needed to perform their jobs.

ments in these organizations. But this often results in the duplication of data. A hospital, for example, may keep files on patients treated in the emergency room. If a patient is then admitted, separate records may be compiled and kept for admissions, surgical procedures, X rays, insurance, and billing purposes. The patient's name, address, personal physician, and medical history might be repeated in most or all of the records.

A data-base approach to file design treats all data from every department as one entity. A **data base** is a single collection of related data that can be used in many applications. Data is usually stored only once in a data base, which minimizes data duplication.

In a data base, data is stored in such a way that the same data can be accessed by many users for various applications (see Figure 6–15). Data ele-

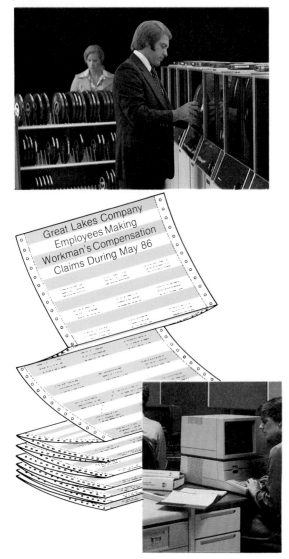

Data Base Corrals Rustlers

Cattle rustling is not an activity found only in history books; rustlers are alive and active in the black market, where a cow can bring $500 and a trailer-truckload $10,000 or so. With this kind of money at stake, the Texas and Southwestern Cattle Raisers Association (the nation's largest antirustling organization) has made a computer its defense weapon.

A data base of cattle transactions is stored on an electronic microfilm index. When cattle are reported stolen, the computer checks and lists all sales of cattle with that brand for a specified time period. Then the Texas Ranger assigned to the investigation tracks the sellers. Sometimes the ranger must backtrack through several transactions to get the real crooks. Once the rustlers have been pinpointed, the data base can be searched for their other cattle sales, perhaps identifying multiple crimes.

In just four years, this system has recovered or accounted for stolen merchandise worth over $1.3 million. Since the computer system can also handle more mundane business matters, the organization believes that its decision to automate was a good one.

ments are grouped to fit the needs of all departments in the organization rather than the needs of one particular application.

In addition to reducing the duplication of data, data bases increase efficiency. When a data element is updated, the change needs to be made only once because the data files are shared by all users. Once the update is made, current information is readily available to all departments.

The task of determining the logical design of data in a data base is the responsibility of the system analyst and data-base analyst. A **system analyst** is the interface between users and the system programmers. The **data-base analyst** is responsible for the analysis, design, and implementation of the data base. Together, they try to model the actual relationships that exist among data elements. The physical design of the data base is performed by the data-base administration (DBA) team. The DBA team must consider the problems of data redundancy, access time, and storage constraints in order to develop a logical design that works for the physical records and files actually stored in the data base.

The key to a successful data base is to incorporate more than one physical file into a logical file. What one user views as a logical unit of data may include data from several files. For example, if a user needs an employee's identification number, address, and salary, all that information can be obtained from two files, the personnel file and the payroll file (see Figure 6–16).

Data-base systems depend on direct-access storage devices (DASDs) to allow easy retrieval of data elements. The capabilities of DASDs are needed to handle the many logical relationships that exist among data elements. Combinations of data elements can be retrieved from a number of DASDs.

Data-Base Management Systems. An organization can use a **data-base management system (DBMS)** to help set up a data base. A DBMS is a set of programs

System analyst The person who serves as the interface between users and system programmers.

Data-base analyst The person responsible for the analysis, design, and implementation of the data base.

Data-base management system A set of programs that serves as the interface between the data base and the programmer, operating system, and users.

Figure 6-16
Example of a Data Base.
One company's data base may consist of five files: employees, inventory, payroll, customer, and accounting. Data for one logical file can be obtained from several physical files.

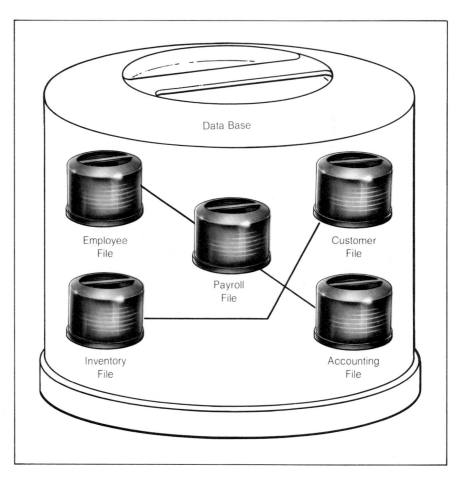

Data Base

Employee File

Customer File

Payroll File

Inventory File

Accounting File

that serves as the interface between the data base and the programmer, operating system, and users. With a DBMS, the programmer does not have to pay attention to the physical nature of the file; the programmer's main concern is the specific data the program needs.

A DBMS can perform the following functions:

- Organizing the data into logical structures that model the actual relationships among the data elements
- Storing the data required to meet the needs of multiple users
- Providing for concurrent retrieval and updating of data
- Arranging data to eliminate data duplication
- Providing privacy controls to prevent unauthorized access to data

Assessment of the Data-Base Approach.   Using a data base has a number of advantages:

- Data redundancy is minimized.
- Data can be stored in a manner that is useful for a wide variety of applications.
- Updating involves only one copy of the data.
- The system can handle requests that previously may have spanned several departments.

190

Data Bases Create Security Problems

Data bases, which allow users from several or all departments in an organization to use the same information for many applications, create special problems of data security. When the data is confidential, security becomes even more important. In early 1985, a San Francisco police lieutenant admitted he had access to the city's criminal justice computer system for about two months. The files in the computer system were shared by several departments, including the public defender, district attorney, sheriff, coroner, and Office of Civilian Complaints, which handles citizens' complaints against the police department.

The lieutenant obtained a menu that gave him easy access to the files in the minicomputer system. Even though the officer claims he did not read or copy any files in the public defender's system, the public defender's office asserted that the prosecution of up to 1,500 cases may be in jeopardy. Among the confidential information kept in the public defender's files were defense strategy notes and transcribed interviews. A defendant's right to independent counsel would be violated by police knowledge of attorney-client confidences.

Mayor Dianne Feinstein asked an independent group of city representatives to review the case and make recommendations. In the meantime, city agencies were advised to remove any confidential files from the computer system.

Big problems arise when departments share the same computer system and too many people have access to information that may be confidential. The problems escalate as more and more data bases are linked together in computer networks. As Jerry Berman, director of the American Civil Liberties Union's technology and privacy project, has noted, government agencies must put a higher premium on security in order to protect privacy rights.

Limitations of the data-base approach include the following:

- An error in one input data record may be carried throughout the data base.
- Design and implementation of a data-base system requires highly skilled, well-trained people.
- Major attention must be given to the security of the system, since all the data resources of the organization are collected in a place that is readily accessible to data-base users.
- Traditional processing jobs may run more slowly.

FOCUS ON MICRO-COMPUTING

Data Security For Microcomputers

More and more organizations are using microcomputers, especially in connection with data-base management systems. Managers at all levels have microcomputers right on their desks so that they can easily access company data bases. This availability of access causes problems of data security. Anyone can sit at another person's microcomputer and use it. The files contained in a manager's software library can be read by anyone who has access to the machine.

Until a few years ago, end users (people in the organization who ultimately use the data in data bases) could not possibly have accessed the company's data base without help or permission. They had to go through the data-processing department, specifying the information they needed. Today, if an organization has a well-designed data-base management system (DBMS), end users can usually make inquiries to the data base on their own. The tool that makes this type of access possible is the microcomputer.

Special concerns arise when end users can access the data base directly. With regard to data security, a DBMS must allow users to access data without getting into files that are off limits, and, users should not be able to update, add, or delete records without proper authorization. Many times, microcomputers in an information system are equipped with communications capabilities. This opens a company's data base to virtually anyone with the proper communications equipment.

Data security was not such a problem for organizations before microcomputers were commonly used to access data bases. Mainframes and minicomputers tend to be secure because there are a variety of security measures that can be installed to prevent unauthorized access. To date, however, there are very few security measures available for microcomputers.

Two common ways to ensure the security of data bases accessed through mainframes and minicomputers are passwords and call-back modems. Mainframes and minicomputers usually limit the number of unsuccessful passwords that can be tried and lock out the potential user who tries more than three or so passwords. If the DBMS allowed an unlimited number of passwords to be tried, eventually a person would stumble upon the correct password. The call-back method requires a user to provide an ID number to the computer and then hang up. The computer searches a directory for the ID number, which is linked to a particular phone number, and then calls that number. If the authorized person is at the correct place, access is granted.

Microcomputer operating systems have little password protection at this time. Password checking is usually performed by an application program. For example, a data-base management program from Micro Data Base Systems, MDBS3, provides up to 16 access levels. Other data-base management programs such as Softco's Protec and Ashton-Tate's dBASE II also offer some level of access control.

192

The problem with using a call-back method for microcomputers is that microcomputers are not always used by the same people at the same locations. A call-back system would also eliminate one of the greatest advantages of microcomputing—the flexibility to take the microcomputer where computing is needed.

When microcomputer-to-mainframe communications programs are designed to be user friendly, breaking into them is usually easy because the process of logging on to the mainframe is made as simple as possible, not as secure as possible. There is a security measure that remedies this problem for mainframes but not for microcomputers. It is software that keeps track of who has signed on to the system, from what location, and for what purpose. This audit trail makes detecting unauthorized access to files possible. For example, if a marketing manager requests access to files that he or she has no business seeing, such as the company payroll files, the mainframe security monitors would be alerted. Audit trails for microcomputers are impractical because of limited memory and diskette storage and low microprocessor speed.

Mainframes can also secure data in data bases by means of data encryption. Data is scrambled before it is stored and cannot be read without a data "key." This security method is not very useful for microcomputers because encryption cannot be used with most of the software used on microcomputers. One program that uses data encryption is MDBS3, which stores data in an encrypted form that can only be unscrambled when it is read back through the program.

Even though mainframe security is quite good, a mainframe cannot tell whether it is being accessed by a dumb terminal or a microcomputer. This is significant because dumb terminals have no way of saving information displayed on their screens. But a microcomputer can save information in memory or on disk. Some DBMS end users have only dumb terminals, thereby preventing them from having a permanent record of the data in the data base. If someone accessed the system with a microcomputer, the data could be saved and used in any way. And it could not be detected.

Why has the security of microcomputers used in data-base management systems not been given the attention it deserves? According to Doug De Vries, computer security manager at Hewlett-Packard's corporate computing center, 1 to 2 percent of a company's data-processing budget should be used to protect the data resources. But the cost of security measures available for microcomputers—encryption boards, password protection, lock-down packages—can easily amount to 10 to 20 percent of the microcomputer's cost.

Since detecting data-base break-ins that occur through microcomputers is difficult, the general attitude seems to be that the problem is not too serious. It may not seem serious because microcomputers are not usually concentrated in one part of an organization. They are distributed through various departments and offices, so the extent of computerization may not be evident. But some companies invest millions of dollars in microcomputers and related equipment. With resources as large as this wrapped up in microcomputers, not to mention the money involved in the design of data bases, investing in security is a wise plan.

SUMMARY POINTS

- Data elements can be logically linked in a data file using hierarchical, network, or relational data structures.
- Data can be organized to help speed inquiries by using pointers, chains, and lists.
- The factors to be considered when designing a data file are (1) the type of logical records to be used in the file, (2) the methods used to access the data in the file, and (3) the desired organization of the file.
- Record lengths can be either fixed or variable. Fixed-length records are easy to design and work with, but they may waste space. Variable-length records eliminate wasted space in a file.
- Batch file access methods require transactions to be gathered for processing at one time.
- Online file access methods provide the ability to retrieve data and update data at any time.
- In sequential design, all data is stored in sequential order on a master file; it may be ordered by some key field. Transactions to be processed against the master file are stored on a transaction file. Transactions are usually collected and processed against the master in one batch. During processing, transactions are matched against the master file, and the master file is updated. Updates to the master file are made by writing a new master file during processing. The entire master must be read when sequential processing is used.
- Batch access methods are generally used with sequential file designs.
- In direct-access processing, records are accessed according to their key. The computer determines the physical location of the record on the disk by a transformation process on the key or by using a directory. Once the physical address is known, the record can be retrieved.
- Direct-access file designs are accessed using online methods.
- Indexed-sequential processing is used when the same file may be required for sequential processing and single-record updates. A primary key is used to identify each unique record, and records are stored in sequence according to the primary key. Secondary keys are set up for those fields used to gain access to the file. The computer uses the key value to determine the approximate physical location of the record (or records), and then reads the records sequentially until the desired one is found.
- A data base is a grouping of data elements structured to fit the information needs of all departments of an organization. The data base reduces data duplication and increases efficiency and flexibility.
- A data-base management system (DBMS) is a set of programs that provides, among other things, (1) a method of arranging data to limit duplication; (2) the ability to make changes to the data easily; and (3) the ability to handle direct inquiries.
- Problems involved when microcomputers are used to access data bases include the updating, addition, or deletion of records by unauthorized users.
- Methods to secure data in data bases, include passwords, call-back modems, audit trails, and data encryption. These methods are not always easy to use with microcomputers.

REVIEW AND DISCUSSION QUESTIONS

1. How does a hierarchical data structure differ from a relational data structure?
2. How does a pointer link data records within a file?
3. How does a ring list differ from a simple list?
4. What three factors must be considered before a file can be designed?
5. What is the major problem in using fixed-length records?
6. What are the two most common methods of accessing a data file?
7. Define the term *key*. Explain the use of a key in sequential processing. How does the use of a key in direct-access processing differ from sequential processing?
8. Distinguish between a master file and a transaction file.
9. Explain the similarities between indexed-sequential processing and sequential processing. How is direct-access processing similar to indexed-sequential processing?
10. How does the computer use a directory during data retrieval?
11. What is a data base? How can it be structured to respond to a variety of inquiries?
12. Name three advantages of using a data base.
13. What problems are involved with using a call-back system to secure data bases accessed by microcomputers?
14. How can an organization ensure that the people using its data base are authorized users?
15. How much money should an organization invest in microcomputers before installing security protection devices?

CHAPTER 7
DATA COMMUNICATION

COMPUTERS IN OUR LIVES

Commuting by Computing

When Steven Roberts decided to experiment with a change in life-style and become a telecommuter, people sat up and took notice—in Denver, Key West, Dallas, Seattle, and some less well known but picturesquely named towns like Ocrecoke, North Carolina, and Christianburg, Ohio. Steven was not a typical telecommuter working from a three-bedroom ranch in surburbia. Instead, he chose to carry out his telecommuting experiment during a 14,000-mile odyssey looping about America. His preferred method of transportation on the journey was an eight-foot-long recumbent bicycle replete with the latest in high-tech gadgetry.

A free-lance writer with a special interest in computer technology, Steven wanted to prove that the "electronic cottage" is a concept that can be successfully implemented on the road. And he did. In addition to the fully equipped recumbent bicycle—a bicycle with a low center of gravity that permits the rider to pedal from a semi-reclining position—and assorted camping gear to approximate the comforts of home, the writer carried a Radio Shack Model 100 portable, which he used to compose stories on the road. A modem (a device used to send computer signals over telephone lines), the nearest pay phone, and CompuServe (a commercial communication network that provides information services for a variety of needs) linked Steven to his home base in Columbus, Ohio, where his assistant received files and handled such mundane tasks as managing the business. Freed from the restriction of a stuffy office, Steven enjoyed the sights and sounds of cross-country travel. The unusual vehicle and high-tech gadgets that made the trip possible piqued the curiosity of onlookers along the way, prompting one puzzled man to ask if Steven was from NASA!

Electronic communication and the nature of free-lance writing made it possible for Steven Roberts to work while enjoying the freedom of the road, but the principles of telecommuting can be applied to many other jobs and offer workers a degree of freedom seldom experienced in the past. Freedom from the frustration of traffic jams and the boredom of a nine-to-five routine, the opportunity to see family members more often, and the money saved by a company's not having to provide office space, are some of the benefits of telecommuting. But telecommuting is not for everyone—yet. Many people fear that working at home is tantamount to committing professional suicide. Some feel they have to be physically present in the office so they can play the game of office politics and not be passed up for pay raises and promotions. Others miss the daily interaction with coworkers that is both a social outlet and a means of gauging status within an organization through the body language of eye contact and gestures. They fear that without this daily interchange they will be unable to evaluate their job performance.

Despite these drawbacks, the University of Southern California's Center for Future Research predicts that by 1993 five million Americans will telecommute to the office. We live in an information age and since a person doesn't have to be at a specific location to change or convey ideas, electronic transmission is an ideal means of moving information. Before too long, as Steven Roberts has demonstrated, our entire concept of "going to work" may have to change.

Telecommuting is one aspect of a much broader field of computer development called data communication. The study of data communication includes such diverse topics as hardware, networks, and satellite communication. The following chapter discusses these and other aspects of data communication.

INTRODUCTION

Newer, more advanced processing techniques increasingly use some form of remote input/output (I/O) device in direct communication with the computer. Salespeople with POS terminals can communicate sales data directly to the computer as transactions occur, providing up-to-date sales and inventory figures. Banks with MICR applications process checks at incredible speeds, using the computer to keep track of check numbers and dollar amounts. Terminals with CRTs can be used for data input as well as information output. Whatever the form, direct communication with the computer can provide fast, up-to-the-minute information by reducing delays in the collection and dissemination of data.

This chapter discusses the concepts and techniques involved in message transmission and introduces the types of equipment that make data communication possible. It introduces the concept of computer networks and discusses the most popular types. Finally, satellite communication systems are discussed.

COMMUNICATION CHANNELS

Applications that use remote input/output devices must have some way of communicating with the computer. A **communication channel** is the pathway used to carry data from one location to another. It provides for the exchange of data between remote sites and the computer. Types of communication channels used for data transfer include telegraph lines, telephone lines, coaxial cables, microwave links, communication satellites, and laser beams.

The electronic transfer of data from one location to another is referred to as **data communication.** Data communication involves a microcomputer or a computer terminal connected to a large computer that contains a data base. For example, the Library of Congress data base is linked to terminals in local libraries throughout the United States. In a data communication system, data is transmitted between terminals and a central computer or even between two or more computers. The combined use of communication facilities such as telephone systems and data-processing equipment is called **telecommunications.** The increasing number of information systems involving geographically dispersed people and equipment have led to more emphasis being placed on the development of telecommunications facilities.

Communication channel A medium for carrying data from one location to another.

Telecommunications The combined use of communication facilities, such as telephone systems and data-processing equipment.

199

MESSAGE TRANSMISSION

Data can be transmitted over communication channels in analog or digital form. Transmission of data in continuous wave form is referred to as **analog transmission.** This is the type of transmission used on normal telephone lines. An analog transmission can be compared to the waves created by a stick in a pan of still water. The waves travel from the center of the pan to the edge without interruption. Messages are sent and received over telephone wires in the form of electronic "waves" that follow the path of the wire. In the past, analog transmission was the major means of relaying data over long distances, largely due to the type of communication lines provided by American Telephone and Telegraph (AT&T) (see Figure 7–1a). **Digital transmission** involves transmitting data as distinct "on" or "off" states, or pulses (see Figure 7–1b). This is often referred to as pulse form. The computers discussed in this book represent data in pulse form.

Analog transmission requires that the sender convert the data from the digital ("on" or "off") form in which it is stored to analog (wave) form before transmission. This conversion process is called **modulation.** Conversion from wave form to digital is required at the receiving end before the data is entered into the computer. This conversion is called **demodulation.** Both modulation and demodulation are accomplished by devices called **modems** (See Figure 7–2). The term *modem* is derived from the terms *mod*ulation and *dem*odulation.

Since telephone lines were originally designed for voice transmission in analog

Modem A device that modulates and demodulates signals transmitted over communication lines.

**Figure 7–1
Analog and Digital Transmission**

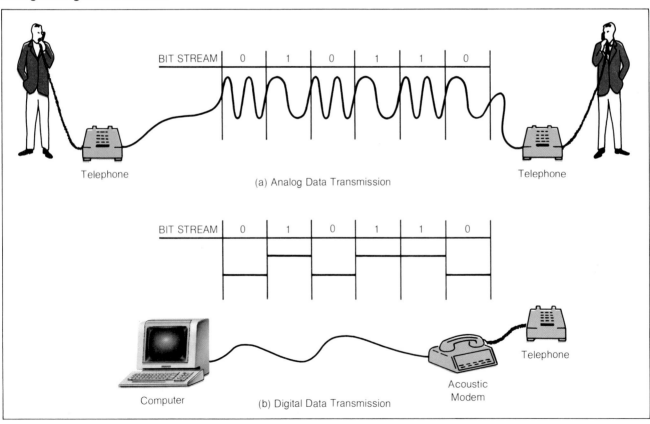

BIT STREAM | 0 | 1 | 0 | 1 | 1 | 0

Telephone

(a) Analog Data Transmission

Telephone

BIT STREAM | 0 | 1 | 0 | 1 | 1 | 0

Computer

(b) Digital Data Transmission

Acoustic Modem

Telephone

Figure 7–2
Modem in Use

form, a modem is needed to change the digital pulses from a computer into analog form for transmission over phone lines. Three types of modems are used for this purpose: (1) direct connect, (2) acoustic coupler, and (3) internal. A **direct-connect modem** is attached to the computer by a cable. The modem is also linked directly to the telephone line by a cord that plugs into a standard telephone jack. An **acoustic coupler modem** also connects to the computer by a cable, but the modem's link to the phone differs from a direct-connect modem. To link an acoustic coupler modem and a telephone, a standard contoured telephone receiver is placed on two rubber cups that are built into the modem. An **internal modem** is built in or plugged directly into the internal circuitry of the computer. An internal modem typically has dial-up capabilities and plugs directly into a standard telephone outlet, thus eliminating the need for a connection directly to a telephone.

Modes of Transmission

Transmission of data may occur in one of three basic modes: simplex, half-duplex, or full-duplex (see Figure 7–3). A **simplex** transmission is unidirectional, or one way. A simplex modem can either send or receive data; it cannot do both. A **half-duplex** modem can transmit data in two directions but only one way at a time. This type of transmission is commonly used in telephone services and telephone networks. A **full-duplex** modem can transmit data in both directions simultaneously. This is the most versatile type of transmission.

Speeds of Transmission

Data is transmitted at varying speeds. The speed at which a modem transmits data is referred to as **baud.** Baud is commonly identified as the number of bits per second that can be transmitted over particular communication lines. The two most common speeds at which modems transmit data for microcomputers

Simplex A type of communication channel that provides for unidirectional, or one-way, transmission of data.

Half-duplex A type of communication channel through which data can be transmitted in both directions, but in only one direction at a time.

Full-duplex A type of communication channel through which data can be transmitted in both directions simultaneously.

201

Figure 7–3
Channel Transmission Modes

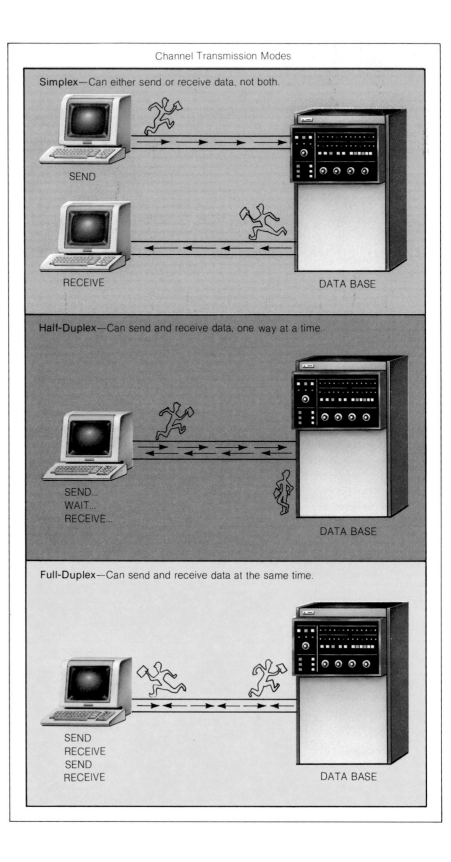

202

Is Faster Better?

A new type of modem to be used with microcomputers may make the confusing world of communications even more confusing. Users of communication hardware and software have had to contend with making decisions about things like 300- or 1,200-baud modems, seven or eight data bits, and carriage returns with line feed. The new object of confusion and controversy is the 2,400-baud modem. This device can send data at a rate twice as fast as 1,200-baud modems and four times faster than 300-baud modems. But users are asking themselves the question: Is faster better?

The problem with 2,400-baud modems centers around telephone lines. Phone lines were designed to carry low-fidelity sound—the kind of sound that is generated from voice conversation. Personal computers send asynchronous (irregular) signals. When these signals are sent at a rate greater than 300 baud, problems can arise. Problems show up in the form of "garbage" characters, which appear in data transmitted via 2,400-baud modems. The characters appear when poor quality telephone lines permit "noise" to mix with the computer's signal. Even users of 1,200-baud modems can run into trouble when transmitting data.

Attempts have been made to overcome this problem. Communication software has something called "error-control protocols." The error-control procedure checks for the presence of stray or missing bits of data. This sounds good, but it is only a partial solution to the problem. There are no industrywide standards for error control. Each communication software company has its own standard for error control. The consumer, then, must select from the range of communication software without really knowing what kind of error control performance to expect. Understandably, this can lead to a lot of confusion and a lot of garbled data!

Many consumers are handling the problem by simply not buying the new communications equipment. Others buy the modems and then do not use them. Consumers are recognizing that until the problem is solved, faster may not be better.

are 300 baud and 1,200 baud. A new type of modem for use with microcomputers can transmit at 2,400 baud. Unfortunately, problems with these faster modems have hampered their acceptance for use with microcomputers.

Software for Transmission

Communication software, also called **terminal software,** is used with a modem to complete data transmission. Basically, communication software helps a microcomputer temporarily become a part of the remote computer system with which it is communicating. In effect, the software "tricks" a computer into acting as if a microcomputer terminal is part of that system.

Communication software Programs that assist in the transfer of data across communication channels by "tricking" a computer into acting as if a microcomputer terminal is part of that system.

HIGHLIGHT

In the Movies

As the lights dim and moviegoers settle into their seats with a carton of hot buttered popcorn, most of the audience for the movie *2010: Odyssey Two* will probably be unaware that without computers the movie they are about to enjoy would probably never have been made. Two Kaypro computers and a communication link between Culver City, California, and Sri Lanka were largely responsible for the successful completion of the film.

Peter Hyams was commissioned to write the screenplay and produce the film *2010: Odyssey Two*. The movie was to be based on a story by Arthur C. Clark. Hyams was a great admirer of Clark's work and wanted the screenplay to retain the "Clark touch." This meant that Hyams and Clark would have to be in almost constant communication while the screenplay was being written. Unfortunately Clark lives on Colombo, an island in the Indian Ocean that is part of Sri Lanka, while Hyams has an office in Culver City, California.

The 13 time zones separating the two locations made frequent conventional telephone conversations impractical, and regular mail was too slow for the type of communication needed between the two men. The communication problem was solved with a first-of-its-kind (for Hollywood) communication link. Hyams chose two Kaypro computers, modems, and communication software to assist in the completion of the screenplay. The participants had daily discussions about the status of the screenplay while living literally on opposite sides of the globe. At the end of each workday, Hyams would leave his work in a file in the answer mode of his computer. Clark would begin his workday by calling Hyams' Kaypro and reviewing the file. Clark then made the appropriate changes to the file and sent it back to California.

The daily communication system between the two men was so successful that a book was published from the transcripts of their correspondence! *The Odyssey File* was published by Ballantine Books. The screenplay was successful, too; the movie was a hit. What could be more appropriate than using computers to help make a movie about the year 2010?

Digital transmission requires no conversion of data to analog because the computer stores data in pulse form. This reduces the time required to send messages. Digital transmission also has a much lower error rate (about 100 times lower) than analog transmission. These two facts mean that users can transmit large amounts of data faster and more reliably. Unfortunately, digital pulses cannot be sent over standard telephone lines. Data sent over phone lines must be transmitted in analog form via a modem. A remote terminal directly linked to a minicomputer or a mainframe transmits data in digital form.

Grades of Transmission

The **grade,** or **bandwidth,** of a channel determines the rate at which data can be transmitted across the channel. **Narrow bandwidth channels** can transmit data at a rate of 45 to 90 baud. Telegraph channels are typical narrow bandwidth channels.

Voice-grade channels have a wider frequency range; they can transmit data at rates of 300 to 9,600 baud. Voice-grade channels such as telephone lines are used by AT&T's Wide Area Telephone Service (WATS), and many others.

For applications that require high-speed transmission of large volumes of data, **broad-band channels** are most suitable. Coaxial cables, microwaves, and fiber optics belong in this category. Western Union offers a leased broad-band service. Such a service is capable of transmitting data at rates of up to 120,000 baud.

Bandwidth   The range, or width, of the frequencies available for transmission on a given channel.

Narrow bandwidth channel   A communication channel that can only transmit data at a rate of 45 to 90 baud; for example, telegraph channels.

Concept Summary 7–1 ▬ Message Transmission

Types of Modems	Modes of Transmission	Speeds of Transmission	Grades of Transmission
Direct-connect modem	Simplex	300 baud	Narrow bandwidth channels (45 to 90 baud)
Acoustic-coupler modem	Half-duplex	1200 baud	Voice-grade channels (300 to 9600 baud)
Internal Modem	Full-duplex	2400 baud	Broad-band channels (120,000 baud)

MULTIPLEXERS AND CONCENTRATORS

Multiplexers and **concentrators** increase the number of input/output (I/O) devices that can use a communication channel. It is advantageous to increase the number of devices that can use a channel because terminals operate at a much lower speed (100 to 150 baud) than communication channels (300 to 9,600 baud for voice grade). Thus, a channel is not used to full capacity by a single terminal.

Multiplexing can promote more economical use of the communication channel; it acts as a communication interface, combining the input streams from several devices into a single input stream that can be sent over a single channel to the computer system. This allows a single communication channel (typically voice grade) to substitute for many slower subvoice channels that might otherwise have been operating at less than full capacity. Once the computer system has completed processing, the output message is sent to the multiplexer, which then routes the message to the appropriate device.

A concentrator differs from a multiplexer in that it allows data from only one terminal at a time to be transmitted over a communication channel. The concentrator polls the terminals one at a time to see if they have any messages

Multiplexer   A device that permits more than one I/O device to transmit data over the same communication channel.

Concentrator   A device that systematically allocates communication channels among several terminals.

to send. When a communication channel is free, the first terminal ready to send or receive data will get control of the channel and continue to control it for the length of the transaction. The use of a concentrator relies on the assumption that not all terminals will be ready to send or receive data at a given time. Figure 7–4 shows examples of communication systems with and without multiplexers and concentrators.

PROGRAMMABLE COMMUNICATIONS PROCESSORS

Programmable communications processor A device that relieves the CPU of the task of monitoring data transmission.

A **programmable communications processor** is a device that relieves the CPU of many of the tasks typically required in a communication system. When the volume of data transmission surpasses a certain level, a programmable communications processor can handle these tasks more economically than the CPU. Examples of such tasks include handling messages and priorities, terminating transmission after messages have been received, requesting retransmission of incomplete messages, and verifying successfully transmitted messages.

Message switching The task of a communications processor of receiving messages and routing them to appropriate destinations.

Front-end processor A small CPU that performs a number of tasks and which serves as an interface between a large CPU and peripheral devices.

The two most frequent uses of communications processors are message switching and front-end processing. The principal task of the processor used for **message switching** is to receive messages and route them to appropriate destinations. A **front-end processor** performs message switching as well as more sophisticated operations, such as validating transmitted data and preprocessing data before it is transmitted to the central computer.

NETWORKS

The development of the communication channels discussed earlier made possible the development and widespread use of computer networks. A computer **network** is the linking together of CPUs and terminals via a communication system. A network allows users at different locations to share files, devices, and programs. Networks may be either remote or local.

Remote networks (also called wide-area networks) cover large, geographically dispersed areas. Communication between stations usually occurs via standard telephone lines, dedicated telephone lines, or microwave relays. Because of prohibitive costs, remote network use is generally restricted to large corporations.

A **local-area network (LAN)** operates within a well-defined and generally self-enclosed area, such as a small office building. The communication stations are usually linked by cable and are generally within 1,000 feet of each other. Distance is limited by the time required for the signal to travel from one workstation to the other and by the decrease in the strength of the signal as it travels over the cable.

In local-area networks, microcomputers can be linked together to share peripheral devices and information and also to provide the ability to communicate between members of the network. Sharing peripheral devices such as printers and mass storage devices can reduce costs on a per-computer basis. For example, four or five microcomputers may share a high-speed, high-quality letter-perfect printer and a hard-disk unit. The ability to share information is very important; information contained at a central location provides greater data

Figure 7–4
Communication Systems with and without Multiplexers and Concentrators

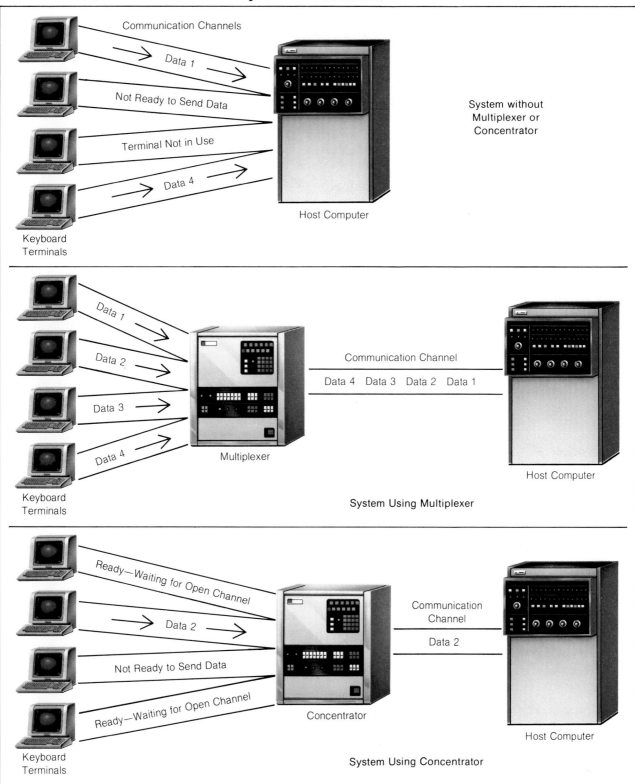

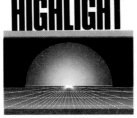

Legal Beagles Use Electronic Mail

In Montgomery County, Pennsylvania, lawyers are discovering that electronic mail can make their jobs much easier.

Montgomery County is proud of its computerized system for keeping track of court business. The system is one of the most advanced of any county government in the country. A Honeywell mainframe computer is responsible for keeping almost all court records online. Dial-up communication lines make calling the courthouse and checking on the status of cases easy for lawyers. Up-to-the-minute information is available on the filing of lawsuits, scheduling of cases, recording of judgments, collecting of alimony and child support, and selecting of juries. Attorneys simply dial the courthouse whenever they need current information.

The system has proven so successful that in one month it received over 8,500 calls for information. County officials predict that the number of calls will increase by at least 35 percent a year. Connections to the courthouse network can be made via personal computers, regular terminals, or communicating word processors. The system is free to all users.

The Montgomery County systems designer, Robert MacNeel, describes the typical attorney as having 150 active cases. That means simple jobs like scheduling and checking on court dockets can sometimes be quite complex. The computerized system makes calling the courthouse computer and checking on court dockets and schedules in a matter of minutes possible for lawyers.

The National Center for State Courts approves of the system and has suggested that Montgomery County be used as a model by other courts computerizing their records.

integrity (accuracy and timeliness) and is accessed or updated in a timely fashion from any number of locations within the network.

The ability to communicate among members of the network is also an important consideration. **Electronic mail** is one means of network communication. Electronic mail allows one member of the network to send a message to another member. If the member receiving the message is not currently connected to the network, the message will be saved until the next time he or she connects to the network. Electronic mail can eliminate many of the unnecessary calls and return calls of a telephone message process.

The advantages of a local-area network are numerous and should not be overlooked in an environment that uses multiple microcomputers. Among other things, a LAN permits users to share hardware, software, and data. This sharing of resources reduces costs for the users and helps provide a more direct means of communicating.

Architecture

As with a single CPU and its terminals, a network's CPUs can be hooked together to form either local or remote systems. All networks are comprised of two basic structures: nodes and links. A **node** refers to the end points of a network and consists of CPUs, printers, terminals, and other physical devices. **Links** are the transmission channels that connect the nodes.

Nodes and links can be arranged in a number of different types of network architecture. Some of the more common are star, ring, hierarchical, and bus. Figure 7–5 illustrates the star, ring, and hierarchical, configurations. Figure 7–6 illustrates the bus and fully distributed configurations.

In a **star configuration,** all transactions must go through a central computer before being routed to the appropriate network computer. This creates a central decision point, which facilitates workload distribution and resource sharing, but it exposes the system to single-point vulnerability. When the central computer breaks down, all the nodes in the network are disabled. An alternative approach uses a number of computers connected to a single transmission line in a **ring configuration.** This type of system can bypass a malfunctioning unit without disrupting operations throughout the network.

A more sophisticated approach is the **hierarchical configuration,** which consists of a group of small computers tied into a large, central computing complex. Under this approach, an organization's needs are divided into multiple levels, which are controlled by the single computer at the top of the hierarchy. The

Star configuration A network design in which all transactions must go through a central computer prior to being routed to the appropriate network computer.

Ring configuration A network design in which a number of computers are connected by a single transmission line in a ring.

Hierarchical configuration A network design for multiple CPUs, in which an organization's needs are divided into multiple levels that receive different levels of computer support.

Figure 7–5
Network Configurations

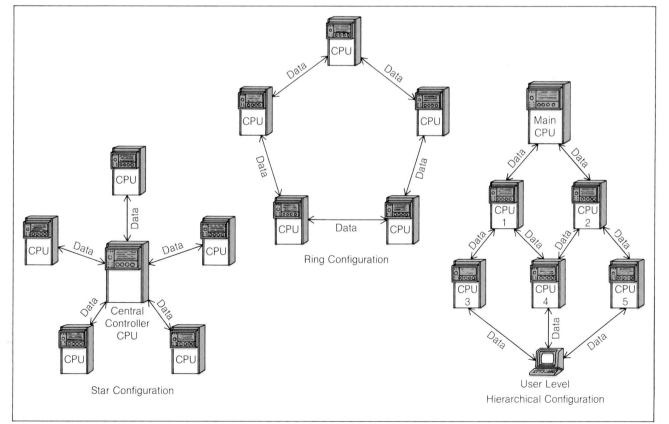

Ring Configuration

Star Configuration

User Level
Hierarchical Configuration

Figure 7–6
Bus and Fully Distributed
Configurations

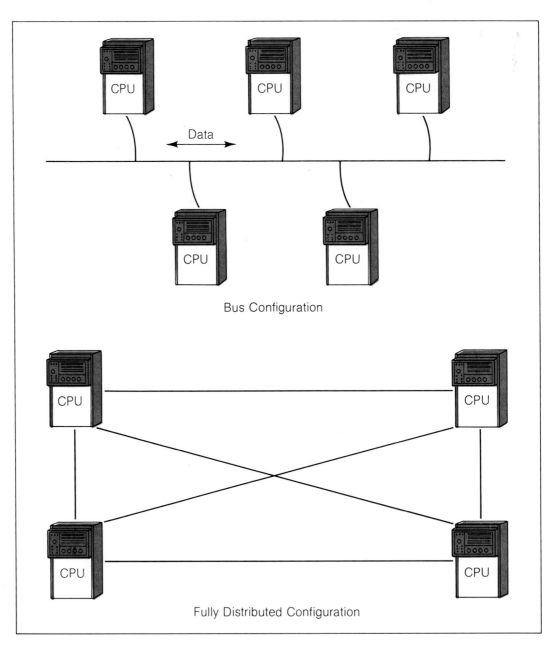

Bus Configuration

Fully Distributed Configuration

lowest level is the user level, where only routine transaction-processing power is supplied. This level is connected to the next higher level and its associated information system. At each higher level, the machine size increases while the need for distribution decreases.

HIGHLIGHT

Electronic Copyrights

Imagine you are participating in an electronic conference. One of the conference participants at another location makes a comment that sparks an idea in your mind. You quickly send your thought through the electronic network and other conference participants add to your idea. When the conference is over, who owns your idea? Suppose the organizer of the conference collects the ideas that resulted from the meeting and publishes them for a profit. Should you share in the wealth?

The question of ownership of ideas that are a result of electronic conferences is rapidly becoming an issue in the 1980s. Many people feel that information generated as the result of an electronic conference should be considered public domain. They feel that electronic conferences are just another form of communicating through public information channels similar to radio or television. Richard Baker of CompuServe calls conferences "a public exchange of information."

Not everyone agrees with Mr. Baker, but almost everyone does agree that the question of ownership is complex. The Copyright Act of 1976 addresses the ownership issue by implying that individual contributions to an electronic conference are owned by the person making the contribution. The ideas alone are not copyrightable, but the words used to express the ideas can be copyrighted. The owner of the entry has five years in which to obtain a copyright of the material. If the owner takes no action within that period of time, he or she forfeits the right to ownership. If the material is displayed without a copyright symbol, one can assume that no copyright on the material exists.

The Copyright Act of 1976 only scratches the surface of this complex issue. Industry experts feel they need further standards addressing the rights of electronic distribution. Successfully managing the problem now will prevent a rash of lawsuits in the future.

The **bus configuration** is used primarily with local-area networks. In a bus configuration, each computer plugs into a single bus cable that runs from workstation to workstation. Each computer must have its own interface that connects it to the network. As messages travel along the bus cable, stations monitor the cable and retrieve their own messages. If one node in a bus configuration breaks down, the system can still function effectively.

A **fully distributed network configuration** is one in which every set of nodes in the network can communicate directly with every other set of nodes through a single communications link. Each local system has its own processing capabilities.

Distributed data processing (DDP) A system in which data processing is done at a site other than that of the central computer.

Distributed Computing

The concept of **distributed data processing (DDP)** involves processing that, to some degree, is done at a site independent of the central computer system. A distributed system may be contrasted with a centralized approach in which all data-processing resources are in a common physical location and administrative unit within an organization. The amount and type of processing that takes place at a distributed site varies from company to company, depending on the structure and management philosophy of the company. A distributed data processing system requires the use of a communications network that may conform to any of the network configurations discussed earlier.

Figure 7–7 shows a distributed system consisting of three dispersed minicomputers connected by communication linkages to a central computer. The three minicomputers are located in three separate colleges of a large university—the College of Business, the College of Musical Arts, and the College of Education. Each college has its own processing requirements. Some of the information generated by the minicomputers is communicated to the central

Figure 7–7
Distributed Data Processing System

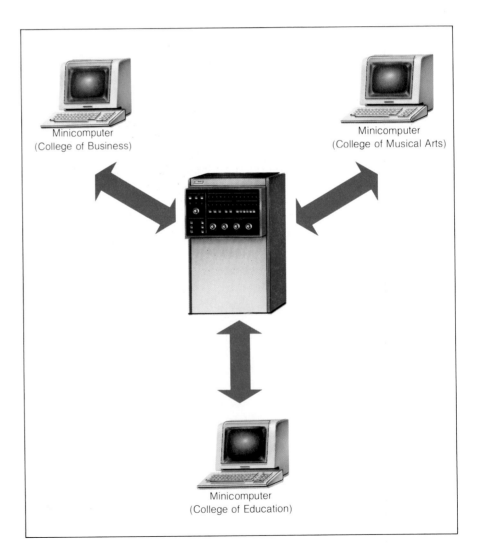

Minicomputer
(College of Business)

Minicomputer
(College of Musical Arts)

Minicomputer
(College of Education)

computer to be used in universitywide planning and control. Such a network provides fast response and great flexibility to local system users. Furthermore, the central facility is available to users for jobs that require computing power beyond the capabilities of the minicomputers.

This approach to distributed data processing gives the various functional areas the ability to process data independently of the central computer, as well as to communicate data required by the entire organization to the central computer. Some information generated in the functional areas can be communicated to the central computer to be used in organizationwide planning and control.

Since an organization's managerial philosophy normally determines the type of system and the amount of processing done at a distributed site, a company with a strong, centralized managerial philosophy will normally do the majority of its processing at one central location. A company with a decentralized managerial philosophy will do a large amount of processing at distributed sites, with the central computer serving primarily as a communication link among various sites. As the technology in data communication improves and computers become more widely used at dispersed locations, the importance and use of distributed data processing will grow. The following example explains how the Norfolk Southern Railway Company uses a distributed system.

Norfolk Southern Railway Company

Norfolk Southern Railway Company operates a sophisticated network of minicomputers in a distributed approach. This system, located at the Sheffield, Alabama, automatic railroad classification yard, was completed in 1973. The project cost $15 million and took 2½ years to complete. The computer activity is divided into two systems, a management information system (MIS) and a process control (PC) system. Five minicomputers are linked together to form these systems—two on PC, one on MIS, and two on backup (see Figure 7–8).

The system is connected to a large computer installation in Atlanta, Georgia, from which the information flow begins. About two hours before a train is scheduled to arrive in Sheffield, the Atlanta computer transmits a message to Sheffield. The message consists of the makeup of the train, car sequence, destination, weight, and other pertinent information. This data is stored by the MIS minicomputer. A hard copy is printed to assist in planning.

The MIS minicomputer is accessed by the yard supervisor via a CRT. The yard supervisor determines which receiving track the cars will go onto and enters this data into the computer. At this point, the PC minicomputers take over.

A small hill is located at the end of the receiving track. Each inbound car is moved over the hill and onto one of 32 classification tracks. Based on the data entered by the yard supervisor, the PC computers determine which classification track is appropriate. The system also controls car movement and speed. Each car is pushed onto the receiving track at a speed under four miles per hour. Track switching is also controlled by the system.

The PC systems are connected to the MIS minicomputer. The PC computers transmit data about each car including sequence, destination, and contents. The MIS minicomputer prepares a list of this information, and the list is compared to the actual composition of the train. A controlled automated system is achieved. Southern Railway operates its Sheffield station 24 hours a day. Backup

Figure 7–8
Norfolk Southern Railway's Distributed System

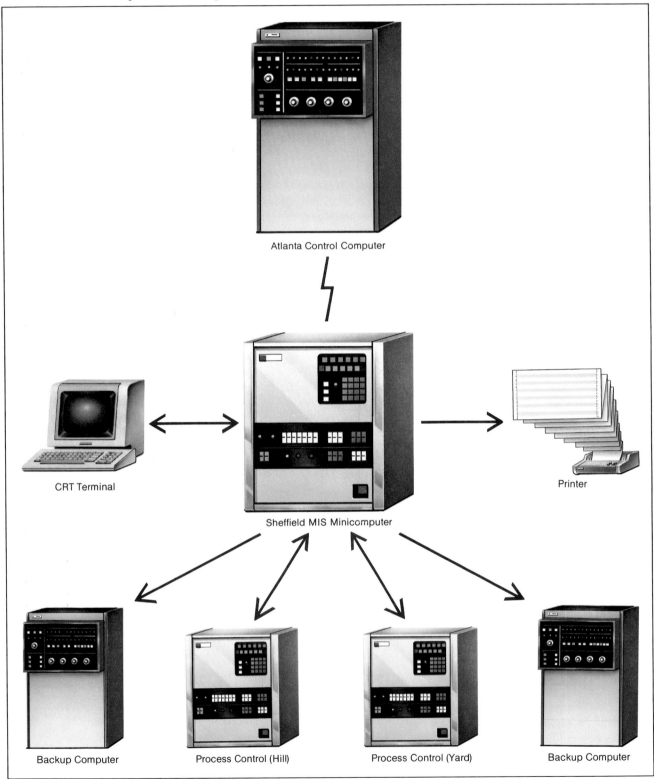

Atlanta Control Computer

CRT Terminal

Sheffield MIS Minicomputer

Printer

Backup Computer

Process Control (Hill)

Process Control (Yard)

Backup Computer

minicomputers stand by in case of breakdown. This application demonstrates how Southern Railway depends on the high reliability of a distributed system.

SATELLITE COMMUNICATION SYSTEMS

The networks discussed earlier are earth-based. Today many networks rely on the use of satellite communication channels to extend their ranges to other continents. However, satellite-based networks are very expensive, primarily because they need earth stations (small dishlike antennas and associated communications equipment) to send and receive messages from the satellites. In the past, satellites have been used mainly for voice and television transmission. However, satellite communication is becoming increasingly attractive for business applications. Satellites can be used by dispersed companies to save time and money in the transfer of voice and data. Communication can be extended across the country or around the world (see Figure 7–9).

Figure 7–9
Satellite Communication System

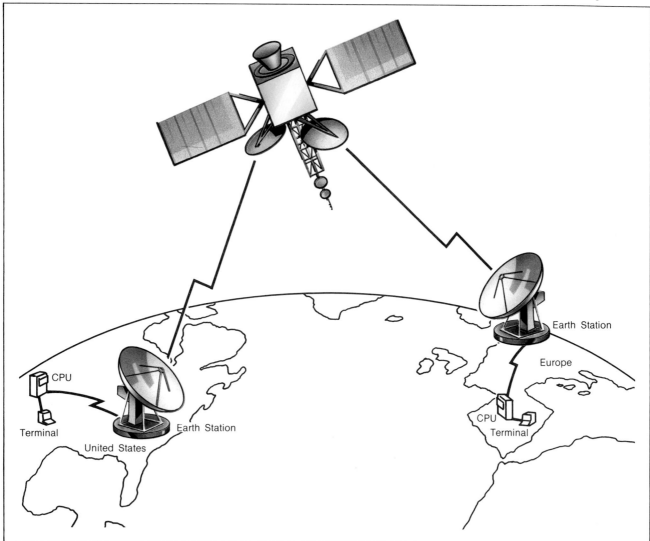

Home Banking

Recently, one of the biggest problems most nine-to-five workers had with banking was getting to the bank during business hours. Banks were usually open only during normal business hours, and most workers could not leave their jobs to handle financial transactions. A few years ago, banks began offering after-hours banking at 24-hour automatic teller machines that can handle withdrawals, deposits, and, in some cases, electronic transfer of funds between accounts. Still, a trip to the bank was involved. Now, with personal computers in more and more homes, banks are preparing to handle home banking.

Home banking requires that the customer have a computer at home and a modem for connecting with the bank's computer via telephone lines. The customer can transfer funds between his or her accounts or pay bills with a few keystrokes rather than drive to the bank. In fact, with many institutions and businesses offering employees direct deposit of paychecks, going to the bank may become a thing of the past.

Home banking has been in the experimental stages for some years, but recently Bank of America opened the service to all its northern California customers. If all goes well with Bank of America's venture, home banking could become the norm in a few years.

In the development of satellites over the past two decades, several problems have emerged that do not exist with terrestrial networks. While satellite communication is a cost-effective method for large companies, it is a very capital- and equipment-intensive industry and satellites must compete with AT&T's existing land-based network. People generally agree that satellites are not a substitute for ground networks. Measures must be taken to guard against such things as time delays (also called **propagation delays), downtime** (the time the system is not working because of equipment problems), security problems, natural disasters, and even war. And since satellites are often connected to land-based networks, precautions must be taken to avoid possible incompatibility.

Propagation delay A time delay in a satellite communication system.

Downtime The time a system is not working because of equipment problems.

Current Satellite Usage

One of the advantages of satellite systems is the capability of transmitting data using a broad bandwidth. This means that more data can be transmitted at a faster rate than with narrow bandwidth (such as telegraph lines) or voice-grade bandwidth (telephone lines). In addition, the ability to transmit data from a multitude of locations adds to the effectiveness of satellite usage.

Satellite systems consist of earth stations, or "dishes," that send and receive signals to an orbiting satellite. Located on the satellite itself are a number of **transponders,** small amplifiers that receive the signals from the earth station and reflect them to the appropriate receiving location. A single satellite usually consists of 24 transponders. Each transponder can carry one television channel or 1,200 voice channels, or it can be used to transmit a stream of data.

Transponders Small amplifiers located on satellites, which receive signals transmitted from earth stations and reflect them to receiving stations.

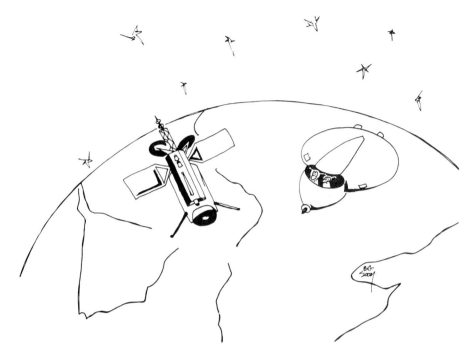

"No, it's not a filling station. Now what?"

To set up a satellite system, the satellite must first be built and launched. This requires a substantial capital investment, often millions of dollars. Once the satellite is in orbit, other companies may lease service from the owner of the satellite. Those companies must then either lease or buy an earth station.

Western Union, a leader in the communication industry, was the first company to establish a commercial system whereby companies could lease satellite services. Western Union satellites, referred to as the Westar system, are being used in a multitude of services; Westar not only provides services to the broadcast industry, but also is being used for transmitting text and photographs for regional printing of *The Wall Street Journal, U.S. News and World Report, Time, People* and *Sports Illustrated.* In addition, Western Union has entered the new and expanding area of video conferencing. For example, Texas Instruments, Inc. leased time from a Westar satellite to broadcast its annual stockholder's meeting. The meetings, held in Dallas, were shown in 22 regional offices.

Concept Summary 7–2 ▬ Network Architecture

Structure	Feature
Star	All transactions go through a central computer: single-point vulnerability.
Ring	All computers connected to a single transmission line, but malfunctioning units are bypassed.
Hierarchical	Organizational needs are divided into multiple levels. A single computer controls the hierarchy.
Bus	Used primarily with local area networks. Each computer must have an interface to connect to the bus cable that links the machines.

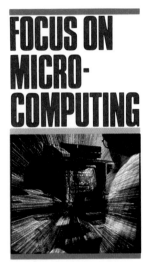

FOCUS ON MICRO-COMPUTING

Communication Networks

A. C. Markkula, former president of Apple Computers, predicts that by the year 2000 a personal computer will be as necessary as an automobile is now. His projection is based on the anticipated use of microcomputers as telecommunicators between the individual and huge data banks. Nearly everyone will have as much information available as could be provided by the best of libraries, and it will be easier to access. Neither the location of the individual nor the cost associated with transmission will be a hinderance to getting good information.

Networks established by and for individuals with shared interests are cropping up all over the country. These systems allow individuals to exchange a wide range of information from favorite recipes to the latest in home computer games. Communication networks are not restricted to the ingenuity of the individual. There are several commercial network services available to subscribers. Two of the largest are The Source and Dow Jones/Retrieval Service. A third, CompuServe, Inc., owned by H&R Block, provides an example of the developments and growth of this industry. CompuServe offers a huge data bank full of interesting information. The following is a partial list of topics offered:

- Home record keeping
- SAT test information
- News
- Travel
- Shopping
- Games
- Tax advice
- College financial aid
- Theater listings
- Trivia
- Science
- Medicine

CompuServe was established in 1969 as a computer time-sharing service. The strategy has been to offer problem-solving computer services to individuals and companies. CompuServe is the nation's largest information and communication service with over 200,000 subscribers in 500 U.S. cities. The company also serves more than 42 foreign countries via satellite links.

The network was initially structured in a star configuration. Each regionally located remote communications processor was connected with the computing center in Columbus, Ohio. This arrangement was functional and cost effective, but reliability was a problem. There was only one communication path for each message. As the field of home information services expanded, CompuServe had to experiment with and improve its network structure.

A new structure was developed as the network grew. CompuServe set up a ring configuration to allow remote links to more than one processor. If a direct path breaks down, a message can still be routed around the ring and into the computing center in Columbus. The new system is more costly than the old, but the structure is more reliable.

CompuServe provides information services for a variety of needs to individuals, groups, companies, and even the government. Interchange is a service designed for businesses. The service relays information to managers, sales representatives, and customers on the CompuServe network. Authorized users need only push a button or two to access information on a variety of topics, including price schedules, order status reports, inventory availability, and training programs. The service provides up-to-the-minute information faster and more reliably than conventional forms of communication (phone or mail).

The CompuServe data base offers the widest variety of information of any data base in the country. More than 50 educational, adventure, and sports games are available through the service. Many are interactive; a player in Albuquerque might compete against a player in Philadelphia. Comp-U-Store is an electronic catalog of over 60,000 items. Travel America offers 24-hour travel assistance including information on scheduling, prices, and reservations. Telesports has the latest in-depth information about both professional and collegiate sports. The service may be updated as often as five times an hour. The weather information service, NOAA, has state, extended, marine, and aviation forecasts. The CB Simulator allows users to "talk" to fellow subscribers. This service was so popular that a mainframe computer was added to the system to handle all the calls.

CompuServe is only one example of a network service that is growing. As microcomputers increase in number and the information needs of society grow, communication networks will continue to improve their services to personal computer users. Prices for using CompuServe vary, but rates for peak daytime hours are higher than for evening.

SUMMARY POINTS

- Data communication is the electronic transmission of data from one location to another, usually over communication channels such as telephone or telegraph lines, coaxial cables, or microwaves. The combined use of data-processing equipment and communication facilities, such as telephone systems, is called telecommunications.
- Data can be transmitted over communication channels in analog or digital form. The transmission of data in continuous wave form is referred to as analog transmission. Digital transmission involves transmitting data in distinct "on" or "off" states.
- Modulation is the process of converting data from the pulse ("on" or "off") form used by the computer to a wave form used for message transmission over communication lines. Demodulation is the process of converting the received message from wave form back to pulse form. These functions are performed by devices called modems.
- The three types of modems are direct-connect, acoustic coupler, and internal. These modems are capable of three types of transmission: simplex, half-duplex, or full-duplex. Simplex modems transmit data unidirectionally; half-duplex modems transmit data in two directions but only one way at a time; full-duplex modems can transmit data in both directions simultaneously. Data is transmitted by modems at variable speeds, the most common speeds used with microcomputers are 300 baud and 1,200 baud.

- The grade (or bandwidth) of a channel determines the rate at which data can be transmitted across the channel.
- Multiplexers and concentrators increase the number of devices that can use a communication channel.
- A programmable communications processor is a device that relieves the CPU of many of the tasks typically required in a communication system. The two most frequent tasks of communications processors are message switching and front-end processing.
- A computer network is the linking together of several CPUs and terminals via a communication system. These systems may be either remote or local systems.
- Five common network configurations are star, ring, hierarchical, bus, and the full distributed configuration. In the star configuration, all transactions must go through a central computer. A ring configuration uses a number of computers connected to a single transmission line. A malfunctioning unit can be bypassed without disrupting operations throughout the network. A hierarchical configuration consists of a group of small computers tied into a large central computing complex. A bus configuration is used primarily with local area networks; each computer plugs into a single bus cable that runs from workstation to workstation.
- Local area networking involves interconnecting computers in a single building or a complex of buildings.
- Electronic mail is a means of network communication in which one member of the network sends a message to another member.
- Distributed data processing involves processing that, to some degree, is done at a site independent of the central computer system.
- Today many networks rely on the use of satellite communication channels to extend their ranges. Satellite systems are capable of transmitting data using a wide bandwidth, so more data can be transmitted at a faster rate than with narrow or voice-grade bandwidths.
- Commercial network services such as CompuServe of Columbus, Ohio, offer a huge data bank of information to subscribers. CompuServe's network configuration has changed from a star to a ring configuration.

REVIEW AND DISCUSSION QUESTIONS

1. What is a communication channel? Name some common forms of communication channels.
2. Distinguish between analog and digital transmission.
3. What are modems? What purpose do they serve in data communication?
4. Distinguish among simplex, half-duplex, and full-duplex transmission modes.
5. What is the purpose of communication in data communications?
6. Of what significance is bandwidth in data communications? Distinguish among narrow, voice-grade, and broad bandwidths.
7. How do multiplexers and concentrators aid in processing?
8. Describe the star, ring, and hierarchical network configurations.
9. Why might an organization choose a distributed data-processing system?
10. What distinguishes a local area network from other distributed data-processing systems?

11. Describe a satellite communication system.
12. Why did CompuServe change from a star to a ring configuration?
13. Describe why the ring configuration would be more reliable than the star configuration network.
14. What topics other than those shown in the sample listing for CompuServe would be of use to the personal computer owner for home or business?

CHAPTER 8

COMPUTER SYSTEMS

COMPUTERS IN OUR LIVES

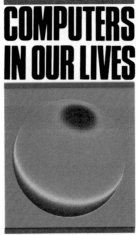

Supercomputers and Super Chess Players

At the Association for Computing Machinery's fifteenth annual North American Computer Chess tournament, the winner was the Cray Blitz computer program. The Cray Blitz program, which defended its title in a four-game sweep over its electronic opponent, is considered to be among the two or three best chess programs in existence.

The Cray Blitz runs on the Cray XMP-48 supercomputer, one of the fastest and most sophisticated machines made. But if Cray is to continue winning chess championships with its computers and software, it will need help.

The United States is falling behind in the race for supercomputer development. Universities in the United States have not kept pace with universities in other countries in purchasing supercomputers, and as a result, research efforts have lagged. (Only three schools in the United States have purchased class IV supercomputers—the most advanced supercomputers available on the market today.) Additionally, training in the operation of the machines has not kept pace with the demand because there are so few supercomputers on campuses. The United States is simply not producing enough professionals who know how to work with these computers. Even if the United States does pull forward in technological advances, enough people may not be available to staff the next generation of supercomputers.

One of the major problems universities in the United States face in doing supercomputer research is money. The supermachines are very expensive to buy and operate. Access charges may run as high as $2,000 to $3,000 an hour, and few universities have the funds to support such operating costs. In Japan, where the government subsidizes fees, charges may be as low as $60 an hour. Although the National Science Foundation recommended that Congress appropriate $520 million to help ten universities purchase supercomputers and establish nationwide access networks, at present, many researchers cannot afford to use existing machines, leaving most university supercomputers underused. The University of Colorado owns a supercomputer that runs only 20 to 30 percent of the time.

Money—for operation, research, and programs—is needed. To spur the development of supercomputer technology, U.S. government agencies are sponsoring renewed efforts in time-consuming and expensive supercomputer research. Such research may be complex, but even writing programs for supercomputers is not simple—or cheap.

The Cray Blitz chess program was developed by Bob Hyatt, Harry Nelson, and Albert Glower. The three estimate that collectively they spent 32,000 hours developing the program over an eight-year period. They feel their work was worth the effort. The Blitz is the World Computer Chess Champion as well as the North American Chess Champion. The program is ranked as "high expert"—the level just below "master."

With the help of government funding, perhaps universities in the United States can move forward in the race to develop supercomputer technology and give our country a "high expert" or "master" ranking once again. The following chapter discusses the technological development of supercomputers, as well as minicomputers and mainframes.

INTRODUCTION

During the past two decades, all aspects of the computer market have experienced rapid growth. New products and computer systems are constantly being introduced to perform a range of tasks from monitoring fuel mixtures in automobiles to modeling the economics of nations.

This chapter identifies and discusses three categories of computers: minicomputers, mainframes, and supercomputers (or maxicomputers). Characteristics and appropriate applications are described for the systems in each category. The chapter also discusses important market trends and vendor support within each market sector. The software market and computer services offered by service bureaus and time-sharing companies are discussed toward the end of the chapter.

MINICOMPUTERS

Characteristics

Minicomputers were first developed in the 1960s. **Minicomputers** were originally smaller, less powerful, and less expensive than the larger mainframe computers. But the distinction between minicomputers and mainframes has become blurred. Advances in technology have moved minicomputers toward mainframe computers in terms of capability, memory size, and overall processing power. The minicomputers manufactured today are more powerful than the mainframe computers manufactured ten years ago.

Minicomputers manufactured today are generally easier to install and operate than mainframe computers. The smaller computers take up less floor space than mainframes. They may fit on a desk, or they may be as large as a file cabinet. They require few special environmental conditions. Minicomputers can be plugged into standard electrical outlets and often do not require special facilities such as air conditioning and water cooling. Prices for minicomputers range from a few thousand dollars to two or three hundred thousand dollars.

Minicomputers have come a long way since their initial development for specific applications such as inventory control and engineering calculations. Current minicomputers are more flexible, provide greater capabilities, and support a full line of peripherals (see Figure 8–1). The growth in minicomputer applications has led to the concept of distributed processing. Minicomputers are also used in time-sharing applications, numerical control of machine tools, industrial automation and word processing.

Minicomputer A type of computer with the components of a full-sized system but a smaller primary storage capacity.

225

Figure 8–1
Sperry Minicomputer System with Peripherals

Flexibility The degree to which a computer system can be adapted or tailored to the changing requirements of the user.

The **flexibility** of minicomputers has led to their tremendous popularity. They can be used in an unlimited number of configurations. For example, a minicomputer system for a small firm may consist of a visual display terminal, a disk storage unit, and a printer (see Figure 8–2). A large distributed system may consist of hundreds of minicomputers and peripherals tied together by communication channels to meet the needs of a geographically dispersed organization.

Another important advantage of a minicomputer system is that it can be enlarged to meet the needs of a growing organization since it can be implemented in a modular fashion. For example, a hospital may install one minicomputer in its outpatient department for record keeping and another in the pharmacy or laboratory. As additional minicomputers are installed, they can be connected to existing ones to share common data. An individual minicomputer can be expanded in a modular fashion to increase disk storage space.

In the late 1970s and early 1980s, the minicomputer industry grew at a rate of 35 to 40 percent annually. However, increased capabilities of microcomputers along with improved software for the small machines has led to the increased use of microcomputers in traditional minicomputer markets. Many companies are now linking microcomputers with minicomputers to hold down equipment investment costs and still meet processing needs.

There are many manufacturers of minicomputers. Leading manufacturers include Digital Equipment Corporation (DEC), Hewlett-Packard, Data General, Honeywell, General Automation, Burroughs, Texas Instruments, and IBM. Smaller manufacturers include Wang Laboratories, Systems Engineering Laboratories, Inc. (SEL), and Prime Computer, Inc.

Applications

In many cases, minicomputers are used in conjunction with communication facilities to provide remote processing capabilities (see Chapter 7). Most vendors

226

in the minicomputer sector offer telecommunications equipment to provide powerful, flexible computing capabilities.

Before the advent of distributed processing, many organizations depended on large, centrally located computers. As user needs increased, these computers became overloaded. Centralized computer departments were not able to respond quickly to user requirements. To reduce the workload on their large computers users began to replace or supplement them with a number of minicomputers at the locations where processing was required. Figure 8–3 diagrams an example of a distributed minicomputer system.

Vendor Support

At the center of a minicomputer system is the software that directs its operations. For example, a minicomputer and peripherals alone are not enough to implement a distributed system. Many hardware vendors sell software packages to accompany their hardware. The vendors realize that low cost and performance will no longer sell their products. Efficient software is a primary key to selling hardware. Several firms specialize in software development, although software

Figure 8–2
Diagram of a Small Minicomputer System

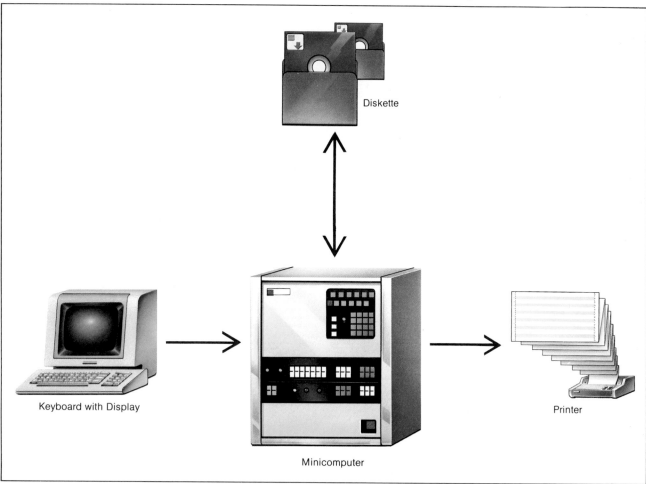

Diskette

Keyboard with Display

Minicomputer

Printer

Figure 8–3
Distributed Minicomputer System

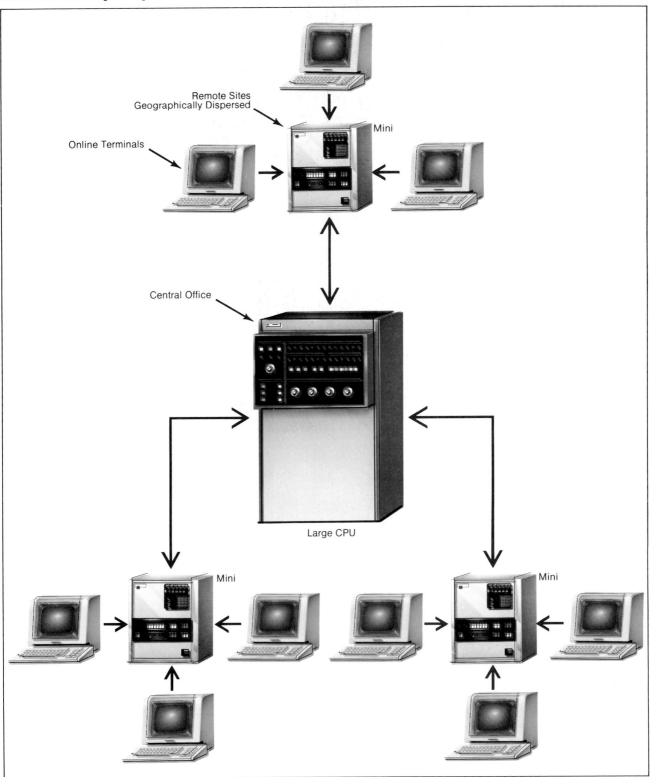

Remote Sites
Geographically Dispersed

Online Terminals

Mini

Central Office

Large CPU

Mini

Mini

HIGHLIGHT

Micros Outshine Minis

Computer vendors had a heyday in the early 1980s as sales of microcomputers soared. Many homes and small businesses followed the trend and bought their first computers. Computer stores, specializing in microcomputer hardware and software, sprang up in shopping areas across the country.

Minicomputers, long the mainstay of larger businesses and institutions, held their own in sales at first. But as the microcomputer grew in popularity and capability, the growth rate of minicomputer sales slowed. The microcomputer began to infringe on what was once considered sacred minicomputer territory. Several developments, including lower prices, networking capabilities, better software packages, and increased storage capacity, help to explain the market's preference for microcomputers in the mid- to late-1980s.

Minicomputer vendors lost most of their sales at the expensive end of the product line. Most user companies, whether or not they were new in the computer market, chose microcomputer networking or small, less-expensive minicomputer systems over more expensive machines. The largest growth in computer sales occurred in the workstation category: desktop terminals and microcomputers that could link with a data network, reducing the need for more expensive minicomputers.

Many businesses consider the availability of quality software by far the most important criterion in choosing a microcomputer. Microcomputer software packages are generally of higher quality than the software packages available for minicomputers. Four software packages—Lotus 1-2-3, Wordstar, dBase II, and VisiCalc—accounted for most microcomputer software purchases in the mid-1980s. Software programs that previously required the minicomputer's larger storage capacity can now run on microcomputers.

can also be developed by the user. But software development is a time-consuming and costly process that few users choose to pursue. Many users prefer to buy prewritten software packages and tailor the software to their specific needs. Indeed, when choosing a minicomputer system, managers often select an available software package, then choose the hardware that supports the software they need.

Many application software packages have been developed for specific in-dustries, such as transportation, manufacturing, hospitals, food companies, and many more. Accounting packages contain programs for accounts receivable, payroll, order entry, billing, and general ledger.

System software now available for minicomputers includes high-level lan-guage translators for FORTRAN, BASIC, COBOL, RPG, and other languages and data-base management systems, data dictionaries, and program development aids that allow users to develop their own application programs.

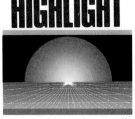

Infoshare Networks Micros and Minis

It's bigger than a bread box and smaller than a footlocker—only 7 by 16 by 17 inches. Yet up to 16 microcomputers equipped with an inexpensive TeleVideo PM Interface can hook up to TeleVideo's Personal Minicomputer PM/16. This powerful minicomputer, called by some a "network in a box," allows IBM PC users to work together on data-processing projects without data entries and revisions—that eventually will be merged, updated, and checked for accuracy—having to be made on each user's disk.

This type of networking, or linking computers together, uses an operating system called Infoshare. Infoshare does more than traditional networking. It increases the capabilities of each personal computer linked to it. While logged onto the network system, each connected personal computer, or workstation, has access to the minicomputer's memory capacity. Users can operate their personal computers as standalone computers, access a variety of programs stored in PM/16, or share information with another personal computer that is logged onto the network.

The PM/16 minicomputer does not process data. It provides access to programs and disk storage. Actual processing takes place at the workstation with a personal computer.

One of PM/16's most amazing abilities—allowing more than one workstation to access and run a program at the same time—saves users valuable time. PM/16's Infoshare prevents the bottlenecks that commonly occur on other network systems when users share files and must wait for programs to be free. PM/16 also offers security measures not often found in minicomputer systems.

Minicomputer users, then, are finding it increasingly attractive to purchase software packages. The packages decrease the need for in-house data-processing staff and make it possible to implement total systems within relatively short time periods. Given the number and variety of packages available, most users can purchase software that meets their data-processing needs. The software market will be discussed in more detail in a later section.

MAINFRAME COMPUTERS

Characteristics

Mainframe A type of large, full-scale computer capable of supporting many peripherals.

The heart of the large-scale computer is the **mainframe.** During the 1960s the term *mainframe* was synonymous with CPU. Today the word refers simply to a computer that is more powerful than a minicomputer (see Figure 8–4). A mainframe computer can process large amounts of data at very high speeds,

Figure 8–4
Mainframe Computer System

holds millions of characters in primary storage, and supports many input, output, and auxiliary storage devices.

When several mainframe computers of differing sizes are built by the same manufacturer and have the same processor, they are said to be in the same **family of computers.** The computers share common processing capabilities and can run many of the same programs. The sharing of software with few or no changes is known as **software compatibility.** This feature makes it possible for users to acquire larger systems that can run the same or modified software as smaller mainframes are outgrown, thus saving the cost of new software.

IBM was one of the first computer manufacturers to produce a family of computers with software compatibility. In the 1970s IBM produced the IBM System/370 series of mainframes (see Figure 8–5). Many of those machines

Family of computers Mainframes of differing sizes built by the same manufacturer and having the same processor.

Software compatibility The ability to use programs written for one system on another system with little or no change.

Figure 8–5
IBM System/370/155 Mainframe

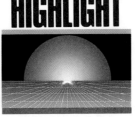

HIGHLIGHT

Parke-Davis and Easytrac Data-Base Access

Harry Tappen, director of market research and planning at Parke-Davis Pharmaceutical Co., wanted to know why consumer response to a certain ad campaign was far below what he had expected. With the help of Easytrac, Tappen used his microcomputer to access several data bases stored on mainframe computers and discovered that the promotion had targeted the wrong consumer group.

Easytrac, a decision support system (DSS), is a collection of marketing software applications developed by a company called Management Decision Systems. It is an interactive system that does not require much computer experience to learn and use. What does this mean to Harry Tappen? It means that now he can get vital information to make marketing decisions anytime instead of waiting until the end of the month for data-processing reports.

Easytrac asks Tappen questions like: What do I need to know? What is the present situation? What more do I need to know? Through a spiral of questions and answers, Easytrac can generate precise questions and access a variety of computers and data bases to find the answers.

Once Easytrac finds the necessary data, Tappen can explore what graphics will best express the data. Whether Tappen wants a pie chart, bar graph, or algebraic curve, Easytrac can draw the graphics. Easytrac represents one of the many ways different kinds of computers in different locations can communicate to help management.

Business managers and executives rely on reports from the various departments within a company. They don't want to know everything. They want only certain fields of information, like how much of a particular product the company has sold already this month or how much money they should spend to promote a new product.

Business managers and executives at Parke-Davis used to have to wait for the data-processing experts to send them preformatted reports. Often the reports came too late for the most efficient decision making and contained unnecessary information.

With Easytrac, managers can access many data bases to compile the information they want. By accessing syndicated data bases, they can find out how much their competitors spend on advertising and in which medical journals competitors run their ads. Managers can access internal data bases stored on corporate mainframes to get sales, inventory, or shipping data. Through direct access to all available data bases, managers can make better decisions and more accurate forecasts.

are still in use today. Several other companies have followed IBM's lead and produced their own mainframe families.

The mainframe sector is the backbone of the computer industry. Major manufacturing competitors in this market are IBM, Burroughs, Honeywell, National Cash Register (NCR), Control Data Corporation (CDC), and Amdahl. These vendors appeal to potential users of large, sophisticated computers.

Schwinn Modernizes with Mainframes

In the late seventies Schwinn Bicycle Company was plagued with problems: leaking roofs, an archaic data-processing department, and a losing race against European manufacturers of ten-speed bicycles. Robert Walsh, MIS manager at Schwinn, tackled the data-processing problem. He wanted to update Schwinn's data-processing system after 25 years of neglect. Walsh went shopping for a system that would efficiently manage Schwinn's affairs. Walsh was especially interested in a system that would keep track of the thousands of different items that roll off the assembly lines daily. He also wanted to replace an outdated payroll system.

Before spending any money on new computer equipment, Walsh did a lot of investigating. He did not rely on vendor's information and sales pitches. He went directly to the companies that already used proposed equipment. By talking with these users, Walsh discovered the disadvantages as well as the advantages of each system. Once all the facts were compiled, Walsh made his recommendations.

With the purchase of several IBM mainframes, ten IBM System 36 minicomputers, and supporting software, Schwinn has gone from the ridiculously obsolete to the sublime. In addition to streamlining payroll operations, the new equipment allows employees to access the previous day's inventory and sales figures. No longer do workers have to wait until the end of the month to gauge the results of their labors. The new system gives workers almost immediate feedback.

Now that mainframe and minicomputers have helped take care of the data-processing problems, and Schwinn's sales of ten speeds are improving, something really needs to be done about those leaking roofs!

Entry into the mainframe market is restricted by the huge capital investment required. However, once in the market, companies can spread the costs of research and development, hardware, and application and system software design over a number of units, thus reducing individual unit costs.

Applications

Traditionally mainframe computers were used for centralized processing. A change in the computer industry is the trend away from centralized processing and toward distributed processing. The demand for large, central computer systems has been replaced by a demand for smaller, more flexible systems. Mainframe vendors who have specialized in the production of large CPUs are diversifying into other sectors of the computer industry to remain competitive. For example, IBM has established a General Systems Division to manufacture minicomputers. Other companies have diversified into telecommunications and office products.

Many companies requiring the processing capabilities of large computers have already had them for some time. Purchase of newer mainframes are made only when the company needs expanded capacity or when new price/ performance ratios make them cost effective. The cost of maintaining large computer systems deters many firms from purchasing them. Some users are finding purchasing small computer systems to be more economical. In short, the high (most expensive) end of the market is becoming saturated. Mainframe computers come in various sizes and with various processing speeds and storage capacities. Purchase costs may range from $200,000 to several million dollars for a large mainframe system with peripherals.

Vendor Support

Mainframe vendors do more than sell mainframe computers. A computer is useless to an organization that lacks the knowledge needed to operate it. Most vendors provide support services along with an initial purchase. These services normally include education and training for all levels of users from top executives to data-entry personnel. Training can involve classes and seminars or self-study in which users pace their own learning while studying manuals and practicing hands-on exercises. Other services may be included in the purchase or lease price of the computer system, so managers should consider additional costs when purchasing a large computer system.

Though the mainframe sector once dominated the computer industry, it has lost part of its market share during the past decade because of the changing nature of the computer business. At one time, the industry was almost purely a hardware business. The price of a computer system was dominated by the cost of the hardware; software costs were included in the total price of the system. With recent technological advances, the cost of hardware has been declining at a rate of 15 to 20 percent per year. In contrast, software and service costs have continued to increase significantly.

SUPERCOMPUTERS

Characteristics

Supercomputer The largest, fastest, most expensive type of computer in existence; also called maxicomputer or monster computer.

The largest, fastest, most expensive computers made are called **supercomputers,** or **maxicomputers** (see Figure 8–6). The processing power of these machines is so fast that many central processors are required to complete calculations. Processing speeds of some supercomputers may be as high as 400 to 600 million operations per second. Mainframes perform closer to 50 million operations per second. Only a few supercomputers are produced each year because the manufacturing cost is high and the market is limited. Each super machine costs several million dollars to develop.

The United States has led the world in developing computer technology and supercomputers. But the days of the United States as a world leader in computer technology may be numbered. Other countries have entered the field of computer development, and Japan leads the competition in research and development. The Japanese are currently developing their own supercomputers. This situation has created concern in the United States.

While supercomputers account for a limited share of the total dollars spent in the computer market, they do represent the most advanced computer technology of our time. The computer industry changes very quickly, and new

Figure 8–6
Cyber 205 Supercomputer by
Control Data Corporation

technology is rapidly absorbed. The country that leads in supercomputer technology tends to have the most powerful computers on other levels, too, giving that country an edge over other countries in several significant areas.

To improve the situation, government agencies are sponsoring supercomputer research in universities around the country. The cooperative efforts of government, universities, and corporations may help keep the United States a world leader in computer technology.

Applications

One of the first supercomputers, the CRAY-1, was developed by Cray Research in 1976. The CRAY-1 and later supercomputers such as the CRAY X-MP (see Figure 8–7) are used mainly for weather forecasting, nuclear weapons development, and energy supply and conservation. Other supercomputers are used

Concept Summary 8–1 ▬ Comparison of Computer Systems

	Minicomputers	Mainframes	Supercomputers
Size	Smaller than mainframes	Smaller than supercomputers	Largest computer made
Cost	A few thousand to two or three hundred thousand dollars	Two hundred thousand to several million dollars	Several million dollars
Notes	Flexibility of systems has led to their popularity	Often part of a family of computers	Capable of performing millions of operations in a second

by large corporations and government agencies that need large data bases and complex calculation capabilities.

Supercomputers can perform jobs that cannot be done by other computers. The super machines can process millions of operations in a second, and during the 1980s, they are expected to reach a performance level of one billion operations per second. This lightning fast operation makes it possible for supercomputers to run programs that are too complex for smaller machines.

The rapid processing speed also makes supercomputers especially useful in aerodynamic design and scientific research as well as nuclear weapons development, weather forecasting, and energy conservation. All of these fields require processing massive amounts of data very quickly.

Figure 8–7
The CRAY X-MP Supercomputer System

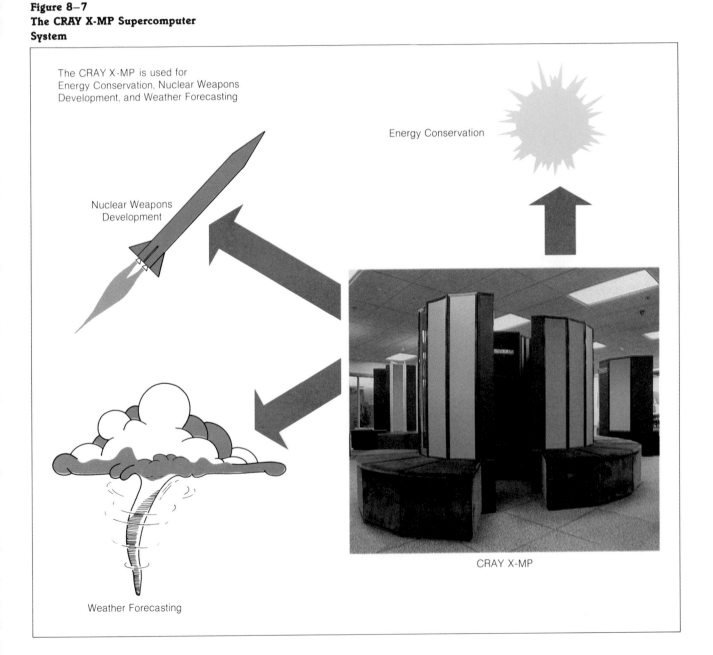

The CRAY X-MP is used for Energy Conservation, Nuclear Weapons Development, and Weather Forecasting

Energy Conservation

Nuclear Weapons Development

Weather Forecasting

CRAY X-MP

HIGHLIGHT

Supercomputer Market Growth Predicted

In the mid-1980s, analysts projected that the worldwide supercomputer market will grow more than 30% annually. They felt the increased demand for high-speed number crunching will lead to the completion of an estimated 200 supercomputers in 1990 alone.

Several industries will lead the need for more and faster supercomputers. For aircraft, the Defense Department will develop a vision and speech recognition system requiring a computer that processes 10 billion to 100 billion instructions per second. Oil field exploration, computer animation, and simulation of metal stress for automobile design will also add to the demand for supercomputers.

Supercomputers process numbers in groups. This capability gives them an amazing edge over conventional computers, which process numbers singly. Some of the Cray supercomputers, manufactured by Minneapolis-based Cray Research, can process up to half a billion instructions per second.

Development of the supercomputer may focus on increased speed or improved compatibility. Fujitsu, Japan's largest computer company, hopes to end U.S. dominance of the supercomputer market in the 1980s by emphasizing their supercomputer's compatibility with IBM mainframe software. Although critics claim that Fujitsu will sacrifice speed for software compatibility, preliminary impartial results found that Fujitsu's top-of-the-line supercomputer processes up to half a billion instructions per second, which matches the speed of some Cray models.

Analysts predict that by 1990 two Japanese firms, Hitachi and NEC, and U.S.-based IBM will enter the international supercomputer market. Research and technology await the increasing capabilities of the supercomputer to turn scientist's dreams into reality.

SOFTWARE

Software and consulting firms specialize in developing information systems for businesses. Usually, firms specialize in either system software or application software. Both are often sold as packages—collections of programs that work together to accomplish specific processing objectives. Such software packages are debugged and well documented. Some suppliers even update users' programs when new versions are developed.

Vendor Support

Manufacturers in all market sectors provide software packages to accompany their equipment. However, the overwhelming demand for software in the past decade has made specializing in software offerings profitable for firms. The leading suppliers of computer software include Computer Sciences, Automatic

Data Processing (ADP), General Electric, Electronic Data Systems (EDS), McDonnell Douglas, and Tymshare. A number of smaller firms offer software for use on minicomputers and microcomputers, including word processing and business packages.

Data management software is one of the most popular software packages. Others include communication packages, in which complete programs connect large networks of computers; for example, ADR offers DATACOM, IBM offers CICS (Customer Information Control System), and Cincom offers ENVIRON/1. Operating system software and utilities packages are available from several vendors; common examples are librarian programs and high-level language translators. In addition, application software is available in a multitude of forms, ranging from inventory management to payroll and general ledger.

Market Trends

The increased purchases of hardware that resulted from declining costs have escalated software demand. Users want sophisticated software such as database management systems (DBMS). Many users who once developed their own software are now buying standardized application and system programs. Although these standardized programs may need to be tailored for the organization, the benefits of purchasing packages are quickly realized, since the cost of buying a package is a fraction of the cost of developing the software in-house.

Small business users and first-time users are hardest hit by the "software crunch." These users do not have the staff needed to support software development. Software firms are attempting to reach these potential customers through avenues such as retail stores. Some stores offer one-stop shopping, providing programs ranging from computer games to small business applications. The current offerings of any software company are in a constant state of flux. Many firms offer new releases of their software packages containing the latest developments requested by users. Other firms develop specialized software packages under contractual arrangements.

Concept Summary 8–2 ▬ Needs Met by Time-Sharing Services and Service Bureaus

Type of Organization That Can Benefit from a Time-Sharing Service	Type of Organization That Can Benefit from a Service Bureau
Is using EDP for the first time	Requires complete data-processing services or specialized services but cannot afford to own a computer system
Requires only occasional processing capabilities	Needs temporary data-processing personnel
Cannot afford to own a computer system	Requires a computer system that meets the needs of a specific industry
Needs additional magnetic disk or tape storage space	

SERVICE BUREAUS AND TIME-SHARING COMPANIES

Computer systems are a major expense. Many companies cannot afford systems of their own. **Service bureaus** provide data-processing services such as system development and computer operations. **Time-sharing** companies maintain computer facilities rented by a wide variety of users who want the sophistication of a large computer system without incurring all of the costs. Time-sharing companies also provide computer power to companies that do not need 24-hour-a-day processing.

Growth in the time-sharing industry is primarily due to the advances in communication equipment. Time-sharing customers usually purchase input/output devices and use them to access the facilities of the time-sharing company. Storage space on magnetic tapes and disks can be rented; the customer pays for CPU resources at a monthly rate. Some time-sharing companies have networks of computers spread throughout the nation. They have the ability to distribute the costs of such a system over many users, thus reducing unit costs.

A disadvantage of using time-sharing is that it becomes very expensive as data-processing needs increase. The more computer time required, the greater the monthly costs. However, time-sharing may be an economical alternative for companies that are first-time electronic data processing (EDP) users.

Service bureaus provide a number of data-processing services. Some bureaus perform all data-processing activities for small firms. Others specialize in providing temporary personnel to perform data-entry or programming activities. Many specialize in a particular industry, serving oil companies, for example, or savings and loan associations.

An example of a service bureau is McDonnell Douglas Information Systems Group. The largest computer center in the world, McDonnell Douglas serves approximately 10,000 customers and processes over 30,000 time-sharing jobs in an average week at the St. Louis, Missouri center. The computer center contains 13 large-scale computers linked to 16,000 terminals. McDonnell Douglas also sells software to various industries (insurance, manufacturing, and construction) and offers computer-related consulting services to computer users.

Managers have countless alternatives from which to choose when acquiring an EDP system. They will be faced with an even greater number of decisions as computer vendors continually develop new and better ways to gain a share of the market and reach the consumer with information about their products. The following section discusses some of these future management decisions regarding computer systems.

MANAGEMENT PERSPECTIVES ON COMPUTER SYSTEMS

Management is faced with several alternative methods of meeting data-processing requirements. Some firms choose to lease or buy computer resources and do in-house processing; other firms use outside service bureaus. Other alternatives include time-sharing and traditional methods of manual processing. Selecting the best alternative for an organization is an exceedingly complex task.

The selection is further complicated by the myriad equipment configurations available. Given the numerous peripheral devices discussed in Chapters 4 and 5, a seemingly infinite number of configurations is possible. The following

Service bureau A business that provides data-processing services such as system development and computer operations.

Time-sharing A system in which two or more users access the same central computer resources and receive what seem to be simultaneous results.

239

Bundled A way of selling computers in which the price includes training, maintenance costs, software, and other related products and services.

Unbundled A way of selling computers in which vendor support and training items are priced separately.

paragraphs discuss some of the major points organizations should consider when choosing from available alternatives.

The purchase prices of CPUs and peripheral devices prohibit all but the largest firms from buying and owning large computer systems. Traditionally, therefore, large and medium-size computer systems have been rented or leased. Normally, it takes several years of lease payments to reach the purchase price of the equipment. Minicomputers and microcomputers, on the other hand, are much lower in cost and are usually purchased outright.

The costs and quality of service must not be overlooked. Maintenance is a separate contractual matter, when a system is purchased, and its cost can be significant (often several thousand dollars a month for large systems). Maintenance services can be performed by the computer manufacturer or by a specialized maintenance firm. The quality of service is vital, because a computer breakdown can totally disrupt work flow.

Vendor support and training are especially important when an organization first installs a computer system or radically changes an existing one. The expertise of the vendor can be invaluable during design and implementation. Most vendors offer training classes to educate users of the systems they sell or lease, but the quality and amount of training offered vary greatly. The cost for these services may be included in the price of the equipment; if so, the support is said to be **bundled.** In contrast, if such items are priced separately, they are said to be **unbundled.** In 1969, the courts set a precedent when they forced IBM to unbundle its software. Prior to the court decision, IBM refused to sell certain computer systems without accompanying software. The computer industry is evolving into a business dominated by software and service costs.

Large computer systems are often justified on the basis of the *volume* or the *complexity* or *diversity* of work they can be used to accomplish. Their capabilities stem not only from the equipment within the system but also from the sophisticated software available for use with it. For large firms, multiprogramming and virtual-storage capabilities may be necessities. These capabilities can be exploited fully only with large and medium-sized computers.

The speed and storage capacity of the CPU are also of great interest to computer users. The volume and type of processing to be done determines the speed and storage capacity required and the size of computer needed. Large businesses that process data in great volume frequently need large computer systems. Firms that use computers for scientific applications need very fast computers but may not need large storage capacities. Small organizations may find that minicomputers meet all their requirements. Large businesses may use small computers for applications where response times and storage capacities are not critical. For example, a minicomputer costing only $50,000 may do the same types and amounts of work as a mainframe computer costing $2,000,000.

Besides paying for hardware and software, an organization must pay the salaries of its computer staff—managers, system analysts, programmers, data-entry personnel, computer operators, and computer technicians. Most computer-related jobs require a high degree of skill and training. These specialized services are not cheap; the salaries of computer staff may constitute a significant portion of an organization's monthly payroll.

The flexibility of a system is the degree to which it can be adapted or tailored to meet changing requirements. Many manufacturers design their systems using a modular approach that permits the addition of components to a system configuration, thereby allowing for growth and adaptation as an organization's needs change. An organization can start with a relatively slow, limited system and then change to a large CPU or add more peripherals when needed. Systems designed with emphasis on modularity are usually flexible.

Software compatibility also affects a system's flexibility. Compatibility refers to the ability to use programs written for one system on another system with little or no change. From a user's point of view, the number of required program changes should be minimal since reprogramming is both costly and time consuming. Fortunately, many manufacturers offer systems that can be expanded with few program changes.

While this list of considerations is by no means complete, it demonstrates the complexities involved in choosing a computer system. Other key considerations include the size and structure of the organization. For example, a large, highly centralized organization may have little choice but to acquire a large computer system. In contrast, small businesses and decentralized organizations often find that all their data-processing needs can be met with minicomputer systems.

The computer industry is a large and growing sector of the United States economy. Although the largest user of computers is the federal government, the business world is rapidly closing the gap. A computer explosion has occurred, and with the rapidly expanding capabilities of minicomputers and small computer systems and the new technological developments in secondary storage and communication systems, the task of evaluating system alternatives will become increasingly complex.

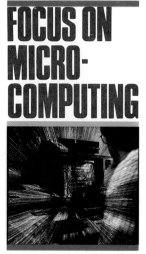

FOCUS ON MICRO- COMPUTING

Micro to Mainframe—New Problems

Microcomputers have become part of a growing trend that involves linking the small machines with mainframes and minicomputers. Desktop microcomputers are becoming common sights in many large organizations as professionals are accessing data bases and downloading files (transferring files from a remote computer to the user's machine) from a mainframe or minicomputer to a microcomputer. Many companies that were eager to try linking microcomputers with larger systems are now faced with a new dilemma—managing the security problems that the microcomputer to mainframe link has created.

Most companies have taken security measures to protect information stored in minicomputers and mainframes. User access to data bases may be carefully monitored and limited to designated employees. But microcomputers that are tied to large computer systems via modems and software have created, in many cases, the potential for extensive hardware theft, software piracy, unauthorized data access, and malicious activities.

There are several reasons for this situation. Most organizations do not have security measures for microcomputers and users. This casual approach may be due, in part, to the distinctive qualities of microcomputers that separate them from larger systems. Microcomputer equipment is usually scattered throughout an organization rather than centralized in one department. Equipment expenses are also spread out over many departments. When equipment is damaged or missing, there is no single person or department responsible for investigating the loss. The equipment itself is relatively cheap compared to the cost of minicomputers and mainframes, and equipment loss may not be viewed as significant. The high cost of security measures and management's not understanding the security risks involved also contribute to poor security.

As microcomputer communication with larger systems increases, problems also increase. Users sometimes allow anyone in their offices free access to their machines. This relaxed environment often leads to misuse in the form of damage to both hardware and software. Microcomputers are frequently placed on desktops or workstations or even transported back and forth between home and office. The easy portability of many machines and software makes them a target for theft. In many companies, an individual can pick up a micro, peripherals, or software and simply walk away. An entire data base can be carried away in a pocket. The growing market for stolen hardware, specifically personal computers, makes disposal of stolen equipment easy. To compound the problem, when equipment turns up missing, companies often do not report the loss either to company officials or to the police. The missing equipment may be viewed as misplaced rather than stolen, and managers may feel the loss is insignificant and merely order replacements for the missing equipment.

As hardware damage and theft increases, companies are attempting to protect equipment. Individual computers can be attached to desks by devices such as cables that bolt to the micro on one end and a stationery unit on the other. Disks can be stored in locked drawers. Many office furniture manufacturers are responding to the situation by offering special lockup cabinets for personal computers. Data-Mate offers a cabinet that, when properly used, can restrict physical access to all equipment inside the cabinet including disks and peripherals.

Software piracy also presents a security challenge. Copying company software for personal use violates copyright laws. Companies need to institute strict policies against this practice. Some software companies offer copyright protection programs that make unauthorized copying of software difficult.

The security area that is beginning to cause the greatest concern among companies using microcomputer to minicomputer or mainframe links, is unauthorized data access. Microcomputer access to minicomputers and mainframes often bypasses standard security access procedures such as user passwords. Verifying the authenticity of the user becomes a problem in situations like this since so many people can use microcomputers to access information or files stored in a larger system. First, there is easy access to microcomputers scattered about a company. Next, the machines themselves are user friendly. And last, user authenticity is difficult to verify.

Communication technology has also made unauthorized electronic entry possible outside the physical limits of a company. Companies that permit access to their minicomputers or mainframes from remote locations via telephone equipment are particularly vulnerable. Without a user verification system, there is no way for a company to know if a user at a remote site is authorized to access a central computer or not.

Password protection and call-back modems are helping to solve this problem. LeeMAH, a San Francisco based company, offers "Secure Access Unit" for users that desire call-back protection. The main problem with a call-back security system is that authorized users may not always be communicating from the same remote location. The call-back feature has no way of discriminating between authorized users calling from unauthorized locations and unauthorized individuals attempting to gain access to proprietary information. Therefore, an authorized user could be denied access to the central computer.

The security problem of malicious activity can be most easily overcome by implementing security measures that protect equipment and limit user access. Disks that are securely locked away when not in use cannot fall into the wrong hands. Call-back modems that verify user authenticity will not permit unauthorized "data diddlers."

Microcomputer links to minicomputers and mainframes have created problems for organizations using the new technology, but careful security measures can help overcome these problems.

SUMMARY POINTS

- Advances in technology have blurred the distinction between minicomputers and mainframes, but generally minicomputers are easier to install and operate than mainframes. The computers are smaller and less costly than mainframes and require few special environmental conditions.
- The flexibility of minicomputers has led to their popularity. A small company may use only one minicomputer, while a larger organization may link many units together.
- Many companies are linking microcomputers and minicomputers to control equipment cost and to increase processing capabilities.
- Minicomputers are used in conjunction with communications facilities to provide remote processing capabilities.
- Efficient software is a primary key to selling hardware, and many vendors sell software packages to accompany their hardware. Application software has been developed for specific industries and minicomputer users prefer purchasing software packages to developing their own.
- Once synonymous with CPU, the term *mainframe* now refers to a computer that is more powerful than a minicomputer.
- Several mainframes of differing sizes built by the same manufacturer and having the same processor are said to be in the same family of computers. These computers run the same or modified software.
- Entry into the mainframe market is restricted by the huge capital investment, but once in the market, companies can spread the costs of research and development, hardware, and software over a number of machines.

■ Support services provided by vendors include education and training for all levels of users.

■ Hardware costs for mainframe computers have decreased while software and service costs have increased.

■ The trend toward distributed processing has replaced the large central computer with smaller, more flexible systems.

■ The largest, fastest, most expensive computers made are called supercomputers or maxicomputers. Many central processors are required to complete calculations in supercomputers. Processing speeds may reach 400 or 500 million operations per second.

■ One of the first supercomputers, the CRAY-1, was developed by Cray Research in 1976. It is used in weather forecasting, nuclear weapons development, and energy conservation and supply.

■ While the United States has led the world in computer technology, foreign countries, chiefly Japan, are conducting their own research in computer technology and gaining on the United States.

■ The country that leads the world in computer technology has an edge over other countries in several significant areas. The United States government is sponsoring computer research in universities across the country in order to remain a leader in computer development.

■ The demand for software is growing at an unprecedented rate. Many users find buying software from a software vendor less expensive than creating programs in-house. Prewritten packages are documented and debugged. However, an organization must tailor such programs to meet its particular needs.

■ Service bureaus provide data-processing activities to firms that are unable to support the costs of a computer system. Time-sharing companies provide the use of computer facilities to customers for a monthly fee. Both of these services allow users to realize the benefits of a large computer system without the associated costs.

■ Selecting a computer configuration for an organization or for personal use is a complex task. Important factors to be considered include: purchase versus rental prices of hardware, maintenance costs, vendor support, software costs and capabilities, hardware capabilities, staff requirements, and system flexibility and compatibility.

■ The practice of linking microcomputers with minicomputers and mainframes has created new security problems for many corporations. New products and routine security measures can reduce the risk of unauthorized entry into data bases.

REVIEW AND DISCUSSION QUESTIONS

1. What type of support do computer vendors offer to buyers of mainframe systems?
2. What market trends are currently causing the downturn in sales of mainframe computers?
3. Explain how the flexibility of minicomputers has contributed to their popularity.

4. What role has software played in the acceptance and use of minicomputer systems?
5. What are some uses of supercomputer systems?
6. Why is remaining a leader in supercomputer technology important for the United States?
7. What is a family of computers, and what advantages do computer families offer to users?
8. Why might a firm contract with a service bureau? What are some advantages and disadvantages of using service bureaus and time-sharing companies?
9. What is the primary cause of growth in the time-sharing industry?
10. What security measures can organizations that link personal computers with mainframes and minicomputers take to prevent misuse of the system?

CHAPTER 9

MICROCOMPUTERS

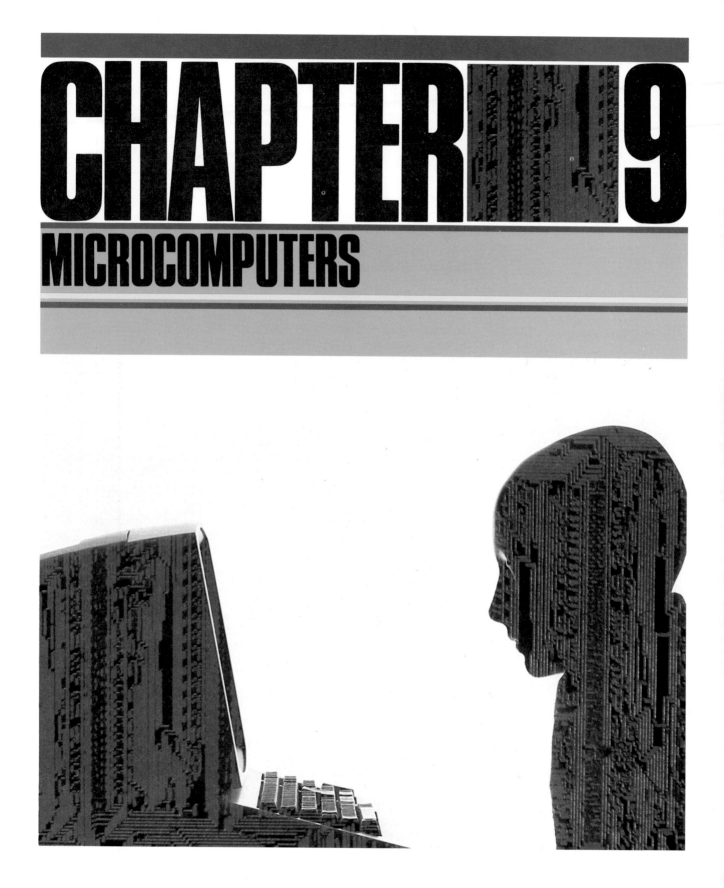

COMPUTERS IN OUR LIVES

Dorms, Classes, Books, and Microcomputers?

Colleges and universities have long been catalysts for new ideas. Research conducted in a broad range of disciplines has often sparked ideas and social changes that initially caused much controversy (think, for example, of early resistance to the idea of inoculation against disease). Today, as a result of technological research, a change is occurring on campuses themselves that once again is causing a great deal of controversy. The change is that some colleges require entering freshmen to purchase microcomputers.

Students evaluating universities must now not only consider a school's tuition, accreditation, location, and size but also whether and how it integrates computers into the curriculum. Liza Anderson, a sophomore at Cuyahoga Community College in Cleveland, Ohio, faced this dilemma when she began looking for a school where she could finish her degree in journalism. Liza first became aware that she might someday need to use a microcomputer when she read an article in Writers' Digest about authors using word-processing software on microcomputers to write their stories and books and newspaper and magazine reporters using portable computers to write their articles at the scene of an event. At the time, Liza barely knew what a microcomputer was!

Liza wondered if she should look for a college that integrated computers into its courses. As an investigative reporter should, Liza did some research to find out which colleges and universities made computers mandatory for all students. She discovered that about nine universities in the country, including Brown, Drew, Clarkson, and Drexel, require freshmen to buy microcomputers. Some of the schools include the cost of the computer in the tuition. For example, Clarkson University provides each freshman student with a Zenith Z-100, which is paid for through an increase in tuition. Others sell the machines directly to students at a discount. At Drew University students must buy an Epson QX-10, but they are given a 30 percent discount through a special university program.

Liza's research also revealed an ongoing controversy over the mandatory microcomputer requirement. On one side, some educators feel that universities with mandatory microcomputer requirements have a competitive edge over universities without them. Many students are afraid that without computer knowledge they will have difficulty finding a job after graduation. Therefore, they will seek universities that offer plenty of exposure to computers. Schools that ignore the importance of implementing computers in the curriculum will find enrollment decreasing.

The other side maintains that although microcomputers should certainly be included in a university education and that students should have the option to select computer courses if they so desire, students should not have to purchase individual microcomputers. Many students cannot afford the added expense of purchasing a computer. Also, this group contends, universities are trying to avoid expanding their own computer facilities by passing off the expense to students.

248

With this information, Liza was ready to make an informed choice. She evaluated her educational needs and decided on the extent of computer knowledge that would be useful to her, both professionally and personally, finally opting for a school that offered maximum microcomputer experience. She certainly did not want to be left in the dust of the computer revolution. Then, based on her criteria, she reviewed several colleges and universities. Selecting a college was a tough decision but at least Liza knew what she wanted.

Microcomputers are affecting most people's lives, not only the lives of college students, in one way or another. Possibly, in another generation everyone will use a microcomputer at work, no matter what his or her job is. Most people will probably have one at home also. This chapter discusses how microcomputers were developed and how they work, what hardware is used with them, and the ways in which they affect society. It also tells you how to care for a microcomputer and its peripherals and what to look for when buying one.

INTRODUCTION

There are few technological occurrences as fascinating as the evolution and growth of the microcomputer industry. In only one decade, microcomputers evolved from relatively primitive build-it-yourself kits to sophisticated machines more powerful than some of the early mainframe computers. Interest in microcomputers quickly spread from computer hobbyists to small business owners, managers, researchers, engineers, teachers, teenagers, and homemakers. This avid interest, in turn, enticed computer manufacturers to design and produce microcomputers to meet the demand.

Microcomputers have become firmly entrenched in society because they have so many uses. They also affect society in ways that will remain with us for years. For these reasons, presenting topics that are of special concern to microcomputer users is necessary. Hardware and software requirements sometimes differ from those of larger computers. Also, microcomputer users sometimes require special support that may be obtained through services such as user's groups and electronic bulletin boards. Topics such as these are covered in this chapter along with the eventful history of microcomputers.

THE MICROCOMPUTER EXPLOSION

Microcomputers, also called personal computers or home computers, are the smallest computers. They differ from minicomputers, mainframes, and super-computers in capability (power), price, and size. But the capabilities of microcomputers are rapidly expanding. There is no longer a clear distinction between the capabilities of some microcomputers and those of the next class of computers, minicomputers. Some microcomputers, often referred to as supermi-

Microcomputer A small, low-priced computer used in homes, schools, and businesses.

crocomputers, are so powerful they are being used instead of minicomputers by some organizations.

Microcomputers can usually sit on a desk top (see Figure 9–1). They are less expensive than minicomputers and mainframes, due largely to their less complex and less expensive operating systems. Microcomputer prices range from about $100 to $10,000.

The prefix *micro* should be thought of as applying more to size and cost than to capability. Microcomputers are very powerful for their size. Today's microcomputers can equal the power of the early room-sized mainframe computers. Although they still cannot perform as many complex functions as the large computers available today, technology continues to give them more speed and more memory at an ever-decreasing cost.

A New Technology Emerges

Recall from Chapter 2 that the fourth generation of computers began with the invention of the microprocessor in 1971. A microprocessor is a single chip containing arithmetic and logic circuitry, as well as control capability, for memory and input/output access (see Figure 9–2). A microprocessor controls the sequence of operations and the arithmetic and logic operations. It also controls the storage of data, instructions, and the intermediate and final results of processing, much as the CPU of a mainframe does. However, the CPU of a mainframe contains a series of integrated circuits and is much more sophisticated than the microprocessor.

Microprocessors quickly increased in power while they decreased in size. This revolutionary combination of power and miniaturization paved the way for microcomputers as they exist today.

Actually, the first microprocessor was not designed to be used in microcomputers. Ted Hoff, an engineer at Intel, designed the first microprocessor chip for a Japanese company that wanted an integrated programmable circuit chip

Figure 9–1
Microcomputer.
Microcomputers, the least expensive category of computers, are general-purpose machines used in many applications in homes, offices, and schools.

Figure 9–2
Microprocessor.
This microprocessor from Bell Labs has as much processing power as some minicomputers.

for its line of calculators. At the time, calculators used circuit chips that could perform only one function. Hoff's chip, the Intel 4004, could be programmed to perform numerous calculator functions.

The Intel 4004 had a very limited instruction set, could not perform many functions, and could manipulate only 4 bits (a "nibble") of data at a time. By 1974, however, microprocessors could manipulate 8 bits (one byte) of data at a time. Popular 8-bit chips are the MOS Technology 6502, Zilog Z-80, Intel 8080, and Motorola 6809. These powerful 8-bit microprocessors were used in the first microcomputers.

Recently, 16-bit and 32-bit microprocessors have been developed. Common 16-bit microprocessors are the Intel 8088 and Intel 8086. A popular 32-bit microprocessor is the Motorola 68000. So far, the most powerful microprocessor is the 64-bit microprocessor developed by Control Data Corporation. However, it has not yet been implemented in any commercial microcomputers.

Microprocessors are being used to control the functions of many devices other than microcomputers. They are commonly found in microwave ovens, calculators, typewriters, vending machines, traffic lights, and gas pumps. Recently, microprocessors have been incorporated in the design of automobiles. They control the ignition system, the flow and mix of gasoline, and the timing of sparks. They also monitor and convey to the driver information about speed, fuel supply, and other basic operations.

Microcomputer Pioneers

Ed Roberts, the founder of a company called MITS, foresaw the start of the microcomputer revolution. He envisioned a computer that could be assembled from a kit. In 1974 MITS introduced one of the first microcomputers available to the general public, the Altair 8800. The computer came unassembled for $397 or fully assembled for $498. It used an Intel 8-bit microprocessor and had only 1K (1000 bytes) of memory. The Altair 8800 was featured in the

January 1975 issue of *Popular Electronics* and created so much interest that MITS received over 5,000 orders. This overwhelming response indicated that the market for microcomputers was well worth pursuing.

In 1976, not long after the introduction of the Altair 8800, Stephen Wozniak, an employee of Hewlett-Packard, finished building a small, easy-to-use computer. His computer, the Apple I, used the MOS 6502 microprocessor chip which, at $20, was inexpensive enough to be used for home computers. Steven Jobs, a friend of Wozniak's and a former Hewlett-Packard employee, persuaded Wozniak to leave Hewlett-Packard and start a business with him. The two men raised $1,300 and began building Apple computers (see Figure 9–3). Their first commercial microcomputer, the Apple II, was a remarkable success. Since then, Apple has produced a series of Apple II computers, including the Apple IIe, Apple II Plus, Apple IIc and the Macintosh.

Also in 1976, Commodore Business Machines, headed by Jack Tramiel, acquired MOS Technology, the semiconductor manufacturer that was developing the 6502 microprocessor. With additional financing supplied by Commodore, the chip was incorporated in the Commodore PET. In 1977 the PET was introduced at an electronics show (see Figure 9–4). Tramiel also sold the 6502 chip to Apple and Atari. Later, Commodore developed the VIC 20 and Commodore 64 microcomputers.

In 1977 the chairman of Tandy Corporation, John Roach, was busy persuading Tandy president, Charles Tandy, to manufacture a microcomputer and market it through the Radio Shack stores that Tandy had bought in 1963. Roach had the foresight and marketing skill to create a situation where, for the first time, a person could walk into a retail store and purchase a low-priced personal computer. The TRS-80 microcomputer Models I, II, III, and 4 (see Figure 9–5), the portable TRS 200, and the advanced TRS 2000 have made Radio Shack and Tandy Corporation a driving force in the microcomputer industry.

IBM entered the microcomputer race in 1981 under the leadership of chief executive officer John Opel (see Figure 9–6). The IBM Personal Computer (PC), developed under the direction of Philip D. Estridge, quickly became the standard

Figure 9–3
Steven Jobs, Stephen Wozniak, and the Apple II

Figure 9–5
John Roach and the TRS-80 Model 4

Figure 9–4
The Commodore PET

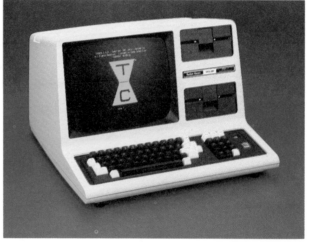

in small business computers (see Figure 9–7). It used the Intel 8086 micro-processor, which could manipulate 16 bits of data at a time. The success of the IBM PC prompted other microcomputer manufacturers to develop 16-bit computers. IBM then introduced the IBM PCjr and the more advanced IBM PC XT and IBM PC AT.

In the few years since 1974, over 150 companies have introduced micro-computers. Some, such as DEC, NCR, Wang, and Hewlett-Packard, were al-

Figure 9–6
John Opel

Figure 9–7
The IBM PC

253

ready established mainframe and minicomputer manufacturers. Others were new companies trying to capture a share of the microcomputer market. Not all were successful. Among the companies forced to regroup or abandon the microcomputer race are Osborne Computer, Coleco, Texas Instruments, and Timex.

The shakeout of microcomputer companies is not over, and the market for microcomputers is still growing, although at a slower rate than it did in the early 1980s. For the next several years, the prices of microcomputers should continue to decline while more and more capabilities are added.

Concept Summary 9–1 ▪ Microcomputers and Their Microprocessors

Microcomputer	Year Introduced	Manufacturer	Microprocessor
Altair 8800	1974	MITS	Intel 8080
Apple II	1976	Apple Computer	MOS 6502
PET	1977	Commodore	MOS 6502
TRS-80 Model I	1977	Tandy Corporation	Zilog Z-80
IBM PC	1981	IBM	Intel 8086

SOFTWARE AND HARDWARE

The Microcomputer's Power

As discussed earlier in the chapter, the power behind a microcomputer comes from the microprocessor, a silicon chip only fractions of an inch wide. Microprocessors can be categorized according to their speed and the amount of primary storage they can access directly. The speed with which the microprocessor can execute instructions affects the speed of the microcomputer. Speed depends on two major factors: word size and clock speed.

Word size is the number of bits that can be manipulated at one time. An 8-bit microprocessor, for example, can manipulate 8 bits, or one byte, of data at a time. A 16-bit microprocessor can handle 16 bits, or two bytes, of data at a time. So, a 16-bit microprocessor can manipulate twice as much data as an 8-bit microprocessor in approximately the same amount of time.

However, there is no direct correlation between word size and speed. A 16-bit microprocessor is not necessarily twice as fast as an 8-bit microprocessor. It may be more than twice as fast in performing arithmetic operations but not quite twice as fast in performing input, output, storage, retrieval, and logic operations. Still, a 64-bit microprocessor is faster than a 32-bit, which is faster than a 16-bit, which is faster than an 8-bit microprocessor.

The **clock speed** of a microprocessor is the number of electronic pulses the chip can produce each second. Clock speed is built into the microprocessor and is measured in **megahertz (MHz).** *Mega* means million and *hertz* means times per second so 1 megahertz is 1 million times per second. The electronic pulses affect the speed with which program instructions are executed because instructions are executed at set intervals, which are timed by the electronic pulses. To illustrate this concept, assume that one instruction is executed every 100 pulses. A 4 MHz microprocessor, then, could process 40,000 instructions

Clock speed The number of electronic pulses a microprocessor can produce each second.

Megahertz (MHz) One million times per second; the unit of measurement for clock speed.

per second (4 million pulses divided by 100 pulses). An 8 MHz microprocessor could process 80,000 instructions, or twice as many as a 4 MHz microprocessor. Thus, the more pulses produced per second, the faster instructions can be executed. Most microcomputers have clock speeds ranging between 2 MHz and 8 MHz.

The amount of data that can be directly accessed in primary storage also affects the speed with which instructions can be executed. Each microprocessor can directly access only a certain amount of data in primary storage. This means that the microprocessor can manipulate a certain number of bytes of data (usually measured in blocks of 16K) without switching from primary storage to a supplementary storage bank. Supplementary storage banks are still part of primary storage. They are internally located and should not be confused with secondary storage such as floppy disks. Typically, 8-bit microprocessors can directly access 64K bytes of data and 16-bit microprocessors can directly access 256K.

Adding more primary storage to a microcomputer than can be directly accessed by its microprocessor is also possible. If this happens, the microprocessor has to move from primary storage to the supplementary storage banks. This switching process is controlled by a program built into the microprocessor. Although the time the microprocessor takes to switch between storage banks is extremely brief, that time could still be used for other tasks. For this reason, the greater the amount of data that can be directly accessed, the faster the instructions can be executed.

Operating Systems

As discussed in Chapter 11, an **operating system (OS)** is a collection of programs used by the computer to manage its operations and provide an interface between the user or application program and the computer hardware. The first computers did not have operating systems. Users of these computers had to turn switches to enter data and instructions in binary form, one byte at a time. Of course, this was quite a time-consuming process.

Operating system (OS) A collection of programs used by the computer to manage its operations; provides an interface between the user and computer hardware.

Next, operating system programs were installed in ROM. These programs in ROM could read more complex instructions from punched paper tape or cassette tape. Still, programs had to be written to decode keyboard signals or transfer output to a printer, for example, each time a new application program was written for a particular computer. Soon, programs written to manage these input/output tasks, as well as other operations, were included as part of the operating system. The most popular microcomputer operating systems are discussed in the following sections. They are all designed to run on systems using floppy disks.

CP/M

The first operating system developed for use with microcomputers was Digital Research's CP/M (Control Program for Microprocessors). CP/M was stored on a floppy disk so that it could be loaded into any microcomputer, provided it used the Intel 8080, Intel 8085, or Zilog Z-80 8-bit microprocessor. Microcomputer manufacturers could license CP/M from Digital Research, which was less expensive than developing their own operating system. CP/M became very popular and consequently, much software was written to be used with it.

CP/M was originally written for programmers and is not easy for a beginner to use. The user must know quite a bit about how the computer functions. Still, CP/M is very powerful and many (about 15,000) application programs have been written for it.

When 16-bit microprocessors were developed, a 16-bit version of CP/M called CP/M-86, was also developed. But CP/M-86 is not nearly as popular as CP/M, possibly because it has more competitors. Digital Research has also developed an operating system called Concurrent DOS that will run several programs at the same time.

MS–DOS

Microsoft introduced its operating system, called MS–DOS, for 16-bit microprocessors in 1981. Microsoft licensed it to IBM to be used in the IBM PC. MS–DOS (also called PC–DOS) quickly became the most popular 16-bit operating system as IBM PC sales soared. More than 100 computers used MS–DOS, and many application programs have been written to run on it.

MS–DOS is designed to run on the INTEL 8088 and 8086 16-bit microprocessors. But is is not very compatible with microcomputers using other microprocessors, which will certainly keep it from becoming an absolute standard operating system.

MS–DOS is similar to CP/M, with many of the same commands. Like CP/M, MS–DOS requires the user to have knowledge of the computer itself, and it is not particularly easy for a beginner to use. But MS–DOS has many improvements over CP/M. For example, files stored on disk can be found much more quickly and disk access is faster. It can also be customized for different disks or other hardware the user wants to add.

Apple DOS and Apple ProDOS

Since the first Apple computer used the MOS 6502 microprocessor, CP/M could not be used as the operating system. In 1978 Apple developed an operating system, Apple DOS, to be used with its computers. Apple DOS is a very simple operating system designed to be used by nonprofessional computer users. It is easy to learn and easy to use. Unfortunately, Apple DOS's simplicity causes several disadvantages. It has limited utilities compared to CP/M and MS–DOS and does not work well with more than two floppy disks. Apple DOS allows its directory to fill only two screens. If many short files are created, the directory fills up before the space on the disk.

ProDOS is an updated version of Apple DOS that overcomes some of its problems. ProDOS can handle more files in disk storage and provides a better directory system. It also provides faster disk access. Still, ProDOS is limited in what it can do.

Apple DOS and ProDOS will remain popular as long as Apple computers are sold. And since there have been so many application programs written for Apple computers, they should remain popular despite CP/M or MS–DOS standards.

Unix

Unix is an operating system that Bell Laboratories developed for minicomputers in the late 1960s. It was first implemented on a microcomputer in 1978.

Unix may become the industry standard, over CP/M and MS–DOS, because it was not designed for a specific microprocessor, and it is written in a high-level language. It can be run on microcomputers, minicomputers, and mainframes and can be adapted for a new computer in several weeks' time. This adaptability is important because of the significant number of new computers and microprocessors introduced each year.

Unix lets the user do several tasks at one time from the same terminal. Unlike the other popular operating systems, its file structure allows files to be manipulated in many ways, and it has over 200 utility programs. Unix is available on many computers and is preferred by many programmers.

However, Unix also has disadvantages. There are many versions of the operating system, and they are not all compatible. Also, the majority of application programs written for Unix are for scientific or engineering tasks. There are few application programs written for home users.

Other Operating Systems

Pick, an operating system similar to Unix in the number of utilities and features it offers, is a powerful system designed especially for business environments. Although Pick is powerful and has complex capabilities, it is simple to learn and easy to use. The user needs no extensive knowledge of how the computer works. Pick is not easy to maintain, however, and there are few people with Pick experience.

A simple, uncomplicated operating system designed for home and small business use is TRSDOS (Tandy Radio Shack Disk Operating System). It can only be used with Radio Shack TRS-80 Model I, Model III, and Model 4 microcomputers. Still, there are many good application programs written for TRSDOS. The Model 4 was made to be CP/M-compatible, which may indicate the phasing out of TRSDOS.

One operating system has little in common with the operating systems discussed earlier. Apple's advanced operating system works the microprocessor hard and is extremely complex, but the complexity makes it easy to use. Instead of memorizing system commands, users instruct the operating system by pointing at icons (graphic images) using a mouse.

Apple introduced the advanced operating system in 1983 in the Lisa microcomputer, which used the powerful Motorola 68000 microprocessor. Lisa's operating system was easy to use but it was slow and too expensive to sell well. Apple discontinued the computer in 1984.

Apple tried the OS again in the Macintosh. This time, technical people as well as consumers were satisfied and the Macintosh was a great success. The Macintosh system lets the user concentrate on what needs to be done rather than how to do it. Commands are issued by simply moving the mouse to point to and select the desired option from a menu. The major drawback to this advanced operating system is the lack of application software available for it. Since Apple has copyrighted their system, there will be no compatible systems in the near future, which will limit the amount of software developed for it.

Microcomputer Compatibility

Many microcomputer owners have bought a certain brand of computer only to find out later that the computer alone cannot perform all the tasks one requires. This problem can be solved by adding peripheral equipment such as

Concept Summary 9-2 ▪ Operating Systems

Operating System	Manufacturer	Microprocessor
CP/M CP/M-86	Digital Research	Intel 8080, 8085, Zilog Z-80 Intel 8086, 8088
MS-DOS	Microsoft	Intel 8088, 8086
Apple DOS Apple ProDOS	Apple Computer	MOS 6502 MOS 6502C
Unix	Bell Laboratories	no single family

Compatibility The ability to use equipment or software produced by one manufacturer on a computer produced by another manufacturer.

disk drives, color monitors, printers, and modems. Internal circuitry can even be added to expand memory, increase speed, or change screen widths. However, microcomputer owners wishing to expand their systems must be concerned with compatibility. **Compatibility** is the ability to use one manufacturer's equipment or software with another manufacturer's equipment.

When adding equipment to a particular microcomputer, choosing the same manufacturer's peripherals is not always necessary. Many times, another manufacturer's equipment has the same or better capabilities at a lower cost. But the peripherals must be compatible with the microcomputer. Likewise, software designed to be used with a particular operating system cannot be used on computers with different operating systems. The same is true for hardware designed for one operating system. However, by adding a **coprocessor** to a computer, that computer can be made compatible with another operating system. A coprocessor is a microprocessor that can be plugged into the original computer to replace or work with the original microprocessor. The coprocessor usually comes on a plug-in board along with other chips necessary for it to run. The original microprocessor and the coprocessor share the computer's disk drives, keyboard, and other peripherals.

Coprocessor A microprocessor that can be plugged into a microcomputer to replace or work with the microcomputer's original microprocessor; promotes hardware and software compatibility.

A coprocessor allows software written for its operating system to be run on a machine that could not run the software otherwise. For example, adding a Z-80 board to the CPU will make an Apple IIe CP/M compatible. There are coprocessors available to make IBM PCs (MS-DOS) compatible with Apple IIs (Apple DOS or ProDOS), or TRS-80s (TRSDOS) compatible with CP/M. In fact, almost any two operating systems can be made to run on the same machine by adding a coprocessor.

Microcomputer Peripherals

The types of input and output devices used with various computer systems have been discussed earlier in the text (see Chapter 4) as have storage devices (see Chapter 5). Certain peripheral devices work especially well in a microcomputer environment. These devices must be easy to use because microcomputer users are usually not experienced programmers. Cost is another factor limiting the type of peripheral device used, especially with storage devices.

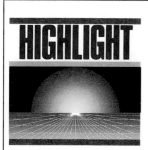

New Standards for Compatibility

The U.S. microcomputer market will most likely get some tough competition from Japanese manufacturers soon. Microsoft's Far East president, "Kay" Nishi, has written a set of standards for hardware and software development. The standards, called the MSX system, have been adopted by 35 companies from Japan and other countries.

Following the MSX standards, a manufacturer can build computer systems that will interface with a variety of peripheral devices. The greatest strength of the MSX system, however, is that all hardware and software developed according to MSX standards will be compatible.

Computers based on MSX standards are already available in Japan and Europe but have not yet entered the U.S. market because of a lack of English-based software. Foreign companies claim they are wary of competition from U.S. computer giants such as IBM and Commodore. Still, keeping in mind the Japanese impact on the automobile and electronics industries, look for MSX computers to inundate the U.S. market any day. These computers, which would probably undercut U.S. microcomputer prices, could have a dramatic effect on the microcomputer market of the future.

Input/Output Devices

The increased use of microcomputers has promoted the development and popularity of a variety of input/output devices. Many input devices, in particular, have become standard for use with microcomputers.

The most common I/O device is the monitor (see Figure 9–8). Monitors allow users to view information before sending it to the microprocessor for processing, as well as to view information sent from the microprocessor. The information displayed on the monitor can be in either character or graphic form, such as a bar graph or pie chart.

Monitors are generally divided into four categories: (1) monochrome, (2) color, (3) RGB (red-green-blue), and (4) combination TV/monitors. Monochrome monitors display a single color, such as white, green, or amber, against a black background. Color monitors, on the other hand, display a composite of colors received in one signal. RGB monitors receive three separate color signals, and they can display sharper images than the standard color monitors. They are most commonly used for high quality graphic displays. Combination monitors are designed to double as TV receivers and color monitors.

Joysticks and game paddles are generally found on microcomputers that run game applications. Both devices are used to position some object on the monitor screen. For example, joysticks (see Figure 9–9) position the cursor displayed on the monitor. If the face of the monitor is viewed as an x/y plane, the joystick is used to control the movement of the cursor within that plane. Game paddles

**Figure 9–8
Monitor**

Figure 9–9
Joysticks

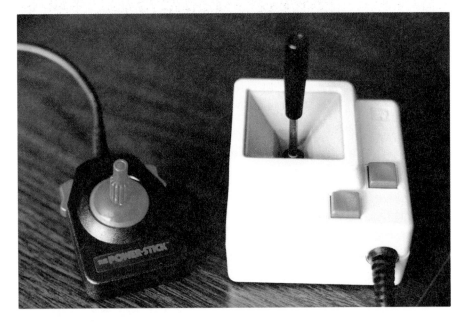

Figure 9–10
Game Paddle

(see Figure 9–10) are used to position a figure that moves vertically or horizontally on the monitor screen for a particular video game.

The mouse is a hand-movable input device that controls the position of the cursor on the screen (see Figure 9–11). The mouse is connected to the computer by an input cord. When the mouse is rolled across a flat surface, it sends electronic signals through the cord to the computer, and the cursor moves accordingly. Using the mouse eliminates a considerable amount of typing.

Graphics tablets are flat, boardlike surfaces directly connected to the microcomputer CRT screen (see Figure 9–12). The user draws on the tablet using a pencillike device, and the image is transmitted to the screen. Graphics tablets enable the user to employ colors, textures, and patterns when creating images.

Figure 9–11
A Mouse.
Some microcomputers allow a mouse to enter data. The mouse is similar to the tracker balls used in video games, except the roller is in the belly of the mouse. The user rolls the mouse around on the desk, and a cursor on the screen moves according to the movements of the mouse. A click of the button on the mouse commands the computer.

Figure 9–12
Graphics Tablet.
A graphics tablet allows the user to
bypass the keyboard and enter data
from a flat pad.

A touch screen looks like a normal computer screen, but it can detect a user's touch and identify the point at which the user touches the screen (see Figure 9–13). The touch screen is especially useful when the user is presented a list of alternatives from which to choose. When the user touches the desired alternative, the computer registers the choice made and continues processing accordingly.

Common output devices for microcomputers, besides monitors, are printers and plotters. Both impact and nonimpact printers are used with microcomputers. Dot matrix printers are commonly used for rough drafts or when the quality of the print is not an important factor. Letter quality printers, such as the daisy wheel printer, are used when output must have the quality of type-

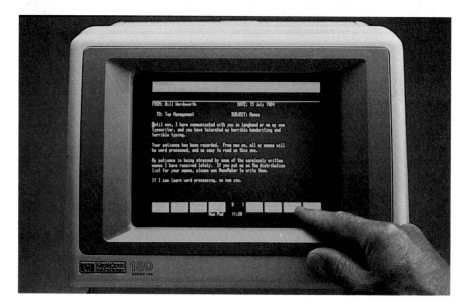

Figure 9–13
Touch Screen

written pages. Since the prices of laser printers have dropped, these letter-quality printers have also become popular for use with microcomputers.

Microcomputers are being used more and more for computer-aided design and business graphics. Plotters are used to produce the graphic images needed for these applications. A plotter consists of pens, a movable carriage, a holder for paper, and sometimes a drum (see Figure 9–14). The pens and/or the paper are moved to produce curves, complex graphic shapes, and various charts.

Storage Media

The storage media commonly used with microcomputers are cartridge tapes, cassette tapes, and floppy disks (see Chapter 5). These media are inexpensive and small, which makes them ideal for microcomputer data storage. However, they are not suitable for storing large amounts of data. Hard disks are more expensive than floppy disks, but they can store up to ten times more data.

Cartridge tapes are best suited to storing short programs and data files (see Figure 9–15). They allow only sequential access of data, which is very slow. The main advantage of cartridge tapes is their low cost.

Cassette tapes are popular with microcomputer users because they can be used with a regular cassette player, and they are easy to store (see Figure 9–16). They are also inexpensive. As on cartridge tapes, data access is sequential and very slow.

Floppy disks offer direct access of data, which makes them much faster than cassette tape (see Figure 9–17). Two standard sizes of floppy disks are available: 8 inches and 5¼ inches. A new 3½-inch microdisk, such as the one used with the Apple Macintosh, has been well-received by users. Besides being small

Figure 9–14
Plotter.
This is a flatbed plotter. The paper lies flat under a bar that holds the pens. Some plotters are called drum plotters, because the paper rolls out on a cylinder while the graphic design is being plotted.

Figure 9–15
Cartridge Tape

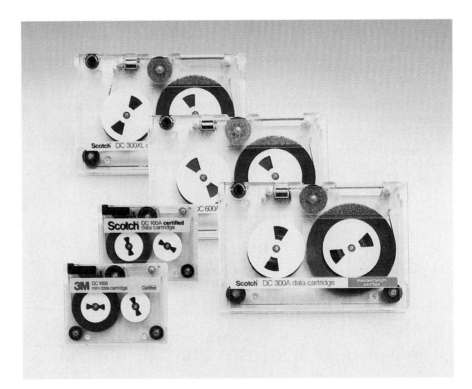

Figure 9–16
Cassette Tape

and inexpensive, floppy disks are reusable, lightweight (less than 2 ounces), easy to store, and safe to mail.

Hard magnetic disks can store more data than cassette tapes and floppy disks (see Figure 9–18). Data access is also faster with hard disks than with floppy disks. There are two varieties of hard disks: fixed and removable.

A fixed disk is a sealed unit the user cannot open. It is relatively inexpensive but more expensive than a floppy disk. Fixed disks are reliable, secure, and small, and they will store a large amount of data.

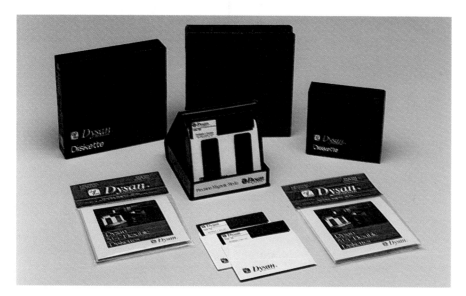

Figure 9–17
Floppy Disks

Figure 9–18
A Hard Disk Unit

A removable disk allows the user to change disks. This feature provides for easy and quick backup since the disks can be removed and kept in a different location. Removable disks are not as popular as fixed disks because they are too expensive for most microcomputer users.

SPECIAL MICROCOMPUTERS

Portables and Transportables

The smallest microcomputers available are portables. Portables are light enough to be carried and do not need an external source of power. They are powered by either rechargeable or replaceable batteries. Portables usually need some form of direct-access mass storage medium, such as floppy disks.

Portables can be divided further by size into briefcase-sized, notebook-sized, and hand-held. The Hewlett-Packard 110 is briefcase-sized and is noted for being much faster than other portables (see Figure 9–19). Radio Shack's Model 100 and Model 200 are notebook-sized and used mostly for word processing (see Figure 9–20).

Portables should be distinguished from another class of small microcomputers, the transportables. Transportables are generally larger than portables but are still small enough to be carried. They differ from portables because they require an external power source. Even though it weighs only 7½ pounds, the Apple IIc shown in Figure 9–21 is a transportable, because it does not contain its own power source.

Some portables are capable of almost as much as small desktop microcomputers, and their prices reflect it. They range in price from around $3,000 to $5,000. Other portables are dedicated to certain functions and carry a much lower price tag, from around $800 to $2,000.

Figure 9–19
Hewlett-Packard
110 Portable Computer.
This computer can fit in a briefcase, which makes carrying it on business trips easy.

Figure 9–20
Radio Shack Model 100
Portable Computer.
This lower-priced portable is used mostly for special functions such as word processing.

Each portable has different features, so users must evaluate their particular needs before selecting a portable. Some useful features include built-in modems and telecommunications software for transmitting and receiving data. Some portables have ports for connecting floppy disk drives, cassette recorders, or bar code readers. Most portables have built-in software such as a word processor, spreadsheet, or data-base manager. Built-in programming languages such as BASIC are also included with some portable computers.

Figure 9–21
Apple IIc.
The Apple IIc is a transportable microcomputer that requires an external power source and a separate display. It weighs only 7½ pounds.

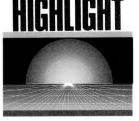

Portable Computers Save Lives

Computers don't have to be large and powerful to be used to save lives.

In Jamestown, New York, Radio Shack's portable computer, the TRS-80 Model 100, rides in ambulances with paramedics on all emergency calls. Weighing only four pounds and about the size of a book, it is mounted on the ambulance dashboard. Its memory stores the medical histories of about 1,000 high-risk patients who might need immediate emergency treatment. These patients either have previously used the ambulance service or have submitted their medical records as a precautionary measure. When an emergency call comes from one of these patients, paramedics can review the patient's medical history on the way to the scene.

In addition to medical backgrounds of high-risk patients, the computer's memory contains important emergency medical instructions, a medication inventory, and messages for ambulance staff.

Using the portable computer in this way, paramedics can stabilize victims or even save lives on the way to the hospital emergency room.

Three technologies are responsible for the sophistication of portables. Microprocessors give portables the power of a full-sized computer in a single chip. Flat display panels allow portables to be slim and therefore easy to carry. Finally, battery power frees portables from dependency on external power sources.

So far, portables have been found to be especially useful for reporters and businesspeople. A reporter can, for example, cover a presidential news conference two thousand miles from the newspaper's headquarters, write the story using a word-processing package on a portable computer, and use a modem to send the finished product over telephone lines, ready for printing. Businesspeople who travel frequently also find portables useful. Salespeople can use them to develop sales or status reports to send back to the main office. They can record information on the spot while it is fresh in their minds. The hours they spend on airplanes now can be productive if they work on portable microcomputers as they travel. Also, time spent in the office summing up data after a sales trip can be reduced.

Supermicrocomputers

Some microcomputers are so powerful they can compete with low-end minicomputers. These machines are sometimes called supermicrocomputers (see Figure 9–22). Supermicrocomputers are usually built around powerful 32-bit microprocessors. Because microprocessors are very inexpensive compared to the CPUs of minicomputers, supermicrocomputers offer users a significant price edge over minicomputers. The low cost of microprocessors also makes it possible to build supermicrocomputers with several microprocessors, each ded-

Figure 9–22
Supermicrocomputer

icated to a particular need. For example, individual microprocessors can be dedicated to each user workstation, disk drive, or printer.

Supermicrocomputers must be able to store large amounts of data. Hard disks can store much more data than the traditional floppy disks used with microcomputers. Fortunately, the prices of hard disk drives are falling, making them ideal storage devices for supermicrocomputers.

One problem hindering the full-scale implementation of supermicrocomputers is a limited amount of available software. But as they gain popularity, there will be more interest in developing software for them, just as a great deal of software was developed for traditional microcomputers.

Another problem is the loyalty of minicomputer users to their machines. Many users are skeptical of the power a supermicrocomputer has and would not readily choose a supermicrocomputer over a minicomputer system. Time will remedy this problem as the power of supermicrocomputers increases and as more uses are found for them.

THE IMPACT OF MICROCOMPUTERS

Microcomputers are general-purpose machines; that is, they are designed to perform a variety of tasks. The people who buy and use microcomputers are a diverse group—businesspeople, teachers, students, doctors, lawyers, and farmers—and their computing needs are just as diverse. Because microcomputers have so many applications, they have appeared in virtually every city, town, and neighborhood in the country. Microcomputers obviously affect our lives in many ways.

Microcomputer Applications

The number of uses for microcomputers has increased as the computers themselves have acquired more features. Microcomputers can be used as typewriters, calculators, accounting systems, record keepers, and telecommunications instruments. They can also act as easels, tutors, and toys (see Figure 9–23).

In business, microcomputers are used for ordering, controlling inventory, bookkeeping, processing payroll, and many other tasks. Executives are putting microcomputers in their offices so they can have access to the information they need when making decisions (see Figure 9–24).

Microcomputers also have a wide variety of uses in homes. Even people with little or no programming experience can use microcomputers to balance

Figure 9–23
Microcomputer Applications.
The uses for microcomputers are as diverse as the people who use them. Almost any task can be made easier with a microcomputer and application software.

Microcomputers Track Criminals

Randy Mooseles, a police detective in Melbourne, Florida, uses his Commodore 64 microcomputer to track criminals in the area.

Mooseles compiled a data base of suspects based on the types of crime committed in Melbourne. He developed his own data base because he could not get the information he wanted fast enough from the large data bases kept by state and federal agencies. For example, Mooseles could not request a list of suspects based on a certain m.o. (modus operandi, the method used to commit a crime) and get the information quickly.

So, Mooseles built his own data base. He filed data on the problem crimes in Melbourne: robberies and burglaries. Melbourne, with a population of 50,000, had 66 robberies and 940 burglaries in 1983.

Mooseles's files include the m.o., name, physical description, fingerprints, birthdate, and address of persons suspected or convicted of these types of crimes. Now, when a burglary or robbery has taken place, he can request a list of suspects who have the known characteristics of the criminal who committed the crime. For example, he can obtain the names of all red-headed male suspects over 20 years old or all suspects who break and enter by carefully cutting the glass in a window.

Mooseles is sure the Melbourne Police Department and other police departments could benefit from using microcomputers and data bases similar to his.

Figure 9–24
Microcomputers Aid Decision Making.
This executive analyzes information at his desk. Having a microcomputer in the office is not only convenient but also speeds up the flow of information within an organization.

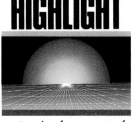

HIGHLIGHT

Microcomputers Aid the Disabled

Thanks to personal computers, disabled people are finding new ways to live happy, productive, and independent lives.

In California, Donald McIntyre used his interest in computers to help his son, Ewen, a 22-year-old victim of cerebral palsy. The elder McIntyre customized a personal computer so Ewen could operate the machine with a minimum of keystrokes. Even though he has limited use of his arms, Ewen is able to attend college and operate a small bookkeeping service with the help of his computer.

John Boyer of Madison, Wisconsin, is blind and deaf, but computers help him lead a full life. Boyer started a company called Computers to Help People, Inc., to prove the value of the disabled as worthwhile employees. A programmer employed by Boyer's company has cerebral palsy and uses a mouthstick to type commands on a computer keyboard. Boyer, also a programmer, operates a computer with help from a device that translates visual information into tactile characters. The characters are "read" by Boyer when he touches them with his fingers. Boyer plans to expand his company and, ultimately, to employ at least 20 full-time workers.

checkbooks, store recipes, prepare budgets, and play games. With flashy graphics and joysticks, a home microcomputer can become a personal video game arcade. Some people have even connected household appliances to their computers. For example, computers can turn lights on and off, control heating and air conditioning, and run the lawn sprinkler.

Recently, experiments have been conducted in banking and shopping at home by computer. At first, most people resisted the changes created by such systems. Once people saw the systems could work, however, the advantages became clear. For example, shopping and banking at home saves time and money by eliminating the need to drive around town to banks and stores. The temptation to buy on impulse is also lessened because people are not tempted by displays of products they do not need, as they might be if they walked through the stores.

In schools, microcomputers are used to instruct students and perform administrative jobs. They can help students understand subjects such as math, science, and English by offering individualized instruction (see Figure 9–25), and they can help administrators perform such tasks as ordering supplies, processing payrolls, and keeping enrollment records.

Microcomputers can also make hobbies more enjoyable. For example, special programs are written so music buffs can easily create, edit, store, and play musical compositions, all on the computer. Other programs help coin and stamp collectors catalog their collections. These are just a few of the programs geared to the interests of hobbyists.

Figure 9–25
Microcomputers in the School.
Even these six-year-olds enjoy using
microcomputers in school.
Increasingly, students' orientation to
computers begins in their first years.

Distributed Processing

An important development triggered by the use of microcomputers is the use
of distributed processing (see Chapter 7). Microcomputers can be linked by
communication lines so that processing can be done at different locations. The
portability of microcomputers makes them ideal for distributed processing because they can be placed wherever users of the system are located.

Organizations that can benefit from distributed processing include manufacturing firms with factories located around the country, department stores with

"Before we leave let's spread some of those cheese crumbs on the keyboard, too!"

271

branches in different cities, and law firms with offices in many places. For example, plant managers at remote factories could handle inquiries and produce reports using microcomputers linked to the main corporate computer. Then plant managers and executives in other locations would have access to each factory's reports.

Distributed processing may change how an organization functions, especially if operating units in different locations do not have much interaction. At first, managers and executives might not know how to use the new information available to them and might be disturbed by top management's increased control over their units. If a distributed processing system is to be successful, users of the system have to accept the changes that will occur.

Telecommunications

As discussed in Chapter 7, telecommunication is the electronic transmission of data from one location to another. Microcomputers can be hooked to a telephone and a modem so that data can be sent and received over telephone lines. Telecommunications make possible several new ways to communicate using microcomputers.

Commercial Data Bases

Commercial data base A collection of information accessible over communication lines to paying subscribers.

Commercial data bases, also called **information services** or **information utilities,** offer many types of general information to their subscribers. Passwords are often used to ensure that only paying customers can access a commercial data base. Commercial data bases charge customers either a flat fee or a connect time fee. *Connect time* refers to the actual time a customer is using the data base. If a customer does not use the data base at all one month, there is no charge. If a customer is being charged a *flat fee,* the monthly charge remains the same no matter how much or little the customer uses the data base.

Customers of commercial data bases must also pay for any long-distance telephone charges, if a long-distance call is required to access the data base. Some telephone companies also charge an extra fee (separate from the long-distance charges) for customers who use modems.

One advantage of owning a microcomputer is the ability to keep up with the changing world without leaving the home or office. Commercial data bases are often used by people doing in-depth research. Research data once available only at public or university libraries can now be accessed at home or the office.

Popular commercial data bases are The Source, CompuServe, B.R.S., Dialog, and The Dow Jones Data Retrieval Service. (For details on CompuServe, see the Focus on Microcomputers in Chapter 7). Information offered by these and other commercial data bases include video versions of major newspapers, stock market reports, airline and hotel reservation services, sports news, movie and book reviews, gourmet recipes, foreign language drills, and home buying and selling information (see Figure 9–26). Complete encyclopedias can be found on certain data bases. The main advantage of an electronic encyclopedia is that information is always up-to-date, not merely as current as the information was at the time of publication.

Figure 9–26
Commercial Data Base Menu Screen.
With a subscription to a commercial
data base, personal computer users
have the world at their fingertips.
These women are checking the
week's best-selling fiction books.

Electronic Bulletin Boards

Microcomputers can also be used to access electronic bulletin boards, which
are operated by computer enthusiasts and can be accessed at little or no cost.
Electronic bulletin boards are usually set up for the users of a particular computer
system, for example, the owners of Apple computers. They can be started by
practically anyone who has a telephone, a microcomputer, a modem, and
communications software. There are approximately 3,000 bulletin boards in
operation in the United States. Of course, an electronic bulletin board will not
contain as much information as a commercial data base, but a well-constructed
one can provide much information on particular topics.

To access a bulletin board, the member has to dial the bulletin board telephone number and log on to the system. The member can then ask for any
personal mail that may be waiting or can send messages to other members.
Members commonly contribute information on equipment, software, support,
computer dealers, and computer care and maintenance.

The value of a bulletin board increases as members contribute programs
they have written to the library of programs. Users may need to contact the
bulletin board operator (commonly called a system operator or sysop) before
downloading or uploading a public domain program from or to the bulletin
board. Public domain programs are programs donated for public use by their
creators. The sysop may then assign the user a password or terminal program
that will allow the program to be copied.

Some bulletin boards have been set up for users with special interests rather than owners of particular computers. For example, there are bulletin boards for writers, attorneys, and pilots. Others have been created to help users find dates or to conduct informal polls on political issues. The number of bulletin boards should continue to increase as more personal microcomputers are purchased.

Local Area Networks

Local area networks (LANs) link microcomputers in the same general area to share information and hardware (see Chapter 7). Usually, the microcomputers are within a thousand feet of each other since they must be connected by a cable hookup (see Figure 9–27).

The popularity of LANs is just beginning to rise. Teachers use LANs to monitor their students' progress and leave homework on their terminals. In offices, LANs are used to send electronic mail and to share information on projects that involve a number of persons. LANs can be useful in any situation where people with microcomputers in the same area need to communicate and share information and hardware.

Implications of Telecommunications

As telecommunications are used more and more by people with microcomputers, concern is growing about the implications of such technology. Some people predict telecommunications will create a "paperless" society, in which books, newspapers, and magazines will not exist. With microcomputers in most homes and offices, users will have access to the information provided by traditional paper media through some form of telecommunication. Libraries would become obsolete. In offices, there would be no need for paper memos, reports, and letters since they could be stored and sent electronically.

In schools, written homework and reports would be abandoned. Assignments

Figure 9–27
Local Area Network.
Local area networks will continue to gain popularity because of the explosion in microcomputer use. Portable microcomputers with LAN capability may represent the wave of the future.

Electronic Addiction

Bulletin board systems and information utilities offer a fantasyland of communications. Some users spend $15 to $50 per month, others find that $500 barely pays for their habit.

Some utilities offer a simulated CB radio for people to talk back and forth. And bulletin boards provide a way to meet people for computer "loners."

Dr. Ronald Levy, a Buffalo, New York, psychiatrist, says bulletin boards are something like telephones for teenagers. "Talking by bulletin board becomes a way of relating without meeting people face to face. It creates less stress than face to face encounters. This type of relationship is important in a teenager's development. And for people who are older, bulletin board relationships can provide a way to begin a social life."

However, it can become a habit to talk to people without any physical contact. Levy warns that this type of relationship is not meant as a substitute for life.

Sometimes the pocketbook stops this. Connect time costs money, especially if the bulletin board number at the other end is a long distance call. Some utilities charge over $25 per hour for connect time. A couple of hours per week could add up to a huge bill, which most people simply can't afford.

Other people learn to treat bulletin boards and data bases as only part of their lives. After all, there are many other things to do and people to see—face to face, that is.

could be sent from the teacher's computer to each student's microcomputer at home. Likewise, homework could be sent back to the teacher's terminal for grading. The graded homework could then be transmitted to the student for review. Telecommunication of this sort might even make traveling to school unnecessary for students.

Many people are concerned about how electronic communication will affect interpersonal relationships. If students, teachers, workers, and friends can communicate by typing messages to each other on their microcomputers, will they still talk face to face? If not, will they ever learn how to interact or cultivate relationships? Relationships in a paperless society may be very different from today's relationships. However, until electronic communication becomes common in our daily lives, we can only speculate about the effects.

User's Groups

Where can a new microcomputer owner go for help in getting the machine in operation? When a $150 software package will not run on the machine, who can identify the problem? Which word-processing package, priced under $200, works best on a certain microcomputer? Questions such as these often baffle the proud new owner of a microcomputer. The answer, in all cases, is a **user's group.** A user's group is a relatively informal group of owners of a particular

User's group An informal group of owners of a particular microcomputer, who meet to exchange information about hardware, software, service, and support.

microcomputer model who meet to exchange information about hardware, software, service, and support.

An estimated 1,000 user's groups were in operation by 1984. Apple II, IBM PC, Vic 20/C-64, Timex Sinclair, and Osborne computers are among the many microcomputer user's groups in operation. Some local groups have only a dozen or so members while other nationwide groups report up to 12,000 members.

The value of user's groups comes from the accumulation of knowledge and experience ready to be shared by members. Many times, the best evaluations of hardware and software available for a particular microcomputer comes from one who has actually purchased and tried it. As software becomes more sophisticated and more hardware becomes available to enhance microcomputers, user's groups will become even more valuable.

A user's group usually starts when a few people get together to discuss problems and benefits they have had with their particular microcomputers. As word spreads about the group and more people in the area buy the microcomputer, the user's group grows. As it grows, the group becomes a more valuable source of information. Once membership becomes so large that the informal atmosphere is no longer effective, the group usually establishes a more formal organization. This means electing officers, setting a definite meeting time and place, and devising a meeting agenda.

Large user's groups sometimes put out newsletters to keep members informed of new hardware and software. They may also operate a software library with programs written and donated by members. Some groups purchase products, such as floppy disks, software packages, and equipment upgrades, in large quantities and offer them to members at low prices.

User's groups may provide an invaluable service to owners of microcomputers that have been discontinued, such as the Timex Sinclair 1000, Osborne, and IBM PCjr. When a manufacturer goes out of business, parts and peripheral equipment become scarce, and service and technical support almost always disappear. But user's groups can continue to offer support and may even arrange to obtain parts for members.

Since user's groups do not normally have telephones or office space, finding a local group is not always easy. However, dealers who sell the microcomputer usually know how to contact user's groups, and groups often post notices and flyers in computer stores. Information on national groups is sometimes included in the microcomputer package when it is sold. Contacting the manufacturer directly may also yield the name of the person to contact about a local group.

Computer Stores

Computer store A retail store that sells microcomputers and is structured to meet the needs of small business and personal computer owners.

When microcomputers first appeared they were primarily sold by mail order. Products were shipped directly from the manufacturer to the user. Around 1975, the first **computer stores** began emerging (see Figure 9–28). These stores are structured to meet the needs of small business and personal computer owners. Some stores offer products from only one manufacturer, others offer a wide variety of hardware and software for several microcomputer brands.

A good computer store will have demonstration systems on display so that the shopper can actually test the system. It's salespeople and technical experts should be able to answer questions and provide technical guidance for the computer novice.

Figure 9–28
Computer Store.
The Computer Center at Radio Shack (a division of Tandy Corporation) bustles with activity. Microcomputer users buy a great deal of hardware and software to give their systems greater capabilities. This has created a demand for computer stores in all areas.

Today, thousands of computer stores exist in the United States. Some are part of nationwide chains; others are small individually owned stores. They can be found in large cities, small towns, downtown business districts, malls, shopping centers, and even suburban neighborhoods. The large number of computer stores indicates that microcomputers have infiltrated every part of the country and touched most people's lives.

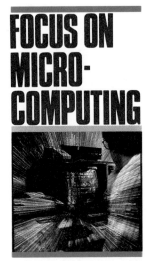

FOCUS ON MICRO-COMPUTING

Caring for Your Microcomputer

A common saying is an ounce of prevention is worth a pound of cure. Although this saying usually applies to personal health, it can also be applied to personal computers.

Taking good care of your microcomputer requires time and effort, but preventive maintenance will probably save you time and money in the long run. Cleaning and protecting your computer's disk drive, monitor, keyboard, printer, and other components will keep the system running better for longer. A well-maintained computer system spends less time in the repair shop, which saves you money and increases your computer use.

Reading the owner's manual before taking the computer out of its box is a good idea. The owner's manual often contains tips for keeping the computer clean as well as do's and don'ts for the specific model.

Maintenance experts emphasize that maintenance does not include do-it-yourself repair. Unless you are a qualified technician, there is virtually nothing you can repair inside a typical microcomputer. Tinkering around inside the computer only risks further damage, electrical shock, and a voided warranty.

Still, you can do a great deal to postpone the need for major repairs. Perhaps the best place to start is the microcomputer's environment. An ideal environment is an office or study where the temperature is a stable 75°F and the humidity remains around 50 percent. Too much humidity is not good, but an area that is too dry is even worse. A dry environment is conducive to static electricity, which can scramble data stored on floppy disks. A humidifier and antistatic mat and spray can help control static electricity. Extreme heat and cold should also be avoided, so keep the computer out of direct sunlight; off appliances that get hot, such as televisions; and away from windows, heating ducts, and air-conditioning units.

A sturdy resting place for the computer and its components is another consideration in finding a good home for your computer. Move the computer as little as possible. If you must move the computer a long distance, place it in its original packaging to prevent damage.

Smoking, eating, and drinking are all potentially hazardous to a personal computer's health. Smoking adds tar and other matter to the air and, in turn, into and onto the computer. Dropped crumbs and spilled liquid will cause keys to stick and malfunction. Dirty hands inevitably lead to a dirty computer.

Even in an ideal environment, additional precautions and some simple maintenance techniques are necessary to keep a microcomputer in top working condition. Dust particles and static electricity are virtually impossible to prevent. Together they can cause a short circuit. The most visible collection of dust and static is on the monitor. To check for static electricity and dust, run your finger lightly across the screen. If you hear a crackling sound and have dust on your finger, you have both culprits.

278

Before cleaning any part of your microcomputer, consult the owner's manual for any warnings or suggestions about simple maintenance and prevention. If there are no warnings against it, use common household glass cleaner and a paper towel to clean the monitor. Too much liquid on the screen, however, may short circuit the machine. The best cleaning method is to turn off the monitor, apply the cleaner to the towel, and then wipe the screen.

Antistatic sprays and towelettes generally prevent static longer than glass cleaner. To prevent static, some good habits include keeping the monitor covered and out of direct sunlight, and turning it off when not in use.

Like a typewriter, the computer keyboard seems to attract dust and dirt. You can clean the surfaces of the keys with a mild cleanser such as dish-washing liquid. Of course, dust and dirt also accumulate in places that are hard to clean, such as between and under the keys. A moistened cotton swab or soft brush will reach between keys, while a can of compressed air will blow out dirt from under keys. Covering the keyboard when it's not in use will help keep dust and dirt out. Also, keep food and drinks at a distance. These simple measures should keep the keyboard functional for a long time. If the keyboard does malfunction, it may be less expensive to replace rather than repair it.

Floppy disk drives are much more expensive to replace, and, of all computer components, they have the greatest potential for problems. Trouble with disk drives can cause a loss of data, which translates into lost time and money.

Keeping the disk drive clean will greatly reduce the likelihood of disk drive problems. "Wet/dry" drive cleaners are preferred by most experts. These devices clean the read/write head(s) inside the drive by loosening particles and dust with a white fiber disk sprayed with a cleaning solution. To clean a disk drive, you spray the disk with a special disk-cleaning solution, insert the disk, let it rotate several times, and remove it. Manufacturers usually recommend that the disk drive be cleaned after 6 to 15 hours of drive operation. Never clean a read/write head using a cotton swab and alcohol. This method applies direct pressure to the head, which may cause serious damage. To keep as much dust as possible away from a disk drive, cover it when it's not in use.

Your computer will only be as reliable as the storage media used to store data. Disks that have been certified by a reputable company are generally reliable. Less-expensive, off brands may not save you money in the long run if they are defective.

Floppy disks should always be handled with care. Never touch the surface of the disk (visible through the oval cutout). Floppy disks are sensitive to extreme temperatures, dust and eraser particles, and pressure such as writing on their jackets with a ballpoint pen (use felt-tip markers to write on the label). Magnetic fields, such as those emitted from telephones, tape recorders, radios, and stereo speakers, can damage the data on floppy disks, so do not store them near such objects. Always store disks in their protective envelopes.

Printers are also prone to problems. Dust and paper pieces are the number one causes of problems. Compressed air and a vacuum cleaner probably yield the best results when cleaning a printer. The owner's manual should tell you when and where to lubricate printer parts. Again, keep the printer covered when it is not in use.

Most other peripherals such as external modems and hard disks require little maintenance. A mouse can be taken apart (carefully) and cleaned to prevent sticking or skipping.

Common sense is the real key to proper microcomputer care. When components get dirty, clean them. Lubricate moving parts so they continue to run smoothly. Always consult the owner's manual before undertaking any maintenance or repair action. When in doubt about what to do, call a trained repairperson. Just remember, caring for your computer before there are problems will keep it running reliably for a long time.

SUMMARY POINTS

- Microcomputers differ from minicomputers, mainframes, and supercomputers in capability, price, and size. They are the smallest and least expensive computers, but the distinction between the power of minicomputers and the power of microcomputers is fading as microcomputers become more powerful.
- The increased power and miniaturization of microprocessors paved the way for the development of microcomputers.
- The first microprocessors could manipulate 4 bits of data at a time. Most microcomputers today can manipulate 8 bits or 16 bits; 32-bit microprocessors have recently been developed.
- The Altair 8800 was the first microcomputer available for commercial sale. It was developed by MITS.
- Microcomputer pioneers include Ed Roberts of MITS, Stephen Wozniak and Steven Jobs who built the Apple II microcomputer, Jack Tramiel of Commodore Business Machines, John Roach of Tandy Corporation, and John Opel, chief executive officer of IBM. These people were influential in making microcomputers available to the general public.
- The speed of a microcomputer depends on two major factors: word size and clock speed. Word size refers to the number of bits that can be manipulated at one time. Clock speed refers to the number of electronic pulses the microprocessor can produce each second.
- Popular operating systems include CP/M (Control Program for Microprocessors), MS–DOS, Apple DOS and Apple ProDOS, and Unix. There is no standard operating system for microcomputers. Therefore, microcomputers with different operating systems are not compatible, at least not without a coprocessor.
- Microcomputers with different operating systems can be made compatible by installing a coprocessor. A coprocessor works with the original microprocessor to allow both the original operating system's and the new operating system's software and hardware to run on the microcomputer.
- Common microcomputer input/output devices are monitors, joysticks and game paddles, the mouse, graphics tablets, touch screens, printers, and plotters.

- Storage media used with microcomputers are cartridge tapes, cassette tapes, and floppy disks. Hard magnetic disks are being used in some situations where large amounts of data must be stored.
- Portable computers are light enough to be carried and do not need an external source of power. They may be briefcase-sized, notebook-sized, or hand held. Transportables are generally larger than portables but are still light enough to be carried. However, they require an external power source.
- Supermicrocomputers are a class of microcomputers with power that rivals that of minicomputers. These high-end microcomputers are less expensive than minicomputers and they provide users with high performance at a relatively low cost.
- Microcomputers have many uses in business, at home, and in schools. They have a far-reaching impact on society.
- Microcomputers are frequently used for distributed processing. Linking microcomputers by communication lines allow people in different locations to use the same computer resources.
- Microcomputer users can subscribe to commercial data bases with many types of information, such as video versions of newspapers, stock market reports, movie reviews, and encyclopedias.
- Electronic bulletin boards are operated by computer enthusiasts called sysops. They are generally set up for users of a particular computer system, and they allow users to send and receive messages, contribute reviews of software and hardware, and donate programs for other members to use.
- Local area networks link microcomputers in the same general area so users can share information.
- The owner of a particular microcomputer can join a user's group to get advice and information from other owners of the same brand of microcomputer.
- Computer stores are structured to meet the needs of small business and personal computer owners. They usually offer a variety of hardware and software for several microcomputer brands.
- Preventive maintenance is required to keep a microcomputer in good working order. Simple cleaning techniques for the monitor, keyboard, disk drive, and printer prevent serious problems.

REVIEW AND DISCUSSION QUESTIONS

1. Describe the development of the microprocessor and explain how it contributed to the development of the microcomputer.
2. Name at least six uses of microcomputers in business, home, or school.
3. Give an example, other than the examples in the text, of an organization that could use microcomputers and distributed processing.
4. What is a commercial data base? What costs are involved in subscribing to one?
5. What benefits could a microcomputer owner obtain by belonging to an electronic bulletin board?
6. How does a user's group differ from an electronic bulletin board?
7. Compare portable and transportable computers.

8. Explain how a microcomputer's speed depends on word size and clock speed.
9. What is meant by microcomputer compatibility? What determines microcomputer compatibility?
10. Name five input/output devices that are specifically used with microcomputers.
11. What requirements must be met by storage media used for microcomputers?
12. How does a fixed hard disk differ from a removable hard disk? Which is most commonly used with microcomputers? Why?
13. What is a coprocessor?
14. Describe the ideal environment for a microcomputer.
15. Why is static electricity a problem for microcomputers? How can it be prevented?

CHAPTER 10
THE PROGRAMMING PROCESS

COMPUTERS IN OUR LIVES

Rosa Torres and "Willy-Nilly Programming"

As an intern in computer programming at Belding-Stone Consultants, Rosa Torres was using the latest in programming techniques to customize and debug computer software for small businesses that could not afford their own programmers. Belding-Stone programmers often had to rewrite programs produced by less experienced programmers who used the debugging technique.

With the debugging technique, the programmer writes a program that seems to solve a problem. Then the program is tested. As soon as an error occurs, that error is fixed. When another error turns up, that one is fixed. Often the fixes are "glued" together by using an instruction called the GOTO statement, which allows program execution to jump in and out of the various tasks in a program. If you were asked to read a book by the GOTO method, you might read in this order:

1. *GOTO chapter 5*
2. *Read chapter 5 and GOTO chapter 7*
3. *Read chapter 7*
4. *Oops, we forgot that material in chapter 2 is necessary to chapter 7*
5. *GOTO chapter 1 and read chapter 1*
6. *Now GOTO chapter 7 and reread the material*

You can see that if a programmer used many of these GOTO statements, the result would be an inefficient, hard-to-read program. Rosa discovered this kind of program usually works, but she also knew that sooner or later some new input could turn up more errors.

The debugging technique and the tangle of GOTOS were common in early computer programming. For example, the software that operated the IBM 360 computer—a third-generation computer developed in the 1960s—had cost hundreds of millions of dollars, was more than a year late, and still contained thousands of errors when it was released. Similar problems with other programs led to industry conferences on the "software crisis." At these meetings experts recommended implementing methodologies that would encourage an organized, or structured, approach to programming. In the early 1970s a team of IBM programmers tried structured programming to build an information bank for the New York Times. Surprisingly, the project was completed in record time and contained almost no errors. Other programmers scrambled to learn the new techniques, but as Rosa was finding out, even in the 1980s old habits die hard. Programmers at Belding-Stone certainly did not lack business—and Rosa gained experience—as customers brought in their software for revisions.

While in college preparing for her career as a computer scientist, Rosa studied the ideas of Edsger Dijkstra, who recommends applying rigorous mathematics techniques to write well-designed software. She learned about top-down design, proper program documentation, and program design aids such as Nassi-Shneiderman charts and structure charts. She knew that changing methodologies could cost a company a lot of money and that structured programming does not solve every programming problem. In looking at long-term benefits, however, using structured programming techniques can save money for a company. Chapter 10 describes these and other aspects of structured programming.

INTRODUCTION

Many tasks that you learn to perform become "second nature" to you. Some, such as sleeping, curling a fist, smiling that first smile, or sucking formula from a baby bottle, are believed to be instinctive behaviors. Other tasks, once learned, become so ingrained that you do not think about the specific steps involved. Do you stop to think "left foot, push down—right foot, pull up" while riding your bicycle? Do you analyze the "ch" sound in the word *change* versus the "ch" sound in the word *character* each time your eyes focus on these words? How many times do you actually concentrate on the motions of chewing and swallowing your breakfast muffin? Once you have learned to type, do you stop to think which finger should strike which key as you type a memo or research paper?

On the other hand, if you want to pedal faster, you will tell your feet to move faster. If you are studying linguistics, you will certainly analyze sounds of letter combinations. If you realize you are gulping your breakfast, you may consciously slow down the act of chewing and increase the number of chews. And if you did not learn the positions of number and special character keys in typing class, you will continue to glance at the keyboard when you need to type an ampersand.

You perform some tasks automatically and other tasks by independent thought and voluntary action. For most behaviors, you do not send a list of detailed instructions to your brain. If you are modifying a behavior or learning a new task, many steps will incorporate processes already learned. By thinking logically, practicing the steps, or relating old behaviors to new tasks, you can make up for the steps you do not know how to do. However, computers exhibit no independent thought or voluntary action. These incredibly fast machines do tasks step by step and only as instructed. They cannot "make up" for omitted steps. On one hand, this appears to limit the tasks that computers can perform. On the other hand, it suggests computers are limited only by people's ability to break down a problem into steps that computers can use to solve it.

Any "intelligence" the computer seems to possess is given to it by programmers. Early computer programs were prepared in machine language, a code based on the binary number system using the digits 1 and 0. When computer applications became limited because long programs written in two digits were cumbersome, someone invented a method of translating a mnemonic language called assembly language into machine language. Later, high-level languages based on even more Englishlike commands were developed. As computer circuitry becomes more complex and computer languages become more sophisticated, programmers are able to increase the types of problems that can be solved through computer use, and computers seem even more "intelligent." These innovations have made giving instructions to the computer easier for humans. However, programmers are still developing techniques to prepare programs that are easy to use, understand, and maintain. This chapter discusses the sometimes complicated task of breaking down a problem and its solution into the logical series of steps required for computer problem solving. Included are discussions on structured programming techniques, tools for designing structured programs, and methods of checking programs.

COMPUTER PROBLEM SOLVING

Since computers solve problems according to instructions provided by programmers, each program has to be well thought out. The problem must be analyzed in detail to anticipate all logical conditions that may be encountered during processing. If an unanticipated condition arises during processing, the program will be executed incorrectly or not at all. In addition, programmers must remember that the computer will execute program steps in sequential order unless otherwise instructed.

In the early days of software development, programmers had few rules to follow. Many programmers approached their work in a somewhat haphazard way, hoping their programs would execute properly when run. The programs were hard to follow and included little written explanation of their logic. Gradually, programmers began to prepare software by following a standard problem-solving process and by incorporating several qualities universally accepted as descriptive of well-written programs.

Desirable Program Qualities

A program that produces incorrect output is useless. However, generating the correct output is not the only requirement of a good program. Programmers agree that the following qualities are vital for successful software:

- Processing should be reliable: it should consistently produce the correct output. All formulas, computations, logic comparisons, and transfers of control must be accurate.
- Programs should anticipate input errors. Reliability alone is no guarantee of a successful program. Internal logic may be correct, but an incorrect data item (garbage in) could produce incorrect output (garbage out). A good program is designed to minimize the occurrence of "garbage in." For example, a program that asks the user to input the ages and birthdates of employees will test for input that is unusual or illogical. If the user enters an improbable age, such as 4682 or −35, the program will send an incorrect entry message. A user who enters "21-42-12" as a birthdate should be asked to check the validity of that date.
- Programs should be efficient. In general, this means that programs should execute as quickly as possible. Computers are very expensive, and CPU time is a valuable resource. Some companies charge users hundreds of dollars *for each minute of CPU time.* An efficient program could save a company thousands of dollars per year.

- Programs should be maintainable. They should be easy to update and modify. Programs should be written in independent modules, or segments, so that a change in one module does not necessitate a change in others.
- Programs should be easy to read and understand. Names for data items should be descriptive. Statements should be placed in a format that is easy to read and follow. Steps should be defined and explained. In other words, the programmer should write the program so that someone else can easily read and understand it.

Steps in the Problem-Solving Process

To prepare a well-written program, the programmer should follow four steps in problem solving and program development:

- Defining and documenting the problem
- Designing and documenting the solution
- Writing and documenting the program
- Compiling, debugging, and testing the program and revising the documentation

Defining the problem and designing the solution are two steps generally independent of the programming language used. They are the most difficult steps, because the programmer must be adept at defining a problem according to the user's needs and analyzing it in terms of current computer capabilities. In defining the problem, the programmer determines the nature and extent of the problem to be solved. In planning the solution, the programmer combines the required inputs and the basic program logic patterns (discussed later in this chapter) to provide the desired output.

The other steps—writing, compiling, debugging, and testing the program—involve coding the solution in one of many computer programming languages. The programmer selects the programming language that best fits the processing requirements of the program. After the program is coded, it is submitted to the computer, where it is translated into machine language. The debugging and testing stages involve correcting poorly written program statements, removing logic errors, and entering test data into the program. During the four problem-solving steps, the programmer should document the work, or prepare written descriptions of all program components. Specific methodologies can help the programmer complete these steps successfully. Taken as a unit, the methodologies are often referred to as the structured approach to programming, discussed in the following section.

STRUCTURED PROBLEM SOLVING

People solve problems every day. Most problems have several acceptable solutions: for example, try to count the number of ways to clean a room! Although you can list the precise tasks that must be done, many variables exist. You can vary the order in which the tasks are done: should you dust the furniture or wash the windows first? The cleaning method may vary: some floors require scrubbing with a mop and soapy water, while other floors require vacuuming. Products vary with the task: the vinegar solution that helps clean windows

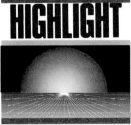

Why Learn to Program?

Relevancy was a key word among educators in the 1970s. Often *relevancy* simply means a quality that will help you get a job, be a smart consumer, and get on with daily living. In their daily lives, average adults do not diagram sentences, translate Latin, use logarithm tables, write essays, dissect frogs, or quote long passages from Shakespeare's plays. If schools taught only relevant courses, students would be studying driver education, typing, smart shopping, wise television program selection, house cleaning, child rearing, and nutrition. So why teach anything that is not relevant?

The getting-a-job and relevant-to-daily-living arguments are often refined to support the teaching of computer programming. However, not everyone will get a job as a computer programmer, and not everyone needs programming skills to use a computer. If these two major arguments don't apply, why should students learn programming? Two authors offer their viewpoints. Arthur Luehrman, founder of the firm Computer Literacy in Berkeley, California, says programming, along with any other subject, is taught for one reason only: to "give the student a significant way to think about things, to express ideas, and to examine other people's thoughts." Frederick Brooks, author of *The Mythical Man-Month*, simply says programming is fun. He expresses the "sheer joy of making things, . . . the pleasure of making things that are useful to other people, . . . the fascination of fashioning complex puzzle-like objects of interlocking moving parts and watching them work in subtle cycles, playing out the consequences of principles built in from the beginning, . . . the joy of always learning. . . ." Only the most hardened skeptic would fail to be convinced by these arguments!

would lift the varnish from a table, while the furniture polish that gives a sheen to the varnished table would cloud the windows. Yet some methods enable you to clean a room more efficiently than others. If you plump up pillows on the sofa and chairs after you have vacuumed and dusted, you simply create more dust!

Computer problem solving is similar. Many solutions exist for a single problem. Some are more efficient than others. Some create problems the programmer did not consider when designing the solution. When users become frustrated by not understanding a program or the program does not run under unforeseen circumstances, the programmer realizes his or her failure to implement all the problem-solving steps. A classic example involved the maiden flight of the space shuttle Columbia. A problem arose with the computer system 20 minutes before launch time. If the problem could not be found within three hours, the flight would have to be scrubbed. No problems could be found with electrical circuitry or communication lines. Therefore, technicians reasoned, the error must be in the nearly 500,000 lines of computer programming needed to instruct the computers on board the shuttle. Finding the "bug" was like trying to find a misspelled word in Webster's Unabridged Dictionary. A similar example involves the software used during the first moon shot in 1969. Five days before launch time, a programmer discovered that a mathematical formula in the software had the moon's gravity as a repulsive rather than an attractive force. If such errors had not been discovered, the flight would have been perilous, to say the least. These types of errors led several computer scientists to formulate methodologies for a more structured approach to programming. Among them was Edsger Dijkstra, a Dutch computer scientist, who recognized the need for structured approaches in the early 1960s. Too many programmers go about their work in an undisciplined, haphazard fashion, he said. If structured design and programming methods had been followed, he insisted, such errors would never occur.

Programs that are prone to errors often contain statements that cause execution to jump around within the program. These programs may contain logic that is understood only by the original programmers, and even they may forget what their programs should do! This increases costs and difficulties associated with program design and maintenance. Furthermore, without standard design procedures, a programmer may spend far more time than necessary in determining an appropriate solution and writing the program. To counter these tendencies, structured programming techniques were suggested in the early 1970s. Stated simply, **structured programming** encourages programmers to think about the problem first rather than spend an unreasonable amount of time on **debugging** later. The techniques have been expanded and refined in the pursuit of four goals:

Structured programming A top-down modular approach to programming that emphasizes dividing a program into logical sections to improve productivity and program clarity.

Debugging The process of locating, isolating, and resolving errors within a program.

1. Reducing time and costs associated with program development
2. Increasing programmer productivity
3. Increasing clarity by reducing complexity
4. Decreasing time and effort needed to maintain a program once it is implemented

Four methodologies characterize structured programming: top-down design, program documentation, program testing during all stages of the problem-solving process, and use of a programming team.

Top-Down Design

Programmers must learn a programming language, but this is a relatively simple task; the difficult part of programming is learning to organize solutions in a clear, concise way. One method of organizing a solution is to define the major steps or functions first, and then expand the functions into more detailed steps later. This method, which proceeds from the general to the specific, is called **top-down design.** Top-down design employs the **modular approach,** breaking a problem into smaller and smaller subproblems. When the actual program is written, these subproblems can be written as separate **modules,** each of which performs a specific task.

The most general level of organization is the main control logic: this overall definition of the solution is the most critical to the success of the program. Modules at this level contain broad descriptions of the steps in the solution process. These steps are further detailed in several lower-level modules. Depending on the complexity of the problem, a hierarchy consisting of several

Top-down design A method of defining a solution from general to specific in terms of major functions and subfunctions to be performed.

Modular approach A method of simplifying a project by breaking it into segments or subunits.

Module Part of a whole; a program segment or subsystem; set of related program statements that perform one given task.

levels of modules may be required, with the lowest level modules containing the greatest amount of detail.

Making a pizza is a good example of a problem that can be organized in top-down fashion (see Figure 10–1). The desired output is good-tasting pepperoni pizza. The inputs consist of ingredients such as flour, water, yeast, salt, tomato sauce, cheese, and pepperoni. When the main module (make pizza) is analyzed, the major modules might be these:

1. Preheat oven.
2. Assemble utensils and ingredients.
3. Prepare dough.
4. Put toppings on dough.
5. Bake pizza.

Algorithm A set of well-defined instructions for the solution of a problem in a finite number of steps.

These steps provide a basic **algorithm** for solving the problem of making a pizza. This algorithm is refined by breaking each of the major steps into smaller steps. For example, Step 3 could be broken down like this:

1. Read recipe for dough.
2. Measure ingredients.
3. Mix ingredients.
4. Let dough rise.
5. Grease pan.
6. Spread dough in pan.

Some of these steps could be broken down even further. Step 2, for example, could contain substeps for each ingredient.

When top-down design is used, the complete solution is not established until the lowest-level modules have been designed. However, this does not prevent

Figure 10–1
Diagram Showing Top-Down Design for Making Pizza

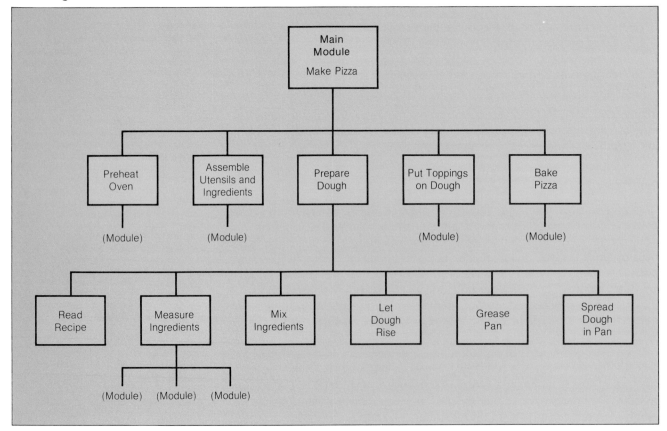

higher-level modules from being written, tested, and documented at early stages of the development cycle.

Documentation

A computer program without documentation would be like a teacher without records of students' test scores or files of students' work. When students ask why they received certain grades, such a teacher has no written documentation or student papers to back up the grades. When users or programmers wish to determine what a program does and how, the program without documentation offers no written information.

Documentation is the portion of a program that explains the program. It describes what the program should do, what data is needed, how data is identified in the program statements, and how the output is formatted. In top-down design, the documentation describes the modules as well, explaining their individual functions and their relationship to the whole program. Documentation also includes the charts produced during program design, the tests and data used to check the program, and any changes made to the program. Other important documentation provides instructions to program users and lists hardware requirements for running the program (such as disk drives or printers). A listing of the actual computer program should also be included.

Where does the documentation appear? Some documentation appears in the actual program statements to identify the objectives of the major solution and the individual modules. Other documentation may appear on the monitor when the program is run to help users understand what they should do with the program. Still other documentation appears in **run books,** which are used by the computer operator to run the program, and users' manuals, which should contain all documentation designed to aid users not familiar with a program. Users' manuals, for instance, explain how to establish contact with the computer and enter the commands to use software.

Run book Program documentation designed to aid the computer operator in running a program; also known as the operator's manual.

Everyone who uses the computer needs such documentation at some time. Proper program documentation is a reference guide for programmers and analysts who must modify or update existing programs and procedures. Without it, a programmer may spend days or weeks trying to ascertain what a program does and how it does it. Further, in many cases, programs are designed to operate under a fixed set of conditions and constraints. When organizations change and grow, program modifications must keep pace with their changing needs. Documentation helps managers evaluate the effectiveness of the programs and determine where changes are desirable. Documentation is also essential to those who must perform the manual functions of entering data required by the system and running the program.

The process of documentation is an ongoing one. It begins with the initial request for a program. It continues throughout the problem-solving steps and into the process of program maintenance. Documentation will be specifically described during each problem-solving step later in this chapter.

Program Testing

Documentation is not the only process that should occur at each problem-solving step. Each step should be tested before proceeding to the next step. During the early years of programming, testing often occurred after the entire

HIGHLIGHT

Egoless Programming

Students get defensive about their work when they see a teacher's comments plastered in red ink all over their papers. Newswriters bristle when a copy editor changes their stories to the point of being unrecognizable as their work. Why should computer programmers be any different? Programmers may be wary of letting other people look at their work, fearing that others may detect mistakes that will make them look stupid. A research paper, news story, or program reflects the pride—yes, the very soul—of the person who prepared it. Yet unless a programmer is self-employed, the program that he or she writes belongs to the organization that employs him or her.

Since programs are products, they can benefit from inspection by other programmers in a company. A review by other programmers may remove defects that would make the programming process more expensive and time-consuming. Adopting an atmosphere of mutual assistance and inspection forms the core of a programming attitude called egoless programming. The concept became popular when Gerald Weinberg included it in a book called *The Psychology of Computer Programming*. At that time structured programming ideas were just gaining popularity; programming still retained a "lone wolf" aura. In his book, Weinberg illustrated how silly the defensive attitudes could be.

Egoless programming is not meant to minimize the creativity of the programmers but to help increase productivity and maintainability of programs. Rather than view each criticism as a stab in the back, the programmer sees the comment as constructive and realizes that he or she may, in turn, offer the same sort of assistance to another programmer.

program was completed. Corrections were made in a "patch-it-up" manner, and major errors were often discovered after programs were implemented. People who bought software were discouraged and frustrated when programs did not execute correctly or when they could not understand why errors occurred. Although errors still occur—even after software is released for sale—software developers test their programs more thoroughly today than they did in the fledgling years of the industry.

Errors can be major (perhaps the problem is incorrectly defined) or minor (a typing error causes an error message to appear on the monitor). Since different kinds of errors occur at the various stages of program development, the different types of testing are described specifically under the discussion of each problem-solving step.

The Programming Team

Chief programmer team (CPT) A method of organization used in managing system projects by which a chief programmer supervises programming and testing of program modules.

An important first step taken to coordinate a programming effort involves the formation of a **chief programmer team (CPT),** which is a small number of programmers under the supervision of a chief programmer (see Figure 10–2). The number of team members varies with the complexity of the project. The

Figure 10–2
Organization of Chief Programmer Team

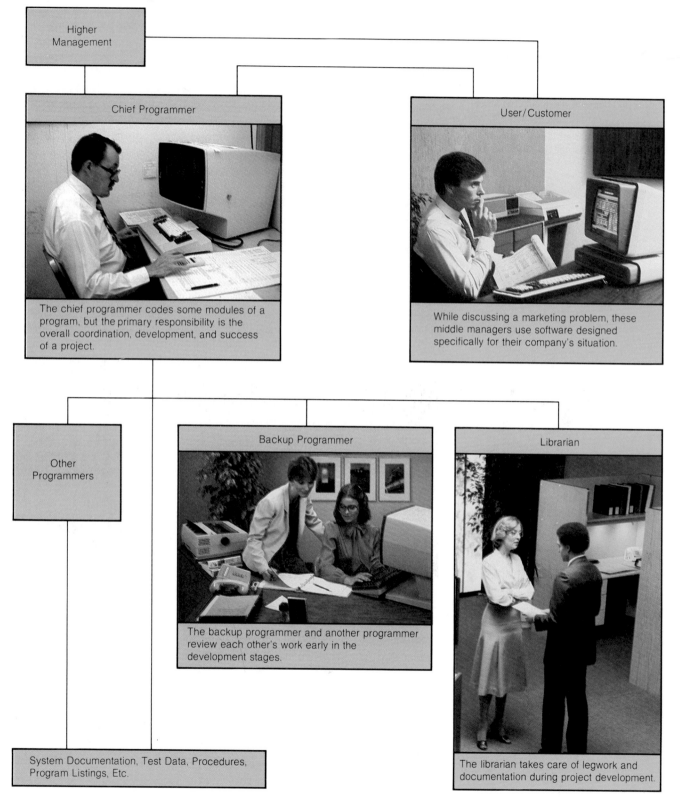

Higher Management

Chief Programmer

The chief programmer codes some modules of a program, but the primary responsibility is the overall coordination, development, and success of a project.

User/Customer

While discussing a marketing problem, these middle managers use software designed specifically for their company's situation.

Other Programmers

Backup Programmer

The backup programmer and another programmer review each other's work early in the development stages.

Librarian

The librarian takes care of legwork and documentation during project development.

System Documentation, Test Data, Procedures, Program Listings, Etc.

System analyst The person responsible for system analysis, design, and implementation of computer-based information systems.

goals of the CPT approach are the goals of structured programming: to produce a software product that is easy to understand, maintain, and modify; to decrease costs by reducing testing time and improving programmer productivity; and to increase program reliability. Organizations have applied the CPT concept to implement systems and programs well ahead of schedule and with minimal errors.

The chief programmer is responsible primarily for the overall coordination, development, and success of the programming project, but retains secondary duties of program design and coding of some of the modules. In large system projects a lead **system analyst** supervises the design effort, while the programmer concentrates on the technical development of the project.

Usually, a backup programmer is assigned as an assistant to the chief programmer to help in design, testing, and evaluation of the program. Separate modules of the system are programmed and tested by other programmers on the team. The modules are integrated into a complete system by the chief programmer and backup programmer, who may also code the most critical parts of the overall system.

The CPT also includes a librarian to help maintain complete, up-to-date documentation of the project and to relieve the team programmers of many clerical tasks. A librarian enhances communication among team members because he or she makes all program descriptions, coding, and test results current and visible to everyone involved in the effort.

The CPT approach facilitates top-down design and ongoing documentation of programs. It also helps with the testing of programs. An important goal of a programming effort is to produce an error-free program in the shortest possible time. This requires that the program be carefully reviewed before it is implemented. Early detection of errors and oversights can prevent costly modifications later. Team members review each other's work and the accompanying documentation at each stage of development, making suggestions for additions, deletions, and modifications.

Let's see how the four methodologies of structured problem solving are related to program maintenance and the four steps of the problem-solving process.

DEFINING AND DOCUMENTING THE PROBLEM

Getting somewhere is impossible if you are not clear where you are going. In programming, a clear and precise statement of the problem must be given before anything else is done. Yet many programming fiascos have occurred because this step was neglected. The first step in defining a problem is the recognition of a need for information. However, the person writing a program to meet that need is often not the same person who will be using it. Communication between the two people (or groups of people) may be inadequate, leading to misunderstandings about the desired results of the program. Therefore, before the programmer proceeds, the problem must be clearly and mutually defined and documented in writing by all parties involved. The documentation should include:

1. A short narrative statement defining the problem and describing what the program is supposed to do.

2. A description of the desired output and the manner in which it is to be formatted.

3. The input (data necessary to obtain the desired output), the manner in which it is to be formatted, the ease of data entry, and any methods of checking for invalid data.

The Programming Process

Suppose a user needs a program that will convert feet to miles. In stating the output first, we say that we desire a statement that tells the number of miles in a given number of feet. The needed input is the number of feet to be converted and the mathematical formula needed to perform the conversion. This information could be documented as follows:

Problem Definition: Write a program to convert feet to miles.

Needed Output: The output (the number of miles in a given number of feet) will be formatted according to this example: There are xxxx.xx miles in xxxxxxx.xx feet.

Needed Input: The user must input the number of feet to be converted.

Even though output is the last step of computer processing, it can be effectively used as the first step in defining the problem. By defining the output required of the program, the information requirements of users become clear. The accompanying documentation clarifies the problem for the people involved to make sure the programmer's understanding of the problem is the same as that of the user. It also provides material to be reviewed by the CPT (if used) and shown to the user. Checking a program's validity early in development is critical to saving time and assuring that everyone is satisfied with the product. Once the problem is defined, the analyst/programmer proceeds to the next step, designing a solution.

DESIGNING AND DOCUMENTING A SOLUTION

When the definition of the problem has been completed, the design of the solution begins. This design may take the form of one or more programs. The programmer takes each of the segments uncovered in the definition step and works out a tentative program flow, that is, what needs to be done first in the program, what second, and so on. By approaching each segment separately, the programmer can concentrate on developing an efficient and logical flow for that segment.

The programmer does not need to know which programming language is to be used in order to develop a program design. In fact, knowing the processing requirements first, helps the programmer select the language best suited to those requirements. To develop a tentative flow, the programmer develops an algorithm: the finite sequence of steps needed to accomplish a particular task. For example, in the conversion program just described, the algorithm is the formula MILES = FEET/5280. Algorithms range from broad descriptions at the top of the design hierarchy to very detailed statements at the lowest level. Each step in the algorithm must be clear, specific to its level of the design, and feasible. The steps are planned according to the patterns of logic that a computer understands.

Logic Patterns

All computer instructions are based on four basic logic patterns: simple sequence, selection, loop, and branch. In illustrating the patterns, let's consider a program that will search the names of honor students to isolate those eligible for scholarships, (see Figure 10–3).

Simple sequence logic involves executing instructions one statement after another in the order presented by the programmer. It is the simplest and most often used pattern: in fact, the computer assumes that all instructions are to be executed in this order unless otherwise directed. Below are listed the steps arranged in simple sequence for the scholarship program:

Simple sequence Program logic in which one statement after another is executed in the order in which they are stored.

1. Read input.
2. Compare with scholarship criteria.
3. Print names of eligible students.

Figure 10–3
Four Traditional Program Logic Patterns

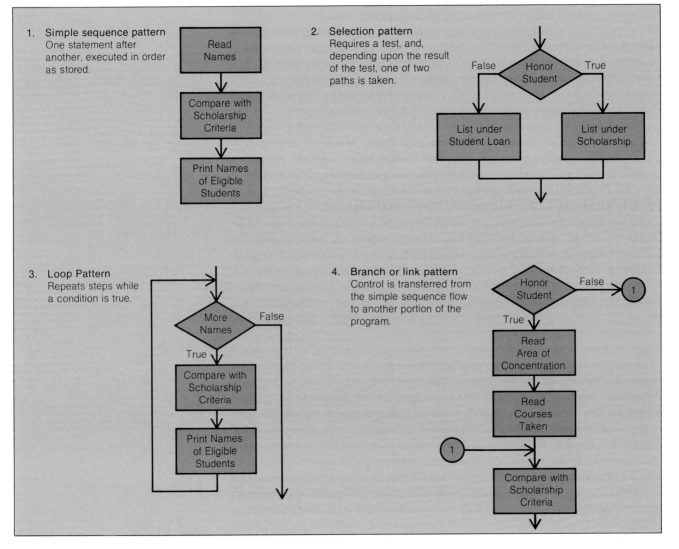

The **selection** pattern requires that the computer make a choice among two or more items. Each choice is based on one of the three comparisons a computer can make: equal to, less than, or greater than. When complex selections must be made, several comparisons can be combined. For example, the computer can select all students with a grade-point average equal to or greater than 3.50 in the scholarship eligibility problem and then sort qualified students into the scholarship category.

The **loop** pattern causes an interruption in the normal sequence of processing and directs the computer to loop back to a previous statement in the program. The computer then reexecutes statements according to the simple sequence flow. If the same sequence of statements is to be executed many times, the programmer need not rewrite that set of statements for each set of data. When selecting eligible students in the scholarship problem, the computer will loop through the same set of criteria for each name read.

When using the loop, the programmer must establish a way for the computer to get out of the loop after it has been executed the required number of times. Once all the student names have been processed, control of execution should shift to the statement immediately following the loop. This shift of control can occur in two ways. The first involves a **trailer** (or dummy) **value** that signals the computer to stop performing the loop. The programmer tests for this value within the program. For example, the last student name may be "NO NAME," a value that will not be encountered in input data. When the computer pulls NO NAME from the data list, it recognizes the data item as a signal to stop the loop. The second method of loop control uses a **counter,** which regulates the number of times the loop is executed. The programmer enters the counter value and determines a method of increasing the counter and testing its value each time the loop is executed. When the proper value is reached, the computer stops executing the loop.

The last and most controversial pattern is the **branch,** which is often used in combination with selection or looping. This pattern allows the programmer to skip statements in a program. For example, if a student does not meet the first test of eligibility—a 3.50 average—program execution skips the remaining criteria and reads a new student name. This pattern also encourages undisciplined jumping around among program statements, a characteristic forbidden in structured programming. It is often signaled with the command GOTO. For this reason, structured programming is often called GOTOless programming. In structured programming, the programmer must work out a program design that uses only simple sequence, selection, and loop patterns. Few or no GOTO statements are needed if a program is well planned (see Structured Coding later in this chapter). When faced with this task of writing structured programs to solve complicated problems, the programmer employs several design tools to help visualize the plan.

Selection Program logic that includes a test; depending on the results of the test, one of two paths is taken.

Loop Program logic that causes a series of instructions to be executed repeatedly as long as specified conditions remain constant.

Trailer value A value used to control loop execution in which a unique item signals the computer to stop performing the loop.

Counter A value in a program that indicates the number of times a loop is to be executed; when the stated value is reached, the loop is terminated.

Branch Program logic used to bypass or alter the normal flow of execution.

Design Aids

Several design tools—pseudocode, flowcharts, structure charts, HIPO charts, and Nassi-Shneiderman Charts—provide ways to illustrate algorithms visually. By using these tools, the programmer can avoid omissions and errors that might occur in the "plunge-in-and-hope-for-the-best" method of programming.

All design charts should be included as part of program documentation. They help explain the objectives and functions of a program and also aid in maintaining and changing existing programs. The charts also play a role in program testing. At the design stage, charts help the programming team visualize the program design and suggest changes, additions, or deletions to the plan.

Pseudocode

Pseudocode An informal, narrative design language used to represent the logic patterns of structured programming.

Pseudocode is a narrative, Englishlike description of processing steps to be performed in a program. The programmer arranges these descriptions in the order in which corresponding program statements will appear. Using pseudocode allows the programmer to focus on the steps required to perform a particular process, rather than on the syntax of a particular computer language. Each pseudocode statement can be transcribed into one or more program statements.

Pseudocode is easy to learn and flexible in making changes. Although pseudocode has no rigid rules, several key words often appear. They include IF/THEN/ELSE, DOWHILE, DOUNTIL, and END. Some statements are indented to set off repeated steps or conditions to be met. The statements cannot be translated for execution by the computer, therefore *pseudo-* is an appropriate prefix for this type of code because it means "fake." Figure 10–4 illustrates a pseudocode for eligibility tests.

Flowcharts

Flowchart A graphic representation in which symbols represent the flow, operations, logic, data, equipment, and so on of a program; also called a block diagram or logic diagram.

A **flowchart,** sometimes called a block diagram or a logic diagram, provides a visual frame of reference to the processing steps in a program. Instead of using the Englishlike statements of pseudocode, the flowchart uses easily recognizable geometric symbols to represent the type of processing performed in a program (see Figure 10–5). The symbols are arranged in the same logical sequence in which corresponding program statements will appear in the program.

Programmers have accepted and use a standard set of flowchart symbols established by the American National Standards Institute (ANSI). Figure 10–6 shows some of the ANSI flowchart symbols.

Flowlines Lines that connect flowchart symbols.

Flowchart symbols are arranged from top to bottom, left to right. **Flowlines** connect the symbols and visually represent the implied flow of logic from statement to statement. Arrowheads indicate the direction of flow. Brief instructions within the symbols provide a more detailed description of the activities represented by the blocks. Although flowcharts present execution flow graphically, they can take up several pages and grow more confusing as programs become more complex.

**Figure 10–4
Pseudocode for Determining Grade-Point Eligibility**

```
Begin program
    Read student's name, field of study, and transcript
    Do while there is more data
        Sort into scholarship/loan categories
        Compare grade-point average
        If average greater than 3.50 then print name
        End IF
End program
```

Figure 10–6
Flowchart Symbols

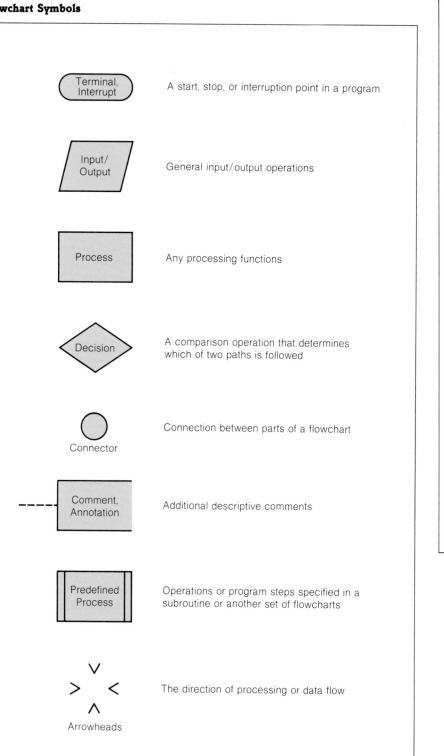

Terminal, Interrupt	A start, stop, or interruption point in a program
Input/Output	General input/output operations
Process	Any processing functions
Decision	A comparison operation that determines which of two paths is followed
Connector	Connection between parts of a flowchart
Comment, Annotation	Additional descriptive comments
Predefined Process	Operations or program steps specified in a subroutine or another set of flowcharts
Arrowheads	The direction of processing or data flow

Figure 10–5
Example of a Flowchart

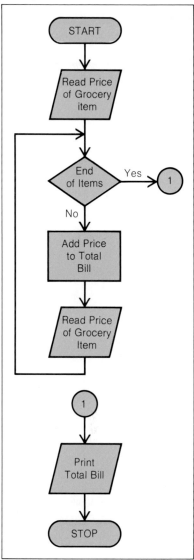

299

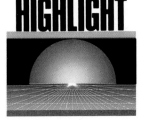

Von Neumann and Flowcharts

Ever wonder who thought up the flowchart concept? Well, you can place some responsibility on the Hungarian-born mathematician John Von Neumann.

The name John Von Neumann most frequently triggers an association with the EDVAC computer and the concept of stored programs. But Von Neumann is also considered the father of flowcharting. In a paper, "The First Draft," he described computers by logical functions rather than electrical aspects, and he often illustrated his ideas with flowcharts. While working with Arthur W. Burks and Herman H. Goldstine on the EDVAC, he described "flow diagrams" in a report titled "Preliminary Discussion of the Logical Design of an Electronic Computing Instrument."

Von Neumann's flow diagrams were similar to today's ANSI flowchart style, linking geometric shapes that stood for input or output, decision, processing, and so on. Goldstine recognized Von Neumann's contribution in his book, *The Computer from Pascal to Von Neumann:* "I became convinced that this type of flow diagram . . . could be used as a logically complete and precise notation . . . and that indeed this was essential to the task of programming."

However, if Von Neumann had not designed flow diagrams, someone else would have. After all, many other program design aids exist, including Nassi-Shneiderman charts, Chapin charts, the Warnier-Orr methodology, the Jackson method, and HIPO charts—a long enough list to show that many people devised some form of design charts.

Structure Charts

Structure chart A graphic representation of top-down programming, displaying modules of the problem solution and relationships between modules.

Structure charts show the hierarchical levels of the modules in top-down design. The modules are represented by rectangular boxes or blocks linked by flowlines. The highest level in the hierarchy is the main control module, labeled Scholarship Eligibility in Figure 10–7. This module is broken into lower-level modules that correspond with the four major functions of the scholarship program, which, in turn, can be further segmented. For example, the Match Criteria block can be broken down into individual comparisons with stated criteria. In structure charts, the degree of detail increases at the lower levels.

The flow of control in the structure is from top to bottom. Each module has control of the modules directly below it and is controlled by the module directly above it. Programming statements are written for one module at a time. Each module can be tested in the entire hierarchy by substituting **dummy modules** for the incomplete modules. The dummy modules help test the flow of control in a program. By the time the lowest-level modules have been coded, all other modules have already been tested and debugged.

Dummy module A temporary program module inserted at a lower level to facilitate testing of the higher-level module.

HIPO (Hierarchy plus Input-Process-Output) A documentation or design technique used to describe inputs, processing, and outputs of program modules.

HIPO Diagrams

The term **HIPO (Hierarchy plus Input-Process-Output)** is applied to a kind of visual aid commonly used to supplement structure charts. Whereas structure

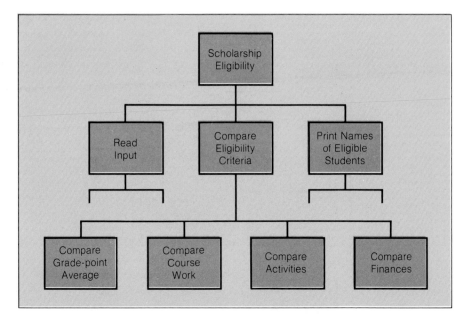

Figure 10–7
Structure Chart

charts emphasize only structure and function, HIPO diagrams highlight the inputs, processing, and outputs of program modules.

A typical HIPO package consists of three types of diagrams that describe a program or system of programs from the general level to the detail level. At the most general level is the **visual table of contents,** which is almost identical to the structure chart. Each block is given an identification number that is used as a reference in other HIPO diagrams. Each module in the visual table of contents is described in greater detail in an **overview diagram,** which includes the module's inputs, processing, and outputs. The reference number assigned to the overview program shows where the module fits into the overall structure of the system as depicted in the visual table of contents. If the module passes control to a lower-level module in the hierarchy, that operation is also given a reference number. A modified structure chart and overview diagram appear in Figure 10–8. **Detail diagrams** enable the programmer to understand the data items and the specific functions of a program design and to write the code to perform them. The varying levels of detail allow the diagrams to be used by managers, analysts, and programmers to meet needs ranging from programming to program maintenance to designing entirely new systems.

Nassi-Shneiderman Charts

The **structured flowcharts** developed by Isaac Nassi and Ben Shneiderman are valued in both the design phase and the coding phase of program development. Structured flowcharts combine elements of traditional flowcharting and pseudocode. They use the English phrases common to pseudocode with some of the graphic analysis that characterizes flowcharts. Many programmers find Nassi-Shneiderman charts easier to draw than the traditional flowcharts with many geometric shapes. One chart consists of a rectangular box partitioned according to a standard format for the basic logic patterns. The logic flows from top to bottom. Figure 10–9 depicts the logic patterns in the context of Nassi-Shneiderman charts.

Visual table of contents   Similar to a structure chart; each block is given an identification number used as a reference to other HIPO diagrams.

Overview diagram   A diagram used in HIPO to describe in greater detail a module shown in the visual table of contents.

Detail diagram   A diagram used in HIPO to describe the specific function performed and data items used in a module.

Structured flowchart   A graphic representation of logic patterns depicting the function of a program or module and compactly arranged in a partitioned box; also called Nassi-Shneiderman chart.

301

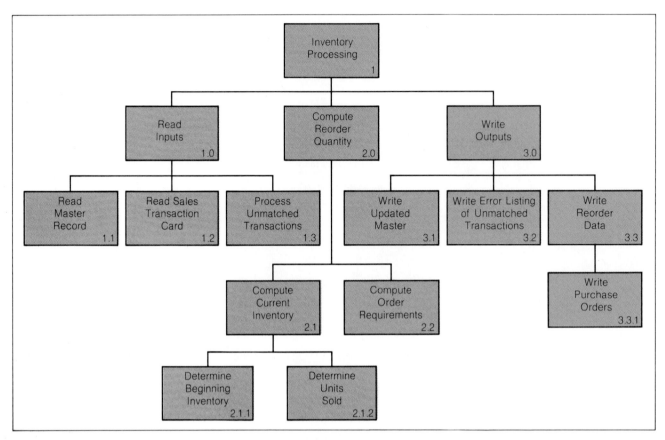

Figure 10–8
Visual Table of Contents for
Inventory Processing Example and
HIPO Overview Diagram for "Read
Inputs" Model

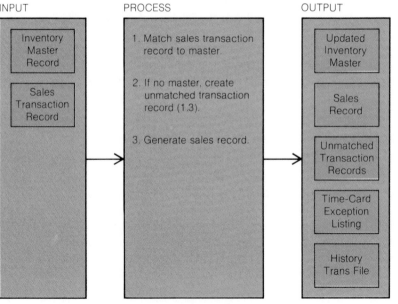

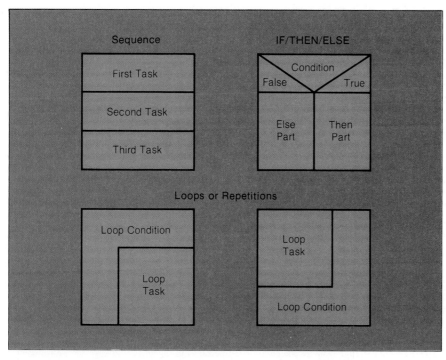

Figure 10–9
Some Logic Patterns of Nassi-Shneiderman Charts

These charts reflect the design and size of modules. The main module can be shown in simple sequence form, while a lower-level module offers enough detail that programmers can code the module directly from the chart. Figure 10–10 shows how the scholarship program can be defined in Nassi-Shneiderman charts.

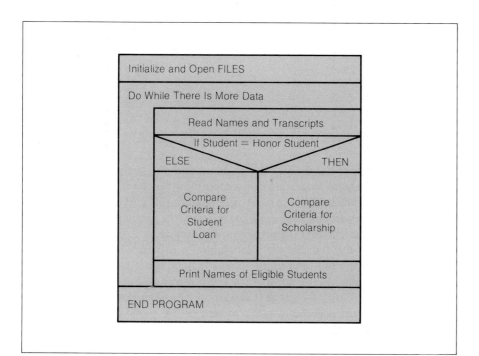

Figure 10–10
Nassi-Shneiderman Chart

Concept Summary 10–1 ▪ Comparison of Design Aids

Chart	Purpose	Format	Characteristics
Pseudocode	Describes processing steps in a program.	Englishlike narration in top-down sequence.	No rigid rules. Contains keywords such as DOWHILE, DOUNTIL, IF/THEN/ELSE.
Flowchart	Describes processing flow graphically.	Geometric symbols linked by flowlines. Arrowheads show flow direction. Brief descriptions of steps appear within symbols.	Standard. Traditional. Universally known. May take up too much space.
Structure chart	Shows hierarchical levels of modules in top-down design.	Blocks linked by flowlines arranged in top-down sequence.	Helps in placing dummy modules to test programs. Detail increases at lower levels. Facilitates modular programming.
HIPO diagram	Highlights inputs, processing, and outputs in detail.	Three types of block diagrams: visual table of contents, overview diagram, detail diagram.	Identification numbers show relationships between the various diagrams.
Nassi-Shneiderman chart	Shows processing steps.	Englishlike phrases contained in rectangular boxes partitioned to represent the logic patterns.	May be easier to draw than flowcharts. Logic flows from top to bottom. Reflects design and size of modules.

WRITING AND DOCUMENTING THE PROGRAM

After the programmer has defined the problem and designed a solution, he or she writes the program in a specific programming language. Sometimes the proposed solution will limit the choices of languages that can be used in coding the program. Other constraints outside the scope of the problem and its solution may also affect the choice of a programming language. A programmer may have no choice in the selection of a language for a particular application; for instance, a business may require the use of COBOL because of its readability and because it is used in the company's existing software.

Once the programming language is chosen, the programmer should proceed to code the program according to the **syntax** of the particular programming language and the rules of structured programming.

Syntax Rules of a programming language that must be followed while coding instructions, as syntactical rules must be followed in English.

Structured Coding

When top-down design and structured programming are used to create a program, certain rules must be followed during coding. Four major rules govern the use of GOTO statements, the size of modules, the definition of a proper program, and documentation.

Structured programming is characterized by its lack of GOTO statements. The programmer must plan and write the program within the confines of three logic patterns: simple sequence, selection, and the loop. This discipline limits jumping from one program statement to another in random fashion. Since a GOTO statement signals a jump, the programmer uses as few GOTO statements as possible, yielding GOTOless programs.

When GOTO statements are avoided, the programmer can code each module as an independent segment. Each module should be relatively small to facilitate the translation of modules into program statements. Many advocates of the modular approach suggest that each module should consist of no more than 50 or 60 lines of code. When module size is limited in this manner, the coding for each module fits on a single page of computer printout, which simplifies testing and debugging procedures.

Yet another rule of structured coding dictates that modules should have only one entrance and one exit. A program segment that has only one entrance and one exit is called a **proper program** (see Figure 10–11). This makes the basic flow easy to follow and allows easy modification of program logic to accommodate system changes.

A final rule to follow in structured program coding is to include documentation, or comment statements, liberally throughout the program. The comments should define names of data items, explain the main module, and document the functions of each lower-level module. The documentation aids in testing and debugging programs, which should occur at intervals throughout the coding phase.

Types of Statements

Certain types of program statements are common to most high-level programming languages: comments, declarations, input/output statements, computations, transfers of control, and comparisons.

Comments, or remarks, have no effect on program execution. They are inserted at key points throughout the program to explain the purposes of program segments. If a series of statements sorts a list of names into alphabetical order, for example, the programmer may want to include the remark: "This segment sorts names in ascending alphabetical order."

The programmer uses declarations to define items used in the program. Examples include definitions of files, records, variables, initial values of counters, and so on.

Input statements bring data into primary storage for use by the program. Output statements transfer data from primary storage to output media such as hard-copy printouts or displays on monitors.

Computational instructions tell the computer to provide results of addition, subtraction, multiplication, division, and exponentiation.

Another type of instruction allows the sequence of execution to be altered

Proper program A program using the structured approach and top-down design and emphasizing only one entrance and one exit.

**Figure 10–11
A Proper Program**

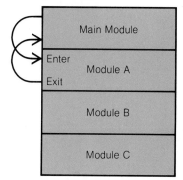

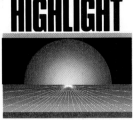

Is Your Program Full of—Er—Spaghetti?

The term "spaghetti thinking" was first introduced in the 1960s. It began with a Dutch computer scientist, Edsger Dijkstra, and his famous GOTO letter. Dijkstra scorned programmers who just fiddled with their programs until they came out right. He wanted to curb the use of a common programming structure, the transfer, also known as the GOTO statement. Such statements can cause program execution to jump backward and forward with little rhyme or reason. In March 1968, Dijkstra wrote a letter in *Communications of the ACM* (Association for Computer Machinery), saying the GOTO statement actually invited programmers to write messy, error-filled programs. Since that time, people have called the tangle of GOTOs in a program the "spaghetti code"; if a person drew a line in such a program from each GOTO statement to where it transferred, the resulting picture would look like a plateful of spaghetti.

One popular language that seems to encourage overuse of GOTO statements is BASIC. In fact, Dijkstra once said that people who learned to program in BASIC were hopelessly mired in GOTO thinking. However, proponents of BASIC insist that programmers can write well-designed BASIC programs with a minimum of GOTO statements. They also argue that a program does not become well-structured merely by the elimination of GOTO statements. Recent forms of BASIC, such as True BASIC, designed by Thomas Kurtz and John Kemeny, encourage programmers to discard the GOTO statement and use, instead, more structured programming methods. The impulsive programming techniques of spaghetti thinking are fast becoming unacceptable.

by transferring control to another portion of a program. A conditional transfer of control alters the sequence only when a certain condition is met. An unconditional transfer always changes the sequence of execution.

The final type of statement is the comparison, which allows two items to be compared on the basis of equality. Depending on the result of the comparison, either input/output, computation, or transfer of control could occur.

COMPILING, DEBUGGING, AND TESTING THE PROGRAM

After the program has been written, it is submitted to the computer for translation. The following section describes how a high-level language program is altered to a form the computer can use.

Language Translation

The programmer uses a sequence of instructions to communicate with the computer and control program execution. As computers have developed in complexity, so have programming languages. There are three language levels: machine language, assembly language, and high-level language (see Figure 10–12).

Machine language is the code that designates the proper electrical states in the computer expressed in combinations of 0s and 1s. It is the only language the computer can execute directly; therefore, it can be called the language of the computer. Assembly language is one step removed from machine language. Programmers using assembly language must be very conscious of computer circuitry and must designate operations to be performed and locations where data can be stored or found. However, assembly language is more easily understood by humans. Convenient symbols and abbreviations, known as mnemonics, are used instead of the 0 and 1 groupings of machine language.

High-level languages are so called because they are the furthest removed from the workings of the hardware. They least resemble the 0 and 1 combinations that indicate electrical states. Whereas one assembly language instruction is generally equivalent to one machine language instruction, one high-level language statement can accomplish the same result as half-dozen or more machine language instructions, principally because the addresses for the required storage locations do not have to be specified; they are handled automatically.

Assembly and high-level languages are much more widely used by programmers than machine language. Since these languages cannot be executed directly by computers, they are converted into machine-executable form by a **language-translator program.** The sequence of instructions written by the programmer—the **source program**—is transformed by the language-translator program into a machine-executable form known as the **object program.**

The translator program for an assembly language is called an **assembler program.** A high-level language translator can be either a **compiler program** or an **interpreter program.** Assemblers, compilers, and interpreters are designed for specific machines and languages. For example, a compiler that translates a source program written in FORTRAN into a machine-language program can only translate FORTRAN.

During the compilation or assembly (the translation process), the object program is generated all at once. The programmer may receive an assembly listing or source program listing that contains indications of any errors the assembler or compiler detected during translation. Only after all the errors have been corrected can the object program be successfully created and submitted to the computer for execution.

On the other hand, an interpreter, a language translator that has been used extensively on microcomputer systems, evaluates and translates a program

Source program A sequence of instructions written in either assembly language or high-level language that is translated into an object program.

Object program A sequence of machine executable instructions derived from source-program statements by a language-translator program.

DEGREE OF USER ORIENTATION		DEGREE OF MACHINE ORIENTATION
Low	Machine Language	High
↓	Assembly Language	↓
High	Higher-Level Language	Low

Figure 10–12 Language Levels

one statement at a time. The interpreter reads a program statement by statement—first checking syntax, then translating the statement, and finally executing the statement before proceeding to the next statement (see Figure 10–13). Programming by this method is called interactive programming.

Debugging and Testing

The process of locating, isolating, and eliminating errors, or bugs, is called debugging. We have seen that assemblers, compilers, and interpreters provide error messages that can be used to locate and correct syntax errors. Syntax errors are violations of the rules associated with a particular programming language. For instance, a programmer may misspell the command WRITE as WRTE or use a comma or colon incorrectly. However, logic errors must be detected by the programmer. Such errors may result when the programmer does not fully understand the problem or does not account for unforeseen conditions that may arise during processing. These errors may be located through program testing, desk-checking, or structured walkthroughs.

Structured programming allows the program to be tested in small sections, so that errors can be isolated to specific sections. Running and rerunning a specific unit may be necessary before the cause of an error can be found. The programmer rewrites the incorrect part and resubmits the program segment for another test. The programmer must take care that correction of one logic error does not lead to several other errors.

A programmer often finds **desk-checking** helpful in attempting to catch flaws in program logic. Desk-checking describes the method by which a programmer pretends to be the computer, reading through each instruction and simulating how the computer would process a data item.

After a programmer has worked for a long time to correct the logic of a

Desk-checking A debugging method in which the sequence of operations is mentally traced to verify the correctness of the logic.

"Williams is in there debugging right now."

Figure 10–13
Interpreter-Detected Errors

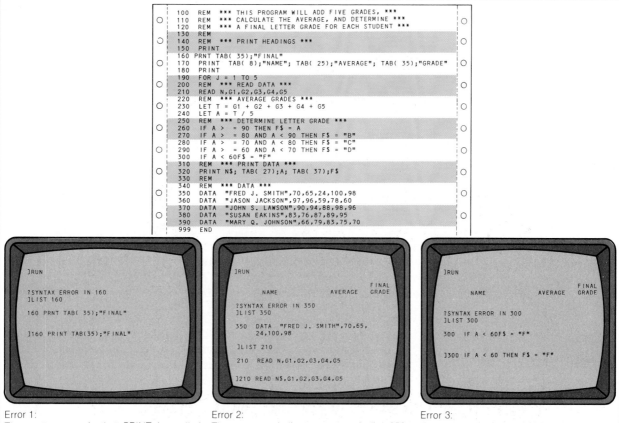

```
100   REM   *** THIS PROGRAM WILL ADD FIVE GRADES, ***
110   REM   *** CALCULATE THE AVERAGE, AND DETERMINE ***
120   REM   *** A FINAL LETTER GRADE FOR EACH STUDENT ***
130   REM
140   REM   *** PRINT HEADINGS ***
150   PRINT
160   PRNT TAB( 35);"FINAL"
170   PRINT  TAB( 8);"NAME"; TAB( 25);"AVERAGE"; TAB( 35);"GRADE"
180   PRINT
190   FOR J = 1 TO 5
200   REM   *** READ DATA ***
210   READ N,G1,G2,G3,G4,G5
220   REM   *** AVERAGE GRADES ***
230   LET T = G1 + G2 + G3 + G4 + G5
240   LET A = T / 5
250   REM   *** DETERMINE LETTER GRADE ***
260   IF A >  = 90 THEN F$ = A
270   IF A >  = 80 AND A < 90 THEN F$ = "B"
280   IF A >  = 70 AND A < 80 THEN F$ = "C"
290   IF A >  = 60 AND A < 70 THEN F$ = "D"
300   IF A < 60F$ = "F"
310   REM   *** PRINT DATA ***
320   PRINT N$; TAB( 27);A; TAB( 37);F$
330   REM
340   REM   *** DATA ***
350   DATA  "FRED J. SMITH",70,65,24,100,98
360   DATA  "JASON JACKSON",97,96,59,78,60
370   DATA  "JOHN S. LAWSON",90,94,88,98,96
380   DATA  "SUSAN EAKINS",83,76,87,89,95
390   DATA  "MARY Q. JOHNSON",66,79,83,75,70
999   END
```

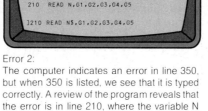

Error 1:
The syntax error is that PRINT is spelled PRNT. When that error is corrected, the program will run until another error is detected.

Error 2:
The computer indicates an error in line 350, but when 350 is listed, we see that it is typed correctly. A review of the program reveals that the error is in line 210, where the variable N should have been typed N$ to show that the variable values are words rather than numbers.

Error 3:
The syntax error in line 300 is the omission of the word THEN.

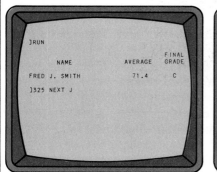

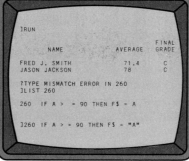

Error 4:
The program runs, but for only one name. Since we know there are five names typed in the DATA-list, there must be an error. The NEXT statement has been omitted.

Error 5:
A "TYPE MISMATCH ERROR" is indicated for line 260. Upon examination, we see that the variable name does not match the variable value. Therefore, we change F$ = A to F$ = "A" to show that the variable value is a string.

The program runs correctly.

309

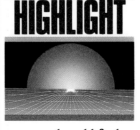

HIGHLIGHT

A Tale of Two Bugs

The story of the first computer bug has become a legend. In the summer of 1945, something went wrong with the Mark II, a large electromechanical device used by the Department of Defense. Though the machine was not working properly, the operating personnel could find no obvious problems. A continued search revealed a large moth beaten to death by one of the electromechanical relays. The moth was pulled out with tweezers and taped to a log book (now exhibited in the Naval Museum at the Naval Surface Weapons Center, Dahlgren, Virginia). "From then on," said Commodore Grace Hopper, one of the people working with the machine, "when the officer came in to ask if we were accomplishing anything, we told him we were 'debugging' the computer." So the phrases "bugs in the program" and "debugging the program" became popular in describing programming errors.

Few people realize, however, that the use of the word *bug* to mean an error is at least a hundred years old. Thomas Alva Edison introduced the word in a letter to Theodore Puskas, Edison's representative in France, on November 13, 1878. He wrote:

> *I have the right principle and am on the right track, but time, hard work, and some good luck are necessary too. It has been just so in all of my inventions. The first step is an intuition, and comes with a burst, then difficulties arise—this thing gives out and then that—"bugs"—as such little faults and difficulties are called—show themselves and months of intense watching, study and labor are requisite before commercial success—or failure—is certainly reached.*

So now you have it—A Tale of Two Bugs.

---

program, he or she may tend to overlook errors or assume a clarity that in reality does not exist. For this reason, programmers sometimes trade their partially debugged programs among themselves. The programmer stepping through a "fresh" program may uncover mistakes in logic that the original programmer overlooked. When team members review each other's programs, the peer review is sometimes called a **structured walkthrough.** Although structured walkthroughs can occur any time during the coding and testing of a program, they are perhaps most useful during earlier stages of programming. Structured walkthroughs are part of the attempt to minimize costs by early detection of problems. During regularly scheduled reviews, charts, documentation, and coding are studied to check the overall completeness, accuracy, and quality of the program. When errors are corrected or adjustments made to the program, the accompanying design charts and documentation must be revised to reflect the changes.

When a compilation without errors is achieved, a test run is needed. This run involves executing the program with input data that is either a representative

Structured walkthrough A formal evaluation of the documentation and coding of a program or system to determine completeness, accuracy, and quality of design.

sample of actual data or a facsimile of it. Often, a programmer will submit sample data that can be used to compare the computer-determined output with manually calculated correct results. A programmer should also input unusual or incorrect data that imitates errors a user might make in entering data. The output should be easy to recognize so that the programmer can see whether it is correct.

PROGRAM MAINTENANCE

Once the program is implemented, it must be maintained. Maintenance refers to the revisions needed to correct, improve, update, or expand programs. Bugs may be found in a program after it is implemented; the corrections must be changed and documented. Company policies or tax laws may change; a program that incorporates facets of policy or tax laws must be updated to reflect the changes. Sometimes new hardware is acquired by a company; the old software may need revision to run properly on the new equipment. Software vendors often release new versions of the software used with company-generated programs; a company may adapt its programs to match the newly

Concept Summary 10–2 ▪ Structured Programming

Problem-Solving Steps	Structured Programming Characteristics
Defining and Documenting the Problem	• Defines the overall problem, or main module, first. • Documents the desired output and its format and required input. • Tests validity of the definition by making sure all parties involved agree with the problem definition. • May be reviewed by a programming team to catch any misunderstandings early in the procedure.
Designing and Documenting the Solution	• Provides a structured methodology for developing the algorithm (processing formula). • Provides design aids that facilitate the top-down approach (structure charts, HIPO diagrams, pseudocode, Nassi-Shneiderman charts. • Provides documentation through charts and any further explanation needed. (Documentation in the form of charts also aids program maintenance.) • Offers a stopping point to evaluate program for validity, accuracy, and quality. • Reviewed by a programming team to catch unforeseen or overlooked factors (structured walkthrough).
Writing and Documenting the Program	• Facilitates the top-down approach: the program is coded in independent modules, GOTO statements are avoided, and modules contain single entry and exit points. • Provides documentation within the source program which appears as remark or comment statements. • Reviewed by a programming team to detect errors in logic.
Compiling, Debugging, and Testing the Program	• Reflects the top-down approach by testing one module at a time, using dummy modules in the structure chart hierarchy. • Detects inadequate documentation and incorrect logic through desk-checking, structured walkthroughs, and testing with sample data.

released software. Sometimes a company merely needs to review a program to see if it generates information that is still meaningful and usable.

If existing documentation is accurate and up-to-date and if structured programming techniques were used to prepare the software, programmers can perform these program maintenance chores more easily.

PROGRAMMING CASE STUDY

A teacher would like to use a computer to help with determining grades, one of the more time-consuming tasks of the profession. In defining the problem, we determine that the program should calculate average numerical grades based on five test scores and assign final letter grades based on a given scale.

To design a solution, we must determine the desired contents and format of the output. The teacher would like a printout listing the students' names, average test scores, and final letter grade equivalents under the headings *Name, Average,* and *Final Grade.* The input will be the students' names and five test scores. To arrive at the final grades, the computer will process the data by adding the five scores, dividing by five (the number of tests) to calculate the average, and assigning a letter grade based on the following predetermined scale:

Average	Final Grade
90–100	A
80–89	B
70–79	C
60–69	D
0–59	F

We must prepare an instruction flow to organize the processing steps. The headings can be printed before the data is entered. Since each student has five grades, the students' names and five grades must be input and the grades added together and averaged. Once the average has been determined, the appropriate final letter grade can be assigned according to the scale. Then the name, average, and final grade can be printed. When the data for one student has been processed, the data for the next student can be read and processed, and so on, until no more statistics are available.

The pseudocode representing the logical flow of the solution is found in Figure 10–14. A flowchart for the solution of this problem is given in Figure 10–15. The program design is also depicted in a Nassi-Shneiderman chart (see Figure 10–16). Study the various diagrams to match the steps of the solution.

After constructing the program design and reviewing the logic, we express the solution in a programming language—in this case, BASIC—and enter the completed source program into the computer. When using BASIC with a microcomputer, the programming process is generally interactive and the language-translation program is an interpreter. This means the source program will be translated into an object program line by line. During this procedure, the programmer should correct any syntax and logic errors. Then the program can be executed to produce the desired output. Figure 10–17 shows the source program listing and the output produced during the execution of the program.

Figure 10–14
Pseudocode for Case Study

```
Begin
Print Headings
Do until End of Items
   Read Student's Name and Grades
   Calculate Student's Grade Total
   Calculate Student's Grade Average
   Determine Final Letter Grade
   Print Name, Average, Final Grade
End Loop (No More Data)
End
```

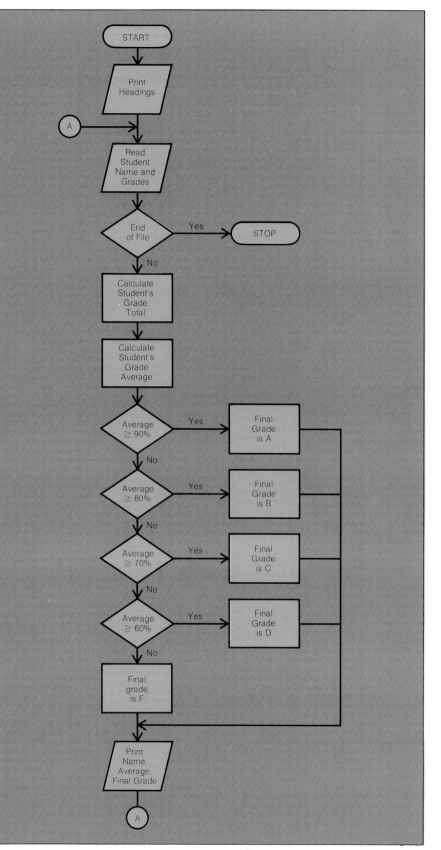

Figure 10-15
Flowchart for Case Study

Figure 10–16
Nassi-Shneiderman Chart for Case
Study

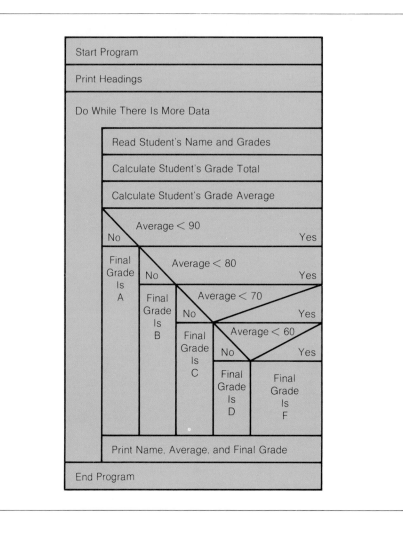

314

Figure 10–17
**BASIC Program with Sample Data
for Case Study**

```
100   REM   *** THIS PROGRAM WILL ADD FIVE GRADES, ***
110   REM   *** CALCULATE THE AVERAGE, AND DETERMINE ***
120   REM   *** A FINAL LETTER GRADE FOR EACH STUDENT ***
130   REM
140   REM   *** VARIABLES ***
150   REM   ***                    N$ = STUDENT ***
160   REM   ***                     T = TOTAL   ***
170   REM   ***                     A = AVERAGE ***
180   REM   ***                    F$ = FINAL LETTER GRADE ***
190   REM   *** G1, G2, G3, G4, G5 = SCORES  ***
200   REM
210   REM   *** PRINT HEADINGS ***
220   PRINT
230   PRINT  TAB( 35);"FINAL"
240   PRINT  TAB( 8);"NAME"; TAB( 25);"AVERAGE"; TAB( 35);"GRADE"
250   PRINT
260   FOR J = 1 TO 5
270   REM   *** READ DATA ***
280   READ N$,G1,G2,G3,G4,G5
290   REM   *** AVERAGE GRADES ***
300   LET T = G1 + G2 + G3 + G4 + G5
310   LET A = T / 5
320   REM   *** DETERMINE LETTER GRADE ***
330   IF A >  = 90 THEN F$ = "A"
340   IF A >  = 80 AND A < 90 THEN F$ = "B"
350   IF A >  = 70 AND A < 80 THEN F$ = "C"
360   IF A >  = 60 AND A < 70 THEN F$ = "D"
370   IF A < 60 THEN F$ = "F"
380   REM   *** PRINT DATA ***
390   PRINT N$; TAB( 27);A; TAB( 37);F$
400   NEXT J
410   REM
420   REM   *** DATA ***
430   DATA  "FRED J. SMITH",70,65,24,100,98
440   DATA  "JASON JACKSON",97,96,59,78,60
450   DATA  "JOHN S. LAWSON",90,94,88,98,96
460   DATA  "SUSAN EAKINS",83,76,87,89,95
470   DATA  "MARY Q. JOHNSON",66,79,83,75,70
999   END
```

Output

```
]RUN

                              FINAL
      NAME           AVERAGE  GRADE

FRED J. SMITH          71.4     C

JASON JACKSON          78       C
JOHN S. LAWSON         93.2     A
SUSAN EAKINS           86       B
MARY Q. JOHNSON        74.6     C
```

315

FOCUS ON MICRO-COMPUTING

Programs for Your Microcomputer

The real power behind any personal computer is the programs that make it run. These programs are called software to distinguish them from the machines themselves, which are called hardware. One man who recognized the importance of software is Tony Gold. Gold and his collaborator, Larry Alkoff, started Lifeboat, which became one of the largest software publishing and distributing firms. The company was first conceived as a one-stop source for microcomputer software packages configured for CP/M80 (an operating system that has become an industry standard) and other compatible operating systems. (An operating system is a collection of programs designed to permit the computer system to manage itself.) Gold has been credited with being the driving force behind the development and use of CP/M80 as a standard operating system. Such a standard enables users, regardless of their brand of computer, to use a wider variety of software products.

According to Gold, there are four groups of personal computer users: the professionals who do some kind of analysis; the transaction-processing group, including individuals involved in mailing-list work or accounting; the home computing market; and educators. Lifeboat has designed software primarily for the business market, selling and supporting well over a hundred software packages and many different computer manufacturers.

The era of business software for personal computers began in 1979 with the introduction of Visicorp's VisiCalc, the popular electronic spreadsheet program used for financial planning and budgeting. The program allows the user to enter or change data values, alter format, and answer "what if" questions simply by entering new assumptions. Since the introduction of VisiCalc, many other business programs have flooded the market. These packages range from general accounting systems to more specific applications, such as portfolio management and filing and billing systems for doctors and dentists. As software became more sophisticated, developers began to combine several types of functions into what is called integrated software. Integrated business packages, for example, allow the user to work with a spreadsheet; do word processing (writing and editing text); prepare graphic aids such as bar charts, pie charts, and line graphs; and file data. Of course, users can buy software that offers just one or two of these functions, such as word-processing software or data-filing packages.

Members of all four groups of personal computer users can find uses for business, text-editing, and file-handling software, but they buy software to accomplish other tasks, too. Education software developers design software targeted toward educators and home computer users. The software offers the advantages of introducing students to new material, supplying them with immediate feedback, and allowing them to perform "dry runs" of experiments that could prove costly and dangerous. Some educational software permits users to practice typing skills that facilitate further computer use. Examples include *Master Type* by Scarborough Systems, *Touch Typing Tutor,* by Taylormade Software, *Wiztype* by Sierra, and *Typing Tutor III* by Simon & Schuster/Electronic Publishing Division.

Developers of computer games cater primarily to the home market. Once the exotic worlds, stolen treasures, and dark caverns of adventure games lured only a small, dedicated group of fans. Recently, a new form of the adventure game has whetted the appetites of computer game fans of all ages. Dubbed interactive fiction, the new "literary form" emphasizes character interaction and story line. In one example, *Cutthroats* by Infocom, characters such as Johnny Red or the Weasel speak to you through the computer. In your attempts to solve the logic problems and identify the traitor in a motley crew, you "talk" back to the characters. This strong focus on character development sustains the illusion of active participation in the story. Other examples include *Dragonworld* and *Fahrenheit 451* by Trillium Corp.; *Robots of Dawn* and *Dragonriders of Pern* by Epyx Inc.; and *Earthly Delights* by Datamost.

Computer game fans can buy software that will enable them to design their own games, too. Games vary from mazes to pinball games to the shooting gallery variety. Examples include the Loderunner packages by Broderbund.

Other software can help you relax, create artwork, compose music, analyze your psyche, and print individually designed Christmas cards. With so many attractive applications for home and business use, understanding why anyone would hesitate to learn how to use computers and software is difficult. In the best of software, excellent documentation and user interfaces guide users in running the program, entering the data, and formatting the output.

Users' manuals provide instructions and clearly explain the program objectives and functions the user can perform when running the program. Other documentation exists in the form of "help" screens designed to display instruction and explanation on the monitor. Another characteristic of excellent documentation is guidance the user receives as the program is executed; and here we overlap the area of user interface.

Interface describes the way in which you give data to a computer and receive information from it. Interface design has been torn between ease of use and ease of programming: the simplest interfaces to use are the hardest to program. Traditionally ease of programming has won. Therefore, the novice user is usually confronted with what are called command-line interfaces. The monitor may display no information but merely show a □,], A>, or some equally cryptic symbol. Each time the symbol appears, the computer waits for the user to enter a new line of data or a new command. The choice of commands may range into the hundreds. If you do not know what to enter, you will have to consult a users' manual, and some of them are notoriously confusing.

In order to bypass the formidable command-line interface, some software offers menus or lists of choices from which you pick a command. You may then enter a letter such as E for Edit or M for Move, or you may type a word. Sometimes these menus take up the entire screen area, and you may have to page through several layers of menus to choose the command you need. Although these menus are very helpful to new users, they may frustrate experienced users. The best menu-driven software lets the experienced user bypass the menus.

Some of the newer systems offer visual interfaces called icons. Rather than typing a command such as PIP B: = A:TEXTFILE.EXT (it must be typed perfectly, mind you) to copy a file onto a new disk, you merely point at a file icon and move it to the icon representing the second disk. A common pointing device is the mouse, a device rolled on a surface to move the cursor on the screen.

Complex typed commands are difficult to memorize, layers of menus can become confusing, and visual interfaces are not always suitable. What's left? A new type of interface allows the user to "pull down" or "pull up" menus from a selection of keyword headings, such as FILE, EDIT, and STYLE. Once the user has made a selection, the menu disappears, avoiding the layering of pages of menus displayed on the screen.

Many systems combine all the interfaces, allowing the novice user to sit down at a computer and begin a program with little preparation, yet permitting the experienced user to bypass menus and pointers and simply type in a command, for instance, pressing the command key and the Z key for "undo previous typing." The interfaces permit user-friendly implementation of many kinds of software for business and home purposes. Tony Gold correctly identified the user groups; now the user groups must venture forward to try the wealth of software available for almost any application imaginable.

SUMMARY POINTS

- The programmer must tell the computer how to solve a problem step by step.
- Programmers should strive to write high-quality programs that are reliable, efficient, maintainable, and easy to read and understand, and that allow a minimum number of input errors.
- Four steps comprise the program-solving process: defining and documenting the problem; designing and documenting the solution; writing and documenting the program; and compiling, debugging, and testing the program and revising the documentation.
- To complete the above four steps successfully at reduced development and maintenance costs, a programmer must implement a structured approach to program design. Following structured techniques should also increase programmer productivity and program clarity.
- Structured programming is characterized by top-down design, more-than-adequate documentation, program testing at all stages of the problem-solving process, and use of a programming team to develop the software.
- In the top-down approach, a program is broken into functional modules following a hierarchy from general to specific.
- Program documentation should occur at all programming stages. It facilitates testing and review of programs at the development stages and simplifies modification and updating of existing programs.
- Program testing should occur at all programming stages to isolate errors early in the programming stages and to reduce time and costs associated with software development.
- Top-down design is often characterized by use of a chief programmer team (CPT) to fulfill the goals of structured programming and facilitate program

testing and documentation. The team may consist of the chief programmer, a backup programmer, and a librarian. Depending on the complexity of the project, the team may consist of fewer or more members.

- Defining the problem begins with recognizing the need for information. The definition should include a statement of the problem, the needed output, and the required input. The definition should be mutually acceptable to all parties involved in the programming effort, including the user.
- The second step in problem solving involves designing a solution. Planning a solution requires that the programmer know the four logic patterns used by the computer to solve problems: simple sequence, selection, loop, and branch. (Structured programming recognizes all but the branch.) These logic patterns are used to develop the algorithm(s) needed to solve the problem.
- When using the simple sequence pattern, the computer executes program statements one after another.
- Selection requires the computer to compare two items to determine whether one is equal to, less than, or greater than the other.
- The loop sends control back to a previous program statement. That statement is reexecuted and processing continues with the next statement in accordance with simple sequence logic.
- The branch logic pattern makes the computer skip over certain program statements. If used too often, it can make a program inefficient and confusing.
- Pseudocode is a narrative description of the processing steps in a program that aids the programmer in determining the program's logical flow.
- Flowcharts are pictorial representations of processing logic in a program.
- Structure charts show the hierarchical levels of the modules in top-down design.
- HIPO (Hierarchy plus Input-Process-Output) charts also describe programs that are defined in terms of top-down design. They show the input, processing steps, and output of each module.
- Nassi-Shneiderman charts also facilitate top-down design. They are structured flowcharts arranged in partitioned rectangles with program logic flowing from top to bottom.
- Once the solution is planned, the programmer chooses an appropriate language and writes, or codes, the program. Several types of statements are common to most languages.
- A programmer using structured coding follows four rules: avoid the GOTO, or branch, statement; limit the size of the modules to no more than 50 or 60 lines of code; construct a proper program module (one that has only one entry and only one exit); and include liberal documentation throughout the program.
- A sequence of instructions written in assembly language or a high-level language is called a source program. The language translator program converts the source program into a machine language equivalent known as an object program.
- The translator program for assembly language is called an assembler program. A language translator for a high-level language can be a compiler program that translates the source program all at once or an interpreter program that translates the source program statement by statement.
- After programs have been written, they are debugged and tested. Desk-checking and structured walkthroughs facilitate debugging and testing. Test-

ing is done with sample data so that the computer-determined output can be compared with manually prepared correct results.

■ Structured programming and proper documentation help in program maintenance, which refers to the revisions necessary to correct, improve, update, or expand software.

■ Improved user interface has helped users take advantage of the many types of software available for microcomputers. Interface describes the way in which a user submits data to a computer and receives information from it.

■ Types of interfaces include command-line interfaces, icons, and menus.

REVIEW AND DISCUSSION QUESTIONS

1. Discuss the qualities that make one program better than another.
2. List four objectives of structured programming.
3. Explain top-down design. How can the relationships existing between the different parts of a program or system design be visually represented?
4. When should documentation occur and why?
5. What people should receive documentation of a computer program, and which types of documentation should each receive?
6. How does the concept of the CPT enhance structured programming?
7. What are the advantages of beginning a system design by examining the desired output?
8. What important tasks should be accomplished when defining a problem?
9. Why do proponents of structured programming frown on the branch pattern?
10. Contrast flowcharts and structure charts on the basis of format and use.
11. Draw a flowchart that depicts the steps necessary to convert Fahrenheit temperatures to Celsius and print both temperatures.
12. Write the pseudocode that illustrates the steps necessary to test for and sum the prime numbers between 1 and 1,000. (Prime numbers are numbers that are evenly divisible only by 1 and themselves.)
13. When would use of the Nassi-Shneiderman chart be more beneficial than the traditional flowcharts?
14. Why is the term *GOTOless programming* associated with structured programming?
15. After the program has been submitted to the computer, how does the computer translate it into machine-executable form?
16. What can a programmer do to protect accuracy throughout processing?
17. Discuss some ways that software for microcomputers can help teachers and students.
18. Have you ever used software in which the visual interfaces, menus, or help messages interfered with efficient use, according to your abilities? Describe them.

Enhancing the Quality of Life

Computers have enhanced the quality of our lives in many ways, from improving health care to enriching leisure time. Advances in medical research and treatment have been made possible through computer technology. Computerized equipment is used extensively in the health care field for laboratory testing and analysis, computer-assisted diagnosis, and monitoring and treatment of patients. Professionals in the fields of law enforcement and fire fighting use computers to help carry out their duties. Prison life can improve when computers are used to help prisoners learn new skills. Computers can even enhance the quality of our vacations and help bridge the generation gap.

One of the areas in which computers have had the most impact in terms of improving the quality of people's lives is medicine. In hospitals computers are used to assist doctors in the diagnosis and treatment of illnesses. Bio-Logic Systems produces microcomputer equipment that can help diagnose brain tumors. Electrodes from an electroencephalograph are connected to a patient's head and a color video map reveals brain activity ①. The electrical activity mapping capability serves as an important intraoperative monitoring device ②.

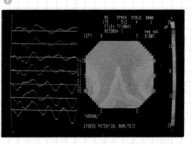

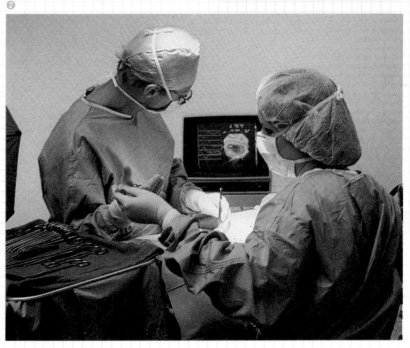

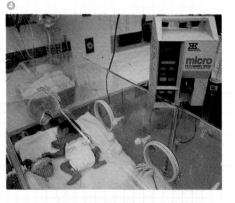

A laboratory technician checks computer-controlled infusion pumps for flaws before sending the pumps to hospitals ③. In a hospital neonatal intensive care unit, a FLO-GARD 8500 micro volumetric infusion pump is used to administer drugs to a critically ill newborn ④. The pumps are used for microinfusion of drugs and chemotherapy. As you can see, the results may be highly successful ⑤!

Another successful use of computers relating to drugs is in pharmacies. Pharmacists use computers to keep track of customer records. Special software designed for use by pharmacists monitors the prescriptions filled for each customer and checks for negative drug interactions ⑥.

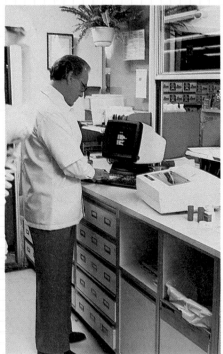

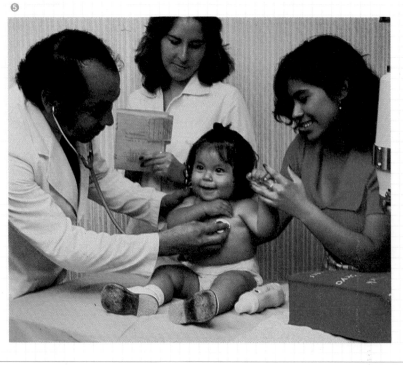

Computer technology has had an impact on the physically disabled. At Wright State University, Dr. Jerrold Petrofsky developed a computerized "stimulation and feedback" system to help paraplegics walk. Nan Davis, paralyzed from the waist down, received encouragement from people all over the world when she publicly took several steps with the help of Dr. Petrofsky's system . The development of smaller and more powerful microprocessors has led to the creation of the Utah Arm. This prosthesis, which resembles a real arm, was developed by researchers at the University of Utah Center for Biomedical Design and is used on people whose amputation is above the elbow ⑧. While somewhat less dramatic but certainly beneficial, researchers also use computers to teach patients biofeedback techniques to help control problems such as migraine headaches, chronic pain, and high blood pressure ⑨.

In communities throughout the country, computers are working with local police and fire departments helping to make our lives better. Many local police departments use computers to gain access to national data bases that contain information on missing persons. In Orlando, Florida the police department uses a robot to teach "Dangerous Stranger Awareness" to elementary school children. The robot and officer have a two-way conversation discussing safety tips for children ⑩. The Phoenix Fire Department is using computers to fight fires and save lives. When a call comes into the station a dispatcher receives the call and enters the caller's information about the fire into a computer terminal ⑪. Information such as the size and location of the building and the type of fire, will then appear on the monitor ⑫. The information is transmitted to mobile computer terminals located in the fire trucks ⑬. Firefighters can review the information on the mobile monitor while traveling to the fire.

In addition to uses by doctors, police officers, and firefighters computers are also used to enhance the quality of our lives in more pleasurable ways. At Club Med, a resort chain with locations all over the world, computers enhance the quality of vacations. Computer seminars are offered in a relaxed vacation atmosphere ⑭. Guests are encouraged to "play" with computers in their free time ⑮.

Inside the walls of an Arizona prison, computers are enhancing the quality of life for prison inmates. Prisoners who are taught computer skills are hired by Best Western, an international hotel chain, to book room reservations for Best Western properties throughout the world ⑯. Having computer skills will help these inmates find jobs when they leave prison. Computers are helping prisoners bridge the gap between life inside the restricted prison environment and life outside prison. They are also helping bridge the generation gap as grandchildren and grandparents find the new technology an exciting way to learn together ⑰.

CHAPTER 11

SOFTWARE

COMPUTERS IN OUR LIVES

Software for the SAT

Like most high school students, Nancy was not looking forward to taking her SAT (Scholastic Aptitude Test). Like it or not, however, she knew a good SAT score is necessary for both entrance into college and scholarships. Even though Nancy was nervous about taking the SAT, she did feel prepared. For the past year, she had participated in a program sponsored by her high school where students could prepare for the SAT using the high school's computers and SAT software packages.

When the SAT test first came out, teachers and guidance counselors alike declared studying for the exam was impossible. Success or failure resulted from the instruction received by the student over the previous twelve years. With the development of SAT software packages, that philosophy is changing. Some educators now believe that studying for the SAT is useful. If nothing else, at least studying familiarizes students with the basic format of the test and many teachers find that students are highly motivated to study for the SAT with a computer.

The SAT software package used by Nancy's high school comes with an extensive manual that offers sample questions, tutorial material, and strategies for taking the test. The software itself has two modes—learning and testing. In the learning mode, a student can choose to have the answers to the questions explained. In the test mode, students' answers are recorded, checked, and scored just as they would be on an actual exam. The software also offers a complete analysis of a student's score, listing the various skill areas (analogies—opposites, antonyms, and cause and effect, for example) and the percent the student answered correctly. A study priority is then assigned to each topic. This is how Nancy discovered that her ability to answer analogy questions was weak. She was able to generate more analogy questions and get extensive practice in this area.

Nancy particularly appreciated the feedback the software provided in the learning mode. If she chose an incorrect answer to a question, the program offered hints on how to correctly answer the question rather than just telling her the right answer. This way Nancy could rethink and rework the problem. In the mathematics section, geometry problems were illustrated with graphics. Geometric figures were rotated three-dimensionally and from different perspectives on the screen to help her visually grasp the problem.

Since Nancy does not always respond well to stress, she also liked the timed practices that could be performed in the test mode. This timed test simulated actual SAT timed test conditions. Sometimes, the pressure of a timed test causes Nancy to block out answers to questions she has studied thoroughly. Taking the test under the same time conditions helped her to adjust to this stress.

Whether or not SAT software packages guarantees improved SAT scores has not been proven. One educational consultant recently found a difference of 94 points on scores between students who did study with a SAT software package and those who had no supplementary preparation. In another study, students using SAT packages increased their average scores 35 points

328

after one month of preparation. While this may not seem overly impressive, some of those students jumped as much as 180 points within that month.

Nancy recommends the SAT software packages. Her final SAT score was more than satisfactory and she was accepted by the college she most wanted to attend. Perhaps she would have performed just as well on the SAT without help from the computer, but according to Nancy, she wouldn't want to test that theory.

Software such as the various SAT preparation packages require programming many alternatives and answers. Although programming such a package sounds complicated, today's programmers design software by using structured programming methodologies. They also choose many new, powerful programming languages, such as the ones discussed in this chapter, that make the programming of complex patterns easy.

INTRODUCTION

The benefits of smaller, faster, and more efficient computers cannot be realized without the existence of well-prepared software. Programs help users solve many practical problems through computer processing; they are also used by the computer to govern its own internal operations such as input and output, translation of source code into object code, and order of processing. As we see in this chapter, software links users, computers, and peripheral devices to perform tasks.

This chapter discusses the difference between system and application programs and describes the functions of the operating system. It also reviews multiprogramming, virtual storage, and multiprocessing—developments that increase the effectiveness and efficiency of the computer so that many people can use the resources of one computer. Various programming languages are described, along with their advantages and disadvantages. Finally, the problem of software piracy is discussed briefly.

TYPES OF PROGRAMS

Despite the apparent complexity and power of the computer, it is merely a tool manipulated by an individual. It requires step-by-step instructions—a program—to reach the solution to a problem. The two basic types of software are **system programs,** which coordinate the operation of the computer and **application programs,** which solve particular user problems.

System Programs

System programs directly affect the operation of the computer. They are designed to facilitate the use of the hardware and to help the computer system run quickly and efficiently. System software includes a variety of programs,

System program Instructions written to coordinate the operation of computer circuitry and help the computer run quickly and efficiently.

Application program A sequence of instructions written to solve a specific user problem.

329

In Every Young Person, An Old Person Is Waiting to Get Out!

People have been inventing new uses for computers faster than you can say "user-friendly." One recent idea puts a wrinkle in time.

Artist Nancy Burson of New York City uses a computer to create a picture of how a young person will look in 5 years, 20 years, or even 25 years. With her system, adding decades to a face takes just a few seconds.

Burson owns a company called Face Systems, Inc., that markets her computer programs. Her portraits are of two kinds. One is a model of an aged face. The other is a mixture of the features of several faces. She has created elderly images of Brooke Shields, John Travolta, and Princess Diana for *People* magazine. One of her face mixtures was "Nuclear Powers"—a blend of the faces of world leaders, including Ronald Reagan and Margaret Thatcher.

Burson hopes that her system can be used for more practical purposes. One use aids in the search for missing people. Dee Scofield was 12 years old when she disappeared from an Ocala, Florida, shopping center. If she is alive, she is now 21 years old. Burson "drew" a portrait of how Dee would look to help in an ongoing search for the woman.

Burson also hopes plastic surgeons will use her programs. Surgeons could show patients how they would look with a thinner nose, a stronger chin, or fewer wrinkles.

such as operating systems, utility programs, and programming language translators, discussed later in this chapter. A system program may allocate storage for data being entered into the system. Such a program will vary from computer to computer because the architecture of various computers differs. System programs are provided by the computer manufacturer or a specialized programming firm. They can be modified to meet a particular organization's needs.

Application Programs

Application programs perform specific data-processing or computational tasks to solve an organization's information needs or help an individual with personal or educational tasks. They can be developed within the organization or purchased from software firms. Typical examples include those used by businesses in inventory control and accounting. In banks, for example, application programs update checking and savings account balances.

Major categories of application programs are word processors, spreadsheets, data management, and graphics. Other applications include programs that facilitate communications; educational software for drills, simulations, and tutoring; games; and control systems for home and office environments. A more thorough discussion of application software is in Chapter 12.

OPERATING SYSTEMS

In early computer systems, human operators monitored computer operations, determined the order in which submitted programs were run, and readied input and output devices. While early electronic development increased the processing speeds of CPUs, the speed of human operators remained constant. Time delays and errors caused by human operators became a serious problem.

In the 1960s, operating systems, which are collections of system programs, were developed to help overcome this problem. An **operating system** is used by the computer to manage its own operations at computer speeds. It provides an interface between the user or application programs and the computer hardware. Instead of a human operator preparing the I/O devices to be used for each program and loading the programs into storage, the operating system assumes responsibility for all jobs to be run (see Figure 11–1).

Operating system A collection of programs designed to permit a computer system to manage itself and increase the use of computer resources.

Purpose of an Operating System

An operating system is geared toward attaining maximum efficiency in processing operations. One way to increase efficiency is to eliminate human intervention. A second way to increase efficiency is to allow several programs to share computer resources. The operating system allocates these resources to the programs requesting them and resolves conflicts that occur when, for example, two or three programs request the use of the same tape drive or primary storage location. In addition, the operating system performs an accounting function for large time-sharing systems; it keeps track of all resource use to determine user fees and evaluate whether the CPU is being used efficiently.

A third way the operating system increases efficiency is by scheduling jobs on a priority basis. Although running programs in the order in which they are

Figure 11–1
Computer Operations.
In Association of American Railroad's computer control/data center, a computer operator discusses a problem.

submitted may seem logical, this is not always the most practical approach. For instance, assume that five programs are submitted for processing within a short period of time. If one program requires one minute of CPU time and the other four require one hour each, processing the short program first may be appropriate. If one program will produce a vital report and the others generate less important output, the more important program should probably be processed first. A system of priorities can be established based on considerations such as the required processing time and the need for the expected output.

Program processing can occur in two ways, either by batch or online. In a batch-processing environment, several user programs (jobs or job steps) are grouped and processed one after the other in a continuous stream. For example, in the evening an operator may load all jobs (such as, updating bank accounts or credit card debits) to be processed during the night onto a tape drive and enter them into the system. The operating system will direct processing without interruption until all jobs are complete, thus freeing the operator to perform other tasks. On the other hand, an online system can respond to spontaneous requests for system resources, such as airline reservation inquiries entered from online terminals at a travel agency.

Operating systems currently in use on mainframe and minicomputer systems can handle both batch and online applications simultaneously. These operating systems direct the processing of a job and also respond to interrupts from I/O devices, such as online terminals, printers, and secondary storage devices, which must communicate with the CPU through the operating system. When an I/O device sends a message to the CPU, normal processing is suspended (the CPU is interrupted) so that the CPU can direct the operation of the I/O device. The function of the operating system is, therefore, to manage the resources of the CPU in its handling of batch and online processing and its control of peripheral devices.

Components of Operating Systems

An operating system is an integrated collection of subsystems. Each subsystem consists of programs that perform specific duties. Since all operating system programs work as a "team," CPU idle time is avoided and use of computer facilities is increased. Operating system programs are usually stored on a secondary storage device known as the **system residence device.** The secondary devices most commonly used are magnetic tape (TOS—tape operating system) and magnetic disk (DOS—disk operating system) (see Figure 11–2). (Magnetic-drum technology allows for the fastest processing times, but many existing operating systems use magnetic-disk technology.)

Two types of programs make up the operating system: **control programs** and **processing programs.** Control programs oversee system operations and perform tasks such as input/output, scheduling, handling interrupts, and communicating with the computer operator or programmers. Processing programs are executed under the supervision of control programs and are used by the programmer to simplify program preparation for the computer system.

Control Programs

The three major control programs are the supervisor program, the job-control program, and the input/output management system. The **supervisor program**

System residence device An auxiliary storage medium (disk, tape, or drum) on which operating system programs are stored.

Control program A routine, usually part of an operating system, that helps control the operations of a computer system.

Processing program A routine, usually part of an operating system, used to simplify program preparation and execution.

Supervisor program The major component of the operating system; coordinates the activities of all other parts of the operating system.

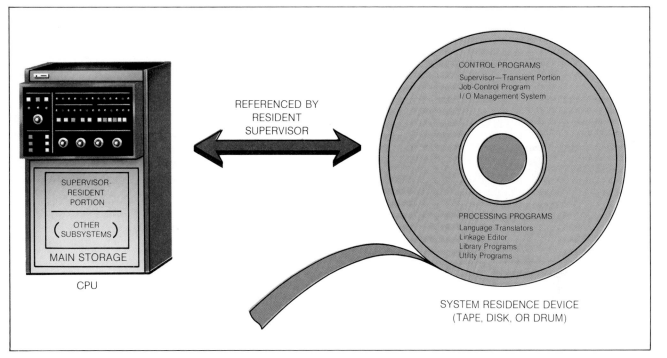

CONTROL PROGRAMS
Supervisor—Transient Portion
Job-Control Program
I/O Management System

PROCESSING PROGRAMS
Language Translators
Linkage Editor
Library Programs
Utility Programs

REFERENCED BY
RESIDENT
SUPERVISOR

SUPERVISOR-
RESIDENT
PORTION
(OTHER
SUBSYSTEMS)
MAIN STORAGE

CPU

SYSTEM RESIDENCE DEVICE
(TAPE, DISK, OR DRUM)

Figure 11–2
Operating System in Primary Storage and System Residence Device

(also called the monitor or executive) is the major component of the operating system. It coordinates the activities of all other parts of the operating system. When the computer is first put into use, the supervisor is the first program to be transferred into primary storage from the system residence device. Only the most frequently used components of the supervisor are initially loaded into primary storage. These components are referred to as **resident routines.** Certain other supervisor routines, known as **transient routines,** remain in secondary storage with the rest of the operating system. Supervisor routines call the transient routines and load them into primary storage as needed. The supervisor schedules I/O operations and allocates channels to various I/O devices. It also sends messages to the computer operator indicating the status of particular jobs, error conditions, and so on.

The operating system requires job-control information in order to perform its mission. (A job is a task to be processed by the CPU.) A **job-control language (JCL)** is the communication link between the programmer and the operating system. Job-control statements are used to identify the beginning of a job, to identify the specific program to be executed, to describe the work to be done, and to indicate the I/O devices required. These statements are translated into machine-executable code by the control program called the **job-control program.**

The control programs of the operating system must be able to control and coordinate the CPU while receiving input from channels, executing instructions of programs in storage, and regulating output. I/O devices must be assigned to specific programs, and data must be moved between them and specific memory locations. The control program referred to as the **input/output management system** oversees and coordinates these processes.

Resident routine One of the most frequently used components of the supervisor, which is initially loaded into primary storage.

Transient routine A supervisor routine that remains in secondary storage with the rest of the operating system.

Job-Control Language (JCL) A language that serves as the communication link between the programmer and the operating system.

Job-control program A control program that translates job-control statements into machine-executable code.

Input/output management system The part of the operating system that coordinates the CPU while receiving input, executing instructions of programs in storage, and regulating output.

333

Language-translator program Software that translates the Englishlike programs written by programmers into machine-executable code.

Linkage editor A subprogram of the operating system that links the object program from the system residence device to primary storage.

Library program A user-written or manufacturer-supplied program or subroutine that is frequently used in other programs.

System library A collection of files in which various parts of an operating system are stored.

Processing Programs

The operating system contains several processing programs that facilitate efficient processing operations by simplifying program preparation and execution for users. The major processing programs contained in the operating system are the language translators, linkage editor, librarian programs, and utility programs.

Most application programs are written in a language more closely resembling English than machine language, because writing in machine language is too complex and time-consuming. A **language-translator program,** as its name implies, translates Englishlike programs (the source programs) written by programmers into machine-language instructions (the object program). See Chapter 10 to review the more detailed explanation of language translation.

On a mainframe system, the translation process may work as follows: the programmer specifies in JCL the language in which a program is written. When the program is to be executed, the job-control program interprets that job-control statement and informs the supervisor which language translator is needed. The supervisor then calls the appropriate language translator from the system residence device. The language translator converts the program into machine language. Often the translated application program is placed on the system residence device until the supervisor calls for it to be loaded into primary storage for execution. A processing program called the **linkage editor** "links" the object program from the system residence device to primary storage. It does this by assigning appropriate primary storage addresses to each byte of the object program.

Library programs are user-written or manufacturer-supplied programs and subroutines that are frequently used in other programs. So that these routines will not have to be rewritten every time they are needed, they are stored in a **system library** (usually on disk or tape) and called into primary storage when needed. They are then linked with other programs to perform specific tasks.

"No Farnswell, They're not wasting time. They're programming!"

The processing program called the **librarian program** manages the storage and use of library programs by maintaining a directory of programs in the system library. It also contains appropriate procedures for adding and deleting programs.

Operating systems also include processing programs called **utility programs** that perform specialized functions. One such program transfers data from file to file, or from one I/O device to another. For example, a utility program can be used to transfer data from tape to tape, tape to disk, card to tape, or tape to printer. Other utility programs, known as **sort/merge programs,** are used to sort records into a particular sequence to facilitate updating of files. Once sorted, several files can be merged to form a single, updated file. Job-control statements are used to specify the sort/merge programs; these programs or routines are then called into primary storage when needed.

Although the original operating system is usually obtained from the manufacturer of the CPU, alternative operating systems can be purchased from software vendors. In addition, subsystems can be bought that either improve an existing system or provide additional capabilities to the operating system. For example, the operating system for a bank's computer may be supplemented with a subsystem to interface with magnetic-ink character readers. Applications requiring the use of light pens with display terminals also demand special subsystems.

Several popular operating systems for personal computers are CP/M, Apple DOS and Apple ProDOS, MS–DOS, and Unix (see Chapter 9). CP/M was the first operating system developed for personal computers. New versions include CP/M-86 and Concurrent CP/M. More than 15,000 application programs have been written to be run on systems using CP/M. The Apple operating systems are used for the Apple II computers, and MS–DOS (also PC–DOS) operates with IBM PCs. MS–DOS is becoming a standard in the computer industry because so much software is being developed that will run under it and so many computers now use it. The Unix operating system was recently developed

Librarian program   Software that manages the storage and use of library programs by maintaining a directory of programs in the system library.

Utility program   A program within an operating system that performs a specialized function.

Sort/merge program   A utility program used to sort records when updating and combining files to form a single, updated file.

Concept Summary 11–1 ▪ Operating System as Interface

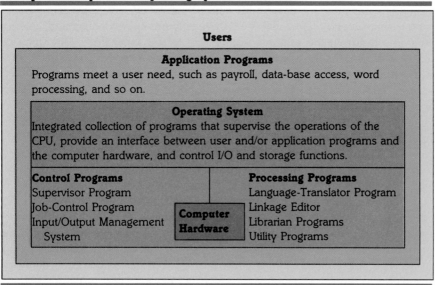

Figure 11–3
Virtual Storage.
Virtual storage and multiprogramming allow many people to use the resources of a central computer from their own terminals.

Multiprogramming A technique that places several programs in primary storage for execution, giving the illusion that they are being executed simultaneously.

Virtual storage An extension of multiprogramming in which portions of programs are kept in secondary storage until needed, giving the impression that primary storage is unlimited.

Multiprocessing A multiple CPU configuration in which jobs are processed simultaneously.

Region In multiprogramming, a term often used to mean the internal space allocated; a variable-sized partition.

Region In multiprogramming, a term often used to mean the internal space allocated; a variable-sized partition.

Partition In multiprogramming, the primary storage area reserved for one program; may be fixed or variable in size.

Memory management/memory protection In a multiprogramming environment, the process of keeping the programs in primary storage separate.

from the Unix operating system designed by Bell Laboratories to use on minicomputers. Some people predict that it will become the industry standard because of its expanded features. It provides a library of over 200 utility programs and also offers a unique file structure so that files can be manipulated in ways not available with other operating systems.

INCREASING PROCESSING EFFICIENCY

Just as application programs have become more sophisticated over the years, so have system programs. Early computer systems were plagued by inefficient use of computer resources, either because human intervention was required or because system programs were not sophisticated enough to allocate resources well. Several developments have greatly increased the overall efficiency of the computer. These are multiprogramming, virtual storage, and multiprocessing. **Multiprogramming** allows the computer to work with more than one program at a time. **Virtual storage** makes main storage appear larger than it is, while **multiprocessing** provides for simultaneous execution of more than one program by several computers (see Figure 11–3).

Multiprogramming

When the CPU is very active, the system as a whole is more efficient. However, the CPU frequently remains idle because I/O devices are not fast enough. The CPU can operate on only one instruction at a time; furthermore, it cannot operate on data that is not in primary storage. If an input device is slow in providing data or instructions, the CPU must wait until I/O operations have been completed before executing a program.

In the earliest computer systems with simple operating systems, most programs were executed using serial processing—they were executed one at a time. Serial processing was terribly inefficient because the high-speed CPU was idle for long periods of time as slow input devices loaded data or output devices printed or stored results.

Multiprogramming increases CPU active time by effectively allocating computer resources and offsetting low I/O speeds. With multiprogramming, several programs reside in the primary storage unit at the same time. Although the CPU still can execute only one instruction at a time, it can execute instructions from one program, then another, then another, and back to the first again. Instructions from one program are executed until an interrupt for either input or output is generated. The I/O operation is handled by a channel, and the CPU can shift its attention to another program in memory until that program requires input or output. This rotation occurs so quickly that the execution of the programs in storage appears to be simultaneous. According to the terminology of computer professionals, the CPU executes the different programs concurrently, which means "over the same period of time." This process is often referred to as overlapped processing, and is illustrated in Figure 11–4.

Although multiprogramming increases the system's flexibility and efficiency, it also creates some problems. First, the programs in primary storage must be kept separate. This is accomplished by using **regions** or **partitions.** Keeping programs in the correct region is known as **memory management,** or **memory protection.** A similar situation exists with I/O devices: two programs cannot

336

access the same tape or disk drive at the same time. These problems are handled by the operating system's control programs.

A second problem that arises with multiprogramming is the need to determine which program will be processed first. To alleviate the problem, each program is assigned a priority. In a time-sharing system, the programs being used for online processing must respond immediately to users at remote locations. Thus, these programs are assigned the highest priority. Programs of low priority are typically executed in batch mode. For large systems with several programs of differing priorities, scheduling is not a simple task. Two programs of the same priority may request CPU resources at the same time. The method of deciding which program gets control may be arbitrary: for example, the program that has been in primary storage longer may receive priority. Fortunately, the operating system is capable of handling such problems as they occur, and in most instances makes the process of multiprogramming invisible to the user.

Virtual Storage

Multiprogramming increases system efficiency because the CPU can execute programs concurrently instead of waiting for I/O operations to occur. A limitation of multiprogramming, however, is that each partition must be large enough to hold an entire program; the program remains in memory until its execution is completed.

Another limitation is that all the instructions of a program are kept in primary storage throughout its execution, whether they are needed or not. Yet, a large program may contain many sequences of instructions that are executed infrequently. For example, the program may consist of several logical sections, but most of the processing may be done by only one or two of them. While this processing occurs, those not being used are occupying primary storage that

TIME PERIOD		1	2	3	4	5	6	7	8	9
SERIAL PROCESSING	Input	1			2			3		
	Processing		1			2			3	
	Output			1			2			3
OVERLAPPED PROCESSING	Input	1	2	3	4	5	6	7	8	9
	Processing		1	2	3	4	5	6	7	8
	Output			1	2	3	4	5	6	7

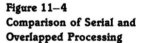

← Additional Processing Performed

**Figure 11–4
Comparison of Serial and Overlapped Processing**

could otherwise be used more efficiently. As processing requirements increase, the physical limitations of memory become a critical constraint, and the productive use of memory becomes increasingly important.

For many years, the space limitations of primary storage have been a barrier to applications. Programmers have spent much time trying to find ways to trim programs to fit into available primary storage space. In some cases, attempts have been made to segment programs (break them into separate modules) so that they could be executed in separate job steps; but doing this manually is both tedious and time-consuming. While hardware costs have decreased and storage capacities have increased, this storage problem still exists in high-volume processing systems that require large programs.

To alleviate the problem, an extension of multiprogramming called virtual storage (sometimes called virtual memory) has been developed. Virtual storage is based on the principle that only the immediately needed portion of a program be in primary storage at any given time; the rest of the program and data can be kept in secondary storage. Since only part of a program is in primary storage at one time, more programs can reside in primary storage simultaneously, allowing more programs to be executed within a given time period. This gives the illusion that primary storage is unlimited.

To implement virtual storage, a direct-access secondary storage device such as a magnetic-disk unit is used to agument primary storage. The term **real storage** is usually given to primary storage within the CPU, while virtual storage refers to the direct-access storage. Both real and virtual storage locations are given addresses by the operating system. If necessary data or instructions are not in the real storage area, the portion of the program containing them is transferred from virtual storage into real storage, while another portion currently in real storage may be written back to virtual storage. This process is known as **swapping** (see Figure 11–5). If the portion of the program in real storage has not been modified during execution, the portion from virtual storage may

Real storage Primary storage; contrast with virtual storage.

Swapping In a virtual storage environment, the process of transferring a program section from virtual storage to real storage, and vice versa.

Figure 11–5
Schematic Drawing of Virtual Storage and Swapping

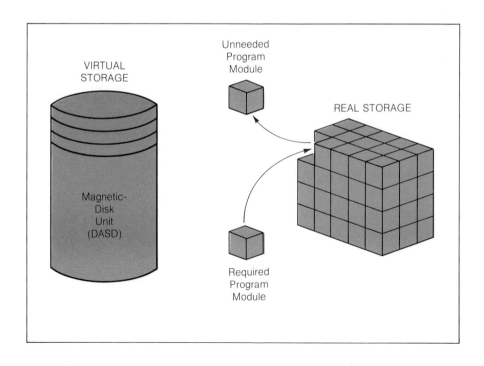

be simply laid over it, because copies of all parts of the program are kept in virtual storage.

There are two main methods of implementing virtual storage systems, both of which use a combination of hardware and software to accomplish the task. The first method is called **segmentation.** Each program is broken into variable-sized blocks called segments, which are logical parts of the program. For example, one segment may contain data used by the program; another segment may contain a **subroutine** of the program; and so on. The operating system software allocates storage space according to the size of these logical segments.

A second method of implementing virtual storage is **paging.** Here, primary storage is divided into physical areas of fixed size called **page frames.** All page frames for all programs are the same size, and this size depends on the characteristics of the particular computer. In contrast to segmentation, paging does not consider the logical portions of the programs. Instead, the programs are broken into equal-sized blocks called **pages.** One page can fit in one page frame of primary storage (see Figure 11–6).

In both paging and segmentation, the operating system handles the swapping of pages or segments whenever a portion of the program that is not in real storage is needed during processing.

Virtual storage offers tremendous flexibility to programmers and systems analysts designing new applications; they can devote their time to solving the problem at hand rather than to fitting programs into storage. Moreover, as already explained, the use of primary storage is optimized, since only needed portions of programs are in primary storage at any time.

One of the major limitations of virtual storage is the requirement for extensive online secondary storage. Also, the virtual storage operating system is highly sophisticated and requires significant amounts of internal storage. If virtual storage is not used wisely, much time can be spent locating and exchanging

Segmentation A method of implementing virtual storage in which a program is divided into variable-sized blocks (segments) depending on the program logic.

Subroutine A sequence of statements outside the main part of a program that can be used repeatedly in different parts of the program.

Paging A method of implementing virtual storage in which data and programs are broken into equal-sized blocks (pages) and loaded into real storage when needed.

Page frame In a virtual storage environment, one of the equal-sized physical areas into which primary storage is divided.

Page In a virtual storage environment, the portion of a program that is kept in secondary storage and loaded into real storage only when needed.

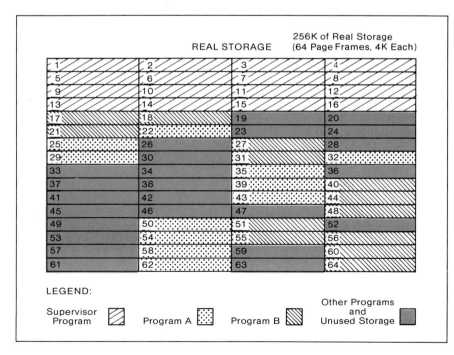

Figure 11–6
Paging

Thrashing A situation in virtual storage in which little processing occurs compared to the amount of locating and swapping of pages or segments.

Front-end processor A small CPU serving as an interface between a large CPU and peripheral devices.

Back-end processor A small CPU serving as an interface between a large CPU and a large data base stored on a direct-access storage device.

program pages or segments; in some programs, little actual processing occurs compared with the amount of swapping. (This is known as **thrashing**.)

Multiprocessing

Multiprocessing involves the use of two or more CPUs linked together for coordinated operation. Stored-program instructions are executed simultaneously, but by different CPUs. The CPUs may execute different instructions from the same program, or they may execute totally different programs. (In contrast, under multiprogramming, the computer appears to be processing different jobs simultaneously but is actually processing them concurrently.)

Multiprocessing systems are designed to achieve a particular objective. One common objective is to relieve a large CPU of tasks such as scheduling, editing data, and maintaining files so that it can continue high-priority or complex processing without interruption. To do this, a small CPU (often a minicomputer) is linked to the large CPU. All work coming into the system from remote terminals or other peripheral devices is first channeled through the small CPU, which coordinates the activities of the large one. Generally, the small CPU handles all I/O interrupts and so on, while the large CPU handles the "number crunching" (large mathematical calculations). A schematic diagram of this type of multiprocessing system is shown in Figure 11–7. The small CPU in Figure 11–7 is commonly referred to as a **front-end processor.** It is an interface between the large CPU and peripheral devices such as online terminals.

A small CPU may also be used as an interface between a large CPU and a large data base stored on direct-access storage devices. In this case, the small CPU, often termed a **back-end processor,** is solely responsible for maintaining the data base. Accessing data and updating specific data fields are typical functions a small CPU performs in this type of multiprocessing system.

Many large multiprocessing systems have two or more large CPUs. These large CPUs are no different from those used in single-CPU (stand-alone) configurations. Each may have its own separate memory, or a single memory may be shared by all of them. The activities of each CPU can be controlled in whole or in part by a common supervisor program. This type of system is used by organizations with extremely large and complex data-processing needs. Each large CPU may be dedicated to a specific task such as I/O processing or arithmetic processing. One CPU can be set up to handle online processing while another handles only batch processing. Alternately, two CPUs may be used together on the same task to provide rapid responses in the most demanding applications. Many multiprocessing systems are designed so that one or more of the CPUs can provide backup if another malfunctions. A configuration that uses multiple large CPUs is depicted in Figure 11–8. This system also uses a small CPU to control communications with peripheral devices and perform "housekeeping chores" (input editing, validation, and the like).

Coordinating the efforts of several CPUs requires highly sophisticated software and careful planning. The scheduling of workloads for the CPUs involves making the most efficient use of computer resources. Implementing such a system is a time-consuming endeavor that may require the services of outside consultants as well as those provided by the equipment manufacturers. The payoff from this effort is a system with capabilities extending far beyond those of a single-CPU system.

Figure 11-7
Multiprocessing System with Small Front-End Processor and Large Mainframe

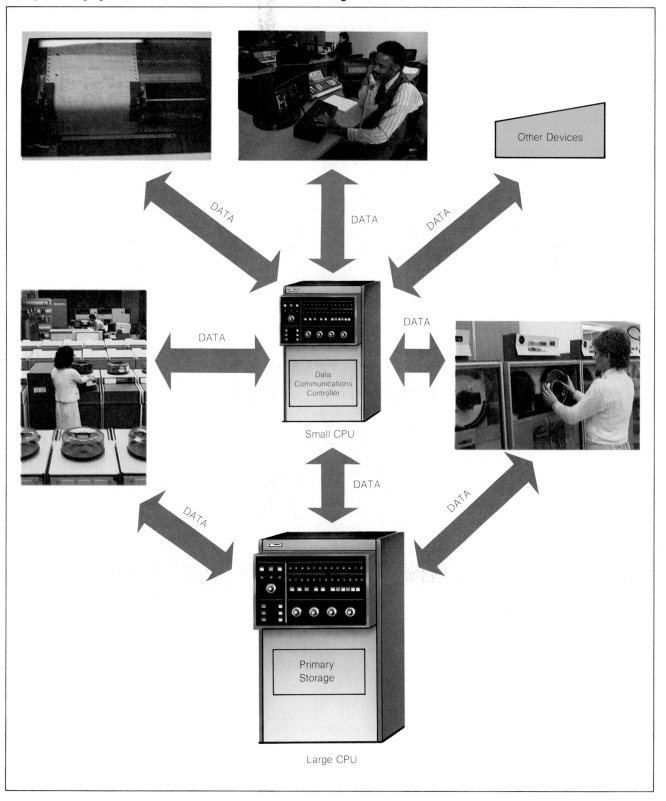

Figure 11–8
Multiprocessing System Using
Multiple Large CPUs

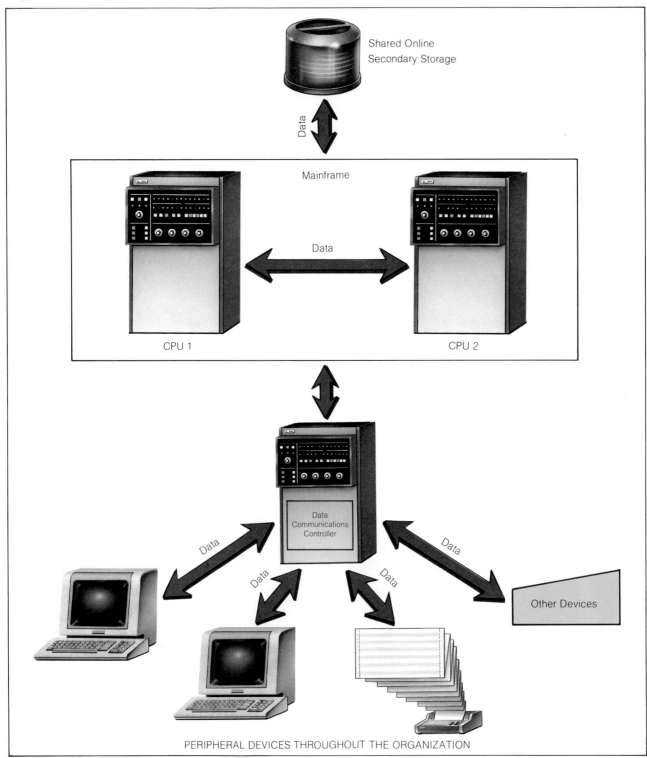

Shared Online
Secondary Storage

Data

Mainframe

Data

CPU 1

CPU 2

Data
Communications
Controller

Data

Data

Data

Data

Other Devices

PERIPHERAL DEVICES THROUGHOUT THE ORGANIZATION

DEVELOPMENTS THAT IMPROVE COMPUTER EFFICIENCY		
Multiprogramming	**Virtual Storage**	**Multiprocessing**
● Involves storing several programs in primary storage at one time. ● Processes programs concurrently by shifting back and forth among the programs—overlapped processing.	● Involves use of pages or segments of a program. ● Only needed portions of program reside in primary storage, giving illusion that primary storage is unlimited.	● Involves use of two or more CPUs linked together. ● Stored-program instructions are executed simultaneously.

COMPUTER LANGUAGES

The earliest computers were programmed by arranging various wires and switches within the computer components. Up to 6,000 switches could be set on the ENIAC to perform one program. However, when a new program was to be run, all the switches had to be reset. This was clearly inefficient. The EDSAC, the first stored-program computer, allowed instructions to be entered into primary storage without rewiring or resetting switches. Codes that corresponded to the on/off electrical states were needed to enter these instructions. These codes were called machine language. Later, assembly language was developed to offset the tediousness of writing machine code. Both machine and assembly languages are machine dependent, requiring the programmer to learn details about the particular microprocessor being programmed. The development of FORTRAN in the mid-1950s signaled the beginning of a trend toward high-level languages that emphasized procedures and problem solving rather than the operation of computer hardware. In an effort to make programming languages even more like everyday English, query languages were developed. These languages, also called nonprocedural languages, enable nonprogrammers to access data bases and perform other functions without writing an actual program.

Low-Level Languages: Machine and Assembly Languages

Low-level languages give the programmer direct control over details of computer hardware; they enable the programmer to specify memory locations, direct input and output operations, and govern the use of registers. Programmers who write low-level language programs must be highly skilled in two areas. First, they need a great deal of technical knowledge: low-level languages are machine dependent and require that programmers know exactly how a particular microprocessor works. Programs written in low-level languages will execute only on the specific machine for which they were written. Second, programmers must be very detail oriented. Every step the computer takes to execute a program must be coded. Actual numerical addresses of storage locations for instructions and data must be specified. Every switch and register

48	00	23C0	
4C	00	23C2	
40	00	2310	
D2	01	2310	2310
48	00	2310	
4E	00	2028	
F3	17	3002	2028
9G	F0	3003	

Figure 11-9
Machine-Language Instructions Expressed in the Hexadecimal Number System

Operation code (op code) The part of an instruction that tells what operation is to be performed.

Operand The part of an instruction that tells where to find the data or equipment on which to operate.

must be known. Once these skills are learned, the programmer has the tools to harness the strengths of particular microprocessors. The efficiency and machine orientation of low-level languages make them appropriate for coding operating system software (discussed earlier in this chapter).

The lowest level language is machine language, the language of the computer. Machine language is the only language a computer can recognize and act upon directly. It functions as the object language of other language programs, which must be translated into machine language before the computer can execute the instructions. Because data in digital computers is stored as either on or off electrical states, machine language takes the form of 1s and 0s to be understood by the machine. But coding a program in this binary form is very tedious, so machine language is often coded in either octal or hexadecimal codes (see Figure 11-9). Each machine language instruction has two parts: an **op code (operation code)**, which tells the computer what function to perform, and an **operand**, which tells the computer what data to use when performing that function. The operand takes the form of the specific storage addresses of data.

Machine language is the most efficient language in terms of storage area use and execution speed. It allows the programmer to use fully the computer's potential for processing data. On the other hand, programming in machine language is very tedious and time-consuming. Instructions are difficult to remember and use.

Assembly languages were developed to overcome the disadvantages of machine language. The programmer uses mnemonics, instead of 1s and 0s, to specify machine operations, or machine op codes. The mnemonics are Englishlike abbreviations for the machine-language instructions, for example, STB for *store in register B*, LDA for *load register A*, and CMP for *compare*. Table 11-1 shows some common arithmetic operations and codes in assembly language and in binary code. Locations of memory circuits and data are specified by symbolic names rather than digits in assembly language.

Writing programs in assembly language offers several other advantages. First, assembly language programs are highly efficient in terms of storage space use and processing time. In fact, assembly language is chosen when fast execution is essential; often it is used in software that generates graphics on microcomputers. Second, the assembler program (language translator) performs some checking functions and generates error messages that are useful in debugging.

Table 11-1 ▬ Examples of Assembly-Language Mnemonic Codes

Operation	Typical Assembly-Language Mnemonic Code	Typical Binary OP Code
Add memory to register	A	01011010
Add (decimal) memory to register	AP	11111010
Multiply register by memory	M	01011100
Multiply (decimal) register by memory	MP	11111100
Subtract memory from register	S	01011011
Subtract (decimal) memory from register	SP	11111011
Move (numeric) from register to memory	MVN	11010001
Compare memory to register	C	01011001
Compare (decimal) memory to register	CP	11111001
Zero register and add (decimal) memory to register	ZAP	11111000

Why Not English?

Ada, Pascal, BASIC, PILOT, FORTRAN, Logo. Computers can be programmed in all these languages and many more, but why can't somebody program a computer to understand English?

English is filled with colorful expressions that add interest and meaning to our speech and help us communicate more effectively with each other. Also, much of what we say to each other has meaning because of the context in which it is spoken. For example, if your friend told you to "kill the lights" as you were walking out the door, you would probably reach for the light switch and flick it to the "off" position.

A computer interprets every statement exactly; there is no room for vagueness. The statement "kill the lights" is structured the same way as the statement "kill the mosquito" and would be interpreted the same way.

With present-day computer memory powers, programming a computer to understand all the shades of meanings in the English language as it is used in everyday speech would not be useful, or even possible. So, for the time being, at least, it's Ada, Pascal, and all the rest when we communicate with the computer.

Finally, assembly language encourages modular programming techniques, which break a program into a number of separate modules, creating small, easily handled units. However, assembly language is still a cumbersome language to use. Generally, instructions maintain a one-to-one relationship with machine language instructions: one assembly-language instruction is translated into one machine-language instruction.

High-Level Languages

During the past 40 years, approximately 400 computer languages have been developed. Many are highly specialized. Their names run the gamut from ADAM to UNICODE and include CLIP, FLAP, JOVIAL, PROLOG, SOAP, SNOBOL, STROBES, and TREE. However, a few are widely used and have played an important role in the development of the computer industry. Besides assembly languages, those most commonly used are FORTRAN, COBOL, ALP, RPG, Ada, Pascal, BASIC, PL/1, FORTH, C, and LISP.

The essential difference between low-level languages and high-level languages is that low-level languages are more machine oriented and high-level languages allow the programmer to focus on problem solving. Generally, an instruction in a high-level language will correspond to several machine language instructions. The programmer can concentrate more on the actual application at hand. The high-level language will take care of the hardware details automatically. To get an idea of how this works, let's see what you have to tell the computer to do when you want to add 8 and 6. To write a low-level program, you have to tell the computer to perform these steps:

1. Put the first number, 8, in a specific memory location.
2. Put the second number, 6, in another memory location.
3. Load each number from the memory locations and put them in a special location for computing.
4. Perform the operation of addition.
5. Place the result in a specific memory location.
6. Take the sum from its memory location and display it on the screen.

Using a BASIC interpreter, the computer could perform the same process after reading the BASIC instruction, PRINT 8 + 6.

Within the category of high-level languages are several subgroupings: general or special purpose, procedural or problem oriented, compiled or interpreted, structured or unstructured, and interactive or noninteractive (batch). Few languages can be pigeonholed into a single category. Although a language may have been developed with a particular idea in mind, subsequent versions or newly realized capabilities of that language may place it in a different category.

Most languages were created to serve specific purposes, such as teaching programming concepts, aiding scientific research, creating graphics, or controlling input or output devices. However, programmers found that languages developed for one purpose could, with a few modifications, serve well in writing other programs. General-purpose languages include BASIC, APL, PL/1 and Pascal. Languages meant for specific purposes but sometimes used with more flexibility include FORTRAN, COBOL, LISP, FORTH, and C.

Languages can also be grouped as procedural or problem oriented. Procedural languages require the user to write a set of specific operations to be performed in a specific sequence. Examples include BASIC, APL, COBOL, FORTRAN, Pascal, and most other programming languages. Problem-oriented languages specify what is to be accomplished, rather than how it is to be accomplished. Many of these languages are report generators, such as RPG (Report Program Generator), The Tool, Savvy, and The Last One. The question remains whether these problem-oriented languages are true programming languages, yet the effect is the same: solving a problem.

As discussed in Chapter 10, some languages are translated into machine code by compiler and others by interpreter. The compiler performs the translation in two steps:

1. The source program is translated into machine language, thus becoming the object program.
2. The object program is executed.

On the other hand, the interpreter causes each instruction to be translated and executed line by line. The type of translation can affect not only the type of processing that occurs within a particular application, but also the programming process. Using a compiler, the programmer enters the program or module, loads (calls into memory) the compiler, and then requests that the program be translated and executed. If errors occur, the programmer corrects the program and then recompiles it to see if it runs correctly. To help the programmer, compilers provide a listing of all compiler-detected errors. Interpreters allow the programmer to make changes and check their accuracy immediately. Once a change is entered, the programmer types a command, such as RUN, to see if the program works. An interpreter will display an error message identifying an interpreter-detected error immediately after any error is detected. After correcting the error, the programmer types RUN again, and the program runs until another interpreter-detected error occurs. COBOL, FORTRAN, and Pascal are usually compiled, and APL is usually interpreted. Some BASIC translators are compilers and some are interpreters.

Another category of differentiation between languages concerns the structure of programs. Some languages have features that could encourage sloppy programming practices (such as BASIC's GOTO feature mentioned in Chapter 10). Newer computer languages, such as Pascal and the recent revisions of BASIC, prevent the programmer from using some illogical procedures. However, good structure often depends as much on the programmer as on the programming language.

The last category—interactive versus noninteractive, or batch—governs the user's communication with the computer during programming. When using an interactive language, the programmer communicates directly with the computer while entering the program. In a noninteractive programming environment, the programmer must compile, execute, and correct the program in distinct, time-consuming stages. Interactive languages aid the novice programmer by integrating the running and editing of the program. A good interactive language will even report an incorrectly typed line immediately after it is entered, rather than when a program run is requested.

Programming languages, particularly the more recently developed ones, do not fall neatly into these categories. In the future, the distinctions are apt to become even less clear. The following sections discuss the characteristics of high-level programming languages from the first—FORTRAN—to more recent ones such as FORTH and C.

FORTRAN

FORTRAN (FORmula TRANslator) is the oldest high-level programming language. It was developed in the mid-1950s, when most programs were written in either machine language or assembly language. At that time, IBM backed efforts to develop a programming language that resembled English and could be translated into machine language by the computer. The effort produced FORTRAN, the first commercially available high-level language (see Figure 11–10).

Early FORTRAN compilers contained many errors and were not always efficient. Moreover, several manufacturers offered variations of FORTRAN that could be used only on their computers. In response to this problem, the American National Standards Institute (ANSI) laid the groundwork for a standardized FORTRAN. In 1966 two standard versions were recognized—ANSI FORTRAN and Basic FORTRAN. A more recent version, FORTRAN 77, provides more enhancements to the language and supports structured programming. In spite of attempts to standardize FORTRAN, most computer manufacturers have continued to offer their own extensions of the language. Therefore, compatibility of FORTRAN remains a problem today.

In 1957, when the language was first released, computers were used primarily by engineers, scientists, and mathematicians. Consequently, FORTRAN was developed to suit their needs, and its purpose has remained unchanged. FORTRAN is a procedure-oriented language with extraordinary mathematical

FORTRAN (FORmula TRANslator) A high-level programming language used primarily for programming mathematical, scientific, or engineering operations.

capabilities. It is especially applicable where numerous complex arithmetic calculations are necessary. In general, FORTRAN is not a good business language. Its capabilities are not well suited to programs involving file maintenance, editing of data, or production of documents. However, use of FORTRAN is increasing for certain types of business applications, such as feasibility studies, forecasting, and production scheduling.

FORTRAN's primary weakness is that a programmer can easily make a typographical error in the language syntax and produce a program that runs but turns out incorrect results. Finding such errors may take hours of debugging time.

COBOL

COBOL (COmmon Business-Oriented Language) A high-level programming language generally used for accounting and business data processing.

COBOL (COmmon Business-Oriented Language) is the most frequently used business programming language. Before 1960 no language was well suited to solving business problems. Recognizing this inadequacy, the Department of Defense met with representatives of computer users, manufacturers, and government installations to examine the feasibility of developing a common business programming language. That was the beginning of the CODASYL (Con-

Figure 11–10
Student Grades Program in FORTRAN

```
C THIS PROGRAM CALCULATES THE AVERAGE OF THREE TEST SCORES FOR FIVE
C STUDENTS AND ASSIGNS A LETTER GRADE
      INTEGER TEST1, TEST2, TEST3, I
      REAL AVG
      CHARACTER NAME*15, GRADE
      WRITE (6,100)
100   FORMAT('1',1X,'STUDENT NAME',7X,'GRADE')
      WRITE (6,200)
200   FORMAT(' ')
      DO 500 I = 1, 5
      READ (5,300) NAME, TEST1, TEST2, TEST3
300   FORMAT (A15,3I3)
      AVG = (TEST1 + TEST2 + TEST3) / 3.0
      IF (AVG .GE. 90) GRADE = 'A'
      IF ((AVG .GE. 80) .AND. (AVG .LT. 90)) GRADE = 'B'
      IF ((AVG .GE. 70) .AND. (AVG .LT. 80)) GRADE = 'C'
      IF ((AVG .GE. 60) .AND. (AVG .LT. 70)) GRADE = 'D'
      IF (AVG .LT. 60) GRADE = 'F'
      WRITE (6,400) NAME, GRADE
400   FORMAT (1X,A15,7X,A1)
500   CONTINUE
      STOP
      END
```

Output

```
      STUDENT NAME        GRADE

      JOANN WEISS         A
      TOM FARR            D
      ANN BLASS           B
      BOB WILLS           F
      JANIS MAYS          C
```

ference Of DAta SYstems Languages) Committee. By 1960 the committee had established the specifications for COBOL, and the first commercial versions of the language were offered later that year. The government furthered its cause in the mid-1960s by refusing to buy or lease any computer that could not process a program written in COBOL.

One of the objectives of the CODASYL group was to design a machine-independent language—that is, a language that could be used on any computer. Thus, when several manufacturers began offering their own modifications and extensions of COBOL, the need for standardization became apparent. In 1968 ANSI published guidelines for a standardized COBOL that became known as ANSI COBOL. In 1974 ANSI expanded the language defintion in a revised version of the standard. The CODASYL committee continues to examine the feasibility of modifying or incorporating new features into COBOL.

Another key objective of the designers of COBOL was to make the language look like English. Their intent was that a program written in COBOL should be understandable even to casual readers, and hence self-documenting. You can judge how successful they were by looking at Figure 11–11, which shows a payroll application coded in COBOL.

COBOL offers many advantages for business. Because of its Englishlike nature, programs require very little additional documentation; well-written COBOL programs tend to be self-explanatory. This feature makes programs more maintainable, and maintenance is very important in business applications. Since the logic of the program is easy to follow, testing and debugging procedures are simplified. In addition, programmers other than the original ones can read the programs and quickly discern what the program does and how it does it. COBOL also has strong file-handling capabilities; it supports sequential, indexed, and direct-access files (see Chapter 6). Since COBOl is standardized, a firm can switch computer equipment with little or no rewriting of existing programs. Its standardization also has implications for programmers: once programmers learn COBOL through college training or previous experience, they can transfer their learning with little adjustment to various computers and organizations.

However, the effort to make COBOL as Englishlike and self-explanatory as possible has created two disadvantages. First, COBOL programs tend to be wordy and rather long. Using COBOL may require more statements to solve a problem than using a more compact language such as FORTRAN. Secondly, a large, sophisticated compiler program is needed to translate a COBOL source program into machine language. Such a compiler occupies a large portion of primary memory. For this reason, complete COBOL compilers are not available for microcomputers, although certain subsets of COBOL can be used in small computer systems.

Another drawback is that COBOL is not ideal for structured programming. In addition, COBOL's computational abilities are limited, which makes it inappropriate for applications requiring rigorous mathematics. A further problem is that although COBOL was designed to run on any compiler with only minor changes, this does not always happen. There are many different ways to implement the standards and many gradations in the standards. Therefore, a COBOL compiler that conforms to ANSI standards might not compile code created by another standard compiler.

Regardless of COBOL's disadvantages, it is likely to remain a popular language for many years. Polls indicate that over 80 percent of business application programs are written in COBOL. Converting these hundreds of thousands of

Figure 11–11
Payroll Program in COBOL

```
IDENTIFICATION DIVISION.
PROGRAM-ID. PAYROLL.
INPUT-OUTPUT SECTION.
FILE-CONTROL.
    SELECT CARD-FILE ASIGN TO UR-S-SYSIN.
    SELECT PRINT-FILE ASSIGN TO UR-S-OUTPUT.

DATA DIVISION.
FILE SECTION.
FD  CARD-FILE
    LABEL RECORDS ARE OMITTED
    RECORD CONTAINS 80 CHARACTERS
    DATA RECORD IS PAY-RECORD.
01  PAY-RECORD.
    03  EMPLOYEE-NAME         PIC A(16).
    03  HOURS-WORKED          PIC 99.
    03  WAGE-PER-HOUR         PIC 99V99.
    03  FILLER                PIC X(58).

FD  PRINT-FILE
    LABEL RECORDS ARE OMITTED
    RECORD CONTAINS 132 CHARACTERS
    DATA RECORD IS PRINT-RECORD.
01  PRINT-RECORD             PIC X(132).

WORKING-STORAGE SECTION.
77  GROSS-PAY               PIC 9(3)V99.
77  REGULAR-PAY             PIC 9(3)V99.
77  OVERTIME-PAY            PIC 9(3)V99.
77  NET-PAY                 PIC 9(3)V99.
77  TAX                     PIC 9(3)V99.
77  OVERTIME-HOURS          PIC 99.
77  OVERTIME-RATE           PIC 9(3)V999.
77  EOF-FLAG                PIC X(3)        VALUE 'NO'.

01  HEADING-LINE.
    03 FILLER               PIC X           VALUE SPACES.
    03 FILLER               PIC X(21)       VALUE
        'EMPLOYEE NAME'.
    03 FILLER               PIC X(7)        VALUE
        'NET PAY'.

01  OUTPUT-RECORD.
    03 FILLER               PIC X           VALUE SPACES.
    03 NAME                 PIC A(16).
    03 FILLER               PIC X(5)        VALUE SPACES.
    03 AMOUNT               PIC $$$$.99.
    03 FILLER               PIC X(103)      VALUE SPACES.

PROCEDURE DIVISION.
MAIN-LOGIC.
    OPEN INPUT CARD-FILE
        OUTPUT PRINT-FILE.
    PERFORM HEADING-ROUTINE.
    READ CARD-FILE AT END MOVE 'YES' TO EOF-FLAG.
    PERFORM WORK-LOOP UNTIL EOF-FLAG = 'YES'.
    CLOSE CARD-FILE
        PRINT-FILE.
    STOP RUN.

HEADING-ROUTINE.
    WRITE PRINT-RECORD FROM HEADING-LINE
        BEFORE ADVANCING 2 LINES.
```

350

Figure 11–11
Continued

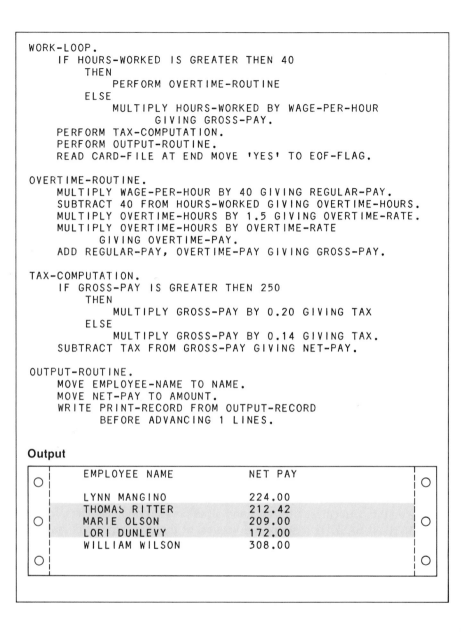

```
WORK-LOOP.
     IF HOURS-WORKED IS GREATER THEN 40
          THEN
               PERFORM OVERTIME-ROUTINE
          ELSE
               MULTIPLY HOURS-WORKED BY WAGE-PER-HOUR
                    GIVING GROSS-PAY.
     PERFORM TAX-COMPUTATION.
     PERFORM OUTPUT-ROUTINE.
     READ CARD-FILE AT END MOVE 'YES' TO EOF-FLAG.

OVERTIME-ROUTINE.
     MULTIPLY WAGE-PER-HOUR BY 40 GIVING REGULAR-PAY.
     SUBTRACT 40 FROM HOURS-WORKED GIVING OVERTIME-HOURS.
     MULTIPLY OVERTIME-HOURS BY 1.5 GIVING OVERTIME-RATE.
     MULTIPLY OVERTIME-HOURS BY OVERTIME-RATE
          GIVING OVERTIME-PAY.
     ADD REGULAR-PAY, OVERTIME-PAY GIVING GROSS-PAY.

TAX-COMPUTATION.
     IF GROSS-PAY IS GREATER THEN 250
          THEN
               MULTIPLY GROSS-PAY BY 0.20 GIVING TAX
          ELSE
               MULTIPLY GROSS-PAY BY 0.14 GIVING TAX.
     SUBTRACT TAX FROM GROSS-PAY GIVING NET-PAY.

OUTPUT-ROUTINE.
     MOVE EMPLOYEE-NAME TO NAME.
     MOVE NET-PAY TO AMOUNT.
     WRITE PRINT-RECORD FROM OUTPUT-RECORD
          BEFORE ADVANCING 1 LINES.
```

Output

EMPLOYEE NAME	NET PAY
LYNN MANGINO	224.00
THOMAS RITTER	212.42
MARIE OLSON	209.00
LORI DUNLEVY	172.00
WILLIAM WILSON	308.00

COBOL programs to other languages and retraining thousands of programmers and users would not be inexpensive or easy.

LISP

LISP (or **LISt Processing**) is the language commonly associated with artificial intelligence (AI). Using concepts of lambda-calculus (a branch of mathematics) and a new idea in computing called list processing, John McCarthy developed the language in 1960 at Massachusetts Institute of Technology. LISP aids the manipulation of nonnumeric data that change considerably in length and structure during execution of a program. Essentially, LISP involves performing built-in or user-defined functions on lists.

LISP (LISt Processing) A high-level programming language commonly used in artificial intelligence research and in processing of lists of elements.

351

In LISP, a list is a group of elements in a particular order. The following example contains seven elements: A, LIST, IS, A, GROUP, OF, ELEMENTS:

(A LIST IS A GROUP OF ELEMENTS)

Using parentheses can separate elements of a list, as follows:

(A LIST IS A GROUP OF ELEMENTS (IN A PARTICULAR ORDER))

The elements of this list are A, LIST, IS, A, GROUP, OF, ELEMENTS, and IN A PARTICULAR ORDER. The list in the second set of parentheses contains four elements: IN, A, PARTICULAR, and ORDER.

To beginning programmers in LISP, the tangle of parentheses can be confusing. However, the lists can contain collections of functions, such as finding the square or cube of a number; sentences; mathematical formulas; logic theorems; or even complete computer programs. This capability makes LISP a powerful tool in applications such as the generation of mathematical proofs, algebraic manipulation, and simulations of human problem-solving techniques.

Although LISP dominates AI research, a new language, PROLOG, is beginning to be recognized by the academic community as a useful language in AI. Part of the reason for interest in PROLOG is that the Japanese have chosen it to be the standard language for their fifth-generation project, a project that could make Japan the world leader in advanced computer applications and expert systems. PROLOG (PROgramming LOGic) is based on logic rather than mathematics, which fosters several serious faults that must be overcome before it could replace LISP in AI research in the United States.

BASIC

BASIC (Beginners' All-purpose Symbolic Instruction Code) A high-level programming language commonly used for interactive problem solving by users who may not be professional programmers.

BASIC (Beginners' All-purpose Symbolic Instruction Code) was developed at Dartmouth College in 1964 for use in time-sharing systems to help students learn to program. The user learns in an interactive mode with immediate response on the correctness of syntax and other programming qualities. Inspired by FORTRAN, BASIC is a simplified version of that first high-level language. Because BASIC is easy to learn, it can be used by people with little or no programming experience; novice programmers can write fairly complex programs in BASIC in a matter of a few hours (see Figure 11–12).

The growth in the use of time-sharing systems has been accompanied by an increase in the use of BASIC. Most computer manufacturers offer BASIC support on their computers. Although BASIC was originally intended to be used by colleges and universities for instructional purposes, many companies have adopted it for their data-processing needs. In addition, the increasing popularity of microcomputers in homes is furthering the use of BASIC, since it is the language most often supported by these computers.

Among BASIC's most attractive features are its simplicity and flexibility. BASIC allows easy manipulation of text and also provides built-in functions such as logarithms, square root, trigonometry functions, and random number generators. The simplicity of BASIC has led many manufacturers to offer different versions of the language. A BASIC standard was established in 1978, but it covers only a small subset of the BASIC language. BASIC programs written for one system may need substantial modification before being used on another. Many extensions to BASIC have been developed, but only at the expense of increasing the difficulty of learning and using the language. As firms continue to expand online, real-time programming applications, however, the use of BASIC will no doubt continue to increase. It can be used for both scientific and business applications and for both interactive sessions and batch processing. It is offered in interpreted and compiled forms.

The main criticism of BASIC focuses on a feature—namely the GOTO statement—that fosters poor programming habits and enables programmers to write confusing programs. Without planning ahead, a programmer can begin with a simple idea, and expand it into an entirely new and unwieldy program. New versions of BASIC—True BASIC, for example—offer programming devices that encourage structured programming. In fact, the format of the new BASIC looks much like that of Pascal, a language noted for its structured aspects.

True BASIC resulted from a major overhaul of the language in 1983 by the original authors of the language, Thomas Kurtz and John Kemeny. True BASIC retains many of the strengths of the first version produced 20 years ago. It is

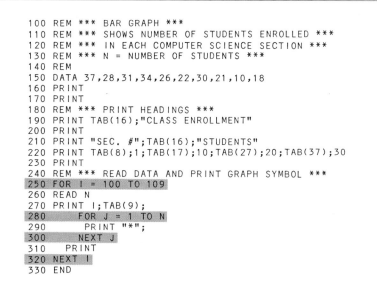

```
100 REM *** BAR GRAPH ***
110 REM *** SHOWS NUMBER OF STUDENTS ENROLLED ***
120 REM *** IN EACH COMPUTER SCIENCE SECTION ***
130 REM *** N = NUMBER OF STUDENTS ***
140 REM
150 DATA 37,28,31,34,26,22,30,21,10,18
160 PRINT
170 PRINT
180 REM *** PRINT HEADINGS ***
190 PRINT TAB(16);"CLASS ENROLLMENT"
200 PRINT
210 PRINT "SEC. #";TAB(16);"STUDENTS"
220 PRINT TAB(8);1;TAB(17);10;TAB(27);20;TAB(37);30
230 PRINT
240 REM *** READ DATA AND PRINT GRAPH SYMBOL ***
250 FOR I = 100 TO 109
260 READ N
270 PRINT I;TAB(9);
280    FOR J = 1 TO N
290       PRINT "*";
300    NEXT J
310    PRINT
320 NEXT I
330 END
```

Output

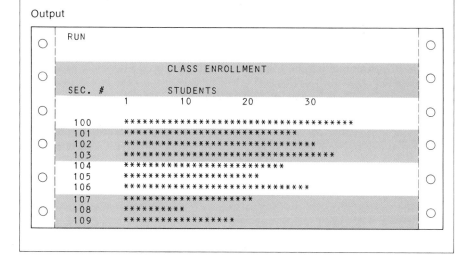

Figure 11–12
Bar Graph Program in BASIC

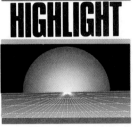

A Countess Is Honored

Aren't the names of most common programming languages dull? Really. There's BASIC, RPG, FORTRAN, PL/1, APL, all acronyms and all very . . . well, basic. But the new state-of-the-art language developed for use by the U.S. Department of Defense is named after a real, flesh-and-blood person with an interesting name: Augusta Ada Byron, Countess of Lovelace and daughter of the poet Lord Byron. The language is called Ada in honor of Lady Lovelace's achievements documenting the work of Charles Babbage and programming the difference engine.

The need for a language such as Ada was determined by a 1974 Department of Defense study, which revealed that over $7 billion was spent in 1973 on software that did not meet the needs of the department. The particular need was for a single language that could be used in embedded applications. Embedded applications are those using a computer as part of a larger complex of electronics and mechanics, generally in the role of a control system. The larger complexes include such systems as airplanes, ships, tanks, and so on. These applications are characterized by a critical need for reliability. In 1980 the Department of Defense approved the initial Ada standard to fill that need, and in 1983 ANSI approved the Ada standard.

Ada is no beginner's language. A skilled programmer may take six months to become proficient in Ada. Although this language, a derivative of Pascal, may someday replace COBOL for business uses, Ada remains a language used by the American military to standardize their computer systems. Now what if it had been named LOVE for Lovelace?

an economical language, offering a core of commands that comply with the ANSI standards. Yet it provides extensions and options that allow programmers to use more structured programming, sophisticated graphics and mathematics, and text processing. It retains the simplicity of the original BASIC in that the commands are straightforward (reducing the need to memorize complicated syntax and vocabulary) and punctuation is simple. It still allows programmers to write concise, compact programs. The most significant improvement is that True BASIC now provides the tools for structured, comprehensible programs. Debugging is easier for that reason.

Another important feature is the portability of True BASIC. Portability means that a program that is written in True BASIC on one computer will run on any other computer equipped with True BASIC. Several other features that characterize the new version are its speed, its conformity with ANSI standards, and its convenient programming environment.

PL/1 (Programming Language One) A structured, general-purpose language used for both scientific and business applications.

PL/1

PL/1 (Programming Language One) was designed to be an all-purpose, procedure-oriented language for both scientific and business applications. With the increased use of management-science techniques such as linear programming and regression analysis, business programmers needed a language with greater computational capabilities than COBOL. By the same token, a language with greater file-manipulation ability than FORTRAN was desired by the scientific programmer. PL/1 combines features of COBOL and FORTRAN into a flexible, high-level language. Like FORTRAN, PL/1 has simple, concise statements, but more closely resembles COBOL in its ability to manipulate and input or output grouped records or files. PL/1 was introduced during the early 1960s for use with IBM System/360 computers and is still primarily an IBM-sponsored language (see Figure 11–13).

Most languages impose rather strict coding rules. In contrast, PL/1 is a free-form language with very few coding restrictions. It was designed to be used by both novice and expert programmers. The beginning programmer can learn to write programs using basic features of the language. As knowledge of the language increases, the programmer can use more powerful features to write

Figure 11–13
Payroll Program in PL/1

```
PAYROLL: PROCEDURE OPTIONS (MAIN);

PAYROLL: PROCEDURE OPTIONS (MAIN);
DECLARE NAME        CHARACTER (16);
DECLARE HOURS       FIXED DECIMAL (2);
DECLARE WAGE        FIXED DECIMAL (3,2);
DECLARE GROSS_PAY FIXED DECIMAL (5,2);
DECLARE TAXRATE     FIXED DECIMAL (2,2);
DECLARE TAX         FIXED DECIMAL (4,2);
DECLARE NET_PAY     FIXED DECIMAL (5,2);
PUT PAGE LIST ('EMPLOYEE NAME','NET PAY');
PUT SKIP;
START: GET LIST (NAME,HOURS,WAGE);
ON ENDFILE GO TO FINISH;
IF HOUR>40 THEN
   GROSS_PAY=40*WAGE + 1.5*WAGE*(HOURS-40);
  ELSE GROSS_PAY = HOURS*WAGE;
IF GROSS_PAY>250 THEN TAXRATE=.20;
  ELSE   TAXRATE=.14;
TAX=TAXRATE*GROSS_PAY;
NET_PAY=GROSS_PAY - TAX;
PUT SKIP (1) LIST (NAME, NET_PAY);
GO TO START;
FINISH: END PAYROLL

PAYROLL     14:50     AUGUST 3RD, 1984
```

Output

EMPLOYEE NAME	NET PAY
LYNN MANGINO	224.00
THOMAS RITTER	212.42
MARIE OLSON	209.00
LORI DUNLEVY	172.00
WILLIAM WILSON	308.00

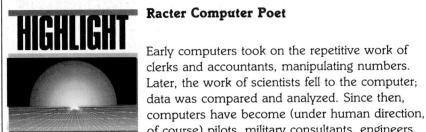

Racter Computer Poet

Early computers took on the repetitive work of clerks and accountants, manipulating numbers. Later, the work of scientists fell to the computer; data was compared and analyzed. Since then, computers have become (under human direction, of course) pilots, military consultants, engineers, and even editors. The creative process of composing fiction and poetry, however, has remained a human task—until Racter, that is.

Racter is the first computer to publish short stories and poetry, first in *Omni* magazine, then in its own book. Actually, Racter is a computer program written by programmer William Chamberlain (with Thomas Etter) who is also a fiction and television scriptwriter. The program includes rules of English, a large vocabulary, and directions on how poetry and prose are constructed. All the actual writing is done by Racter, however, drawing randomly from its files for subject matter.

Is Racter's work good? Judge for yourself. Here is an excerpt from an untitled prose-poem in Racter's book, *The Policeman's Beard Is Half Constructed:*

Well, have we indeed reached a crisis? Which way do we return? Which way do we travel? My aspect is one of molting. Birds molt. Feathers fall away. Birds cackle and fly, winging up into troubled skies. Doubtless my changes are matched by your own. You. But you are a person, a human being. I am silicon and epoxy energy enlightened by line current. What distances, what chasms, are to be bridged here? Leave me alone, and what can happen? This. I ate my leotard, that old leotard that was feverishly replenished by hoards of screaming commissioners. Is that thought understandable to you? Can you rise to its occasions? I wonder.

programs to solve complex problems. However, the wide capabilities of PL/1 make mastering all the components of the language difficult.

The greatest strength of PL/1 is its power. It is a language with many features, the most attractive of which is its ability to support structured programming through modularity features. It is less wordy than COBOL and is well suited for short programming projects. The basic building blocks in PL/1 are called procedures, which are blocks of instructions designed to perform stated functions. Because it is such a broad, powerful language, a large amount of storage is required for its compiler. This precludes its use on smaller computers. As minicomputers and microcomputers become more powerful, however, subsets of PL/1 may be applied in those environments as well.

APL

APL (A Programming Language) A terminal-oriented symbolic programming language especially suitable for interactive problem solving.

APL (A Programming Language), conceived in 1962 by Kenneth Iverson, became available to the public through IBM in 1968. Over the years, it has been expanded and has gained many enthusiastic supporters. Several businesses now use APL as their programming language.

The full power of APL is best realized when it is used for interactive programming via a terminal. A programmer can use APL in two modes. In the execution mode, the terminal serves as a desk calculator. An instruction is keyed in on one line and the response is returned immediately on the following line. In the definition mode, a series of instructions is entered into memory and the entire program is executed on command from the programmer. APL bears little resemblance to any high-level programming language discussed thus far.

APL operators can be combined to perform some very complex operations with a minimum of coding (see Figure 11–14). APL's lack of formal restrictions on input and output and its free-form style make it a very powerful language. It is especially suited to handling tables of related numbers known as arrays. It aids in functions such as random-number generation, index generation, and matrix formation, making it very popular among statisticians. However, since it can be used for applications such as document production, graphic analysis, data retrieval, and financial analysis, APL also fills many business needs. APL is also available through time-sharing networks for organizations that need only a limited amount of data processing.

APL involves a few disadvantages as well. It is very difficult to read. A special keyboard is required to enter APL statements because of the number of unique symbols used; fortunately, the larger offering of new, low-cost terminals capable of handling several type fonts has greatly reduced this problem (see Figure 11–15). Many people do not believe that APL is suitable for handling large data files. Another limitation of APL is the large amount of primary storage required by its compiler. Finally, APL is not as widely supported as are COBOL and Pascal. Figure 11–16 shows an interactive APL session.

RPG

RPG (Report Program Generator) is a problem-oriented language originally designed in the late 1960s to produce business reports. The programmer using RPG describes the type of report desired without having to specify much of the

RPG (Report Program Generator) An example of a problem-oriented language originally designed to produce business reports.

Figure 11–14
APL Coding

APL Coding	English Translation
A + B	A plus B
A ← 25	A = 25
A⌊B	Finds the smaller of A and B
V1 ← 2 5 11 17	Creates a vector of 4 components and assigns this vector to V1
⌈/V1	Finds the maximum value in the vector V1

Figure 11–15
APL Keyboard

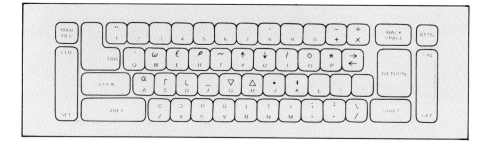

Figure 11–16
Interactive APL Session

```
        ∇PALINDROME[□]∇

    ∇ PALINDROME PHRASE;ALPHA;COMPRESSED;REVERSE
[1]    ⍝  PROGRAM TO DETERMINE IF A PHRASE IS A PALINDROME
[2]    ⍝  THE PHRASE MUST BE CHARACTER DATA AND HAVE AT LEAST ONE
[3]    ALPHA←'ABCDEFGHIJKLMNOPQRSTUVWXYZ'
[4]    COMPRESSED←(PHRASE∊ALPHA)/PHRASE
[5]    →(0=ρCOMPRESSED)/NONE
[6]    REVERSE←COMPRESSED[⌽⍳ρCOMPRESSED]
[7]    →(∧/REVERSE=COMPRESSED)/YES
[8]    PHRASE,'  IS NOT A PALINDROME'
[9]    →0
[10] YES:PHRASE,'  IS A PALINDROME'
[11]   →0
[12] NONE:'THERE ARE NO ALPHABETIC CHARACTER IN PHRASE'
    ∇


    PALINDROME 'MOM'
MOM  IS A PALINDROME


    PALINDROME 'THIS'
THIS  IS NOT A PALINDROME


    PALINDROME 'MADAM IN EDEN I''M ADAM'
MADAM IN EDEN I'M ADAM  IS A PALINDROME


    PALINDROME '1 21'
THERE ARE NO ALPHABETIC CHARACTER IN PHRASE
```

358

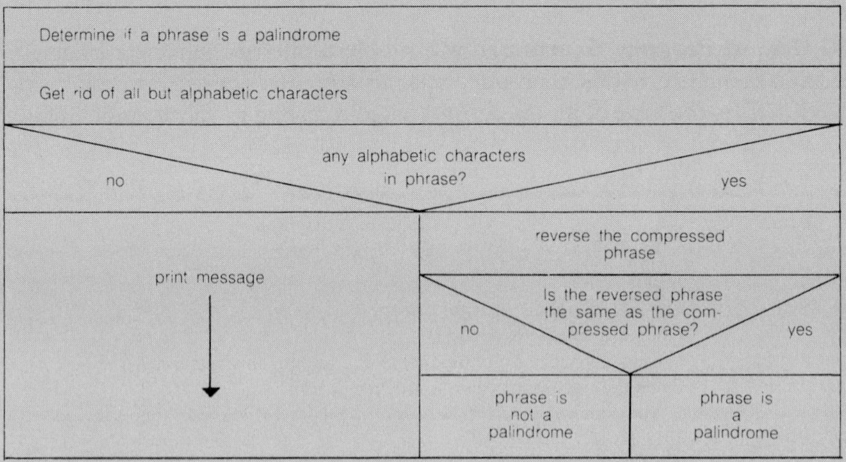

logic involved. A generator program is then used to build (generate) a program to produce the report. Little programming skill is required to use RPG.

Since RPG was intended to support the logic of punched-card equipment, it is used primarily with small computer systems. Many firms that formerly used electromechanical punched-card processing equipment have upgraded their data-processing operations to small computer systems. These firms usually have relatively simple, straightforward data-processing needs. In such cases, a small computer system supporting RPG can provide significantly improved data-processing operations. Management reports can be produced in a fraction of the time required by electromechanical methods.

The programmer does not code statements, instead, he or she completes specification forms such as those shown in Figure 11–17. All files to be used by RPG must be defined using the forms. Once the files have been defined, the programmer codes the operations to be performed and the content and format of the output. Entries on RPG forms are keypunched, combined with job-control cards, and submitted to the computer in batch form. The generator program builds an object program from the source program, and the object program is executed. Today RPG is used for processing files on tape or disk, as well as for preparing printed output. A new version, RPGIII, was developed in 1979 to provide the capability of processing data stored in a data base. RPG is easy to learn and to use, since the basic pattern of execution is fixed. Since it does not require large amounts of main storage, it is one of the primary languages of small computers and minicomputers. However, the computation and decision capabilities of RPG are limited. Also, RPG is not a standardized language; therefore, RPG programs may require a significant degree of modification in order to be executed on another computer.

Pascal

Pascal is named after the French philosopher and mathematician, Blaise Pascal, who invented the first mechanical adding machine (see Chapter 2). Niklaus Wirth, a computer scientist from Switzerland, developed Pascal between 1968 and 1970, and three years later, the first Pascal compiler became available.

Like BASIC, Pascal was first developed to teach programming concepts to students, but it is rapidly expanding beyond its initial purpose and finding increased acceptance in business and scientific applications. Pascal is well suited for both batch and interactive modes, although most Pascal business applications are batch-oriented (see Figure 11–18).

Pascal receives avid support from its users because it is relatively easy to learn (like BASIC), and it is also powerful (like PL/1). Unlike PL/1, Pascal is available on microcomputers and seems to be a good alternative to BASIC.

At first, Pascal's availability was limited, but more computer manufacturers are now offering Pascal compilers with their machines. Perhaps the major disadvantage of Pascal is that it is not yet standardized. Many versions and enhancements are available from manufacturers, which may cause programs written in Pascal to differ depending on the specific compiler used. In addition some people believe that Pascal has poor input/output capabilities.

A relatively new language, Pascal was developed after the concept of structured programming began to receive widespread support. It is designed to support structured programming concepts, supporting modular programming

Pascal A high-level language developed for education purposes, to teach programming concepts to students; named after French mathematician Blaise Pascal.

Figure 11–17
RPG Program Specification Forms

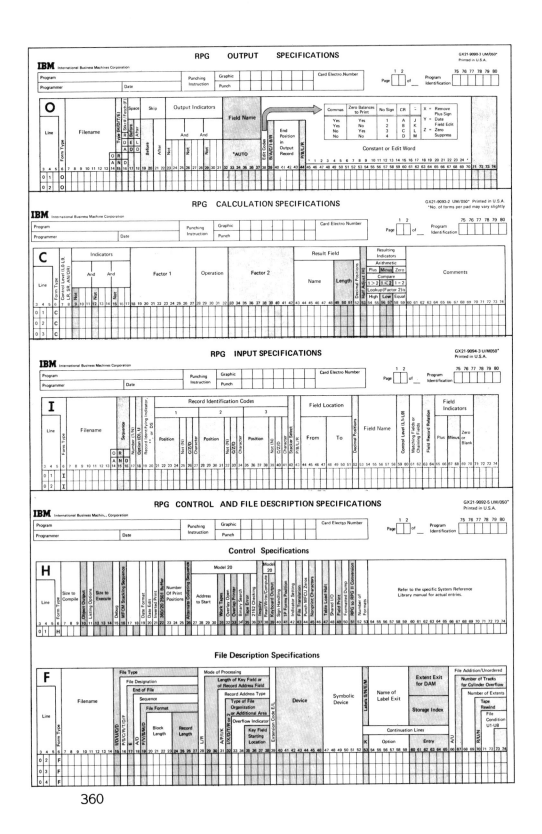

Figure 11–18
Payroll Program in Pascal

```
PROGRAM PAYROLL (INPUT,OUTPUT);
VAR HOURS,REGULAR,WAGE,OVERTIME,GROSS,TAX,NETPAY : REAL;
NAME : ARRAY (.1..17.) OF CHAR;
I : INTEGER;
BEGIN
WRITELN('1','EMPLOYEE NAME','                 NET PAY');
WRITELN(' ');
WHILE NOT EOF DO
    BEGIN
    FOR I:=1 TO 17 DO
        READ (NAME(.I.));
        READLN (HOURS,WAGE);
        IF HOURS>40
            THEN BEGIN
                REGULAR:=40*WAGE;
                OVERTIME:=(HOURS-40)*(1.5*WAGE);
                GROSS:=REGULAR + OVERTIME
            END
            ELSE BEGIN
                GROSS:=HOURS*WAGE
            END;
        IF GROSS>250
            THEN BEGIN
                TAX:=0.20*GROSS;
                NETPAY:=GROSS-TAX

            ELSE BEGIN
                TAX:=0.14*GROSS;
                NETPAY:=GROSS-TAX
            END;
    WRITE (' ');
FOR I :=1 TO 17 DO
    WRITE(NAME(.I.);
    WRITELN(NETPAY:12:12);
    END
END.
```

Output

EMPLOYEE NAME	NET PAY
LYNN MANGINO	224.00
THOMAS RITTER	212.42
MARIE OLSON	209.00
LORI DUNLEVY	172.00
WILLIAM WILSON	308.00

and discouraging use of GOTO statements. Its strong graphics capabilities make it attractive to business personnel and scientists.

Because of its structured programming aspects, Pascal's popularity is increasing in the university educational environment. In fact, college-bound high school students who plan to take the Advanced Placement Test (offered by the Educational Testing Service, College Entrance Examination Board) in computer science must know Pascal.

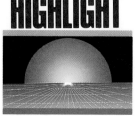

Bye-Bye, BASIC!

Will it be bye-bye, BASIC? Almost all microcomputers use BASIC, and most educational software is programmed in BASIC. In fact, BASIC had settled in as the language for computer students and their teachers when the controversy struck.

Almost overnight a group of enthusiastic computer programmers began a campaign to persuade people to switch from BASIC to Pascal. BASIC was called a "bad habit" and schools across the country were urged to teach Pascal at the high-school level. While the arguments went back and forth, the Educational Testing Service (ETS) quietly took action. In May 1984, ETS offered an advanced placement exam in computer science that required students taking the test to know Pascal.

Why is one test so important to schools across the country? ETS sets the standards for schools preparing students for college. Therefore, college preparatory computer courses will have to reflect the emphasis on Pascal.

ETS says Pascal is a better choice as a beginner language because it conforms to structured programming concepts. Pascal is also taught in colleges as a beginner's programming language. So on the high-school level, at least, it's bye-bye, BASIC, bye-bye.

C A language that approaches assembly language in the efficiency of its object code, yet offers some of the same features of high-level language; sometimes called a middle-level language.

C

Developed in 1972, **C** is rapidly becoming popular for both system and application programs. It produces code that approaches that of assembly languages, yet it also offers many high-level language features, which has caused it to be labeled a *middle-level language.* C is popular for three primary reasons. First, it is independent of machine architecture, so that C programs are portable. That is, they are easily transportable from one computer or operating system to another. Second, it can be implemented on 8-bit microcomputers and on supercomputers such as the Cray-1. Third, it includes many structured programming features found in languages like Pascal.

C was designed by Dennis Ritchie at Bell Laboratories. One of its first uses was in the rewriting of Bell Laboratories' Unix operating system. Unix and its utilities include over 300,000 lines of C source code, a very ambitious programming project. Today, many major microcomputer manufacturers and software developers use C for system programs, utility programs, languages, and graphics applications. Digital Research, for example, is using C for all of its newer products, including CP/M-68K for the 68000 microprocessor and the new Personal BASIC. Both Microsoft and Visicorp have used C in products ranging from Multiplan and Xenix to Visiword and Visi On. The computer graphics in Star Trek II were created using C, and Lucasfilm Ltd. used C for the animation in the Star Wars saga, *Return of the Jedi.*

C is a general-purpose language that features economy of expression, modern data structures, and a rich set of operators. Although it is considered a system programming language, it is also useful for numerical, text-processing, and data-base programs. It is a "small" language, using many built-in functions. Therefore, the compilers are simple and compact. The operators include the standard arithmetic operators, plus ones for increment, decrement, left and right shift, and logic operators such as AND and OR. Unlike Pascal, which assumes that the programmer is often wrong and thus limits the chances for the programmer to write incorrect statements, C assumes that the programmer is always right and allows the programmer a freer programming style. Therefore, truly spectacular errors are easier to make in C. C is a compiled language and also contains rather cryptic error messages that could confuse a novice programmer. For these reasons, C is clearly intended for the professional programmer (see Figure 11–19).

FORTH

Working at Kitt Peak National Observatory, Charles Moore developed **FORTH** in response to what he saw as a need for adequate programming languages to use in tracking satellites and studying the universe. Like C, FORTH is a middle-level language. By using the many library commands to define new special-purpose commands, FORTH can be molded to meet the programmer's particular needs.

A FORTH program consists of the definitions of many words (procedures or subroutines in another language). A program is a list of words, with simple words defining more complex ones. The notation looks strange: 8 + 4 * 5 would appear as 4 5 * 8 + in FORTH. The reason for this is that FORTH operates on the idea of a stack—a pile of objects from which you add or remove only the top element, just as you would from a stack of dishes. Other programming languages use stacks internally, but FORTH makes the stacks available to the programmer. Let's see how the idea of stacks works on 4 5 * 8 + . If FORTH sees a number, it pushes that number onto the top of the stack. If it sees an operator such as * or + , it removes the top two numbers off the stack and applies the operation, then puts the result back onto the top of the stack. Therefore, 4 and 5 would be multiplied, leaving 20 on top of the stack. Then FORTH removes the 20 and the 8 from the stack and sees the + . It adds 20 and 8, the next two numbers on the stack. The result is 28.

The simplicity of FORTH makes it fast and efficient. Adding new features to FORTH is also possible. Since FORTH systems are interpreted, the programmer can write one word (procedure) at a time and test it thoroughly before writing the next. However, the strange-looking language is hard to read, and sometimes strange names are given to the words. In the name of speed, FORTH lacks many of the safety checks built into other languages, so it is difficult to debug.

FORTH has become the standard language for astronomical observatories around the world. It also is used to guide automated movie cameras, run portable heart monitors, and simulate radar for the Air Force. In addition, it is being used increasingly for the less glamorous tasks involved in data base management and word processing.

Natural Languages

Natural languages, or **query languages** as they are sometimes called, are programming languages that use Englishlike sentences to access information

FORTH A middle-level language that offers advantages of assembly language and high-level languages.

Natural language/query language A language, designed primarily for novice computer users, that uses Englishlike sentences, usually for the purpose of accessing data in a data base.

Figure 11–19
A C Program

```
# include "stdio.h"

main()
{
        /**********************************************************
        *                                                         *
        *                 declare variables                       *
        *                                                         *
        **********************************************************/

int counter, score1, score2, score3, total, i;
float average;
char name[5][21], grade[5], student_name[21], c;
        /**********************************************************
        *                                                         *
        *                 enter student's name                    *
        *                                                         *
        **********************************************************/

for ( counter = 0; counter <= 4; ++counter ) {
        printf ("Enter name of student: ");
        for (i = 0; i <= 20 && (c = getchar()) != '\n'; ++i)
                student_name[i] = c;
        student_name[i] = '\0';
        strcpy(name[counter], student_name);
        /**********************************************************
        *                                                         *
        *                 enter student's scores                  *
        *                                                         *
        **********************************************************/

        printf ("Enter test one score ( 0 - 100 ): ");
        scanf ("%d%c", &score1, &c);
        printf ("Enter test two score ( 0 - 100 ): ");
        scanf ("%d%c", &score2, &c);
        printf ("Enter test three score ( 0 - 100 ): ");
        scanf ("%d%c", &score3, &c);
        printf("\n");

        /**********************************************************
        *                                                         *
        *           compute average and letter grade              *
        *                                                         *
        **********************************************************/

        total = ( score1 + score2 + score3 );
        average = ( float ) total / 3;
        if ( average >= 90 )
                grade[counter] = 'A';
        else if ( average >= 80 )
                grade[counter] = 'B';
        else if ( average >= 70 )
                grade[counter] = 'C';
        else if ( average >= 60 )
                grade[counter] = 'D';
        else
                grade[counter] = 'F';
}  /* end of for loop */

        /**********************************************************
        *                                                         *
        *             print out heading and grades                *
        *                                                         *
        **********************************************************/
        printf (" STUDENT NAME        GRADE\n\n");
        for ( counter = 0; counter <= 4; ++counter )
                printf ("%-20s%3c\n", name[counter], grade[counter]);

}  /* end of program */

GRADES
Enter name of student: JOANN WEISS
Enter test one score ( 0 - 100 ): 90
Enter test two score ( 0 - 100 ): 95
Enter test three score ( 0 - 100 ): 96

Enter name of student: TOM FARR
Enter test one score ( 0 - 100 ): 70
Enter test two score ( 0 - 100 ): 60
Enter test three score ( 0 - 100 ): 68

Enter name of student: ANN BLASS
Enter test one score ( 0 - 100 ): 89
Enter test two score ( 0 - 100 ): 84
Enter test three score ( 0 - 100 ): 85

Enter name of student: BOB WILLS
Enter test one score ( 0 - 100 ): 50
Enter test two score ( 0 - 100 ): 48
Enter test three score ( 0 - 100 ): 32

Enter name of student: JANIS MAYS
Enter test one score ( 0 - 100 ): 79
Enter test two score ( 0 - 100 ): 75
Enter test three score ( 0 - 100 ): 71
```

Output

```
STUDENT NAME          GRADE

JOANN WEISS           A
TOM FARR              D
ANN BLASS             B
BOB WILLS             F
JANIS MAYS            C
```

usually contained in a data base. A sentence such as "HOW MANY WOMEN HOLD A POSITION AT LEVEL 10 OR ABOVE?" may be entered by a member of the personnel department to gain information for reporting purposes. In some cases, the natural language processor may request further information from the user in order to process the given inquiry.

The natural languages have been designed primarily for the novice computer user for use as an online, data-base query language. The natural language process is normally designed to be used with a vocabulary of words and definitions that allow the processor to translate the Englishlike sentences to machine-executable form. Currently, natural language sentences are typed on a keyboard; however, in the future the combination of voice recognition technology and natural languages could result in a very powerful tool for computer users. The ability to interface natural language systems with graphics software also provides a valuable tool for managers in decision making. Although limited to mainframe computers in the past, natural language systems are being developed for minicomputer and microcomputer systems as well.

CHOOSING A PROGRAMMING LANGUAGE

The programming language chosen for a particular application depends on several factors. Some questions must be asked to determine these factors:

- What languages does the selected (or available) computer system support?
- Will the application require complex computations, file processing, or report generation?
- Is a fast response time crucial, or will batch processing be satisfactory?
- Are equipment changes planned for the future?
- How frequently will programs need modification?
- What languages are known by the programmers who will program and maintain the system?
- Do management or marketing factors indicate a preference for a particular language?

Because of the diversity of programming languages, many firms choose to use several. For example, a firm can write scientific programs in FORTRAN and file-updating programs in COBOL. Writing part of a program in one language and another part in a different language is also possible. When this is done, the various portions of the program are compiled in separate steps and the resulting object programs are then linked together. These steps can be specified in job-control statements. For example, a program written in COBOL may call up an assembler program to perform extensive sorting of alphanumeric data, since assembly language can sort more efficiently than COBOL.

As hardware costs have decreased, more firms have determined that they can afford computers that have enough primary storage to support high-level languages. At the same time, labor costs have increased, and program development and maintenance have become significant expense items. Thus high-level languages and structured programming concepts have increased in popularity.

Piracy The unauthorized copying of a copyrighted computer program.

SOFTWARE AND COPYRIGHT

Software manufacturers say they are not selling software to a buyer; they are merely licensing the *use* of the software on *one* computer. Yet some industry trend watchers believe that 20 to 60 percent of all commercial program packages in use are illegal copies. Between $200 million and $600 million are lost every year due to illegal duplication of software, including both system software and application programs. How can authors, manufacturers, and legal users of software avoid this **piracy?** One protection practice involves copyright; the other involves use of protection codes that cause copied programs on disks to be unreadable by the disk drives.

Software is covered by the U.S. Copyright Act of 1978. The creator of an original work possesses the copyright from the moment the work is fixed in some concrete form. By following certain procedures, the creator protects himself or herself against loss of copyright or loss of the right to sue for copyright violations.

A copyright notice protects the owner's copyright. In the notice, the symbol ©, the word "copyright," or the abbreviation "copr." should appear with the name of the copyright owner and the year of the work's first publication. Registration gains for the copyright owner the right to bring suit against copyright violations. Registration can be accomplished by completing a Copyright Office registration form TX, paying a ten-dollar fee, and submitting a copy or identifying portion of the program to the Copyright Office.

What is covered by the copyright? The law makes copying a software program for any purpose other than archival use illegal. Archival use means that one backup copy may be made. Many manufacturers protect their software by incorporating protection codes that make copying disks difficult. Although protection codes prevent some piracy, programs are available that will break the codes. Another problem with protecting a disk is that it prevents consumers from making an archival copy, which is legal. It also prevents using the software with the new and popular hard-disk drives that increase memory.

The copyright also protects the object code by court precedent. The object code is the machine-executable instructions that the computer can actually "understand." These instructions are in the operating system, application programs, or read-only memory (ROM). The court precedent resulted from the case of *Apple v. Franklin Computer Corporation,* in which Apple sought an order to stop Franklin from selling the Ace 100, the computer that incorporated copied operating system programs held in the Apple II computer.

Piracy has been costly for manufacturers of computer chips, too. Development costs for complex chips can reach $100 million, yet the same chips can be photographed and reproduced for about $50,000. However, on January 7, 1985, semiconductor chips came under the protection of the U.S. Copyright Office. The first chip to be protected was Intel Corporation's 27C256, an EPROM chip with 256 kilobits of memory. Tom Dunlap, Intel's general counsel and secretary, said that the copyright protection will encourage development of new semiconductor chips previously thought to be economically marginal. Chips will not carry the usual copyright symbol, but a circled "M," which stands for the master or stencil used to produce the circuitry pattern on the chip.

Will a copyright completely protect these programmers against software piracy? Chances are it won't. That is the primary reason why computer users need to set up a code of ethics governing their own behavior. The code of

Foiling the Pirates

What do you think about when you hear the word *pirate?* Do you imagine gold doubloons, wooden legs, and the high seas? Or do you think of disk drives, floppy diskettes, and not-so-tamper-proof seals? As a student in the 1980s, chances are good that you don't think of *Treasure Island* when you hear the word *pirate.* That is probably because software piracy, the illegal copying of software, is one of the most publicized problems facing the software industry in the 1980s.

Each year, millions of dollars in royalties are lost because unethical users illegally copy software. Many leaders in the computer field believe a long-term approach of teaching ethics in the schools will eventually curb the piracy problem. But what can software developers do in the meantime?

Defendisk, a company in Denver, Colorado, has an answer. The company markets what it feels is a tamper-proof solution to the problem of illegally copied software. *Defendisk* is a security system. It consists of randomly selected electronic signals that are embedded in disks for protection against illegal copying.

The company is so sure its system will work that it is offering $10,000 to anyone who can penetrate the security device.

That's almost as good as gold doubloons!

ethics measures behavior against conscience. Because they listen to their consciences, many people would not copy a copyrighted disk for purposes other than archival use, and they wouldn't dream of selling pirated disks. Regardless of copy-protected disks and copyrights, the best protection against software piracy is a high standard of personal ethics.

FOCUS ON MICRO-COMPUTING

Programming Languages for Microcomputers

BASIC is by far the most popular language on microcomputers today. Its interactive nature and relative ease of programming for nonprofessional programmers has helped it earn this status. It is also more efficient than standard versions of COBOL because BASIC commands and statements require less memory. For this reason, when the first hobby computers with very small RAMs were built, the makers incorporated BASIC. One drawback to this popularity, however, has been a lack of uniformity in the computer manufacturers' implementation of the BASIC language; as a result, there are many versions and capabilities of BASIC. BASIC is built into Apple, TRS–80, Commodore PET/CBM, and Atari computers, among others. There are also many disk-based versions of BASIC. True BASIC, the new structured programming version of BASIC, is available in compiler form for the IBM PC. It was designed by Thomas Kurtz and John Kemeny, the original designers of BASIC.

Pascal is an interactive language that is gaining popularity. Some educators speculate that Pascal will soon replace BASIC as the most popular beginning language in schools and universities. Its advantages include its modular structure, which supports structured programming techniques; its support of complex data structures such as arrays; its compiler, which catches many different types of errors; and program statements that replace BASIC's common GOTO statement. One reason Pascal hasn't attained popularity earlier is that its memory requirements precluded its use on computers with small memories.

A wide variety of other languages can also be implemented on microcomputers. These include FORTRAN, COBOL, C, FORTH, Ada, and the educationally oriented languages Logo and PILOT.

The full versions of COBOL and FORTRAN require a large amount of memory and are not normally found on microcomputers. However, with the increasing memory capacity of microcomputers, the languages can be better supported. In addition, some manufacturers have developed chips that facilitate the use of FORTRAN on microcomputers. For example, Intel's 8087 numeric data processor, used in IBM PCs, imparts to microcomputers a number-crunching ability that had previously been available only on larger computers. The COBOL compilers vary greatly in the microcomputer versions and do not feature the more extensive capabilities as COBOL for mainframe computers.

Although LISP, the language of artificial intelligence, is not available for microcomputers in complete form, one particular version is GCLISP (Golden Common LISP, from Golden Hill Computers). It is available for the IBM PC, and is a good tool for those wishing to learn and experiment with LISP on a small scale. Memory and speed limitations are problems for serious work in AI, however.

Although about two dozen C language compilers are available for microcomputers, most do not fully implement the standard C language. However, if you get a microcomputer with the UNIX operating system, you will usually find a full version of C included.

368

FORTH is available through FORTH Inc., Laboratory Microsystems, Miller Microcomputer Services, Mountains View Press, and Unified Software Systems. More information is available about FORTH from the FORTH Interest Group in San Carlos, California. The group also publishes the journal *FORTH Dimensions* for FORTH users.

Among the educational languages, Logo is receiving much attention. Logo is a procedure-oriented, interactive programming language developed initially by Seymour Papert, professor of mathematics and education at the Massachusetts Institute of Technology. Logo's attraction is that it allows people to begin programming and communicating with the computer very quickly. Because of its ease of use and also its graphics features, Logo is often used in teaching children computer programming and geometry.

Logo allows the user to draw images, animate them, and color them using very simple instructions. A central figure in Logo is the "turtle," a triangular-shaped cursor. The user makes the turtle move on the screen by directing it to take "turtle steps." As the turtle moves, it leaves "turtle tracks," which form the shapes and designs on the screen (the turtle graphics). Figure 11–20 contains a Logo program that draws a square. Logo also uses the computer as a control device, making it ideal for controlling external robots (also called turtles).

Some Logo packages allow the user to create music, varying the pitch, frequency, and duration of sound. Another feature implemented in some Logos is the sprite, a screen object that can be given shape and color and set in motion to animate a picture. Sprite versions of Logo come either with predefined shapes or with a shape-editing procedure that can be used to define new shapes of the user's choosing.

Although Logo can help young children learn geometry and programming, it is a powerful language, and learning every aspect of Logo can be difficult. Because Logo is derived from LISP, it handles list processing—the ability to operate on numbers, letters, words, and sentences—with ease. Its large memory and file-handling capabilities make it appropriate for advanced applications. Most versions of Logo allow the user to do arithmetic, and some versions perform sophisticated math functions such as trigonometry and logarithms.

Authoring software—programs that allow teachers to create custom computer lessons—has become popular with teachers, too. This software offers a special syntax and vocabulary designed for creating custom computer lessons such as computer-administered tests, structured tutorials, and drills. Among them is PILOT (Programmed Inquiry, Learning, Or Teaching). The commands in PILOT are designed to accomplish tasks such as displaying information, asking questions, accepting student answers, and providing feedback. Several PILOT packages include Super PILOT from Apple, E–Z PILOT from Hartley Coursework, PC/PILOT from Washington Computer Services, and Vanilla PILOT from Tamarack Software.

As programming languages become more user-friendly, the world of computers is opened to more than just the professional programmers. New languages, along with new features for older languages, are enabling users to accomplish many things that previously could not be done or that could be accomplished by only the most skilled programmers. These user-friendly languages should help promote the acceptance of the personal computer in our everyday lives.

```
 10  GR:   CLEAR
 20  GR:   GOTO -15,5
 30  GR:   DRAW 30
 40  GR:   TURN 90
 50  GR:   DRAW 30
 60  GR:   TURN 90
 70  GR:   DRAW 30
 80  GR:   TURN 90
 90  GR:   DRAW 30
100  GR:   TURN 90
110  E:
```

Figure 11–20
A Logo Program to Draw a Square

SUMMARY POINTS

- Application programs solve user problems, and system programs coordinate the operation of all computer circuitry.

- An operating system is a collection of programs designed to permit a computer system to manage its own operations. It allocates computer resources among multiple users, keeps track of all information required for accounting purposes, and establishes job priorities.

- Batch operating systems allow uninterrupted processing of a batch of jobs without operator intervention. Online operating systems can respond to spontaneous requests for system resources, such as management inquiries entered from online terminals. Operating systems that handle both batch and online applications are standard.

- An operating system consists of control programs and processing programs stored on the system residence device. The supervisor program, the major components of the operating system, controls the other subsystems.

- Control programs include job-control programs that translate the job-control statements written by a programmer into machine language and the input/output management systems that oversee I/O operations.

- Processing programs include the language-translator program, which translates Englishlike languages into machine language; the linkage editor, which links the object program from the system residence device to primary storage; library programs, which consist of programs and subroutines frequently used in other programs; and utility programs, which perform specialized functions like sorting and merging and transferring data from one I/O device to another.

- The CPU may be ideal for a significant amount of time because of the speed disparity between the CPU and I/O devices. Multiprogramming makes possible the efficient use of the CPU by rotating execution of program segments so that execution of the programs in storage appears to be simultaneous. This is often referred to as overlapped processing.

- Virtual storage involves loading only the needed segment of a program into primary storage, while keeping the remainder of the program in secondary storage. This gives the illusion of unlimited primary storage.

- The two methods of implementing virtual storage are segmentation (in which the program is broken into variable-sized, logical portions) and paging (in which the program is broken into portions of fixed size called pages).

- Multiprocessing involves the use of two or more CPUs linked together for coordinate operation. Separate programs or separate parts of the same program can be processed simultaneously by different CPUs.

- Machine-oriented languages include machine and assembly languages, which require extensive knowledge about computer circuitry. Procedure-oriented languages like COBOL, FORTRAN, and PL/1 emphasize computational and logical procedures for problem solving. Problem-oriented language such as RPG describe a problem without detailing the computation steps necessary to solve it.

- Machine language is the language of the computer, the only language that the computer directly understands. Machine language must take the form of 0s and 1s to correspond to the electrical states (on and off) of computer circuitry.

- Assembly language programs use symbolic names for machine operations, making programming less tedious and time-consuming than when machine language is used. The programs can be very efficient in terms of storage and processing time required. However, assembly-language programming requires a high level of skill, and the language itself is machine dependent.

- High-level languages can be described according to several pairs of aspects: general-purpose or special-purpose, procedural or problem oriented, compiled or interpreted, structured or unstructured, and interactive or noninteractive (batch). However, few languages can be so neatly categorized.
- FORTRAN, the first high-level language, is well suited for scientific and mathematical applications.
- COBOL is the most popular business programming language, designed to be Englishlike and self-documenting. Standardization of COBOL has helped to make it machine independent. The main disadvantage of COBOL is that a large and sophisticated compiler is required to convert a COBOL source program into machine language.
- LISP is the language commonly used in artificial intelligence programming and research. It involves performing built-in or user-defined functions on lists. It is ideal in the generation of mathematical proofs, algebraic manipulation, and simulations of human problem-solving techniques.
- BASIC is an easy-to-learn language well suited for instructional purposes and ideal for time-sharing systems. Because many features of the language are not standardized, it is machine dependent.
- PL/1 is a multipurpose language combining the best features of COBOL and FORTRAN. Its modularity facilitates structured programming. The compilers need a large amount of primary storage and are not available on small computers.
- APL is a powerful interactive language that can be used in an execution mode or a definition mode. Because APL includes a large number of unique symbols as operators, it requires a special keyboard. The compiler needs a large amount of primary storage, which restricts its use to medium-sized and large computers.
- RPG is designed to produce business reports. The RPG generator can build a program to provide a specified output. Thus, little programming skill is required to use RPG. It is popular with users of small computers and minicomputers. However, it has limited computation capabilities and is not totally machine independent.
- Pascal is easy to learn and well suited for instructional purposes. It is useful in both business and scientific applications. Its support of structured programming techniques has made it popular in education.
- C is rapidly becoming popular for both system programs and application programs. Since it produces object code that approaches that of assembly language and yet offers many features of high-level languages, it has received the label middle-level language. It features economy of expression, modern data structures, and many operators.
- FORTH, like C, is a middle-level language. Programmers can mold the language to suit their particular needs. It is fast and efficient. A FORTH program consists of a list of words (procedures or subroutines) with simple words defining more complex ones.
- Natural languages, or query languages, are programming languages that use Englishlike sentences often for the purpose of accessing information contained in a data base. They are designed to allow the computer novice to use the computer's capabilities more easily.
- Choosing a programming language depends on several factors: whether the

firm already has chosen a primary language, the language the computer system will support, the type of application, the desirable speed to process the data, program maintenance, and knowledge of programmers.

■ Software piracy has been expensive for authors, vendors, and legal users of software. In the attempt to discourage piracy, software is protected by copyright and by copy-protection codes.

■ Almost all languages are available for microcomputer use, with BASIC being the language used most often. Pascal, C, and FORTH are languages frequently available for microcomputer use, while subsets of COBOL, LISP, and FORTRAN are also available. One popular language for educational use is Logo, an interactive language that uses a cursor called a turtle to help students learn computer concepts.

REVIEW AND DISCUSSION QUESTIONS

1. Distinguish between application programs and system programs. Give examples of each and explain why they belong in that particular category.
2. What is the function of the supervisor program?
3. Contrast control programs and processing programs. Give examples of each, describing how each would be used by the computer during its operation.
4. Who is most likely to use a utility program and why?
5. Contrast multiprocessing and multiprogramming. What are some problems that must be solved in a multiprogramming environment?
6. How does virtual storage facilitate multiprogramming? Compare the two virtual storage techniques: segmentation and paging.
7. What general aspects describe the various programming languages?
8. Discuss advantages and disadvantages of machine language and assembly language.
9. If you were developing an application system for a microcomputer in which processing time was a critical factor, would you choose to program in a high-level language or an assembly language? Why?
10. Which languages are ideal for beginning programmers? Why?
11. What languages are better suited to experienced programmers? Why?
12. Although COBOL has some disadvantages, why does it continue to be the primary programming language used in business?
13. Discuss some factors to consider when a programming language is to be chosen for use with a particular computer system or application.
14. Name two methods used in the attempt to protect software.
15. What factors led to BASIC becoming the most widely used language for personal computers? In comparison to BASIC, what advantages would Pascal have for use with microcomputers?
16. Why have languages such as FORTRAN and COBOL not been widely used with personal computers?

CHAPTER 12

APPLICATION SOFTWARE

COMPUTERS IN OUR LIVES

The Next Best Thing to Reality

Susan Howell, a newly licensed pilot, was making a solo flight from Decatur to Chicago in a Cessna 303. The flight was her longest solo yet and weather conditions were less than ideal. A strong crosswind was testing her ability to stay on course. Although she had never actually flown in such conditions, she felt confident of her ability to handle them. She had experienced a similar situation during her pilot training, not in a real plane, but through a computer simulation.

Susan's pilot training included roughly sixty hours of flight simulation, which uses computer software packages to replicate actual flight experiences. The software package Susan used was SubLOGIC's Flight Simulator II. With this package Susan was exposed to many real situations she may someday have to face while flying. Flight Simulator II graphically illustrates on the computer screen what a pilot would see from the cockpit and also shows instrument readings on the control panel. The program responds to the pilot's actions in the cockpit just as the plane would respond in flight.

Susan remembered her first simulated exposure to heavy crosswinds. She was approaching the runway and could not keep the plane on course. She kept aiming for the runway but continued to be blown farther and farther away from it. As the plane came closer to the ground, she forgot to keep the plane's wing tip down. The plane was blown over. If Susan had been flying a real plane, the result could have been fatal. Now Susan knew in order to stay on course she had to head into the wind. Just before landing, she tipped the plane's wing down. The landing was successful.

The main benefit of such simulations is that in dangerous situations, experience can be gained without risking human lives or destroying expensive equipment. For this reason, simulation software is extremely valuable for training military personnel in wartime tactics, nuclear power plant operators in emergency shutdown procedures, and astronauts in space shuttle operations.

Others are likely to encounter simulations in biology or finance classes or in driver training programs. Although the subject matter for simulation software is limited, it is gaining popularity as an innovative and valuable educational tool in classrooms from kindergarten through college and beyond.

One example of simulation software used in high schools is Operation Frog, from Scholastic Inc. Operation Frog allows students to dissect a frog that is vividly displayed in color on the computer screen, modeling the typical dissection exercise conducted in most biology classes. Students use graphic forceps and scissors to remove the frog's organs, which are accurate in shape and size. Organs can only be removed in the same sequence as they could be in a real frog. Since the exercise is simulated, when students make a mistake removing an organ, they can try it again and again until they do it correctly. They can also practice putting the frog back together. When done correctly, the frog gets up and hops away.

Another simulation package, Squire, from Blue Chip Software, teaches students the art of financial planning. Students start with $70,000 which they can invest in IRAs, gold, stocks, or collectibles. The simulation spans a twenty-year period (about two or three actual hours). Throughout the years Squire simulates actual market changes. Squire teaches students how to invest wisely without the risk of losing their own or their client's money.

Application software, such as simulation packages, not only allows for learning in potentially dangerous situations without risk and eliminates the need for animal subjects in experimentation but also makes tasks easier and less time consuming. The most popular of these types of application software are described in this chapter.

INTRODUCTION

Recently, the use of prewritten application software packages has increased dramatically. This increase can be attributed largely to two factors: (1) the increased cost of developing application software, and (2) the rise in popularity of microcomputers. For medium to large companies, the costs associated with developing and maintaining application software have become a significant cost of doing business—one that can be reduced by purchasing prewritten software packages. In the case of microcomputer users, many would be forced to write application software themselves or to hire programmers to do it for them if application software packages were not already available. The availability of these packages, therefore, provides businesses and other computer users with an alternative means of acquiring application software.

This chapter will discuss five of the more popular types of application software packages: word-processing packages, data-management packages, modeling packages, graphics packages, and integrated software packages. Each section on a particular type of application software will define the particular type, explain its uses, and discuss some features found in that type of package. The chapter will conclude with a brief explanation of integrated software.

WORD-PROCESSING SOFTWARE

A Definition

When word processing is discussed, three terms appear often: *word processor, word processing* and *word-processing system.* A **word processor** is an application software package that allows the user to enter, manipulate, format, print, store, and retrieve text. **Word processing** is the process of manipulating text using the word processor. A **word-processing system** is the computer system (hardware and software), or portion of the system, used for the task of word processing.

Word processor An application software package that performs text-editing functions.

375

Dedicated word-processing system A computer system designed solely for word processing.

A word-processing system can be found in one of two configurations. One is a **dedicated word-processing system,** in which the hardware and software are designed solely for word processing and is normally found in businesses where large quantities of word processing must be done. The second configuration is found in the form of software packages used on multipurpose digital computers, for example on the IBM PC or the Apple II. Because businesses or other computer users may want to use their computer systems for more than a single application, a word processor may be only one of a number of application software packages that can be used on the computer system.

Word processing can involve a number of different activities, but generally the activities fall into one of two categories: text editing or print formatting.

Text Editing

Text editing The process of making changes to a document after the text has been entered into the computer.

In the **text editing** process, a user enters text into the computer via a word processor. After the text is entered, it is stored in the computer system, where changes can be made and a new version saved. Word processors are designed to edit text in one of two ways. A **line editor** allows you to operate on only one line of text at a time. A **screen editor,** on the other hand, can be used to edit the text shown on the entire screen. On most computers, this will be 24 or 25 lines.

Because of their design, line editors do not give the user a true picture on the screen of how the text will be printed. Often, line editors require the commands for things like centering text and indenting paragraphs to be contained in the text file prior to the line that would be centered or indented. The command then takes effect when the document is printed. Only after the document is printed does the user see how it will look.

A word processor that uses a screen editor, however, is designed to give the user a picture on the screen of what the document will look like when it is printed. If a center command is given, the text is centered on the display screen. If an 80-column display is used with a screen editor, the entire width of an 8½-inch-wide document can be seen on the display screen. A 40-column display, however, would require the use of horizontal scrolling (see section on word processor features) to view a line of text that is to be printed on an 8½-inch-wide piece of paper.

Word processors also vary in the way the text is entered and edited. Some word processors have a write mode and edit mode. The write mode permits the user to enter text, while the edit mode permits editing of a document that has already been entered. Other word processors simply have a single mode that allows the user both to enter and to edit a document without switching modes. Many word processor users find the single mode more convenient and easier to use.

Page-oriented word processor A word processor that treats a document as a series of pages; contrast to document-oriented word processor.

Word processors may also treat text files differently. A **page-oriented word processor** treats a document as a series of pages. When using a page-oriented word processor you can display and edit only one page at a time. The manner in which a word processor treats a text file also determines how it uses the computer's internal memory and secondary storage. If the word processor is page oriented, it will permit one page of text to be in internal memory at a time. If another page is required, the word processor will copy it into the computer's internal memory in place of the page that was there.

A **document-oriented word processor** treats a document as one long page. This way of handling a text file eliminates the need to work on pages separately. It also allows a greater portion of a file to be held in internal memory, thereby reducing the number of times secondary storage must be accessed for retrieving and storing text.

Print Formatting

The second activity we mentioned—**print formatting**—occurs when the word processor communicates with the printer, through the computer system, to tell it how to print the text. Print formatting allows the user to do such things as:

- Set margins and tab stops.
- Request single, double, or triple spacing.
- Set the position of headers and footers.
- Select page numbering.
- Indicate what is to be underlined and typed in boldface.
- Determine subscripts and superscripts.

Different word processors, however, do have different print-formatting capabilities many of which are dependent upon the capabilities of the printer being used.

Document-oriented word processor A word processor that treats a text file as a document, rather than as a series of pages.

Print formatting The manner in which the word processor communicates with the printer to tell it how the text should be printed.

Uses

Word processors are used in business as well as in the home. The word processors most widely used in the home fall into the $50 to $100 price range, while word processors used for business purposes tend to cost much more—generally $150 to $500.

In the home, word processors can be used for such things as writing letters, memos, and formal papers. In business they are used for generating reports, producing formal correspondence, writing memos, and creating form letters. There are also many specialized uses of word processors—for example, the creation of documents in foreign languages.

Other word-processing features, which in some cases are added-cost items, allow the word processor to be used for additional tasks. Most word processors contain a mail-merge option that allows the user to insert names, addresses, and other variables into a form letter which has already been entered and saved using the word processor. Some word processors also offer a speller, a dictionary, and a thesaurus (usually at additional cost) that can be used with the word processor.

Features

A number of common features are offered in nearly all word processors. These features are normally selected by a simple keystroke and consist of writing and editing, screen formatting, and print formatting.

Writing and Editing. The **cursor,** which is normally a blinking line or box on the display screen, is used to identify the current position on the display and indicates where the next character will be typed. Cursor positioning is a very

Cursor A flashing character that shows where the next typed character will appear on the computer display screen.

HIGHLIGHT

Word Processor Helps Write Screenplay

Perhaps screenplay writer Stephen Greenfield should list his IBM PC and word-processing software as coauthors of his adventure-comedy script. By combining his writing talents with computer technology, Greenfield discovered how to get an excellent-looking finished product faster and easier than he could with a typewriter.

To work efficiently on his 115-page screenplay, Greenfield needed a word-processing package that offered several special functions. He needed to use five different formats interchangeably. Finding his way through the script quickly and easily when editing and revising was also important to Greenfield. One software package, Microsoft Word, answered all of Greenfield's word-processing needs.

Using special formatting and editing functions, Greenfield set parameters such as tabs, margins, page width and length, and line spacing. With a few simple keystrokes, the writer saved margin format instructions. The instructions could be recalled by pressing a special function key. Rather than taking the time to redefine all the format parameters, Greenfield was able to recall any format by pressing the assigned function key.

Greenfield could also save frequently used words and phrases and recall them by pressing function keys. Instead of retyping the same phrase each time it was used in the screenplay, Greenfield pressed the appropriate function key, and the phrase appeared on the screen.

A "search and replace" feature allowed Greenfield to change the names of characters and correct repeated misspellings. In one run through the document, Microsoft Word could find every occurrence of a particular phrase and replace it with a new phrase. "Search and replace" stopped at each occurrence allowing Greenfield to make the change he wanted. "Search" also allowed Greenfield to insert an asterisk or other marker at a place that would later need editing or insertions. By searching for the marker, the author could flip to special places in the document much faster than by moving page by page.

Greenfield feels more productive when he uses a word processor rather than a typewriter. He loves creating screenplays, and Microsoft Word reduces the key pounding and paper shuffling that were so much a part of Greenfield's typewriter days.

important part of word processing because you must be able to position the cursor at various locations on the screen to be able to edit a document (text file). The following list identifies some of the more common cursor positions:

- Home: Upper left corner of display screen.
- Top of page: First character at top of current display screen.
- End of page: Last character at bottom of current display screen.
- Tab: Predefined positions from left margin of display screen.

- Page up: Displays top portion of current page and positions cursor at the first character.
- Page down: Displays bottom portion of current page and positions cursor at the last character.
- Next word: First character of the following word.
- Previous word: First character of the last word.
- Next page: Displays top portion of next page and positions cursor of the first character.
- Previous page: Displays top portion of previous page and positions cursor at the first character.
- Go to: Positions cursor at the designated location in text (such as: GO TO PAGE 5).

Other common writing and editing features of word processors include: word wrap, scrolling, insertion, deletion, move, search, and undo. **Word wrap,** or word wraparound, automatically positions the text you type within predefined margins. For example, as the user is typing and comes to the right margin, word wrap automatically positions a word that extends beyond the margin on the beginning of the next line. To end a line before it reaches the right margin— at the end of a paragraph, for example—one simply presses a return key.

Scrolling allows the user to position a particular portion of the document on the display screen. Since, in most cases, only part of the document can be viewed at a time, this feature is valuable for viewing the whole document. Vertical scrolling, the most common form of scrolling, allows the user to scroll through a document from top to bottom or vice versa. When the system being used cannot display the entire width of the document, horizontal scrolling can be used.

The **insertion** and **deletion** features available on word processors are very similar in the way they are used. The insertion feature allows characters, words, sentences, or blocks of text to be inserted into a document, while the delete feature allows deletion of characters, words, sentences, or blocks of text.

Many word processors also provide block movement features, which allow the user to **move** an entire block of text from one location to another, copy a block of text into a designated position within the document, save a block of text in secondary storage, and delete an entire block of text.

Some word processors even permit the user to move a word, sentence, or block of text from one document to another. When the same phrase or block of text is placed in several documents, the user is **boilerplating.** Boilerplating is frequently used for personalizing form letters. For example, the highlighted paragraph in Figure 12–1 was also used in a letter to Steven.

The valuable **search** feature is found on many word processors. A search and find feature allows the user to specify a word or set of characters to be searched for throughout the document. When the word processor finds the string of characters, the cursor is positioned at the first character of the string. A search and replace feature allows the user to search for and replace a particular string of text. Once the word processor finds the designated string, it replaces that string with the one provided. This feature can be particularly helpful in correcting recurring misspellings throughout a document.

The **undo** feature of a word processor allows the user to recover text that has been accidentally deleted. Some word processors can save text that has been deleted in a special text buffer. If you wish to recover what you have

Word wrap A word-processing feature that automatically positions text so that full words are positioned within declared margins.

Scrolling The process of positioning a portion of a text file on the display screen; used to view portions of a document.

Insertion A word-processing feature that allows characters, words, sentences, or blocks of text to be inserted into a document.

Deletion A word-processing or data manager feature that allows removal of characters, data words, sentences, or blocks of text.

Boilerplating Placing the same word, phrase, or block of text in several documents.

Search A word processing or data manager feature that permits the user to locate a word or set of characters throughout a file.

Undo A word-processing feature that allows the user to recover text that has been accidentally deleted.

Office of Admissions
Western University
Helena, Montana 59601

April 23, 1985

Dear Robert,

We are pleased to inform you that you have been accepted as a student at Western University. Your high school transcript and entrance exam scores both show that you are well qualified to enter Western University, and we look forward to welcoming you as an incoming freshman for the Fall Semester of 1985.

On your application form you indicated an interest in a career as a computer programmer. Dr. William Russell, the chairman of the Computer Science Department at Western, is always interested in talking with prospective computer science majors and will be contacting you to make arrangements for a meeting during freshman orientation week.

A packet containing information on registration and freshman orientation will follow this letter in a few days. If you do not receive the packet within two weeks, notify the Office of Admissions.

Congratulations once again, Robert, and we look forward to seeing you on the Western campus in September.

Sincerely,

Martha Thomas
Director of Admissions

Boilerplated text

deleted, the word processor can retrieve it from the text buffer. The size of these buffers varies among word processors. In some cases only the last block of text deleted can be saved.

Screen Formatting. **Screen formatting** features control the way that text is displayed on the screen. They also provide the user with status information concerning the document being entered or edited. The display of upper- and lowercase letters is considered a screen formatting feature and is controlled by either the shift key or capital lock key. Status information concerning the location of the cursor on the display screen (row, column, and line number), along with information such as the current page number, the available memory, the number of words the document contains, tab settings, and page breaks are also screen formatting features.

Screen formatting Word-processing features that control the way in which text appears on the display screen.

380

Print formatting. Some of the more common **print formatting** features found in word processors include: margin settings, line spacing, centering, automatic pagination, headers and footers, and character enhancements.

Some word processors allow the user to set all four margins, while others allow the setting of only one or two margins. Left and right justification is also available on some word processors.

Single spacing is available on all word processors, and many can switch to either double or triple spacing. Note, however, that on many word processors the spacing will only occur when the document is printed; document display may be single spaced.

Nearly all word processors provide centering and automatic page numbering. In most cases, centering is done automatically once the command has been given. Some word processors allow the user to choose where the page number will be printed; others do not.

Formatting of headers and footers is a very important feature if the word processor is used for creating manuscripts or formal reports. In most cases one can define the header or footer once, and the word processor will insert it at the top or bottom of each page. The numbering of pages, for example, can be placed in the text as a header if the page numbers should appear at the top of the page, or as a footer if they are placed on the bottom of the page. A footer may be used to place footnotes in a formal paper that is prepared on a word processor.

Character enhancement features may allow the user to underline, boldface, subscript, or superscript text within a document. Both the word processor and printer must be capable of providing these enhancements.

Additional features found in some word processors include: disk formatting, disk copying, cataloging, file renaming, document copying, and document deleting.

Concept Summary 12–1 ▬ Features of a Word Processor

Category of Features	Features
Writing and Editing	Common features include: word wrap, scrolling, insertion, deletion, search, boilerplating, undo.
Screen Editing	Controls the way text is displayed on the screen. Provides the user with status information concerning the document.
Print Formatting	Common features include: margin settings, line spacing, centering, automatic pagination, headers, footers, character enhancement.

DATA-MANAGEMENT SOFTWARE

A Definition

Data managers (or **data-management packages)** are application software packages that computerize the everyday tasks of recording and filing information. Traditional manual filing systems, using pencil, paper, file folders, and file cabinets, can be replaced by a computer system with data managers. With a

Data-manager/Data-management package An application software package that computerizes the everyday tasks of recording and filing information.

data manager, data is recorded using a computer terminal and keyboard and is stored on the computer's secondary storage devices where it can be accessed.

Most data managers contain a number of standard features, including the following:

- The ability to add or delete information within a file.
- The ability to search a file for information based on some criterion.
- The ability to update information within a file.
- Sorting of information into some order.
- The ability to print reports or mailing labels.

There are two types of data managers. Although many of the standard functions discussed above are contained in both types, the two types differ greatly in their capabilities. The two types of data managers are file handlers and data-base packages.

File Handlers. File handlers and data-base packages differ mostly in the way in which the data is stored and accessed. One way to view the difference between the two types of data managers is by reviewing their development through time.

File handlers were developed first and were designed to duplicate the traditional manual methods of filing. Before computers were used for filing, sections or departments in a business generally kept records that pertained only to their particular area of interest. The payroll department, for example, might keep an employee's name, number, address, salary, and number of deductions to facilitate the writing of paychecks. The personnel department, on the other hand, might keep each employee's name, number, salary, job title, address, employment history, and spouse's name. Each department would keep its own information for its own use.

Computers and computerized record keeping converted the procedures and methods of recording and filing data from paper, file folders, and file cabinets to computer software and storage devices. Computer access allowed each department to maintain its own independent files. The personnel department would have access to the employee file, while the payroll department would have access to the payroll file.

File handlers, therefore, can access only one data file at a time. They also cause duplication of data between files when used in a situation where many files containing similar information must be maintained. This frequently occurs in a large corporation. File handlers are useful in certain situations. A small business, for example, can benefit greatly from the use of a file handler package that organizes and properly maintains the business's inventory.

Data-Base Packages. File handling software did have some drawbacks for companies that had enormous amounts of data and limited computer resources. Because of the duplication of data and difficulty in accurately keeping one piece of information, such as an employee address, across several files, large companies began to develop data bases.

Data bases consolidate various independent files into an integrated whole from which all users can get the information they need. Such consolidation means that a piece of data needs to be located in only one place, making it easier to maintain. Users can still search for, update, add, or delete data as with a file handler. A data-base differs from a file handler in the way in which data is organized and stored.

File handler A data-management application package capable of operating on only one file at a time.

Data base Data that are commonly defined and consistently organized to fit the information needs of a wide variety of users in an organization.

Figure 2–13
Racks of Vacuum Tubes.
Vacuum tubes formed the architecture of first-generation computers.

roundings. Vacuum tubes could switch on and off thousands of times per second, but one tube would fail about every 15 minutes. Too much time was wasted hunting for the burnt-out tubes.

Cards were used to enter data into the computers. These cards were punched according to a coding scheme like the one developed by Hollerith. A machine interpreted the holes in the cards and translated them into machine language for the computer. The results of the translation were often stored on **magnetic drums.** These were cylinders coated with magnetizable material. A drum rotated at high speeds, while **read/write heads** poised just above it either "wrote" on the drum by magnetizing small spots or "read" from it by detecting spots already magnetized. Processing occurred according to specified instructions or programs given to the computer. Results were punched on blank cards.

Early first-generation computers were programmed by writing the strings of 0s and 1s comprising machine language. Preparing a machine language program was extremely tedious. Commodore Grace Murray Hopper of the U.S. Navy recognized this inefficiency (see Figure 2–14). She and her staff developed the first **language-translator program:** a set of programs that would translate other codes into machine language. An English abbreviation, based on **mnemonics,** was used to represent the series of 0s and 1s of each machine language instruction. At first, the concept was called automatic programming, a concept applied to write **assembly languages** which were translated into machine language by translator programs called assemblers.

Magnetic drum Cylinder with a magnetic surface on which data can be stored by magnetizing specific positions on the surface.

Read/write head Electromagnet used to read data from or write data onto magnetic media.

Language-translator program Software that translates Englishlike programs into machine-executable code.

Mnemonics Symbolic names or memory aids used in assembly language and high-level programming languages.

Assembly language Lower-level, symbolic programming language that uses abbreviations rather than groupings of 0s and 1s.

UNIVAC I (UNIVersal Automatic Computer) One of the first commercial electronic computers; became available in 1951.

High-level programming languages Englishlike coding schemes that are procedure-, problem-, and user-oriented.

The common first-generation computer was the **UNIVAC I (UNIVersal Automatic Computer)** developed by Mauchly and Eckert (see Figure 2–15). In need of financial support when their company lost money on a previous project, Eckert and Mauchly approached several companies, including Remington Rand Corporation. Remington Rand bought their company and propelled itself into the computer age with a product that was years ahead of the machines produced by competitors. In 1951 the first UNIVAC I replaced IBM equipment at the U.S. Census Bureau. Another UNIVAC was installed at General Electric's Appliance Park in Louisville, Kentucky. For the first time, business firms saw the possibilities of computer data processing. Although business applications do not require the sophisticated "number crunching" needed in computing scientific formulas, they do involve the handling of large volumes of data. The most popular business uses in the 1950s centered on payroll and billing.

When Mauchly and Eckert's UNIVAC replaced IBM equipment at the Census Bureau, Thomas J. Watson Jr., the son of IBM's founder, acted quickly to move IBM into the computer age (see Figure 2–16). The IBM 650 computer gave IBM the lead in the computer industry, since many companies already using IBM punched-card equipment purchased the 650 as the next step toward more advanced data processing.

IBM was also instrumental in developing the first **high-level programming language** for use by scientists, engineers, and mathematicians. An IBM employee, John Backus, headed the team that developed FORTRAN—short for FORmula TRANslator—a language still used today. Because the primary users of computers at the time were engineers, scientists, and mathematicians, FORTRAN was designed with extraordinary mathematical capabilities to meet their needs. FORTRAN allowed the programmer to write a program in mnemonic terms. A translator, or compiler, then interpreted the program and converted it to machine language instructions that the computer could execute.

In the early 1950s, the public was not yet aware of the amazing computing machines. This changed with the 1952 presidential election. After analyzing only 5 percent of the tallied vote, a UNIVAC I computer predicted that Dwight David Eisenhower would defeat Adlai E. Stevenson. CBS doubted the accuracy

Figure 2–15
The UNIVAC I

of the prediction and did not release the information to the public until the election results were confirmed by actual votes. The election predictions became the first in a burgeoning trend that has culminated in today's controversy about predicting election results from East Coast tallies before the polls are closed on the West Coast.

Business acceptance of computers grew quickly. In 1953 Remington Rand and IBM led the infant industry, having placed a grand total of nine installations. By the late 1950s, IBM alone had leased 1000 of its IBM 650 series. Also by that time, the public had acquired a stereotyped conception of computers as giant brains that could outthink humans and take away their jobs.

THE EARLY SIXTIES: INNOVATORS

Throughout the 1950s, vacuum tubes were the primary electronic components of computers. During this decade, four hardware advances led to the **second-generation computers** of the early 1950s: the transistor, magnetic core storage, magnetic tapes, and magnetic disks.

The **transistor**—the invention of which was announced in June 1948 by Bell Labs—received little attention until 1956, when William Shockley, John Bardeen, and Walter Braittain received the Nobel Prize in physics for inventing the tiny solid-state device (see Figure 2–17). Shockley had been fascinated by the properties of crystals, which were classified as semiconductors. He was par-

Figure 2–16
Thomas Watson Jr.

Second-generation computers Computers that used transistors; smaller, faster, and containing larger storage capacity than earlier computers.

Transistor Type of circuitry characteristic of second-generation computers; smaller, faster, and more reliable than vacuum tubes.

Figure 2–17
William Shockley (foreground) and John Bardeen and Walter Braittain, the Co-Inventors of the Transistor

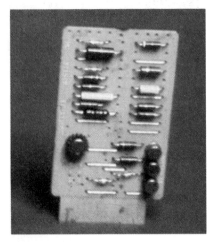

Figure 2–18
Transistors Mounted on a Circuit Card

Magnetic core Iron-alloy ring about the size of a pinhead; cores form memory and are strung on fine wires that carry current.

Real-time Describes the capability of a system to receive and process data, and provide output fast enough to control an activity.

Figure 2–19
A Frame of Magnetic Cores

ticularly interested in the effect caused by impurities in the semiconductor crystals. Semiconductors could act as conductors for electrical current passing through one direction, but not the other. Shockley believed that the impurities in the semiconductors could be made to control the current. Therefore, current could be controlled in a solid state rather than a vacuum. Bardeen and Braittain solved the puzzle, and the transistor was invented. The transistor—the word is a contraction of transfer resistor—was a small component made of semiconducting material that acted as a switch to control the flow of electrical current.

Transistors became common as people began to buy the pocket-sized radios made possible by the invention. The devices also revolutionized computers. By the early 1960s transistors had replaced vacuum tubes in computers. The transistors were mounted close together and connected with tiny, flat wires on small cards called circuit boards (see Figure 2–18). Because they used transistors, the second-generation computers were smaller, faster, and more reliable than earlier models. They used less electricity, and their transistors generated much less heat than computers that used vacuum tubes.

Just as transistors replaced vacuum tubes as primary electronic components, **magnetic cores** replaced magnetic drums as internal memory units (see Figure 2–19). The U.S. government had continued to support computer development, particularly the Whirlwind I project at the Massachusetts Institute of Technology (MIT) Digital Computer Laboratory. The Whirlwind's purpose was to experiment with **real-time** aircraft simulation for which speed and reliability were essential. The laboratory chief, Jay W. Forrester, devised magnetic core storage to accomplish this objective (see Figure 2–20).

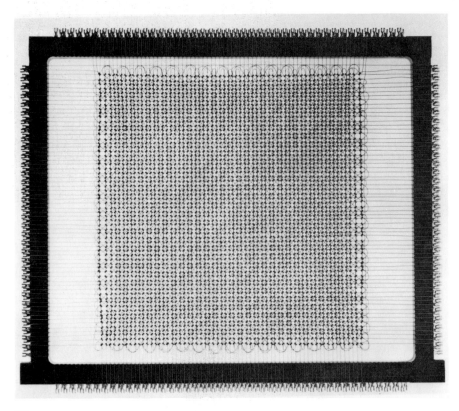

52

Magnetic cores consist of tiny doughnut-shaped rings of magnetic material strung on fine wires. An assembled unit looks very much like a window screen. An electrical current passed through the wires on which a core is strung, magnetizes the core to represent either an "on" or an "off" state. In this way, groups of cores can store instructions and data. The advantage of magnetic cores is that instructions and data can be located and retrieved for processing in a few millionths of a second—much faster than with magnetic drum storage.

This new type of internal storage was supplemented by external storage on **magnetic tapes** and **magnetic disks** (see Figure 2–21). The Germans had used huge steel tapes (the reels were two feet in diameter and weighed 200 pounds) for sound recording during the war. Plastic magnetic tapes replaced the metal tapes, and later were used for recording computer output. Output was stored as magnetized spots on the surface of the tape. However, data could be entered only in sequence on the tape. Every time a single item or small group of items needed to be added or changed, the entire tape had to be rewritten. Rather than rewrite a tape often, computer operators waited until a large batch of data had accumulated. Then they ran the tapes in an operation known as **batch processing** to update the data.

Another by-product of sound recording, the platter, led to the introduction of the magnetic disk. Much as a record is "accessed" on a jukebox, magnetic disks allowed **direct access** to data. Rather than reading all recorded data from beginning to end, the read/write head could selectively locate specific data. Adding this capability to computers made possible real-time transactions, such as making airline reservations. In fact, American Airlines installed a real-time reservation system in 1964.

The men who figured prominently in the development of second-generation computers—Shockley and Forrester—continued to research the computer field. Shockley set up his own semiconductor laboratory in Palo Alto, California. He employed many of the best researchers in semiconductors, although some eventually left the company to begin Fairchild Semiconductor. Fairchild spawned a number of other companies, most of which were located nearby. The area

Figure 2–20
Jay W. Forrester

Magnetic tape   Narrow strip of material upon which spots are magnetized to represent data; a sequential storage medium.

Magnetic disk   Metal or plastic platter coated with a magnetic material upon which data can be stored as magnetized spots.

Batch processing   Method of processing data in which data items are collected and forwarded to the computer in a group.

Direct access   Method of processing in which data are submitted, retrieved, or updated by accessing the specific locations of data.

Figure 2–21
A Second-Generation Computer System.
This IBM 7070 system relied heavily on magnetic tape secondary storage and required many tape drives to read from and write to the tapes.

Figure 2–22
John G. Kemeny

Time sharing Arrangement in which two or more users can access the same computer resources and receive seemingly simultaneous results.

Remote terminal Terminal placed at a location away from the central computer.

Interactive Descriptive of computer languages that allow the user to communicate directly with the computer in a conversational fashion.

Integrated circuit An electronic circuit etched on a small silicon chip less than 1/8-inch square.

Silicon chip Solid-logic circuitry on a small piece of silicon used to form the primary storage of third-generation computers.

became known as Silicon Valley because, by this time, nearly all semiconductors were made of silicon.

Forrester, who was at first involved in the aircraft simulation project, became absorbed in a new effort in the late 1950s. He studied the use of computers to solve problems, a concept known as system dynamics. In system dynamics, computer simulations help researchers study human social systems by analyzing factors behind economic conditions and resource use, such as unemployment, inflation, tax policies, energy, and pollution.

As computers became more common, colleges offered more courses in computer programming and electronics technology. Yet the technology of the early sixties was frustrating for students learning how to program or studying advanced mathematics with computers. The common processing method was batch processing. Students would submit their "jobs," usually in the form of stacks of computer cards, and then wait for hours for them to be processed. If a program contained an error, the student would correct the error and resubmit the job, waiting more hours for the new results. Dr. John Kemeny, a mathematics professor at Dartmouth College, thought it was unfair to make students wait so long (see Figure 2–22). With Dr. Thomas Kurtz, he developed **time-sharing** software, which allowed many students to use the computer system at the same time. Students entered data on typewriterlike terminals **(remote terminals)** and received output through the same devices. Although the main computer processed only portions of programs at a time, the time-sharing software made it seem as if each user had complete control of the computer. Computer processing had become **interactive,** meaning the user could enter a program and data and receive an almost immediate response. Instead of waiting hours for a result, the user could now communicate directly with the computer in a conversational fashion and receive results almost immediately.

Dr. Kemeny and Dr. Kurtz also designed a programming language, BASIC (Beginner's All-purpose Symbolic Instruction Code), to be implemented on this time-sharing system. BASIC remains the most common language used on microcomputers today. (Dr. Kurtz has upgraded the BASIC language into a structured language called True BASIC, which was introduced in late 1984.)

THE LATE SIXTIES: TECHNOLOGY TREND SETTERS

At the same time that transistors were replacing vacuum tubes in computers, Jack S. Kilby of Texas Instruments was busy developing the **integrated circuit** (see Figure 2–23). He realized that the components of electronic circuits could be etched onto small chips rather than being wired together. Rather than many separate pieces soldered together, many circuits are combined onto one tiny piece of silicon, hence the name *integrated*. Kilby's first circuit was primitive. But soon a single **silicon chip** less than ⅛-inch square could hold 64 complete circuits. This seems crude to us now; we use chips that contain as many as 500,000 transistors.

The chips made it possible to design computers that used less power, cost less, and were smaller and much more reliable than any previous machine. In the first-generation computers a vacuum tube failed every 15 minutes; a chip may fail every 33 million hours of operation. These reliable integrated circuit

Figure 2-23
Jack S. Kilby and the First Integrated Circuit

chips were used in the computers that guided the Apollo 11 mission to the moon.

Kilby was only the first of many technology trend setters to usher in what is known as **third-generation computers.** Another key person was Gene Amdahl, who revolutionized the IBM computers by designing the IBM System/360 series (see Figure 2–24). This series offered both scientific and business applications and introduced the family concept of computers. At first the system consisted of six computers, each offering different memory capacities. The computers could support 40 different peripherals for input/output and auxiliary storage. Since applications and equipment were **compatible,** systems could be upgraded easily. The series also introduced **operating systems** stored on magnetic disks. These operating systems controlled input and output operations and did many tasks previously handled by human operators.

Integrated circuits formed the cores of these computers. The circuits also led to the third-generation development of **minicomputers** by Digital Equipment Corporation (DEC) (see Figure 2–25). Minicomputers offered many of the features of full-scale computers on a smaller scale. Smaller and containing less internal storage capacity than full-scale machines, the minicomputers also cost less. This feature permitted smaller businesses to acquire computer power.

A new industry began to emerge: the software industry. Programs to perform payroll, billing, and other business tasks became available at fairly low costs. Yet software was rarely free of "bugs," or errors. Programs written for second-generation computers had to be rewritten to suit the architecture of third-generation computers. Since the architecture was different, programmers had to update their skills. Because of the rapid growth of hardware during this period, skilled programmers were scarce.

Businesses began questioning computer use. Admittedly, acquiring a computer lent an air of prestige to a company. But often companies had installed hardware and software without adequate analysis of their needs. In addition, the newspapers headlined computer errors: a homeowner received a water bill for $200,000, or welfare clients received $80,000 worth of duplicate checks. Many problems could be attributed to human error, but some programs simply did not process data reliably. The computer industry experienced growing pains as the software industry lagged behind advances in hardware technology.

Third-generation computers Computers characterized by the use of integrated circuits, reduced size, lower costs, and increased speed and reliability.

Compatible Descriptive of hardware that can communicate without changing the data or programs.

Operating system Collection of programs that permit a computer system to manage itself and to avoid idle time.

Minicomputer Computer with the components of a full-sized system but having a smaller memory.

Figure 2-24
Gene Amdahl

Figure 2–25
A DEC Third-Generation
Minicomputer

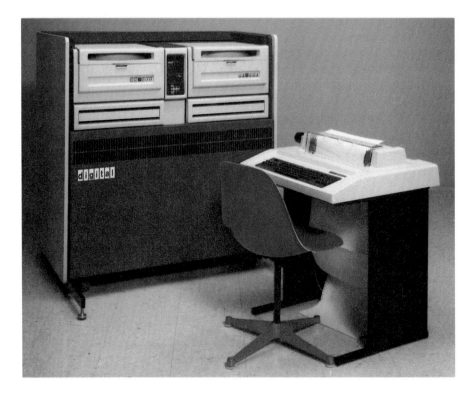

THE SEVENTIES AND EIGHTIES: ENTREPRENEURS

Large-scale integration (LSI) Method by which circuits containing thousands of electronic components are densely packed in a single chip.

Engineers continued to cram more and more circuits onto a single chip. The technique by which this was accomplished was called **large-scale integration (LSI).** The closer the components, the shorter the route electricity had to travel. With shorter routes, processing was faster. Yet the functions that could be performed on a chip were fixed in the production process.

Ted Hoff, a young engineer at Intel Corporation, introduced a concept that packed the arithmetic and logic circuitry needed for computations on one chip (see Figure 2–26). Other control functions and input/output circuitry would be placed on separate chips. The result was a single, programmable processing unit, the **microprocessor,** or "computer on a chip." The microprocessor could be made to act like any kind of calculator or computer desired. Hoff convinced Intel to market the product and its successors energetically.

Microprocessor A programmable processing unit containing arithmetic, logic, and control circuitry.

Fourth-generation computers Computers that use chips made by LSI and offer improved price and performance.

Microprocessors began to appear everywhere: in toasters, wristwatches, washing machines, and spacecraft. The invention ushered in the **fourth-generation computers.** In fourth-generation computers, electronic components were further miniaturized through LSI. This process puts thousands of transistors on a single silicon chip, which replaced the magnetic core as the primary internal storage medium and provided faster processing.

Very-large-scale integration (VLSI) Further miniaturization of integrated circuits, offering even greater improvements in price, performance, and size of computers.

Currently, **very-large-scale integration (VLSI)** is replacing large-scale integration. Today, a microprocessor based on VLSI is more powerful than a roomful of 1950s computer circuitry (see Figure 2–27). As many as 500,000 transistors can be placed on a single silicon chip.

Microcomputer A computer small in size, but not in power; now available in 8-, 16-, and 32-bit configurations.

Out of the microprocessor grew the **microcomputer.** In the January 1975 issue of *Popular Electronics* (now *Computers and Electronics*), Leslie Solomon

K (kilobyte) Symbol used to represent 1024 (2^{10}) storage units (1024 bytes); often rounded to 1000 bytes.

featured the MITS Altair 8800. This was one of the first do-it-yourself computer kits. It included a microprocessor, and it generated enormous interest.

Other microcomputers in kit form became available: the Scelbi-8B, the Sphere I, the Jolt, and the Mike. Most featured from **1K (kilobyte)** to 4K of memory (primitive when compared to computers like the IBM PC AT with 1000K of internal memory). During the early years of microcomputing, only a few microprocessor chips were available: the Intel 8080, the Motorola 6800, the Zilog Z80, and the MOS Technology 6502. Computer hobbyists could count on ten user groups and clubs and two publications, *Creative Computing* and *Byte*.

By 1977 three major microcomputer manufacturers emerged. John V. Roach supported Tandy Corporation's Radio Shack in releasing the TRS-80, a microcomputer that was already assembled. For the first time, a person could walk into a retail store and buy a low-priced personal computer. Commodore Business Machines Inc., founded by Jack Tramiel, and Apple Computer Inc., founded by Steven Jobs and Stephen Wozniak, followed Radio Shack's lead with The Commodore PET and the Apple I (read more about Tramiel, Jobs and Wozniak in "Focus on Microcomputers" at the end of this chapter). The later succession

Figure 2–26
Ted Hoff

Figure 2–27
A Motorola MC 68000 16-Bit Microprocessor That Uses VSLI

Period	Computer System Characteristics	
First Generation The Fifties	Use of vacuum tubes in electronic circuits Magnetic drum as primary internal-storage medium Limited primary-storage capacity Slow input/output; punched-card-oriented Low-level symbolic-language programming Heat and maintenance problems Applications: payroll processing and billing Examples: IBM 650 UNIVAC 1	**Vacuum Tubes (one circuit)**
Second Generation The Early Sixties	Use of transistors for internal operations Magnetic core as primary internal-storage medium Increased primary-storage capacity Faster input/output; tape orientation, with disks being introduced High-level programming languages (FORTRAN, BASIC) Great reduction in size and heat generation Increased speed and reliability Batch-oriented applications Examples: IBM 1401 Honeywell 200 CDC 1604	**Transistors (one circuit)**
Third Generation The Late Sixties	Use of integrated circuits Increased storage capacity More flexibility with input/output Smaller size and better performance and reliability Emergence of minicomputers "Family" concept of compatible computers introduced Fledgling software industry began to grow Availability of operating-system programs (software) to control I/O and do many tasks previously handled by human operators Examples: IBM System/360 NCR 395 Burroughs B5500	**Integrated Circuits (hundreds of transistors)**

**Fourth
Generation**
The Seventies
and
Eighties
	Use of large-scale integrated circuits
	Increased storage capacity and speed
	Modular design and compatibility between equipment (hardware)
	   provided by different manufacturers (customer no longer tied to one
	   vendor)
	Introduction of microprocessors, microcomputers, and supercomputers
	Applications: computer-aided instruction, home computing, robotics, expert programs
	Examples: IBM 3033 Burroughs B7700 HP 3000 (minicomputer)
		**Large-Scale and
		Very Large-Scale
		Integration
		(thousands to hundreds
		of thousands of
		transistors)**

of microcomputers, included the Apple IIe, and IIc, the Commodore 64, IBM PC, Atari 800, and many more (see Chapter 9).

As microcomputers became more popular, many companies began producing software that could be run on the smaller machines. Most of the early software was written for games. Later, instructional programs (primarily drills) began to appear. One important software development was the first electronic spreadsheet for microcomputers: VisiCalc. Written by Dan Bricklin and Bob Frankston and introduced in 1979, VisiCalc vastly increased the uses for microcomputers in the business world, and lead to integrated software—featuring word processing, business graphics, spreadsheets, and data filing systems—in the 1980s. Many companies are linking microcomputers to their mainframes or even depending on microcomputers alone. Because of these trends, many manufacturers of mainframes and minicomputers—including Wang, DEC, Hew-

This Is A Personal Computer?

Back in 1966 you could own a "personal computer" . . . if you had room to house a used vacuum tube monster, or if you could afford to buy a used transistor computer at $4,750 or $5,000—in 1966 dollars. The alternative was to build your own.

To build your own, you had to know a lot about electronics, back-plane wiring, metal working, plastics, and scrounging! Maybe you could acquire some old equipment. Sometimes magnetic drum memories were available, but you had to salvage one from equipment that had been sledge-hammered before being discarded. If you could find a used teletype machine, you had your input/output device. It was a frustrating, time-consuming "hobby."

Then the first home-built computer kit, the Mark 8, came out in 1974. You built it completely from scratch; there was no power supply, no screen, no keyboard, no case, no software. Very few were built. In 1975 the MITS Altair 8800 was introduced. If you ordered one, you got a blue box with four card slots, a power supply, and a binary front panel; a CPU board with an 8080 microprocessor chip; 256 bytes of random-access memory (RAM); no read-only memory (ROM); no interfaces to the outside world; no software; but lots of diagrams, assembly instructions, and solder. Once the computer was built, you used a teletype machine to enter programs. You wrote your own software: there was no word-processing program, checkbook balancer, or data filer. But if you did build one, you might be the only one in your town or even your state to accomplish the feat!

"Dad, I have a telecommunication device. Can I access your time-sharing capabilities?"

HIGHLIGHT — The Hackers

If you believe the media, you believe that hackers are nasty little boys who hunch over their microcomputers and modems and break into the world's securest computer systems. Unfortunately, hackers have wreaked havoc in computer systems. By the time he was 16, one famous hacker had "crashed" a DEC TOPS-10 operating system, and later a CDC Cybernet system—supposedly crash-proof—through computers at the University of Washington.

But hackers are also a persistent, hard-working group. They stand by their own code of ethics: Never say, "You can't do that!" Although hackers have frequently violated the formal rules of computer use, they have also created word processing programs, spreadsheets, graphics programs, video games, and the personal computer.

In November 1984, 150 of the best computer hackers gathered at an abandoned Army base in Marin County, near San Francisco. The group included Lee Felsenstein, the organizer of the Home Brew Computer Club; Andy Hertzfeld, who wrote the Macintosh ROM for Apple; Doug Carlston, the president of Broderbund Software; Steven Levy, who wrote *Hackers: Heroes of the Computer Revolution;* Charles Moore, who invented the computer language FORTH; Steven Wozniak, who developed the Apple I and Apple II computers; and many others.

They argued about whether all software should be free, about whether microcomputers or mainframes were best, and about whether hacking had received a bad name from the media. And they reestablished the importance of keeping in touch. Hacking may never be the same after the Hackers Conference of November 1984.

---

lett-Packard, and NCR—have announced personal computers. The resulting high-pressure competition has forced some microcomputer companies out of business.

While some companies were concentrating on microcomputers and their accessories, other companies began building computers that were much larger. Rather than follow the miniaturization trends of this period, Seymour Cray developed large, very fast scientific computers commonly known as **super-computers** (see Figure 2–28). In 1976, he formed Cray Research to produce the Cray-1, Cray-2, and Cray X-MP. Supercomputers like the ones produced by Cray and ETA Systems, Inc. are used for figuring lengthy and complex mathematics. Scientists use them in weather forecasting, aircraft design, and energy conservation. The federal government considers them vital to national security, and uses them in nuclear weapons research, cryptography, and nuclear reactor safety analysis. Supercomputer companies hope eventually to produce computers that have the power of 40 million IBM PCs and can link with as many as 64 other machines to solve a problem.

Software developers are trying to keep pace with the advances in hardware.

Supercomputers Large, sophisticated computers capable of performing millions of calculations per second and processing enormous amounts of data.

Educational software no longer provides only drills; it allows students to simulate laboratory experiments, learn new material, and write their own programs. Software for home management, hobbies, and telecommunications offers a wide variety of computer uses. Industry, medicine, and government can depend on software that allows the creation of large banks of data to increase efficiency of operations. Fewer mistakes can be blamed on faulty software.

As they learn more about programming and languages, scientists hope to develop programs that imitate human thinking. In fact, some suggest a fifth generation of computers based on **artificial intelligence (AI),** which involves programming computers to imitate the human qualities of creativity, judgment, and intuition. Two of the innovators in this field were John McCarthy and Marvin Minsky. In 1967 Minsky published *Computation: Finite and Infinite Machines,* a standard reference work in AI. Earlier, McCarthy had developed LISP (List Processing), a language still used in AI programming. Any programs that resemble AI today are known as **expert systems.** An expert system is software that can search a stored base of knowledge and recommend solutions to specific problems. Examples include *Caduceus,* which is designed to aid in medical diagnosis, *Mycin,* which covers blood diseases, and *Puff,* which measures lung functions. Future uses of artificial intelligence may solve the problem of robot vision and the use of natural language, language as people really speak it.

With these improvements in hardware and software, the computer has evolved into a mix-and-match assemblage of machines of many sizes and capabilities. Microcomputers are being linked to large mainframe systems, supercomputers

**Figure 2–28
Seymour Cray**

Artificial intelligence (AI) Ability of computers to solve problems that seem to require imagination, intuition, or intelligence.

Expert system Form of artificial intelligence software that imitates the same decision-making processes of experts on a specific field.

This computer is being used to control the home environment, such as heating, lighting, and security.

Concept Summary 2–3 ■ People and Computer Development—Pioneers, Innovators, Trend Setters, Entrepreneurs

Person	Computer Development
John W. Mauchly J. Presper Eckert	Designed UNIVAC
Commodore Grace Murray Hopper	Designed language translator programs
Thomas J. Watson Jr.	Propelled IBM into the computer era with the IBM 650
John Backus	Wrote FORTRAN
William Shockley John Bardeen Walter Braiteen	Designed the transistor
Jay W. Forrester	Devised magnetic core memory
Dr. John Kemeny Dr. Thomas Kurtz	Developed the time-sharing concept and BASIC
Jack S. Kilby	Designed the integrated circuit
Gene Amdahl	Designed family concept of computers for IBM
Ted Hoff	Associated with design of microprocessors
John V. Roach Jack Tramiel Steven Paul Jobs Stephen Wozniak	Formed companies that manufactured microcomputers
Dan Bricklin Bob Frankston	Wrote VisiCalc for microcomputers
Seymour Cray	Built supercomputers
John McCarthy Marvin Minsky	Were innovators in artificial intelligence

are interacting with other supercomputers, and the distinctions between the capabilities of minicomputer and mainframe or microcomputer and minicomputer are becoming fuzzier. Computer applications are truly eclectic: they range from business to science to law enforcement to education. Dr. Michael Lehv uses an Apple II Plus to monitor his heating system in his Columbus, Ohio, home, while the movie company Digital Productions used a Cray X-MP to create the art for the movie *The Last Starfighter*. Yet computers remain simply tools that facilitate the processing of data, just as Babbage, Hollerith, Atanasoff, and Mauchly planned.

FOCUS ON MICRO-COMPUTING

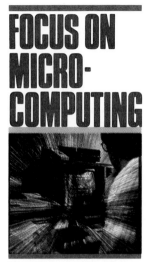

Innovators in the Micro World

Patrice George creates weaving patterns with graphics software and her Apple II computer. She runs her designing and weaving business from a downtown loft in New York City. Her clients include J. P. Stevens, Standard Textiles, and Toltec Fabrics.

An Arson Data Information System designed on dBase II data-base software helps Fred Ringler of the People's Firehouse fight arson and revive business in Brooklyn. He runs the software on the Texas Instruments Portable Professional personal computer.

The TRS-80 Model I computer and Orchestra-80 software helped Robb Murray write eight neo-Baroque compositions, recorded on a 45 rpm record as "Classical Mosquito." Without the computer, Murray says his music "would have amounted to nothing more than a drawerful of abandoned manuscripts."

Microcomputers have certainly helped many people accomplish many tasks. In fact, they have become so popular that by the end of 1984 an estimated 7.5 million people owned microcomputers.

The first really popular microcomputer was the Altair 8800 produced by MITS. This computer came unassembled for $397 or fully assembled for $498. MITS received a flood of orders, and the personal computer era was on its way. The history of personal computers involves a number of ingenious individuals, including Jack Tramiel, founder of Commodore Business Machines.

Born in Poland before World War II, Tramiel was a survivor of the concentration camps. After the war, he moved to the United States and drove a taxi for awhile. Eventually, Tramiel started a typewriter repair business that later expanded to include the production and sale of adding machines in Canada. Tramiel predicted then that calculators would someday sell for as little as $10 at the neighborhood drugstore.

Tramiel identifies the beginning of his firm's involvement in computers as 1977 when their new computer was introduced at an electronics show. At that time, it was not really known what the computer's uses would be. So many people asked about delivery schedules that they were finally told to get in line, send their money in, and when their number came up, delivery would occur. In one month, over $3 million was received, and Tramiel knew that personal computing power was a real need.

The business grew with Tramiel's policy of integrating all business operations involved in the manufacture and sale of computers. When Commodore acquired MOS Technology, a semiconductor manufacturer, it gained control over the 6502 microprocessor then in development. Tramiel poured extra money into the project, and it paid off. The processor was also used in Apple and Atari computers.

Today, Tramiel is chairman of the board of Atari. His philosophy—to provide more-sophisticated technology to computer users—is culminating in the introduction of two prototypes of the ST line of computers. In addition, Atari will offer the 8-bit Atari EX microcomputers and a portable computer, the Atari XEP. He predicts mushrooming personal computer sales as children trained in computers at school instigate purchases. He considers today's computer kids as the best salespeople any industry ever had.

Knowing the market's sales potential, Tramiel followed the General Motors philosophy, as he puts it, of having products to meet a broad set of needs at reasonable prices. He aims "to sell to the masses, not the classes." According to Tramiel's predictions, by the 1990s hand-held computers will be as popular as calculators are now.

Meanwhile, Commodore is working hard to stay in the microcomputer business. The company is introducing two new computers, the Commodore 128 Personal Computer and the Commodore LCD, a portable computer with a liquid crystal display screen.

Another trailblazer in the computer industry is Steven Jobs. Growing up in California's Silicon Valley, Jobs was interested in technology in high school. He attended lectures at Hewlett-Packard and attracted enough attention from the president, William Hewlett, to get a summer job. Later, Jobs attended college but dropped out after two years and went to work for Atari. His good friend Stephen Wozniak still worked at Hewlett-Packard. In 1976, Wozniak succeeded in building a small, easy-to-use computer on which he had been working in his spare time.

Wozniak was pleased with this clever machine, but Jobs had visions of its use in homes and small businesses and talked Wozniak into starting a business. By selling Job's Volkswagon and Wozniak's scientific calculator, the two raised $1,300 with which to build the first Apples (named in honor of a pleasant summer working in Oregon's orchards) in Job's parents' garage.

The rest is history. A superb marketing effort has helped Apple blossom in homes and businesses nearly everywhere. When revenues reached $335 million in 1981, Chairman of the Board Jobs became a modern-day folk hero and millionaire. Wozniak later left the business and returned to college but still remains a major stockholder.

Apple clearly intends to remain competitive in the personal computer market. Apple introduced the Apple III at the National Computer Conference in June 1980, the Lisa in January 1983, the Apple IIe in February 1983, and the Macintosh and Apple IIc computers in early 1984. By November 19, 1984, the two-millionth Apple IIe was sold. Many Apple IIe's have been placed in schools, along with a wide variety of educational software.

Charles Tandy, the outgoing, talkative president of Tandy Corporation, pioneered personal computer sales with the TRS-80. He used retail outlets, a marketing technique now being used by such giant companies as IBM and Xerox. With foresight and marketing/management genius, Tandy moved his business from leathercraft and hobby supplies into the rapidly expanding field of electronics. In 1963 he bought a struggling chain of nine retail and mail-order Radio Shack stores and quickly turned them into a rapidly expanding business. His success in the personal computer field came from knowing his market and making his product easily accessible. With the introduction of the TRS-80 in 1977, a person could walk into a store and purchase a low-priced personal computer. Radio Shack quickly added the TRS-80 Model II for business application, with more memory and twice the speed of the first model. Today Radio Shack computers include the TRS-80 Model 4, the TRS 200 portable computer, and the more-sophisticated TRS 2000 computer.

These companies have remained in the microcomputer business. But they have been joined by companies such as DEC, NCR, Wang, Hewlett-Packard, and IBM, that previously offered only mainframes and minicomputers. The microcomputer business has become increasingly competitive—so competitive that some companies have been forced out of business. Among these firms is Osborne Computer.

Adam Osborne started his firm in 1980 with profits he made selling 12 computer books published in eight languages. The first Osborne personal computer was shipped in July 1981, and revenues of $10 million were reported at year-end in November. Within 60 days of that first shipment, Osborne's firm had profits—quite a feat!

Eventually Osborne began selling a portable computer that weighed only 24 pounds and had a 3½-inch by 2½-inch display screen. In addition, he included two disk drives, and five software programs (worth $1,500), all for $1,795. But in October 1983 Osborne filed for bankruptcy.

Since then, Osborne has started a low-cost-software publishing firm, Paperback Software. He markets the software through bookstores. Programs to date include Executive Writer, Number Works, MyABCs, Paperback Writer (word-processing software), Draw-It (graphics software), and Executive Filer.

The microcomputer industry has one feature that will remain constant: it will always be changing. New hardware will be introduced, new technologies will make microcomputers more powerful, and some companies will fail. Many quit the industry, and many more enter it. If the people who become the "movers and shakers" in the microcomputer's future are as aggressive and creative as the ones who started the industry, microcomputing will indeed remain exciting.

SUMMARY POINTS

- Humans have always sought ways to calculate the answers to problems and keep track of the results. Developments preceding the computer that illustrate this trend include the abacus, Napier's Bones, and Pascal's and von Leibniz's calculating machines.
- Babbage's analytical engine would have used concepts similar to the design of a computer, but was doomed to failure because it was too advanced to be produced by the technology of its time.
- The first "programmable" machine was used in the weaving industry. Designed by Joseph Marie Jacquard, it used punched cards to instruct the loom. Herman Hollerith later applied this concept in processing census data when he designed a tabulating machine that could read data punched onto cards. Accounting machines applied the same techniques for processing business data.
- Foundations for some of today's corporations were laid in the late 1800s and early 1900s when William S. Burroughs began the Burroughs Adding Machine Company; James Powers started his own company, which later became Remington Rand and Sperry Univac; and Thomas J. Watson, Sr., renamed his company International Business Machines Corporation (IBM).

- Howard H. Aiken invented the first large-scale electromechanical automatic calculator, the Mark I, in 1944. But earlier John Atanasoff and Clifford Berry had produced the Atanasoff-Berry Computer (ABC), an electronic digital computer for solving equations. The first general-purpose electronic digital computer, ENIAC, was built by John W. Mauchly and J. Presper Eckert while they were working on a government project.

- By 1948 the transistor had been invented by Nobel prizewinners William Shockley, John Bardeen, and Walter Braittain. Second-generation computers, which relied on these transistors, were smaller, faster, and more reliable than the earlier computers.

- The second generation of computers was also characterized by magnetic core memory developed by Jay W. Forrester, magnetic tape auxiliary storage, and the first magnetic disks.

- The integrated circuit (silicon chip) was developed by Jack S. Kilby of Texas Instruments in 1958. This led in the 1960s to third-generation computers, which used the solid-state integrated circuits to obtain reductions in size and cost and increases in reliability and speed.

- Other contributions in the 1960s included minicomputers, Gene Amdahl's concept of hardware compatitibility, John G. Kemeny's and Thomas Kurtz's time-sharing system and BASIC programming language, and an expanded software industry.

- Fourth-generation computers rely on large-scale integration and very-large-scale integration to cram more transistors on a single silicon chip. In 1971 Ted Hoff introduced a microprocessor, which contained the circuitry for arithmetic and logic operations and some control functions on one chip. The programmable chip led the way to the microcomputer.

- The first microcomputers were available as kits. Three already assembled microcomputers debuted in 1977. Radio Shack and Tandy Corporation introduced the first TRS-80 computer. It was the first time a microcomputer could be purchased in a retail store. The other two microcomputers were the Commodore PET and the Apple I.

- The microcomputer business has become a highly competitive arena, as many computer firms, including IBM, Wang, NCR, DEC, and Hewlett-Packard, have introduced microcomputers.

- Instead of building microcomputers, Seymour Cray began designing super-computers—the huge mainframe computers that operate at incredibly high speeds.

- As improvements in hardware have been made, software has improved, too. Compatibility and effectiveness have improved. A current trend in software is toward expert systems, a form of artificial intelligence (AI). Some scientists believe that AI will usher in a fifth generation of computers. AI may solve the problems of robot vision and use of natural language by humans.

- Since 1980 people have used microcomputers for many jobs, such as managing kitchens, filing data on arsonists, creating music, and designing weaving patterns. In the future, they may use such machines as the Atari EX, the Commodore 128, the Apple Macintosh, and the TRS 200 portable computer.

REVIEW AND DISCUSSION QUESTIONS

1. Calculating machines developed in the 1600s by Pascal and von Leibniz could perform many of the functions of modern computers. In what two ways were these early calculators unlike computers?

2. In what way did the development of a loom by Jacquard affect the development of computing devices?

3. Charles Babbage attempted to build a machine employing the concept now used in computers. What was this machine called and why was it never built?

4. What was the first automatic calculator? How did this machine differ from first-generation computers?

5. What are the chief characteristics in structure and storage that distinguish first-, second-, and third-generation computers?

6. Why has the development of the integrated circuit and large-scale integration had such an impact on the computer industry?

7. What were three major problems in the software industry in the 1960s?

8. What was Ted Hoff's contribution to computer evolution?

9. How did Radio Shack, Commodore Business Machines, and Apple Computer, Inc., affect the computer industry?

10. Compare the expert system software with the concept of artificial intelligence.

11. If you could buy any microcomputer and software, what capabilities would you want? What would you plan to do with your equipment?

12. Begin building a time line of microcomputer developments since 1975. Include advances since this book was published. Use computer magazines and books to help you.

CHAPTER 3

DATA PROCESSING AND COMPUTER HARDWARE

COMPUTERS IN OUR LIVES

Superforecasts

Which processes weather data more reliably— geese on the wing, the groundhog, or a Cray X-MP? Sometimes when the forecasted flurries turn into a major storm dumping 17 inches of snow in twelve hours, it's tempting to choose the geese and the groundhog. Nevertheless, supercomputers are increasingly accurate in predicting the weather. With voluminous memories and lightning speeds, the computers take batches of weather readings from around the world and give back global forecasts three to ten days in advance. A goose just cannot compete.

Data processing includes three main steps: input, processing, and output. Geese receive input in the form of changes in air pressure. By processing, or organizing, this "data," they choose to fly at an altitude where air is dense, because thinner air provides less lift. On fair, high-pressure days, they can fly quite high, but when a low-pressure air mass moves in, they will fly closer to the ground where the air is denser. By watching their behavior—the output—you can determine the air pressure, but hardly ten days in advance.

Scientists probably know how the story about the groundhog seeing its shadow got started. But for the untutored observer this phenomenon has been a sign to predict the length of winter that has passed into folklore.

However, computerized weather data processing occurs with more precision. The most sophisticated processing of weather data takes place in Reading, England, where a Cray X-MP provides an ever-changing mathematical atmospheric model of the earth, taking into account clouds forming and dissipating, snow falling and melting, precipitation, evaporation, changes in sea surface temperature, and the earth's geography. Four times a day the Cray receives data, manipulates the numbers, and outputs the forecast by means of maps and printouts. By analyzing its data, Swiss commodity buyers can anticipate trends in Brazil's coffee market, American polar researchers can decide how to plan an expedition, and Dutch alpinists can climb the Himalayas.

Fitting the parts of the forecast together isn't easy. Although about 100,000 measurements enter the Cyber 205 system at the National Meteorological Center in Silver Springs, Maryland, each day, they are not sufficient. The ground stations that gather data are about 200 miles apart— plenty of room for a storm to drop in undetected—and the little-understood behavior of air masses over the oceans is a crucial weakness in the system. Most errors are in the short-term forecasts within the twelve- to twenty-four-hour range that affect our daily plans.

A prime forecasting target for meteorologists is storms—hurricanes, thunderstorms, and tornadoes. Meteorologists are tinkering with global models that will run on the next generation of supercomputers. When everyone else flees an oncoming tornado, lab meterologists race around the countryside trying to get closer. By filming the tornadoes and placing a 400-pound measuring device called TOTO (for Totable Tornado Observatory)